Linguistic Minorities in Western Europe

MEIC STEPHENS

Linguistic Minorities
in Western Europe

GOMER PRESS
1976

First Impression October 1976
Printed by J D Lewis & Sons Ltd
Gomer Press   Llandysul   Dyfed   Wales

SBN 85088 362 8

er mwyn fy merched
LOWRI   HELEDD   BRENGAIN
a holl blant Ewrop

CONTENTS

MAPS

PREFACE

This book describes the cultural and political situations of over fifty linguistic minorities in sixteen States of Western Europe. By 'linguistic minority' is meant a community where a language is spoken which is not the language of the majority of the State's citizens. The purview has been extended slightly, however, to include Norway and Luxembourg where the linguistic circumstances are in some ways exceptional. Ethnic groups such as the Cornish and Manx, whose languages are more or less extinct as spoken tongues but continue to be considered as part of their cultural identities, have also been included.

The term 'linguistic minority' should be taken, for the purposes of this book, as referring to indigenous and, in some cases, to autochthonous populations, or to communities so well established that they can be properly regarded as the historic occupants of the territories in which they live. It therefore excludes all refugees, expatriates and immigrants. The Jews and the Rom have also been omitted, because in Western Europe their situations are *sui generis* and their problems neither linguistic nor territorial.

Within this broad definition there are two main types of linguistic minority in Western Europe today. The first comprises those communities whose language, whether it is accorded a certain status or none at all, is certainly not the official language of any State. French ethnologists like Guy Héraud know this type as *'les ethnies sans état'* and the Italians, in Sergio Salvi's words, as *'le nazioni proibite'*. Writers in English have recently begun to follow the French example of calling these communities 'internal colonies'. As examples may be cited the Bretons in France, the Frisians in the Netherlands, the Basques in Spain and the Welsh in Britain. They are, for the most part, nations in their own right which do not look beyond their own territories to ethnic homelands elsewhere.

Whether or not the languages of this first type can all be described as 'national' must depend on the extent to which their speakers have demonstrated a consciousness of being nations. Lacking this awareness, some of them—the Ladins of the South Tyrol, for example—will have to be content to have their languages described as 'regional' in this book. But whenever there is a pejorative sense to the word, as in the French Government's use of *'les parlers régionaux'* when referring to Basque and Breton, this connotation will usually be made clear. The term 'minority language' is also less than satisfactory because some of these languages, such as Faroese and Catalan, are spoken by the majority of the population in the areas with which they are associated. The use of 'ethnic language' has been avoided because it tends to equate a person's ability to speak the language with membership of the ethnic group, which is not always the case, and—in the work of certain writers—the term has acquired racialist overtones.

The second type of linguistic minority consists of communities which, while in a numerical minority within the States of which they are citizens, speak languages which are official, State languages elsewhere. Examples of this numerous group are the French-speakers of the Aosta Valley in north-west Italy and the Danish-speakers of Schleswig-Holstein in West Germany. The main difference between these and minorities of the first type is that, while the former have developed over the centuries as complete, self-contained peoples, the latter usually owe their existence to comparatively recent alterations in State frontiers. The degree of recognition accorded to the languages of the second type may vary between the full official provision made for Italian in Switzerland and the total lack for Finnish in Sweden or Dutch in France. One of the few advantages which such minorities sometimes have over those of the first type is that, as do French in Switzerland and Swedish in Finland, their languages may enjoy a cultural prestige out of proportion to their numerical strength.

The only States in Western Europe today which do not have a linguistic minority belonging to one or other of these two types—leaving aside the very small communities of Andorra, San Marino, Liechtenstein, Monaco and the Vatican City—are Iceland and Portugal. Even if the proportions of this book had allowed the inclusion of Yugoslavia, Greece, Malta and Cyprus the same would have been true.

Although it may not be usual for both types of linguistic

minority, as identified here, to figure in a single study, they are to be considered in this book because, insofar as they exist within the context of a State, most of them share a common predicament. They are communities which have retained their own languages despite the powers of the State and the threat of assimilation by the majority populations which by its centralism the State encourages.

Some minorities might object that the adoption of this method results in their being treated in the context of a State which they regard as oppressive or, at best, neglectful of their special identities. It may also seem to them that the State frontiers which divide their homelands have thus been recognised. This approach has been used, however, not only because there is much to be gained from facing present realities but also for the reason that it reveals the nature and extent of their problems in a manner which is generally advantageous to minorities. After all, their basic dilemma arises from the rival, often mutually exclusive claims made upon their allegiances by Nation and State. It is one of this book's purposes to demonstrate, as the writer Denis de Rougemont has put it, 'The State is not the Nation, nor the Nation the State'.

There are other problems of terminology which must be noted now. While it is possible to refer to 'the Faroese' or 'the Catalans' without fear of ambiguity, it is not so easy to avoid confusion when dealing with, say, the German-speaking inhabitants of Denmark or Belgium. The English language does not always offer a readily acceptable equivalent of the French and German expressions which are commonly to be found in ethnic and linguistic studies. The reader is therefore asked to bear in mind that when these minorities are described as 'the Germans of North Slesvig' or 'the Germans of the Eastern Cantons' it is to their language that reference is being made and not to their citizenship, which is Danish or Belgian. There is less difficulty, of course, when the minority is known in English by its own name as are the South Tyroleans, the Alsatians and the Piedmontese, for example.

Each minority will be described by facts from the external history of its language; philological explanation will be kept to a minimum, except when it throws light on the language's present circumstances. Apart from geographical location, numbers and distribution, there will be details of the language's status and use in such sectors as education, law, government, religion, the mass media and literature. Also described will be many of those factors common to almost all minorities: rural decline and depopulation, urbanisation and industrial exploitation, tourism and immigration, and so on. It is therefore with the community in all its aspects, not with its language alone, that this book is concerned. If this book pays particular attention to the literature written in the languages under consideration, it is not merely that the author is indulging his own interests but that writers have usually been in the vanguard of national movements and their work among the most illustrious and permanent expressions of their people's culture,

Unfortunately, it is difficult to draw meaningful comparisons between minorities because there is often a lack of precise data which can be used to establish a set of hierarchical scales. Even the Census is not altogether reliable, since the questions relating to the language often vary from decade to decade and from State to State. But if the reader will accept that the description of linguistic minorities on the scale undertaken here, far from being an exact science, can only be impressionistic and incomplete, then the picture drawn will be of interest.

The information presented in this book has been compiled from a variety of sources. It includes material taken from a large number of books, magazines, newspapers, pamphlets, manifestoes and official documents which have been gathered over a period of about ten years. Other facts have been elicited from individuals, organisations and institutions, particularly those mentioned in the text and listed in the acknowledgements. My heavy debt to other authors is acknowledged explicitly in footnotes or implicitly in the bibliography. The most comprehensive study of ethnic groups in Europe remains *Handbuch der Europaïschen Volksgruppen,* edited by Manfred Straka and published for the Federal Union of European Nationalities in 1970. The present work is also intended as a handbook, a guide or introduction to this vast subject.

Written over a period of eighteen months beginning in July 1974, this book follows events up to the end of December
xvi

1975. As a result, several important developments which took place between its completion and publication have not been described. These include, for example, the plans for European union announced by Leo Tindemans, the Belgian Prime Minister, the political crisis in Italy, the further deterioration of the situation in Northern Ireland, the debate on devolution in the United Kingdom, including *Plaid Cymru*'s successes in the District Council elections, and the Spanish Government's reforms, all of which took place during the first half of 1976.

Finally, because I am neither a professional historian nor a qualified socio-linguist, I owe it to the reader to make my general viewpoint clear: I am a Welshman of socialist convictions who supports the national movement in my own country. The spirit in which I undertook the writing of this book was similar to that of George Orwell in his *Homage to Catalonia:* 'I have tried to write objectively about the Barcelona fighting, though obviously, no one can be completely objective on a question of this kind. One is practically obliged to take sides, and it must be clear enough which side I am on. Again, I must have made mistakes of fact, not only here but in other parts of this narrative. It is very difficult to write accurately about the Spanish war, because of the lack of non-propagandist documents. I warn everyone against my bias, and I warn everyone against my mistakes. Still, I have done my best to be honest.'

Meic Stephens
Cardiff 1976

INTRODUCTION

Language has not always been the principal criterion by which nations are identified. Up to the nineteenth century the national consciousness of most European peoples was based upon a number of factors among which religious belief, feudal tradition, social class, ethnic stock and cultural heritage, including language, had all been predominant at one time or another. After 1840, however, there occurred what appears now to have been a sudden shift in the emphasis of nationalist ideologies: language, for good or ill, became the decisive factor and the symbol of nationality.

The example of Hungary serves to illustrate this general point. Before 1840 the Hungarian nation consisted of peoples who spoke Hungarian, Slovak, German, Rumanian, Croat, Ruthenian and Slovene. They found a common identity in the traditions of a kingdom which was nearly a thousand years old. The official language of government was Latin, while the medium of trade, education and science was German. Hungarian replaced Latin in 1844 after the vernacular had been re-shaped to meet the requirements of the modern world. The concept of a multi-lingual Hungarian nation was then abandoned and the way prepared for a mono-lingual Magyar State. Over the next twenty years, under a resolute policy of Magyarisation at all levels, the linguistic rights of those citizens who spoke languages other than Hungarian were seriously impaired.

Among the first to adopt the spirit of Hungary's linguistic policies was Prussia. Up to 1860 the Polish-speakers who formed some 10% of Prussia's population enjoyed a wide measure of cultural autonomy, on condition that they behaved as loyal subjects of the Prussian State. The province of Posen even had its own political institutions, as the Grand Duchy of Poznan, within an otherwise strongly centralised system. But by 1870, when Prussia had become the leader of a new Germany, there was no longer place for languages other than German within its borders.

Linguistic nationalism among European States is a product of the nineteenth century. Its earliest manifestations were largely the result of that complex phenomenon known as Romanticism which had taken root in the liberal circles of Germany during the previous decades. Romantic concepts of People, Nation and State were concentrated by German patriots into the single basic ideal of a society finding solidarity in a common language. Johann Gottfried Herder (1744-1803) and Johann Gottlieb Fichte (1762-1814) were among the pioneers of German Romanticism. Another thinker typical of his day was Wilhelm von Humboldt (1767-1835). A friend of the writers Schiller and Goethe, Humboldt produced important works on aesthetics, literary criticism and political theory, but his most lasting achievements were in linguistic philosophy. According to Humboldt, who equated language with spiritual energy, those who spoke a common language were destined to become sovereign peoples with their own States, the frontiers of which would correspond with linguistic boundaries. The new nationalism was given its classic expression when he wrote, 'The true homeland is really the language'. This idea had grown out of Germany's recent experience: divided as it was into scores of small, powerless, feudal states, it had failed to match the growing nationalism of its rival, France. Humboldt's view therefore found a quick response among nationalist politicians in Germany and he went on to win fame as the Prussian civil servant who reformed Germany's education system and founded the University of Berlin. Although his liberalism came to be detested in Metternich's day and he was obliged to resign in 1819, Humboldt's concept of *Heimat* survived—not in the way he had intended but as the justification for German imperialism between 1870 and 1945.

The linguistic philosophy of the German Romantics was soon to find acceptance elsewhere in Europe during the course of the nineteenth century. The Pan-Slav and Pan-Nordic movements learnt from it and used it for their own purposes. In England, John Stuart Mill (1806-73) wrote in *Representative Government* (1861), 'Free institutions are next to impossible in a country made up of different nationalities . . . the boundaries of governments should coincide in the main with those of nationalities'. Mill's view was contested, however, when Lord Acton (1834-1902) argued in an essay published the following year that 'the combination of different nations in one state is as necessary a condition of civilised life as the combination of men in society'. Acton, of course, was primarily concerned with the British and Habsburg Empires and fearful of what effects Mill's assertion might have had on their stability. It occurred to neither that their views could have had relevance for the Celtic peoples of the United Kingdom, the British Confederation dominated by the English hegemony.

In France too, German Romanticism found its disciples. If it is true that democracy and nationalism were the twin children of the Revolution of 1789, the French were now inspired with a sense of national mission which could be fulfilled only at the expense of the other peoples living within the Republic. For Romantic writers like Francois-René de Chateaubriand (1768-1848), Alphonse de Lamartine (1790-1869) and Ernest Renan (1823-92), despite their enthusiasm for the Celtic spirit, the 'regional speech' of France's provinces was good only for folk-loric purposes. The sole language permissible in the public affairs of the highly centralised State was French. Among the results of this Jacobin view is the French education system which excludes all other languages spoken within the Republic; it was introduced in the 1850s and has been defended by all French Governments ever since. A comparison of French and German nationalism during the nineteenth century leads to the conclusion that they were different only in one respect: whereas the fostering of 'the national language' was but the point of departure for the Germans, it was always the implicit aim of the French.

It was not long before the two were inextricably linked, however. Napoleon, intent upon making France the mistress of a multi-national, French-speaking Empire, aroused the national sentiments of all its neighbours, including Germany. After 1815 the same forces were at work among the peoples of the Austrian-Hungarian, Turkish and Russian Empires. None of these was linguistically homogenous. Franz Josef, the Emperor of Austria-Hungary, ruled over a vast conglomeration of peoples which included Czechs, Slovaks, Croats, Slovenes and Ruthenians, all resentful of their subjection, as well as Poles and Italians who enjoyed certain privileges as land-owners. All were dominated by the

xxi

Austrians and Hungarians who had formed the Dual Monarchy in 1867. Yet even these did not share a common language: half the population of Hungary consisted of minorities, while Austria's minorities amounted to a numerical majority.

By the end of the nineteenth century there were still about 45 million people belonging to linguistic minorities in various parts of Europe. The map had been substantially altered. On the one hand, Italy had been united and the greater part of the Balkans liberated from the Turkish Empire. On the other, the persistence of Austrian and Russian imperialism, and the emergence of a new Germany, were about to revive the Napoleonic dream of dominating the entire continent.

Meanwhile, in the rest of Europe, the nineteenth century had seen a resurgence among what Karl Marx called 'the unhistoric nationalities'—the Celtic peoples of Britain and France and the non-Castilian peoples of Spain. For them too language had become a symbol of nationality. Even among peoples without their own language there were attempts to create a national form of speech which would express their sense of separate identity. Norway nurtured *Landsmål* because the official *Riksmål* had too much of a Danish character. The Faroese followed the example of N. F. S. Grundtvig (1793-1872), who taught the Danes to withstand German expansionism, by developing a language different from Danish. In Switzerland the Swiss-German dialects were used for literary purposes by writers like Jeremias Gotthelf (1797-1854) and in Provence the poets of the *Félibrige,* including Frédéric Mistral (1830-1914), strove to make a new medium out of *la langue d'oc.*

Language, its dialects and orthography, had also become a banner around which disputes of other kinds were waged. Flemish challenged Dutch in Belgium. In Yugoslavia and Czechslovakia Croat competed with Serb, Slovak with Czech and the Cyrillic alphabet with the Latin. Many Lutherans among the Poles and Lithuanians preferred German to their own languages because it was the language of their faith; some Slovene Protestants chose to use Hungarian for similar reasons. Other minorities, lacking sympathy for the ideologies of the States where their ethnic homelands lay and where their languages had become official symbols, made deliberate attempts to cultivate differences in their speech. In

xxii

Germany and Austria some Slavonic peoples such as the Memellanders, the Masurians, the Kashubs, the Water Polacks and the Schlonsakians, altogether some 2 million people, kept themselves aloof from the nationalism of Poland, Czechoslovakia and Slovenia, to which they were ethnically related. Most of the minorities of this type, however, are by now hardly recognisable as distinct communities: in their case the loss of a distinct linguistic identity was followed either by assimilation into the majority population of the host State, or later, by re-unification with their homelands to the east.

It was little wonder that the First World War was fought, according to the slogan of the day, 'for the rights of small nations': there was hardly any part of Europe which could fail to respond. At the War's end there was widespread hope that some of the problems arising from Europe's linguistic heterogenity would at last be solved. Indeed, several new States created out of old national aspirations were now recognised by the Treaties of Versailles and St Germain in 1919 and 1920. Out of imperial Russia came an independent Finland and the Baltic States of Estonia, Latvia and Lithuania. From the western marches Poland was reborn. President Wilson's famous Fourteen Points for Peace, presented to the Congress of the United States of America on 8 January 1918, included the central principle of self-determination. There was to be autonomous status for all the subject peoples of the Habsburg and Turkish Empires. But the Allies' intentions proved impossible to realise. Italy insisted on as much territory as possible at the expense of Austria and Yugoslavia. The Rumanians had claims to press against Hungary, Bulgaria and Russia, the Greeks old scores to settle with Turkey. Czechoslovakia, a new State, was in conflict with Hungary and Poland, while all its neighbours contested Poland's frontiers. When Poland was given access to the sea via the Polish Corridor, from General Foch was drawn the prophetic comment, 'There lies the root of the next war'.

By 1939 minority problems had reached serious proportions in almost every European State. There were minorities of up to 40% of their populations in Poland and Czechoslovakia. In Spain the Catalans and Basques had fought for their autonomy in the name of the Republic overthrown by Franco in the Civil War of 1936-9. In France, Belgium and Italy, the Bretons, Alsatians, Flemings and South Tyroleans had suffered because their commitment to the State had proved to be less than total. For most Europeans during the inter-War years, especially with the rise of National Socialism in Germany and Italy, language was still the crucial test of nationality and a symbol of political allegiance while, for most governments, use of the State language was assumed to imply loyalty to the State.

The Second World War solved only a few of the minority questions caused by the treaties which concluded the First World War. Whereas, prior to 1939, there had been approximately 30 million Europeans (excluding citizens of the Soviet Union) who lived under foreign government, by 1945 their number had been reduced to about 10 million. The rest had either fled or, under German occupation, had been deported or exterminated, often so that political frontiers could be re-drawn in closer proximity to linguistic boundaries. Yet the principle of self-determination found no wider support in 1945 than it had in 1920. Relations between States continued to reflect controversies in which language was the central or predominant issue. But there was no attempt in the Charter of the United Nations to enunciate any principle which might have proved useful to States with 'border problems'. Omitting all reference to the autonomy of ethnic or linguistic groups, the Charter deals only with 'a principle of equal rights and self-determination of peoples', leaving the question of what constitutes 'a people' undefined. The Governments of Western Europe have usually interpreted this clause as signifying peoples in their entirety, always refusing to grant the right of self-determination to fragments of peoples and invariably for reasons to do with the State's territorial sovereignty. Nor is there much in international law which can be used to end such conflicts as those between Austria and Italy over the South Tyrol or Italy and Yugoslavia over Trieste. It is therefore left to the Governments of the States involved to approach the problem in their own way, usually with unfortunate results for the minority. Denmark and West Germany are rare exceptions in the success of their reciprocal arrangements over Schleswig; Germany and France have been more typical in their rival claims to Alsace.

It is in an attempt to win recognition for the special problems of ethnic minorities at an international level that the Federal Union of European Nationalities campaigns. Previous to the Second World War the minority question had been the responsibility of the Nationality Congresses which worked under the auspices of the League of Nations but, with the advent of Hitler, their work had proved impossible to continue. The F.U.E.N. was formed in Paris in 1949 under the presidency of the Walloon writer Charles Plisnier and with the Breton Joseph Martray as its secretary. At present the Union's membership consists of organisations representing minorities in Austria, Belgium, Britain, Denmark, Finland, France, West Germany and Italy. According to its statute, a minority (or 'nationality' as the F.U.E.N. prefers) is 'a national group which manifests itself by criteria such as its own language, culture or traditions and which constitutes in its native soil no proper State or is domiciled outside the State of its nationality'. The Union, with a secretariat in Denmark, supports the work of the United Nations and the Council for Europe, making representations to these and other bodies such as State Governments, in favour of a federal structure for Europe in which minorities' rights would be recognised. At its seventeenth congress, held in 1967 at Abenra in Slesvig, the Union adopted a list of twelve 'Basic Principles of a Law of Nationalities' and now seeks to have them accepted as part of international law. Among these principles are recognition of the minority's right to use its language in education, religion, law, administration and the mass media and its right to cultural, legislative, economic and political autonomy. The F.U.E.N. has no official status, however, and most of its attempts to seek the ear of such bodies as the Council for Europe have so far been in vain. It is nevertheless the only organisation which is concerned with all ethnic minorities in Europe and as such it continues to make a valuable contribution to the study of their problems, especially in the publication of its quarterly journal *Europa Ethnica,* and to draw the attention of Governments to their responsibilities in this respect.

Now if a minority's fate is to be settled neither by international law nor by the State where its ethnic homeland is situated, it follows that it can be decided only by what might be called the host State. It is up to the host State to realise that the protection of minorities is as much an economic, social and political problem as it is linguistic. For if the minority is to maintain its language and culture, it needs to be able to compete effectively with the majority. It also requires a number of institutions which will compensate for its initial disadvantages such as a peripheral location, a neglected economy and a lack of educational facilities. Special provision for minorities should not end there, however. It is not enough to base protection only on the citizen's rights as an individual member of the State, as usually happens in Western Europe. The minority needs to enjoy equality of opportunity in all fields, not only as citizens of the host State but also as a minority; that is to say, it must have corporate minority rights, preferably within its own territory. Otherwise, inequality in economic and cultural terms will be perpetuated, disaffection among the minority will spread and alienation, whether psychological, linguistic. economic or political, will follow.

The possibility of compromise or co-operation between States, and between Governments and their minorities, is sometimes made more difficult by the fact that the minority speaks a dialect, as in Alsace, or an archaic form of a language, as in Carinthia. Further complications arise where the situation generally known as bilingualism does not prevail for all purposes and to the same extent over the whole area under dispute. The several forms of bilingualism may belong to one of two broad types. The first, heterogenous bilingualism, in which two languages are used by different peoples in one territory, can be further divided into geo-bilingualism in which each language has its own separate geographical area inside one territory within which mono-lingualism prevails, as in Belgium, and bipart-lingualism in which two languages are spoken in one area by different peoples, as with German and Czech in Czechoslovakia before 1918. The second type, homogenous bilingualism, in which two languages are used by the same people in one territory, can be divided into diglossia, in which two languages or a high and low variety of the same language operate in one area for the same people, each language having its own domain,

as in the German-speaking cantons of Switzerland, and ambi-
lingualism in which two languages operate for the same
people in one territory but where both are used at the official
level as well as for everyday purposes, as in Finland. The
degree of official recognition accorded to the languages of
minorities often has to take account of such circumstances.
Other minorities, such as the Lapps and Greenlanders, or
those whose languages are virtually extinct, like the Manx and
Cornish, present their own unique problems.

Because Switzerland learnt the lessons arising from its
linguistic heterogeneity in time to prevent serious conflict between its parts, it is often cited as an example of how multi-
lingual States may be planned or re-organised. It should be
noted, however, that Switzerland owes its reputation for
linguistic harmony to a highly decentralised system of government in which its four communities have been concentrated
for a long time in separate cantons with full cultural and
political autonomy. Nevertheless, in cantons where more than
one language is spoken, friction has developed for linguistic
reasons. Also, the precarious situation of Romansch suggests
that even in Switzerland the protection of linguistic minorities
is far from being completely effective. It remains true,
however, that—except for the Jura question—the Swiss have
been saved from bitterness over minority problems by the
prospect of an early settlement which their system affords,
and by their steadfast refusal to expand their frontiers during
the last hundred years.

Yugoslavia too is a good example of cultural co-existence.
There, besides the Serbs, Croats, Slovenes, Macedonians,
Moslems and Montenegrins who form about 87% of the total
population, live also nine nationalities who include
Albanians, Bulgarians, Czechs, Italians, Hungarians,
Rumanians, Ruthenes, Slovaks and Turks, about 11% of the
population in all, as well as smaller groups of Rom, Germans,
Poles, Ukrainians, Russians, Austrians and Vlachs. The
Socialist Federal Republic of Yugoslavia has not been without
its tensions since 1945, notably in threats by right-wing
separatist groups in Croatia. But, decentralised in six
republics and two autonomous provinces, Yugoslavia has had
real success in basing its very existence as a State on the principles of political and cultural self-management, albeit in the

context of its own form of Marxist-Leninism, for all its peoples and ethnic minorities.

Among the States of the European Economic Community, on the other hand, the problems arising from their linguistic heterogeneity have not been tackled with the same resolution as the Swiss and Yugoslavs have shown. Yet since the Treaty of Rome, it has become more and more apparent that, if European union is to be achieved before the end of the twentieth century, the existence of linguistic minorities and regional cultures will have to be taken into account as a part, an increasingly important part, of the question, what kind of United Europe is it to be? Indeed, it is by now quite evident that, although the founders of the E.E.C. were devoted to the Napoleonic ideal of a centralised European State, since the nine members agreed on direct elections to the European Parliament there has been a rapidly growing demand for more devolution of power from the centre to the regions within a federal system.

The reason which used to be offered as an explanation of why Western Europe has been gripped by centrifugal forces since the Second World War was that regional discontent is caused by economic neglect. This is certainly the case in regions like Brittany and it remains true for many peripheral areas today, but the explanation has become less convincing since about 1962 when differences in statistics for unemployment and income per head between the centres and the regions of most States began to narrow slowly. The areas which have suffered most from recent crises have been not the poor, agricultural regions like the south of Italy but those which depend on heavy and manufacturing industries like the Ruhr, the Lowlands of Scotland, central France, northern Italy, Alsace and Wales. It can therefore be argued that it is not poverty but wealth, or the prospect of wealth as in the discovery of oil off Scotland's shores, which creates the new circumstances in which autonomist movements find fresh support. Regions like the *Mezzogiorno,* where industrial development continues to be slow, show less enthusiasm for running their own affairs than Catalonia, where much of Spain's industry is concentrated. It is when economic progress co-incides with political dissatisfaction that the demand for devolution grows stronger. The remoteness and inefficiency of

xxviii

central government, as in Britain, Spain and Italy, are primary causes of disillusionment and anger in the regions, especially when as a result of economic development there is a threat to the survival of local cultures and institutions.

It is no coincidence that, among the States which now form the E.E.C., it was West Germany which first took up the cause of a united federal Europe—while putting its own house in order by re-organising itself on decentralist lines. Germany had been divided into *Kleinstaaterei* for centuries—under the Holy Roman Empire through the Confederation of the Rhine to Bismarck's customs union—before Hitler based the Third *Reich* on centralised government from Berlin. Soon after 1945, following the isolation of Berlin in East German territory, Willy Brandt saw that 'the Nation State has to become a thing of the past' and that, inasmuch as National Socialism had suppressed the older regional loyalties for the sake of the Nation State, to oppose one was to oppose the other. From its creation in 1949 the Federal Republic (unlike the Democratic Republic of East Germany which is highly centralised) became the most decentralised State in Western Europe, its government based on the *Länder,* or Regions, and its industry, finance and culture spread among its main cities. Each of the ten *Länder* has its own Parliament, cabinet, and Prime Minister, the Federation at Bonn being responsible only for such matters as foreign affairs, defence and currency while, in the *Bundesrat* or Federal Parliament, the representatives of the *Länder* exercise their right to legislate. One result of this system, which has 'centres everywhere', is that there is no call for separatism or more devolution anywhere in West Germany and that its only substantial indigenous linguistic minority, the Danish-speakers of South Schleswig, enjoy political and cultural autonomy to an extent which is a model for the rest of Europe. Furthermore, under Helmut Schmidt, West Germany has extended the principle of polycentrism to the E.E.C. as a whole. In 'the Europe of the Regions', for which the West Germans are the keenest advocates, the Nation States would be gradually dismantled and power removed from Bonn, Paris, London and Rome to assemblies in the capitals of the regions and to the European Parliament in Brussels.

France, geographically the largest State in the E.E.C., on

the other hand, is also the most centrally administered and Paris the capital with the biggest concentration of power. At the same time it is the French who have argued most consistently in favour of 'a Europe of the States', united for economic, political and military purposes against the U.S.A., a Europe in which State power, particularly France's, would be supreme. In this De Gaulle—whose influence on the E.E.C. was predominant in its early years—was followed by Pompidou who believed in European union for much the same reason, and by Giscard d'Estaing who now manoeuvres between the Gaullist legacy and his own pragmatic form of European integration. All three are the heirs of the Jacobin tradition and it is against their view of France and Europe that the regionalist movements are ranged. Decentralisation has had a certain vogue in France for many decades. But there has been no real dimunition of the capital's powers. Since 1972 France has been divided into ninety-five departments, grouped into twenty-two regions, which are run by Prefects appointed or dismissed by the Minister of the Interior in Paris. Each region is also controlled by a Prefect presiding over a regional council half of which consists of indirectly elected representatives—the region's deputies and senators—and the other half of co-opted local authority officials. The regional councils are consultative bodies with no legislative functions and no more than derisory budgets for economic and cultural affairs. Nor is it expected that Olivier Guichard, the Gaullist deputy who headed a Government body set up in 1963 to supervise De Gaulle's economic policies in the regions, will advocate any measure of devolution when he reports in July 1976. However Giscard d'Estaing decides to re-act, the Government's funds will no doubt be appointed through the Prefects. The French President's arguments are mutually contradictory but they never change: France already has enough devolution and to strengthen the regions would destroy the unity of the State. Recent polls have shown that about 71% of the population want their regional councils to be directly elected, but the Government remains unmoved: 'Only the Nation State can be the guarantor of liberty', says Jacques Chirac, the Gaullist Prime Minister, on its behalf. Meanwhile, autonomists from Brittany and Corsica are imprisoned without trial for 'threatening to endanger the unity of the French State'. But although the Government resists political devolution, it supports economic decentralisation. Since 1960 there have been attempts to develop, for example, the ports of Dunkirk, Brest, St Nazaire and Bordeaux, and to encourage industry to move out of the congested Paris area into the provinces to the west and south-west. Already this policy has begun to achieve some success. Paris lost about half a million of its inhabitants between 1962 and 1975. But the gap between incomes in Paris and the rest of France is still enormous. Herein lies, perhaps, a reason for hope that the day of the regionalist movements in France is drawing near. For as the wealth of the provinces increases so may the demand for more political power. Giscard d'Estaing may yet share the fate of De Gaulle who, in 1969, retired from the Presidency because he claimed (though this was not the only reason), that the French had rejected his proposals for regional reform. It seems certain that devolution will be one of the major issues in the presidential elections due in 1981, much more than it was in 1974. Meanwhile, it is significant that the regionalist movements of France have declared themselves in favour of a federal Europe, or, as the Breton leader Yann Fouéré has called it, 'the Europe of a Hundred Flags', and that the Gaullists have anticipated the report by Leo Tindemans, the Belgian Prime Minister, on European unity by describing it as 'bad news for Europe and for France'.

France and Germany are 'the strong men of Europe', and much will depend, in the Europe of tomorrow, on which exerts the greater influence. But theirs are not the only approaches to the question of decentralisation in the modern State. Outside the E.E.C., Spain, for example, remains intransigent towards what Franco condemned as 'the traitor provinces' because they dared to oppose him in the Civil War. The violent resistance of the Basques and Catalans, caused by the dictator's brutally repressive methods, will no doubt continue there for as long as Juan Carlos or his successors refuse to concede at least some of the minorities' demands. Certainly not until democracy and civil rights are fully restored can Spain be accepted as a member of the European Community.

Belgium too has seen violence resulting from the Government's failure over the last twenty years to secure a permanent truce between Flemings and Walloons. A highly centralised State up to 1960, the very existence of Belgium has been endangered on several occasions by mutual antagonism between the two peoples. This tension has obliged successive Governments to re-write the Constitution, devolving power to both communities by the establishment of regional councils with legislative powers in the fields of language, culture, education and, in 1975, the economy. If they are eventually approved by Parliament these councils will also assume spending powers over a wide area, their budget including finance for the health service and industrial development. A late convert to the principle of domestic federalism, Belgium is now favourably disposed towards a united, federal Europe and Leo Tindemans is one of its most committed supporters.

A similar conversion to federalism has taken place in Italy. The Constitution of 1947 gave the nineteen regions, at least on paper, a generous measure of administrative autonomy and five—four of which had linguistic minorities—were granted special statutes. But the rest of Italy had to wait until 1970 before the plans for devolution were implemented. The main reason for this delay were the fears of the dominant Christian Democratic Party that the regions would be taken over by the Communists (as happened in some regions at the elections of 1975) and Rome's refusal to allow the process of devolution to the regional assemblies. Not surprisingly, while the central Government hung on to power, the South Tyrolean problem flared up again and other autonomist movements found new support. But in 1970 regional elections took place and two years later the new authorities began to operate. In theory the regions have fairly wide powers, with responsibility for the health service, agriculture, public works and road transport, but in practice they are under-financed and not yet free from interference by Rome. A new law passed in August 1975 required the Government to extend the scope of regional autonomy within twelve months and a committee is at present trying to decide what further powers should be devolved. Italy is not yet a federal State, and has still not solved the immense problems which arise from its regional variations in wealth, politics and culture. But it is among those States where the notion of federalism, both internal and in the European context, has won more and more ground in recent years.

The same can be said for the Netherlands and Denmark, particularly the latter which has already granted home rule to the Faroe Islands and is preparing to do the same for Greenland by 1978. Even in metropolitan Denmark there has been devolution from Copenhagen. The radical reforms of 1970 reduced the number of local councils from 1,400 to 300 and county councils from twenty-five to fourteen. The new, bigger county councils can now raise their own taxes and are responsible for a wide range of services including roads, hospitals and education. Recent polls have shown that a majority of Danes want more devolution and further integration into the European Community which, with the Dutch, they see as a guarantee of protection against domination by the larger States.

As for Britain, the United Kingdom continues to be one of the most centralised States in Western Europe, and to have serious problems in governing its constituent parts. In Northern Ireland every attempt by Westminster during the last ten years to find a formula for sharing power between the Unionist, Protestant majority and the Republican, Catholic minority has failed. Intransigence on both sides and a floundering Government have plunged the province into violence of an exceptionally tragic kind. The experience of the Stormont Parliament at Belfast has doubtless given regional government in Britain a bad name. Yet it can hardly be claimed that the Labour Party's plans for establishing elected assemblies in Scotland and Wales were announced, in 1975, for reasons of good government. For, as the Scottish National Party and *Plaid Cymru* have pointed out, neither assembly would have control of the economy and, in Wales, there would be no legislative powers. As *The Economist* (London) has said, 'Their primary purpose has been to save Labour's electoral hide in Scotland and Wales, providing elected assemblies in Edinburgh and Cardiff with wide powers over domestic matters in an attempt to dish the nationalists. Whether a spot of constitutional tinkering will blunt the nationalists' appeal, particularly in Scotland, remains to be seen. It might simply play into their hands. In a stagnant or slumping Britain, devolution could turn out to be the slippery slope to separatism'.

Meanwhile, since the Government's announcement of its plans for Scottish and Welsh Assemblies, the national parties of Scotland and Wales, both committed to the establishment of Parliaments, have made substantial progress in membership and at local elections. It now seems inevitable that if the Labour Party, already in a minority position at Westminster, is to command support in Scotland and Wales at the next General Election, it will have to offer more than the White Paper on Devolution published in 1975.

Britain re-affirmed its wish to be a member of the European Community in 1975. It may very well happen from now on that its view of Europe will prove decisive in the choice between the federal solution, as envisaged by West Germany, and the confederal European State as preferred by France. It is difficult to say with any certainty where the two main British political parties stand on this crucial issue. In 1973, when the Conservatives were in power, it seemed that—despite his efforts to please both Brandt and Pompidou—Edward Heath was moving toward the French, confederal view of a European State. Following the Labour Party's return to office in 1974, Harold Wilson set about renegotiating new terms for Britain's membership of the E.E.C. and led the pro-Market campaign in the referendum the following year. But neither the Labour Party nor the Conservative has ever set out in detail the kind of European union which Britain stands for. The debate has been entirely parochial and economic: could Britain afford to withdraw? Indeed, it can be concluded that the British Government's procrastination over the problems of its own Constitution, and its ambivalent attitude towards Europe, have gone hand in hand and that, if a clearer view of this question had been expressed by the Government and Opposition at the referendum on Britain's membership of the E.E.C. in 1975, it is possible that the Scots and the Welsh would have voted differently. In the event, there were majorities in both Scotland and Wales in favour of remaining in the Common Market, but they were significantly smaller than the majority in England. Since then, although the nationalist parties of Wales and Scotland were officially opposed to British membership, they have worked for the improvement of regional policies in the E.E.C. and, through such agencies as the Bureau for Unrepresented Nations in Brussels, have joined with their Alsatian, Breton and Basque counterparts in pressing the federalist case.

The European dimension of Scottish and Welsh nationalism was defined as long ago as the 1920s when the leaders of the national parties in those countries argued that by winning self-government, they would recover their ancient links with Europe, 'the world's leader and its centre', and that 'to bring political and economic unity to Europe should be one of the first priorities of our century'. Today an increasing number of Scots and Welsh are anxious and determined that their countries should play a part in the formation of the new Europe. With many of the other minorities to be considered in the following chapters they believe, in the words of the Swiss philosopher P. J. Proudhon (1809-65), one of the fathers of socialism, that 'the twentieth century will open the era of federations or mankind will once more begin a purgatory lasting a thousand years' and that, as the century enters its last quarter, it is now time to move towards a united but federal Europe which, across State frontiers, will permit and encourage the free development of all its regions and peoples.

1 AUSTRIA

Constitution: Federal Republic

Area: 32,374 square miles

Population: 7.456 million (1971)

Capital: Vienna

Administrative divisions: 9 provinces

Present Government: The Social Democratic Party *(S.P.Ö);* elected 1975

Language of majority: German

THE SLOVENES OF CARINTHIA

Carinthia is Austria's southernmost province. It has an area of about 3,200 square miles, consisting of Upper Carinthia in the west, on the border with Italy, and Lower Carinthia to the east, on the border with Yugoslavia. The principal towns are Hermagor, Villach and Klagenfurt, the provincial capital. Timber and agriculture are the main industries but there are also deposits of iron ore, lead and zinc in the mountains. The Carinthian Riviera, around the province's two hundred lakes, is a popular tourist area. The total population of Carinthia in 1971 was 525,728.

In Lower Carinthia, mostly to the south of the river Drau, there live about 21,906 speakers of Slovene and its dialects, according to the State Census of 1971.* However, for reasons described below, the methods and results of the language Census in Carinthia are often the subject of disagreement. Some estimates put the number of Slovenes at around 45,000.

The Slovenian people settled in their present territories, the larger part of which now form the Yugoslav Republic of Slovenia, after they left their homelands between the rivers Weichsel and Dnieper in the sixth century and travelled westwards, uniting under their chieftain Valuk in a Slavonic tribal alliance. The principality which they established was known as *Karatania,* a name which has survived only in the Austrian province of *Kärnten.* In the year 745 the Slovenes lost their independence to Bavarian invaders and in the thirteenth century they fell under the rule of the Habsburgs. Despite peasants' revolts in the fifteenth and sixteenth centuries and a cultural renaissance in the nineteenth, they remained within the Holy Roman Empire until 1806 and under the Austro-Hungarian Empire until 1918.

At the end of the First World War, the Treaty of St. Germain in 1920 brought the national aspirations of the Slovenian people near to fulfilment. The majority were able to

---

*As there are also smaller numbers speaking languages other than German in all the provinces of Austria, the total number of Croats is around 32,413, Slovenes, 28,000 Magyars 19,117 and Czechs 10,317. In Styria (population: 1,179,810) there were, in 1971, 3,169 Slovene-speakers, 1,074 Croats and 1,028 Magyars, while in Lower Austria (population: 1,379,926) there were 1,296 Czechs and 2,088 Magyars.

join their compatriots among the Southern Slavs in the Kingdom of Yugoslavia and go on, during the Second World War, to see the establishment of the first Slovenian Republic, formed on 5 May 1945. However, when the political map of Europe had been re-drawn, there remained 400,000 Slovenes in Italy and about 90,000 in Austria. The Slovenian minority of Lower Carinthia is therefore an isolated remnant of a nation which, in the neighbouring State of Yugoslavia, has achieved full recognition. Separated by the Karawanken Mountains from the Yugoslav Slovenes, who total 1,735,088 (1971), the Austrian Slovenes speak a language which is an archaic form of Slovene, heavily influenced by German.

In recent years the Yugoslav Government has shown interest in the existence of Carinthia's Slovenes and the Institute for the Study of Ethnic Problems at Ljubljana has published a number of papers on their problems. Central to the Yugoslav view is the fact that in the Republic of Slovenia the linguistic minorities—Croats (31,000), Serbs (13,500), Magyars (10,500) and Italians (3,000)—enjoy fundamental rights under the Constitution and have flourished far more than have the Slovenes of Lower Carinthia.

It is sometimes claimed by the Carinthian Slovenes that the province was Germanised by force of arms. But there is little evidence to suggest that the autochthonous Slavs were driven out or subjected to serfdom, since throughout the centuries this sparsely settled area had room and sustenance for all. It was subjugated by the Romans in 35 B.C. and was crossed by many Germanic tribes in the age of their great migrations across Europe. The Slavs arrived later, only to fall before the Bavarians who converted them to Christianity and improved their economy. The region was thus recognisably German for many hundreds of years and the Slavonic past was almost completely forgotten by its inhabitants. Only in the nineteenth century was it re-discovered, often by German writers and philologists of the Romantic Movement, and not until 1848, under the influence of Pan-Slavism, did the Slovenes of Lower Carinthia show any measure of communal identity.

Under the Treaty of St. Germain the plebiscite of 10 October 1920 was organised to give the Carinthian Slovenes an opportunity of deciding whether they wished to join Austria or the Southern Slavs. Although 70% of them belonged to the Slavonic ethnic group and despite Austria's economic distress at this time, a total of 22,025 (59%) voted to join defeated Austria and 15,279 (41%) in favour of Yugoslavia. Austria was obliged by the Treaty to make provision for its linguistic and religious minorities by agreeing to a number of clauses ensuring equality of rights for all its citizens, including the Croats and Magyars of Burgenland and the Slovenes of Styria, as well as those of Carinthia. Most of these provisions were made and the minorities had little cause for complaint. Even after Austria's annexation by the Third *Reich* in 1938 the Slavs remained unmolested, at least for a while.

When the Germans declared war against Yugoslavia in 1941, however, the fate of the Slovenian population became clear. Among the first moves was the deportation of about 300 families to the interior of Germany, ostensibly to protect them from the Yugloslav communists but in fact to incarcerate them in Nazi camps. These arrests caused bitter indignation among the Slovenes. Many fought as partisans against the German occupation—Carinthia was the only Austrian province where there was armed resistance—and later joined Tito's advancing troops during the closing stages of the War. Parts of Lower Carinthia were then occupied by Yugoslavs and transportation began in the opposite direction, although on a much smaller scale: according to Austrian investigators, 263 persons were arrested in this way, of whom ninety-eight did not return to their homes after the War. At the same time some Slovenes joined right-wing groups, who opposed communism on separatist and often fascist grounds. The accusations of fascism and communism to be heard in Lower Carinthia today date from this period.

After 1945 Yugoslavia hoped to lay claim to the southern parts of Carinthia. But in the State Treaty of 15 May 1955, by which the Republic of Austria was re-established, the Allied Powers decided to restore Austria to its borders of 1938, believing that as it had lost South Tyrol to Italy this part of its territories should be retained. Once again the map of Europe was re-drawn without regard for the linguistic character of the population on either side of the new frontiers.

The Austrian State Treaty included a number of articles specifically intended for the protection of the Slovenian and Croatian minorities' linguistic, administrative, judicial, educational and cultural rights, most of which were immediately implemented by the Government of the reconstituted Austrian Republic after the War. Since 1955 the Slovenes enjoy the right to have their children educated in their mother-tongue at State schools, to speak Slovene in courts of law and for all official purposes within the province of Carinthia. Discrimination against them for linguistic reasons is expressly prohibited.

Despite this legislation, tension between Slovenes and the German-speaking majority has been caused during the last five years because one clause of the Treaty remains only partially carried out. This is the clause (Article 7, Section 3) which recognises Slovene as a second official language for use on place-name signs in Lower Carinthia. There has been an unaccountable delay in the Provincial Government's implementation of this clause, with unfortunate results. The controversy, which came to a head in 1972, escalated to include explosions caused by activist groups on both sides. These acts of violence, such as attacks on Government property by Slovenes and in 1973 the dynamiting by German-speakers of a memorial to anti-fascist partisans, are reported as the work of no more than a handful of people, but the entire population of Lower Carinthia is involved in the controversy.

More significantly, it is clear that behind the debate over bilingual place-name signs (the official signs at the entrance to towns, not road-signs) there lie deep fears and, it is claimed, even secret ambitions. On the German-speaking side the organisation *Kärnter Heimatdienst,* founded in 1957, wants complete assimilation of the Slovenian population as soon as possible. In its newspaper *Ruf der Heimat* for October 1970 it proclaimed, 'Carinthia as a whole is a province belonging to the German language area, to the German cultural sphere and to the history of the German nation!' On the minority's side, a small number—perhaps a few hundred in all, mostly socialists and communists—are calling for a

Slovenian Carinthia, preferably linked with the State of Yugoslavia.

It is evident that the greatest obstacle to the progress of the Slovenes' interests since 1955 has been not so much the Federal Government of Austria as the attitudes of the Carinthians themselves. The first problem arises from the numerical weakness and distribution of the minority. Only in twenty-six parishes do they form more than 20% of the population and over 30% in no more than seven. They are in a majority in only two parishes: Zell and Radsberg (Slovene: *Radise)*. Nevertheless, the Slovenes often invoke the territorial principle in support of their demands. It should not be left, they claim, for the citizen to decide to which linguistic group he belongs but to 'the popular group', a new principle which means in practice the group's leaders and spokesmen. For this reason they reject any kind of official census or investigation into the minority's wishes, presumably because such enquiries would doubtless reveal their numerical weakness, but also because in their view the State's treatment of linguistic minorities should not depend on their numbers alone.

Despite their relatively slow numerical progress in the officially bilingual districts, the Slovenes have recently extended their claims to include not only those valleys where they are most numerous—the Gailtal, the Rosental and the Jauntal—but also such completely German-speaking towns as Klagenfurt, Villach and Hermagor where they do their shopping and have their cultural and recreational facilities. The disagreement over precisely what are the Slovene-speaking districts continues at the present time, thus preventing the implementation of the laws of 4 March 1964 which were intended to re-inforce the legislation of the State Treaty of 1955.

The situation is complicated further by the fact that since the year 1880 the Census in Carinthia has asked a number of different questions about the languages spoken in the province. In 1880, under the Austro-Hungarian Empire, a total of 91,927 claimed Slovene as their mother-tongue *(Muttersprache);* this number had decreased to 85,311 in 1900 and to 74,210 in 1910. At the Census of 1923 the citizen was asked to state his 'thinking language' *(Denksprache)* and in

1934, when 'the language of the cultural circle' *(Kult-urkreissprache)* was requested, 31,703 gave Slovene. In 1951, 42,095 described Slovene as their 'language of everyday use' *(Umgangssprache)*, and in 1961, 25,472 claimed it as 'the language of their homes' *(Haussprache)*.

The apparent decline in the number of Slovene-speakers is contested by the leaders of the minority, not only because the principles of enumeration have varied but also because the Census has not always included among the Slovenian group those Slavs who speak a number of dialects known collectively as Windisch. This idiom is of Slavonic base but thoroughly mixed with a large number of German words. It is considered by philologists to be a bastardized form of Slovene, or of German, usually according to the observer's ethnic sympathies.

The name *Windische,* with *Winden* and *Wenden* (Latin: *Veneti),* was originally used by Germans to denote all the Slavonic peoples, such as the Lusatian Sorbs of present-day East Germany, formerly known as Wends, who settled in their territories. Among the Windisch up to the end of the nineteenth century the word was always synonymous with Slovene. But an artificial pseudo-philological difference was created between the two with the rise of Nazism—the term Windisch was first used in the Census of 1939—which by now has been more or less accepted by the Windisch themselves, with the result that they have stoutly refused on several occasions to be included in the Slavonic ethnic group.

The Slovenian separatists would like to include the Windisch among their numbers but they have found no enthusiasm for their overtures so far. A significant trend is that while the number of inhabitants in the linguistically mixed districts who declared themselves to be Windisch fell between 1961 and 1971 from 11,357 to 3,914, the Slovenian group increased from 13,857 to only 15,615 while the German-speakers increased from 78,783 to 91,183. It is generally agreed that these statistics are to be interpreted as signifying that the speakers of mixed dialects are joining the other two groups, but mainly the German-speakers.

The Windisch also join the German-speakers in their conviction that the demand for a Slovenian Carinthia is unreasonable, in view of the numerical weakness of Slovenes almost everywhere, and that it carries the threat of renewed Yugoslav irredentism. In 1957 the *Bund der Kärnter Windischen* (Union of Carinthian Windisch) was formed by Dr Valentin Einspieler, a member of the Conservative *Ö. V.P.* The German-speakers of Carinthia already had a number of 'patriotic' organisations co-ordinated by the *Kärnter Heimatdienst*. It was this body which claimed responsibility for terrorist attacks in the early 1970s and which forced the repeal of the Bilingual Schools Act when it organised a school strike in 1958.

In 1972 the Austrian Government, in an attempt to show continuing goodwill towards the minority, rushed through a bill to legalise bilingual place-name signs. A total of 205 parishes in Lower Carinthia were provided with signs and instructed to erect them without delay. But members of the *Kärnter Heimatdienst* removed or defaced the signs over-night. When the Government proceeded to set up a Commission on Place Name Signs it was boycotted by the Slovenes because the *Ö. V.P.* had appointed a member of the *Bund der Kärnter Windischen* as its representative. During the unrest which followed there was an exchange of diplomatic notes between Austria and Yugoslavia. More recently still, the German-speakers and the Windisch of these two organisations pressed in 1974 for an independent enquiry to be carried out in order to ascertain the numerical strength of the Slovenian minority. They are confident that such a survey would reveal that Lower Carinthia is not, in fact, a region of solid Slovenian settlement but that its population also includes German-speakers and Windisch. The Austrian Government is known not to favour the proposal for a counting of heads because it would inevitably reveal the precarious situation of the Slovenes and suggest to the more unsympathetic sections of the German-speaking population that the facilities provided for the minority are already over-generous.

Meanwhile, it cannot be denied that the Slovenes are guaranteed full linguistic rights under the State Treaty of 1955 and that, unlike in Italy where such rights have tended to exist only on paper, the Federal Government has done everything in its power to remove all obstacles to their progress as a separate ethnic group. The Slovenes are encouraged, for example, to have their own political and cultural organisations. Most support the *Narodni svet Koröskih Slovencev* (Council of Carinthian Slovenes) which is Catholic and associated with the *Ö.V.P.* The Council was founded in 1949 in opposition to the Marxist *Zveza Slovenskih Organizacij na Koröskem* (Union of Slovenian Organisations in Carinthia). There are also two cultural bodies, the *Krščanska Kulturna Zveza* (Christian Cultural Union) which supports the Council of Carinthian Slovenes, and the *Slovenska Prosvetna Zveza* (Slovenian Cultural Union), a Marxist organisation. All four groups are in close contact with one another, meeting regularly to discuss their joint approaches to the local authorities, and the cultural organisations receive financial support from the Provincial Government.

The cultural groups publish their own weekly newspapers: the religious *Naš Tednik* (Our Weekly Paper) and the socialist *Slovenski Vestnik* (Slovene News). There is a Cultural Centre for Carinthian Slovenes at Klagenfurt and seven other Slovenian periodicals published in Lower Carinthia, of which *Kladivo* and *Mladje* are the principal cultural reviews. All are subsidised by State funds, as are the small number of books which appear every year. Klagenfurt Radio broadcasts forty-five minutes a day in Slovene but there is no television in the language. Instruction at monolingual Slovenian schools is in Slovene; in bilingual schools tuition for the first three years is in German and Slovene, and in upper grades in German only, while Slovene is taught as a compulsory subject. The Slovenian secondary school at Klagenfurt (Slovene: *Celovec)* had 424 pupils in 1970. All parishes in the officially bilingual districts have priests who are able to speak Slovene. The language is used regularly in the law-courts of Eisenkappel *(Zelezna Kapla),* Bleiburg *(Pliberk)* and Ferlach *(Borovlje).*

Despite the provision for the minority in Lower Carinthia, many Slovenes have demonstrated their belief that it is too late in the day to foster their culture in the province, by deliberately choosing paths towards early and complete assimilation. Already the Windisch have gone over to the German-speaking majority and many Slovene-speakers are now following them, especially in the tourist areas where their language seems to have little resistance to German. Only a small proportion are not content with their situation and are pressing for more. There is no widespread movement for unification with Yugoslavia, however, and even the Slovenian activists regard themselves as Austrian citizens. Yugoslavia, as a co-signatory of the Austrian State Treaty, is bound by international law to guarantee the existence of its northern neighbour.

A major step towards normalisation of relations between Austria and Yugoslavia appeared to have been reached on 29 December 1975 when the Austrian Chancellor Bruno Kreisky met Marshall Tito at Brdo in Slovenia for discussion of the minority problem. Following the settlement of the Trieste dispute with Italy in November 1975, the Yugoslavs are now clearly resolved to restore good relations with their northern neighbours. Like the Austrians, they fear that minority and border problems in southern Europe might benefit the Soviet Union. The talks between the two premiers were reported as highly satisfactory, Kreisky announcin g that he intended co-operating closely with the ipposition parties in an attempt to avoid the repetition of past blunders in the Government's treatment of the Carinthian Slovenes.

Until 1970 the goodwill resulting from the 1920 Constitution's recognition of the Slovenes, re-inforced by mutual sympathy with the German-speakers under the Nazi occupation and by the State Treaty of 1955, was the principal feature of the relationship between the minority and the majority. It only remains for Article 7 of the State Treaty to be completely implemented before the Slovenes' position is fully protected. The Austrian Government might also encourage more cultural links with the Slovenes of Yugoslavia.

Even then, it is expected that their numbers will continue to decline. It therefore seems likely, given their small numbers and the wish of many for assimilation, that the Slovenes of Carinthia will suffer the same fate within the next few decades as those of Styria, who total 3,169, or the Hungarian-speakers

of Burgenland who have been reduced to numbers so small
that it is almost impossible to cater for their linguistic and
cultural character.

THE MAGYARS AND CROATS OF BURGENLAND

The province of Burgenland (population: 272,119) is Austria's youngest and easternmost province. Situated between Vienna and the border with Hungary, it was formed after the Treaty of St. Germain, in 1921, from predominantly German-speaking areas of what had previously been Hungarian territory. An agricultural province, it produces wheat, maize, vegetables, fruit and a variety of wines. Eisenstadt (population: 10,059), where the composer Josef Haydn is buried, is the provincial capital.

Of the 19,117 Hungarian-speakers enumerated in Austria by the 1971 Census, 8,413 lived in the province of Vienna and 3,116 in Lower Austria and Styria; there were 5,673 Magyars in Burgenland (2·1%). Their numbers have declined since 1910, when they were 26,225: in 1923 14,931 were left, the rest having emigrated to Hungary after Burgenland became part of Austria two years before, and in 1934 only 10,442, mainly because the estates where most of them found employment had been liquidated. Reduced to 7,669 in 1961, by today the Magyars are confined to enclaves in the districts of Unterwart, Siget-in-der-Wart and Oberpullendorf, near the border with Hungary.

Until 1921 the Hungarian language, or Magyar, was recognised as the only official language in these districts. Although it is still used on some public occasions, German has replaced it for all everyday purposes except in the home. Many officials know Magyar and facilities for translation are provided in law-courts and Government offices, according to the terms of the St. Germain Treaty. The province's education laws of 1937 allow the language to be taught at primary level but only the schools of Unterwart and Siget-in-der-Wart, where there were 420 pupils in 1970, are conducted bilingually. Magyar is taught in the secondary schools as an optional subject. The reformed Church and the Roman Catholic Church use the language regularly. There is no local press in Magyar and all books have to be imported from Hungary. The quarterly journal *Integratio*, published in Vienna, is devoted to the area's Magyar culture which consists for the most part of poetry written in the nineteenth century by poets such as Franz Faludi, the countess Maria Elis, Georg von Gaal and Ludwig von Doczy, and of folk-songs and dances.

The only organisation representing the Magyars of Burgenland is a cultural organisation formed in Oberland in 1968. They have no political party of their own but support the two main Austrian parties. Magyars are to be found in all vocations and they enjoy full civic rights as Austrian citizens. They are recognised by the majority as loyal citizens of the State and, since 1938, there have been no further attempts by the Hungarian Government at revision of the border. Cultural groups are not only subsidised by the Burgenland Government but they are allowed to maintain contact with their counterparts in Hungary. Relations between the Magyars and Croats in the province are entirely friendly.

The Magyars of Burgenland enjoy no specific minority guarantees under the Austrian State Treaty of 1955 but are treated in the same way as the Croats, and the Slovenes of Carinthia, at least as far as education and the law are concerned. With their numbers declining, however, it is not expected that they will continue to maintain themselves as a recognisable ethnic group for longer than a few more decades.

The situation of Burgenland's inhabitants who, at the 1971 Census, claimed Croat as their 'colloquial or everyday language' is only a little more hopeful. In 1951 they numbered 34,339 (12.7%), in 1961 28,242 (10.4%), but ten years later they were reduced to 24,526 (9%). These figures refer, however, not only to speakers of Croat but also to those who speak hybrid forms composed of Croat and German.

The area in which the Croat-speakers live stretches for about eighty miles from Kittsee near the river Danube (German: *Donau)* in the north to Reindersdorf in the south. They are to be found mostly in scattered pockets, like those around Oberpullendorf, in about forty-eight parishes, but are in the majority only in about thirty, or perhaps forty villages. In the north of this area the Croats are mostly industrial workers, whereas in the south they are farmers and small tradesmen.

The ancestors of the Burgenland Croats arrived in the area during the Turkish Wars of the sixteenth century, mostly from various parts of Croatia. About 100,000 are believed to have settled also in the unpopulated parts of western Hungary between the rivers Raab and Danube (Hungarian: *Dunai*), around Bratislava, and in the Leithapart and Marchfeld districts of Lower Austria. Only in Burgenland were they not absorbed by subsequent Germanic immigration. They are sometimes called, pejoratively, *Wasserkroaten* (Water Croats), probably because they are presumed to have come from the shores of the Adriatic, from what is today the Yugoslav Republic of Croatia. During the nineteenth century they resisted all attempts at Magyarisation and from about 1870, under their Habsburg rulers, they developed their own distinctive culture in their own language. They suffered a loss of about 5,000 of their number, however, in the first decade of the present century, following emigration to the United States and the attraction of Vienna, where about 3,528 still live. By today, the form of Croat spoken in Burgenland differs extensively from that spoken by the 3,630,000 Croats (1971) of Croatia. During the visit in 1974 of the President of the Republic of Slovenia, all attempts to communicate with them in modern Croat failed.

The legal position of the Croatian minority is based on Austria's Federal Constitutions of 1920 and 1934, the Treaty of St. Germain, the provincial school laws of 1937 which became Federal Law in 1962, and Article 7 of the State Treaty of 1955 which ensures that, in theory at least, their linguistic rights are guaranteed along with those of three of Austria's other minorities. Austria also ratified in 1959 the European Convention for the Protection of Human Rights and Fundamental Freedoms and, in 1974, the International Covenant on Economic, Social and Cultural Rights.

Under the Federal Law of 18 July 1962 instruction in Croat is to be given in primary schools in those areas where at least 70% of the population use it as their mother-tongue. Where between 30% and 70% have the language, instruction is normally given in both Croat and German, and in other areas parents have to ask the Provincial School Board for special provision to be made. About forty primary schools teach through the medium of Croat and German. Within the Croat-speaking community there is a division of opinion over to what extent the language should be the teaching medium, the *S.P.Ö.* favouring the teaching of Croat as an optional subject only. The bilingual schools have their own inspector and most of the teachers are Croats. A number of text-books in Croat are published by the Austrian Federal Publishing House, and the magazine *Mladost* is published for the pupils. As an optional subject, Croat is taught in seven secondary schools and in four colleges of education; there are also courses for adults and plans to open nursery schools.

Almost all the Burgenland Croats, if they attend places of worship, belong to the Roman Catholic Church. In the diocese of Eisenstadt there are twenty-nine parishes where Croat is the sole language of church affairs and four of these are bilingual, but elsewhere the language of religious instruction and preaching is decided by local circumstances; the bishop of the diocese, Dr Laszlo, is a Croat. The Church publishes hymnals, missals and prayer-books and other devotional works in Croat, as well as *Crickveni Glasnik* and *Nalog,* news bulletins with monthly editions of 5,000 copies each.

The principal organisation in which the Croats defend their culture is *Hrvatsko Kulturno Društvo u Gradišcu* (Croatian Cultural Council of Burgenland). This body dispenses Federal funds for publications in Croat, for libraries and museums, and ensures that the provincial authorities carry out the legislation specifically intended to provide the minority with linguistic and cultural facilities. Among the provisions for which it has pressed, so far unsuccessfully, is an adequate amount of broadcasting in Croat on radio and television, which up to now has been confined to matters of folkloric interest only.

As an official language Croat is used only in a few districts. Place-names are in German almost everywhere, but street-names and local government notices are sometimes in both languages. There are also music and folklore societies, all supported by subsidies from the province, particularly the tambourine bands for which the Croats are famous in Austria, as well as Croatian student and cultural clubs in Vienna. The anthem of the Burgenland Croats is *'Hrvat mi je otac'* (My father is a Croat) which was composed by the priest and poet Mate Meršić Miloradić, with words by Ivan Vukovich. An independent weekly newspaper in Croat, *Hrvatske Novine* (Croatian News), has been published in Eisenstadt since 1910, and there is a smaller weekly newspaper. A few novels and poems have been written since 1945 by Croatian authors living in Burgenland, but there is no significant literature.

Although a Croatian Party won 2,454 votes in 1923, since then the Croats have supported the two main Austrian parties, the *Ö.V.P.* and the *S.P.O.,* about equally. The Croat Lovro Karall, from 1938, was elected as a member of the *Ö.V.P.* and spokesman for the Croatian community, and at present there are two Croats in the Provincial Parliament. There is no discrimination against Croats in the local administration. In the districts where Croat is spoken by the majority the mayor is usually a Croat, and the minority is represented on most public bodies. There is no autonomist Croatian party. Cultural contacts with the Croats of Yugoslavia are unhampered by the Austrian authorities, but usually take the form of musical and folkloric exchanges.

In these respects the Croats of Burgenland exist in a situation which is quite different from that of the Slovenes in Carinthia. Only rarely has there been friction between the minority and the German-speaking majority, and it has always been short-lived. On the other hand, given their already depleted numbers and present rate of decline, and despite full legal protection, it seems unlikely that the Croats of Burgenland, any more than the Magyars, will survive as an ethnic group into the next century.

2 BELGIUM

Constitution: Kingdom

Area: 11,7801 square miles

Population: 9·695 million (1971)

Capital: Brussels

Administrative divisions: 9 provinces

Present Government: The Christian Social Party *(P.S.C./ C.V.P.)* in coalition with the Party for Liberty and Progress *(P.L.P./P.V.V.)* and the Walloon Front; elected 1974

Language of majority: Dutch

THE FLEMINGS AND THE WALLOONS

The Kingdom of Belgium is a State which consists mainly of two linguistic communities. Flanders, the lowland region in the north where Dutch is spoken, comprises the provinces of West Flanders (Dutch: *West-Vlaanderen*), East Flanders *(Oost-Vlaanderen)*, Antwerp *(Antwerpen)*, Limburg and most of Brabant, excluding the capital Brussels. The provinces of Hainaut, Namur, Liège, Luxembourg and part of Brabant make up the French-speaking region of Wallonie in the hilly south. Brussels (French: *Bruxelles*, Dutch: *Brussel)* is a bilingual but predominantly French-speaking city in the province of Brabant where Dutch is the majority language. There are also two much smaller German-speaking areas in the Eastern Cantons of Liège, on the border with West Germany.

It was Julius Caesar who declared that of all the Gauls the Belgians were the bravest, but *Belgae* and *Belgica* were applied in his day to the whole of the population and territory of the Low Countries. Indeed, the name *Belgium* was not used in its modern, political sense until the end of the eighteenth century. Furthermore, since the Flemings speak Dutch and the Walloons French, there is no such thing as a Belgian language, or a Flemish or Walloon language, although the dialects formally spoken in these regions used to be called Flemish and Walloon. There are, however, Flemish and Walloon accents and what strikes the francophone's ear as a Belgian accent *par excellence* is almost always the accent of Brussels.

Although the boundary between Flanders and Wallonie has remained more or less unchanged since the fifth century, conflict between Flemings and Walloons dates from the founding of the Belgian State in 1830. The beginning of outright antagonism on a wide scale was marked by the publication in the *Mercure de France* for April 1897 of an article by the French-speaking poet Albert Mockel who declared, 'Wallonie for the Walloons, Flanders for the Flemings and Brussels for the Belgians!' Several times since then Belgium (French: *Belgique*, Dutch: *België)* has come close to being torn asunder by the antagonisms which exist between the two ethnic groups, most recently in 1968 when the Government collapsed as a direct result of the language question.

The linguistic division of Belgium's territory occurred after the Romans withdrew under threat of invasion by the Goths. The Franks then crossed the Rhine and settled in areas as far south as a line running from Maestricht in the east across what is now Belgium, passing to the south of Brussels and Lille and reaching the North Sea near Boulogne, in present-day France. Unlike the Franks who, led by Clovis, poured into Gaul and were absorbed by superior numbers, becoming French-speaking, those who settled in the sparsely populated areas to the north of the Maestricht—Boulogne line were able to establish their own civilisation and their Low German speech.

Throughout the Middle Ages the French language gained prestige all over northern Europe, becoming in the fifteenth century the language of the Flemish bourgeoisie, the clergy and the administrative classes. Nevertheless, the French and Dutch spoken in what is today Belgium did not become standards around which the opposing political and religious factions of the time rallied. Each new prince of the Burgundian and Habsburg houses took his oath in Dutch and Emperor Charles V spoke the language fluently. French came to be used as the sole language of government in both Flanders and Wallonie under Philip II of Spain (1527-1598). The revolt of the Netherlands against Spanish oppression led to the secession of the mainly Protestant Northern Provinces, formally recognised by the Treaty of Westphalia in 1648 as an independent Holland, while the Southern Provinces, mainly Catholic, were linked first to Spain, then to Austria and, from 1792 to 1815, to France. French culture enjoyed great favour during the eighteenth century, even under Austrian rule, and soon became the predominant language among the educated classes.

In 1815 the United Netherlands were created by the unification of the Northern Provinces with the Southern. Having existed separately for two centuries, divided in their political and religious allegiances, they had little in common. The next fifteen years saw a new interest in the culture of

Holland on the part of the Southern Provinces, and the beginnings of a Flemish Movement. King William of Holland, as ruler of the United Netherlands, encouraged this revival, as a Dutch-speaking Calvinist, by authorising the Dutch language in the schools of Flanders and in the universities opened at his request. But his attempts at nurturing a new pride in the Dutch language among the Flemings had an unexpected effect: they intensified the differences between the Flemish way of life and the Dutch, alienated the French-speaking bourgeoisie and caused the clergy to suspect a Protestant plot to infiltrate the traditionally Catholic areas.

The revolution of 1830 which ended in the establishment of an independent Belgian State was led by the bourgeoisie who were mostly French-speaking and admirers of all things French. Their first aim, after dissolving the political union with Holland, was to cut the linguistic and cultural links too: French thus became the language of the new Kingdom. The rest of the nineteenth century was to be a period of profound humiliation for the Flemings.

Although not in a numerical minority (except in Brussels), the Flemings are to be considered here because, for over a hundred years, they were ruled by Walloons and denied their linguistic rights, and also because the fortunes of the Walloons, who are in fact numerically weaker in Belgium today, are inextricably mixed with those of the Flemings, to such an extent that neither can be considered without reference to the other.

In 1830, when French became the language of the Belgian State, the response of the Dutch-speakers was realistic and moderate. Although at the first Census, held in 1846, they numbered 2,471,248 against 1,827,141 Walloons, the Flemings accepted that the variety of Dutch spoken by the common people was divided into a large number of dialects and was largely unsuited for use in government and administration. Foremost among the philologists and writers who now set about the task of creating a standard form and a favourable climate for the Dutch of Flanders were Hendrick Conscience (1812-83) and Jan Frans Willems (1793-1846). Official recognition of a new unified standard form of Dutch

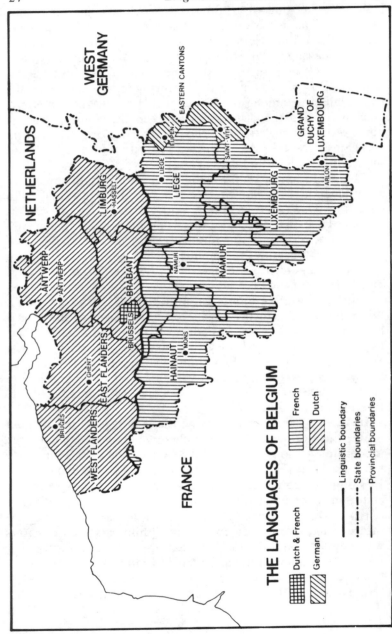

THE LANGUAGES OF BELGIUM

was secured in 1844, and Conscience was later appointed
Dutch tutor to the children of King Leopold I. By 1849 it had
become possible to hold philological conferences with the
Dutch and to publish a dictionary with the aim of stabilising
orthography, grammar and syntax. Despite opposition from
the Flemish writers of the day, who lamented the passing of
colourful dialect forms, over the next generation the language
of Flanders—at least in its written form and as educated
speech—became indistinguishable from the Dutch of
Holland. By today there are no sections of the population
where the language spoken differs in any way, except in local
accent.

Now that the Dutch of Flanders was standardised, the next
step was to secure parity with French. In 1873 the use of
Dutch was made obligatory in all Flemish law-courts and in
public administration five years later. Although the teaching
of Dutch as a second language in all State secondary schools
had been introduced in 1850, a shortage of qualified teachers
caused delay in the implementation of this law until 1874
when Dutch-speakers began to leave the universities in sufficient numbers. In 1883 teaching through the medium of
Dutch became compulsory in all the schools of Flanders and
in 1898 Dutch took its place besides French as an official
language of the region.

All these measures in favour of Dutch were due to the
defeat of the Liberals by the Catholics in the elections of 1884,
a defeat which kept the Catholics in power until after the First
World War. The Catholics owed their triumph during these
years to the massive support of the Flemish provinces which
were bitterly opposed to the French radicalism of the day. It
was thus that political issues and questions of religious belief
became inter-mixed with the language problem. Radicalism
flourished in the heavily industrialised Walloon provinces
while the Flemish provinces remained largely agricultural and
essentially conservative. The great famine of 1847-50, due to
the failure of the potato crop, and the decline of the linen industry, the basis of the Flemish economy, had left Flanders
impoverished and bitter. Flemish society was dominated by
the clergy, the landowners, all French-speaking, and by the
Liberal Party. It was not until the end of the century in the

Linguistic Minorities in Western Europe

textile districts of Ghent that the Socialists came to the fore. There was no Flemish National Party at this time. Such was the dominance of French over all sectors of Flemish life that H. G. Wells in 1900 forecast the doom awaiting numerically small languages like Norwegian and Italian by drawing attention to the situation prevailing in Flanders, where Dutch was being swamped by 'a world language', French.

The tide began to turn in favour of the Flemings with the emergence of a literary movement based on the discovery of the Flemish past by Willems and Conscience. Soon this movement had its own magazine, *Van Nu en Straks* (Of Today and Tomorrow) around which there gathered a group of young writers including Stijn Streuvels (1871-1969), Herman Teirlinck (1869-1967), and Felix Timmermans (1886-1947), much of whose work was regionalist in inspiration and frankly propagandist in intent.

The greatest handicap of the Flemish movement in the early years of the present century was the lack of a university of its own. The struggle to convert the University of Ghent (French: *Gand),* which still taught in French, into a Dutch-speaking institution was long and bitter. Attempts to provide separate French and Dutch sections failed in 1911 because militant Flemings insisted on a complete change to Dutch or nothing. During the First World War the German occupying forces tried to woo the Flemings by opening an exclusively Dutch-speaking University of Ghent but because a number of militants collaborated with the Germans as a result, 'the German University' was closed after the War and trials followed. Much controversy, compromise and negotiation resulted in 1923 in a bilingual arrangement for the University, but this satisfied few. It was only in 1930 that Ghent received its Flemish charter.

During the 'twenties and 'thirties the Flemish cause made rapid progress. Among the factors which contributed to its success were the introduction of the universal franchise and the bitterness of Flemish soldiers who had been commanded by French-speaking officers in the Great War. Many thousands had died, it was claimed, in the confusion caused by orders given in French to monoglot Flemings. But the decisive factor was the emergence of political leaders who had overcome the complexes of their predecessors—young professional men who spoke Dutch for all purposes and for whom French culture had lost its prestige. They were organised in the *Vlaams Nationaal Verband* (Flemish National Party), founded in 1926 under the leadership of Staf de Clercq. By 1933 this party had 60,000 members and seventeen Members of Parliament in 1939. With its slogan *Weg mit Belgie!* (Away with Belgium!) and its para-military wing, the *V.N.V.* was opposed to the structure of the Belgian State in general principle and in all particulars. Although not all its members wanted to substitute a right-wing alternative—and from 1935 it concentrated far more on purely Flemish nationalist demands—the collaboration of some members with the Germans and the obvious military nature of its organisation and behaviour throughout the 'thirties were to attract charges of fascism in the years before the Second World War.

Under mounting pressure from the *V.N.V.*, the Belgian Government passed a number of laws between 1932 and 1938 which achieved virtually full recognition of the Flemings' linguistic demands. Dutch was made the only official language for administration, law and education in Flanders and in the Army separate Dutch-speaking units were formed. The two free Universities of Louvain and Brussels were obliged to offer parallel courses in the two languages so that Belgium now had one French University at Liège, one Dutch University at Ghent, and two bilingual Universities. A law of 1935 allowed the defendant in court-cases to be heard in his mother-tongue in all parts of Belgium, no matter where the alleged offence was committed. In 1937 full cultural autonomy was conceded to Flanders. By the outbreak of the Second World War the Flemish movement was left with few substantial grievances, save that complete separation from Wallonie and the establishment of an independent Flemish State, which many wanted, had not taken place.

The collaboration of a significant number of Flemish nationalists, although by no means the movement as a whole, during the German occupation of Belgium in the Second World War brought the *V.N.V.* into disrepute up to about 1958. Since then a new Nationalist Party, the *Volksunie,* has taken its place. This party had two seats in the Belgian

Parliament in 1958, five in 1961, twelve in 1965, twenty in 1968 and twenty in 1971. Despite its more or less right-wing past, the presence of former *S.S.* men in its ranks and a paramilitary wing, the *Vlaamse Militanten Orde,* the *Volksunie* by today is no longer a neo-fascist organisation. Within its membership there is a broad spectrum of opinion, including a substantial left-wing which welcomes contacts with federalist groups in Wallonie.

Nevertheless, it is the militancy of the Flemish movement's tactics which appears to be most characteristic. Although not confined to the Flemish side, a special feature of the confrontation between them and the Walloons since 1960 has been the violence of the clashes in which Flemish nationalists have been involved. As well as mass demonstrations in the streets, there have been riots in which cars were burned and railway lines destroyed; twenty-four plastic bomb attacks occurred between 1963 and 1966, almost all the work of the Flemish movement. Many of the most serious incidents, at the time of the crisis in the Belgian Congo and the general strike which crippled Belgium, took place during 1961 and 1963 when Flemish demonstrators, estimated at 70,000, clashed with the Walloons at Diksmuide, in West Flanders. It is here, since 1920, that Flemish nationalists have gathered to honour their dead at the Ijzer memorial tower with its huge inscription *A.V.V.—V.V.K.* (All for Flanders, Flanders for Christ) in the form of a cross. The tower was erected in memory of King Albert's troops who fell in the First World War but, owing to these rallies, it has become a symbol of specifically Flemish nationalism. Other incidents have been less violent but no less provocative. In 1962 a hundred Flemish students were expelled by police from a church in Ghent for telling their rosaries, loudly and in Dutch, during a French Mass. In 1966 a Belgian primate was chased from his cathedral by several hundred students singing the Flemish national anthem *De Vlaamse Leeuw* (The Flemish Lion), as part of the campaign against the presence of French-speaking students at the University of Louvain (Dutch: *Leuven).* It should be added, however, that the escalation of violence in 1963, when hand-grenades and bombs exploded in Brussels,

was later revealed to be the work of right-wing extremists un-
connected with the Flemish movement, who, when brought to
trial, admitted that they had committed these outrages in the
hope that the Flemings would be blamed.

French has been the language of the Walloons since the fifth
century and all their dialects are dialects of French. But the
name *Wallonie* dates from documents of 1844. It was invented by J. Grandgagnage to denote the homeland of French-
speaking Belgians, and its use spread as the Dutch name
Vlaanderen came to mean not only the old province of
Western Flanders but the territory under the control of the
growing Flemish Nationalist Movement. Before 1844, Belgian
painters were commonly known as Flemings while Belgian
soldiers were described as Walloons—regardless of the
language they spoke. The name of Charles de Gaulle, for
example, who came from a family with roots in the Dutch-
speaking vicinity of Lille, is derived from the Dutch *de Waele,*
meaning a francophone inhabitant of Belgium. The word
Wallon, however, is older than *Wallonie* by four centuries:
with its root in *Volcae,* the name of a Celtic tribe, its first use
dates from chronicles of the fifteenth century, while in
German *die Walen* was first used in writing to describe a
battle which took place in 1302.

The Walloons are naturally sensitive about the name by
which they choose to be known, having suffered centuries of
misunderstanding on this point from the rest of Europe. It is
remembered, for example, that when Napoleon's troops
entered their territory he ordered the appointment of Dutch-
speaking interpreters so that he could communicate with the
local population, who were francophones to a man.

Inspired by French ideals of centralisation and their ad-
miration for French culture in all its forms, it was the Walloon
generation of 1830 which was foremost in creating the State of
Belgium. During the Revolution of that year the Walloons
offered the crown to Louis-Philippe and, when he declined, to
his son, in an attempt to be incorporated with France. Tension between the Walloons and Flemings grew from
this moment, especially after England imposed Leopold of
Saxe-Coburg, an uncle of Queen Victoria, on the Belgian

throne. For the next fifty years the Walloons hankered after unification with France, to no avail.

One result of this thwarted desire was that Paris continued to exercise a very pervasive influence on Walloon culture, so that Belgium was slow in providing facilities for its artists and writers. With very few exceptions, most Walloon culture is either hardly known in the rest of Europe or it is presumed to be French. Despite a regionalist literary movement in the 1880s, led by Camille Lemonnier and the magazines, *La Jeune Belgique* and Mockel's *La Wallonie,* the emigration of Belgian writers to Paris began with Albert Mockel (1866-1945), Charles Plisnier (1895-1952) and Henri Michaux (born 1899). Walloons who are taken as French writers are represented to day by Françoise Mallet-Joris (born 1939) and Georges Simenon (born in Liège in 1903) who moved first to Paris and later to Switzerland. The same is true of many actors, film-makers, composers and painters, such as René Magritte (1898-1967).

Although Walloon writers, unlike their counterparts in Flanders, never had a major influence on the political development of their region, except in so far as Albert Mockel caused a furore in the *Mercure de France,* the Walloon movement got under way at the same time as many writers began to make their reputations at home and abroad. It was for Mockel's formula for the solution of Belgium's linguistic problems that the Walloon activists strove to win support from about 1912 on. At their congress in that year, led by the powerful personality of the socialist deputy Jules Destrée (1863-1936), the Walloons prepared a programme for the separation of Wallonie from Flanders. Also in 1912, the Walloon flag—a red cockerel bearing the words *Liberté* and *Wallon toujours*—was adopted, and Jules Destrée published his famous 'Letter to the King' which remains a fundamental text for both Walloon and Flemish movements to this day: 'Let me tell you the truth—there aren't any Belgians, only Flemings and Walloons . . .' According to Destrée's analysis, the growth of the Flemish movement had frightened the Belgian Government into granting Dutch-speakers their every demand. Official historians, he claimed, had neglected the

Walloon past and glorified the anti-French exploits of the Flemings, while Walloon art had been taken over by Flemish critics. Public posts were being filled by monoglot Flemings, Wallonie was paying more to the State in taxes than it received as subsidies. The Walloons, Destrée concluded, were beginning to find themselves in the position of a beaten and exploited people.

At its congress of 1945, planned during the War by the clandestine resistance movement *Wallonie Libre,* the Walloon movement gathered to vote on its future. The number of delegates in favour of Belgian unity was seventeen, those for complete independence were 154, for Walloon autonomy within Belgium 391 and for reunion with France 486. The result was a victory for the Walloons as much as for the Flemings: not only was the relative majority in favour of reunion with France but the absolute majority, as both sides noted, opted for the destruction of Belgium. At the second vote, however, there was an almost unanimous decision in favour of autonomy within a Federal State which was seen as a *vote de raison* replacing the previous *vote sentimental.*

Although there was no Walloon autonomist in the Belgian Parliament at the time, the first being elected only in 1965, the effect of the 1945 congress was immediate and substantial. The coal-mining industry of Wallonie was given financial assitance by the Government and commissions were set up to consider the difficult nature of the linguistic boundaries as revealed in the 1947 Census. A succession of Governments—thirteen in all between 1945 and 1960—coped as best they could with mounting discontent from Wallonie and intransigence from Flanders. Many reforms proposed in favour of the Walloons were obstructed by the Flemish majority in Parliament. So, in 1961, the Walloons founded their own organisation, the *Mouvement Populaire Wallon.* When, following the death of its leader André Renard the following year, this organisation failed to progress from being a pressure group to becoming a political party, the movement splintered into a number of socialist groups. These included the *Parti Wallon des Travailleurs* (Walloon Workers' Party), the *Front Commun Wallon* (Walloon Common Front), the

Front Démocratique des Francophones (Democratic French-speakers' Front) and the *Rénovation Wallonne*. The *F.D.F.* which won three seats in Parliament in 1963, was organised to attack what the Walloons considered to be the arbitrary nature of the linguistic boundaries in Brussels which had been decided that year. The representation of these parties in Parliament did not fully reflect the growing discontent in Wallonie where, in a referendum held in 1963, 650,000 signatures in favour of a Federal State were collected. But in the elections of 1968 the Walloon parties achieved an unprecedented unity under the banner of the *Rassemblement Wallon* which was formed to rally Catholics, Socialists, and Liberals against 'the rising tide of Flemish Nationalism', winning six seats.

By 1966 the Walloons were acutely aware that they were less numerous than the Flemings, although this had been the case since 1947, when the first linguistic Census to be held after the War took place. According to the laws of 1932-1938 the enumeration of Belgium's three ethnic groups was to have been held every ten years, in order to determine policies in local government along the main language boundary and in the bilingual conurbation of Brussels. But the Census was delayed until 1947 because, the Flemings argued, social pressures exercised by the French-speaking bourgeoisie were still so great that the small but decisive numbers who were able to speak both languages could not always be expected to give as their 'customary language', as the Census asked, the one which was in fact their mother-tongue. When, at last, the Census was held, it took place amid chaos and acrimony resulting from disputes as to which villages on the boundary between Flanders and Wallonie should be considered bilingual or monolingual. The results, when published, came as a blow not to the Flemings, however, who had feared the worst, but to the Walloons. For the Census revealed that 51·3% of the Belgian population spoke Dutch, 32% French, 15·7% French and Dutch (mainly in Greater Brussels) and 1% German. For the first time since the creation of the Kingdom of Belgium, the Flemings were in a majority and the Walloons in a minority. This trend has continued up to the present. In 1970 the population of Flanders had increased to

5,432,800 (56% of Belgium's population, and Wallonie's to 3,124,900 (32%); a further 62,100 German-speakers were enumerated in the Eastern Cantons of the province of Liège.

In Brussels, on the other hand, the Walloons are in a two-thirds majority among the 1,071,200 inhabitants of the city. No exact, reliable statistics are available on the respective strength of Dutch and French-speakers in Brussels, and those which are available are contested by both sides. It is mainly for this reason that Brussels is the kernel of Belgium's linguistic problem. Officially bilingual, as the street-signs and public notices remind the visitor, the city's life is conducted mainly in French. The increasing internationalisation of the capital in recent years has made the problem even more acute. Over 650 foreign firms now have their European headquarters in Brussels, which also houses the headquarters of the European Economic Community and N.A.T.O. French is well established as the usual language of businessmen, diplomats, Eurocrats and journalists, while Dutch has been relegated to a socially inferior role in a city which was for-merly the principal town of Flanders and is still surrounded by Dutch-speaking areas. The extent of the Brussels conur-bation is, in fact, the most sensitive point of the dispute. The Flemings refuse to surrender further districts to a bilingual régime while the city is constantly spreading as more houses are built in the suburbs, so that more and more French-speakers are moving into the more attractive Dutch-speaking areas on the city's limits. The problem has crystallised around the six peripheral boroughs of Drogenbos, Kraainem, Linkebeek, Rhode-Saint-Génèsius, Wemmel and Wezem-beek-Oppem. The Walloon minorities living here have tried to have their suburbs incorporated in the Greater Brussels area, against opposition by Flemings who insist that they must adjust to the legally defined status of these districts, as Flemings usually do in Wallonie. The Flemings argue that in any legal system there are always limitations on freedom and that when the interests of the community clash with those of the individual it is the general interest which must prevail.

The reasons for the Walloons' decline, except in Brussels, are economic. Their leaders usually correlate increased in-dustrialisation in Flanders with economic crisis in Wallonie, especially in the coal mining and steel industries. They claim that their industrial apparatus is outmoded, their system of communications inadequate and that the bureaucrats of Brussels favour the Flemings by establishing new technological projects and attracting foreign investment in the Campine area of Flanders. They also argue that, whereas most Flemings learn French as their second language, it is a nonsense to be compelled to teach Dutch as a second language in their schools in preference to the languages of modern technology such as German, English and Russian. This reluctance to learn Dutch has unfavourable repercussions for the Walloons. Since executive positions in official and private organisations are being granted increasingly to bilingual citizens, a larger number of candidates are chosen from the Dutch-language community.

The Language Question in Belgium, often called 'the community problem' because it is ideological as well as linguistic, is influenced by pressure groups representing the interests of Flanders and Wallonie but responsibility for political decisions rests, of course, with Parliament.

The three main traditional parties are those of the Christian Social Democrats, the Socialists and the Liberals. The first is divided into the *Christelijke Volkspartij (C.V.P.)* for Flemings and the *Parti Social-Chrétien (P.S.C.)* for Walloons; until recently these two factions formed a single party but are now virtually autonomous, their political action co-ordinated in a national consultative committee. The Socialist Party, the *Parti Socialiste Belge / Belgische Socialistische Partij,* still has a unitary structure and is led by two presidents, one Fleming and one Walloon. The Party of Liberty and Progress, the *Parti pour la Liberté et le Progrès (P.L.P.) / Partij voor Vrijheid en Voorutigang (P.V.V.),* the former Liberal Party, has a national chairman but is organised in two autonomous sections. In 1970 a number of Brussels representatives of the *P.L.P.* re-grouped to form the *Parti Libéral Democratique et Pluraliste (P.L.D.P.),* now called for short the *Parti Libéral.* The Communist Party, organised on a federal basis with a single national chairman, also has members in the Lower and Upper House. Of the parties whose activities are confined to one of the two main linguistic communities, the *Volksunie* still represents the Flemish Nationalists while the Wallons have the *cartel* of the *Front Démocratique des Bruxellois Francophones (F.D.F.)* in Brussels and the *Rassemblement Wallon (R.W.)* in Wallonie, which were joined in 1968 by the *Front Wallon (F.W.)* and the *Parti Wallon des Travailleurs* (Walloon Workers' Party).

In 1961 the Lefèvre-Spaak Government, a coalition of the Catholic Christian Socialist Party *(P.S.C.)* and the Belgian Socialist Party *(P.S.B.)* which was to last until 2 May 1965, decided to attempt a settlement of Belgium's language question. The language Census was abolished, mainly to placate the Flemish movement, and the language boundary was to be amended by transferring for administrative purposes the largely French-speaking district of Mouscron-Comines, about 50,000 people in all, some of them Flemings, from West Flanders to Hainaut and the six communities of the largely Dutch-speaking Fourons (Dutch: *Voer)* region from Liège to Limburg. The first was accomplished with only minor difficulties but the second, involving about 5,000 people and the transference of their districts from a Walloon province to a Flemish, was stoutly resisted by the Walloons. At the same time, facilities for the recognition of minorities living on either side of the language boundary, and in Brussels for francophone immigrants, were introduced against stiff opposition from the Flemings.

In 1962 a new law was passed which declared Brussels to be bilingual, insisted that all schools in the clearly defined Flemish areas must teach in Dutch and that, in Brussels, the decision as to whether a child attended a French or Dutch school would henceforth depend on the language spoken by the father. In linguistically mixed marriages, which amount to about 30% of all marriages in Belgium, French is usually spoken at home by the children, especially in Brussels where there is also a tendency for Flemings to learn French in order 'to pass' as Walloons.

The following year another attempt was made to adjust the frontiers of the nine provinces, giving the Walloons a further 86,439 inhabitants, the Flemings 20,377 and Brussels 2,886.

It was this arrangement, by which predominantly Dutch-speaking communes were to be administered in Dutch, while any French-speaking minority could demand to have its documents presented in French, which created a furore of such bitterness that Lefèvre threatened to resign, being persuaded against doing so only by the personal intervention of King Baudouin. A compromise was found when it was agreed to abolish schools which gave parallel classes in French and Dutch and to replace them with schools where all staff and children would speak the same language. A dual Ministry of Education was created with each French-speaking official and employee matched by his Dutch-speaking counterpart.

This attempt at solving the language question by means of providing two of almost everything for the rival communities has become a characteristic feature of life in Belgium, so that the term 'the two cultures' has a somewhat different meaning here than elsewhere. For example, although viewers in some provinces have a choice of nine different television channels, including two each from Germany, France and the Netherlands, and one from Luxembourg, there are two run by the Belgian State itself: *Radio Télévision Belge / Belgische Radio Televisie* were both founded in 1953. There is no commercial television, mainly because with such an *embarras de richesses* it is feared that the large number of newspapers, which are taken rather more seriously, might lose advertising revenue. Radio transmissions are also split into two language networks. There is, however, little evidence to suggest that broadcasting has much effect on the traditional attitudes of either community towards the other.

The main source of information and comment for most Belgians is the press. It has always been free, lively and one of the main bulwarks of democracy, especially during the World Wars when many clandestine newspapers flourished. In 1970 there were forty-three daily newspapers in all, twenty-seven in French, fifteen in Dutch and one in German, of which twenty-three were Catholic or Christian Democrat, nine Liberal, seven Socialist and four non-party. The total circulation of these dailies was 2,815,000 copies: 1,600,000 for French-language newspapers and 1,200,000 for Dutch. There are no 'national papers' in Belgium for very few have any significant sales outside their own language community. The only exception in this respect is the pro-French, pro-Catholic daily *La Libre Belgique,* which sells 26·5% of its 180,000 copies in Brussels, 43·5% in Wallonie and 30% in Flanders. The circulations of *Le Soir* and *Het Laatste News,* each serving its own region, are much higher. There are, in addition, twenty-one weekly newspapers and magazines in French and twenty-two in Dutch.

Following the reforms of 1963, the Belgian Government took further steps to tackle the language question by revising the Constitution and the number of seats in Parliament according to the increase in population. Up to now, the number of seats had been regularly increased to give one for every 40,000 voters, the last increase being in 1947 when the number was raised to 212. The increase in the population by about 750,000 between 1947 and 1964 necessitated new amendments but, in view of the greatly increased population of Flanders, it was expected that the new seats would be filled by Flemish members, thus increasing their majority over the Walloons. After the Walloons had received assurances that the Constitution could be amended in such a way as to protect them in this respect, a conference of representatives of the *P.S.C.* and the *P.S.B.* (the Liberal opposition walked out before it was over) agreed on three amendments. First, a new article would be inserted, listing the linguistic regions by name, thus making a constitutional recognition of the language boundary; second, the language laws of 1961 would also be written into the Constitution; third, Article 38 would establish procedures for investigating any subject likely to affect relations between the two communities.

All these various conciliatory measures, well-meaning and in some respects ingenious, satisfied neither side and incensed the million citizens of Brussels, especially the francophone majority. The reaction of Brussels confirmed the Flemish and Walloon movements in their conviction that the capital had for too long had too large a say in the affairs of the eight million citizens in the rest of the State. Both sides now pressed for complete autonomy, the Walloons mainly on political and economic grounds, the Flemings on linguistic, administrative, judicial and cultural grounds. A temporary stale-mate was broken when the quarrel was resumed in 1965 over the language of higher education. The Flemings, in particular, were impatient at the Government's attempts to freeze the language question and at the bishops' reluctance to declare unequivocally that the University of Louvain must be Flemish. Student riots occurred in the town in 1965 and again in March 1966 at the same time as up to 45,000 Flemings marched through the streets of Antwerp. Louvain had taught in French for over three hundred years and had become bilingual only when the University of Ghent had received its Flemish charter. The bishops now decided that from the 1966-7 session the Flemish departments of Louvain University should become autonomous. They failed, however, to spell out precisely how this autonomy was to be achieved or how the Flemish faculties were to be administered.

It was the unresolved problem of Louvain University which led to the *débâcle* of 1968, ending in the fall of Prime Minister Paul Vanden Boeynants and his Government—the first time in Belgium's history that a Government had been brought down by the language question. As the French faculties at Louvain were now seriously over-crowded, they announced their intention of moving into the area between Louvain and Brussels. But Flemish academic staff and students protested as one man because, in their view, the French-speaking majority of about 800 teachers and 10,500 students who had dominated the University up to then, were now planning to extend the French language's territory over a good part of Flemish Brabant. When the Flemings called for the exodus of the French faculties into Wallonie, bitter fighting broke out in the streets in January 1968 and demonstrations took place all over Flanders. Vanden Boeynants refused to announce that the French faculties would be moved without delay to Walloon territory, only ten miles away, on the grounds that the revered traditions of one of the most distinguished of Europe's universities would be destroyed. At this declaration eight members of the *P.S.C.*, Flemings all, resigned from the Cabinet. Their spokesman, speaking in impeccable French, summed up their view at a press conference: 'We will not have peace in this country as long as the French-speaking community refuses to adapt itself to the reality of Belgium as it is today, as long as French-speaking citizens demand language facilities whenever they settle in Flanders, and as long as bilingualism continues to mean that Flemings have to speak French'. All attempts to find a solution to this problem failed and the King dissolved Parliament on 2 March 1968.

At the General Election of March 1968 it was widely agreed that the poll was, in reality, a referendum on whether Belgium should remain a State. In the words of Frans van der Elst, a leader of the *Volksunie*, 'The basic issues in this country are now finally brought into the open. The very structure of Belgium is at stake and no lasting solution will be possible on the basis on the unitary State we have had so far'. The results of the election were as follows: the *P.S.C.* (Christian Socialist) retained sixty-nine seats, (a loss of eight), the *P.S.B./B.S.P.* (Socialists) fifty-nine seats (a loss of five), the *P.L.P./P.V.V.* (Liberals) forty-seven seats (a loss of one). The Flemish Nationalist Party, the *Volksunie,* and the Walloon Federalists, the *Rassemblement Wallon* and the *Front Démocratique des Francophones,* almost doubled their strength by taking twenty and twelve seats respectively, but the *Front Wallon* and the *Parti Wallon des Travailleurs* both lost their single seats. The Communist Party kept its five seats and the *Union de la Gauche Socialiste* won seven. In the Upper House, the Senate, the Christian Socialists won sixty-four seats, the Socialists fifty-three, the Liberals thirty-seven, the *Volksunie* fourteen, the *F.D.F* and the *Rassemblement Wallon* four each and the Communists two. The Prime Minister, who had scored a huge triumph in Brussels, was asked to form the next Government, but he first had to restore unity between the Flemish and Walloon wings of his party and in this he failed. Before any kind of federalism could be introduced, a two-thirds majority was essential. However, the Dutch and French-speaking wings of the *P.S.C.* proved to be as suspicious of one another as the Flemish nationalists and the Walloon federalists were. Vanden Boeynants failed to form his Government.

Over a month later, on 17 June 1968, the former Catholic leader, Gaston Eyskens announced that he was able to form a coalition between the *P.S.C.,* the *C.V.P.* and the Belgian

Socialist Party. His cabinet was painstakingly divided between fourteen Flemish and fourteen Walloon ministers with
Eyskens himself, a moderate Fleming, as a go-between. To
satisfy pressure for more autonomy for both regions the
Eyskens-Merlot Government immediately set up separate
Ministries, each with two Ministers for Education, Culture
and Regional Development, as well as two new Ministries for
relations between the two communities. Provision was also
made for the transfer of the French faculties of Louvain to
Ottignies in the Walloon part of Brabant and in 1969-70 it
was decided to establish a complete Dutch-language University at Brussels alongside the existing French-language University. In 1971 laws for the establishment of Cultural Councils
for Flanders and Wallonie were passed. What the Government did not have was the two-thirds majority needed for implementing reforms of the Constitution which would have
allowed it to re-organise Belgium on federal lines. Nevertheless, the collapse of Vanden Boeynants' Government and
the initiative of Eyskens made it quite clear that the
traditional concept of a highly centralised, unitary State
governed from Brussels would in due course be replaced by a
form of federalism acceptable to both Flemings and
Walloons.

The essential characteristic of the new Constitution passed
in July 1971 was that it transformed the unitary Belgian State
into a community State. The principal provisions among its
many clauses were parity between the communities in the
composition of the Government, continuous adjustment of
seats according to population, protection of ideological
minorities, the establishment of Cultural Councils for Flanders, Wallonie and the German-speaking Eastern Cantons, of
regional institutions elected to look after such matters as
economic development, housing, health, tourism and employment, together with recognition of Brussels as a special
region in its own right in these respects.

However, the work of revising the Constitution came to a
stop after the summer recess of 1971 following severe tensions
between coalition parties, caused largely by the unfinished
business in the dispute over Fourons/Voer, the conclusion of
a cultural pact between all parties represented in Parliament

and the delimitation of the economic regions. It was therefore decided to precipitate the general elections from May 1972 to 7 November 1971, the results of which were as follows: the Christian Socialists lost two seats (sixty-seven), the Socialists gained two (sixty-one), the Liberals lost thirteen (thirty-four), the Walloon Federalists gained twelve (twenty-four), the *Volksunie* gained one (twenty-one) and the Communists retained their five. Of the 212 members in Parliament, the Flemings now had 117, a loss of two, and the Walloons ninety-five, a gain of two. In the Senate the Christian Socialists had sixty-one seats, the Socialists forty-nine, the Liberals twenty-nine, the Walloon Federalists, and the *Volksunie* nineteen each and the Communists one, the Flemings having a total of ninety-six against eighty-two Walloons. It was clear from these results that both regional parties had made substantial gains, particularly the Walloons in Brussels at the expense of the Liberals, so that the major parties were denied the consolidated joint majority which would have enabled them to implement regionalisation. Crisis followed after the local elections in Brussels in which a new group, the *Rassemblement Bruxellois,* composed of the French-speaking Liberals and the *F.D.F.,* won a sweeping victory, thus preventing all consultation between the other parties. Eyskens gave up on 22 December 1971, to be replaced by Edmond Leburton, chairman of the Socialist Party.

A new Government, a coalition of the *P.S.C./C.V.P.* and the *P.S.B.* led by Eyskens and Cools, took the constitutional oath on 21 January 1972. Little progress was made, however. Still lacking the necessary majority, the Ministers (nine for each group) had to take account of fundamental divergences between Flemish, Walloon and Brussels representatives, particularly of the 'maximalists' and the 'minimalists'. The regional parties and the Communists take an unequivocal stand in pressing for federalism but differ in their view of how it is to be implemented. The *C.V.P.* is far more inclined to regionalisation than its Walloon partner, the *P.S.C.,* while the inclination towards federalism among Walloon Socialists is opposed by the unitary views of their Flemish colleagues. The Walloon Liberals favour federalism more than the Flemish *P.V.V.* does although the latter would accept a measure of regionalisation. And in all these parties the Brussels politicians favour a unitary State. The Eyskens-Cools Government was paralysed and collapsed in November 1972.

The next Government, formed on 26 January 1973, was a coalition between Edmond Leburton's Socialists, Leo Tindemann's Christian Socialists and Willy de Clercq's Liberals. The new team numbered no less than twenty-two ministers and fourteen Secretaries of State, equally divided among Flemings and Walloons. For the first time there were Ministers for Flemish, Walloon and Brussels affairs. At last empowered by its majority to start implementing regionalisation, the Government also dealt with the problems of cultural autonomy, the Fourons/Voer area, the Eastern Cantons and linguistic legislation in Brussels in a series of laws passed during 1973. Despite this progress, the new bodies thus constituted could not agree and fresh disputes over detail broke out once again. During the months which followed, however, the language problem was over-shadowed by other difficulties which included the debate on reducing military service, the abortion controversy, the scandal in the *R.T.T.* (State Telegraphs and Telephones), the rate of inflation and the oil crisis of 1973. It was the failure of negotiations with the Government of Iran over oil supplies, in January 1974, that caused the Socialist Ministers and Secretaries of State to resign. The King dissolved Parliament on 29 January 1974.

At the last general election, held on 10 March 1974, the Christian Socialists *(P.S.C./C.V.P.)* won a majority under Prime Minister Leo Tindemann with seventy-two seats in Parliament and sixty-six in the Senate. The Socialists *(P.S.B.)* won fifty-nine seats (fifty in Senate) and the Liberals *(P.L.P.)* thirty-three seats (thirty in Senate). The *Volksunie* increased to twenty-two (sixteen in Senate) and the *Front des Francophones* in alliance with the *Rassemblement Wallon* won twenty-two (eighteen in Senate). The Communists lost one seat, holding four (one in Senate). In the cabinet at the present time are Willy de Clercq *(P.V.V.)* as Finance Minister, and Paul Vanden Boeynants *(P.S.C.)* as Minister for National Defence and Brussels Affairs. There are eighteen other Ministers and six Secretaries of State, equally divided between Flemings and Wallons. The Government is a coalition between the Christian Socialist Party, the Liberals and the *Rassemblement Wallon.*

It is impossible to reach any conclusion in this brief description of Belgium's linguistic problems, especially as the present situation is not likely to remain unchanged for long. Up to 1971 it was clear that if the survival of the State was not to be seriously threatened Belgium was obliged to alter the structure of its Government, along federal lines. Despite strife and continuous friction between the two communities, the first steps towards such a solution have been taken. Since 1971 there has been widespread agreement that the need is for greater regionalisation, but there is still no concensus of opinion as to the required degree of reform. The institutions created four years ago are only now beginning to function, and their short-comings to become clear. Whether or not the Belgian State can rely on what has already been done, or whether it will evolve further towards a truly federal solution, only time will tell. What is clear is that Belgium's problem, as defined by the Eyskens-Merlot Government of 1968, remains unsolved: 'We believe that the maintenance of a Belgian nation founded on the union of communities is our only chance of achieving progress for all in a strong Europe. We are convinced that the vast majority of the people in this country think likewise. But this Belgian nation must at the same time be more regional and more European in character. More regional, since economic and cultural regionalism, far from heralding a return to antiquated particularism or hindering progress towards the creation of larger entities, actually places economic and social development at the service of man'.

THE GERMANS OF THE EASTERN CANTONS

The existence of a German-speaking minority in the modern State of Belgium is primarily attributable to the Treaty of Versailles by which the cantons of Eupen and Malmédy, Prussian since 1815, were awarded to Belgium. In this area, which is part of the Walloon province of Liège, there live 62,100 inhabitants (1970) whose mother-tongue is German. There is another German-speaking community in the province of Luxembourg, around the town of Arlon (German: *Arel*), which has been part of Belgium ever since the State was founded in 1830. The total number of inhabitants in these two areas of the Ardennes who speak German or its dialects is approximately 97,000, about 1% of Belgium's population.

Although in political terms the German-speaking area of Belgium is a fairly recent creation, the boundary between the French and German languages in Liège (German: *Lüttich*), fixed in Roman times, has remained intact with only a few French intrusions up to the present. The parish of Herzig, near Arlon, has for centuries been the westernmost of all German-speaking districts. The Duchies of Limburg and Luxembourg joined the Duchy of Burgundy in the fifteenth century and were subsequently ruled by the Habsburgs. During the Napoleonic era they belonged for a while to France but the Congress of Vienna in 1814 partitioned the areas by giving the eastern half of Limburg, including the towns of Eupen, Malmédy and Saint Vith which until then had belonged to the Duchy of Luxembourg, to the Prussian province of the Rhine; the western half, including Arlon, went to the United Kingdom of the Netherlands. The revolution of 1830, by which Belgium was created, re-united these areas but the London Conference of 1839 obliged the new Kingdom to relinquish the northern part of the Duchy of Limburg, and the greater part of Luxembourg which then became a Grand Duchy, while the western parts remained as a province of Belgium. For these historical reasons the twenty-two districts around Arlon in the south, where German is spoken today, became known as German Old Belgium, while the thirty-four districts in the north-east around the town of Eupen, Malmédy and Saint Vith (German: *Sankt Vith*), re-united with Belgium only in 1919, were to be known as German New Belgium. The effect of these territorial adjustments was that, of the 250,000 German-speakers in both areas during the middle of the nineteenth century, there now remained in Belgium only about one-third.

The districts known as German Old Belgium soon grew accustomed to their status as part of the new State, without losing their linguistic identity. In 1898 they organised a petition with nearly 10,000 signatures asking for the teaching of German in their schools, without success but also without rancour. When, on the other hand, they were occupied by Germany during the First World War, it was much against their will. By then the German language had been deliberately neglected and assimilation into the French-speaking majority had begun to take place. The German-speakers of New Belgium, however, maintained their language and their sense of German nationality to a much greater extent. When Eupen was invaded by the Germans on 10 May 1940 a majority of its citizens, relieved from domination by the Walloons, welcomed the opportunity of belonging once more to the *Reich*, having taken the view that they had been annexed in 1919 without their approval. The German language had been banned in these areas in 1918 and there had been growing tension between the German-speakers and the Walloon administration. It is not denied that many German-speakers took the side of Hitler in the Second World War. Of 8,700 from Eupen and Malmédy who joined the *Wehrmacht* between 1940 and 1944, over 2,000 were killed. After the German defeat there was much recrimination and many acts of revenge against alleged collaborators by the Walloon majority.

It was mainly owing to a determined nucleus of democrats among German-speaking Belgians, including Hoen the Regional Commissioner and Zimmermann the Mayor of Eupen, that despite the Nazi years the German-speaking communities were able to begin the slow process of rehabilitation within the Belgian State. At first, progress was slow and a fear of revenge persisted among them. The encouragement of King Baudouin, who asked his Ministers to handle the minority's affairs with utmost sympathy, was decisive in this respect. As early as March 1945 the daily newspaper *Grenz Echo* was allowed to resume publication, although its editor Henri Michel was still in Oranienburg concentration camp at the time. Others also played important parts. The Belgian Foreign Minister Paul-Henri Spaak and the Minister of the Interior Pierre Vermeylen refused, despite recommendations by the Conference of Ambassadors held in Paris in 1949, to annexe further parts of German territory because it would have increased the number of German-speakers inside Belgium. The final border demarcation of 1955 and the Belgo-German Agreement on the Clarification of the Consequences of the War put an end to all dispute between the two States over the German-speaking cantons of Belgium.

After the War prospects for the re-emergence of a German-speaking culture in the Eastern Cantons were poor. In the Arlon area the German language was denied recognition of any kind and there were no demands for it. The traditional Walloon belief in the superior virtues of French remained uncontested by the German-speakers, now numerically much weaker than previously. In the north, however, German and its dialects was still the everyday language of over half of the population of Eupen, Malmédy and Saint Vith. This fact was taken into account by Article 3 of the language law of 30 July 1963 which introduced bilingualism in education, law and administration in the northern areas. But a serious shortage of qualified German-speaking teachers and officials has hampered the use of the language in all spheres. Only the Catholic Church is thoroughly bilingual in practice. Of the German-language newspapers prohibited in 1945, only the *Grenz Echo* has survived, mainly because the authorities approved of its pro-Belgian editorial views. This newspaper has lost many readers in recent years, however, while the *Aachen Volkszeitung*, published in Germany, is more and more read for its daily supplement devoted to the Eastern Cantons of Belgium. Similarly, although the Belgian State radio broadcasts three hours daily 'for our German-speaking compatriots', transmitters situated in Germany are preferred in Eupen, Malmédy and Saint Vith. Cinemas in these towns show German films almost exclusively.

For reasons like these the German-speakers of Eupen, Malmédy and Saint Vith have been suspected since about 1969 of planning moves for reunification with Germany. They have no representatives of their linguistic group in the Brussels Parliament, never having succeeded in forming their own political party. But there is growing discontent among them at the slow rate of economic growth in Wallonie, as part of which they are governed, and at the continuing hostility towards them shown by the French-speakers. If they are to remain within the Belgian State they would prefer to be granted autonomous status or be administered from Flanders, having made common cause with the Flemings in the past against the Walloons.

There have been several initiatives in this direction during the last few years. The most important institution for the promotion of their interests is the *Kulturel Rat für die Ostkantone* (Cultural Council for the Eastern Cantons). This body, first officially suggested by Prime Minister Gaston Eyskens in an interview with the *Grenz Echo* in 1969, was established by a law of 10 July 1973. Its constitution was drafted by Willy Schyns, the first member of the Belgian Government to take his oath of allegiance to the King in German. A member of the Christian Socialist Party, Schyns is also Mayor of the village of Kelinis near Aachen and, since 1973, the Secretary of State for the Eastern Cantons. The twenty-five member Council does not have the same powers as its Flemish and Walloon counterparts, both of which are composed of parliamentarians and exercise legal powers within the now constitutionally guaranteed cultural sovereignty of Belgium's two main linguistic areas. Its functions are to dispense the grants allocated by the Government in Brussels for German cultural affairs in the Eastern Cantons and to play a consultative role in such matters as education and broadcasting.

Among the Council's first decisions was to abandon the use of the terms 'German Belgians' and 'German Belgium' and to replace them with 'German-speaking Belgians' and 'German-speaking areas' in the belief that the old terms were a liability and outmoded. Then, at a special sitting on 9 July 1974 in Eupen, which was attended by Prime Minister Leo Tindemann and Minister of the Interior Joseph Michel, the

Council gave an opportunity for all political groups in the area to express opinions on the region's future. Many members spoke in favour of recognising German as the only official language in education and administration. Others suggested the creation of an 'autonomous eastern zone' where bilingualism would be thoroughly implemented. There are signs that this new regionalist feeling may find acceptance in Brussels. In the long debate in both Houses of the Belgian Parliament on the establishment of Regional Parliaments for Wallonie, Flanders and Brussels which was concluded on 20 July 1974 there were several references to the German-speaking areas. Assurances on representation of the Eastern Cantons in Parliament, the Walloon Regional Council and the Liège Provincial Council were given by Leo Tindemann and the Ministers for State Reform, François Perrin and Robert Vandekerchkove.

It is obviously too early to say whether, after years of acquiescence on account of their sympathies during the Second World War, the German-speakers of the Eastern Cantons may now be beginning to re-assert their corporate identity. But it is clear that, although the Belgian State is more pre-occupied with the divisions caused by the Flemings and Walloons, there is a real desire to include the German-speakers in the reform of the Constitution which now seems inevitable.

3   BRITAIN

Constitution: Monarchy

Area: 94,214 square miles

Population: 55.52 million (1971)

Administrative divisions: England 45 counties, Scotland 9 regions, Wales 8 counties, Northern Ireland 6 counties.

Capital: London

Present Government: The Labour Party (elected 1974)

Language of majority: English

THE GAELS OF SCOTLAND

According to the 1971 Census, there were 88,892 persons living in Scotland who were able to speak the Gaelic language in that year. Of these 477 were enumerated as speaking Gaelic only, but because the figures for monoglot Gaelic-speakers are considered to be of doubtful validity when compared with Census returns for previous decades, the present account will be based on the figure of 88,415 (1.8% of Scotland's population of 5,228,965) who were enumerated in 1971 as being able to speak both Gaelic and English.

The Scottish Gaels live, for the most part, in the north-west Highlands and the islands off Scotland's western coast. The areas of most widespread Gaelic speech are the Outer Hebrides (the Islands of Lewis and Harris, North and South Uist, Benbecula and Barra), the Inner Hebrides (the Islands of Skye, Tiree, Coll, Mull and Islay), together with small districts on the western coast (Ardnamurchan, Wester Ross and West Sutherland); there are also many pockets of Gaelic over the whole of north-western Scotland including in-digenous Gaelic-speaking communities in Perthshire (Gaelic: *Peairt*), central and eastern Invernessshire *(Inbhirnis)*, cen-tral and eastern Sutherland *(Cataibh)*, Ross and Cromarty *(Ros is Cromba)*, Argyll *(Earra-Ghaidheal)*, Nairn *(Narunn)*, and Bute *(Boid)*. The greatest numbers of Gaelic-speakers are to be found, however, in the counties of Ross and Cromar-ty (which includes the Island of Lewis) where 19,510 (35·1%) were enumerated in 1971, and Inverness (including Skye) with 18,740 (22%). Among colonies of Gaels in the Lowlands of Scotland are 12,860 (1·5%) living in Glasgow *(Baile Mór Ghlaschu)*, and a further 25,185 (0·7%) scattered throughout the country. Of the counties with small Gaelic-speaking populations, Argyll has 7,825 (13·7%), Perth 2,060 (1·7%), Sutherland 1,815 (14·5%), Bute 245 (1·9%) and Nairn 175 (2.·2%). This summary shows that there was a slight decrease from 1961 in Inverness, Ross and Cromarty, Argyll and Sutherland with slight increases in Perth, Nairn, Bute and the city of Glasgow. Edinburgh, the capital of Scotland, had 3,340 (0·8%) Gaelic-speakers in 1971, Aber-deen 1,240 (0·7%) and Dundee 830 (0·5%).

There are also speakers of Scottish Gaelic in Canada,

mostly in Cape Breton, Prince Edward Island and Nova Scotia. In 1890, in a speech to the Canadian House of Commons on his motion to make Gaelic an official language, T. R. McInnes claimed that three-quarters of Cape Breton's population of 100,000 spoke Gaelic. By 1940 this number had dropped to about 35,000 and at the 1961 Census only 3,352 people reported Gaelic as their mother-tongue. In 1971 a visiting linguist from Scotland calculated that there were about 1,500 Gaelic-speakers in Cape Breton and it is estimated that, with perhaps 2,500 in Nova Scotia, the total number of Gaelic-speakers in Canada is around 5,000. It was in Cape Breton that the first all-Gaelic newspaper *Mac Talla* (Echo) was published, from 1892 to 1904; the language is still taught at some schools there. No figures for Gaelic-speakers resident in Britain outside Scotland are available.

Despite the slight upward trend of the figures for Gaelic-speakers revealed by the 1971 Census, the story of the language during the present century has been one of gradual decline. In 1891 there were 210,677 bilingual Gaels (5·2%) in Scotland; 202,700 (4·5%) in 1901; 183,998 (3·9%) in 1911; 148,950 (3·1%) in 1921; 129,419 (2·7%) in 1931; 93,269 (1·8%) in 1951; and 80,004 (1·6%) in 1961. There has been an even more rapid decrease in the number of monoglot Gaelic-speakers, of whom 43,738 were estimated in 1891. The bastions of Gaelic in Scotland remain the outer islands making up the area known as the Western Isles, where over 80% of the population are able to speak the language, while on the Islands of Islay, Skye, Tiree and Coll over 50% are Gaelic-speaking and about 30% on the western coast north of Skye, the Island of Mull and the Ardnamurchan peninsula.

The Gaels of Scotland speak a language, called by them *Gàidhlig,* which has also been known at various times in their history as Irish, Erse, Hielans and Gaelic.* Separated from Ireland by the Rhinns of Galway and the Mull of Kintyre (also known as the North Channel), only fourteen miles across at their narrowest points, Scotland was first settled by Gaels from across the water as early as the fourth century A.D. This

---

*The present account of the Scottish Gaels draws heavily on the book by Kenneth MacKinnon, *The Lion's Tongue* (Inbhirnis, 1974), one of the livelier and more realistic accounts of Gaelic to be published in recent years.

Gaelic infiltration into Scotland probably via what is today Galloway, and subsequent settlement, was re-inforced over the next hundred years with the establishment of the Kingdom of Dalriada. By the middle of the sixth century the monastery at Iona, the principal Gaelic foundation in Dalriada, had become a major centre of Christianity and learning from which Columba *(Colum Cille)* was able to work, spreading the influence of Irish/Gaelic civilisation not only throughout the new kingdom, but in the more easterly and northerly lands then ruled by the Picts and to other parts of Europe. The Columban church developed a culture of high standards, symbolised for later centuries by the Lindisfarne Gospels and the Book of Kells, believed to have been made in Iona, and by many hundreds of crosses and other monuments which have survived to the present day.

After the Roman withdrawal from Britain, Scotland consisted of four kingdoms: in the north, Dalriada was the home of the Scots, Irish in origin and Gaelic in speech, who were later to give their name to the whole of Scotland. The Picts were organised in an independent kingdom, north of the Firth of Forth, but speaking a similar language; Strathclyde, the central valley of Scotland, was peopled with Brythonic Celts who spoke an early form of Welsh; and Bernicia was settled by Angles around the mouth of the river Tweed. The Kingdom of Dalriada united with the Picts in the year 730 under Angus MacFergus, a Pict who also annexed the Brythonic kingdom. In 844 the Scot Kenneth MacAlpin became ruler of the united kingdom known as Alba which extended right across Scotland south of the Clyde-Forth line. The Brythonic speech slowly disappeared over the next three centuries, surviving until the reign of David I (1124-53); even the Angles of Bernicia came under the influence of Gaelic. After 1018, when Malcolm II finally conquered the Angles, the Kingdom of Alba was not only united but almost wholly Gaelic-speaking. From these early times a number of chronicles have survived—both Gaelic sagas, shared with Ireland, which relate the exploits of the *Fianna,* armed warrior bands led by heroic chiefs, and 'the oldest Scottish poem', *Y Gododdin,* written in the Old Welsh of Strathclyde, which records the defeat of Celtic forces at Catraeth (Catterick in present-day Yorkshire).

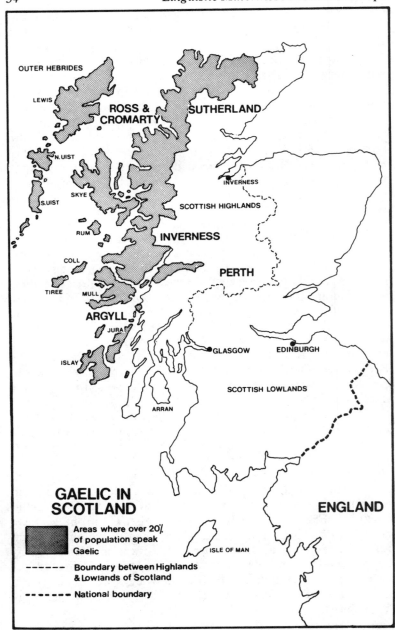

OUTER HEBRIDES

LEWIS

ROSS & CROMARTY   SUTHERLAND

N.UIST

INVERNESS

S.UIST

SKYE   SCOTTISH HIGHLANDS

RUM   INVERNESS

COLL   PERTH

TIREE   MULL

ARGYLL

JURA

ISLAY   GLASGOW   EDINBURGH

ARRAN   SCOTTISH LOWLANDS

GAELIC IN SCOTLAND

ENGLAND

Areas where over 20%
of population speak
Gaelic

ISLE OF MAN

------- Boundary between Highlands
        & Lowlands of Scotland

------- National boundary

Although historians still argue as to whether Gaelic was ever the common language of all Scotland, it is clear from the Gaelic element in place-names that it was spoken over a wide area, first as a prestige language associated with Christianity and later as the medium of political power, to the east, the north and the south, reaching as far as Renfrewshire, Ayrshire, Dumfries and Galloway. Only in the Lothians, where the speech was Teutonic, did Gaelic not become the predominant language. In the Islands of Shetland and Orkney the Vikings established Norse speech which survived into the modern period, but wherever else they settled, for example in the Hebrides, the Vikings were effectively Gaelicised. The influence of Gaelic in the Church survived the Synod of Whitby and the eventual recognition of Rome's supremacy in Scotland, while the bardic orders continued to flourish. By the eleventh century Gaelic was predominant throughout northern Britain as the language of a Scottish State and the major culture of its time, both religious and secular. Through Gaelic the art of writing and scholarship had been restored to a large part of Britain and Europe as far as Italy and Kiev. The Gaels who today live in the Highlands, or what was approximately the ancient Kingdom of Dalriada, are therefore the remnants of a people who once occupied almost all of Scotland, as well as parts of what are now the English counties of Cumberland and Northumberland, perhaps even all the land north of the river Tyne.

How then did the decline of Gaelic begin, or why did Gaelic fail to maintain itself as the national language of Scotland? Up to late medieval times, the fortunes of the language depended on the ebb and flow of power in Scotland and its consolidation in the hands of a French-speaking and, later on, an English-speaking aristocracy. An early blow was struck in the year 1070 when the King of the Scots and Picts, Malcolm Canmore *(Colum Ceann Mór)*, a widower, married the English princess Margaret. She had fled to Edinburgh with her brother, Edward Atheling, a representative of the Saxon royal house, at the time of the Norman invasion of England in 1066. Up to then English was known only to a few Scots who had contacts with kingdoms to the south. But the first linguistically mixed marriage of Gaelic Scotland was to have disastrous consequences. Margaret introduced the English language and English customs, and soon the Scottish nobles were beginning to abandon Gaelic for the new ways. The Kings of Scotland were thus the first to become anglicised and they were followed by the lower classes. Although the Scots remained the enemies of their southern neighbours throughout the medieval period, preserving their military and political independence, they nevertheless abandoned Gaelic and adopted English as the language of their Kingdom.

Following the Scottish King's marriage with Margaret, trade developed between Scotland and England, mainly for the purpose of providing the embellishments which the Queen desired for the churches. A feudal system was gradually established, based on Gaelic tradition but administered first in French and later in English; with this process new social concepts and new terms were introduced. As Norman French gave way to English among the ruling classes in England, a similar move occurred among their kinsfolk in Scotland. For a time, French gained ascendancy in the Scottish court, but there was no sudden shift from Gaelic to English at this level. English arrived in Scotland as the tongue of Flemish merchants who traded in the burghs which began to be established in the eleventh and twelfth centuries. When the court, traditionally located in the Gaelic heartlands of Perth and Fife, at such places as Dunkeld, Scone and Dunfermline, was moved by the royal house of Canmore to the partially anglicised Lothians, there were two classes—nobility and tradesmen—who no longer spoke the language of the people they ruled and served. The situation was exacerbated by the war with England and occupation by English forces of parts of southern Scotland. English refugees fleeing from William the Conqueror settled north of the border and Malcolm brought English prisoners into Scotland. Many of the Gaelic-speaking chieftains of southern Scotland were killed by the English armies and the Gaelic-speaking province of Moray was planted with English settlers.

All these factors provided a variety of language contacts in favour of English. The evolution of Lowland Scots from the Anglian speech of southern Scotland began at this time. Between 1157 and 1400 Gaelic was superseded as the everyday speech of central Scotland, beginning outwards from the burghs along the coastal plain, although in Galloway, Carrick and Fife it was to survive into the sixteenth century and even later. There were only a few rearguard actions against the Anglo-Norman régime now securing its power in the Lowlands, and their principal aim was not the restoration of Gaelic. But Fergus of Galloway led two rebellions during the reign of David I (1124-53) and with support from his Gaelic subjects. Donald Bane *(Domhnall Bàn)* seized the Crown from his brother Malcolm III in 1093. The province of Moray revolted in 1130 and again in 1187 against Norman influences in court and government. In 1138, at the Battle of the Standards, a motley Scottish army under King David I was defeated by the forces of the northern English barons in a disaster which pre-figured the tragedy of Culloden over six hundred years later. By 1234 the Gaelic principality of Galloway was finished and after the death of Aidan, the last lord, its final rebellion was crushed by Alexander II.

The death of Alexander III in 1285 brought to an end the House of Canmore under which Gaelic customs had been maintained, if only partially, up to this time. Gaelic did not suddenly cease to be spoken in affairs of state, however. Most of the mainland of northern Scotland and the western islands remained massively Gaelic-speaking. But by now the Kings of the Scots had become, in language, culture and sympathy, almost wholly French. Only Robert the Bruce gave a place to Gaelic in his court and army. Having won the throne of Scotland with Highland assistance, carrying into battle the *Brecbennach* of Saint Columba, the most sacred relic of Gaelic Scotland, he called a Parliament at Ardchattan in Argyll in which the proceedings were held in Gaelic. He also urged the Irish to make common cause with the Scottish Gaels against the English, reminding them that they shared common origins, customs and language.

Robert the Bruce was correct in his conviction that Scotland and Ireland shared a common language and culture. There was, in fact, one Gaelic civilisation extending from Cork and Kerry to Cape Wrath and the Hebrides throughout the Middle Ages. Differences existed between the Scottish and Irish dialects of Gaelic but until the sixteenth century the literary language had remained more or less unified. There was constant traffic between the Lordship of the Isles, the great homes of the Highlands and the most Gaelic of all the four provinces of Ireland, Ulster. The reputation of Scotland's poets, clerics, judges, musicians and doctors was equally great in Ireland. There existed not only a common literary standard of Gaelic and a mutually intelligible speech but common oral traditions, dress and customs, disrupted only by internecine warfare among the clans. The independence of Gaeldom was to be increasingly threatened by the growing power of the Scottish State, especially after the Reformation, but before this happened the culture transmitted in the Gaelic language showed itself capable of continuous renewal and enrichment. Gaelic society, based upon bonds of kinship and strongly patriarchal, produced new literary and musical forms such as the art of the *piobaireachd* which, as practised by the pipers of the MacCrimmon family under the patronage of the MacLeods, replaced the harp as the musical instrument of the Gaels and became the distinctive pinnacle of their culture.

The Scottish Reformation removed the one institution common to both Gaelic and Lowland Scotland, the Roman Catholic Church, and both areas now became drawn into the same political sphere. After the Treaty of Edinburgh in 1560, it soon became clear that there was bitter feeling on the part of Lowlanders towards the Highlanders, who remained Catholic, and the language of the Gaels came to be considered as alien after this date. The Gaelic language ceased to be known as Scottish and was called Irish or Erse, while Scottish or Inglis came to be the name for the speech of the Lowlands. Gaeldom was equated with barbarity and popery. The Government's aim was to bring about a simultaneous shift from Gaelic to English, from Catholicism to Calvinism, from barbarity to civility, for the reason that a common speech was necessary for the success of the new faith and régime. There was no keener supporter of this policy than the King himself, James VI, whose view of his Gaelic subjects was that they were 'wild savages' who should be 'civilised' and kept under constant vigilance. As in Ireland, where after the Flight of the Earls and the collapse of Gaelic society in Ulster, English and Lowland Scots were planted as a bulwark against Catholicism, Lowlanders were now settled in the Highlands of

Scotland. Contacts between the Gaels of Ireland and those in Scotland were thus interrupted. Gaelic Scotland was thrown upon its own resources and then drawn into the orbit of the Lowlands. After rebellions in 1595 and 1608, it was clear that James, the first King of Scotland, Ireland and England, was intent on pacifying the borderlands between his three realms so that they might become the midland counties of one Kingdom. In 1609 twelve Highland and Hebridean chiefs were tricked into signing the Statutes of Iona, which provided for the introduction of Protestant ministers into Highland parishes, the outlawing of bards, musicians, beggars, the prohibition of traditional hospitality and strong drink, the education of chiefs' heirs in Lowland schools and limitations on the bearing of arms.

This move was the first in a series of measures taken by the Scottish Government specifically directed towards the extirpation of the Gaelic language and the destruction of its culture. The Statutes of Iona were ratified by an Act of the Privy Council in 1616 which stated 'that the vulgar Inglishe toung be universallie plantit, and the Irishe language, which is one of the cheif and principall causis of the continewance of barbaritie and incivilitie amongis the inhabitantis of the Iles and Heylandis, may be abolisheit and removit'. As literacy in Gaelic was not regarded as literacy, the same Act resolved to establish schools for the teaching of English and this policy was followed by the Scottish Government's legislation and the General Assembly of the Church of Scotland over the next two centuries. The remoteness of the Highlands from the Central Lowlands, and their distinct culture, made the spread of new ideas slow and uncertain. What was achieved was the dislocation of the Gaelic language from Scottish nationality and the creation of animosities between Highlanders and Lowlanders. The poet Alasdair MacDonald (Alasdair mac Mhaighster Alasdair) described this hostility as *'mi-rùn mór nan Gall'* (the great ill-will of the Lowlander).

That some change in official attitudes towards Gaelic took place at the beginning of the eighteenth century is clear from the fact that between 1690 and 1717 the General Assembly of the Church of Scotland became conscious of the need to provide Gaelic-speaking Presbyterian ministers in the Highlands. The Church also arranged for the revision of the

Irish Bible into 'the Highland language'. Yet the sole medium of instruction in Highland schools was English and, as a result, Gaelic culture underwent profound changes during the century. The bardic system collapsed and the last exchanges of musicians and poets with Ireland took place. With the demise of the learned orders, the classical culture and patronage were transmuted into folk or peasant culture in the work of such poets as Iain Lom, Alasdair mac Mhaighstir Alasdair, Iain MacCodrum, Donnchadh Bàn Mac-an-t-Saoir, Rob Donn Mac Aoidh and Màiri nighean Alasdair Ruaidh.

The eighteenth century saw the breaking of Gaelic society. Founded in 1701, the Society in Scotland for Propagating Christian Knowledge became the principal agent for the establishment of schools in the Gaelic areas and the promotion of English. By 'Christian Knowledge' this Society meant the Presbyterian religion, church music, arithmetic and English—the sole subjects taught. Despite the provision of the catechism and metrical psalms in Gaelic and a supply of Gaelic-speaking clergy, the Gaelic language and the Irish Bible were banned from the schools opened under the Society's aegis. Only in the hedge-schools, run by Catholic priests, was Gaelic used, despite the fact that the majority of pupils in the S.S.P.C.K. schools were from Gaelic-speaking homes. There was little change in the educational systems until after the collapse of political Jacobinism at the Battle of Culloden in 1745.

Among those responsible for ensuring a more tolerant view of Gaelic was Dr Samuel Johnson, who wrote of the Gaels in 1766: 'Of what they had before the late conquest of their country there remains only their language and their poverty. Their language is attacked on every side. Schools are erected in which English only is taught and there were lately some who thought it reasonable to refuse them a version of the Holy Scriptures, that they might have no monument of their mother tongue'. Although Samuel Johnson also expressed some typically piquant opinions about Scotland, he championed the production of literature in Gaelic and suggested the establishment of a Gaelic press in Skye. It was out of an interest in Gaelic that he uttered his well-known dictum, 'There is no tracing the connection of ancient nations but by language; and therefore I'm always sorry when language is lost, because languages are the pedigrees of nations'. It was Johnson's intervention which, according to his biographer Boswell, obliged the S.S.P.C.K. to produce a Gaelic version of the New Testament. The Old Testament in Gaelic did not appear until 1801.

Resentment at the growing cultural penetration of the Highlands, backed by the Government's coercion in favour of the English schools, was increased, after the Union of Scotland with England in 1707 and the abolition of the Scottish Parliament, by the accession of a non-Scottish dynasty to the British throne seven years later. It was therefore to be expected that the Jacobite Rising of 1715, and more particularly that of 1745, would be supported by the majority of Gaelic chieftains and their clans. The defeat of Prince Charles Edward Stuart, popularly known as Bonnie Prince Charlie, was due, however, as much to ancient feuds among the clans, some of whom fought on the English side, as to the superior military methods of the Duke of Cumberland. Routed at Culloden near Inverness in 1745, the Jacobites were chased into the surrounding countryside with the most ferocious zeal by English troops, their families slaughtered and their property destroyed. As part of the policy of 'pacification' which followed, the Jacobite chiefs were executed and their lands forfeited, or they were driven into exile with Prince Charlie. As preliminaries to the dismantling of the clan-system, the Highlander's dress, arms and bagpipes were forbidden. The surviving chiefs were forced to become landlords employing tenants, the old system of kin relationships was destroyed and then replaced by an economy based on money.

As Derick S. Thompson has pointed out in *Whither Scotland?* (London 1971), from this time on the decline of Gaelic can be explained in the socio-economic terms which are usually applied to the era of the Industrial Revolution. Enforced clearance of the indigenous population was followed by unemployment and emigration on a huge scale from the Gaelic-speaking areas. The Highlands were opened up for commercial exploitation and new trades such as sheep-farming, forestry, charcoal-burning, civil engineering and iron-smelting, were introduced. With the new economy the English language was everywhere predominant: the Gael became alienated from his leaders and from his own culture which grew increasingly redundant, as Scotland became more and more absorbed economically and politically, into the British State.

The disaster of the notorious Highland Clearances went hand in hand with the introduction of new breeds of sheep, especially the Cheviot, to replace the smaller native breeds. From 1790 sheep-farming was so extensive in the Highlands that the landowners went on to clear out people and their cattle for the purpose of making greater profits. Over the next hundred years the pastoral viability of the land was ruined, with wide areas reduced to bracken and moors for deer and grouse. The Gaelic heartlands were thus almost completely depopulated and the Gaelic areas reduced to the fringes of the northern coastal areas and to the Hebrides.

By the beginning of the nineteenth century the situation of the Gaelic language was undergoing substantial changes. Although, out of a Highland population of about 335,000 some 300,000 understood Gaelic only, mainly owing to the S.S.P.C.K.'s failure to promote general literacy in English, the emigration of Gaels had resulted in colonies of Gaelic-speakers in the industrial towns to the south. It was among these emigrants, some of whom had become comparatively prosperous tradesmen, that new attempts were made to promote charitable efforts in their home areas. The Edinburgh Society for the Support of Gaelic Schools was founded in 1811 with the aim of teaching the scriptures solely through the medium of Gaelic and later through English. It is estimated that by 1861 the Society's schools, known popularly as *Sgoilean Chriosd* (Schools of Christ) had taught around 100,000 people to read and had distributed 200,000 Gaelic Bibles. The Gaelic Society of London, established in 1777, contributed to recognition of Gaelic culture in 1782 by securing the repeal of the Disarming Acts of 1746, thus restoring the lawful use of the Highland dress, tartan and bagpipes. This Society, which continues to exist today, also provided a translation service for the Government in London, preparing Gaelic texts for proclamation in the Highland areas, and thus a modicum of official status for the language was regained. A second factor in the preservation of Gaelic during the nineteenth century was the growth of a secular, commercial press. Between 1830 and 1900 about 900 new

Gaelic titles were published by firms based in Edinburgh, Stirling and Glasgow, while Gaelic weekly newspapers such as *An Gaidheal* (The Gael) were established.

Gaelic now became the language of the Church in the Highlands. A strong Protestant tradition had been founded and through the diffusion of the Scriptures and Metrical Psalms in Gaelic and the appointment of Gaels as ministers, the language's place in religious life was secured. At the same time, it was clear that the established church, the Presbyterian Church of Scotland, was an ally of the English Government and the land-owing classes in that it preached a fatalistic, predestinarian theology which taught that the clearances were the will of God in punishment for the Highlanders' sins, particularly those of 1715 and 1745. In 1843, however, there was a secession away from the Church of Scotland, a movement known as the Disruption, on the part of many congregations and ministers in the Highlands. Although usually explained in doctrinal terms, this move was partly caused by the profound unease felt towards the Church in its sanctioning of the clearances. By 1851 the Free Church, despite persecution by the land-owners, had opened 712 schools in which Gaelic was the predominant language. With the Free Presbyterian Church, a further secession, the Free Church remains the principal church of the Gaelic-speaking areas of the Highlands and Islands.

From the end of the nineteenth century Gaelic faced its most serious challenge—the use of the State's schools to eradicate what one Inspector called 'the Gaelic nuisance'. The Education Act (Scotland) of 1872 made no reference to Gaelic. The School Boards which it created took over all the schools previously administered by the S.S.P.C.K., the general Assembly of the Church of Scotland, the Free Church and the Gaelic Schools Societies. Under the new Act the use of Gaelic was actively discouraged in the schools. The *'maide-crochaidh'*, a stick on a cord, was used by English-speaking teachers to stigmatise and punish children speaking Gaelic in class—a device which was to survive in Lewis as late as the 1930s. Protests against the State's policies were few and generally ineffective. The Gaelic Society of Inverness, founded in 1871, canvassed M.Ps in favour of the language but made little progress. *An Comunn Gaidhealach* (The Gaelic

Association), founded in 1891, had more success, but mainly in Lowland areas. Its annual festival, the National *Mod*, and regional *Moid*, became a focus for Gaelic culture and it developed rapidly as a pressure group in education and as a publishing agency. Yet, despite firm recommendations by such bodies as the Educational Institute of Scotland and the Napier Commission on Crofting in 1885 that Gaelic should be fostered in the schools, the language continued to be ignored and received no recognition in the Acts of 1892, 1901 and 1908. As Murdo MacLeod, a Schools Gaelic Supervisor, wrote in 1963, 'The general pattern in the education of Gaelic-speaking children continued to be one of using Gaelic only where necessity dictated its use. As soon as the Gaelic-speaking pupil had acquired a modest acquaintance with English, Gaelic was almost completely discarded until its study was taken up in a desultory manner in the upper primary classes'.

During the first half of the present century, the school became firmly established as an intrusive institution in Gaelic society and a major agent for change in the social structure of Gaelic Scotland. Using only English, it encouraged attitudes towards Gaelic which ran counter to the maintenance of the native language by introducing new forms of knowledge which almost never had any relevance to the surviving elements of the Gael's culture. History was taught from English text-books and thus from an English point of view. The traditional lore of Gaeldom—Ossianic folk-tales, ballads and songs which had survived the opposition of Calvinism—lost its prestige, and was reduced to being the preserve of village bards and scholars. Above all, the schools provided a selection process for the identification of the more gifted children who almost invariably left their homes to seek opportunities elsewhere. Not all those who left the Highlands and Islands were lost to Gaelic culture, however. Many educated Gaels became prominent in such organisations as *An Comunn Gaidhealach* in Lowland areas and from among them has emerged a number of writers who were born and reared in urban areas. Social change, accompanied by its linguistic counterpart, thus transformed Gaelic literature from the medieval 'high culture' into a folk-culture and into a 'metropolitan' culture during the modern period. Although this new culture was relayed back to the Highlands and Islands by such means as *An Comunn Gaidhealach* and broadcasting, the life of the Gaels in the Lowlands developed as a separate unity from that in the Highlands. The rate of assimilation into the English-speaking society of Scotland was, of course, very high. Meanwhile, in the Highlands and Islands, Gaelic became the language of a residual crofter working-class. The small upper-class consisted of English land-owners or anglicised clan chiefs, and the middle-class was similar, so that English continued to be the language of communication outside the croft.

The extent of the decline of the number of Gaelic-speakers was revealed by three reports published between 1936 and 1959. The first of these, commissioned by *An Comunn Gaidhealach,* gathered valuable evidence about attitudes towards the language among fourteen pupils and parents, summed up in the comment, 'The majority of Gaelic-speaking parents are averse to the speaking of Gaelic to their children; they discourage the use of it so that their children have very imperfect English and no Gaelic'. The report concluded with eighteen recommendations urging the use of Gaelic together with the improvement of teaching methods, instruction in Gaelic to non-native-speakers and the appointment of Gaels to administrative posts.

The second survey was carried out by the educationist Christine A. Smith in 1943/4 with the aim of measuring intelligence in Gaelic and English among Gaelic-speaking children in rural Lewis; the survey was sponsored by the Scottish Council for Research in Education and its Committee on Bilingualism. According to her report, the chief cause of the rapid decline of Gaelic in the twentieth century 'has its genesis in the tacit assumption that Gaelic-speaking Scots form such a small minority that no special administration is needed'. She went on to point out that much of the cultural content of the educational system was alien to the young Gael and that such things as circuses, railway-stations, sand-castles, lamp-posts, cricket bats—even pictures and books—were outside his experience. The I.Q. scores of the children interviewed were depressed by temperamental traits, such as shyness, reticence and little attempt to strive against time, which were explained either as products of Gaelic culture or as unsureness in using a second language. Some ten years elapsed between the publication of Christine A. Smith's report and the introduction of Gaelic education schemes in Inverness, followed by Ross-shire and to a lesser extent in Argyll.

The third report was also commissioned by the Committee on Bilingualism of the Scottish Council for Research in Education, in 1957 and 1959. After noting the general decline in the number of Gaelic-speakers between 1881 and 1951, especially among children, and the social distribution of Gaelic, the report described the process of anglicisation within the Gaelic-speaking area of the Hebrides thus: 'The process of anglicisation begins historically around the official centres of transport on the east side of the island opposite the mainland. Thereafter, an English "pale" develops inland from the bridge or pierhead. It may be some time before the development makes any marked advance inland. This is still true of Stornoway in Lewis . . . In Skye, on the other hand, as can be seen around Portree and Kyleakin, the development once begun soon spreads. Before the "breakthrough" occurs there are signs of the times to be seen here and there. What happens is that localities, such as Elgol in Skye at the present time, that were traditionally Gaelic, tend to become anglicised for various local reasons, and then the whole front proceeds to break up. That process is now nearing completion in Mull and Islay'.

Around 1950 there was a turning point in the fortunes of the Gaelic language. Already there had been some resurgence of the language as a literary medium. During the 1930s and 1940s two Gaelic poets had emerged with real claims to be taken seriously as writers of European stature—Somhairle MacGhill Eathain (Sorley MacLean) and Deòrsa Caimbeul Hay (George Campbell Hay) both of whom used new themes, styles and poetic forms. They have been joined by a number of other writers, mainly poets, so that by now there is a substantial, if modest, contemporary literature in Gaelic. Community drama had also been developed and in 1952 the quarterly magazine *Gairm* was launched. At the same time, educated Gaels began to have influence within the Inspectorate of Schools, the county education authorities and the Civil Service.

By now, however, most of the last monoglot speakers of

Gaelic had died—only 974 were enumerated at the 1961 Census, of whom 406 were in the age-group 3-4, 100 in the age-group 5-9 and 309 aged 65 and over. Monolingualism in Gaelic was now no longer possible for by 1960 it survived only among a small number of elderly people, mostly women. From this time on the language has been heard on public occasions only in a small variety of circumstances: in worship, in informal entertainment, at agricultural shows and Highland Games, and so on. It is rare for Gaelic to be used on public platforms in political meetings, or in business, in official communications, advertisements or committees except since 1967 in one or two district councils in the Hebrides.

The first sign that the public authorities were more favourably disposed towards Gaelic was the introduction of the language as a medium of instruction in the county primary schools of the Highlands and Islands from 1958 on. This change was followed in broadcasting, in 1959, when the number of hours on radio in Gaelic increased from two weekly to about three hours weekly over the next eight years and to almost four hours weekly by 1970. The BBC reduced its weekly output in Gaelic to about two-and-a-half hours weekly in 1971, however. At the present time there are three-and-a-half hours of Gaelic on VHF radio every week (out of a total 500 hours broadcast) and occasional short programmes of music, current affairs and drama on television (out of a total 200 hours weekly broadcast by Scotland's three television networks). This coverage has been widely criticised as inadquate but, according to the BBC, is restricted by lack of finance and technical difficulties. The BBC has refused to establish a local radio for Gaelic-speaking areas. It is also a fact that most householders in the Gaelic areas do not possess VHF sets and are therefore deprived of most programmes in their own language. At present there is only one Gaelic programme on Radio 4, a religious service of thirty minutes on Sunday afternoons. On television there is an occasional quasi-Gaelic musical show '*S e ur Beatha* and a monthly discussion programme, *Bonn Comhraidh,* for viewers in the Highlands only. When reminded that its Charter states, 'Each national Broadcasting Council shall be charged with the following functions which shall be exercised with full regard to the distinctive culture, language, interests and tastes of our people in the country for which the Council is established', the BBC in Scotland has usually turned a deaf ear. The Corporation has, nevertheless, recently appointed a Gaelic producer for schools programmes and has opened its Inverness Project which will be extending the present four hours per week of Gaelic broadcasting to about nine in the next year or so. It also presented evidence on the special needs of the Highlands to the Crawford Commission on Broadcasting. Over many years BBC Scotland has fostered a Gaelic Department of specialist staff whose contributions to Gaelic culture has been applauded on many occasions by Gaelic leaders.

The softening of official attitudes towards Gaelic, first apparent around 1950, continued during the 1960s. Increased financial support for *An Comunn Gaidhealach,* the principal language organisation, by the central Government and local authorities, resulted in the appointment of two full-time officers in 1965. In the same year the Highlands and Islands Development Board was established by a Labour Government and went on to give financial assistance to publishing and promotional events in Gaelic. Critics of the Board point out, however, that up to now it has not appointed native Gaelic-speakers to its membership or secretariat and that it has not had an altogether beneficial effect on the language in its area, failing to return the capital generated by tourism to local communities and failing to implement an over-all plan for the solution of their economic and social problems. The National *Mod,* Gaelic Scotland's principal cultural event, has also received financial assistance from local authorities since 1969. The Gaelic Books Council, set up in the same year under the aegis of the Celtic Department of Glasgow University, has stimulated an increase in Gaelic publishing from two or three titles a year from 1960 to 1969, to about forty titles annually since 1970; this body received a grant of 48,500 from the central Government in 1974/5. The Highland Book Club *(Club Leabhar),* an independent organisation, began publishing in 1970 and now produces about seven new titles every year in both Gaelic and English.

Some progress has also been made by Gaelic in the schools during the last twenty-five years. In the bilingual areas of the Highlands and Islands Gaelic is usually the first language of instruction in the infant classes and the medium for most subjects throughout the primary stage. At secondary level English is used for almost all purposes, even for the teaching of Gaelic to Gaelic-speaking pupils, although in other respects the methods of teaching have been substantially improved. Radio broadcasting in Gaelic for schools, started in 1970, has had an excellent influence on the teaching of the language. Gaelic has been introduced as a second language into about two thirds of the primary schools of the mainland in the county of Inverness and, in 1972, it became a subject for learners at the O and A levels of the Scottish Certificate of Education. A survey carried out in 1973/4 by Fionnlaigh MacLeòid, Primary Schools Gaelic Adviser to the Western Islands Council, showed that of the sixty primary schools in the region, there were fifty-six with a total of some 2,700 bilingual pupils, of whom 88% had some knowledge of Gaelic, 68% were fluent Gaelic-speakers and 12% had no Gaelic at all. In the four anglicised schools 68% had a knowledge of Gaelic and only 7% were fluent speakers of the language. Of the 200 teachers in the primary schools of the Western Isles in the same year 158 were fluent Gaelic-speakers, fourteen had a moderate knowledge of the language and twenty-eight had none at all.

At higher level, Gaelic is taught as an important part of the Celtic courses at the Universities of Glasgow, Aberdeen and Edinburgh where there are facilities for taking Ordinary degrees, Honours degrees and Post-Graduate degrees in Gaelic and Celtic Studies; Gaelic is not taught as a subject on its own. The Celtic Departments have been joined by the School of Scottish Studies, the Linguistic Survey of Scotland and the Historical Dictionary of Scottish Gaelic, so that about twenty-four specialist posts are now in existence. The language is also taught at two teachers' training colleges in Glasgow and Aberdeen. So completely does English dominate the educational system, however, that until recently few saw the absurdity of Gaelic-speaking lecturers lecturing in English about Gaelic to Gaelic-speaking students. Courses in Scottish Gaelic are offered at several universities abroad, including those of Oslo, Freiburg, Harvard, St Francis Xavier, Oxford, Trinity College and University College, Dublin.

Although the last few years have seen a more sympathetic and liberal attitude towards Gaelic by Government authorities, particularly in education, very little use of it is made by public bodies outside the language movement. Gaelic has some official status in the Land Court, where the Gaelic-speaking member is statutory, and evidence in Gaelic is allowed but not really encouraged in law-courts within the bilingual areas although the principle of equal validity with English has not been granted.

In religious life, the language is used regularly by the Church of Scotland, the Free Church of Scotland, the Catholic Church, the Episcopal Church and by the smaller denominations. In numbers and ethos the Free Church is nearer to being a Gaelic institution than any other, although many of the Sunday Schools are conducted in English. Its strength lies in Gaelic-speaking districts such as the northern Hebrides and the west coast of Ross-shire and a large percentage of its 25,000 members are Gaels.

The Crofter Commission is strongly sympathetic to Gaelic. The Scottish Central Library and local libraries provide a service of Gaelic books but the National Library of Scotland in Edinburgh has no designated Gaelic post. Gaelic is scarcely used at all on public signs except as street-names in a few places such as Port Charlotte on Islay, Stornoway on Lewis and Ullapool in Wester Ross. The Gaelic Society of London has campaigned for the use of the language on road-signs and in public administration, but with little success. Ten out of sixty-four local authorities agreed to implement a bilingual policy in this respect but none has done so. Among the obstacles encountered by Gaelic enthusiasts are the apathy of Gaelic-speakers and the hostility of English-speaking officials in the local administration.

Of the political parties only the Scottish National Party has made any official commitment to Gaelic, in that it would give the language equal validity with English throughout the bilingual areas; the party also uses it in some of its publications. In the press the use of Gaelic is patchy. The bilingual newspaper of *An Comunn Gaidhealach, Sruth* was discontinued after four years in 1969 and was merged as a supplement in the weekly *Stornaway Gazette* which is now, with the *West Highland Free Press* on Skye, the only newspaper carrying news in Gaelic on a regular basis. There are no Gaelic weeklies, but some Church magazines have monthly supplements in the language. The publishing imprint *Gairm*, founded in 1952 and now with its office in Glasgow, publishes a fairly wide range of books in Gaelic including dictionaries, manuals, prose and verse, history and music, as well as the principal literary quarterly *Gairm* which is edited by the Professor of Celtic at Glasgow University, Ruaraidh MacThómais (Derick S. Thomson), who is also one of the leading Gaelic poets. The Scottish Arts Council supports contemporary Gaelic literature with financial assistance to *Gairm*, the Gaelic Books Council and with prizes and bursaries to writers.

Gaelic literature since the Second World War, and more particularly since about 1955, has passed through a period of stringent re-appraisal. Up to 1940 it was tied to the oral tradition, which still flourishes at the present time. Local bards such as Domhnall Ruadh Chorùna of North Uist contributed to the tradition of village poetry, composing verse on local topics, often in a humorous or satirical or bawdy style. Other writers, like James Thomson, John N. MacLeod, Donald Lamont and Norman MacLeod, all based outside the Gaelic areas, continued to write verse and, to a lesser extent, prose on local topics. From the emergence of Somhairle MacGhill Eathain (Sorley MacLean) in the 'thirties there developed what Derick S. Thomson has called the Modern Coterie of Gaelic writing—these writers live in academic and professional circles, which sets them aside both from their fellow-writers and their public in the Gaelic areas. Sorley MacLean's sequence of poems *Dàin do Eimhir agus Dàin Eile*, published in 1943 and translated as *Poems to Eimhir* in 1971, made it plain that Gaelic was capable once again of dealing with major world themes in an artistic manner. He was soon joined by George Campbell Hay, Donald MacAuley, Derick S. Thomson and other poets rallying around the magazine *Gairm* which played a decisive role in encouraging new work. Among prose-writers who have also published in *Gairm* are Colin MacKenzie and Finlay J. MacDonald and the playwrights Finlay MacLeod and Iain Crichton Smith. Without exception these writers have been bitterly aware of the crisis of the language in which they write and most eminently in the case of Sorley MacLean, have sought political remedies for the problems of Gaelic society.

F. G. Valleé showed in his sociological study of Gaelic on the Island of Barra in the 1950s that the language is primarily used in such communities as the Hebrides at home, in church and for social purposes. In business or when dealing with officialdom, English is invariably used. For example, Gaelic-speakers will count out change in English even after making a purchase in Gaelic; committee and public meetings, minutes and advertisements are usually in English. As Joshua Fishman, one of the leading international figures in the field of sociolinguistics, has pointed out, in cases of cultural contact in which one language is beginning to displace another the speakers of the weaker language are reduced to those who are less typical of the society as a whole. In Scotland today Gaelic is maintained in fringe areas by a crofter working-class, mostly older people, and by the village bards and 'scholars'. Writers and the leading figures of the language movement tend to be those who have left the Gaelic area to enter the professions. Fishman's 'third generation return' is to be observed in the efforts of young Scots of Gaelic descent who are seeking to acquire the language which their parents did not hand on to them.

Foremost among the organisations which today attract young Gaels is *An Comunn na Canain Albannaich* (The Scottish Language Society) which was founded in 1971, on the model of *Cymdeithas yr Iaith Gymraeg* (The Welsh Language Society) in an attempt by methods of militant but non-violent civil disobedience to accelerate the polarisation of attitudes for and against Gaelic in the Highlands and Islands. This Society has brought pressure to bear on the Post Office to accept Gaelic for such purposes as the addressing of letters, and has kept up continual propaganda in favour of the language. The Gaelic League of Scotland is another organisation devoted to the cause of the language, teaching it in classes and publishing manuals in it.

As part of the renewed energies of the Scottish Gaels in present years there have been several initiatives worthy of note. The first of these was the creation of small-scale economic enterprises on Skye which use Gaelic for business purposes. Under the leadership of Iain Noble these businesses use their Gaelic names— *Tigh-Òsda a'Chidhe, Tigh-Òsda Eilean Iarmain, Muileann Beag a'Chrotail, An Òifig Camus Croise* and so on. The Bank of Scotland has been persuaded to print bilingual cheques, as the Clydesdale Bank has already done, and the language has begun to be used in advertisements and entertainments. Among the new organisations using the language as a matter of course is *Sabhal Mór Ostaig,* the Gaelic College and Community Centre opened in 1973 on the Island of Skye. The objectives of the College, which belongs to Iain Noble but is administered as a charitable trust, are to promote education and the study of Gaelic-speaking communities in Scotland and throughout the world, and to act as a Gaelic social centre for residents and visitors on the Island. It has a collection of Gaelic books, the only comprehensive Gaelic library in the west of Scotland, it organises language classes and summer schools, as well as social and commercial activities. In 1974 the Scottish Arts Council appointed Catherine Montgomery as the first resident poet at *Sabhal Mór Ostaig.* In such ways the centre is re-invigorating Gaelic culture on Skye.

The second significant development was the founding in 1972 of a new radical community newspaper *The West Highland Free Press.* Published from Kyleakin, Skye, and serving the Outer Islands, Skye and the north-west coast of Scotland, this newspaper provides a forum for the whole community and has given a sympathetic hearing to the problems facing the Gaelic language, including two columns in Gaelic every week in addition to news and advertisements in Gaelic.

The third hopeful sign is the progress made on Gaelic's behalf in the schools. Under the new regional and island authorities set up in 1975, re-organisation of secondary education in Lewis and Harris has resulted in the up-grading of rural junior secondary schools to the status of comprehensives. This innovation is expected to have a strengthening effect on Gaelic in that the brighter Gaelic-speakers will no longer be sent to board at Stornoway, Portree or Inverness but will from now on stay in their local schools. A senior secondary school is also planned for Uist. It is also hoped that with the appointment in 1973 of an adviser for Gaelic and Primary Education, the new Western Islands Authority will implement a thoroughly bilingual policy in the schools. There are signs too that *An Comunn Gaidhealach* is about to form a new Gaelic youth movement to take the place of *Comunn na h-Oigridh,* which is now defunct.

Another growth-point has been in the realm of entertainment. Badly served by public transport, with bitter weather in the winter months, and deprived of local radio and television in their own language, the Highlands and Islands have enjoyed only the occasional road-show in the tourist season and the traditional arts of dances, ceilidhs and amateur drama. There was therefore a tremendous welcome for the visits of two non-commercial touring companies to the Gaelic-speaking areas: the 7-84 Company and its production of *The Cheviot, the Stag and the Black, Black Oil* and the Glasgow Ossianic Society's *Air Thurus.* The 7-84 Company's purpose is to entertain, in which it succeeds brilliantly, but it is also partly didactic in that it relates, from a Marxist point of view, the story of Gaelic society from the time of the Highland Clearances to the discovery of oil off the Scottish coast.

The likelihood of large-scale industrial and commercial development of the Highland area, due to the discovery of oil, holds serious implications for the future of Gaelic. Adressing the 1974 conference of *An Comunn Gaidhealach,* Derick Thomson said, 'There may be some people about who still say that this development should be resisted. But you can be assured that these people are not looking for jobs or needing jobs to support their families. In any case, there is no possibility of stifling oil development; there may still be a chance of controlling and using it. But surely our basic attitude should be one of welcome: a welcome for the opportunity of prosperity, and a welcome to growth, to the prospect of young people staying in the Gaelic area. If we cannot welcome that prospect we had better go into the undertaking business . . . What matters is what we do next. If the development is left to the laws of the commercial market only, there will certainly be ugly development . . . What we need is an authority, government or local and *ad hoc,* that will plan development with the total needs of communities in mind . . . We have listened to pious policies for the Highlands for a century'. Among the facilities which could follow the spin-off from prosperity based on oil, in Derick Thomson's view, are better roads, recreational facilities, libraries, schools, cultural centres, printing works, a design centre and so on. He went on, 'There is no need for *An Comunn* to turn party political. That would no doubt be dangerous and disruptive. But if the Gaelic movement is to mean anything it must become political in other senses. That means more than talk and especially more than talk on narrowly cultural topics. It means action and particularly action to change the system that is stifling the industrial life of the Gaelic people, and to change it to a system which actively encourages that individual life . . . When we know clearly what our policy is we should walk out on to the streets with it, and walk into the district and regional councils and into committees, on to platforms, into the press. We should brand and boycott and shame the people who advocate foreign policies in the Gaelic areas. If they run hotels we should never darken their doors, if they run garages we should use others. If they voice their loud, foreign voices in our public councils we should answer them firmly in our own accents and tongue, and turn the whole nation's accusing finger at them. For, do not forget, in this matter we have the Scottish nation behind us more and more as each day passes . . . If we do not destroy the system it will continue to destroy us, as it has been doing for generations'.

Derick Thomson concluded his address, which introduced a new militancy to the society's proceedings, by noting a number of areas in which an immediate start could be made. They included the setting up of a Government working-party to take over the neglected functions of the Highlands and Islands Development Board and to make comprehensive, detailed plans for these areas in relation to oil and other industrial development, especially insofar as this development will impinge on the Gaelic communities. *An Comunn Gaidhealach,* he suggested, should also press for action by the Scottish Education Department on a new policy for Gaelic education in the Western Isles, and for a study to be made on the use of Gaelic in public business, technology, tourism, advertising and in such areas as bilingual typography on letter-heads, posters, cheque-books, road-signs and official forms.

The new resolve of the Gaelic areas to assert themselves has had an effect on *An Comunn Gaidhealach,* which up to 1970 had not had much success in the Highlands and Islands. Its annual *Mod* had seemed to many to be pre-occupied with

Gaelic song. Only in 1965 did the society shift its headquarters from Glasgow to Inverness and its provincial festivals had
never really taken root in the Gaelic heartlands. In 1972 the
society launched its Western Isles Regional Council, which
became the first of its committees to hold all its meetings in
Gaelic. At the *Mod* of that year it issued a press release
calling for a basic minimum of official recognition for the
language and its promotion. During the last four years it has
also engaged in a number of practical activities intended to
improve the position of Gaelic in public life. In 1973, both *An
Comunn Gaidhealach* and *Comunn na Cànain Albannaich*
adopted a detailed policy and programme for the language. A
new militancy became apparent, although little has yet been
done in practical terms. Perhaps the most serious obstacle
encountered by the society remains the extremely conservative nature of the Gaels themselves. Over the last three
hundred years Gaeldom has been made economically,
politically and administratively dependent on English. So
many decisions affecting Gaelic society have been taken from
outside, thus arousing the suspicion and often the opposition
of Gaels in the Highlands and Islands. Furthermore, the Gael
has been taught to respect the *status quo,* frequently making
common cause with anglicised landlords and businessmen
who resent or fear the restoration of Gaelic. It is in bringing
about a confrontation between the enemies of Gaelic and
those who wish to see it flourish in better circumstances that
such organisations as *An Comunn Gaidhealach* and *Comunn
na Cànain Albannaich* have their vital role.

It remains true, however, that the status of Gaelic has not
become a political issue in Scotland, like that of Welsh in
Wales; it has not been regarded as such since the struggles of
the Land League in the latter part of the nineteenth century
when it was used to secure the election of Crofter Party M.Ps.
to each of the Highland seats. Despite the success of the Scottish National Party in recent years, and as Scotland proceeds
towards self-government, Gaelic in recent times has not
united Scots not even within the Gaelic areas, and much
remains to be done before this is achieved. Nevertheless, the
Western Isles was the first constituency to return a Nationalist
M.P. to Westminster at a General Election when Donald

Stewart was elected. A Gaelic-speaker, Donald Stewart seconded a resolution put before the S.N.P's Annual Conference in 1974 which required the party to produce a detailed policy for Gaelic both within the Gaelic-speaking areas and in Scotland as a whole. It therefore seems likely that, after devolution of power from London to Edinburgh and the establishment of a Scottish Assembly, as promised and planned by the Labour Party and the British Government in November 1975,* the first steps towards a new, effective policy for Gaelic will be taken.

The survival of Gaelic as a community language into the present century is a remarkable case of language-maintenance in the face of powerful pressures. Unlike Irish, Scottish Gaelic has had no political or cultural movement to champion its cause and there has been little official support for it by either central or local government. Throughout centuries of persecution, neglect, clearance and prejudice, Gaelic has shown a tenacity which cannot be explained merely in terms of culture-lag. That it should not remain on the fringes of Scotland's national life but should be restored as 'the Scottish language' is the conviction of a significant and growing number of Scots at the present time. It remains true, however, that the survival of Gaelic depends on the survival of the Highland community. Today the Gaelic areas, where they are not completely depopulated, are the locations of winter-sport centres, tourist chalets and recreation complexes for the industrial population of the Lowlands of Scotland and the English cities. On present trends, the generation born during the last ten years may be the last for whom Gaelic is a native and community language: the millenium of decline seems close to being accomplished. The circumstances for Gaelic are desperate, and its future will no doubt be decided during the next ten years.

---

* The British Government's plans for the establishment of Assemblies for Scotland and Wales are described in more detail in the section on the Welsh.

THE LOWLAND SCOTS

The Lowlands of Scotland have no precise boundaries but they may be taken to include the southern parts of the country as far as the border with England, the central conurbation which runs for twenty-four miles between the estuary of the Clyde to the Firth of Forth, including Glasgow and Edinburgh, together with large areas on the north-eastern coast. They therefore comprise the old counties of Wigtown, Kirkcudbright, Dumfries, Roxburgh, Berwick, Selkirk, Peebles, East Lothian, West Lothian, Mid Lothian, Fife and Clackmannan, as well as parts of Ayrshire, Lanarkshire, renfrewshire and Stirlingshire, and on the eastern seaboard the counties of Angus, Aberdeen and even Caithness, the most northerly point of mainland Scotland. About four-fifths of Scotland's population of 5,228,965 (1971) live in the Lowlands, mostly in the industrial belt of Glasgow (population: 897,458) and Clydeside, and in the cities of Aberdeen, Dundee and Edinburgh, the capital.

Like the Gaels of the Highlands and Islands, the vast majority of Lowland Scots also speak English, often to a standard which is admired in England. English, whether good or bad, is the language of formality and as the need for formality arises more frequently in urban areas, the inhabitants· of Scotland's cities and industrial areas use English most of the time. But many—precise figures are not available, for reasons which will become clear—are also able to speak another language, Scots.

There remains a good deal of confusion about the origins and nature of this language. It has sometimes been described, incorrectly, as a Gaelic language which has become mixed with English, or as standard English corrupted by the Scottish peasantry and proletariat, or even as 'a kind of slang'. Gaelic-speakers refer to it simply as 'English', often adding an epithet like 'broken' to show that they recognise it as being different from the norm of the Highland lairds and other notables who have either been educated in England or have assumed the anglicised accents of their class. More accurately, this language—for that is what it is—has been known as 'Inglis' and as 'Lallans', as 'the Doric' and as 'braid Scots'—and by detractors of its literary forms as 'synthetic Scots'. This confusion and variety of names for Scots has been caused by a number of factors, including deliberate political obfuscation, social prejudice, the unenlightened teaching of Scotland's history and by the very nature of the language itself.

Scots began as a dialect of Anglo-Saxon, the language brought across the North Sea by Germanic tribes in the sixth century A.D. The northern dialect of Anglo-Saxon became established during the following century in Lothian where—unlike in the rest of Scotland with its Gaelic and Brythonic past—the majority of place-names bear witness to Anglo-Saxon settlement. By the tenth century the Gaelic-speaking kingdom of Alba had been secured over most of the country but this sovereignty was seriously impaired a hundred years later when the Norman Conquest of England brought immigrants from northern England into Scotland, following the Princess Margaret who had married King Malcolm Canmore. The centralising power of the feudal system and the Church spread out from the Forth area around Edinburgh and, under French-speaking barons and their agents who spoke Northern English, soon took in large parts of the Lowlands. The native population, particularly in the burghs, were not militarily conquered but were over-run by this well-organised system, becoming more and more obliged to learn the language of authority and business. In time the variant sometimes known as Early Northern English was adopted by the peasantry, who up to now had spoken Gaelic, and by the upper classes who had spoken Gaelic and Norman French. This form gradually assumed a dominant position in the Northern Kingdom, just as the language of London developed into the official standard English of southern England. It is essentially the old dialectal differences emerging at this time which still distinguish Scots from English.

These differences increased over the next three centuries. Borrowings from Latin, French, Icelandic and Gaelic, as well as independent philological change, the accumulation of new senses and connotations around the parent Germanic vocabulary and the growth of a distinctive idiom, all prepared Scots to be raised from the status of a dialect to that of a

language. For as long as Scotland maintained its political independence, Scots grew into a truly national language, the official speech of the Kingdom of Scotland. For another century
it was called Inglis, the northern word for English, and it was
not very different from the speech of those parts of England to
the north of the river Humber.

The main difference was that in Scotland the lang-
uange became the vehicle of a substantial literature
written by such poets as John Barbour (c. 1320-95),
Robert Henryson (fl. 1480) and William Dunbar (c. 1460-
1520). The first of these, John Barbour, wrote for a courtly
audience and is remembered for his masterpiece *The Brus,* a
biographical poem on the exploits of King Robert the Bruce
written in the style of the French romances but expressed in
'English as spoken and written in Lowland Scotland'. He was
followed by the author of *The Kingis Quair* (The King's
Book), which is usually attributed to King James I (1394-
1437) and which relates incidents in his life, and by the even
more mysterious person known as Blind Harry or Henry the
Minstrel who composed the heroic romance of *Wallace*
around 1460. Robert Henryson, author of *The Testament of
Cresseid* and described by the critic Alexander Scott as 'one of
the very greatest narrative poets ever to practise his art within
these islands', composed beast-fables in the European
tradition, often basing his Scots versions on French or Latin
originals. In the work of William Dunbar there is extraordinary variety of style and content, varying from the
richest allegory through masterly use of the French ballads,
and Latin hymns and the older alliterative metres, to the
profound and profane contemplations of his later years. The
enrichment of the Scots tradition by means of translation was
now well established and continued with Gawain Douglas (c.
1475-1522) whose Scots version of Virgil's *Aeneid* was the first
great translation of classical Latin verse into a European vernacular. In extending the vocabulary of Scots by borrowing
from other languages, Douglas was helping to make it
adequate for all literary purposes, just as writers like Lydgate,
Sidney and Elyot were doing for English. Douglas was also
among the first to give the name 'Scots' to the national speech
and after him the term 'Inglis' was gradually abandoned in

recognition of the fact that there were by now two distinct languages.

The first serious blows to the progress of Scots were struck around 1560, when the Church of the Reformation had only the English Bible at its disposal. Scots now had a powerful rival in its own territory and one which had the authority of the word of God behind it. The ideological unity of the Lowlands Scots was already shattered and now their linguistic unity was assailed. From now on the influence of the English Bible became more and more apparent in the language of the poets, such as Alexander Mongtomerie (c. 1545-1615), William Fowler (died 1612) and Alexander Hume (c. 1557-1609). English became associated in the minds of Scots with what was solemn and dignified, while the native tongue was reduced to use for everyday, familiar, emotional and comic purposes. To the spiritual prestige gained by English was added the social prestige which followed the Union of the Crowns in 1603 and the departure of the Scottish court for London, when King James VI of Scotland became King James I of England. James, who was no mean poet and a patron of other poets, adopted English speech and manners and was imitated by the poets and courtiers who accompanied him to London. Documents from this period show that the language of authority in London soon became the language of authority at home. Although the majority of Scots continued to speak their own language in their everyday affairs, the literary language now fell into desuetude.

Throughout the late medieval period Lowland Scotland had had a distinct cultural identity, with aristocratic art-forms interacting with the popular tradition. But after 1603, when the educated took up English, the language of the élite was no longer that spoken by the ordinary people. For the next century, while Scottish poets followed English fashions, the art of the great *makars,* as the poets were called, was ignored and forgotten while the country people and the townsfolk, at work and at play, went on singing the old folk-songs and ballads in Scots.

Finally, as the last blow to the survival of Scots as a fully curial and national language, the Union of Parliaments in 1707 gave English political prestige when it became the language of legislation for all the countries of Britain. The first Scots to take their seats in the London Parliament were mocked by their English colleagues for the way they spoke. This and similar experiences led them to adopt southern speech partly by imitation and partly by means of elocution lessons designed to eradicate Scottish vowels from their phonemic system and all Scottishness from their vocabulary. In a letter to his brother the philosopher David Hume (1711-76) wrote concerning the education of his newphew, 'The question is, whether he had better continue his education in Scotland or in England. There are several advantages of a Scots education but the question is whether that of the language does not counter balance them and determine the preference to English. He is now of an age to learn it perfectly but if a few years elapse, he may acquire such an accent as he will never be able to cure of . . . The only inconvenience is, that few Scotsmen that have had an English education have even settled cordially in their own country and they have been commonly lost ever after to their friends'. Many Scots now began compiling lists of Scots words and phrases which they believed to be 'contaminating' their speech. Fanatical in this was James Beattie who wrote of the Scots language in 1771, 'For more than half a century it has even by the Scots been considered as a dialect of the vulgar'. Beattie published a collection of Scotticisms in 1779 'designed to correct improprieties of speech and writing'. He was followed by John Sinclair who wrote in *Observations on the Scottish Dialect* (1782), 'Such as wish to mix with the world, and particularly those whose object it is to have some share in the administration of national affairs, are under the necessity of conforming in the taste, the manners, and the language of the public. Old things must then be done away with, new manners assumed and a new language adopted'. The irony was, of course, that although English had been taught in Scotland's schools since the beginning of the seventeenth century, it had been taught by people who for the most part had never heard an Englishman speaking.

By the end of the century, however, there was a number of books on English pronunciation, many by Scotsmen, which ultimately succeeded in bringing at least the vowel sounds of the two languages into nearer approximation—although this has not yet been completely achieved despite the advent of radio. Soon the ruling classes were sending their sons to public schools in England to acquire an English accent and an English education prior to entering Oxford or Cambridge. Writing in the symposium *Whither Scotland?* (London, 1971), Duncan Glen describes the cultural sell-out of Scottish standards which followed the Union as 'the crux of Scotland's present-day troubles. Its failure to be itself and the failure of its political and cultural leaders to be their Scottish selves has created the intellectual and cultural void which is at the centre of Scottish affairs . . . There is a void in the nation and, as a nation suffering from a sense of inferiority and from a withdrawal from involvement in its affairs, Scotland becomes a parochial region of the United Kingdom and its people second-class citizens whose birthright of Scottishness is a handicap to be overcome rather than an asset to be put to the creation of a virile, active culture'.

The revival of verse in Scots which took place during the eighteenth century was largely the result of patriotic gestures against the Union of Parliaments in 1707. At first the poets followed the style of the preceding hundred years, most of which were rural and local. Allan Ramsay (c. 1884-1758) portrayed a series of Edinburgh worthies in vigorous verses and wrote a pastoral play, *The Gentle Shepherd*. Robert Fergusson (1750-74) also wrote on both rural and urban themes, including satire of contemporary politics, a good example of the American poet Robert Lowell's definition of the most effective literary style—'the tongue of the people in the mouth of the scholar'. The ballad, folk-song and comic verse flourished as parts of a popular culture based on oral tradition by people who were for the most part illiterate.

Without the models of poets like Ramsay and Fergusson and the popular tradition from which they sprang, Robert Burns (1759-96) could not have become the world-famous poet who was to give Scots a new lease of life for another century and a half. Burns brought a more telling irony, more rumbustious comedy, more tenderness and passion to verse in Scots, but he added only a little to its forms and themes.

Although greater than Fergusson's, his work was superior to his predecessor's in that while Fergusson had mastered the art of intellectual discussion in Scots, treating ideas with the self-confidence of a scholar, Burns took refuge from his deficient education in a jocularity in Scots or, more often, turned to English whenever he wished to write philosophically. It was as a poet whose verses were meant to be sung that Burns captured the hearts of his compatriots and became famous all over the world as 'the poet of love, liberty and labour.'

The evangelical revival inside the Free Church caused his audience to over-look the more provocative satires and his radical attack on religious conservatism and to concentrate on his domestic idylls, love-lyrics and character-sketches. Although advised by his mentors to drop his 'uncouth Scots' and to write in English, the effect of Burns on the Scots language was sudden and all-pervasive. Restored to an honoured place among the poetic languages of the world, Scots was now taken up by hundreds of poets, and thousands of versifiers, who used and re-used his vocabulary, themes and ideas. Many of the poems in successive editions of the *Whistlebinkie* anthology, first issued in 1832, reduced the range of Burns's genius to 'a lowest common denominator of amorous alcoholism', as Alexander Scott has said. The literary quality of their work was very poor and hardly a name stands out from among this horde of scribblers, but the zeal which Burns inspired in them was to last throughout the nineteenth century, and even up to the First World War.

Furthermore, Burns's success inspired Scotland's other literary genius, Walter Scott (1771-1832) to emulate his predecessor in prose. Writing to James Ballantyne, Scott commented, 'Burns by his poetry has already attracted attention to everything Scottish, and I confess I can't see why I should not be able to keep the flame alive, merely because I write Scotch *(sic)* in prose, and he wrote it in rhyme'. It should be added, however, that Scott confined his Scots to the dialogue of his humbler characters such as Edie Ochiltree, Dandie Dinmont and Jeanie Deans, but turned to English for narrative purposes.

Great as they were, Burns and Scott failed to restore Scots to the standard of the sixteenth century, especially because the prose they wrote was lacking in serious, philosophical vocabulary and the poetry was on a less intellectual level than the *makars* of earlier times. The poetry had no epic, no metaphysical verse, the vocabulary was restricted, more realistic and thus more regional, encouraging the use of local dialects in the absence of a standard, national literary form. Whereas Addison, Steele and Johnson had refined English, the efforts to extend the range of Scots begun by Douglas had long been abandoned. In Burns's poem 'The Cotter's Saturday Night', for example, the difference in scope between Scots and English is apparent: the formal dedication, the formal worship and the moralising are in English, while the description of domestic scenes and action are in Scots; in particular, when the Bible is brought out, the poem slides into English, thus representing the historical association of the Bible in Scotland with the English language. It was not until the present century that attempts were made to translate the scriptures into Scots. The most recent, due for publication in 1976, is the work of William Laughton Lorimer, Professor of Greek at St Andrews until his death in 1967, and his son Robin.

Many of the attitudes towards Scots still prevailing at the present time grew out of the tremendous vogue for the work of Burns and Scott. The loss of political status meant that Scots was no longer used in any formal or official way, so that no attempt was made to think abstractly in the language, to expound new ideas or re-cast old ones. It became limited, in the words of David Murison, 'to the expression of the ephemeral emotion, the incidental anecdote, the proverbial platitude, the simple statement, and if someone were really determined to keep his Scots at all costs and in all circumstances he would find his thinking very circumscribed or the utterance of it woefully inadequate'. The language was not taught in the schools, either as a medium of instruction or as a subject in its own right, the acquisition of it being left to chance. Its quality deteriorated, the grammar was mixed with English, so that for instance the plural of *cow* became *coos* which is neither English *cows* nor Scots *kye,* and the vocabulary began to be impoverished. The process of assimilation was accelerated by universal State education after 1872 when the schools continued 'to chase the Scotticism to its death'.

This policy of suppression and uniformity, based on a naive view of language and social pretensions, failed in its aims but came very close to complete success. It was based on the fallacy that a person can have only one language which he must abandon if he wishes to acquire another, and on the ill-informed assumption that Scots was a kind of bad English which ought to be restored to its original purity. The result of this ignorance, which took no no account of bilingualism, or what is now known as register—the types of speech which almost every speaker possesses and adapts to suit the occasion—was the near-destruction of Scots but not its replacement by good English, for it is generally the case that where bad Scots is spoken the English is also poor. According to David Murison, editor of *The Scottish National Dictionary* since 1946 and Senior Lecturer in Scottish Language in the Universities of St Andrews and Aberdeen, it is probable that the common complaint about the inarticulateness of Scottish children is due not to the fact that they naturally speak Scots but that they have been strongly discouraged from doing so. It is a sobering conclusion that the present situation of the Scots language, which has decayed as a spoken language over the last century, cannot be considered without reference to the psychological complexes instilled in the children who spoke the language universally admired in the poetry of Burns and the prose of Scott.

The First World War marked a turning point in the fortunes of Scotland, its language and its literature. Among the young men who came home in 1918 after fighting for 'the rights of small nations' were many who saw their country as a cultural desert, a land in danger of losing its national identity. They recognised education in Scotland as having been almost completely anglicised, the country's history and literature almost entirely neglected. There was little drama or music or art produced by Scotsmen and, in their view, what passed for Scottish literature was unworthy of the country's literary tradition, a mere appendage of English literature. Rejecting the popular image of Scottish culture, these young writers expressed their opinion that the only way to re-create an independent culture was to revive the indigenous languages of Scotland, Gaelic and Scots. They were also convinced that they had to build not on what Scotland and England had in common but on the differences between them; this aim was described by one of their number as 'at once radical and conservative, revolutionary and reactionary'. The impact of the War thus shocked Scots verse into a contemporary awareness, reversing the trend towards parochialism which had dominated the literary scene since the days of Burns. The transformation is to be seen in the work of Charles Murray (1864-1941) whose *Hamewith* (1900) was concerned with a rural society and its past, but whose *A Sough o'War* (1916) was a fierce denunciation of the War and its aftermath. The new writing was not immediately admired. While Scottish literature remained parochial, preoccupied with the past and the romantic image of Scotland as in Burns and Scott, there was little objection to it and little interest in it. But as soon as this idea of a modern, independent literature gained acceptance, the conservative among Scotland's critics and politicians quickly rose to denounce it especially as it was linked to the progress of Scottish nationalism, long growing but now crystallising into action.

During the latter part of the nineteenth century Scotland had tried to regain its independence by legislation. There had been seven Home Rule motions proposed at Westminster between 1889 and 1895 under the Radical Liberals and a further fourteen Home Rule Bills were to be presented between 1908 and 1927, all defeated by the English majority in the London Parliament. The Scottish Labour Party had been founded in 1888 with Home Rule for Scotland as one of its policies. The first Home Rule Association was founded in 1886, the second in 1917 and others in the 1920s. They had been joined between 1885 and 1928 by a number of other bodies seeking self-determination for Scotland, including the Scots National League, the Scottish Party, the Scottish National Convention, the Scottish National Movement, the Scottish Home Rule Council and the Young Scots Society. In 1928 most of these organisations came together to form the National Party of Scotland and four years later this party merged with the Scottish Party to become the Scottish National Party; this Party, known as the S.N.P., is the one which has led Scottish nationalism to the present time.

The driving-force of the nationalist movement during the 1920s was provided by the writers and by one writer in particular, Christopher Murray Grieve. Born in 1892 at Langholm in Dumfries-shire, six miles from the border with England, Grieve had served in the War and was typical of his contemporaries when he wrote, 'It took the full force of the War to jolt an adequate majority of the Scottish people out of their old mental, moral and material ruts. In retrospect it will be seen to have had a genesis in kin with other post-war phenomena of recrudescent nationalism all over Europe'. More pessimistically, the novelist Lewis Grassic Gibbon added, 'It was the old Scotland that perished then, and we may believe that never again will the old speech and the old ways, the old curses and the old benedictions, rise but with alien efforts to our lips'.

Between 1920 and 1922 Grieve edited three issues of an anthology, entitled *Northern Numbers*, of 'representative selections from certain living Scots poets'. At the same time the Vernacular Circle of the London Burns Club was campaigning for the revival of Scots. Grieve became editor of a new literary review, *The Scottish Chapbook*, which was dedicated to the concept 'Not Traditions—Precedents!' In the first number the editor wrote, 'In my opinion, for several generations Scottish Literature has neither seen, nor heard, nor understood what was taking place around it. For that reason it remains a dwarf among giants. Scottish writers have been terrified to appear inconstant to established conventions. They have stood still and consequently been left behind in technique and ideation. Meanwhile the Scottish nation has been radically transformed in temperament and tendency. Scottish life has been given a drastic re-orientation with the result that Scottish Literature today is in no sense representative or adequate'. At the beginning of his career Grieve had opposed the contemporary movement towards the revival of Scots, believing it to be a back-water. But Scots was his native tongue and the current propaganda in its favour led him to experiment with it. During his investigations of the potential of Scots, C. M. Grieve adopted the pseudonym (he prefers *nom de guerre* to *nom de plume)* of Hugh MacDiarmid.

The first task of Hugh MacDiarmid was to undo the image and influence of Burns. In his book *Albyn* (1927) he wrote, 'The Burns influence has been wholly bad, producing little save puerile and platitudinous doggerel and reducing the whole field of Scottish Literature to a kail-yard (vegetable patch)'. For MacDiarmid Burns was a country-poet of genius but nevertheless a late representative of a rural society, which had been destroyed by the Industrial Revolution. With the new slogan 'Dunbar—not Burns!' the poets were exhorted to study the work of the great *makars* of the fifteenth century—Dunbar, Henryson and Douglas.

MacDiarmid's next task was the restoration of Scots as a medium for expressing the new Scottish sensibility, 'capable of addressing the full range of literary purpose'. As a preliminary, he wrote in *Albyn*, 'No revival of Scots can be of consequence to a literary aspirant worthy of his salt unless it is so aligned with contemporary tendencies in European thought and expression that it has with it the possibility of eventually carrying Scots work once more into the mainstream of European literature . . . If there is to be a Scottish literary revival the first essential is to get rid of our provinciality of outlook and to avail ourselves of continental experience. The prevalent indifference in Scotland to foreign literature is itself one of the causes of the continued domination and subversion of Scottish literature to English literature'. The problems involved in the reviving of Scots were immense. It had kept humble company for so long that it had suffered impoverishment of its vocabulary and taken on associations too homely, trivial and vulgar for high poetry. MacDiarmid therefore had to do for Scots what Spenser did for English: he had to create a new poetic diction. His method was to use words from the various Scots dialects and from all periods of the language's history and to borrow words from other languages, including Gaelic, explaining, 'The course taken in Norway in fashioning the Landsmal on the basis of Old Norse was one of the models I had in mind for Scotland and I was also influenced by the example of Mistral and the subsequent Provençal and Catalan developments'. Like Ezra Pound, James Joyce and T.S. Eliot in English, MacDiarmid was attracted to vocabularies which had not been used for centuries, turning to the language of his boyhood, his people's past and his own class: *'And by my sangs the rouch auld Scots I ken / E'en herts that ha'e nae Scots'll dirt richt thro' / Wi' datchie sesames, and names for nameless things'*. Among the English 'things' the poet rejected at this stage in his career was the English language, commenting in *At the Sign of the Thistle* (1934), 'The English language has vastly out-grown itself and is becoming more and more useless for creative purposes. It is suffering from a kind of imperial elephantiasis'.

The language created by MacDiarmid in his earliest volumes of verse, *Sangschaw* (1925), *Penny Wheep* (1926) and in his masterpiece *A Drunk Man Looks at the Thistle* (1926) became known as 'synthetic Scots' or, even more pejoratively as 'plastic Scots'; later, in the 'forties and 'fifties, it was known as Lallans to distinguish it from the spoken forms of Scots. Among the first writers to rally to its banner, but who later turned against it, was Lewis Spence (1874-1955) who said of MacDiarmid's lyrics as early as 1926, 'The Scotsman who cannot take to the new Scots resembles the Irishman who objects to Dublin street-names being lettered in Gaelic uncial'. Defending his view against Spence's attacks in 1934, MacDiarmid wrote in 'The Case for Synthetic Scots', 'It cannot be too strongly emphasised that it is absurd to debate whether Scots affords as good a medium as any other language for literary purposes. Any language, real or artificial, serves if a creative artist find his medium in it. In other words, it does not depend at all upon any other considerations, but wholly upon the *rara avis,* the creative artist himself'.

Unlike so many theorists in other minority languages, MacDiarmid had the genius, the industry and the opportunity required to write great poetry in illustration of his linguistic principles. In *Sangschaw* and *Penny Wheep* the short lyrics possessed intensity of passion, audacity of imagery, original rhythms and an emotional force of extraordinary strength. With them he became the first Scots poet to express a post-Romantic sensibility and to show himself acutely aware of the contemporary world. But it was with *A Drunk Man Looks at the Thistle* that it became clear that a new era in Scots literature was opening up. The first major poem in Scots for over a century, it ranges widely over time and space in exploration of the fundamental mysteries of love, death and human destiny. In form it is a dramatic monologue by an intoxicated reveller who has fallen into a ditch on his way home from the pub; his meditations are grotesque, satirical, obscene, lyrical, absurd, documentary, mystical, tragic, terrifying, comic and beautiful. The thistle which he contemplates represents both Scotland and humanity, *'The World and Life and Death, Heaven, Hell ana''* as the poet tries to reconcile the contradictions of man's experience. The poem is essentially modern, drawing on Rilke, Blok, Mallarmé and Joyce for its own purposes, and for this reason it caused a furore when it was first published. After hundreds of years Scotland had produced a great poet and the Scottish Renaissance was under way.

Throughout the 'twenties and 'thirties, Hugh MacDiarmid led the field of Scottish writing in an astonishing variety of roles—as poet, propagandist, editor, public speaker, reviewer (under more than one pseudonym and sometimes of his own books), essayist, short-story writer, journalist, translator, broadcaster, prominent member of the Scottish National Party and then of the Communist Party (he was expelled from both, from the S.N.P. on account of his Communism and from the C.P. because of his Nationalism)—a self-confessed anglophobe and extremist in literature and politics alike. During the 'thirties he published, besides other works, nine volumes of poetry, including *To Circumjack Cencrastus* (1936), *First Hymn to Lenin* (1931), *Scots Unbound* (1932), *Stony Limits* (1934) and *Second Hymn to Lenin* (1935); in the 'forties there appeared his biography *Lucky Poet* (1943), *A Kist of Whistles* (1947) and the outstanding poem *In Memoriam James Joyce* in 1955.

Work of such stature was bound to influence others and around MacDiarmid there gathered a number of writers who also produced work of lasting quality. They included William Soutar (1898-1943), A. D. Mackie (born 1904), Robert Garioch (born 1909) and Sidney Goodsir Smith (1915-74), all of whom revitalised the medieval Scots verse tradition. Others, having made their own important contributions, fell silent like Douglas Young (1913-73), or concentrated on writing in Gaelic like George Campbell Hay (born 1915), or reverted to English like Maurice Lindsay (born 1918). MacDiarmid occasionally turned to English in some of his later works, having found that Scots was not adequate for the intellectual kind of poetry he wished to write. But to Mac-Diarmid is owed the fact that, after a century of slavish imitation of Burns, Scots had survived and been revived as a language fit for poetry in the modern world.

Meanwhile London had begun to respond to the growing pressure of Scottish nationalism. In 1926 the Scottish Secretary had become the Secretary of State for Scotland with a seat in the Cabinet at Westminster and new powers; in 1939 the office was moved from London to Saint Andrew's House in Edinburgh and given wider responsibility in home affairs, health, agriculture and education. The S.N.P., despite a split in 1940, after its President Douglas Young refused conscription, calling on members not to fight for England, gained its first seat at Westminster five years later when Robert McIntyre won a majority of 617 votes over the Labour candidate at a by-election in Motherwell. Later that year, however, Labour fought on the Home Rule issue and regained the seat. For some years the S.N.P. was beset by factions such as those caused by Ronald E. Muirhead, 'the Grand old Man of Scottish Nationalism', who at the age of 82 broke away to form the Scottish National Congress in 1951, and by Wendy Wood and her Scottish Patriots. In 1950 Scottish nationalism leapt into the headlines following the removal from Westminster Abbey of *Lia Fail* (The Stone of Destiny), the stone on which Scottish Kings had been crowned over the centuries; the stone was found a year later at Arbroath Abbey wrapped in the Saltire, Scotland's national flag—a white diagonal cross on a blue background. Further incidents followed: the Scottish Liberation Army came to the fore in a campaign of blowing up post-boxes which bore the inscription 'E. II.R.' after pointing out that, while Queen Elizabeth is the second of her name to rule England, there was no previous Queen Elizabeth in Scotland; for this reason the Post Office's pillar boxes in Scotland are inscribed only with 'E.R.'

The idea of an independent, Scottish Scotland was the vision of the writers of the Scottish Renaissance who emerged after the First World War. However, it should not be assumed that because these writers were determined to restore Scots to its former literary status that the language was the central or predominant factor in the growth of political nationalism in their country. Not even Gaelic has been given that importance in the Scottish consciousness and neither Scots nor Gaelic is ever likely to prove the catalyst which, say, the Welsh language is in Wales. As David Murison has said, 'Any idea which may lurk in the mind of an ultra-Nationalist of a Scotland which may someday speak nothing but Scots, is a mere chimera'. It is nevertheless true that Scots is one factor among several, not pre-eminent perhaps but certainly important, which has gone to the making of Scottish identity and it has played a continuing role in Scottish life.

Until the advent of the Scottish Renaissance in the 1920s the world knew little of modern Scotland, its character and aspirations, except insofar as Scots people who had been absorbed into English society filled positions of responsibility as engineers, doctors and administrators in England and British territories overseas. Yet even now, when so many of the principles enunciated by MacDiarmid and the Scottish Renaissance have been implemented, the idea of restoring Scots as an integral part of the Scottish personality is not easily accepted by the large number of Scots who have been educated to English standards and are isolated between the popular Scottish culture and what Duncan Glen has typified as 'the polite English'. Thus it was that the poet Edwin Muir (1887-1959), a spokesman for the anglicised Scot, took the pessimistic stance that the process of anglicisation had proceeded so far that the only choice was to be absorbed into the dominant English culture and so become, as Muir admitted, second-class cultural citizens never likely to make a major contribution to that culture.

Other Scots have believed that they can use the Union with England to their own personal advantage, and have done so with huge success. J. M. Barrie the dramatist and Harry Lauder the music-hall star, for example, gave the English stage what it expected of Scotsmen, just as Ramsay MacDonald, the only true Scot to become Prime Minister of Britain, is generally believed to have sold himself to the English Establishment. Even the rebels of 'the Red Clyde' in the 1920s, men like Maxton and Kirkwood who accepted a peerage, played 'the wild Scot' to the delight and, later, the tedium of England. Comments Duncan Glen, 'They were not, finally, taken seriously by the English who would, and did, give short shrift to Northern working-class rebels. Scotland, and the Scots, are largely a fantasy world to the Southern English Establishment, indeed to Englishmen generally and, sadly, the Scots have done much to make this fantasy real. They have become great imitators and compromisers. This is the tragedy of the second-rate Scot'.

The two hundred years of neglect and betrayal of Scottish standards following the Union of 1707, which was largely responsible for the anti-Scottish attitudes of many Scots, is to be seen most clearly in the schools. Like the Church, the legal system and the Scottish Trades Union Congress, the educational system in Scotland is an administratively autonomous organisation with the status of a distinctive national institution. The schools, nevertheless, have until recent times generally neglected the history and literature of Scotland. History has usually been taught from an English point of view and English has been the language of education throughout the whole country. When in 1946 the Advisory Council on Scottish Education recommended that one period a week should be devoted to Scottish subjects, this specific point was discussed at such great length that, eventually, the decision taken was to express the vague hope 'that all Scottish education might be infused with Scottish sentiment'. David Murison comments, 'Nothing less than the introduction of Scottish literature as an integral part of teaching in the examination structure will do. In Scotland things are so arranged that Scottish subjects, even if on the curriculum, can always be avoided in examination . . . What is more, the unpalatable fact has to be faced that there are very many teachers who in their own day never had the chance or inclination to study Scottish subjects at school and are quite incapable of teaching them'. Some progress to this end has been made in the colleges of education, however, where Scottish history and literature take their place in the syllabus.

By now English is well-established as the socially superior

language of Scotland, despite the fact that few Scots educated in Scotland can use in speech a purely English vocabulary, far less an English pronunciation. Scots, on the other hand, has been seen as a handicap to advancement in the country where the best jobs were to be found, that is to say England, as well as at home. The Scottish Department of Education now acknowledges the revival of national consciousness, and the Scottish Renaissance which put Scots back into use as the language of major poetry, by advocating the retention of Scots forms within the English language and has prepared lists of Scots words which the child may be 'permitted' to use. But many Scots feel that repentance has come too late. Snobbery is not easily overcome and most teachers still regard Scots as a barbarism; many are illiterate in the language, except for a few ballads and parts of Burns and Scott. Yet some progress has been made: Scots Literature is studied in the Universities of Scotland and in some Universities abroad.

There are powerful social and economic pressures working against the use of Scots. The upper classes have not spoken it since the eighteenth century. This is how David Murison describes the language's status: 'It is the language of rustics, servants, lay-abouts, stick-in-the-muds, backward-looking sentimentalists *et hoc genus omne* who have made no headway in the rat-race, and anyone who uses it except to make a joke must take the consequences of his social backwardness, in betraying his vulgar origins or his inability to benefit from comprehensive education . . . The haunting fear of every Scots Mamma is that her dear offspring at an interview for some consequential position, in the south of course, should perpetrate a Scotticism or utter a rather broad *a* and so slam the door to advancement in his own face. This explains why in so many Scottish homes, Mamma is constantly on guard on the speech front against infiltration into the redoubt of what she thinks is pure English'.

In such circumstances the deterioration of Scots has proceeded apace during the last thirty years. An inquiry into the language of school-children in Aberdeenshire around 1930 revealed that about a sixth of the words in the local Scots dialect had been lost in a generation, and more recent studies have confirmed the loss of another sixth since then and suggested the loss of about half the vocabulary before the end of this century. It is only the rural minority in the areas which are rapidly losing their population which keeps its Scots with any degree of vitality. Although of great dialectal variety, in the rural areas where it persists in its richest and least adulterated forms, it is still capable of delicacy, subtlety and power of expression. Elsewhere, in the valleys of the Forth and Clyde, miners and industrial workers are reducing Scots to a gross, malformed and inexpressive variety of English. In Edinburgh there are schools where Scots is not understood at all, let alone spoken, by either teacher or pupil and where even the distinctive trilled *r* and *wh* of the Scots accent is reported to be on the way out. This impoverishment is to be heard in the Scots spoken on radio, television and the stage where an over-emphasis on accent, with a few glottal stops, is intended to pass for modern Scots. The distinctive form of English spoken in Scotland is not, after all, Scots. Middle Scots of the medieval period fares even worse on radio because the readers, never having heard it spoken correctly, anglicise the consonants and reduce the vowels beyond recognition in the belief that Scots is nothing more than a peculiar version of English. Nevertheless, it is clear that most Scots understand more of the language than they actually speak, as the reaction of theatre audiences proves. The fact remains that Scots as a language is in a serious state of decay and is soon to pass into a vestigial condition prior to its total disappearance.

As for written Scots, the situation is not quite so desperate but is far from healthy. The language has no official status and no public inscriptions appear in it. The weekly columns in Scots of many local newspapers have almost all disappeared. The debased industrial variety of the language appears from time to time in novels but this can hardly be described as Scots. Entries in Scots for literary competitions have decreased in number over the last twenty years to about 5%. In prose the language has not become a literary medium, so that all criticism of Scots poetry has to be written in English. Among prose-writers who have used the language consistently and as an integral part of their art, two stand out: Lewis Grassic Gibbon (1901-35), who wrote the greatest Scots novel of the twentieth century, the trilogy *A Scots Quair* (1946), and John Galt who experimented with a half-Scots, half-English style in *The Annals of the Parish, The Provost* and *Ringan Gilhaize.* Among the dramatists, Robert MacLellan, Sydney Goodsir Smith and Robert Kemp are the most successful to have tackled the job of writing prose in Scots.

The chief problem is that, in contrast to poetry, continuity in Scots prose was broken in the sixteenth century and there are no reliable models after that date. Having missed the development which English underwent over the last four centuries, it is difficult to adopt the Scots of a feudal, rural society to meet the demands of modern, industrial life. Yet, inspired by the example of Norway and the Faroes, the Scots have begun work on two large-scale dictionaries in the language. The first of these, *The Dictionary of the Older Scottish Tongue,* edited by J. Aitken and begun in the 1920s, deals with the language prior to 1700 and has reached the letter p. The second, David Murison's *The Scottish National Dictionary,* begun in 1927, is to be completed in 1976 with the publication of the last two parts of its tenth and final volume; the work lists about 50,000 words currently used in Scots or recorded since 1700. The Scots are, nevertheless, aware that there is not much hope for or much point in written Scots which is not supported by spoken forms and that a Scots created out of dictionaries will be little more than a dilettante exercise. In criticism of the Lallans experimenters, David Murison makes the following point: 'The mistake made by so many has been in an unskilful, indiscriminate and, too frequently, unidiomatic splashing about of Scots words taken at random from a dictionary, or concocted, not always correctly, out of their own heads or incongruously asserted from a variety of dialects. Two things should be borne in mind about literary Scots: firstly, that it has the same origin as English, that its differences from English are regular and not haphazard, and numerous as these are, the similarities are still more so, and that English and Scots have roughly the same relationship and should have the same degree of mutual intelligibility as Dutch and German, Spanish and Portuguese, and Polish and Czech or

Russian; secondly that a metropolitan Scots still exists, decayed though it is, and should be restored as a standard'.

To some extent, the decay of Scots is inevitable in the present circumstances and to revive it as a standard language for all purposes is clearly impracticable. There are, however, some serious consequences to the language's decline which need consideration. First of all, the literary heritage of Lowland Scotland is passing from memory as the language in which it was written declines: the work of the medieval *makars,* the ballad poets, Burns and others, becomes gradually less vital and significant; even Scott, Carlyle and Stevenson lose something of their original character. More seriously perhaps, there is a weakening of the individuality, confidence and spontaniety which grow from the free and eloquent use of what is, after all, the mother-tongue of many Scots. The Scot who preserves his native speech, together with his acquired English, has a reservoir of expression on which he draws spontaneously in times of happiness, sorrow, love, hatred and so on. Those who, despite the accent and vocabulary of their native tongue, in turning from Scots to English, are choking the springs of expression in these categories of experience which come to matter most in adult life. This is to be discerned in the habit of older people, too old to worry about their social status, who tend to revert to the older forms of speech they learnt as children. Furthermore, the loss is greater than that in the standardisation of dialect in, say, Yorkshire or Somerset. The Scots language is an integral part of a distinctive national tradition. It has carried the sentiment, heroism and love of country, of a civilised people through a long and turbulent history.

The charge of writing in a synthetic language unrelated to the vernacular is made against the poets still writing in Scots, the so-called *Lallans Makars.* During the Second World War the literary and political movement inaugurated by MacDiarmid continued with the work of a new generation for whom Scots was an acquired language. They have been followed by a number of younger poets who continue to write from much the same position. The principal magazine for contemporary writing in Scots is *Akros,* founded in 1965 by Duncan Glen (born 1933), himself one of the better poets in the language. To join the veterans who, besides Hugh Mac-Diarmid, Robert Garioch and Sydney Goodsir Smith, included J. K. Annand (born 1907), Tom Scott (born 1918) and Maurice Lindsay (born 1918), there now came such poets as Alexander Scott (born 1920) and Edwin Morgan (born 1929) and a host of even younger poets. It remains true, despite the number of poets now writing in Scots and the quality of their work, that English is the language of most Scottish writers today. Most of the Scots poets who made their names in the years up to 1950 are either dead or silent.

Only Hugh MacDiarmid has continued to publish poetry of the standard of his earlier work. His seventieth birthday in 1962 was celebrated by the publication of his *Collected Poems* in New York. Subsequent collections like *A Lap of Honour* (1967), *A Clyack-Sheaf* (1969) and *More Collected Poems* (1970), have consolidated a reputation so formidable that most critics have hesitated before its superlative brilliance and versatility. After over a century of creative effort, during which his work was neglected and attacked by all except a few critics, MacDiarmid has now become 'an institution', Scotland's first citizen and the subject of critical attention which has become an industry. Part of the irony is, as Alexander Scott has suggested, that MacDiarmid has become famous at the very moment when many—though by no means all—of the younger generation of Scottish poets, those born in the later 'thirties, 'forties and early 'fifties, have begun to discuss his achievement as being no longer relevant to their aim which is the creation of a national literature in English rather than in Scots.

It is perhaps more in the field of politics that the ideas of the Scottish Renaissance have come nearest to fruition. During the 'sixties the S.N.P. won more and more public support, especially at local elections, and became the principal party representing the national aspirations of the Scots. In 1966 the Liberal Party, mainly in an attempt to create publicity, supported the twenty-second Home Rule for Scotland Bill when Russell Johnson, M.P. for Inverness, proposed domestic self-government for Scotland within a British federal system. The motion met the same fate as the Home Rule for Wales Bill of 1967. The S.N.P. refused to co-operate with the Liberals, re-asserting that its aim was not a federation but 'to restore Scotland to the position of a free nation with full equality through self-government in the British Isles, the Commonwealth and other associations of nations'.

Following the abortive Liberal move to obtain Home Rule, the S.N.P. made rapid progress. Its first major success was the victory of S.N.P. candidate Winifred Ewing, a lawyer, who polled 18,397 votes at a by-election in Hamilton, Lanarkshire, in November 1967, against 16,598 votes for Labour and 4,986 for the Liberals. This was a staggering blow to the Labour Party, the majority party in Scotland, for Hamilton had been regarded as a safe seat, having been retained by Tom Fraser, Secretary of State for Scotland, with a majority of 16,576 at the General Election. Mrs Ewing joined Gwynfor Evans, the leader of *Plaid Cymru*, who had been elected at a by-election in Carmarthen in July of the previous year.

Since then the S.N.P. has made remarkable progress at both local and general elections. At the General Election of June 1970, at which the Conservative Party led by Edward Heath was returned to Westminster, Donald Stewart won the Western Isles for the S.N.P., the first candidate to win a seat for the party at a general election, although Hamilton was temporarily lost to the Labour Party. The S.N.P. contested sixty-six out of Scotland's seventy-one seats in 1970, in forty-six of which it lost its deposits. On the other hand, the party polled approximately 308,000 votes against 130,000 in 1966, 64,000 in 1964, 22,000 in 1959, 12,000 in 1955 and 7,000 in 1951. The most disappointing results were in the industrial belts of the Lowlands, where the party hoped to win several seats. Out of the twenty-six constituencies of Glasgow, Edinburgh, Dundee and Aberdeen, the party contested twenty-three and lost its deposits in twenty. It did better in the non-industrial areas of the North-West and the Borders, coming second in many seats and cutting the Conservative majorities substantially. The Liberal Party, which contested twenty-six seats in Scotland, lost eighteen deposits and won only three seats. At a time when England was clearly swinging to the right, Scotland moved only slightly in that direction (2·8% against 5% in the southern parts of

England). Labour, holding forty-four out of seventy-one seats, remained Scotland's principal political party, with 46% of the votes cast; the Conservatives received 38%, the Nationalists 11% and the Liberals 4·5%.

At the General Election of February 1974 it became clear that the S.N.P. was now a major party which had made rapid progress during the previous four years. The principal factor in its phenomenal growth is generally considered to be the discovery of oil off Scotland's shores. Campaigning with the slogan 'It's Scotland's oil', the party won seven seats: Aberdeenshire East, Argyll, Banffshire, Clackmannan and East Sterlingshire, Dundee East, Moray and Nairn, and the Western Isles. The total vote cast for the S.N.P. was 633,130 (21·93%), while the Labour Party polled 1,057,601 votes (36·63%) and the Conservatives 950,901 (32·93%), with forty seats and twenty-one seats respectively. The Liberals won three seats with 229,099 votes.

At the second General Election held in 1974, on 10 October, when the Labour Party was returned to Westminster, the S.N.P.'s progress was even more remarkable. It won eleven seats: apart from the seven gained in the previous February, the constituencies which elected a Scottish Nationalist were Angus South, Dumbartonshire East, Galloway and Perth and East Perthshire. The Labour Party won forty-one seats and polled 943,361 votes, the Conservatives sixteen seats and 701,289 votes, the Liberals three seats and 230,894 votes. The total number of votes cast for the S.N.P. was 840,589. The party's strength was now only second to the Labour Party's: given a 5% swing in favour of the Nationalists, the S.N.P. would become the biggest single party in Scotland and, with an 8% swing, the majority party.

When, in November 1975, the British Government announced details of its plans for establishing elected Assemblies for Scotland and Wales, its proposal was for a Scottish Assembly with legislative powers in addition to those proposed for its Welsh counterpart. This difference was defended by the Labour Party on the grounds that Scotland already had its own legal system whereas Wales did not. The S.N.P. criticised the White Paper as offering no more than a sop to nationalist feeling in Scotland, an opinion confirmed when it went on to win seats in local elections and to attract many supporters of the Labour Party, now in disarray, to its ranks. The 'great debate' called for by Edward Short, the Minister responsible for the Government's Devolution plans, began in Scotland during the autumn of 1975 with speculation as to how many more seats the S.N.P. would win at the next General Election and how far it would lead Scotland on the road to independence.

Writing in *Whither Scotland?*, Duncan Glen sums up prospects for Scotland after a measure of self-government has been achieved in the following words: 'The solution is obviously not simply political independence—that will only change the seat of government—but the difficult assumption of a cultural independence which will give a new dynamic to the country. It may be that political independence is essential to cultural independence, but the vision of Hugh MacDiarmid and those other cultural leaders who have fought for the idea of a Scottish Scotland is not a plan to have the same Scotland under new and better (economic) management but of a new Scotland which will be the intellectual, cultural and social equal of the best in Europe. And despite the continuing betrayals by the anglicised, the conservative and the timid, the last fifty years of literary renaissance suggest that an educational and cultural revolution has begun in Scotland and that the country is at long last moving towards achieving the unity, common purpose and maturity to be fully itself again—a Scottish Scotland with a European outlook. That is a vision seen by the renaissance poets of the last fifty years and seen most clearly in the poetry of Hugh MacDiarmid whose work alone, without other fine poets who gave him support, gives the lie to those who believe that Scotland is culturally and nationally dead'.

THE GAELS OF MAN

The Isle of Man is situated in the Irish Sea, more or less equidistant from Northern Ireland and the coast of Cumberland in England, but nearer to Scotland which is about twenty miles to the north. Most of the Island, which has an area of 227 square miles, lies under 1,000 feet but Snaefell, the highest point, rises to 2,036 feet. Its economy is based mainly on agriculture, with some fishing and light industry. But the most important source of income is tourism. About half a million holiday-makers visit the Island every year, attracted not only by its magnificent scenery but by such attractions as a casino and a motor-cycling race for which the place is famous. At the 1971 Census the Isle of Man's population was 56,289, of whom 20,389 lived in the principal town, Douglas, and about 11,000 in the small towns of Ramsey, Peel and Castletown.

The Manx language is no longer spoken in the Island, either as the mother-tongue of any person or as the every-day medium in any community. The two or three hundred people who claim a good knowledge of spoken Manx have learned it as a second language, usually in adult life. An official of *Yn Cheshaght Ghailckagh* (The Manx Language Society) commented recently, 'There are a few of us who could get through a day without speaking English, but it would be difficult and we would have to stop and think for the Manx equivalent of some English words'. Nevertheless, despite the extinction of their language for everyday purposes, the Manx Gaels are to be considered here for reasons similar to those offered for inclusion of the Cornish.

Manx belongs, with Irish and the Gaelic Scotland, to the Goidelic branch of the Celtic languages. That it is Q-Celtic, rather than P-Celtic like the Brythonic branch, is illustrated by the Manx word for *five,* which is *quig* (Welsh: *pump)*, and by many characteristic surnames beginning with Q or hard C or K, an abbreviation of the original *mac* which meant 'son of' as in Irish and Scottish Gaelic. There is much evidence that the existence of this Gaelic speech dates from as early as the fifth century A.D. It is also likely that some Brythonic speech was also present on the Island at this time but that it did not survive. In the tenth century and afterwards Manx Gaelic was temporarily subordinated to the Norse language as a result of conquest by Vikings but after 1266 it was gradually re-established as the principal speech of the Manx people. Norse survives only in a high proportion of place-names throughout the Island.

No satisfactory explanation has ever been given for the name of the Island. The earliest form of Man was *Manu,* of which the genitive was *Manann* and from which are derived *Mannin* and the common form *Ellan Vannin* (Isle of Man). Part of the confusion is caused by the fact that there are other ancient island-names in western Britain which are similar. *Erin* for example, derives from *Eriu* (genitive *Erenn),* while *Arran* is from the genitive of *Aru.* It seems likely that the name is of pre-Celtic origin, perhaps an early tribal name as in Clackmannan in central Scotland which borders on the old British territory known as *Manaw Gododdin.* Another source of controversy is a description by Julius Caesar, made after his brief visits to Britain in 55 and 54 B.C., in which he refers to 'an island called Mona which lies midway across the sea separating Britain from Ireland'. This position can only be that of the Isle of Man. But the name *Mona* (Welsh: *Môn),* was applied in Roman times to the island of Anglesey in Wales. Furthermore, although there is no proof that the Romans ever settled in the Island, they certainly knew of its existence, for Pliny referred to *Monapia* in A.D. 77 and Orosius to *Mevania* in A.D. 416. To complicate matters more, the Icelandic sagas give the name of Man as *Mön,* while in the Island itself the earliest form occurs in the tenth century as *Maun.* What seems certain is only this: that the mythological character known as Mananann, who figures in many guises in Manx folk-lore, did not give his name to the Island but was, rather, named after it.

That Man was linked with Ireland, chiefly Ulster and with the west of Scotland throughout pre-historic times is illustrated by the legends which they have in common. Dating from about the first century B.C., they have, as their principal heroes, Manannan, Conchobar and Cuchalain. The first of these was known as Manannan mac Lir (Son of the Sea), prob-ably in acknowledgement of the sea-links between the three territories of Gaeldom. The exploits of Conchobar, a mythical king of Ulster, and the belief that Cuchulain lived in Man, illustrate the Island's links with that province. Other stories of later date concern the adventures of a hero called Finn and his son Ossian. Much of this early epic literature has been lost but remnants were collected in the eighteenth century from oral tradition as part of the interest in James Macpherson's Ossianic poems.

Contacts between Man and the rest of the Celtic world during the early Christian period, up to the ninth century, are to be seen from the five ogham stones discovered in the Island. The names on these stones are Irish but the form in which they are cut shows the influence of British pronunciation, a process which implies the presence of Goidelic and Brythonic Celts living in contact with one another. It has been concluded by R. H. Kinvig in his book *The Isle of Man** that the Island 'was originally British (in modern terms, Welsh-speaking) not Irish, but that here, as in Gaelic Scotland, the Irish immigrants eventually absorbed the previous population, whereas their colonies in Wales and Cornwall were absorbed by the population they found there'.

It is not known precisely when Christianity was introduced in Man, but many churches and shrines were built in honour of Celtic saints, including St Patrick, St Brigit and St Columba. The most important religious centre during the period 450-800 A.D. was the monastery built by Maughold in the seventh century. This period was remarkable for the wealth of its art and the quality of its learning. Although little of Manx metal-work and calligraphy has survived, the Norsemen having destroyed many religious books, there is abundant evidence that the Islanders excelled as sculptors. The Manx Museum at Douglas has a splendid collection of stone crosses, many in the traditional Celtic form. Throughout this period there were trade and cultural contacts with Ireland, Scotland, England and northern Wales, while Christianity took firm root all over the Island.

Towards the end of the eighth century the prosperity of

*The present account draws heavily on this work, R. H. Kinvig: *The Isle of Man* (Liverpool, 1975).

Man was shattered by the arrival of Vikings, who saw in the Island not only a rich source of plunder but a strategically important base for their raids on the near-by coasts. In the *Orkneyinga Saga* it is stated several times that they would set off from the Island in early summer and 'fare home to Man' as winter approached. Evidence of their settlement in Man has been discovered in a number of burial places. All districts conquered by the Vikings were claimed by the King of Norway but, in practice, the rival chieftains fought over the land they occupied. Man was ruled from Dublin, for a time the centre of Norse power in the area, and later by the Earls of Orkney. As time passed, however, the Island was linked with the other Norse islands of the Hebrides off the west coast of Scotland which became known as the Kingdom of Man and the Isles. The first known ruler of this territory was King Godred Crovan (known to the Manx as King Orry) whose conquest in 1079 is described in the *Chronicle of Man and the Isles* compiled by the monks of Rushen Abbey. He reigned for sixteen years until his death in 1095 and his descendants until 1265.

The Scandinavian settlement was very important in Man's history. Although it began with plunder and destruction and a partial return to paganism, the Vikings brought a new life to the Island and developed what they found there. Marriage between the invaders and the Manx took place on a large scale, to such an extent that since the Vikings were known to the Gaels as *Galls* (strangers) the mixed population of Man was called Gael-Galls by the other Gaelic peoples in areas unaffected by Scandinavian settlement. Norse became the language of government and the ruling classes, but Gaelic remained in the homes. But by the time when the Kingdom of Man and the Isles was coming to an end, Gaelic re-established itself. Owing to the close connection between the Island and the western parts of Scotland, Manx Gaelic was now heavily influenced by the Scottish form, so that from this time on the Island's language developed further away from Irish. Surprisingly, Norse had little effect on Manx, except in a few words used in administration and in place-names.

It was in government that the Norse influence was heaviest. An essential feature of Norse life was the open-air assembly, held every year, at which laws were announced and disputes settled. It was known as a *thing*, a word which forms the first part of the Manx term *Tynwald*, and of which the second part derives from *Völlr*, the Norse for field or meeting-place. *Tynwald* is the meeting still held in Man on 5 July each year for the purpose of announcing new laws. The House of Keys, which is the Island's Parliament, also owes some of its characteristics to the Norsemen, especially to King Godred and the system he devised for governing his maritime kingdom. The Manx name for this body is *Yn Kiare-as-feed* (The Four and Twenty), in reference to the number of seats fixed since 1156. This name was anglicised to Keys, an appropriate corruption since the function of the Parliament was to 'unlock the difficulties of the law'. Other customs, such as the spreading of rushes on the path to Tynwald Hill, and the division of the Island into sheadings, parishes, treens and quarter-lands, are older than the Norsemen.

The Vikings also had an effect on the Island's religious life. At first the development of Christianity was seriously impaired but towards the end of the tenth century it revived and the Norsemen began to give up their pagan beliefs. Their full conversion was a slow progress, and many of the old gods and heroes are depicted on the memorial crosses of the Island. Links with the Irish Church were broken in the eleventh century and the first Bishop of Man, Roolwer (Norse: *Hrólfr*, English: Ralph) owed allegiance to the Archbishop of Canterbury. During the reign of King Olaf (1113-53) the Cistercian monks of Furness built Rushen Abbey, which became a cultural centre of great significance; they also introduced Roman forms of ritual against the opposition of Irish monks based on the island of Iona. From 1153 until the fifteenth century the bishopric of Man and the Isles was under the control of the Archbishop of Trondheim in Norway. Since 1542 it has belonged to the English province of York.

The last King of Man and the Isles was Magnus, who died in 1265. A year later, a treaty was signed between Norway and Scotland by which the Western Isles and Man were handed over to the King of Scotland, Alexander III. There followed a period of conflict between Scotland and England, both sides being anxious to gain possession of Man for its strategic importance. The Manx rebelled against the Scots but were put down. On the death of Alexander's grand-daughter, Margaret 'the Maid of Norway', King Edward I of England claimed Man as an English possession. Who actually governed the Island between 1313 and 1333 it is difficult to say, the Scots, English and Irish fought over it. It was not until 1346, when the English defeated the Scots at the battle of Neville's Cross near Durham, that the Island came under their jurisdiction. The Island was subsequently given to a succession of English nobles and finally, by Henry IV to Sir John Stanley in 1405. Stanley's descendants, the Earls of Derby, were destined to be rulers of Man for the next three hundred years, until 1736.

It is from this period of upheaval that the official armorial bearing of the Island—'the three legs of Man'—survives. This symbol is known to be ancient, being found on Greek vases from the sixth century B.C. Like the swastika and fylfot it is derived from a design based on the spokes of a wheel or the sun's rays, for it was associated with sun-worship. The design was taken from Greece to Sicily and was used on coins made in Syracuse as a symbol of dominion over that island. It is less likely that the Manx emblem has links with Sicily, however, than that is based on the triple knot on the coins used by the Norse-Irish kings of northern England in the tenth century. The first reference to the three mailed legs in Man dates from the thirteenth century, when they were attributed to the Kings of Man. In the following century the symbol was carved in stone and incorporated in the Lord of Man's seal. The Latin motto, *Quocunque Jeceris Stabit* (Whichever way you throw, it will stand) was added later and was first seen on Manx coins dated 1668.

The gift of the Island to Sir John Stanley marked the beginning of a new era in the history of Man. Although this powerful English family, who became Earls of Derby after helping Henry Tudor to defeat Richard III at Bosworth in 1485, rarely visited the Island, they appointed responsible governors and a period of stability followed. The power of the Church and barons was curbed, the ancient constitution of the Island restored and laws codified. The second Earl of Derby (1504-21) gave up the title of King to become Lord of Man, but the third Earl, who held power from 1521 to 1572 and was a devout Catholic, obstructed the cause of the Reformation in the Island.

The slowness with which the Reformation penetrated Manx society was also due to the Island's remoteness, to the people's ignorance of English and to the lack of any books in Manx. The first book in Manx, a translation of the Book of Common Prayer, was translated in 1611 by Bishop John Phillips (1605-33), a Welshman appointed to the bishopric of Sodor and Man in 1605. Unlike many of his predecessors, Bishop Phillips took the Manx language seriously and according to an account written twenty-five years after his death, 'out of zeal to the propagating of the Gospel attained the knowledge of Manx so exactly that he did ordinarily preach in it'. It seems likely that the majority of the population spoke Manx at this time, excluding only the wealthier land-owners, clergy and merchants in the towns. What is equally likely is that most were illiterate in Manx and that even those who could write did not do so in the language. For by now the Gaelic tradition in the Island had been broken. The long absence of native rulers, or any learned class among the Manx, had meant that even place-names and personal-names were written according to English or Latin orthography. It was against this background that Bishop Phillips worked. Not knowing Scottish Gaelic, he based the orthography of his translations on English and his native Welsh.

Throughout the reign of the Stanleys the Island was more or less sealed from contact with the outside world. No tenant was free to leave the Island without special permission from the Governor and, if any succeeded, their land was confiscated. Constant watch was mounted against incursion from Scotland and all Scots landing on Manx shores were ordered to be shot. Conditions for the working-class were atrocious and many illiberal laws remained in force. As a result, Manx Gaelic—still the language of the majority of the population at this time—began to diverge from the dialects spoken in Ireland and Scotland. Whereas the Island had been on the circuit of peripatetic bards and singers, bearers of the old culture common to the whole of Gaeldom, Man now lost contact with its neighbours to the west and north as they ceased to find patrons on the Island. Manx lost much of its traditional vocabulary and whatever remained became the preserve of an uneducated peasantry. The language was impoverished in its use of the genitive and dative forms, except in a few stock-phrases, the structure of sentences was reduced in complexity and prepositions lost much of their original significance. English words were borrowed on a huge scale and the orthography became more and more anglicised.

During the English Civil War Man was drawn into closer contact with England by the seventh Earl of Derby, who was known in the Island as *Yn Stanlagh Mooar* (the Great Stanley). The head of a great Royalist family, he supported Charles I against Cromwell. But the sympathies of many Manxmen who had for long had grievances against their rulers, were with Parliament. There was bitter fighting on and around the Island between Royalists and Roundheads over several years, and popular discontent was fanned by the heavy burden of increased taxes to pay for the Earl's forces and his defence of Man. Eventually, the Great Stanley was defeated at Wigan and executed in 1651 after the battle of Worcester. The Manx then rose in rebellion against the Earl's wife, Charlotte, who had been left in charge of the Island. They were led by William Christian, known in Manx as *Illiam Dhone* (William the Brown Haired). Christian helped the Parliamentary forces to gain possession of the Island in the name of the Manx people. With the restoration of Charles Stuart came the restoration to power of Charles Stanley, the eighth Earl of Derby, as Lord of Man. On his return to the Island, wrongly believing that the amnesty extended also to Man, Christian was arrested. Brought to trial, he refused to plead and when several members of the House of Keys refused to condemn him they were replaced. His speech from the dock, together with an account of the whole episode, is to be found in the introduction to Sir Walter Scott's novel *Peveril of the Peak*. After being found guilty Christian was shot. It is said that he refused a blindfold and that most of the firing squad deliberately shot into the air, only one aiming true. Before his trial Christian had sent an appeal to the King but it did not reach London until after he was shot. It was later upheld, Christian's name was cleared, his land restored to his family and three other leaders of the rising released from prison. Christian was mourned by the Manx as a martyr and a ballad *Baase Illiam Dhone* commemorates him to this day.

The eighteenth century saw the last of the Stanleys and the coming of British rule in the Isle of Man. Under Bishop Barrow and later Bishop Wilson the power of the Church was restored and attempts made to provide a system of education through English for the common people. Congregations outside the towns still understood only Manx, however, and there were no books in the language for use in church, until Bishop Wilson commissioned the printing of the Bible in 1748; he had published a Catechism in Manx in 1707 and began the printing of a Manx Bible in 1748.

The lexicographers of the eighteenth and nineteenth centuries provided valuable information about attitudes to Manx in the prefaces to their translations, dictionaries and grammars. Whereas Bishop Barrow in the seventeenth century had been well aware of apathy and opposition towards it, concluding that the cure for the Manx people's ignorance and irreligious ways was to teach them English, Bishop Hildesley in the eighteenth century recognised the existence of Manx as the language of the majority and sought to make provision for them: 'The Manks people, in general, are naturally shrewd, of quick apprehension, and very apt to learn: and they would be, I am confident, extremely fond of perusing the Scriptures, if they had them, and were taught to read them, in their own tongue, as they are the English Bibles; which latter numbers can do very roundly, whilst they scarce understand the meaning of a single sentence; nay, I might say, I believe, of some, a single word!' Not that Bishop Hildesley was unaware that some of his clergy lacked enthusiasm for Manx; he asked of one, 'Has he made a Manks sermon yet? If he has not, 'tis fit he should, unless he is one of those geniuses of the South, who think the cultivation of that language unnecessary . . . This, I believe, is the only country in the world, that is ashamed of, and even inclined to extirpate, if it could, its own native tongue'.

In 1805 John Kelly, the author of a grammar and two dictionaries, was to write to Bishop Hildesley and Wilson that 'they studied it with a higher view—to render it by publication instrumental in removing

ignorance, communicating truth and obtaining a knowledge of English. Their motives were religious and
moral; but the present state of the empire holds out to government and individuals another motive at this time not less im-
perious, that unity of language is the surest cement of civil as
well as of religious establishments . . . When there shall be
one national language, then only will the union of the empire
be completely established . . . It is true that in process of time
this cultivation of the Gaelic language will destroy the
language itself, as a living language; but it will have produced
the knowledge of a better, and will descend to posterity by
means of the press in a more perfect state, than if it should be
found only in the conversation of unlettered individuals.
There would be no more cause of regret, then, that it was not
a living language, than there is at present, that the Hebrew,
Greek and Latin are no longer such'. As R. L. Thomson
remarks on Kelly's views in his Sir John Rhŷs Memorial Lecture (1969), *The Study of Manx Gaelic:* 'the linguist and the
patriot must alike be affronted by his attitude. It makes me
angry every time I read it'.

It was left to Archibald Cregeen, who compiled the first dictionary of Manx around 1835, to contest Kelly's view. In his
preface are the words: 'I am well aware that the utility of the
following work will be variously appreciated by my brother
Manksmen. Some will be disposed to deride the endeavour to
restore vigour to a decaying language. Those who reckon the
extirpation of Manks a necessary step towards that general
extension of the English, which they deem essential to the interest of the Isle of Man, will condemn every effort which
seems likely to retard its extinction . . . That a language so
venerable for its antiquity and so estimable on many accounts
should be so generally neglected is much to be lamented . . .
Despised and neglected, however, as the language appears to
be at present, it is susceptible of high improvement, and justly
entitled to the attention of the scholar'. Unlike Kelly, Cregeen
was hopeful for the future of Manx, 'At the present period,
then, this interesting little Island promises to become once
more the abode of science and literature, it is hoped that
Gaelic learning will revive, and that every facility will be
afforded for the acquisition of a language so essentially

necessary within the precincts of Mona to the students of Divinity, and the students of law . . . Amongst the numerous literary advantages which King William's College is expected to afford the sons of Mona, it is devoutly to be wished that the cultivation of the vernacular tongue be not overlooked. The establishment of a professorship for that specific object would be highly desirable'. The college, opened in 1833, did not take heed of Cregeen's words and there is still no university on the Isle of Man.

At the level of higher education, Manx is not studied to the same extent as other Celtic languages. T. F. O'Rahilly, the Irish authority, wrote in 1931 that 'it is, perhaps, too much to expect that Manx, that Cinderella of Gaelic tongues, should ever attract many students'. Quoting this comment in his Sir John Rhŷs Memorial Lecture, R. L. Thomson remarked, 'Indeed she is a Cinderella among the Celtic ones as a whole, for Cornish, her counterpart in the British group, has, by reason of possessing some generally rather late medieval remains, appeared more glamorous in the eyes of historically minded students of Celtic than Manx, which can boast of nothing of more certain antiquity than the sixteenth century'. Thomson reminds us that among distinguished philologists who have, nevertheless, shown an interest in Manx are Edward Lhuyd, 'the father of Celtic philology', who brought Manx to the attention of the learned world by describing it in his *Archaeologica Brittanica* (1707), Sir John Rhŷs whose interest was aroused on a visit to the Island in 1886, and Professor K. H. Jackson of Edinburgh University. The only Celtic scholar to have been born in the Island was E. C. Quiggin.

The Manx Bible was followed by a hymn-book in the language, which was published for the Methodists in 1795. About the same time much religious verse was composed in Manx. These *carvals* (carols) are the only original literature composed in the language. Methodism had an enormous success in the Island after visits by John Wesley in 1777 and 1781, by when there were about 2,100 members of Methodist societies out of a total adult population of some 15,000. Wesley recorded his satisfaction in his journal: 'What a fair proportion is this! . . . The local preachers are men of faith and love, knit together in one mind and one judgement'. His impressions of the Island were less enthusiastic: 'it is shut up from the world and having little trade, visited by scarce any strangers . . . The natives are a plain, artless, simple people, unpolished, that is, unpolluted; few of them are rich or genteel; the far greater part moderately poor; and most of the strangers that settle among them are men that have seen affliction'. On the Manx language Wesley was even clearer in his view; asked by a preacher to publish a hymn-book in Manx, he wrote to him in 1789: 'I exceedingly disapprove of your publishing anything in the Manx language. On the contrary, we should do everything in our power to abolish it from the earth, and persuade every member of our Society to learn and talk English'.

The tenth Earl of Derby died without an heir and was succeeded by a relative, the Duke of Atholl. The Atholl dynasty lasted only thirty years, however, although their connection with the Island as land-owners and Governors-General lasted for another sixty years. In 1765 the third Duke sold the lordship to the British Crown which was anxious to be rid of the smuggling trade centred there. By the Revesting Act of that year, and payment of the sum of £70,000, the sovereignty of Man which the King of England had granted to Sir John Stanley in 1405, passed once more to the King. Under the fourth Duke of Atholl, the remainder of his rights was purchased for £417,000 in 1828. Meanwhile heavy taxes had been inflicted on the Manx people, the trade of smuggling wiped out and the Island's economy badly neglected. Although the House of Keys, a self-elected body with no legislative powers, remained, Man was deprived of all authority over its own affairs. Edmund Burke, in one of his famous speeches, compared the British Government's conduct in the Isle of Man with its conduct in America. The Revesting Act of 1765 was known to the Manx as *Yn Chialg Vooar* (The Great Deception).

During the rest of the nineteenth century the Isle of Man suffered from the Revesting Act. Poverty and disease were widespread, prices increased rapidly and emigration began on a large scale. In the 1820s there were tithe disputes and potato riots. The Island was settled at the end of the Napoleonic Wars by retired army and navy officers from

England; debtors also found a haven there. After a passenger-steamer service between Douglas and Liverpool was opened in 1829, the first English holiday-makers began to arrive, and the Island's economy was improved by the beginnings of a tourist industry. At the same time, there was agitation for reform of the House of Keys and financial control of the Island's affairs by a democratically elected body. This was achieved in 1866 when, led by the Governor, Lord Loch, Tynwald passed two Acts for the defence of Manx interests. The century also saw a rapid increase in the Island's population. At the first Census, in 1821, there were 40,081 inhabitants whereas a hundred years previously there had been approximately 14,400. Despite bad conditions in agriculture and the failure of the potato crop, which caused emigration to America, the population grew to 52,387 in 1851 and to 54,752 in 1901.

The constitutional relationship between the Isle of Man and the United Kingdom, together with the Island's present system of internal government, date from the reforms of 1866. In evidence submitted by Tynwald to the Royal Commission on the Constitution in 1970, it was admitted that there is no entirely satisfactory answer to the question, 'What is the government of the Isle of Man?' For a population the size of a fairly small town's, the Manx have devised an unusually complicated system. But it can be summarised as follows: the Government of Man consists of the Lieutenant-Governor who represents the British Crown; the Legislative Council or upper house, with ten members; the House of Keys or elected chamber, with twenty-four members; and Tynwald which consists of the Governor and the two branches of the legislature.

As the supreme Head of Government, it is the Lieutenant-Governor's duty to ensure that the Island does not run into debt. In this he is assisted by a Finance Board and a Police Board, although he retains ultimate authority. He presides over the legislative Council and over Tynwald and has considerable control over most other public bodies in the Island. The consent of the Legislative Council is necessary before any law can be passed. Up to 1919 this upper house was composed entirely of officials, most of whom were appointed by the British Government, but by the Isle of Man Constitution Amendment Act of 1919 under Lord MacDonnell this was

amended to admit four members elected by the House of Keys
and two appointed by the Governor. In the House of Keys
there are twenty-four members elected by universal suffrage
every five years. The only political parties in the Island are the
Manx Labour Party and the nationalist *Mec Vannin* (Sons of
Man). But the majority of members in the Keys are Independent and government is not conducted on party lines.
As members are not paid a living wage, they are drawn mainly
from business and agricultural circles, especially from among
persons of retired age, and there is no Opposition as such.
Tynwald is unique in the British Isles in that it consists of two
legislative bodies sitting together. Its main functions are to
levy·taxes, to decide how the Island's revenue is to be spent
and to administer the various departments of government.
The latter include boards which have responsibility for
education, roads, harbours, airports, health, the social services, fishing, agriculture, water, electricity, forestry, advertising, culture and the arts, town and country planning. As
government is not organised on political lines, however, there
is more discussion about methods than about policies at Tynwald. All Manx laws require Royal assent but, according to
tradition, they have to be proclaimed in both English and
Manx at Tynwald Hill before they are effective.

The MacDermott Commission of 1959 presented a comprehensive survey of the outstanding questions affecting the
Manx Constitution and, since then, several important Acts
have been added to the Statute Book, one of which set up an
Executive Council. The Commission also expressed the view
that the essential features of the Island's relationship with the
United Kingdom should remain unaltered. The Isle of Man is
a dependency of the British Crown under the jurisdiction of
the Home Office. The United Kingdom Government is
ultimately responsible for the good government of the Island,
having power to legislate for it. This view of 'ultimate responsibility' and the consequent impossibility of independent action on any question of real importance has caused anxiety in
connection with the United Kingdom's decision to join the
E.E.C. A Select Committee of Tynwald was set up in
April 1970 to examine the probable consequences of Common
Market membership and to explore possible alternatives.

Relations between Tynwald and Westminster were also strained in 1967 when the British Government banned the pirate radio ship Caroline, moored near the Island, against the wishes of the Manx. More recently, in October 1975, the U.K. Government had to defend the Isle of Man's birching laws before the European Commission on Human Rights at Strasbourg on behalf of the Manx Government, despite the fact that corporal punishment was banned in the United Kingdom some years previously. The Commission's condemnation of birching caused resentment on the Island. The Chairman of the Manx Cabinet, Percy Radcliffe, announced that if the British Government intervened against birching, which he claimed has almost total support from Tynwald and the Manx public, then it was time for the Island to seek 'a new relationship' with the United Kingdom.

The other main difference between the Isle of Man and the rest of the United Kingdom is in the Island's tax structure. Indirect taxation in Man is similar to that on the mainland and has continued to be so after the introduction of Value Added Tax in 1972. But in direct taxation, Manx income-tax is raised at a standard rate of $21 \cdot 25\%$, a good deal lower than in the United Kingdom; there are also higher personal allowances, no surtax, no capital gains tax, and no estate duty. The Manx justification of this relatively low rate is based on the isolation of the Island and its lack of natural resources. Manufacturing industries have to be encouraged to invest in Man by higher regional incentives and wealthy residents, who provide a powerful stimulus to the economy, are also attracted by the low rates and high employment. In 1974/5 the Chairman of the Manx Government's Finance Board, John Bolton, who is known as the Island's Exchequer, reported a surplus of £2·6m. out of a budget of £31 million; unemployment was running at only 1 to 2%.

It was against the influx of outsiders attracted by a more favourable tax system that protests were made in 1973 by small groups of Manx nationalists. During that year there were several cases of arson in which the property of the so-called 'come-overs' was destroyed, and many slogans painted in public places. The chairman of the Government's Finance Board was sent a bullet through the post. These protests coincided with the emergence of a militant group calling itself

Fo Halloo (Underground). In a two-page, duplicated news-sheet this group made allegations of corruption in Government circles and announced, 'We intend to publish what we believe to be the truth about the treasonable conspiracy against the Manx people, in which gangs of alien profiteers and prominent local politicians are obviously engaged, and we will take whatever measures we deem necessary to put a spoke in their wheel'. Although there is no evidence to connect *Fo Halloo* with the burning of property in the Island it is widely assumed to have been responsible. Later, the slogan 'No New Residents' was burnt into a field with the initials '*F.H.*' under the flight-path of aeroplanes arriving from the mainland. Two young people have been convicted for helping a third and unknown person to paint nationalist slogans. Another militant splinter-group in the nationalist movement is *Irree Magh* (Rebellion) which distributed leaflets during 1975 calling for the expulsion of all 'come-overs' and independence from the United Kingdom.

Very little information is available about the membership of *Fo Halloo* and *Irree Magh* but it is believed to consist almost entirely of young people and to be led by a former Scottish nationalist; almost certainly they will not prove to be of lasting significance. What is more clear is that they are more militant wings of the principal Manx nationalist movement *Mec Vannin*. Founded in 1964, mainly through the efforts of Douglas Fargher, a teacher of Manx Gaelic, and Lewis Crellin, *Mec Vannin* today claims about 500 members but has no official representatives in the House of Keys or at local level. Its aim is to revive and foster interest in all forms of Manx culture and to work for the establishment of 'a fully autonomous State' economically and politically separate from the United Kingdom.

Whoever is responsible for the militant activity of the last three years, there is general agreement among the various nationalist groups, including *Mec Vannin*, that the rate of settlement by non-Manx, mainly English people, since the mid-1960s has not been an entirely unmixed blessing. The nationalists are prepared to put up with the tourists who visit Man each summer. Tourism is a long-established industry: in 1901 over 418,000 tourists visited the Island, 593,000 in 1937 and since then the total number has remained around half a million; they spend about £12 million in Man annually. It is against those who return to buy up land and property that the nationalists are bitter. Since 1965 almost a thousand English people have settled in Man every year, so that by today only about 35% of the population is ethnically Manx. The newcomers have pushed up land-price to the point where it is difficult for young Manx people to buy homes and good agricultural land has been used for building purposes. The community is more and more divided between wealthy newcomers and comparatively poor Manx people. The allegations of corruption made on the Island recently arise from the many land-deals between politicians and developers. It was the bungalow of one of the chief developers, who owns 2,000 acres of land as well as hotels and a casino, which was burned down in 1973. Shortly afterwards the Manx Government, which lends a sympathetic ear to charges of corruption, began seeking ways of clearing the air and ensuring that only the wealthiest could settle in the Island. In September 1975 it passed a Finance Act which stated that, as from December 1974, all those who emigrate to the Isle of Man shall be treated as domiciled in the United Kingdom for the rest of their lives. This measure, and the implementation of a Capital Transfer Tax, has begun to slow down the influx of new arrivals—thus pleasing the nationalists but angering the business community.

The revival of national consciousness in the Isle of Man since the Second World War has its roots in the writings of Arthur W. Moore (1853-1909) who for many years was Speaker of the House of Keys. Moore completed a history of the Isle of Man in 1900 and led a Manx delegation to the first Celtic Congress in 1901. Others associated with him were Sophia Morrison and William Cubbon. The principal organisation devoted to Manx at the present time, *Yn Cheshaght Ghailckagh* (The Manx Gaelic Society), dates from this period. Founded in 1899, the Society specialises in the preservation and teaching of Manx Gaelic. Its motto is *Gyn chengey, gyn cheer* (Without a language, without a country), but it has none of the militancy of its Welsh, Irish or Scottish counterparts. Among the devices it employs to encourage the use of Manx is a *fainey,* a pin worn in the lapel in the style of the Irish *fainne.* A youth movement known as *Aeglagh Vannin* flourished in the 1960s, under the leadership of Mona Douglas but is not now very active.

The Society is well aware of the reasons for the decline of Manx. In the first place, the language lacked a Bible until late in its history, as well as a literature of any scope or quality. Methodism did nothing to foster it. Manx was modelled in its written forms on English rather than on Irish or Gaelic, so that T. F. O'Rahilly in 1932 was drawn to declare that it 'hardly deserved to live because it had surrendered to foreign idiom'. English made rapid head-way in the Island around 1700. Up to then, under the Stanleys, and even up to the Revesting Act, Manx was the language of the majority of the common people, about 13,000 in all. But pressure upon them to speak English soon increased. During the eighteenth century the influence of Lancashire and tourism grew. Manx declined over the next two centuries from decade to decade, a process hastened by the schools in which it had no place after the Education Act of 1870. By 1874 there were still 12,000 speakers of Manx but by 1901 it was spoken by only 4,419 people (8·1%) out of a total population of 54,752. Ten years later the number of Manx-speakers was halved and by the 1920s the language was hardly to be heard anywhere. At the Census of 1961 only 160 speakers of the language remained, and few of those were native-speakers. The last person for whom Manx was a mother-tongue was Ned Maddrell, a fisherman-crofter of Cregneash, the language's final stronghold in the south of the Island; he died, aged ninety-seven, in 1974.

Despite this decline, there has been a revival of interest in the Manx language during recent years. Since the Manx Education Act of 1949 the Island's education system is the same as in the rest of the United Kingdom as established by the Butler Act of 1944. But scant attention has been paid to the Manx language up to the present time. The language is taught as an extra-curricular subject in about half of the Island's primary schools but in only one of the Island's secondary schools. The Manx Government's Board of Education provides facilities for learning the language in evening classes, however, in three of the main towns. It was estimated that there were about 500 people learning the language in this way during 1975.

A serious lack among those interested in Manx is the shortage of written texts. A weekly column in Manx appears in *The Manx Star* but none is published in *The Examiner* or *The Times,* the other two weekly newspapers run by the Island's Development Corporation at Douglas; there is no daily newspaper published on the Island and no regular periodical in Manx. The two principal magazines published on the Island, *Manx Life* and *The Manxman,* rarely pay attention to the language. A few issues of a duplicated broadsheet *Coraa ny hGael* (Voice of the Gaels) have appeared recently however. The only grammar is still J. J. Kneen's *A Grammar of the Manx Language.* Only a handful of Manx books have been published since the Second World War; these include *Recortys Reeaghyn Vannin as ny hEllanyn* (Chronicle of the Kings of Man and the Isles), translated from the original Latin and published in 1973, a few stories translated from the Welsh by A. S. B. Davies and a volume of about a hundred short stories and anecdotes which went to press in 1975. Some old books such as Bishop Wilson's *Coyrle Sodjeh* (Principle and Duties of Christianity) have been reprinted. A map of the Island in Manx has also been produced as well as a gramophone record for language-learners together with two records of traditional songs sung by Brian Stowell and Claire Clennell. Stories are sometimes written by Manx teachers for use in class, but are rarely published. On radio there are only five minutes of news in Manx Gaelic, broadcast at nine o'clock on Sunday mornings from a low-power radio station under Government control by volunteers from the Manx Language Society.

No law has ever been passed against the Manx language either by the Government of the United Kingdom or by Tynwald. It has equal validity in the courts of law and in business. Defendants can plead in Manx if they so desire and at least one merchant banker, Slater Walker, transacts business in it and issues bilingual cheque-books. In practice, however, outside Tynwald, where it is used only for ceremonial purposes, the language has no real role in government or administration. Religious services are held in Manx from time to time, in both Anglican and Methodist churches. The Island's material culture is in the keeping of the Manx Museum, Library and Art Gallery, opened at Douglas in 1922.

It is ironic that the Isle of Man, enjoying as it does a large measure of control over its own affairs, to an extent greater than many other minorities in Western Europe, should seem incapable or undesirous of restoring its national language. But that appears to be the case at the present time. Even Lewis Crellin, one of the most respected leaders of the nationalist movement in Man and a Manx-speaker, has written, 'I cannot believe that the language has any future, except as a minority hobby. The process of anglicisation has almost completely wiped out our national identity, a process now greatly hastened by immigration. And in any case, why struggle to keep our language if our country is lost?' Such a hopeless view would no doubt be contested by a few of the young people now striving to re-awaken the national spirit of Man, but even they have to face the reality on which this view is based.

THE GAELS OF NORTHERN IRELAND

The six counties of Ireland under British rule are those in the north-east of the country: Antrim, Londonderry (Derry), Tyrone, Fermanagh, Armagh and Down. This region is sometimes called Ulster but its boundaries do not coincide with the historical province of that name, for they exclude the counties of Donegal, Monaghan and Cavan, which are also parts of Ulster but belong to the Republic of Ireland. The total land area of the six counties is 5,452 square miles, about a sixth of the whole of Ireland, and their population at the 1971 Census was 1,536,065, of whom 416,679 lived in Belfast, the capital.

Although there are no longer any traditionally Irish-speaking or *Gaeltacht* districts in the six counties of Northern Ireland, as there are in the Irish Republic, the Irish language is spoken by a substantial minority of the population. In the absence of official statistics relating to the language, as the Census does not enumerate Irish-speakers in Northern Ireland, it is impossible to estimate the number of people able to speak Irish in the province. Few are native-speakers, anyway. Excepting immigrants from the *Gaeltacht* districts of the Republic, particularly those from neighbouring Donegal, a stronghold of Irish, and a small number who were reared in Northern Ireland in Irish-speaking homes, most have learned the language at school or as adults.

But however they may have acquired Irish, the most important fact to be borne in mind about the language's position in Northern Ireland is that the vast majority of Irish-speakers in the region are Roman Catholics among whom the language has long been an essential part of their Republican consciousness. Only very rarely is it spoken or learned by Protestants, although there are notable exceptions, and almost never by Unionists for whom Irish is inextricably associated with Roman Catholicism and the Republican cause.

At the 1971 Census a total of 477,919 Roman Catholics were enumerated. The Protestants numbered 811,272 of whom 405,719 were Presbyterians, 334,318 belonged to the Church of Ireland and 71,235 were Methodists;

a further 230,449 professed other religions or no religion at all.

With these facts in view, it is necessary to give at the outset, in the broadest outline, an account of how six of Ulster's nine counties came to be separated from the twenty-six counties of what is now the Irish Republic.

With Leinster, Munster and Connacht, Ulster was for centuries one of the provinces of independent Ireland—'my four beautiful green fields' as W. B. Yeats had Cathleen ni Houlihan describe them in his play of 1902—and its history was shared with all Ireland. Indeed, in the early period, Ulster was the predominantly Celtic, political heartland of Ireland. It was the home of Cuchulain, hero of the Ulster cycle of epic tales, and there St Patrick, Ireland's patron saint, who arrived from Wales in A.D. 432, did most of his work after establishing his see at Armagh. Throughout the Middle Ages Ulster produced its share of scholars, poets and rulers such as the great dynasty of the O'Neills, Gaelic-speaking kings who ruled an autonomous province during the fourteenth and fifteenth centuries. Even after the conquest of Ireland, Ulster continued to contribute richly to the Irish tradition. Many of the patriots who took part in its liberation, such as Wolfe Tone (1763-98), Thomas Davis (1814-45), James Connolly (1868-1916), and some of the earliest members of the Gaelic League like Eoin MacNeill (1867-1945), who founded the Irish Volunteers, were Ulstermen; and some, up to the present century, were Protestants.

It was not until 1609, when King James I of England began planting a colony of English and Scottish farmers, mostly Lowland Scots and Presbyterians, on land confiscated from the native Irish, that the first serious blow to the political and cultural life of Ulster was struck. The province then suffered 'pacification' by Oliver Cromwell who, by his butchery, banished all Catholics 'to Hell or Connacht' in the year 1654, rewarding his troops with large tracts of land in Ulster. In 1688 Catholics rose in support of the Stuart cause and besieged the town of Derry, but two years later were defeated by William of Orange, popularly called King Billy, at the Battle of the Boyne. Those Catholics who survived fled abroad where, known as 'the Wild Geese', they joined the French army and took revenge by beating the English at Fontenoy.

But with the defeat of James II England's conquest of Ireland seemed complete and in this Ulster was no exception.

It is important to remember, however, that the majority of Ulster's population in the seventeenth century was Irish-speaking. According to the 1659 Census, out of a total population in the nine counties of 103,923 the native Irish numbered 63,272; 40,651 were listed as 'English and Scots'. The non-Gaelic-speakers comprised two groups—speakers of English and speakers of Lowland Scots. The English-speakers came from England and left their mark on the mid-Ulster dialect spoken in the central areas extending east from enniskillen almost as far as Belfast. But as a result of neglect by Church and State the development of Lowland Scots in Ulster was hampered and its speakers soon turned to English. There is, on the other hand, some evidence to show that the plantations and migrations of the seventeenth century were within what had been a single cultural area, for Gaelic had been the common language of Ireland and Scotland up to this time. It is therefore probable that many immigrants from Scotland were obliged to accomodate themselves to Irish society, especially those who were Gaelic-speaking. The Church made strenuous efforts to appoint Gaelic-speaking bishops in Ulster and pursued a policy of publishing in Irish.

But England's power in Ireland depended on the descendants of those Protestants who had been brought to garrison the country and it was strongest, outside Dublin, in Ulster. The Irish Parliament, in defiance of the treaty under which the Catholic armies had surrendered, stripped Catholics of their civil rights by a series of laws known as the Penal Code. All attempts at protest were most brutally put down. Ulster, where resistance to the Crown was particularly determined, suffered the full force of the English army's terror.

Throughout the eighteenth century Ireland was ruled by the Protestant Ascendancy class. The centre of political life was Dublin, where the Irish Parliament sat, and where in 1765 about 120,000 people lived. But as the century wore on, Belfast, with its linen industry, began to flourish more rapidly than the agricultural south so that by 1800 its population had grown to around 24,000. Although Ulster, the only province where the Protestant faith had spread through every social class, now enjoyed a prosperity unknown in the rest of Ireland, there was still widespread discontent among its people. The Penal Code was repealed and some Catholics were given the vote in 1793 but there was no move to give them full equality with the Protestants. As Henry Flood, one of the leading parliamentarians of the day, put it, 'We will give all toleration to religion but we will not give them political power', or as Henry Grattan told the Protestants of Dublin, 'I love the Roman Catholic. I am a friend to his liberty, but it is only inasmuch as his liberty is entirely consistent with your ascendancy and an addition to the strength and freedom of the Protestant community'. Strife between Protestants and Catholics in Ulster now became more frequent and more bitter, each side anxious to win possession of land holdings in the province. It was after a sectarian struggle at Armagh in 1795 that Protestants formed the first Orange Order, a society for the protection of their religion and rights. At the same time, while many Protestants, mainly Dissenters from the Established Church, left Ulster for America, about 250,000 crossing the Atlantic up to 1800, many Catholics turned to secret organisations and eventually to armed rebellion.

English began to spread throughout the east of the province during the eighteenth century, mainly as a result of pressure from the civil administration. In 1710 Parliament ignored a resolution from one of its committees for the provision of Irish-speaking ministers. Despite growing opposition, Irish continued to be used for religious purposes, however, and poets went on writing in it. It was the educational system which had the most pernicious effect on Irish in Ulster—the charity schools inaugurated in 1712, the charter schools of 1731 and later the national schools from around 1831.

The decline of the language evoked interest in its revival and to the various societies engaged in its study many Protestants belonged. Under the auspices of the Belfast Harp Society there was a revival of singing and composing in the language. In 1795 the first Irish magazine, *Bolg an tSolair,* was founded 'to recommend the Irish language to the notice of Irishmen'. Although the United Irishmen's risings of 1798 and 1803 cost this revival movement many of its sympathisers, the work continued throughout the nineteenth century.

The Catholics were not alone in their opposition to the Protestant Ascendancy, at least not at first. It was Wolfe Tone, a Protestant, who in 1791 founded the Society of United Irishmen, in Belfast. The new society's aims were described thus: 'Our provinces are ignorant of each other—we must unite them'. Up to now Ulster had not entertained any separatist ideals, the link with the English Crown having been the central point in its political thinking and northern Protestants looking to England as their ally and protector. The rebellion of 1798, led by the United Irishmen, although mostly Catholic, was the first in which Irish Protestants from the north had taken part. What began as an attack on the English Establishment by the Irish Establishment soon became an attempt to grant full civil rights to all Ireland's people regardless of their religion. The Ulstermen were different from their compatriots only in one aspect of their zeal: while the southerners were primarily interested in winning relief from appalling agrarian conditions, the northerners—who were comparatively prosperous from their industry—were inspired by the ideals of the French Revolution of 1789. But the military leadership of the two groups was unco-ordinated and the expected help from France, with which England was at war, failed to arrive in time. Lord Edward Fitzgerald, leader of the Ulstermen, was arrested almost immediately. Only in Antrim did they succeed in rising but there, under Henry Joy McCracken, they were soon defeated. At Ballynahinch too, in County Down, the United Irishmen under Henry Munroe were quickly crushed, while in the south, Father Murphy led his men to annihilation at Vinegar Hill. By the time the French fleet appeared off the Irish coast the fighting was over. Tone was captured on board the French flag-ship and died while awaiting trial. The following year William Pitt, Prime Minister of England, convinced that there was no way of solving Ireland's problems other than by union with England, passed the Act of Union by which the Parliament of Ireland was abolished.

In the early years of the nineteenth century, whereas the earlier leaders of Irish opinion—men like Grattan and Tone—had been Protestants and in some instances Ulstermen, Irish nationalism as expounded by Daniel O'Connell became almost completely associated with the Catholic Church. The immense popularity of 'The Liberator', as he was known to Catholics, now placed the Protestants of Ulster in a difficult position. As a reaction to O'Connell's attempts to gain emancipation for Catholics, the Orange Order began to grow in numbers and influence. If Ulster's Republicanism began to wane after the defeat of Napoleon and the return of the exiled Bourbons to the French throne, the Protestants' interest in the rights of Catholics vanished after O'Connell's election at Clare in 1829. When he proposed the repeal of the Union with England shortly afterwards he lost the support of the Protestant north completely. In 1835 he wrote, 'The scoundrel Orangemen, always enemies to Ireland, now place all their claims to England and government support. I have two objects—to overthrow the Orange system and to convince the most sceptical that nothing but a domestic parliament will do Ireland justice'. Eight years later, when he went to Belfast to seek Ulster's support for his second object, he found that the Protestant majority had fully accepted union with England and he returned to Dublin with nothing gained. After O'Connell's death in 1847 a new nationalist movement, the Young Irelanders, split the Repeal movement by advocating more militant methods and with the Fenians, almost wholly Catholic, went on to alienate the northern Protestants still further from the cause of Irish independence.

During the Great Famine of 1845-50 Ulster suffered less than the rest of Ireland, mainly because Tenant Rights were in force and it depended more on its linen industry than on the potato crop. Even so, about 33,000 died of typhus fever in the province as people swarmed into the towns in search of food and shelter. By now Ulster was enjoying comparative prosperity. King William III had settled about 500 families of Huguenots, Protestant refugees, around the town of Lisburn who had brought new skills for the modernisation of spinning, weaving and bleaching linen. Fairs sprang up in towns like Dungannon, Dromore, Ballymoney and Bangor; the Lagan Valley became the centre of an expanding industrial area. Belfast's trade increased with the introduction of the cotton industry and its population grew from 24,000 in 1800 to 100,000 in 1850. Industries like Thomas Gallagher's tobacco factory, the ship-yards of Harland-Wolff and the Belfast Ropework Company were the other principal sources of employment. The first railway was built in 1839, from Belfast to Lisburn, and—whereas in the previous century the main roads from the north all led to Dublin—by 1850 the most important trade route ran from Belfast up the Lagan Valley to Armagh. With this new prosperity the Industrial Revolution also brought disease, poverty, execrable living conditions and rabid sectarianism.

The nineteenth century also saw the decline of the Irish language in Ulster which proceeded at a rate even more rapid than in the other three provinces of Ireland, except that—save for Donegal where the language had a stronghold—not one of the nine counties had more than 8% of Irish-speakers among its population in 1851. The decline had been underway since before the beginning of the century, but parish registers and the accounts of such observers as Whitley Stokes in 1806, Daniel Dewar and Edward Wakefield in 1812, show that Irish was widely spoken in rural and mountainous districts of the western districts of Ulster at that time. But by 1851 it became clear that Irish had lost ground everywhere, even in Donegal where over half the population in 1810 had been Irish-speaking.

The total number of Gaels in Ulster according to the Census of that year was 136,164. Donegal had the biggest Irish-speaking population with 73,258 (28·7%), Armagh had 13,736 (7%), Cavan 13,027 (7·5%), Tyrone 12,892 (5%), Monaghan 10,955 (7·7%), Derry 5,406 (2·8%), Antrim 3,033 (1·2%), Fermanagh 2,704 (2·3%), and Down 1,153 (0·4%). By 1891 the total had fallen to 83,226. Donegal still had the most Gaels with 62,037 (33·4%), but in other counties the Irish-speaking population had been drastically reduced: Tyrone had 6,687 Gaels (3·9%), Armagh 3,486 (2.4%), Cavan 3,410 (3%), Monaghan 2,847 (3.3%), Derry 2,723 (1·8%), Antrim 885 (0·4%), Down 590 (0·3%) and Fermanagh 561 (0·8%). Whereas in 1851 there had been 35,783 monoglot Irish-speakers, of whom 34,882 lived in Donegal, there were only 7,053 by 1891, of whom 7,037 were in Donegal. The number of Irish-speakers in Ireland enumerated by the 1851 Census was 1,524,286, or 23% of the population.

Despite this decline, there was still interest in Irish among the scholars and ministers of Ulster. In 1840 there were ninety-eight schools in Tyrone and twenty-five in Antrim where pupils were taught to read the Bible in Irish and it was claimed by the Presbyterian Church in 1845 that over 17,000 adults had been taught in this way. A curious fact is that the Catholic priests of the time were not as enthusiastic for Irish as the Presbyterians, whose Synod of Ulster in 1833 made the language essential for ministers in Irish-speaking districts. Meanwhile, the revival was centred mainly on Belfast and among Protestants, who founded the *Cuideacht Gaoidheilge Uladh* (Ulster Gaelic Society) in 1830. The collection of manuscripts and translation of foreign classics like *A Pilgrim's Progress* were essential parts of the Society's work, which continued up to 1843, when Queen's University at Belfast took over some of its functions, a Chair of Irish being established there six years later. But by 1850 it had become clear that Irish was under serious pressure. In 1853 Robert MacAdams wrote in his magazine, *The Ulster Journal of Archeology,* 'We are on the eve of great changes. Society in Ulster. seems breaking up . . . That which conquest and colonization failed to effect in centuries, steam and education are now accomplishing peacefully and rapidly'.

The change in the position of Irish in Ulster can be seen in the fact that, whereas up to about 1850 it was normal for a member of the Protestant middle-class to belong to, say, the Belfast Harp Society or the Ulster Gaelic Society, after 1860—as a result of growing political tension—Irish had come to be associated in the public mind with Catholicism and Republicanism. While Irish continued to be spoken in some districts of Ulster, it was regarded with suspicion by people who had no first-hand knowledge of it and who seldom met Irish-speakers. Furthermore, MacAdam, who had been responsible for having the question about language included in the 1851 Census, commented, 'It is well known that in various districts where the two languages co-exist, but where English now largely predominates, numbers of individuals returned themselves as ignorant of the Irish language either from a sort of false shame or from a secret dream that the Government in making this enquiry (for the first time) had some concealed motive, which could not be for their good'.

By the end of the century, when Belfast's population had swollen to 350,000, it was clear that the province's links with Britain were strong and cherished by the majority of its people. The British sentiments of the Ulster Protestants were expressed in opposition to Gladstone's numerous proposals for granting Home Rule to Ireland. While Parnell's Irish Party won the support of the Catholics in the north and south, from 1885 the Protestant's faith in the British Liberal Party had been destroyed. The Unionists saw in British rule of Ulster a means of sharing in Britain's economic boom and of avoiding the distress now widespread in the rest of Ireland. For them Irish nationalism had a predominantly Catholic following and Home Rule was synonymous with 'Rome Rule'. Furthermore, they were proud of the place Ulstermen held in the British Empire, then at its zenith. At an Orange convention attended by 12,000 delegates on 17 June 1892 the following resolution was carried: 'We solemnly resolve and declare that we express the devoted loyalty of Ulster Unionists to the crown and constitution of the United Kingdom; that we avow our fixed resolve to retain unchanged our present position as an integral part of the United Kingdom, that we declare to the people of Great Britain our conviction that the attempt to set up such an all-Irish Parliament will result in disorder, violence and bloodshed . . .'

During the next twelve years, the Orange Order made strenuous attempts to unite Ulster Protestants of every class in a new organisation, the Ulster Unionist Council. The province now turned to the Conservative Party which was already opposed to Liberal policies in Ireland and which had declared itself totally in favour of the Union, taking the name Conservative and Unionist Party from this time on. The Orange Order was given a new respectability by Lord Randolph Churchill's remarks, 'The Orange card is the one to play' and 'Ulster will fight and Ulster will be right'. Thousands of Protestants flocked to join the Order which, with its sashes, banners, marches, drums and sectarian violence, its cry of 'No surrender!' recalled from the siege of Derry in 1688, has remained a permanent feature of life in the province up to the present time.

If, from this point on, the present account seems to deal

more with the Protestant majority than with the Catholic minority, it is because the Orange Order gained the upper hand and became the principal force in determining that in a British Ulster the Catholics, and the Gaels among them, would be forced to accept the position which they have occupied, more or less, ever since. Without considering this background it is difficult to understand why the Irish language in the six counties of Northern Ireland today is identified almost totally with the Catholic faith and the Republican cause.

The Census of 1911 revealed that in Ulster, as nowhere else in Ireland, the descendants of the Protestant colonists—who were by now of Irish nationality but jealous of their British citizenship—were in a majority over the native Catholics, who wished to match their Irish nationality with citizenship of an independent Ireland. As part of the total population of Ireland, the Protestants made up little more than a quarter. But in the city of Belfast they had a majority of two to one. The Catholic population of Ulster's nine counties was as follows: Antrim 20·5%, Armagh 45·3%, Down 31·6%, Derry 45·8%, Fermanagh 56·2%, Tyrone 55·4%, Cavan 81·5%, Monaghan 74·7% and Donegal 78·9%. At the same time, the percentage of Irish-speakers in Ulster at the 1911 Census, the last time they were to be enumerated, had risen to 2·3% from 1·3% in 1891; there were approximately 8,000 native-speakers of Irish in Belfast in 1913. This slight increase was largely attributable to the foundation of *Conradh na Gaeilge* (The Gaelic League) in 1893. The population of Ulster in 1911 was 1,581,696 (Ireland's was 4,390,219), of whom 890,108 were Protestants and 690,134 Catholics.

The Ulster Unionists are described by Dorothy MacArdle in her official history, *The Irish Republic* (Dublin, 1937), thus: 'They bore little resemblance to the Northern men who had been leaders of the national struggle in 1798. Their adherence to the Union was tenacious in the extreme, for to the Union, and to their status as agents and garrison for Britain, they owed their position of power . . . They were dependent on the British connection, while Britain's hold over Ireland was in part dependent on them. The maintaining of the cleavage between Catholic and Protestant was to the interest of British and Ulster Unionists alike . . . They were the employers of labour; any alliance between the Catholic and non-Catholic workers would have been a menace to the propertied class. Religious antagonism between Catholics and Protestants in the factories, docks and ship-yards enabled the employers, like the Empire, to divide and rule . . . That this small, compact Unionist majority should dread any form of self-government for the Irish was natural enough. For generations they had opposed and exploited the people and a redressment of the balance seemed to them a thing greatly to be feared. It would leave them a mere minority in the country with only a minority's rights. To these real causes for apprehension they added extravagant, imaginary terrors, seeing a thousand bogies of revenge and reprisal lurking under the shadow of Home Rule'.

In 1911, under its leader Sir Edward Carson, a Dublin lawyer and Member of Parliament, the Ulster Unionist Council announced plans for the setting up of a Provisional Government for the province in the event of Home Rule becoming law. On 28 September 1912 half a million Protestants signed a Solemn League and Covenant, some in their own blood, swearing to defeat Home Rule by all necessary means. When, early in the same year, Winston Churchill, at the time a Liberal, visited Belfast to persuade the Unionists that they were wrong, he had to be protected by five battalions of infantry and two squadrons of cavalry. He wrote later, 'The Ulster menace is nothing but melodramatic stuff and the Unionist leaders would be unspeakably shocked and frightened if anything came of their foolish and wicked words'. But the Unionists were now drilling with the Ulster Volunteer Force and, on orders from Prime Minister Asquith, British forces stationed at Dublin moved into Ulster in a show of force. A few weeks later the U.V.F., now claiming 100,000 members, landed 35,000 German rifles and five million rounds of ammunition. This gun-running was matched by similar preparations on the part of the Irish Volunteers. The two organisations were formed to fight not against each other, it should be noted, but against the British Government, the one to maintain the Union and the other to destroy it. Meeting at Buckingham Palace in London in 1914, their two leaders Carson and John Redmond, Parnell's successor as leader of the

Irish Nationalist Party who was committed to winning Home Rule by peaceful means, failed to reach agreement. Then, just as it seemed as if Ireland was on the brink of bloodshed, the First World War was declared. Many Irishmen, both Protestant and Catholic, enlisted in the British Army in the belief that Ireland's problems would be solved after the Kaiser had been defeated. Others, mostly Catholics but from north and south, were not willing to wait that long.

Following the Easter Rising of 1916 and the proclamation of an Irish Republic, the execution of its leaders, the electoral success of *Sinn Fein* and the War of Independence, the British Government under Lloyd George passed a Government of Ireland Act which set up two Parliaments in Ireland, one in Belfast and one in Dublin. The Ulster Unionists accepted this Act for it removed their greatest fear—that the province would be governed from Dublin—and ensured that at least the six, mainly Protestant counties would remain under British rule. But the Treaty signed in London in 1921 by those who accepted the partition of Ireland, led by Arthur Griffith and Michael Collins, was not approved by 'the die-hards' like De Valera who objected to partition and the oath of allegiance to the British Crown: they now engaged the Free Staters in a bitter Civil War during which erstwhile comrades found themselves on opposing sides.

Meanwhile, the Parliament of Northern Ireland met for the first time in June 1921, at Belfast's City Hall. At the opening ceremony King George V said, 'I speak from a full heart when I pray that my coming to Ireland today may prove to be the first step towards an end of strife amongst her people, whatever their race or creed. I appeal to all Irishmen to forgive and forget and to join in making for the land they love a new era of peace, contentment and goodwill'. But the King's hopes were not to be realised. The agreement of 1921 had given Northern Ireland, among other things, the right to vote itself out of the Free State and this it did at the earliest opportunity. It had also provided for a boundary commission to decide finally where the border between the Free State and Northern Ireland would be drawn. Some Free Staters like Michael Collins had no doubt that the North would eventually have to join the South for economic reasons, especially if only the minimum of territory was conceded to Britain. But Sir James Craig (later Lord Craigavon) was determined to give away 'not an inch' of the six counties still under Belfast rule and it was the Unionist view which was up-held. In 1925 the Commission announced that Fermanagh and Tyrone would not be given to the Free State, despite the Catholic majorities in these counties. Winston Churchill foresaw what was bound to happen when he wrote in his book *The World Crisis: the Aftermath* (London, 1929), 'The whole map of Europe has been changed. The position of countries has been violently altered. But as the deluge subsides and the waters fall we see the dreary steeples of Fermanagh and Tyrone emerging once again. The integrity of their quarrel is one of the few institutions that have been unaltered in the cataclysm which has swept the world'.

Having described how Ireland came to be partitioned, it is not the purpose of the present account to follow the events which since 1925 led to the present crisis in Northern Ireland, but perhaps some of the principal developments need to be noted.

In the Free State, which in 1949 became the Republic of Ireland, De Valera made the abolition of partition one of the two chief aims of *Fianna Fail,* the party he founded in 1928, and its continued existence the reason for the Republic's neutrality in the Second World War. In the six counties bitterness and conflict between Protestants and Catholics increased and the Irish Republican Army, banned on both sides of the border, began its campaign of armed attacks in the hope of hastening the end of British rule. After the War Northern Ireland continued to be run by an exclusive Protestant upper-class dominated by an extra-parliamentary force, the Orange Order. Almost every Unionist M.P. since 1925 has been a member of the Order and no Catholic has ever been among its members. In 1949 Westminster passed the Ireland Act by which Northern Ireland's status as part of the United Kingdom could not be altered without Stormont's consent. This could not be given while Stormont was dominated by a Protestant Unionist majority which refused to share power with Catholic representatives. During the 1950s, at a time of economic depression and high unemployment, there was much criticism of the undemocratic nature of the Stormont system and numerous accusations of gerrymandering in the interests of Protestant victories at elections. Discrimination against Catholics also continued in the most blatant manner in such sectors as education, jobs, housing and the social services.

Following raids in the six counties by *Saor Uladh* (Free Ulster) between 1953 and 1956, the 'Border War' of 1956-61 produced 600 major incidents, mainly the destruction of British military installations, bridges and police barracks. About a thousand I.R.A. men were engaged in these activities, against 5,000 British troops, 5,000 territorials, 10,000 B. Specials (an auxilary police force recruited from among Protestants), 3,000 members of the Royal Ulster Constabulary, and 2,000 special security police. Yet no more than twelve people were killed, six on either side, thirty-eight were wounded and the damage to property was estimated at only about £1 million. In 1961 *Sinn Fein,* the political wing of the nationalist movement, lost its four seats in the Dublin Parliament and its vote in the six counties was cut from 152,310 to 63,415 in 1959. In that year the party was banned by the Government of Northern Ireland, but the Nationalist Party, led by Edward McAteer, continued to fight elections, holding about a quarter of the fifty-two seats at Stormont in 1967.

Hope for co-operation between South and North after Sean Lemass, the Republic's Prime Minister, and Terence O'Neill, Prime Minister of Northern Ireland, met in January 1965—the first time this had happened in forty years —came to nothing. Up to now relations between Governments north and south of the border had been improving quietly over the previous two decades, particularly since all constitutional parties in the Republic condemned any efforts to achieve the reunion of Ireland by force. But these improved relations were not popular among more extreme Ulster Unionists and soon, under Ian Paisley, a Presbyterian minister with demagogic talents, they protested and so vociferously that O'Neill was replaced by Major Chichester Clark. In 1971, under the pressure of increased threats by the I.R.A., Clark was obliged to give way to Brian Faulkner who remained as Prime Minister of Northern Ireland until Stormont was suspended in 1972. It was against this background that the Civil Rights Movement, led in its early days by Bernadette Devlin and later by the Social Democratic Labour Party, emerged during the 1960s and that the I.R.A. was to resume its campaign of armed attacks on the British Army and other instruments of British rule in the six counties.

While it remains true that the conflict in Northern Ireland is principally between Irishmen with two different religious faiths, Protestant and Catholic, and two political convictions, Unionist and Republican, it is clear from the opinions expressed by representatives of both sides that one factor in the quarrel is the Irish language which is seen as a basic tenet of the Catholic, Republican viewpoint and is therefore attacked by the Protestant, Unionist community. The northern politicians interviewed in the supplement *An Ghaeltacht Inniu* (The *Gaeltacht* Today) of *The Irish Times* (2 April 1975) are fairly typical. The Ascendancy's attitude to Irish is represented by Lord Brookborough of the Northern Ireland Unionist Party: 'There is absolutely no reason why Irish should not be studied as an academic subject. I wouldn't necessarily like to see-it disappear as a culture. I have been to the western *Gaeltachts* many times and always thoroughly enjoyed my visits. I delight in any language or culture as long as it is not aggressively employed but all my life the promotion of Irish has been divisive. I used to take *The United Irishman* which I enjoyed reading. It had a series of phrases in Irish described as useful in everyday life and the one which sticks in my mind is the Irish for "Don't throw the hand-grenade yet".' An even more bitter view is that of John Baird, a member of the Loyalist Coalition: 'The forced feeding of Irish and the frantic preservation of the Gaelic Twilight is the cancer eating away at the Republic of Ireland . . . It was the Ulster Unionist who created the State of Ulster in the first part of this century. But it is the Irish Nationalists, backed by the Irish language, who have ensured that Ulster endured for fifty years. However, from my point of view, long may the corpse of Gaelic receive the kiss of life—long may it be spared to divide'.

Commenting on such views, the journalist Andrew

Boyd, correspondent of *The Irish Times* in Northern Ireland but not an Irish-speaker, writes: 'What I most deplore is the ignorant hostility of those Ulster Loyalists who refer to Irish as "a foreign language" and regard it as a facet of either Catholic theology or Papal politics. No doubt Padraig Pearse must take the blame. It was he who made the language a matter of Republican politics. And in the opinion of almost every Orangeman, Republican politics, Papal intrigue, Catholic theology, the Gaelic League and the Gaelic Athletics Association are all one and the same thing. Add to that mixture a strong dose of McAliskey (the married name of Bernadette Devlin, now a member of the Irish Republican Socialist Party) Marxism and the compound of the Loyalist man's bugbears is complete . . . Many Loyalists regard Irish as a seditious language that could endanger the constitutional position of Northern Ireland'.

There is, of course, some basis for this last belief since the Irish language plays an important part in the activities of Republicans in Northern Ireland. It is said that in the I.R.A. *(Oglaigh na hEireann)* drill-commands are given in Irish, that some of its leaders like Rory O'Brady are able to speak it fluently and that at least one hut in the Longkesh internment camp was entirely Irish-speaking. But apart from in such contexts, Irish is also used regularly by many thousands of Catholics in Belfast, especially those who during the last six years have taken part in the Civil Rights Movement. For example, the people who re-built Bombay Street, burned in August 1969, were members of the Irish-language movement. Indeed it is sometimes claimed that the largest *Gaeltacht* in the whole of Ireland is in Belfast. By this is meant not that entire communities speak the language on an everyday basis but there are thousands of native Irish-speakers, some of the third generation, together with others who have learned the language at school or as adults, living in the city.

One such group are the residents of Shaw's Road, Belfast, ten families who built themselves a housing estate where Irish is the only language spoken. Their primary school, where all instruction is given in Irish by its two teachers, receives no financial assistance from either Stormont or Westminster but is paid for by the parents and supporters, and is not linked to any

Church. The same militants have opened a shop selling Irish-language books and a grocery.

The principal language organisation in Belfast is *Cumann Chluain Ard*, with about 400 members and a hard core of sixty workers. Its chairman, Albert Fry, is typical of Northern language militants in his scorn for both the Dublin Government's policies for Irish and what he considers the pusilanimous views of bodies like *Conradh na Gaelige* (The Gaelic League). 'The only way to revive Irish', maintains Albert Fry, 'is to decide to speak nothing else and let anyone who wants to communicate in English pay an interpreter. This might sound extreme but the position is an extreme one and there is no room for half-measures'. It is claimed that the children of Republicans like Albert Fry hear nothing but Irish at home, that their radios are turned to *Radio na Gaeltachta* only and their television sets are used once a week, for Irish programmes. Even the graffiti and political slogans on the walls of the 'no-go' areas, where the British Army are from time to time unable to penetrate for fear of attack by the I.R.A., are in Irish.

The Irish language enjoys no official status of any kind in the six counties of Northern Ireland. Whatever position it has attained in education and religion is more the result of historical circumstances than of any encouragement from the authorities. There is one Catholic service in Irish every Sunday in Belfast and once a month in other towns such as Derry, Armagh and Dungannon. Four of the Catholic Bishops are fluent Irish-speakers and many of the priests are active in Irish-language activities, especially in the Gaelic League and in *Cumann na Sagart*, the Irish-speaking priests' association. No Protestant services are held in Irish and no minister of the Church of Ireland or the Presbyterian and Methodist Churches is active on the language's behalf. No political party places the Irish language very high on its programme, although the encouragement of Irish figures in the programme of the S.D.L.P. The language has no status in law and no defendant has ever asked to be tried in it. No official forms are provided in the language and the use of Irish is discouraged by such bodies as the Post Office and the Registrar of Births. Irish is never used as a spoken language on programmes on the BBC (Northern Ireland) or Ulster

Television. The main Catholic daily newspaper, *The Irish News (Belfast)*, carries a short column in Irish from time to time and some of the provincial weekly newspapers do the same.

The defiance of localities like the Shaw's Road has developed in recent years in response to the continuing failure of the Department of Education in Northern Ireland to provide a full system of the teaching of Irish in the State schools. The question asked by Andrew Boyd seems apposite here: 'Integrated education is the sally-rod with which the Unionists and their fellow-travellers are now beating the Catholics of the North, but why don't the State schools themselves make a contribution to better understanding by encouraging the study of Irish, if only as an optional subject—wouldn't that help to break down the cultural barriers that now divide Catholics from Protestants?' The situation has not changed much since the publication of the Commission on the Restoration of Irish in 1964. Irish is treated as a foreign language in the State Schools. Out of a total of 1,529 primary schools and 193,952 pupils in the six counties in 1960, in only 140 schools (9·1%) were 15,001 pupils (7·7%) taught the language and only 3,000 pupils were learning it in grammar schools. Irish is taught as a compulsory subject only in Catholic schools. In 1966 only 6·4% of pupils in primary schools were being taught Irish and in January 1968 it was being taught only in 156 schools out of a total of 1,332. According to the Department of Education, some sixty-seven secondary schools were teaching Irish in 1957, all of them Catholic. Examinations are provided at C.S.E. and at G.C.E. 'O' and 'A' levels.

In addition, around 900 pupils are sent annually to summer courses organised by *Conradh na Gaelige* (The Gaelic Leage) in the *Gaeltacht* districts of Donegal. The League, which has about eighty branches in the six counties and publishes a monthly magazine called *An t-Ultach* (The Ulsterman), also holds evening classes in the language in some parts of the regions. It is said that among Irish-learners in the six counties the standard of competency and commitment to the language is much higher than in the Republic. At the higher level of education, Irish is studied at the Celtic

Department of Queen's University, Belfast, where books have been published in the language during recent years, and as part of an Irish Studies course at the New University of Ulster in Coleraine, where a quarterly literary magazine *Dánta Aduaidh* (Poems from the North) is published.

Outside Belfast, the Irish language is in greatest evidence in the counties of Fermanagh and Armagh, on the southern border with the Republic. Crossmaglen *(Crois Mhic Fhloinn),* for example, a town in south Armagh with a population of 1,300, won two of the Gaelic League's *Glor na nGael* prizes for promoting Irish in 1975, first prize for the North and second for a town of its size in Ireland. The district, only two generations ago, was a *Gaeltacht* famous for its Irish poets and musicians; the last native-speaker died in the 1930s but many have a knowledge of the language still. Among its distinguished sons is Mgr. Tomais Ó Fiaich, who became President of St Patrick's College, Maynooth, the most famous seminary in the Republic, in 1974. In many of the town's shops the goods are marked in Irish and the language is spoken every night in several pubs. Irish classes are held for children and adults, with financial aid from *Comhaltas Uladh* (The Ulster Association) and the language is taught in all the primary schools of the area as well as the town's Catholic secondary school. Mass is held in Irish once a week, while *Radio na Gaeltachta* and *Telefís Eireann* have many listeners and viewers. A news bulletin, *Glor na Fheadha,* is also published. The *fleadh cheoil,* a local festival, is held annually and traditional music groups flourish under the aegis of *Comhaltas Ceoltoiri* (The Irish Music Society). The political sentiments of Crossmaglen, where there have been numerous instances of violence during the last ten years and where the I.R.A. is known to have a base, are displayed—despite the presence of a British garrison—in the Republican tricolour which flies from the burned-out shell of the town's courthouse.

It is beyond the scope of the present account to follow the complexities of political events in Northern Ireland over the last six years. But some idea of the scale of the violence into which the region has been plunged since 1969 may be had from the number of deaths which have occurred as the result of sectarian violence, whether at the hands of the various Loyalist para-military organisations or the Official and Provisional wings of the I.R.A., or else as a result of shootings by the British Army. In 1969, when the British Army was sent to Northern Ireland following the riots in Derry and Belfast on 12 August, thirteen civilians died. Twenty-five were killed in 1970 and by June a total of 11,000 British troops were stationed in the region. The internment of Republican suspects began on 9 August 1971 and during that year 173 people died, 130 of whom were civilians. After the events of Bloody Sunday, 30 January, when thirteen civilians were shot by troops, and a two-day strike by Protestants paralysed the province, the abolition of Stormont and direct rule from Westminster followed on 30 March 1972. The number of British troops was increased to 20,000 in August 1972 in an effort to combat the I.R.A. and enter the 'no-go' areas of Belfast. By the end of that year 469 people had been killed, including 103 soldiers. In the border plebiscite of 8 March 1973, 591,820 voted in favour of retaining Northern Ireland's link with Britain and 6,463 voted against, a total of 61% participating. In 1973 the number of deaths was reduced to 249, of whom fifty-eight were soldiers, and to 215 in 1974, including twenty-eight soldiers, after a power-sharing Executive Council had been introduced at Stormont. But following the Loyalist strike of 15 May 1974, the resignation of Brian Faulkner as Chief Minister and the collapse of the Executive on 29 May the death-roll increased again. In 1975, despite a ceasefire by the I.R.A. in February and the election of a Convention in May in which the United Ulster Union coalition won an overall majority, there were 245 violent deaths, including those of fourteen soldiers. It was announced in December 1975 that over a thousand civilians and 246 British soldiers had been killed in Northern Ireland since August 1969. Many thousands more had been seriously injured. Explosions in London, in which twenty-eight people lost their lives, were claimed as the work of the I.R.A. During the autumn of 1975, Merlyn Rees, the British Minister for Northern Ireland, continued to say, as he did on 26 August, 'There can be no question of the Government at Westminster abdicating their responsibilities in Northern

Ireland'. At the same time, over 15,000 British troops were on active service in the six counties, internment without trial continued until November 1975, both the Republican and Loyalists were engaged in retaliatory and internecine murders of the most appalling kind and many hundreds on both sides were serving prison sentences.

There is, of course, no solution to the Northern Ireland problem which is acceptable by all parties or even by the main protagonists whose mutual hostility has for so long been the source of the discord and violence. Indeed, the conditions prevailing in the province make impossible any attempt at stable government. Political debate concerns the very existence of the province's allegiance to the State, whether British or Irish. But there is no constitution and no consensus and no body with a monopoly of force with which to implement its policies. Civil government is non-existent and the British Army is the only effective source of authority, not the Northern Ireland Office which now has merely a nominal status. In these circumstances there is no hope of a compromise at the present time. There are, nevertheless, a number of alternative forms of government which have been mooted in an attempt to break the deadlock.

The first alternative is that the six counties will continue to be ruled directly from London, either as at present with a Secretary of State for Northern Ireland in the Cabinet at Westminster who is formally responsible for administering the province, or after their full integration with the United Kingdom. The second alternative is an independent State of Northern Ireland, with Unionists relinquishing their links with Britain and Republicans theirs with Ireland; this could be achieved either by a unilateral declaration of independence by Loyalists or by negotiation. The third alternative is the re-unification of the six counties within an all-Ireland Republic, either on a federal basis with Parliaments in all four provinces, or by means of a British-Irish condominion rule with the States sharing responsibility for government, or by the transfer of Northern Ireland to the Republic following, possibly, a plebiscite in which a majority of citizens in the United Kingdom and the Republic voted for such a solution. In practical political terms, however, this move could not be achieved peacefully. The Republic would hesitate to incorporate a million Protestants without their consent in a new State inhabited by 3 million Catholics: there would probably be armed resistance by Protestants considering themselves 'sold' to the Republic despite repeated pledges that this would not happen by the British Government. The fourth group of alternatives includes repartition by local option and the consequent moving of the border; but this would mean that some predominantly Catholic districts in the east of the province would be in the Protestant sector while some Protestants would find themselves in the Republic, for there is an admixture of Catholics and Protestants in almost all parts. The destruction of Northern Ireland might also result from military action, perhaps following the withdrawal of British troops, if para-military forces on both sides engaged one another; such a holocaust might be sparked by a pogrom by Protestants or by a Republican uprising. The fifth alternative is self-government within the United Kingdom, and the province ruled either by a Loyalist majority or a broad Unionist coalition or by power-sharing between Catholics and Protestants. It goes without saying that all these alternatives present enormous difficulties and that all have been rejected by one side or the other.

As a result, there seemed little hope at the end of 1975 that Northern Ireland was any nearer to finding ways of solving its political problems, or even of stopping the slaughter, than it was in 1969. It was in that year, writing in the newspaper *The Observer* (London) on 24 August, that the journalist Patrick O'Donovan made this comment on the bloody feud between the people of Northern Ireland: 'They are all Irish. All cursed by their history. And they are still working out the destiny ordained by one of the most tragic of national stories'.

THE WELSH

Wales, situated in the west of Britain, is a largely mountainous country bounded on two sides by the Irish Sea and by the Bristol Channel on the third. It has an area of 8,006 square miles, about one twelfth of the United Kingdom's and its population in 1971 was 2,731,204 (4.9%). As a result of local government reform, the counties of the Principality—as it is known for ceremonial purposes—were reduced in number from thirteen to eight in 1974. About two-thirds of the population lives in the connurbation which lies between Newport, on the border with England, and Swansea to the west, mostly in the valleys of Gwent (formerly Monmouthshire) and in the three divisions of the old county of Glamorgan, especially on the coastal belt. The traditional occupation of coal-mining and steel-making have declined in recent years but this industrial region of southern Wales continues to make a major contribution to the British economy. The other counties, all largely agricultural, are Dyfed (formerly Carmarthenshire, Pembrokeshire and Cardiganshire), Powys (formerly Breconshire, Radnorshire and Montgomeryshire), Gwynedd (formerly Merioneth, Caernarfonshire and Anglesey) and Clwyd (formerly Denbighshire and Flintshire). Cardiff, the capital city of Wales, has a population of approximately 284,000.

At the Census of 1971 a total of 542,402 (20·84%) persons living in Wales were enumerated as being able to speak the Welsh language. Given the uneven distribution of population, it was predictable that Glamorgan (Welsh: *Sir Forgannwg*) would have the greatest number of Welsh-speakers, about 141,000. The county of Carmarthenshire *(Sir Gaerfyrddin)* had 103,000, Caernarfonshire *(Sir Gaernarfon)* 73,000, Denbighshire *(Sir Ddinbych)* 49,600, Anglesey *(Sir Fôn)* 37,000, Cardiganshire *(Sir Aberteifi)* 35,800, Merioneth *(Sir Feirionydd)* 24,900, and Flintshire *(Sir y Fflint)* 24,400. The counties with the smallest Welsh-speaking populations were Pembrokeshire *(Sir Benfro)* with 19,500, Breconshire *(Sir Frycheiniog)* with 11,700, Montgomeryshire *(Sir Drefaldwyn)* with 11,600, Monmouthshire *(Sir Fynwy)* with 9,300 and Radnorshire *(Sir Faesyfed)* with 700.

It can be concluded from these statistics that the areas which are predominantly Welsh in speech are still in the western and northern parts of the country, with nuclei in Anglesey, the Llŷn peninsula and Meirionydd in Gwynedd, and the northern and eastern districts of Dyfed. All these are mainly rural areas and they are surrounded by others where the process of anglicisation has accelerated during the last decade. The separation of the nuclei in Gwynedd from that in Dyfed, as a result of inroads made by English following the development of tourism along the coast of Cardigan Bay, is especially significant in an analysis of the distribution of the Welsh language. Among the towns and industrial districts where Welsh is spoken are Caernarfon, Bangor, Aberystwyth, Llanelli, Ammanford, the Swansea valleys and Merthyr Tydfil. The number of Welsh-speakers in Cardiff (Welsh: *Caerdydd)* is approximately 13,000.

The total number of Welsh-speakers enumerated by the 1971 Census showed an over-all decline. Indeed, at every Census since 1891, when 880,000 (54%) Welsh-speakers were recorded, the number of Welsh-speakers in Wales has decreased. In 1901 there were 929,800 (50%), 977,400 (43%) in 1911, 922,100 (37%) in 1921, 909,300 (37%) in 1931, 714,686 (28·9%) in 1951 and 656,002 (26%) in 1961. There was also a steady fall in the proportion of persons speaking Welsh only, from 280,900 (15%) in 1901 to 97,900 (4%) in 1931 and to 32,700 (1·2%) in 1971.

The Welsh language belongs, with Cornish and Breton, to the Brythonic branch of the Celtic languages. It derives from the language of a people, called the *Celtae* by classical authors, who had conquered large parts of Western Europe during the centuries which preceded the Christian era. These continental Celts were defeated by the Romans and their language disappeared in Gaul, leaving traces only in place-names throughout what are today France, Austria, Switzerland, Italy, Spain and the Balkans. Their language would have disappeared completely if the Britons (Welsh: *Brythoniaid)* and the Goidels had not settled in Britain and Ireland. By the year 55 B.C., when the Romans first arrived in these islands, the two Celtic languages had been well established for about a thousand years. Brythonic was the language of what are today Wales, England and southern Scotland, while Goidelic was the language of Ireland and parts of north-western Scotland. But in the first century A.D. the insular Celts, after fierce resistance, led by the druids from their base in Anglesey, were conquered by the Romans under Ostorius and, for the next four hundred years, Britain was to be a frontier province of the Empire.

On the withdrawal of the Romans in A.D 410, however, the Britons emerged as a free people, Romanised and Christianised, with their language and customs intact. Cunedda, who had come to Wales from Scotland soon after the Romans' departure, founded the royal dynasty of Gwynedd, while Welsh self-government was recognised by the Emperor Magnus Maximus (Welsh: *Macsen Wledig*). It is from this post-Roman period that Welsh nationhood has developed, and these two are generally considered to be the fathers of the nation. According to archeologists and proto-historians who have studied the Celtic territories of this period, a situation is envisaged of a society of free tribesmen and serfs who worked both pastoral and arable land, the former being descendants of the Celtic settlers of the Iron Age and the latter the Iberian survivors of the late Bronze Age now ruled by their Celtic masters.

In the post-Roman period the Britons formed a Celtic confederation which stretched from Cornwall to the Clyde. By the middle of the sixth century those who were to become the people known today in English as the Welsh had become conscious of their unity in face of growing threat from Anglo-Saxon aggression. They called themselves *Cymry* (fellow-countrymen), their country *Cymru* and their language *Cymraeg*. To the Anglo-Saxons they were known as *Wealas* (foreigners), from which the modern English form of their name has developed.

Cut off from the Cornish by the Saxon victory of 577, but not from their northern compatriots until the Battle of Chester in 716, the language of this people developed into Old Welsh. Their material culture was not extensive, but great emphasis seems to have been placed on the spoken word, especially their language in its resistance to Anglo-Saxon. This too was the Age of Saints when contacts between Wales

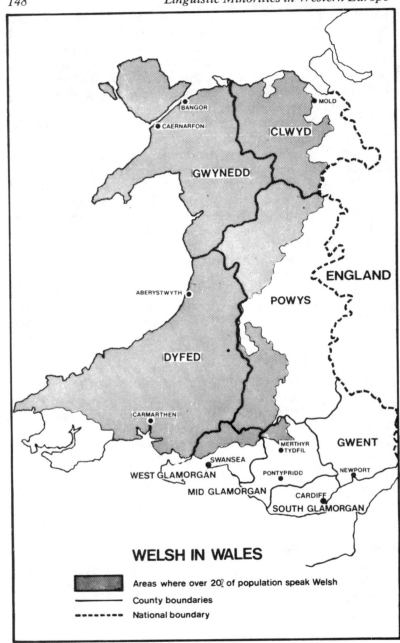

WELSH IN WALES

and its Celtic neighbours to the west and south were close and fruitful, with art and music flourishing and the monasteries keeping alive the scholarship which had been extinguished by the barbarians in the rest of Europe. At the same time the Welsh were continuously under attack from their neighbours. At last, around 740, the border between Wales and England was marked by the dyke built by Offa, King of Mercia. Still the Welsh were obliged to defend their territory from the Norsemen, which they did valiantly under Rhodri Fawr, King of Gwynedd and ruler of two thirds of Wales.

The earliest Welsh literature dates from this time, the end of the sixth century, although it was not written down until three hundred years later. The poet Taliesin tells of the prowess in battle of Urien, King of Rheged, a province in southern Scotland, and refers to the respect paid by him to the bards at his court. Another poem, *Y Gododdin,* attributed to Aneirin, praises the heroes of a tribe whose capital, Caer Eiddyn stood in the neighbourhood of modern Edinburgh: their war-band was wiped out by Saxon forces at Catraeth, Catterick in modern Yorkshire. The courage of the Welsh in defending their land is celebrated in the lament of Llywarch Hen who lost all but one of his twenty-four sons in wars against the invaders. Unlike Breton, Welsh thus became a literary language at a very early stage in its history. The Welsh literary tradition, unbroken and nearly fourteen centuries old, is therefore among the most ancient in Europe.

It has often been remarked that, from the sixth century to the present time, the history of Wales is the history of the Welsh language. Indeed, in medieval times the Welsh word for 'language', *iaith,* was used synonymously with *cenedl,* 'nation'. From its beginnings and throughout the period of Welsh independence Welsh was the language of government, administration and law. Several historians have shown that Welsh in Wales enjoyed a higher prestige than any of the other vernacular languages of Europe in the same period. Down to the time of the Norman Conquest of England, the Kingdom of Wales retained its political and legal independence. The laws of Hywel Dda, a tenth century prince, were administered in the courts and Welsh, with Latin, was the language used. From these laws it is clear that the status of the bard and the language he employed was high in medieval Welsh society. The language was enriched and purified by the bardic schools which flourished for over a thousand years, to disappear only in the sixteenth century. Theirs was a courtly poetry, enjoying the patronage of princes, conservative but not closed to influences from abroad, technically accomplished, often meant to be accompanied by music, and written in praise of traditional Celtic virtues such as prowess in battle, natural and personal beauty, hospitality and honour. The emergence of a prose tradition during the medieval period indicates that the spoken language, more associated with everyday life, was also treasured. By the famous prose masterpiece known in English as the Mabinogion and its contribution to the Arthurian Romances, Wales belonged to the mainstream of European culture.

After 1066, however, Norman lords who had settled along the frontier between Wales and England began to encroach on the lands of the Welsh. By 1100 they had over-run large areas of eastern and southern Wales, establishing in the Marches their own authority. The law in these areas, from Gloucester to Chester, was Anglo-Norman and the languages used in the records were Latin and French, with Welsh admitted in evidence. Hywel Dda's laws survived only where Welsh princes maintained their independence—in Gwynedd in the north-west and Deheubarth in the south-west—and there Welsh was the language used in the courts and, with Latin, the language of record as well. Resistance to the Normans was long and determined. Gerald the Welshman (Latin: *Giraldus Cambrensis*), himself partly Norman, wrote of the Welsh, 'Their mind is wholly on the defence of their country and its freedom; it is for their country that they fight, for freedom they labour; for these they think it sweet not only to fight with the sword but also to lay down their lives'.

Welsh independence came to an end with the death of the last native prince Llywelyn II, known in Welsh as *Llywelyn ein Llyw Olaf* (Llywelyn our Last Prince) in 1282. Following the military successes of Edward I, the Statute of Rhuddlan in 1284 provided for the administration of English law in those parts of Wales ruled directly by the Crown. But no attempt was made to proscribe the Welsh language in the courts. Interpreters into Latin or French, later English, were employed in the higher courts and in the commotes, or lower courts, the language still normally used was Welsh. The language therefore held its own not only in domestic and literary usage but in legal matters throughout the Middle Ages. Not even after the rising in 1400 of Owain Glyn Dŵr (c. 1354-1416), was there any legislation against the Welsh language. He it was who revived the spirit of national independence, albeit briefly, by proclaiming an independent Church, two Universities and a Parliament. For this he is remembered by the Welsh to this day as their national hero.

After Owain Glyn Dŵr's rebellion, with the exception of the establishment of a Council of Wales and the Marches by Edward IV in 1471, the political, territorial and economic life of Wales became increasingly integrated with that of England. During the Wars of the Roses western Wales supported the House of Lancaster and eastern Wales the House of York. The battle of Bosworth in 1485 had ironic results for Wales. It was a largely Welsh army which put Henry, who could boast of his descent from the Tudors of Penmynydd in Anglesey, on the English throne. For now began the disintegration of those foundations on which Welsh independence had been built. This destruction was carried out by the Tudors and its core was the anglicisation of the Welsh nobility and their alienation from their own people. London, with a Welshman on the throne, became the focus of all their ambitions. They sent their sons to be educated at grammar schools and universities in England, and later opened schools in Wales where education on the English model was given. By 1585 the process had gone so far that Gruffydd Robert (c. 1522—1610) could write in *Y Drych Cristionogawl* (The Christian's Mirror), 'The nobility and others neglect and despise the Welsh tongue' and 'the greater part of the nobility neither can read nor write Welsh, which is a shameful thing'. With the demise of the bardic schools and the dissolution of the monasteries in the 1530s, Wales thus lost the only two systems of education in the Welsh language which the country could call its own.

The clearest expression of Tudor intentions was the Statute of Wales, usually called the Acts of Union, which were passed in 1536 and 1542. Now, for the first time, the Welsh language was formally recognised as a symbol of Welsh national independence. By this Act, Wales was 'incorporated, united and annexed' into the English State by Henry VIII. With the loss of political independence, and with the decline of the Roman Catholic Church throughout the country, Welsh links with Europe grew fewer. From Tudor times onwards, most of the influence on Welsh culture came from or through England and the influence of Wales on the literary life of Europe almost ceased altogether. Critical changes were now effected in government and law: the country was divided into shires, so that English law could be administered in a uniform way, the Lords of the Marches were deprived of their privileges and English was introduced as the sole language of officialdom.

The preamble of the Act of 1536 referred—for the first time in any statute—to the existence of the Welsh language thus: 'the people of the same dominion have and do daily use a speche nothing like ne consonaunt to the naturall mother tonge used within this Realme'. It went on to announce its intention 'utterly to extirpe alle and singular the sinister usages and customs' of Wales which differed from those of England. Whether or not this clause referred to the Welsh language is debatable. But the same Act provided, in Clause 20, the so-called 'language clause', that the language of law-courts in Wales must be in English: 'all Justices . . . and all other officers and ministers of the lawe shall proclayme and kepe . . . all courtes . . . in the Englisshe Tongue and also from hensforth no personne or personnes that use the Welsshe speche or langage shall have or enjoy any maner office or fees within the Realme of Englonde, Wales or other Kinges dominions . . . onles he or they use and exercise the speche or langage of Englisshe'.

The Acts of Union did not expressly prohibit the Welsh language, but from now on the law was to be administered in English and all records were to be kept in that language; it followed that officials who were to administer the law and maintain records must know English. The government of Wales was thus entrusted to the minority, about 5% of the population, who knew English. Nevertheless, from 1536 until the eighteenth century, while the law was administered in English, Welsh was undoubtedly widely used in the courts, at the highest level of the Council in the Marches and the Court of Great Sessions down to the hundred and manor courts. At the Quarter Sessions many of the magistrates were Welsh-speaking and evidence was given before them in Welsh. The language of record, however, continued to be Latin and later, English, with Welsh incorporated only when the words used were alleged to be of a treasonable or slanderous nature. English was also the main language of administration, as the correspondence of deputy-lieutenants, justices of the peace, sheriffs and other officials which has survived from this period show. Welsh was used only on special occasions, such as when James I was proclaimed in Welsh in 1603, although in a few areas of Gwynedd it was used at Quarter Sessions and in the parish records.

As late as 1798 Thomas Roberts (1765-1841), author of the pamphlet *Cwyn yn erbyn Gorthrymder* (A Complaint against Oppression), made it clear what confusion there must have been among a largely monoglot population when brought before the law: 'But the judge speaks English, and the lawyers too, while the witnesses testify in Welsh; certainly they have a translator who is on oath to declare the witnesses' words as faithfully as he can; yet everyone who understands both Welsh and English knows that it is very difficult to translate in such a way that the words have as full an effect on the jurors in the one language as in the other . . . So we can easily see that justice can only occasionally be done in this country, and that by accident: because the laws and the language in which they are expressed are beyond the understanding of the jurors who have to give judgement'. A further effect of the use of English in law and administration was to relegate Welsh to an inferior status, unworthy for official purposes in the eyes of the wealthier and better-educated classes. Thus began one of the root causes of the decline of the language up to the present time.

The Tudor period was also to have lasting effects on Welsh as the language of religious worship. During the Middle Ages, in both Wales and England, Latin had been used in church services but the vernacular for religious instruction and in private devotions. English became the language of worship in England after the promulgation of the English Book of Common Prayer in 1549 and after the Act of Uniformity enforced its use in all parish churches. No similar provision was made for Welsh at this time, though William Salesbury (?1520-?1584) published a Welsh translation of the Epistles and Gospels, on his own initiative, in 1551. It was not until the reign of Elizabeth I that specific permission for the translation of the Book of Common Prayer and the Bible into Welsh was given. Under the Act for the Translating of the Bible and the Divine Service into the Welsh Tongue, passed in 1563, four Welsh bishops and the Bishop of Hereford (part of whose diocese was then Welsh-speaking) were required to have the Bible and Prayer Book translated, and copies placed in any parish church where Welsh was commonly used, before St David's Day, 1 March 1566, and to see that the clergy in all such parishes were to conduct divine services in Welsh. The Act also laid it down that a copy of the Bible and of the Book of Common Prayer should be placed in every parish church, so that 'such as do not understand the said language, by conferring both tongues together, the sooner attain to the knowledge of the English tongue'. It has been argued that this provision indicates that the purpose of the Act providing for the translation of the Bible into Welsh was, in fact, the furtherance of a knowledge of English, but from the wording this remains arguable. What is certain is that it was not so much from a love of the language that the Welsh Bible was authorised but from the Tudor desire to secure religious uniformity and political stability throughout England and Wales.

The translation of the Bible into Welsh was the crowning achievement of scholarship in Renaissance Wales. The work was done by Bishop William Morgan (c.1545-1604) and published in 1588. He it was who asked his fellow countrymen, 'Do you think that you need no better words nor wider expressions to discuss learning and philosophy and the arts than those you normally use for buying and selling and eating and drinking? If you think so, then you deceive yourselves. And take this therefore as my warning to you: if you do not save and correct and perfect the language in the lifetime

of the present generation it will be too late'. The authorised
version of William Morgan's Bible was edited in 1626 by Dr
John Davies (c. 1537-1644) of Mallwyd, one of the greatest
scholars of the day and an authority on the older literary
language which had been perfected in the bardic schools. The
Welsh Bible, 'the historic blunder' of the Tudors, thus set a
standard which most writers have followed ever since—an
enormous advantage for any language and one certainly not
shared by any of the other Celtic languages.

It was the status accorded to Welsh by the Act of 1563, and
its regular use as the official language of worship in the
Established Church, and later among Nonconformist
congregations, which appear to be the principal reasons why
Welsh held its ground so successfully in comparison with the
more rapid decline of languages like Irish, Gaelic, Manx and
Cornish. Nor did Welsh, unlike the other Celtic languages
degenerate into a number of dialects because the Bible
produced a common literary standard, giving the language a
cohesion which it had never known before. Its style, based on
the ancient poetic traditions, had a dignity which pervaded
almost all literature subsequently written. The translation of
the Bible co-incided with the development of printing and so
gave the Welsh a substantial number of books to read in their
own language. At the same time, it was the virility of the
spoken language which enabled the people to take full advantage of the translation of the Scriptures into Welsh.
Thrown almost entirely upon their own resources, and
deprived of patronage by the anglicised upper classes, the
common people of Wales held tenaciously to their language
and to their social, cultural and religious traditions which
were expressed through it.

From the middle of the eighteenth century Wales, still
almost wholly Welsh in speech, was an economically poor
country, mainly pastoral and governed by a land-owning class
by now completely anglicised, but its largely peasant culture
was given a tremendous impetus by the religious revivals of
this period. The Celtic Church had been replaced by the
Roman in the eleventh century, when Wales had been
organised in four dioceses owing a grudging allegiance to
Canterbury. In turn the Roman Church had been swept away

by the Anglican Church under the Act of Union in 1536. From the earliest days of the Reformation this Established Church had grown estranged from the common people and many had been attracted by Calvinism, the stern doctrines of which had a special appeal to a people without leaders of its own. By the 1840s, while John Wesley's cause made progress in England, the majority of the Welsh supported the Protestant Nonconformist sects—Baptists, Congregationalists, Calvinistic Methodists, Wesleyans and Unitarians. The legal and educational disabilities they suffered in consequence were readily identified with their inferior national status which generated pressure for social reform and deeply influenced the character of their radical politics.

After nearly a century of controversy the Anglican Church in Wales was disestablished and disendowed in 1914 but still exists as one religious body among many in an atmosphere of mutual tolerance. Conducting its activities in the Welsh language and in a warm emotional atmosphere congenial to the national temperament, Nonconformity has been a factor of immense importance in strengthening the culture of Wales and centuries of Puritanism have had a permanent effect on the Welsh character. Most of the social leaders of Wales have been products of the Chapel, which has usually played a radical role in politics.

The fact that the Nonconformist revival was both religious and social is attributable to the work of Griffith Jones (1683-1761) of Llanddowror. Assisted by the philanthropist Madam Bevan of Laugharne (1698-1779), he organised the Welsh Circulating Schools which spread to all parts of the country. Here young people and adults were taught to read the Bible and Book of Common Prayer, and other religious works translated into Welsh by the Society for the Promotion of Christian Knowledge. Their primary aim, according to Griffith Jones, was 'to teach the scholars to read the word of God'; no attempt was made to teach writing. At the time of Griffith Jones's death in 1761 there were 3,495 Circulating Schools in Wales and over 158,000 pupils—over half the total population—had attended them. In this way the reading of Welsh remained dominant for many generations afterwards.

The religious revival made the common people of Wales articulate in their own language for the first time. Later in the century the revival of preaching and the hymns of writers like William Williams of Pantycelyn (1716-91) helped to perpetuate the spoken word in Welsh, as did the Sunday Schools started by Thomas Charles (1755-1814) of Bala, at which children were taught to read and recite from the Bible.

The coming of the Industrial Revolution during the last decades of the eighteenth century led to a rapid transformation of the social and economic scene in Wales. Many of the new industrialists, and the thousands of workers who poured into the valleys of southern Wales, were not Welsh; English tended to become the language of business and industry. But with the influx of Welsh-speaking workers from rural areas, the language was strong enough to resist the new threat to its existence. Indeed, although the Education Act of 1870 created a system of elementary education in which Welsh was completely ignored, while the Act of 1899 provided secondary education on an English pattern, the language was so well established that the full effect of this educational policy was not felt for a generation or so. Even so, Welsh was prohibited in most schools and pupils caught speaking it were physically punished and obliged to suffer the shame of wearing the 'Welsh Not' around their necks—a humiliation which was inflicted on all the Celtic peoples, and others, during the nineteenth century. In 1851 Welsh was the language of 90% of Merthyr Tydfil, the biggest town in Wales at this time with a population of 63,000 and a centre of publishing in the language. Welsh was also the language of Dic Penderyn (1807/8-31) executed for his part in the Merthyr Riots of 1831, and of the Chartists, men like John Frost (1784-1877) and Zephaniah Williams (1795-1874), who led the growing working-class movement of the day, and of the Daughters of Rebecca who attacked toll-gates in western Wales.

Economic growth was matched by the equally rapid advance, in town and country, of Nonconformity which was expressed almost wholly in Welsh. The number of books published in the language increased and Welsh journals and newspapers appeared for the first time. Among the vigorous aspirations of political and social consciousness in Wales at this time there was a growing awareness of national identity and of the fortunes of the language and culture which were its principal tokens. Movements like the Society for the Utilization of the Welsh Language, and individuals like Dan Isaac Davies (1839-87), strove to give the language an honourable place, but it was not until the turn of the century that it was used as a medium of instruction as a subject in education. The valiant efforts of O. M. Edwards (1858-1920) as Chief Inspector of Schools in Wales led to a new attitude towards the language on the part of the Board of Education and later the Welsh Department of the Ministry of Education. By contrast, the formal and official use of Welsh had become more and more neglected and, on some occasions, repressed.

The most notorious incident was the report of the Commissioners sent to Wales to inquire into the state of education in 1846-7. Because the report condemned the use and survival of Welsh as the cause of all backwardness and immorality in Wales, it became known as *Brad y Llyfrau Gleision* (The Treachery of the Blue Books): 'The Welsh language is a vast drawback to Wales and a manifold barrier to the moral progress and commercial property of the people . . . the Welsh element is never found at the top of the social scale . . . his language keeps him under the hatches'. In this the Commissioners were appealing to the belief, cherished at this time, in the importance of 'getting on in the world' where English was the language of success, wealth, power, prestige, Queen Victoria and the British Empire. Their report, which condemned the National Schools and failed to appreciate the quality of education given in the Sunday Schools of Wales, was warmly received at Westminster where William Williams, a Welshmen representing Coventry, concluded for the Government: 'Send the English schoolmaster among them . . . a band of efficient schoolmasters is kept up at much less expense than a body of police or soldiery'. Mathew Arnold, as an Inspector of Schools at this time, wrote in 1852, 'It must always be the desire of a Government to render its dominion, as far as possible, homogenous . . . Sooner or later the difference of language between Wales and England will probably be effaced . . . an event that is socially and politically so desirable'. *The Times* in 1866 declared that 'the Welsh language is . . . the curse of Wales . . . its prevalence and the ignorance of the English language have excluded the Welsh people from the civilisation of their English neighbours'.

It was against such attitudes, and in an attempt to establish a free Welsh society, that Michael D. Jones (1822-98) founded *Y Wladfa,* a colony in Patagonia where Welsh was to be the sole official language of law, religion and education. The venture was a brave one, and, despite great hardships, met with success. By today, however, the Welsh language in Patagonia is spoken by only a few thousand people, descendants of the first settlers. Emrys ap Iwan (1851-1906) was another lone voice who preached a nationalism far in advance of its day: 'In order to appreciate how odious is our attitude, let us imagine that the English behave towards us as we do to them; at meetings held in the heart of England they turn to Welsh or half-Welsh because two or three monoglot Welsh-speakers are bold enough to cry out "Welsh, Welsh!"'.

The position of Welsh was strengthened, however, by the enthusiasm of many exiles in London who, in the late eighteenth and early nineteenth centuries, became active in promoting an interest in the language and its literature. Organised in the Honourable Society of Cymmrodorion, which had been founded in 1751, they did much to revive the *eisteddfod*—a local festival, at which adults and children sang, recited and competed in the composition of Welsh prose and verse; held all over Wales, they culminated in the National *Eisteddfod.* The Welsh national anthem, *Hen Wlad fy Nhadau* (Old Land of my Fathers), was also composed at this time—in 1856 by the weavers Evan James (1809-78) and his son James James (1833-1902) of Pontypridd. The anthem, which the Bretons and Cornish have adopted, is sung frequently on public occasions in Wales, such as rugby matches, *eisteddfodau,* and other public gatherings, and has a cherished place in the affection of the people. Further development of interest in Welsh culture took place with the establishment of the first College of the University of Wales at Aberystwyth in 1872, the foundation of the National Library in the same town and of the National Museum in Cardiff, both granted charters in 1907.

In 1889 the Welsh Intermediate Education Act was passed, resulting in an increase in the number of grammar schools. The three University Colleges at Aberystwyth, Cardiff and Bangor were federated to form the University of Wales in 1893 and the Central Welsh Board was established to examine the grammar schools in 1896. The Welsh Disestablishment Act of 1914 disendowed the Church of England in Wales. These initiatives were largely the fruits of the Home Rule Movement led by Gladstone's Liberal Party and *Cymru Fydd* (Wales of the Future), an organisation founded in 1886 and seeking to obtain a national legislature for Wales. David Lloyd George, Member of Parliament for Caernarfon, was the national hero and all save one of the Welsh seats belonged to his party after the General Election of 1900. The Government at Westminster agreed in principle to Home Rule for Wales in 1895. But the *Cymru Fydd* movement, apparently more concerned with Disestablishment and the Land Question than self-government, collapsed shortly afterwards. Lloyd George became a Cabinet Minister in 1906. E. T. John presented a Bill for Welsh Self-Government, but there was little support for this move. There were some gains, however: following the creation of the Welsh Department of the Board of Education in 1907, a Welsh Board of Health and a Welsh Department of the Ministry of Agriculture were established in 1919.

The Welsh language in the course of its history has faced many crises but none so serious as those which have occurred during the present century. The decline is reflected by the Census: in 1901 just over half the population, some 929,800 persons in all, were Welsh-speaking but fifty years later their numbers had fallen to 714,686 or 28·9%. Apart from the loss of political independence and the concomitant factors already mentioned, the reasons for this decline are mainly economic and social. The period from 1760 to 1914 saw a great shift from a predominantly agricultural economy to dependence on the metal and coal industries, in which over a third of the people were employed. Between 1851 and 1911, while the rural population declined, the population of Wales as a whole doubled from 1·2 million to 2·4 million. The influx of workers from England and Ireland transformed the structure of Welsh society. Between the World Wars the effects of economic depression were tragic in Wales. The number of unemployed rose to 10% of the entire population, reaching its peak in 1932 when 38% of the work-force were registered as unemployed, despite the fact that about 25,000 people had left Wales in every year over the previous decade. By 1938 about 430,000 people had left Wales. The Welsh economy, even the Welsh personality, have hardly recovered from the damage done during those years.

The economic position of Wales improved during and after the Second World War. Hundreds of new enterprises were started and an ambitious programme of redevelopment was undertaken in one of the most successful exercises in regional development ever attempted in Britain. Since 1960, however, Wales has suffered from a decline in some of its main industries, including coal, steel and agriculture. Between 1960 and 1970 the numbers employed in the extractive industries (agriculture, forestry, fishing, mining and quarrying) fell from 138,000 to 70,000. The rate of unemployment has remained well above that in the United Kingdom as a whole, once more reaching 10% in some towns. The economic growth of Wales during the last decade has been slow. The manufacturing industries now employ more than a third of the labour-force but this has not been sufficient to off-set the loss of jobs in older industries. The run-down of the coal and steel industries in the industrial valleys of the south-east has had grave consequences for the national economy. The number of males in employment fell from 670,000 in 1960 to 608,000 in 1970.

The transformation of the Welsh economy has not been without its effects on the national language of Wales. Inter-marriage on a large scale after 1945, together with industrial development in areas which had been Welsh-speaking up to then, resulted in further dilution and a loss of community spirit. The appointment of persons unable to speak Welsh to executive and technical posts in the larger industries meant that the language could no longer be used to the same extent as in the older, smaller industries. The decline of the Non-conformist chapels, formerly a stronghold of the language, was a major blow. The advent of radio was a threat to Welsh until, after much agitation, a Welsh Region of the BBC was established in the 1930s, while the influence of English television in homes where only Welsh is spoken continues to this day. Small farms are disappearing as a result of amalgamation, the spread of forestry or the demands of mineral prospecting. In the rural and coastal areas the volume of visitors and 'holiday homes' grows from year to year.

More alarming still is the influx of English people, mainly the retired, into the rural areas which have been the traditional bastions of the Welsh language. The population of Wales increased by 87,000 between 1961 and 1971—some 3·3% as compared with 5·3% for the United Kingdom as a whole. During the year 1970/1 a total of 42,490 people moved into Wales from other parts of Britain, while 41,000 left—a net gain of 1,450 but a huge, over-all loss of the indigenous population. In the five years up to the Census of 1971 about 33,600 people from north-west England moved into Wales, while 17,800 left Wales for north-east England—a net increase of 15,800, but again a substantial loss of Welsh people. Similar statistics show that the influx of population into Wales is also from the West Midlands of England. The number of immigrants to Wales from the rest of Britain was up by 16% on the figures revealed by the 1961 Census. The majority of the new-comers were over the age of forty-five. The Census of 1971 also revealed that 81% of the population of Wales had been born in Wales, 15% in England and 4% elsewhere.

During the years between the two World Wars the Welsh were more concerned with economic problems than with the fate of their language. Socialism in Britain had gained its first Member of Parliament in 1900 when Keir Hardie won a seat at Merthyr Tydfil for the International Labour Party. By 1920 the British Labour Party had replaced the Liberal Party, as the representative party of the Welsh people. Aneurin Bevan, architect of the National Health Service and Member of Parliament for Ebbw Vale, was the most famous of the many Welshmen who have played important roles in the British Labour Movement. The natural radicalism of the Welsh, and their loyalty to trade unions during the severe economic crisis in the coalfields in the 'twenties and 'thirties, have ensured for the Labour Party a paramount place in Welsh life up to the present, especially in southern Wales. At the General Election of October 1974 it won twenty-three out of the thirty-six seats in Wales, polling 761,447 or 49·5% of the votes cast.

The other thirteen seats are at present divided between the Conservatives who hold eight and polled 367,647 votes (23.9%) in Wales at the General Election of October 1974, *Plaid Cymru* which polled 166,259 votes (10·7%) and won three, and the Welsh Liberal Party which polled 239,057 votes (15.5%) and won two; the Welsh Communist Party polled 2,941 votes (0.15%) in three constituencies but won no seats.

It was the Labour Party which, during and after the Second World War, reviewed the process of administrative decentralisation which had began at the turn of the century, but which had come to a halt around 1920. In 1940 the Welsh Board of Health took over responsibility for housing, water supplies and other local government services. By 1945 there were fifteen Government departments in Cardiff. The Education Act of 1944 provided for a Central Advisory Council for Education in Wales and in 1948 the same Act established the Welsh Joint Education Committee, a committee of local education authorities with advisory and executive functions. The Council for Wales was set up in 1949 and continued until 1966 when its work has taken over by the Welsh Economic Council, which in turn was replaced by the Welsh Council two years later. There were also significant developments in the allocation of ministerial responsibility for Welsh affairs. In 1951 the office of Minister for Welsh Affairs was created; this post was held by the Home Secretary until, in 1957, it was transferred to the Minister of Housing and Local Government. A Minister of State for Wales to assist the Minister for Welsh Affairs was appointed in 1957.

It was not until October 1964, in fulfilment of an election promise, that the Labour Party—which had been out of office for thirteen years—created a Secretary of State for Wales with a seat in the Government at Westminster. At the outset the executive functions of the Secretary of State for Wales—James Griffiths, M.P. for Llanelli, was the first to hold this post—were those which had been administered by the Welsh Office of the Ministry of Housing and Local Government, mainly town and country planning, housing, water and other local government matters, including economic planning and roads. Since then the Welsh Office has taken over responsibility for the health service, national parks, forestry and agriculture (with the Ministry for Agriculture), ancient monuments, tourism, child care, primary and secondary education, the National Museum and the National Library and in the summer of 1975 the power to administer financial assistance to industry. The staff of the Welsh Office increased from 225 in 1964 to 990 in December 1972 and to 1,500 in 1975, and its budget from £48,000 to over £240 million. In addition to those already mentioned, the Secretary of State is at present responsible for the following: arts and culture (except the Welsh Arts Council, local museums, libraries and galleries), environmental services, rural development, social work, sport and recreation, transport and the urban programme.

Wales is represented in the House of Commons by thirty-six members, a little under 6% of the total. There is no separate peerage of Wales but a number of Welsh people hold peerages of the United Kingdom. A one-day debate on Welsh affairs, in each parliamentary session, is held in the House of Commons. The Speaker, a Welshman and former Secretary of State for Wales, is George Thomas, Labour member for Cardiff West. Welsh affairs are also debated by the Welsh Grand Committee, established in 1960.

It was recognised soon after the Second World War that local government in Wales was in need of reform. The system of thirteen county councils, four county borough councils and 164 county district councils, included too many small and poor authorities for the economical and efficient administration of local affairs. The Local Government Act of 1972, which applied to England and Wales, provided for a two-tier system of local government consisting of eight counties and thirty-seven districts. This Act took effect from 1 April 1974. The main functions of the new county councils are roads, the fire service, education, youth employment, the social services and consumer protection, while the district councils are responsible for housing and share with the county authorities responsibility for such matters as recreation and town and country planning. At the local level, provision was made for about a thousand community councils with more or less the same functions as the parish councils which they replaced. Serious doubt has been expressed as to the wisdom of these reforms, especially in the light of the Government's recent proposals for devolution of power from Westminster to Cardiff by the creation of a fourth tier of government—an elected Assembly for Wales.

Although since the days of Keir Hardie the Labour Party has been committed, at least in theory and especially at election times, to the principle of granting more devolution for Wales, and has in fact implemented many of its proposals for bringing more power to Cardiff from Westminster, the demand for self-government has been led, since 1945, by *Plaid Cymru* (The Party of Wales), known in English as the Welsh Nationalist Party. Political nationalism had made little progress in the years following the First World War. From 1921 on there was a succession of Home Rule Bills at Westminster, all defeated either by the Tories or by lack of commitment on the part of the Welsh Labour members who won eighteen out of the thirty-six seats in Wales at the Election of 1922.

Only a handful of Welsh patriots were of the opinion that there could be no Home Rule without a party based in Wales and owing its first allegiance to the Welsh people. These young men, incensed by the Government's refusal to consider even the most modest innovation for Wales, were further humiliated when they saw Ireland attaining self-government in 1922. For them the lesson was clear: meeting during the National *Eisteddfod* at Pwllheli in 1925 they formed *Plaid Genedlaethol Cymru* (The National Party of Wales). The Party's original aims were threefold: to establish a Parliament for Wales, to ensure the separate representation of Wales at the League of Nations and to win recognition of Welsh as the official language of Wales. An early pamphlet stated, 'Our immediate ambition is a government for Wales which shall be for the good of Wales', and went on to list a number of fields, including education, transport, health, housing and the economy, which the party considered to need separate administration.

The most outstanding personality in the new party, which

attracted its first members mainly from the academic world, was Saunders Lewis. Born in Liverpool in 1893, the son of a Calvinistic Methodist minister, but later a convert to Roman Catholicism, Saunders Lewis had served in the First World War and had been wounded in Flanders. As the party's leading theorist, as a literary critic and dramatist, he was to have the primary influence on the formulation of its philosophy and aims over the next few decades.

The party contested its first General Election in 1929 when Lewis Valentine, a minister, won 609 votes, against 38,000 cast for the other three parties. The early electoral efforts of *Plaid Cymru* were not attended with much success. Even during the 'twenties and 'thirties its candidates won little support. The electorate continued to look to the Government in London, seeing no prospect of work in a self-governing Wales.

It was with Lewis Valentine and the writer D. J. Williams that Saunders Lewis was to take direct action against the Government's policies in Wales. In 1935 plans were announced by the Air Ministry to build three aerodromes, two in England and one near Penyberth in the Llŷn peninsula of north-western Wales. The first two sites were abandoned in the face of local protest by preservationists, ornithologists and English writers but public opinion in Wales, unanimous in its opposition, was ignored. On the night of 6 September 1936 Saunders Lewis and his companions set fire to some buildings at Penyberth and then reported their action to the police. At their trial in Caernarfon, Saunders Lewis delivered an eloquent defence of their symbolic act of civil disobedience: 'We are in this dock of our own will, not only for the sake of Wales, but also for the sake of peace and unviolent, charitable, relations now and in the future between Wales and England'. What was at stake in Llŷn, they argued, was 'the irreparable loss of a language, of purity of idiom, of a home of literature, of a tradition stretching back fourteen hundred years'. Saunders Lewis went on, 'We were compelled to do serious damage to the bombing school buildings. Only serious damage could ensure that we should appear before a jury of our fellow countrymen, in a last desperate and vital effort to bring the immorality of the Government's actions before the

judgement of Christian Wales'. Saunders Lewis founded his
defence on the argument that 'the moral law is binding on
governments just as it is on private citizens' and that 'justice,
not material force, must rule in the affairs of nations'.

The jury at Caernarfon failed to agree on a verdict. At the Old
Bailey, however, where they refused to plead, the three were
sentenced to a year's imprisonment each. On his release from
Wormwood Scrubs Saunders Lewis was dismissed from his
post as lecturer in the Department of Welsh at University
College, Swansea, but became the hero of *Plaid Cymru* which
was now attracting many intellectuals to its ranks. Over the
next fourteen years, supporting his family by journalism,
Saunders Lewis wrote some of his most important work, including the play *Buchedd Garmon*. Since then, although no
longer active on behalf of *Plaid Cymru,* Saunders Lewis has
continued to make a major contribution to Welsh letters. He
has often been described as 'the greatest Welshman since
Owain Glyn Dŵr' and is revered as such by younger militants
in the nationalist movement today. In 1971 *Yr Academi
Gymreig* (The Welsh Academy) nominated him for the award
of the Nobel Prize for Literature.

After the Second World War, *Plaid Cymru* began to make
electoral progress at both local and national level. At by-
elections in Carmarthenshire and Neath in 1945 its candidates won over 6,000 votes each, and four years later it won
a seat on Carmarthenshire County Council. The growth of
Welsh national feeling in these years also found expression in
the activities of *Undeb Cymru Fydd* (The New Wales Union).
By 1956 this organisation had collected some 250,000
signatures of people in favour of a Welsh Parliament and it
was reported that eight out of every ten persons approached
had agreed to sign the petition. Under the leadership of
Gwynfor Evans, its President since 1945 to the present, *Plaid
Cymru* defined its long-term aims as self-government
for Wales within the Commonwealth, a seat in the United
Nations for Wales and 'to safeguard the culture, language,
traditions and economic life of Wales'. The party nevertheless
campaigns for an elected Parliament and supports the principle of official status for Welsh and English. A party which

up to now had appealed mainly to Welsh-speaking intellectuals, it won support in most parts of Wales, including
the industrial valleys of Glamorgan, during the 1950s and
polled a total of 85,000 votes (5%) in twenty constituencies at
the General Election of 1959.

During the early 'sixties *Plaid Cymru* led public opinion
against the drowning by Liverpool Corporation of the
Tryweryn valley in Meirionethshire for the purpose of a reservoir. The village of Capel Celyn, an area of rich Welsh
culture, became a symbol as Penyberth had been in 1936.
Over 125 local authorities in Wales, together with trade
unions, religious bodies, cultural organisations and a
majority of Welsh M.P.s, united in their objection to these
plans. The Government's refusal to take Welsh opinion into
account became yet another example of the way in which
Wales, without its own Government, was defenceless within
the English-dominated British State. In 1962 and 1963 installations on the site were destroyed by young militants and
in 1969, at the time of the investiture of the Prince of Wales,
members of a group calling itself the Free Wales Army were
imprisoned. A considerable amount of damage to Government property was caused during the campaign which
culminated, on the very day of the investiture, in the trial of
the F.W.A. The heaviest sentence on any of the activists found
guilty of causing explosions at this time was on John Jenkins,
a sergeant in the British Army, who was imprisoned for ten
years. Two other nationalists were killed while carrying explosives at Abergele.

But by now, the progress of *Plaid Cymru* as a constitutional, political party opposed to violence was under
way. Gwynfor Evans had been elected Member of Parliament
for Carmarthenshire, with a majority of 2,436 votes, at a by-
election in July 1966, only to lose it by 3,907 votes to the
Labour candidate at the General Election of 1970. Despite this
set-back, *Plaid Cymru* polled over 175,000 votes (11%), with
an average vote in the thirty-six constituencies of over 4,800,
an increase of about 60% on its total vote in 1966. Other
nationalist candidates had done well at by-elections in the industrial constituencies of Rhondda West and Caerffili in 1967
and 1968. *Plaid Cymru,* like the S.N.P. in Scotland, now

became a real alternative to the older parties, especially to the Labour Party which, from a caucus position in many parts of Wales, had lost much of its socialist vision.

At the General Election of 28 February 1974 *Plaid Cymru* won Caernarfonshire and Merioneth while Gwynfor Evans failed by only three votes to recapture Carmarthenshire. In Caernarfonshire and Merioneth Dafydd Wigley and Dafydd Elis Thomas retained their seats in the General Election of 10 October 1974 and Gwynfor Evans won back Carmarthenshire with a majority of 3,640 votes. *Plaid Cymru* has a membership of around 40,000, roughly the same as the Labour Party in Wales, and 290 branches in all parts of the country. It has a full-time staff of fifteen in five offices at Cardiff, Carmarthen, Aberystwyth, Dolgellau and Caernarfon; it publishes a weekly newspaper in English, *Welsh Nation,* and a monthly in Welsh, *Y Ddraig Goch*. Its general secretary is Dafydd Williams, its Chairman Phil Williams and its President Gwynfor Evans.

The growth of *Plaid Cymru* in the 1960s was not the only progress made by the nationalist movement in Wales during that decade. For many nationalists, the drowning of the Tryweryn Valley by Liverpool Corporation, against the wishes of public opinion in Wales, but with the approval of the Government in London, marked a turning-point. In the words of Saunders Lewis, who had for long been politically inactive up to this time, 'the Government has taken the measure of the feebleness of Welsh-speaking Wales and knows that it need not concern itself about it any more'.

In February 1962, Saunders Lewis delivered on BBC Wales a radio lecture entitled *Tynged yr Iaith* (The Fate of the Language) in which he described some of the factors which had caused the decline of Welsh since 1536. The lecture's conclusion was, 'I take it for granted that if present trends continue, Welsh will cease to be a living language early in the twenty-first century'. Coming as it did from the founder of *Plaid Cymru* and the most distinguished literary figure in Wales, the lecture had a startling effect on its listeners. All the close argument, the controlled but biting sarcasm, the appeal to European values so characteristic of Saunders Lewis's writing, were now used to jolt the Welsh into a realisation of the desperate plight of their language.

'Is the situation hopeless?' he asked. 'Of course it is, if we choose to accept despair. There is nothing in the world more comfortable than giving up hope. After that a man can proceed to enjoy life. The political tradition of the centuries, all the economic tendencies of the present time, are against the survival of Welsh. Nothing can change that fact except determination, will power, struggle, sacrifice and effort . . . It is possible to save the Welsh language. Welsh Wales is still a substantial area of the land of Wales and the minority is not yet entirely insignificant . . .' Then came the lecture's main message: 'Go to it in earnest and without wavering to make it impossible to conduct local authority or central government business without the Welsh language . . . This is not a haphazard policy for isolated individuals . . . It is a policy for a movement, and that movement should be active in areas where Welsh is the everyday spoken language, demanding that all election papers and every official form relating to local or parliamentary elections in Wales be in Welsh, raising the Welsh language to be the main administrative medium of district and county. Perhaps you will say that this can never be achieved, that it is impossible to get sufficient Welshmen to agree and to organise such an important and energetic campaign. Perhaps you are right. All I maintain is that it is the only political question deserving of a Welshman's attention at the present time. I am aware of the difficulties. There would be stormy reactions from all quarters. It would be argued that the campaign was destroying our chance to attract English factories to the Welsh rural areas, and this would doubtless be so; it is easy to predict that the scorn and contempt of the English gutter press would be poured forth daily . . . The fines in the courts would be heavy, and the consequences of not paying them would be costly, though not more costly than fighting purposeless parliamentary elections. I do not deny that there would be a period of hate and persecution and strife instead of the loving peacefulness so remarkable in Welsh political life today. To revive the Welsh language in Wales is nothing less than a revolution. Success can only come through revolutionary methods. Perhaps the language would bring self-government in its wake; I cannot tell. The language is more important than self-government. In my opinion, if we were to have any sort of self-government for Wales before the Welsh language is recognised and used as an official language in all the administration of the state and local authorities in the Welsh areas of our country, it would never attain official status, and the doom of the language would come more quickly than it will come under the English Government'.

The small gains made for the teaching of Welsh up to 1944 had been matched by some successful attempts to win recognition for the language in public life. After the establishment of county councils in Wales by the Local Government Act of 1888, a few authorities had tried to have their records kept in Welsh. During the 1920s *Undeb y Cymdeithasau Cymraeg* (The Union of Welsh Societies) had pressed for equal recognition for Welsh in official usage. The Welsh Language Petition, organised at the National *Eisteddfod* in Cardiff in 1938, presented 360,000 signatures to Parliament three years later and resulted in the Welsh Courts Act of 1942 which provided that 'the Welsh language may be used in any court in Wales by any party or witness who considers that he would otherwise be at any disadvantage by reason of his natural language of communication being Welsh'. This Act also made the provision of an interpreter obligatory and no longer at the judge's discretion. But all proceedings were to continue to be recorded in English. Although it repealed 'the language clause' in the Act of Union of 1536, the Welsh Courts Act of 1942 did not therefore have the effect of making Welsh an alternative language for use in the courts. The situation now began to change, however, in the late 'fifties and early 'sixties, largely as the result of a few individuals. Trefor Beasley and his wife of Llangennech had refused to pay their rates until Llanelli Rural District Council issued bilingual rate demands. Legal proceedings were taken against them on twelve occasions and the bailiffs seized their furniture six times. But in 1960 the Council gave in and bilingual rate forms were made available.

The Beasleys were mentioned by Saunders Lewis in his radio lecture as pioneers to be emulated. The lecture was intended as a call for action and was addressed to *Plaid Cymru*. But the party made no response. Instead, a few months later, in the summer of 1962, a new organisation *Cymdeithas yr Iaith Gymraeg*, (The Welsh Language Society) was formed by a number of young people, students mostly, who—frustrated by *Plaid Cymru*'s refusal to consider unconstitutional methods over the Tryweryn issue— were ready to respond to Saunders Lewis's challenge and to devote themselves to a campaign on behalf of the Welsh language.

For *Cymdeithas yr Iaith Gymraeg*, as for Saunders Lewis, the root cause of the Welsh language's decline had been its banishment, ever since the incorporation of Wales in England by the Act of Union of 1536, from the sphere of ad- ministration and officialdom. Because this prohibition was a political act enforced by English law, because the implicit in- tention was to exterminate the Welsh language, the Society's campaign had to be of a political nature. Saunders Lewis had shown that Welsh must attain official status and that the campaign he envisaged should take precedence over the movement for self-government. Furthermore, in the words of Cynog Davies in *The Welsh Language Today* (1973), the Society's 'latent function would be at once more indefinable and more ambitious: to effect some kind of transformation in the Welsh psychology, to strengthen national consciousness, to inject a new reality into nationalism by bringing to light through the language struggle the hidden oppression in the relationship of Wales with England'.

This second role was defined by J. R. Jones in his conviction that *Cymreictod* (Welshness) and *Prydeindod* (Britishness) are incompatible. Over the next eight years J. R. Jones, Professor of Philosophy at University College, Swansea, became with Saunders Lewis the dominant theorist of Welsh nationalism for *Cymdeithas yr Iaith Gymraeg*. In his writings, the lecture *Cristionogaeth a Chenedlaetholdeb* (Christianity and Nationalism) delivered at the *Plaid Cymru* Summer School in 1962, and his booklet *Prydeindod*, published in 1966, he demonstrated the central importance of the language as being, with land, one of the essential bonds in the for- mation of a people. He showed too the need for emphasis on language as necessary for the avoidance of 'the Fascist per- version' which is based on blood and race. By the time of his death in 1970 J. R. Jones had provided a full philosophical basis for *Cymdeithas yr Iaith Gymraeg,* teaching the young nationalists of Wales that the death of a language was not merely sad or regrettable but a matter of the very highest seriousness, 'a symptom of the crisis of civilisation'.

The crisis of the Welsh language was described by J. R. Jones in the following way: 'It is said of one experience that it is among the most agonising possible . . . that of having to leave the soil of your country forever, of turning your back on your heritage, being torn away by the roots from your familiar land. I have not suffered that experience. But I know of an experience equally agonising, and more irreversible (for you could return to your home), and that is the experience of knowing, not that you are leaving your country, but that your country is leaving you, is ceasing to exist under your very feet, being sucked away from you, as it were by a consuming, swallowing wind, into the hands and the possession of another country and civilisation'. With these words J. R. Jones expressed something of the predicament of contemporary Wales and the agony of other peoples in similar circumstances in Western Europe today.

The present position of the Welsh language cannot be described without giving an account of the activities of *Cymdeithas yr Iaith Gymraeg* during the last thirteen years. The Society's first campaign was organised as an attempt to secure Welsh or bilingual summonses. After a court in Cardiganshire had refused summonses in Welsh, a number of members set out deliberately to break the law by challenging the power of the State and its insistence that English alone was the language of law and administration. A demonstration at the post office in Aberystwyth in February 1963, followed by the blocking of traffic on Trefechan Bridge, called public attention to the inferior status of the Welsh language in law. In July of that year the Minister for Welsh Affairs announced the establishment of a committee under the chairmanship of Sir David Hughes-Parry 'to clarify the legal status of the Welsh language and to consider whether changes should be made in the law'. The Society called a halt to public demonstrations for the next two years, pending the results of this enquiry. Its secretary, John Davies, a research student at the time, carried on a great deal of correspondence with local authorities, the Inland Revenue, the Post Office and commercial interests in attempts to persuade them to use Welsh for official purposes. Parents refused to register the birth of their children unless Welsh certificates were provided, and some were prosecuted. Road-signs in a village in Pembrokeshire, incorrectly spelt as Trevine, were removed and replaced by signs bearing the correct name, Trefîn. A student at University College, Bangor, publicly declined to accept his degree because the college authorities had refused to grant official status to Welsh. A news letter, *Tafod y Ddraig* (The Dragon's Tongue) was launched; it continues as a lively monthly bulletin of the Society's activities.

It was Owain Owain who first used the term *Y Fro Gymraeg* (the Welsh-speaking area), in *Tafod y Ddraig* in January 1964, asserting with Saunders Lewis that the language's remit must be based on its continuance where it is the main normal medium of communication, rather than in the English-speaking areas. The Society's emphasis on *Y Fro Gymraeg*, the Welsh equivalent of the Irish *Gaeltacht*, has remained a central part of its programme up to the present time. Its manifesto, published in 1972, is quite clear on this point: 'We have repeatedly stated that when we speak of the crisis of the Welsh language what we have in mind is the danger that it will cease to be the first spoken language of any part of Wales, that the bond between land and language will be broken. But let no one be misled into believing that because of the emphasis we place on this point, *Cymdeithas yr Iaith Gymraeg* is concerned only with the Welsh-speaking areas. Welsh is the language of all Wales and its retreat from the areas which are today labelled "non-Welsh-speaking" is very recent. It is significant too that many of the most hopeful signs of activity are to be found in these very areas—the pioneering of secondary education through the medium of Welsh is an obvious example. Indeed, many of us believe that it is no longer possible to retain the language in the Welsh-speaking areas unless at the same time it enjoys a revival in the non-Welsh-speaking areas. Most certainly we aim to see it restored to those areas as a living language. Nevertheless it is quite obvious that the maintenance of the language in the Welsh-speaking areas is a matter of fundamental importance

. . . In a word we can do no less and no other than base our efforts to re-establish Welsh as the language of all Wales and its continuance as a living language in the Welsh-speaking areas'.

The year 1965 saw an increase in the militancy of *Cymdeithas yr Iaith Gymraeg*. *Plaid Cymru* had made almost no progress at the General Election of 1964 and only a few small concessions to the language had been granted. In October 1965 the Hughes-Parry Report on the legal status of the Welsh language recommended that Welsh should be admitted in government and administration according to the principle of equal validity with English: 'there should be a clear, positive, legislative declaration of general application to the effect that any act, writing or thing done in Welsh should have the legal force as if it had been done in English'. The report rejected the principle of equal status, however, which would have given the Welsh speaker a legal right to use his own language for all official purposes. While it welcomed the Report's recommendation, and the passing of the Welsh Language Act in 1967, *Cymdeithas yr Iaith Gymraeg* now set out to test the principle of equal validity with a series of campaigns and public demonstrations. A mass occupation by 300 members was held at Dolgellau post office in November 1965 and others at Lampeter (Welsh: *Llanbedr Pont Steffan)* and Machynlleth, followed by a hunger-strike by six members at Merthyr Tydfil. Several members were imprisoned for refusing to tax their cars while road-fund licences were available only in English. Electoral registration forms and Income Tax forms in English were returned with the demand that they be printed in both languages. The Society warned banks that members would take their accounts elsewhere unless bilingual cheques were printed. Electricity bills, pension forms, radio and television licences, motor tax discs in Welsh were also demanded.

In most cases the authorities conceded that these documents should be provided in both Welsh and English, or that both languages should be used on the same document. As a result, a large number of forms are available in Welsh today and the language is seen on an increasing scale on public notices and advertisements all over Wales. The most intransigent of the

Government bodies asked to implement a policy of bilingualism was the Post Office. But the Society's eleven-year campaign against this body ended in October 1975 following the Post Office's decision to meet the demand for bilingualism. The Post Office announced that among the innovations were to be the use of Welsh on post-boxes, in sub-post offices, signs, forms, leaflets and notices at all offices. This decision was reached after the three *Plaid Cymru* M.P.s, with a Labour member and a Liberal member, had asked the Post Office to make a public statement to this effect; the language can also be used for speaking to the operator, addressing letters and in all communications.

The campaign for the use of Welsh in law-courts was more protracted, however. In July 1966 the magistrates at Swansea had declared, 'A summons in Welsh would be a violation of the law. The language of the Queen's Courts is English'. At Cardiff, in 1965, it was announced, 'The Court will not take any notice of what is said in Welsh'. Even after the Welsh Language Act was passed in 1967, some benches and judges refused to hear cases entirely in Welsh. Several members of *Cymdeithas yr Iaith Gymraeg* were imprisoned at Carmarthen Assizes in April 1972 after protesting from a public gallery against the holding of a case in English. In the following July Lord Hailsham asked Judge Edmund Davies 'to enquire into the matter of language in the courts of Wales'; his Committee's Report recommended that equipment for simultaneous translation should be provided in some Crown Courts. The first complete case heard entirely in Welsh in a Crown Court was held at Cardiff in May 1973; by now facilities for instantaneous translation have been installed in two other Crown Courts.

After Gwynfor Evans won the by-election at Carmarthen in July 1966 the activities of *Cymdeithas yr Iaith Gymraeg* had lost some of their impetus but were to regain it with a campaign for the use of Welsh on road-signs and another against the investiture which took place at Caernarfon in July 1969. In that year the Society renewed its attack on both fronts with determination. From January 1969 many hundreds of English-only signs were obliterated, usually with green paint, and over the next five years several hundred members were prosecuted. At a general meeting of the Society in November of the same year it was decided to give the Government a year to implement a bilingual policy. Dafydd Iwan, a well-known folk-singer and chairman of the Society in 1970, was among those imprisoned for three months as a result of his painting activities. Dafydd Iwan's defence was typical of the new spirit of *Cymdeithas yr Iaith Gymraeg:* 'You accuse me of inciting my fellow-members to act; but I am afraid that I do not deserve that praise. They, like me, have been incited, not by any person, nor any committee nor circular. They have been incited by the crisis of their nation and language. They have been incited and terrified by the possibility of the death of that nation and that language. Behind each stroke of the brush on the English road-signs of Wales there are centuries of disgrace and servility and anglicisation. This is what incited them to act'. Fourteen other members were jailed for three months each after interrupting a trial at the High Court in London as a protest against the Government's attitude; a week later eleven were released but three refused to appeal and served their sentences.

At the end of the year, in October 1970, the Society announced its intention of resuming its policy of removing English signs. In the following February eight leading members were arrested and charged with 'conspiracy to destroy road-signs'. At their trial in April 1971 about fifty others were jailed for contempt of court. The Society then set up a committee under Roderic Bowen, Q.C., a former Liberal M.P. for Cardiganshire, to consider the problem in March 1971. Nine middle-aged people were tried at Carmarthen Crown Court in April 1971 for handling stolen road-signs, but were conditionally discharged. In December 1972 the Bowen Report recommended the use of bilingual signs on all types of roads throughout Wales, with the Welsh above the English. The Society then called off its campaign, calling on the Government to implement this recommendation without further delay. But because no official announcement was made, painting began again in May 1973. The campaign continued throughout 1974 and 1975, after the Secretary of State for Wales, while accepting the Bowen Committee's recommendation that bilingual road-signs should be erected, had refused to authorise that Welsh should be placed above English.

The Society's view in the road-signs controversy is described in its Manifesto thus: 'Our definition of the conditions adequate to safeguard the language in Welsh-speaking districts are those that will make it essential for any incomer who wishes to partake fully of the life of the community, to want to and to be able to master it, because of its prestige and status, and because of its practical utility. Nothing less than this will suffice. Secondly, they must mean the restoration of the language to its rightful place of respect and dignity as the national language of Wales. This means that it shall always have symbolic precedence'. The Manifesto quotes Alwyn D. Rees who, as editor of the magazine *Barn* up to his death in 1975, made an important contribution to the Society's work: 'This is a matter of principle, and in the world of principle there can be only one appropriate place for Welsh, namely before or above English'. When Gwynedd County Council began erecting signs which gave the superior position to Welsh, they were ordered by the Welsh Office to be replaced by others with English on top. It was this decision which caused a demonstration by *Cymdeithas yr Iaith Gymraeg* at Llanelltyd, near Dolgellau, on 8 November 1975.

The Society's view was challenged on this occasion, however, by members of *Adfer,* a movement based on a housing society and led by Emyr Llewelyn, which claimed responsibility for removing the bilingual signs the night before the main demonstration and announcing that it is opposed to the use of English, even under the Welsh, on signs in *Y Fro Gymraeg.* A number of bilingual road signs have been erected in various parts of Wales, the Welsh Office still adamant that the English must be above the Welsh for reasons to do with road safety, *Cymdeithas yr Iaith Gymraeg* still insisting that Welsh, as the national language of Wales, must be given priority.

The other campaign which reached its climax in 1969 was the Society's opposition to the investiture of Prince Charles, a campaign which it considered necessary, despite the fact that energy was to be diverted from its principal aim, because *Plaid Cymru* had decided neither to support nor even to declare opposition to the event. *Cymdeithas yr Iaith Gymraeg* saw the symbolism of the investiture as 'the grotesque celebration of the conquest of Wales' which could not be ignored. At first, the Society won widespread support: its rally at Caernarfon on St David's Day, 1 March 1969, was the biggest it had ever organised. But by July, when the ceremony was held, this public sympathy had turned to hostility, as a result of the efforts made by the Government's publicity in favour of the event. Only in the satire of Dafydd Iwan's song *Carlo,* the letters attributed to the Queen in *Tafod y Ddraig,* in innumerable cartoons and poems—and in the explosions which culminated in the trial of the Free Wales Army on the same day as the investiture—was the nationalist view expressed. Encouraged by various public bodies like the Wales Tourist Board, the general mood of the day was adulation, especially when it was announced that the Prince was to spend a term at University College, Aberystwyth, learning about the history and language of Wales. J. R. Jones's comment was, 'The Investiture revealed how complete a cultural devastation has been wrought on the minds of the Welsh'. Gwynfor Evans said later that, in his opinion, the campaign of *Cymdeithas yr Iaith Gymraeg* against the investiture had been the chief cause of his losing his seat at Carmarthen in the Election of 1970.

From now on, the differences between *Plaid Cymru* and *Cymdeithas yr Iaith Gymraeg* grew more obvious, the one concentrating on electoral progress and the other on direct action intended to challenge the authority of the Government in every sphere where the Welsh language was affected. It remains true, however, that the vast majority of the Society's members support *Plaid Cymru* when voting at elections and in other ways. The Society's attitude to the British Government was summarised in its Manifesto: 'The upholders of the United Kingdom in Wales argue that it is possible to safeguard the interests of national minorities and preserve their cultural distinctiveness in union with a greater nation, indeed they say that it is only inside such a union that this is possible. *Cymdeithas yr Iaith Gymraeg* believes that only in a Free Wales can there be any hope of creating the new and fundamental conditions, the creative policies needed to further the revival of the language. We believe the same to be true about the kind of social and economic conditions necessary for the well-being of the nation. We therefore see the struggle for the language and the struggle for national political institutions as one and the same. And we hold that the failure and refusal of London Governments over the last few years to take positive action for the language is powerful evidence for our point of view. Now if the upholders of the British system in Wales wish to prove their standpoint valid, it is their privilege to ensure the creation, through that system, of a favourable environment for the survival and extension of the Welsh language. If the British Government will not create an environment it will have betrayed its responsibilities and forfeited its right to the government of Wales'.

The year 1971 saw an intensification of the Society's militancy in the launching of the campaign for a Welsh-language television channel. There had been a procession through the streets of Cardiff. in May 1968, and television studios in Bangor and Cardiff had been occupied by Society members in October of that year. In December 1970 thirty members had been arrested in London after blocking the highway outside the BBC's headquarters on three consecutive days. Then, in March 1971, the Society called on its members to refuse to pay their television licences. Between September 1971 and June 1973 nearly 200 people were taken to court and charged with this offence. Some who refused to pay fines were imprisoned; about a hundred in all were jailed during 1971 alone. Radio and television licences were burned in public and deputations sent to the Welsh Broadcasting Council and the Welsh Committee of the Independent Television Authority. In July 1971 ten members of the Society climbed television masts in various parts of Wales to focus public attention on the campaign. Three members led by Ffred Ffransis (later to become a son-in-law of Gwynfor Evans) caused damage at Granada Television studios in Manchester. Seventeen members were arrested in April 1971 and accused at Mold of 'campaigning to interfere with television transmissions'. Nine were subsequently given suspended sentences but four were imprisoned, including Ffred Ffransis who was jailed for two years. Demonstrations continued with the occupation of transmitting stations, the BBC studios at Cardiff and the Ministry of Posts and Telecommunications in London. There was limited damage to property, live programmes and a speech by the Minister of Posts at Westminster were interrupted, telephone exchanges blocked and a private radio station started.

The period of direct action was brought to an end in April 1973 and in the following July a conference of movements and councils from all over Wales was called by the Lord Mayor of Cardiff at which the Minister of Posts was asked to give special consideration to Wales when deciding the future of the fourth channel. In 1974 the Crawford Committee on Broadcasting recommended that the fourth channel in Wales should be allocated to a separate service with priority given to Welsh language programmes and operated jointly by the BBC and Harlech Television, the independent commercial company operating in Wales. The Committee also recommended that the BBC should gradually increase its Welsh-language programmes on radio and VHF and English-language programmes of Welsh interest on Radio 4 (Wales) with the object of developing two Welsh series independent of Radio 4 (Medium Wave). These recommendations were accepted by the Government in March 1975 and by *Cyngor yr Iaith Gymraeg* (The Welsh Language Council).

At the same time as the Society's campaign for a Welsh-language television channel, it began its opposition to the 'holiday homes' which have been bought on an increasing scale by English people in the western and northern parts of Wales over the last two decades. The movement known as *Adfer* (Restoration) was founded in 1971, as was *Cymdeithas Tai Gwynedd* (Gwynedd Housing Association), for the purpose of buying property in *Y Fro Gymraeg* which would provide homes and work for Welsh-speakers. In July 1972 an auction of holiday homes at Caernarfon was interrupted by members of *Cymdeithas yr Iaith Gymraeg* and between January and May 1973 about fifty holiday homes in various parts of Wales were occupied for twenty-four hours. In June 1973 the Government, in a White Paper on housing, announced its intention of doing away with all renewal grants for second homes. The existence of holiday homes in the rural Welsh-speaking parts of Wales remains a problem, however, and the Society continues its campaign. Tourism in Wales has all the usual pernicious effects on Welsh society that it has in other scenically attractive but economically neglected regions of Western Europe.

It will be clear from this brief account of *Cymdeithas yr Iaith Gymraeg* that the Society has played a leading role in the struggle to win official status for Welsh since its formation in 1962, and has made an important contribution to the recent progress of political nationalism in Wales. Its success has been such that its example has been followed by similar organisations in Ireland and Scotland. By today the Society has around 4,000 members and an office with a full-time staff at Aberystwyth. Although most of its active members are young people under the age of thirty, the Society has won a wide measure of support among Welsh-speakers who, even when its methods are questioned, approve generally of its aims. On the other hand, it has met opposition from some politicians and attracted bitter comment in the press. The Society has been consistent in its rejection of violence, whether 'of tongue, fist or heart' in confrontation with the law and often under vilification by its opponents, it has followed the principle of non-violence. Emyr Llywelyn, one of the Society's leading members before *Adfer* became its rival, spoke for the whole movement when he said, 'The Welsh language is not worth one drop of innocent blood; it is not worth the pain and suffering of innocent people'. The destruction of property, on the other hand, is not considered as inconsistent with the Society's principles. Ffred Ffransis has said in court, 'Destruction of property may be essential to prevent violence to people . . . in Wales, broadcasting equipment is being used as a means of oppression against the language and personality of the Welsh people. It would be quite wrong to use personal violence against broadcasters or controllers in order to stop this oppression, but it is right, and indeed it is the responsibility of every conscientious Welshman, to destroy property which is being used to oppress the people'.

Dafydd Glyn Jones has made the following assessment of

the Society in *The Welsh Language Today* (1973): '*Cymdeithas yr Iaith Gymraeg* has succeeded in bringing the problem of the Welsh language into public notice on a scale never achieved before. We could have known much earlier, had we faced the situation honestly, the concessions from the authorities, local and central, are granted when it is less trouble to grant them than to refuse them. The truth of this is now borne out by ten years of empiric proof, and it is slowly changing the consciousness of Welsh Wales. The proscribing of the Welsh language, by the Act of 1536, was effective because it applied only to certain key spheres. The task which *Cymdeithas yr Iaith Gymraeg* has taken upon itself is to provoke the system into showing that these few crucial prohibitions still have effect (although the Language Clause of the Act of Union has been officially repealed), and that they constitute a denial of the Welshman's dignity as a human being. It is expected that when this becomes clear to a sufficiently large number of people, Wales will demand or seize the power to determine her own future. Thus, every campaign of *Cymdeithas yr Iaith Gymraeg* has, in addition to the obvious aim of obtaining concessions in the public use of Welsh, a less immediate but equally central aim, which is to awaken a new spirit among the people. This is what Saunders Lewis meant when he spoke of "using the language as a weapon". Official status is, of course, quite essential. It has played a key role in the revival of languages whose plight was far sorrier than that of Welsh. But *Cymdeithas yr Iaith Gymraeg* will readily concede that status will not of itself save a language. Just as important, as part of the broad strategy, is the spirit of determination which the fight for official status calls into being. *Cymdeithas yr Iaith Gymraeg* has assumed that persuasion, to be effective, does not have to be friendly, and that the kind of persuasion which shocks and challenges people, impresses them with a seriousness of purpose, and appeals to the aristocratic instinct in them, eventually bringing more solid results. The courting of unpopularity is a necessary part of this exercise. *Cymdeithas yr Iaith Gymraeg* is still an unpopular minority movement, with an active membership of not much more than a thousand, and is destined to spend many more years in the wilderness before a majority of the people grasp the meaning of the struggle on which it has embarked. But there are small indications that its strategy is working, and that its boldness, persistence and sheer physical courage are making a deeper impress on the Welsh imagination than the immediate evidence suggests'.

Although, in the campaign for official recognition of Welsh, the pace has been set by *Cymdeithas yr Iaith Gymraeg*, the Society is not alone in working on the language's behalf. Indeed, a great deal of effort by many other bodies, both voluntary and official, has resulted in considerable progress by the Welsh language movement since the Second World War.

Perhaps the most significant gains have been made in education. Following the publication of the Government's Report *Welsh in Education and Life* in 1927, primary schools in the Welsh-speaking areas had begun to use Welsh as a medium of instruction for certain subjects and methods for the teaching of Welsh as a second language in the English-speaking had been improved somewhat. But on the whole the schools were generally considered to be failing in their attempts to arrest the language's decline. A historic step forward was taken in 1939 when the first *Ysgol Gymraeg* (Welsh School) opened, with seven pupils, at Aberystwyth. This was an independent primary school, sponsored by *Urdd Gobaith Cymru* (The Welsh League of Youth), at which Welsh was the main medium of instruction for all subjects. After the Education Act of 1944, the school was replaced by another which was maintained by the Cardiganshire Education Authority. Similar schools were then opened in other parts of Wales, particularly in English-speaking counties such as Flintshire and Glamorgan, and in Cardiff. By today there are about sixty Welsh-language primary schools in English-speaking areas. Their work is supported by *Undeb Rhieni Ysgolion Cymraeg* (The Welsh Schools Parents' Association) and, of course, by the local education authorities. Welsh is also taught and used as a medium of instruction at many primary schools in the western and northern counties. The fact that the decline in the number of Welsh-speakers between 1961 and 1971 was not as great as in previous decades is doubtless attributable to the progress made in the teaching of Welsh at primary level in recent years. At the same time, it is known that the number of pupils receiving an education through Welsh is not yet sufficient and a huge effort is currently being made to open more *Ysgolion Cymraeg.*

Nursery education through the medium of Welsh is organised by *Mudiad Ysgolion Meithrin* (The Nursery Schools Movement) which was formed in 1971. In the autumn of 1975 there were about 230 of these play-groups attended by about 3,500 children under the age of five; sixty-eight were in Gwynedd, sixty-one in Dyfed, thirty-six in Clwyd and twenty-seven in Mid-Glamorgan. The movement, which has its own full-time officers and offices in Cardiff, received a grant of £24,400 from the Welsh Office as a contribution towards its administrative costs in 1975/6. With the growth of the *Ysgolion Cymraeg,* the work of this movement is generally considered to be crucial for the future of the Welsh language. It remains true, however, that if the 1981 Census is not to enumerate fewer than 20% of the population as Welsh-speaking, the number of Welsh-speaking children, at present some 12% of the total, will have to be doubled in the near future.

It was Flintshire and Glamorgan, where the first Welsh-language primary schools opened in the 1950s, which also pioneered in the field of secondary education through the medium of Welsh. The first school of this kind, *Ysgol Glan Clwyd* at Rhyl, opened in 1956, was followed by others at Mold in 1961, at Rhydfelen near Pontypridd in 1962, at Wrexham (Welsh: *Wrecsam)* in 1963, at Ystalyfera in 1969, at Aberystwyth in 1973 and at Llanhari near Cardiff in 1974. Similar schools are currently under consideration for Bangor and Carmarthen *(Caerfyrddin).* A total of 5,129 pupils were attending these secondary schools in the autumn term of 1975. The success of all seven has been remarkable and augurs well for the future. Welsh is also taught as a subject at O and A level to pupils for whom it is a first language, and as a second language.

Secondary education through the medium of Welsh has led to a demand for the same facilities at the colleges of the University of Wales. Among subjects in which some teaching is now done in Welsh are Education, Welsh History,

Philosophy, Geography, History, French, English, Social Science and Theology. Welsh is taught (in Welsh) as a degree subject at all five colleges. During the autumn term of 1975 a total of 349 undergraduates were studying Welsh in the University of Wales, nearly half of them at Aberystwyth. The University continues to make a contribution to the cultural life of the country, but in recent years the increasing number of students and teaching staff from outside Wales has had a baneful influence. Many critics have accused the University of failing in its responsibilities towards the national culture.

Welsh is also taught and used as a medium of instruction at the six colleges of education where primary school teachers are trained. Techniques of teaching Welsh as a second language have made great advances as a result of the development of oral methods. Research has been led by the National Language Unit at Trefforest, near Pontypridd, and by the Faculties of Education at the University Colleges, and has been supported by the Welsh Joint Education Committee.

There has been a rapid increase in the number of adults learning Welsh as a second language in recent years. Many courses are run by education authorities and both HTV and BBC Wales have broadcast programmes for learners. Among the more successful courses are those organised on the model of the Ulpan scheme in Israel which consists of teaching a new language by means of an intensive crash-course for five evenings a week over a period of several months. In 1975 there were about twenty centres where the Ulpan method was being used to teach Welsh to adults. At the National *Eisteddfod* in 1975 the writer Bobi Jones called for the creation of a movement for adult learners of Welsh and an intensification of effort in this sector.

The National *Eisteddfod* is the principal cultural event in the Welsh language. The festival, which is held alternately in the north and south of the country during the first week of August every year, celebrates its eighth centenary in 1976. The first gathering which might be called an *eisteddfod* was held under the patronage of the Lord Rhys ap Gruffydd at Cardigan (Welsh: *Aberteifi)* in 1176. During the Middle Ages the *eisteddfod* was a session of poets who met to discuss their craft and the traditional verse metres, but in the eighteenth century it declined to become a contest for versifiers meeting informally in taverns. From 1789, under the auspices of *Y Gwyneddigion* (The Men of Gwynedd), a society of Welshmen living in London, the *eisteddfod* grew in scope and influence: by the 1860s it had become a national festival of poetry and music. It flourishes today, despite financial and administrative crises arising mainly from its determination to remain amateur, as a manifestation of the nation's popular culture, attracting a quarter of a million visitors and having no equivalent in any of the other Celtic countries. The sole official language is Welsh, a rule strictly applied since 1950 with excellent results for the festival's success but with the disapproval of certain local authorities which refuse to make financial contributions towards its maintenance on the grounds that English should be admitted to the programme. When this charge was made in 1967 an open letter signed by a majority of Welsh writers whose work is in English called for the preservation of the Welsh Rule. The National *Eisteddfod*'s programme consists of competitions for poetry, prose, drama, recitation, instrumental and vocal music, dancing and the visual arts. The highlights of the week are the presentation of a chair and a crown to the winning poets in competition for poetry in the traditional metres and in the free metres respectively. The ceremonial aspect of the *Eisteddfod* is the responsibility of *Gorsedd Beirdd Ynys Prydain* (The Assembly of Bards of the Isle of Britain) which, although popularly believed to have descended from the druids, dates from 1791, when it was invented by Iolo Morganwg (1747-1826). The principal ceremonies and competitions are held in a central pavilion but many events—including concerts, films, lectures, plays and exhibitions—take place on the periphery of the *Eisteddfod* field or in a near-by town.

It is at the National *Eisteddfod* that the visitor is reminded of the large number of societies and other bodies which have an interest in the Welsh language. The oldest of these is *Anrhydeddus Gymdeithas y Cymmrodorion* (The Honourable Society of Cymmrodorion), a learned society founded in 1751 which has a membership of around 2,000 and which publishes an annual volume of its transactions. Scholarship is also the field of *Urdd Graddedigion Prifysgol Cymru* (The Guild of

Graduates of the University of Wales) which was founded in 1894 when the University received its charter.

Most of the other organisations are no older than the present century. Foremost among them is *Urdd Gobaith Cymru* (literally, The League of Hope for Wales), the national youth movement founded by Ifan ab Owen Edwards in 1922. About 57,000 children and young people belong to the *Urdd*. With offices at Aberystwyth, a full-time staff of thirty and volunteer officers in all parts of Wales numbering about 600, the movement is recognised as a branch of the Government's Youth Service; in 1974/5 it received an annual grant of £15,570 from the Exchequer and a total of £16,289 from the local education authorities; the movement raised a further £31,918 from its own activities. It organises a wide variety of activities, including three summer camps, regional and national *eisteddfodau,* and the publication of six magazines in Welsh. Non-political but devoted to the principle of Welsh nationhood, the *Urdd* is a highly successful movement with a central place in the cultural life of Wales today.

Another success story of more recent date is that of *Merched y Wawr* (Daughters of the Dawn). A women's movement launched in 1967 with Welsh as its only language, *Merched y Wawr* was a break-away from the Women's Institute which had forbidden the use of Welsh for official correspondence and records at its branch in Parc, near Bala in Merioneth. Its growth has been rapid: by the end of 1975 it had over 200 branches and about 10,000 members in all parts of Wales; its magazine *Y Wawr* has the biggest circulation of any Welsh journal—over 5,000 copies quarterly.

Besides *Cymdeithas yr Iaith Gymraeg,* there are three other voluntary societies directly concerned with the language: *Urdd Siarad Cymraeg* (The League for Speaking Welsh), founded in 1947; *Undeb y Gymraeg Fyw* (The Union of Living Welsh), founded in 1965; and *Sefydliad Cymru* (The Institute of Wales) founded in 1972. All three aim to give help to people wishing to learn Welsh but are rarely in the public eye; they have no political aims and are neither as active nor as successful as *Cymdeithas yr Iaith Gymraeg.* The only professional teachers' organisation for which the Welsh language is a basic consideration is *Undeb Cenedlaethol Athrawon Cymru* (The National Association of the Teachers of Wales), but its membership is only about 2,000—a fifth of the number claimed in Wales by the National Union of Teachers, the body which represents teachers throughout the United Kingdom. Welsh-speaking scientists formed *Y Gymdeithas Wyddonol Genedlaethol* (The National Scientific Association) in 1971 and are served by the magazine *Y Gwyddonydd* (The Scientist), published by the University of Wales Press. The work of seven religious bodies calling for a wider use of Welsh in public life is co-ordinated by *Pwyllgor Cydenwadol yr Iaith Gymraeg* (The Interdenominational Committee for the Welsh Language).

Welsh literature, the art at which the Welsh have always excelled, has flourished since the First World War. Among the major literary figures of the present century are the poets T. Gwynn Jones (1871-1944), T. H. Parry-Williams (1887-1975), R. Williams Parry (1884-1956), D. Gwenallt Jones (1899-1968) and Waldo Williams (1904-71); the prose-writers D. J. Williams (1885-1970), Kate Roberts (born 1891) and T. Rowland Hughes (1903-44); the dramatists Saunders Lewis (born 1893) and John Gwilym Jones (born 1904) and the critic W. J. Gruffydd (1881-1954). Other important writers include the poets Euros Bowen (born 1904), Pennar Davies (born 1911), Bobi Jones (born 1929) and Gwyn Thomas (born 1936); the prose-writers Islwyn Ffowc Elis (born 1924) and Eigra Lewis Roberts (born 1939); and the dramatist Gwenlyn Parry (born 1932). These writers and their contemporaries are the heirs of a literary tradition which is fourteen hundred years old.

But Welsh literature is not only ancient, it is being written today on contemporary themes by more writers than ever before in its history. They are represented, for the most part, by *Yr Academi Gymreig* (The Welsh Academy), a national association founded in 1959. This body has about forty-five members elected to its Welsh-language section and about the same number belong to its English-language section. The Academy, the secretaries of which are officers of the Welsh Arts Council, from which almost all its finances are derived, holds an annual conference, publishes the magazine *Taliesin* and a series of foreign novels translated into Welsh, and in 1975 began work on the compilation of a new English-Welsh Dictionary.

In opening its doors to Welshmen who write in English in 1968, the Academy brought about a rapprochement between writers in the two languages spoken in Wales. Many Anglo-Welsh writers such as R. S. Thomas (born 1913), Emyr Humphreys (born 1919), Glyn Jones (born 1905), Gwyn Williams (born 1904), and Harri Webb (born 1920) are Welsh-speakers who are committed to the cause of the language and the nationalist movement in Wales. The literary magazines published in English have also made an important contribution to a discussion of Welsh culture and society since 1945; they are *Wales* (1937), *The Welsh Review* (1939), *The Anglo-Welsh Review* (1949), *Poetry Wales* (1965) and *Planet* (1970).

The number of books published in Wales has increased annually over the last ten years, to an extent greater than in any other Celtic language. About 300 new titles appeared during 1975. The principal publishers among the twenty or so imprints which belong to *Undeb y Cyhoeddwyr a Llyfrwerthwyr* (The Union of Publishers and Book-sellers) are Gwasg Gomer of Llandysul and Christopher Davies of Swansea; between them they publish about half the titles published in any year. Children's books are the speciality of *Gwasg y Dref Wen* of Cardiff; books in the more scurrilous categories are published by *Y Lolfa* of Tal-y-bont in Cardiganshire, which also produces a bawdy magazine once a year. The University of Wales Press specialises in the publication of works of Celtic scholarship, for which the National Library of Wales at Aberystwyth, an autonomous institution maintained by Government funds, also has a special responsibility.

Few Welsh books sell more than 2,000 copies each and almost all are published with the aid of subsidy. The Government's annual grant to Welsh books for adults has increased regularly to £45,000 in 1976/7; it is administered by the University of Wales Press Board. The Welsh Joint Education Committee has a scheme for the purchase of Welsh children's books by local authorities for use in schools. The Welsh Books Council, based at Aberystwyth, has four departments which offer a service to publishers for the design, editing, publicising and distribution of their books, and also organises book fairs and competitions. It is financed partly by local authorities but mainly by the Welsh Arts Council with grant-aid totalling £50,800 in 1976/7. During the current year the Welsh Arts Council is spending approximately £220,000 on literature in Wales, both Welsh and Anglo-Welsh, about 7% of its total revenue grant; the rest is spent on music (including the Welsh National Opera Company), drama (including the Welsh Theatre Company and its Welsh-language section *Cwmni Theatr Cymru)* and the visual arts (including films and crafts). Part of the Welsh Arts Council's support for Welsh literature is grant-aid to the magazines *Barn* (Opinion), *Y Genhinen* (The Leek), *Taliesin* and *Y Traethodydd* (The Essayist) and to six magazines for children. The principal review of current affairs in Welsh is *Barn* which sells about 3,000 copies monthly. There are, in all, about seventy Welsh-language magazines of various kinds.

Among the by-products of the growth of national feeling in Wales during the last decade has been the opening of bookshops, crafts enterprises, housing associations and other ventures by Welsh-language activists: Gwilym Tudur, owner of *Siop y Pethe* at Aberystwyth, and Carl Clowes, the founder of *Antur Aelhaearn,* a co-operative in the village of Llanaelhaearn in the Llŷn peninsula of Gwynedd, are typical of this new enterprise. Welsh folk-music and pop-music have also enjoyed immense popularity among young people. Dafydd Iwan, one of the leaders of *Cymdeithas yr Iaith Gymraeg,* was among the earliest singers of topical songs and now co-manages *Recordiau Sain* (Sound Records), the leading Welsh record company.

There is no daily newspaper in Welsh. The weekly *Y Cymro* (The Welshman), published from Oswestry (Welsh: *Croesoswallt)* has a circulation of around 7,000 copies. *Y Faner* (The Flag), founded in 1843, is the oldest surviving national newspaper. There are also regional newspapers such as *Yr Herald Gymraeg* (The Welsh Herald) published in Caernarfon, and various denominational journals. There is little Welsh in the *Liverpool Daily Post* which circulates mainly in the

north of Wales, nor in the *Western Mail,* the daily published in
Cardiff which claims to be 'the national newspaper of Wales';
but the latter gives good coverage of Welsh-language events
and other aspects of the cultural and political life of Wales. A
recent development of great importance is the launching by
voluntary groups of *papurau bro* (community newspapers);
about a dozen of these, all published entirely in Welsh, had
been started by late 1975.

Broadcasting in Wales dates from the 1930s when a Welsh
Region of the BBC was established. By today BBC Wales
broadcasts, from its studios in Cardiff and Bangor, about
twenty-six hours a week in Welsh on radio (eighteen hours in
English), and on television about eleven hours a week (six
hours in English). The independent commercial television
company HTV (Harlech Television), also based in Cardiff,
broadcasts about six hours a week in Welsh and three-and-a-
half hours in English. Listeners and viewers in most parts of
Wales can also tune in to stations broadcasting from London
and other parts of England. Following many years of campaigning by *Cymdeithas yr Iaith Gymraeg* and other bodies,
as well as controversy and hostility on the part of non-Welsh-
speakers in Wales, the Government accepted in November
1974 the recommendation of the Crawford Committee on
Broadcasting that a separate Welsh-language television service for Wales, transmitting about twenty-five hours a week in
Welsh, should be provided on the fourth channel soon to
become available. The Committee's report also recommended
that the BBC should increase the number of Welsh-
language programmes on Radio 4 VHF and of programmes
in English of special interest to Wales. These services, to be
run jointly by the BBC and HTV, were expected to be
fully operative before 1980. There was some doubt, however,
as to whether the Government would make an early start on implementing the Crawford Commiteee's proposals after a
Home Office working-party known as the Siberry Committee
reported on 25 November 1975 that the likely cost of setting
up the fourth channel as a Welsh-language service would be
about £9 million and the running costs about £5 million a
year. The Chairman of *Cymdeithas yr Iaith Gymraeg,* Win-
ford James, commenting on the possibility of further delay,

was reported as saying, 'We are looking for a statement from the Government by the end of this parliamentary session that a Welsh channel will come into being. This is the only statement that will avert the implementation of further direct action'.

The Crawford Committee's proposals for the use of the fourth channel in Wales was supported by *Cyngor yr Iaith Gymraeg* (The Welsh Language Council), a body nominated by the Secretary of State for Wales in 1973. This Council has twelve members and exists to advise the Secretary of State on all questions affecting the Welsh language. To date it has published reports on broadcasting, children's magazines and Welsh-medium nursery education. The Council is among the most recent signs that the Government recognises that it has a duty towards the Welsh language but has not yet convinced its critics that it has any but any advisory role to play.

It is nevertheless true, as the preceding account suggests, that during the last two decades the Government has responded, albeit inadequately, to demands made on behalf of the Welsh language. Whether it will now be prepared to meet the growing desire for devolution of political power from Westminster to Cardiff remains to be seen. The two questions are, of course, inextricably related and the present account must therefore end by narrating the events leading up to the publication of the White Paper on Devolution in November 1975.

It was the rise of *Plaid Cymru* in the 1960s which obliged the Government to take the demand for self-government seriously. Following the success of Gwynfor Evans in July 1966 and near-defeats for the Labour candidates at Rhondda West and Caerffili in March 1967 and July 1968, where their majorities were slashed from 16,888 to 2,306 and from 21,148 to 1,874, opinion polls revealed that 60% of the people of Wales were in favour of a Welsh Parliament. In October 1968 Harold Wilson announced a Government enquiry into the whole question of self-government for Wales and Scotland to be chaired by Lord Crowther, former editor of *The Economist*. The Prime Minister said at the time that an important reason for appointing the Commission was 'the strong feeling, not only in Scotland and Wales, but in many parts of

England, of a greater desire for participation in the process of decision making, moving it nearer—wherever this is possible—to the places where people live'.

The Royal Commission on the Constitution 1969-73, from March 1972 under the chairmanship of Lord Kilbrandon after the death of Lord Crowther, reported in October 1973. It was unanimous in rejecting separation and federalism and in recommending directly elected Assemblies for Scotland and Wales and for the regions of England. The Queen's speech on 12 March 1974 said the Government 'will initiate discussions in Scotland and Wales on the Report of the Commission on the Constitution, and will bring forward proposals for consideration'. On 3 June 1974 the Government published a consultative document entitled *Devolution within the United Kingdom:Some Alternatives for Discussion* which summarised the various schemes of devolution put forward in the Kilbrandon Report and posed a number of questions relating to each of the different schemes. On 17 September the Government published a White Paper entitled *Democracy and Devolution* in which it accepted the main recommendations of the Kilbrandon Commission. This document stated: 'The Government, like the Royal Commission, regard it as a vital and fundamental principle to maintain the economic and political unity of the United Kingdom . . . The unity of the country and of the economy is essential both to the strength of our international position and to the growth of our industry and national wealth . . . The Government are firmly convinced, as was the Royal Commission, that the United Kingdom must remain one country and one economy and that constitutional change must be undertaken with the clear objective of strengthening rather than weakening this unity . . . The Government intend to build on what has already been achieved, in order to provide more democratic involvement'. The White Paper also reported that the Secretary of State had had discussions on devolution with a variety of organisations in Wales. The majority of those consulted were in favour of a directly elected Assembly for Wales. About the functions this Assembly should exercise there was no general agreement, however: opinion was divided between those who favoured legislative devolution and those who were for executive devolution. Only a small minority wanted a Welsh Advisory Council or no fundamental change at all. The majority were agreed that the office of Secretary of State for Wales should continue and that there should be no reduction in the number of Welsh Members of Parliament at Westminster.

The White Paper concluded, 'The Government intends to legislate for the establishment of Scottish and Welsh assemblies as soon as possible. Much work still remains to be done and many critical decisions taken on which Government will wish to have the widest consultations. But when detailed schemes have been worked out and implemented the Government believe that this will bring great benefits to the people of Scotland and Wales. They will be able to have a decisive voice in the running of their own domestic affairs'. Announcing the Government's decision to create an executive, elected Assembly for Wales and a legislative Assembly for Scotland, John Morris, the Secretary of State for Wales, was quoted in the *Western Mail* (17 September 1974) as saying that the White Paper on devolution was 'the most important event in the history of Wales since the Act of Union of 1536'.

The Government's decision to establish Assemblies for Wales and Scotland was incorporated into the Labour Party's manifesto at the General Election of October 1974. In February 1975 the Leader of the House of Commons, Edward Short, re-iterated the Government's pledge to establish Assemblies for Scotland and Wales and expressed his hope that a Bill would be ready by the end of the year. By October 1975, however, there were signs that, despite their party's official commitment to devolution, prior to the General Election of February 1974, about ten of the twenty-three Welsh Labour M.P.s were not in favour of the proposed measures. Furthermore, among the Labour Party's thirty-six constituency parties in Wales only twenty-one were known to be in favour of the Government's proposals for an Assembly, while fifteen supported the call for a referendum. The Wales Trades Union Council, on the other hand, welcomed the Government's plans and came out against the idea of a referendum.

It was the lack of unanimity among Welsh Labour M.P.s, together with the traditional opposition to the national aspirations of the Welsh on the part of Conservatives, as well as a back-lash among English M.P.s against the Labour Government's proposals for Welsh and Scottish Assemblies, which caused a lively public debate of the issue throughout the autumn of 1975. According o an opinion survey carried out on 13 November 1975, 51% (of a sample of 500 people in twenty constituencies in Wales) expressed their opinion that there should be no change in the constitutional position of Wales; 27% were in favour of a directly elected Assembly; 12% of a directly elected Assembly with power to raise and spend its own taxes; 10% were in favour of complete independence. Those in favour of a referendum were 62%.

The debate continued with even greater passion after the Queen's Speech on 19 November 1975, in which it was stated *inter alia* that, 'Legislative proposals for the establishment of Scottish and Welsh assemblies to exercise wide governmental responsibilities within the framework of the United Kingdom will be brought forward'. Harold Wilson angered Scottish and Welsh Nationalist M.P.s by adding, 'The Government is not insisting that the House completes the whole legislative processes in this session . . . On the assumption that the Bill is introduced at the earliest time and cannot conclude its passage in this session, it will be the Government's intention to present the Bill with whatever amendments are thought right at the very beginning of the next parliamentary session, and to receive the Royal Assent with all possible speed'. There was need, the Prime Minister hinted, for public discussion of a second White Paper and legislation would therefore have to be delayed by at least a year so that the Devolution Bill would not be passed until the 1976/7 session of Parliament.

The S.N.P. and *Plaid Cymru* threatened to join forces with Conservatives, the Ulster Unionists and Liberals in a bid to defeat the Government. The Labour Party also faced the prospect of a revolt among its own pro-devolution Scottish back-bench M.P.s With a majority of one, the Government was in danger of being defeated on the devolution issue but, in the event, this did not happen. Gwynfor Evans expressed the disappointment of Welsh devolutionists when he described the postponement as 'a complete and cynical betrayal of a promise by Labour to the people of Wales. The debate on self-government has been going on in Wales for a decade. The Wilson statement and the delay shows how totally bankrupt the Labour Government is of any political principle or concern for the real interests of Wales. The Labour Party is trying to slide out of its solemn promise and is using every possible excuse to play for time. This latest demonstration of blatant hypocracy is certain to result in the faster erosion of Labour votes in Wales by *Plaid Cymru'*. For the S.N.P. Douglas Henderson (East Aberdeenshire) announced, 'We want a general election as soon as possible. We are looking for the right opportunity to defeat them', and demanded the resignation of Edward Short. The Government still maintained that it was fully committed to Assemblies for Wales and Scotland, however, and Edward Short flatly denied that the postponement indicated a loss of enthusiasm for devolution on the Labour Party's part.

The Second White Paper on Devolution for Wales and Scotland *Our Changing Democracy*, was published (in Welsh and English) on 27 November 1975. As expected, it set out the Government's proposals for the creation of elected Assemblies for both countries, but a legislative body for Scotland and only executive powers for Wales. The Welsh Assembly, a single-chamber body, would have seventy-two members (two from each constituency) elected every four years and led by a Chief Executive normally the leader of the majority party, and a presiding officer to be known as Speaker. Detailed control of the Assembly's various functions would be given to committees made up of the elected members. The Welsh Office and the post of Secretary of State for Wales would remain. Wales would continue to return thirty-six members to Westminster and the new county councils would continue as at present. Among the fields to be devolved to the Assembly were health, social services, education (excluding the University), housing, roads, water, local government, environmental planning, sport, tourism, forestry, the fire services, social security, transport and the various nominated bodies functioning in Wales. The Assembly would be responsible for an annual budget or block-grant of about £910 million. If devolution was approved by Westminster in 1977, the first

elections were expected to be held in 1978 and the Assembly
would be housed at the Temple of Peace in Cardiff.

The views of the political parties in Wales towards the
Government's proposals were also predictable. The secretary
of the Welsh Labour Party, Emrys Jones, said they marked 'a
new departure in British democracy, a massive step forward
in the democratic involvement of ordinary people, in line with
our views as Socialists and with the radical tradition in
Wales'. The Conservative spokesman, Nicholas Edwards,
M.P. for Pembrokeshire, said the proposals 'would be likely
to lead to the break-up of the United Kingdom'. For the
Welsh Liberal Party, officially committed to the principle of
federalism, Emlyn Hooson, M.P. for Montgomeryshire,
welcomed the proposals but complained that the Government
had not accepted the Kilbrandon Commission's recommendation that election to the Assembly should be by proportional representation. Gwynfor Evans, President of *Plaid
Cymru,* gave a cautious welcome to the White Paper, em-
phasising the party's view that a Parliament for Wales was still
the principal need, and prophesying that the Assembly would
demand and obtain legislative powers within five years, adding, 'the fundamental weakness of the scheme is that it will
have no authority in the fields of industry and the economy'.

Thus began 'the great debate' about the future government
of Wales which is expected to continue, in Wales, Scotland
and Westminster, throughout 1976 and perhaps during what
remains of the present Government's life. It seems probable,
at the end of 1975, that there will be little change in the official policies of the political parties. The Conservatives in
Wales and London will go on arguing against constitutional
reform, rejecting the White Paper because it offers too much,
the Nationalists criticising it because it offers too little, and
the Labour Party struggling to speak with one voice on a
question which has divided its ranks not only in Wales but
also in Scotland and England. Clearly, much is going to
depend on the resolve of John Morris, the Secretary of State
for Wales, and those like him who wish to keep the electoral
pledges made by the Labour Party to the people of Wales over
two decades. It is expected that there will be some form of
devolution before the next General Election. But its nature

and extent will depend on whether the Labour Party can reconcile its dissidents to the principle of more devolution for Wales, and whether it will listen to its own conscience and have the courage to create in Wales the circumstances for a new era in the nation's history.

It was the socialist magazine *New Statesman* (London), commenting on the White Paper on Devolution in November 1975, which summed up the present situation in this way: 'Nobody ever lost money by under-estimating the capacity of what used to be called the Empire. But the way the Queen's Speech this week handled autonomist and now separatist feeling in Scotland and Wales is an exercise in almost Bourbon obscurantism. Having treated our national minorities with alternate neglect and contempt for generations, the Government now proposes to legislate ill-defined Assemblies into existence in order to gratify and assuage a desire whose appetite only increases with the eating. The Labour Party has a special responsibility in this, because as well as forming the present Government it is also the historic majority party in Scotland and Wales, and the desertion of so many voters to another cause must be taken as the most serious development so far in the vacuum left by the last decade's retreat from socialism. . . Typically (and illuminatingly) the current proposal is that a Welsh Assembly should have less power because the Welsh are not so insistent about independence, and thus the carrot need not be so generous. This is the mentality of a central government that has lost any vestige of confidence in its own abilities . . . Those in the Labour Party who now demand a referendum on the issue are fudging it just as much as those who claim that they have been in favour of Home Rule ever since Keir Hardie. The Scots and the Welsh may have to find out for themselves that separation is not the answer, and that the United Kingdom must work out a joint, radical and just solution to the crisis. Labour used to be able to make a claim on that belief. Where does it stand now that the oldest campaigners are drifting away from the colours?'

THE CORNISH

The Cornish are unique among the Celtic peoples of the United Kingdom in that they have no constitutional status which distinguishes them from the English. Cornwall, for administrative purposes, is a county of England. It was described by Henry Jenner in 1904 as having 'a County Council, and a Lort-Lieutenant all complete, as if it were no better than a mere Essex or Herts', and this has continued to be its status up to the present time.

A peninsula seventy-five miles long and forty-five miles broad at its widest point, with a coast-line of about 200 miles and an area (including the Scilly Isles) of 1,357 square miles, Cornwall is divided from the county of Devon in the south-west of England by the river Tamar. Essentially a rural area, Cornwall has no large urban centres; its population of 379,892 (1971) is distributed between small towns like Truro and Bodmin, the former mining districts of Cambourne, Redruth and St Austell, and a number of fishing villages and resorts like Polperro, St Ives and Mevagissey. Apart from small manufacturing industries such as tanning, textiles and paper-making, the chief traditional occupations are farming, fishing and mining.

With the Manx, the Cornish are not a linguistic minority in the same sense as most of the other peoples described in this book. The last native-speakers of Cornish died in the early years of the nineteenth century. For a hundred years previously the language had held the attention of antiquarians and interest in it was to continue throughout the next two centuries. But as a living language or the speech of a community, Cornish had been in decline long before the death, around 1780, of Dolly Pentreath who is sometimes said to be the last monoglot Cornish-speaker. Why then are the Cornish included here?

If confusion is to be avoided, the truth about the present position of Cornish must be clearly stated at the outset. Largely as a result of the Old Cornwall Movement led by Henry Jenner, Robert Morton Nance and A. S. D. Smith during the first half of the twentieth century, there are today some hundreds of people—the precise total is impossible to calculate and is best left thus—who can, with varying degrees

of skill, write and read a revived form of Cornish; a much
smaller number, probably fewer than a hundred, can sustain
a conversation in the language. There are no native-speakers
of Cornish: no adult alive today speaks it as a first language
and no child is being reared with Cornish as the mother-
tongue; it follows that there are no communities where the
language is in use. Furthermore, while no one uses Cornish
for the purpose of everyday living, even among those who have
a knowledge of the language the medium of conversation is
usually English, except on special occasions.

What then are the reasons for considering the Cornish as a
linguistic minority? The first is that, since the purpose of this
book is to present as comprehensive a picture as possible, it
includes a description of minorities which in numbers and
general characteristics are widely dissimilar. If it were
possible to establish an objective set of hierarchical scales, the
Cornish would no doubt have to be placed, with the Manx,
below all others treated in this book, for the simple reason
that the Cornish language is spoken by so few. On the other
hand, Cornish is the historical language of Cornwall: it has
been used there for social, religious and literary purposes
over a period of centuries. And even in the causes for its extinction, one of the few languages in Western Europe to have
suffered this fate during the last three hundred years, there is
interest for the socio-linguist and for other minorities. This is
partly why the Cornish are treated in the present account to a
length out of proportion to the numerical strength of their
language.

But there is a further reason: Cornwall now has a regionalist movement, led by *Mebyon Kernow* (Sons of Cornwall). In this it is no different from many other regions of
Western Europe, of course. But what distinguishes Cornwall
is that the present-day campaign to revive its national
consciousness and to win for it a greater degree of control over
its own affairs is quite evidently based on and inter-mingled
with the knowledge that Cornish was in comparatively recent
times the communal language. The existence of language-
classes and societies devoted to Cornish is also evidence of a
genuine desire to regain for the language something of its
former strength. If only for these reasons, substantial in
themselves, it is clear that the Cornish language has some

relevance to contemporary Cornwall and therefore should not be ignored.*

Cornish belongs with Breton and Welsh to the Brythonic branch of the Celtic languages, among which Irish, Gaelic and Manx form the Goidelic branch. In the first few centuries B.C. Cornwall, together with Devon and parts of Somerset, was the territory of the Dumnonii, a tribe partly of Bronze Age stock and speaking an early form of British. With the Roman conquest of Britain in the first century A.D., Exeter (Latin: *Isca Dumnoniorum*) became the administrative centre of the region. The name of its indigenous people survived through Old Welsh and Old English in the names of *Dyfnaint* and Devon. The word 'Cornwall' is composed of *wealas*, meaning 'foreigners, British, Welsh', as the Anglo-Saxon reminds us, and *Cornubia*, a Latinised form of *Cornuvia* from a still earlier British word *Cornouia*, meaning the land of the *Cornouii*. From this is concluded that in Roman times the area to the west of the Tamar was called *Cornouia* and that the *Cornouii* distinguished themselves from the *Dumnonii* to the east.

Little is known about Cornwall during the Dark Ages. Early historians failed to distinguish clearly between *Kernow* (the Cornish name for Cornwall) and *Kernev*, the Cornouaille district of Brittany to which many Britons had fled during the fifth and sixth centuries from invasion by Angles and Saxons. By the ninth century Old Cornish had emerged as a different language from Old Breton and Old Welsh and Cornwall had been converted to Christianity by missionaries from Ireland and Wales. But by this time the eastern part of Cornwall had been settled by Saxons from Devon and beyond. With the decline of Dumnonia, battles were fought against the Saxons at Camel in the year 721 and at Hingston Down in 825. It was not until 936, however, that Athelstan, King of Wessex, drove the Cornish out of Exeter and defeated Hywel, the last independent King of Cornwall. The river Tamar was fixed as the boundary between the Saxon Kingdom and the territory they conquered at this time. It was during this struggle against Saxon domination that the legends of Tristan and Iseult,

---

*Because the same cannot be said for those districts in Pembrokeshire and in Orkney and Shetland, where Flemish and Norse were once spoken, they have been omitted from the present chapter.

and of that of King Arthur, were born. Both were adapted by French writers in the thirteenth and fourteenth centuries, but the background to each is Cornish. By the tenth century Cornwall had become for administrative purposes a part of England, so that as Charles Thomas, Professor of Cornish Studies at the University of Exeter, has written, in *The Importance of Being Cornish* (1973), 'All its subsequent separatism and idiosyncracies, whether remarked upon externally or boasted about internally, derive from the status and development of the peninsula in the millenium from 100 B.C. to A.D. 900'.

At the Norman Conquest of England, beginning in 1066, Cornwall was ruled by Cadoc, a Cornishman whose black shield with golden bosses later became the Duchy's coat-of-arms. The Domesday Book shows that the Normans settled in Cornwall as baronial land-owners, after which the Saxons formed a middle-class and the native Cornish the lowest class of all. The earliest manuscripts giving Cornish words date from this period and it is clear from other documents that it continued to be the language of the common people in many districts for another five centuries. At an official level, however, Cornish became a casualty in the fierce linguistic struggle which followed the Norman Conquest of England. The irony was that those who supported English in its confrontation with French were led, it seems, by Cornishmen like John Trevisa. English now replaced the Conqueror's language in all parts of England, and Cornwall was no exception. Only among the poor and in the more remote western districts of the peninsula, was Cornish still spoken by the end of the fourteenth century.

From then until the reign of Henry VIII there is little reliable information about the state of the Cornish language as a spoken tongue. In 1542 Andrew Borde wrote in his *Boke of the Introduction of Knowledge*, 'In Cornwall is two speeches: the one is naughty Englysshe, and the other is Cornysshe speche. And there be many men and women the which cannot speake one worde of Englysshe, but all Cornysshe'. As a written language, on the other hand, Middle Cornish was now reaching the peak of its development: there survive from this period a number of religious plays and poems in the language such as *Pascon agan Arluth*, a versified account of

Christ's Passion, the *Ordinalia*, a drama in three parts, and *Bewnans Meryasek*, the life of Saint Meriasek, the bishop of Vannes in Brittany who became a missionary in Cornwall. In the absence of a Cornish Bible, the function of these plays was didactic: to teach the lessons of the Bible to people who could not understand English. But according to the Cornish scholar, A. S. D. Smith, 'the mature Cornish in which the plays are written can only be the outcome of a long tradition of Cornish writing'.

Unlike Wales, Cornwall did not benefit from the Renaissance and the invention of the printing press did little for its language. The Wars of the Roses (1455-85) had caused the death or departure of many of the gentry, or the confiscation of their lands. The Reformation, beginning in 1533, was the turning-point in the fortunes of Cornish. The English Book of Common Prayer was introduced into Cornwall's churches around 1547 by Edward VI, as a blow against Catholicism, and the King's Commissioners were sent to enforce the new law. In 1548 a Cornish force of 6,000 men raised by Humphrey Arundell of Lanherne and Henry Boyer, mayor of Bodmin, marched across the Tamar to defend their Catholic faith and language. Their petition to the King stated, 'We, the Cornyshe men, whereof certain of us understande no Englyshe, utterly refuse thys newe Service'. A. S. D. Smith points out in *The Story of the Cornish Language* (1969) that the rebels were offered the new Prayer-Book in their own tongue but refused to have it in any language. These were the sons of men who, under Michael Joseph, known as *An Gof* (The Blacksmith) and Thomas Flamanck, had marched in 1496 in protest against the payment of taxes, and again the following year under the banner of the Pretender, Perkin Warbeck. *An Gof* had been executed at Tyburn. The Cornishmen of 1548 were again beaten and their leaders killed.

In his *Ancient Cathedrals of Cornwall* (1804), John Whitaker was to write, 'English too was not desired by the Cornish, as vulgar history says . . . but as the case shews itself plainly to be, forced upon Cornwall by the tyranny of England, at a time when the English language was yet unknown in Cornwall. This act of tyranny was at once gross barbarity to the Cornish people, and a death blow to the Cornish language'. The persecution of Catholics which followed *An Gof*'s rising also put an end to the ancient contacts between Cornwall and Brittany. Up to now many Bretons had been living in Cornwall and trade across the Channel had been frequent, but after 1560 their names are no longer to be found in the parish registers. In the same year a Protestant petition asking that 'it may be lawful for such Welsh or Cornish children as can speake no English to learn the Praemise in the Welsh tongue or Cornish language' was refused. From now on, most references to Cornish deride the language.

At the beginning of the seventeenth century there remained only a few monoglot Cornish-speakers, mostly in the extreme west between St Ives *(Porth-ia)* and Ludgvan *(Lodewon)*, Zennor *(Sent-Senera)* and Land's End. The seventeenth century saw a rapid deterioration of the language as an everyday speech and by 1700 Cornish-speakers lived only in the westernmost districts. Despite its decline, the language continued to attract comment from Englishmen, however. Richard Carew claimed in his *Survey of Cornwall* (1602) that the majority of the population were bilingual and John Norden, addressing King James I eight years later, stated, 'And yet (which is to be marveyled) though the husband and wife, parents and children, masters and servants, do naturally communicate in their native language, yet there is none of them in a manner but able to converse with a stranger in the English tongue, unless it be some obscure people who seldom confer with the better sort. But it seemeth, however, that in a few years the Cornish will be, by a little and little, abandoned'. During the Civil War of 1642-6, the young Royalist Richard Symons recorded in his diary for 1644, 'All beyond Truro they speak the Cornish language . . . at Land's End they speak no English'. The only important work of literature which survives from this period, however, is a play entitled *Gwryans an Bys* (The Creation of the World) written by William Jordan in 1611.

Towards the end of the seventeenth century it was becoming clear to scholars that the Cornish language was in danger of total extinction. John Ray prophesised in his *Itinerary* (1667) that 'the language is like in a short time to be lost'. William

Scawen in *Antiquities Cornu-Britanni* around 1680 gave a number of reasons for its decline, including a lack of literature, the loss of contacts with Brittany, the absence of Church services in the language, the lapse of the religious plays and general indifference on the part of the common Cornish people. An attempt was now made by a group of scholars in the Penzance area, led by John Keigwin (1641-1710) to translate parts of the Bible into Cornish in order to revive popular interest, but the task proved too great and only the translation of the Book of Genesis was completed. The most noteworthy of Keigwin's colleagues were Nicholas Boson and his children John, Thomas and Katherine: their writings were to prove of extreme value to later students of the language, especially *Nebbaz Gerriau dro tho Carnoack* (A Few Words about Cornish) published in 1700 and *Jowan Chy an Hor* (John of Chyanhor) written between 1660 and 1670. The latter is one of several folk-tales written by Nicholas Boson for the purpose of teaching Cornish to his sons and was to be used for a similar purpose nearly three centuries later —by Robert Morton Nance in his text-book *Cornish for All* (1929): 'This old tale of the chimney-corner, taking us into the heart of a Cornish-speaking countryside, with familiar place-names to make us feel at home there as we follow John's travels, and repetitions to hammer home so many phrases, must always remain the ideal way-in for Cornish people who would recover what they can of their lost Celtic tongue'. The story was first published by the Welsh antiquary Edward Lhuyd (1660-1709) in his *Archaeologia Britannica* (1707) and republished by the Cornish Language Board in 1969 to accompany a record on which it is read by Richard Gendall. Other scholars associated with the Bosons were William Gwavas, who corresponded with John in Cornish, and Thomas Tonkin who collected folk-songs including *Pela era why moaz, moz, fettow teag?* well-known in English as 'Where are you going, my pretty maid?' The work of such men and the manuscripts they collected was a deliberate attempt to provide Cornish with a written literature, but it was already too late to save the language.

The eighteenth century was the last in which Cornish was in general use. Edward Lhuyd, the eminent scholar from Wales, visiting Cornwall in 1700, found Cornish spoken as a first language in twenty-five parishes but that the gentry did not speak it, 'there being no need, as every Cornishman speaks English'. In his *Archaeologica Brittannica,* Lhuyd—who learned the language from Keigwin and his friends—published a Cornish Grammar, the first text-book ever printed on the subject. It was followed in 1790 by William Pryce's *Archaeologia Cornu-Brittanica* which included, besides Lhuyd's Grammar, the copious vocabulary collected by Gwavas and Tonkin on the coast from Penzance to Land's End in 1735, plus several texts. It was this book which enabled a later scholar, Edwin Norris (1795-1872) to publish his translation of the Middle Cornish plays into English.

While the scholars were busy collecting the last vestiges of spoken Cornish, there was no lack of testimony that the language was now nearing extinction. It was Daines Barrington who was responsible for spreading the belief that the last speaker of Cornish was Dolly Pentreath of Mousehole. During a tour of Cornwall in 1768, Barrington was directed to Dolly Pentreath as a person able to speak the language. 'I desired to be introduced', he wrote, 'as a person who had laid a wager that there was no one who could converse in Cornish; upon which Dolly Pentreath spoke in an angry tone of voice for two or three minutes, and in a language which sounded very like Welsh . . .' Barrington reported this exchange to the Society of Antiquaries which published an account in its Journal in 1776. Dolly Pentreath died in the following year. Barrington contributed another paper to the Society's Journal in 1779, adding a letter written in Cornish in 1776 from a fisherman named William Bodener who claimed to know five persons in Mousehole *(Raginnis)* alone who spoke Cornish, thus disproving the belief that Dolly Pentreath was the last Cornish-speaker.

Whether or not Cornish survived into the nineteenth century is difficult to say. The expansion of industry, particularly mining, and the growth of towns and railways, dealt the final blows to the language. It is believed that a few cases of genuine bilingualism existed for a few decades more, but the evidence is pitifully scanty: John Tremethack, who died in 1852 at the age of eighty-seven, had taught Cornish to his daughter who was still alive in 1875; Henry Jenner's mother-in-law, Mrs Rawlings of Hayle *(Heyl)* who died in 1879 aged fifty-seven, had learned the Lord's Prayer in Cornish at school; Bernard Victor learnt Cornish from his father and passed on a great deal to Jenner in 1875; Dr Stevens of St Ives, talking to the historian J. H. Mathews in 1892, said he had been taught to count in Cornish; and so on. Of John Davey of Zennor (1812-91), a more substantial claim was made: on a plaque to his memory in the village church-yard, are the carefully chosen words 'who was the last to possess any traditional considerable knowledge of the Cornish language'. Davey, it is believed, could converse and sing in Cornish.

The nineteenth century ended in a flourish of scholarship devoted to Cornish. New versions of the medieval plays were edited and manuscripts published. Edwin Norris's *The Ancient Cornish Drama* appeared in 1859, the first comprehensive Cornish dictionary in 1865, the work of a Welshman named Robert Williams . Whitley Stokes published a translation of *Bewnans Meryasek* in 1872, other edited texts appeared in 1879 and W. P. Jago's *English-Cornish Dictionary* in 1887. But by now Cornish was of interest only to Celtic scholars and a few Welsh philologists and little attention was paid to the publication of the Middle Cornish texts. As in other countries, the scholars had applied their energies to the study of Cornish at a time of economic stagnation but, unlike their colleagues elsewhere, they were too late to save the language from its fate. After the passing of the 1870 Education Act, not even Cornish history was taught any longer in schools. Cornwall's mining industry had declined as England found it cheaper to import tin and copper from its Empire overseas, while agriculture and fishing had gone into acute depression. While the population of Britain had increased steadily from about 12 million in 1801 to about 34 million in 1891, Cornwall's had increased from 192,281 to only 322,571, a loss of some 46,819 since 1861. Whereas Cornwall's fishing industry had employed 2,460 men and 1,260 boats in 1870, the entire Cornish fleet numbered only 420 boats and 820 men in 1900. As P. Berresford Ellis comments in *The Story of the Cornish Language* (1971),*

---

*The present account of Cornish draws heavily on the facts used by P. Berresford Ellis in *The Story of the Cornish Language* (Truro, 1971).

'the old Cornish toast, *Pysk, Sten ha Cober!* (Fish, Tin and Copper!) was no longer heard. By 1920 a new toast had replaced it: 'China-clay and Tourists!''

When it began, in the early years of the twentieth century, the Cornish Revival was more concerned with Cornish as a spoken language than as a matter for scholarly and antiquarian pursuit. The Revival was mainly the work of one man, at least at first. Henry Jenner (1848-1934) had read papers to the Philological Society in 1873 and to the British Archaeological Society in 1876 and held a post at the British Museum for many years. He had also followed in the footsteps of Keigwin, collecting the vestiges of Cornish still to be found in some districts. But from 1877, when he organised a public ceremony in memory of Dolly Pentreath in order to draw attention to the language, Jenner was also interested in the possibility of reviving Cornish as a spoken medium. In 1901 he founded *Cowethas Kelto-Kernuak* (The Celtic Cornish Society), the first Cornish language movement, and in the same year joined the *Gorsedd* of Brittany. Two years later he spoke in Cornish at the conference of the *Union Régionaliste Bretonne* at Lesneven in Finistère—the first time for Cornish to be heard in public for a century. In 1904 Jenner had Cornwall admitted to the Celtic Congress which met that year at Caernarfon in Wales. He also published *A Handbook of the Cornish Language* in 1904, in which he asked, 'Why should Cornishmen learn Cornish? There is no money in it, it serves no practical purpose, and the literature is scanty and of no great originality or value. The question is a fair one, the answer is simple. Because they are Cornish'.

Jenner's reply to his own question became the classic reason why Cornishmen now started learning the language. Among the first enthusiasts was Robert Morton Nance (1873-1959) but others were Richard Hall, W. D. Watson and R. St. V. Allin-Collins who wrote short stories in the language; all were able to converse in it. In 1920 Jenner and Morton Nance founded the Old Cornwall Society choosing as its motto *Cuntelleugh an Brewyon us Gesys na vo Kellys Travyth* (Gather the fragments which are left so that nothing be lost). Eight years later the Cornish *Gorsedd, Gorseth Byrth Kernow,* was established, with Jenner as Grand Bard. In 1929 Morton Nance published his *Cornish for All,* an important contribution to the Revival in that it used his unified system of orthography based on the Middle Cornish texts as well as on modern philological and phonetical principles. To this work was added in 1931 *Lessons in Spoken Cornish* by A. S. D. Smith (1883-1950), an Englishman who had already published a text-book, *Welsh Made Easy*, under his bardic name of Caradar in 1930. By 1934, the year of Henry Jenner's death, there were eight Cornish-speaking members of the Cornish *Gorsedd*. Morton Nance's dramatic interlude, *An Balores* (The Chough) had been performed, the Federation of Old Cornwall Societies had classes in a dozen places, a church service had been held in Cornish at Towednack, where the last Cornish services had been held in 1678, and a movement known as *Tyr ha Tavas* (Land and Language) had been launched under the leadership of E. H. Hambly. After the death of Henry Jenner, Robert Morton Nance became the Grand Bard of the Cornish *Gorsedd*. Also in 1934 Nance published his *English-Cornish Dictionary* in collaboration with A. S. D. Smith. The first radio broadcast in Cornish, a programme of choral music, was heard in 1935. Nance published his life's work, a *Cornish-English Dictionary*, in 1938 and in 1939 A. S. D. Smith's complete grammar of the language, *Cornish Simplified*, appeared.

The Second World War—during which leaders of the Revival carried on a correspondence in Cornish (the language was accepted by the military censors)—interrupted the public ceremonies of the Cornish *Gorsedd* but not the writing of books in Cornish. In 1951 the widow of A. S. D. Smith, who had died in the previous year, published his greatest work *Trystan hag Ysolt* (Tristan and Iseult). Interest in learning Cornish also continued to grow: evening classes were started by the education authorities at Falmouth and St Austell and an annual summer school, *Scol Haf Kernewek*, which is still held at Truro *(Trieru)*. A magazine in Cornish, *An Lef Kernewek* (The Cornish Voice) was launched by E. G. Retallack Hooper. Morton Nance went on tirelessly with his work, publishing new editions of his dictionaries in 1952 and 1955, as well as other guides to the language. Shortly before his death, at the age of eighty-six in 1958, Nance remarked, 'One generation has set Cornish on its feet. It is now for another to make it walk'. On his tombstone at Zennor were cut the words

Oberow y vewnans yu y wyr govath (His life's works are his true memorial).

After 1951 the Cornish movement entered a new phase with the founding, on 6 January during the Celtic Congress at Truro that year, of a political organisation called *Mebyon Kernow* (Sons of Cornwall). According to Richard Jenkin, the editor of its magazine *New Cornwall* until it ceased publication in 1972, there were twenty founder-members. The aims of *Mebyon Kernow* were defined as 'to maintain the character and interests of Cornwall as a Celtic nation, to promote the constitutional advance of Cornwall and its right to self-government in domestic affairs, and to foster Cornish studies and culture, including language, literature, history and sport'. At first *Mebyon Kernow*'s progress was slow: by 1960 it had only around a hundred members. But by 1968 it had won a seat on Cornwall County Council and on a number of urban and rural district councils. Two of Cornwall's five Members of Parliament joined the movement and a third declared his support for its principles. The main political principle formulated by *Mebyon Kernow* was Cornwall's right to conduct its affairs, through an assembly to be known as *Cuntelles Kernow* on the same lines as the Manx Tynwald or the States Parliament of the Channel Isles. Its policy for the Cornish language was, while recognising that Cornwall must continue to use English, 'learning Cornish must be an option available to each child' and that 'Cornish must be given examination status'. These aims were revised in 1964 and stated as follows: to maintain the Celtic character of Cornwall and its right to self-government in domestic affairs; to foster the Cornish language, literature, culture and sport, to encourage the study of Cornish History from a Cornish point of view and to demand that Cornish children have the opportunity in school to learn about their own land and culture'.

The first candidate put up by *Mebyon Kernow* in a General Election was Richard Jenkin who fought the constituency of Falmouth-Cambourne in 1971. He polled 960 votes and lost his deposit, while the Conservative candidate was elected with a majority of 1,523. At the two General Elections of 1974 the party's candidate was James Whetter, who polled 850 votes the first time and 350 the second, at Truro. At the present time there are no district councillors elected as *Mebyon Kernow* candidates although about twenty representing other parties, or no party, belong to it. None of the seventy members of the Cornwall County Council were elected as *Mebyon Kernow* candidates, although a few have expressed sympathy for its aims. Cornwall is represented at Westminster by the three Conservatives John Nott (St Ives), David Mudd (Falmouth-Cambourne) and Robert Kicks (Bodmin), and by the two Liberals, David Penhaligon (Truro) and John Pardoe (North Cornwall), both of whom are believed to be members of *Mebyon Kernow*. Charles Thomas comments, 'While local politics still look to the ideals of a non-political (or non-party) structuring, exemplified by our County Council with its majority of Independent members, the depressingly low polls of recent years, and even now the dismal shortage of new or committed candidates, suggest that Cornish people are apathetic about the effectiveness of local representation. This is widely borne out in day-to-day conversations; so many people take it as a matter of course that nothing can be done, that town and district councils contain those who vote openly in their own interests, and that improper influences bring about decisions. Coupled to the wider national mistrust of the two main political parties, and specifically of most politicians, this is as dangerous a trend as it is a depressing one'.

The Chairman of *Mebyon Kernow* is Richard Jenkin, a chemistry teacher at Hayleston, its President Retallack Hooper, editor of *An Lef Kernewek,* and it has about twelve branches with a membership of around 2,500. The party is a member of the Celtic League, the political and cultural organisation to which many organisations in the six Celtic countries belong, and sends delegations to the Federal Union of European Nationalities. It has also presented evidence to the Kilbrandon Commission on the Constitution of the United Kingdom, pressing its case for a Cornish Assembly and opposing any plans for Cornwall's inclusion in a South-West England Region based on Bristol or Exeter. The party's badge is based on the Cross of St Piran, a white cross on a black background, which is used as the national flag of Cornwall. Following a split in 1969, the former secretary Leonard Trelease broke away with others to form the Cornish National

Party but re-joined *Mebyon Kernow* after the General Election of 1971. More recently still, James Wetter—after expressing support for the I.R.A. in the party's periodical *Cornish Nation*—left in 1975 to form the Cornish Nationalist Party; to date he is reported as having succeeded in enrolling only a few friends.

Despite its lack of electoral successes, *Mebyon Kernow* has become the principal pressure-group and is active in several sectors of public life; another of its aims is 'to study local conditions and attempt to remedy any that may be prejudicial to the best interests of Cornwall by the creation of informed public opinion or other appropriate measures'. Its evidence to the Royal Commission on Local Government Reform in 1972 made the following proposals: a Secretary or Minister of State for Cornwall and an elected Council for Cornwall with control over education, including a University and a College of Education, and over planning, a police force and all other powers at present exercised by the County Council and regional boards like the Hospital Board and Rivers Board.

Above all, *Mebyon Kernow* is concerned with the economic problems of Cornwall, and these are acute. As a result of the decline in its fishing and mining industries during the nineteenth century, Cornwall has suffered from depopulation for over a hundred years. Its present population of 379,892 compares badly with the 369,390 inhabitants enumerated in 1861, while the population of the United Kingdom doubled during the same period. Massive emigration began during the copper slump of 1866 when a third of the population left Cornwall, and this was followed in 1874 by a slump in agriculture when cheap wheat imported from America caused a change-over to dairy farming. During the first decades of the twentieth century there were riots by Cornish fishermen against competition by English boats; many followed the miners and farmers to America and the population reached its lowest point of 317,968 in 1931. This emigration has continued to the present time, though not at quite the same rate as previously. On the other hand, the increase in Cornwall's population since 1951, when it was 345,442, is mainly due to the excess of settlers 'from beyond the Tamar'—*emmets* (ants) as they are known in the local dialect—over the number of emigrants.

The process of English settlement which began in the eighteenth century continued with the garrison towns established in the nineteenth and the arrival of the first holiday-makers in Victorian times. By now the county's administration, hospitals, schools, professional and commercial life are almost entirely in English hands. If 'Cornish' is defined as 'born in Cornwall', the 1951 Census gave 69% of the population as Cornish. But if the term is defined further to mean 'born in Cornwall, of parents both of whom were also born in Cornwall', only about 45% of the population qualify. The significance of such statistics is difficult to interpret, however. Richard Jenkin, Chairman of *Mebyon Kernow*, points out that the statistics are invalidated by the fact that there is no maternity hospital in south-east Cornwall, mothers from this area having to go to Plymouth in neighbouring Devon for the birth of their children. His party defines Cornish nationality for membership purposes as the status of anyone who 'considers himself to be Cornish'. The party uses the term 'nation' as a matter of course. This much is certain: Cornwall's indigenous stock has been in a minority for decades. Young people leave in search of educational facilities and jobs, while incomers are mainly retired people attracted by the climate, scenery and what was until recently a comparatively cheap way of life, or else they are small business people intent on making a living from the tourist trade.

The influx of tourists into Cornwall has now reached what Charles Thomas describes as 'nightmare proportions'. Tourism brings about £75 million into Cornwall annually, mainly through resorts like Newquay and St Ives, but only after doing serious damage to the community and environment. The plea of Arthur Quiller-Couch, editor of *The Cornish Magazine* in 1898—'Since we must cater for the stranger, let us do it well and honestly. Let us respect him and our native land as well',—has been largely ignored. Some of the most hideous tourist developments in the United Kingdom are to be found in Cornwall. Local protest at official enquiries is usually led by a preservationist, anti-pollution lobby consisting overwhelmingly of middle-aged English people while the native Cornish are content to find employment at a menial level in the service sectors. Charles Thomas comments, 'In the growing conservationist and environmental circles in

Cornwall, the lead is very often taken by competent, conscientious and outspoken non-Cornish people . . . people who
are prepared to bother. In fact, the Cornish themselves have
by contemporary standards a shocking environmental record,
starting with mining and quarrying, and seen at its very worst
in the short-sighted actions of local councils . . .' Against this
background, perhaps the most extreme example of 'internal
colonialism' to be found in the United Kingdom, *Mebyon
Kernow* carries on a campaign to draw attention to relatively
low incomes, high unemployment figures and a shortage of industry and houses.

Meanwhile, to what extent have the Cornish succeeded in
'making Cornish walk'? The visitor to Cornwall in recent
years may have noticed in a number of instances that the
language is beginning to be used again. Modest though they
undoubtedly are, it is not every minority which can point to
Christmas cards and calendars in its language. In Cornwall
there are also car-plaques bearing the name *Kernow* (Cornwall), shops selling bread described as *Bara an gwella
dyworth Kernow* (the best bread in Cornwall), a post-office at
Cubert with the sign *Lytherva* and a public house at Mabe
Burnthouse called *Tavern Noweth* (New Inn); in 1968 the
Keep Britain Tidy Campaign used Cornish on its posters and
stickers and in the same year a cinema at Truro showing the
musical film *Camelot* advertised it as *Arthur Myghtern a ve
hag vyth* (Arthur, the once and future King). A holiday camp
kept by James Whetter near Mevagissey has Cornish signs at
its entrance and outside its lavatories. Of course, such
instances of the use of Cornish may be dismissed on the
grounds that it is meant to appeal to tourists, as the sale of
items like serviettes and tea-towels with Cornish inscriptions
testifies. But they have also been noted by the Cornish
themselves and are explained to the attentive visitor with
pride.

There are also about six church services held in
Cornish each year. Clearly not intended for tourists
are the patriotic songs written and sung in Cornish by Richard
Gendall, nor does the monthly magazine *Cornish Life* carry a
page in Cornish for the visitors. Cornish is also used in the
motto of some schools and rugby clubs, and is to be seen in
the names of a large number of private houses and hotels.

There is still, however, no Cornish-language programme on the B.B.C. and for more obvious reasons it cannot be used for any official purpose such as in correspondence with local authorities. Some Cornish appears from time to time in *Mebyon Kernow*'s magazine *The Cornish Nation* and the Lodenek Press at Padstow publishes short stories and poems by writers like Donald Rawe. Cornwall has already produced a number of well-known contemporary poets in English like Charles Causley and Denys Val Baker, editor of *The Cornish Review* until its demise in 1974, and in the work of younger writers like Derek Tanguy a new note of Cornish patriotism is to be heard. The most productive young poet now writing in Cornish is Tim Saunders who has published a number of poems in the language with a nationalist and Marxist message for all the Celtic peoples. But perhaps the greatest boost to the language in recent years is the contribution of the folk-singer Brenda Wootton, who has made records in Cornish and leads a duo called *Crowdy Crawn* at folk-clubs and on television. After a concert at Wadebridge in 1975 she told a journalist, 'The reaction I get is fantastic. People are ashamed that they do not know the language of their own country. Singing in Cornish is leading to the young people taking an interest in the language for the first time. When they have children of their own, they will surely ensure that they learn something of the language. I certainly do not think Cornish will ever again be as dead as it was twenty years ago'.

The growing popular interest in Cornish led to the formation in 1967 of *Kesva an Tavas Kernewek* (The Cornish Language Board). This body was set up by the Federation of Old Cornwall Societies, the *Gorseth* and the Royal Institute of Cornwall. It is responsible for all aspects of the study and revival of the language by providing texts, organising classes and conducting examinations to improve the standard of written and spoken Cornish. At the present time there are about 200 pupils in a dozen evening classes sponsored by the Board and the teachers' fees are paid from a grant made by the education authority. In 1974 there were forty-eight candidates at the Board's examinations. Among its most outstanding ex-pupils are the sisters Christine and Mary Truran, daughters of L. H. Truran, Secretary of *Mebyon Kernow,* both of whom are fluent Cornish-speakers and now pursuing Celtic studies at St Hilda's College, Oxford, and Newnham College, Cambridge, respectively. In an interview with the *Sunday Times* (7 April 1974) Mary Truran said, 'What I hope to see is the Cornish language used again by ordinary people, not just an esoteric minority. A first step must be the introduction of the language as an optional subject in schools'. Other language classes have been started in recent years by individuals like John Page at St Austell and Richard Gendall at Helston, while *Scol Haf Kernewek* (Summer School of Cornish) has been held annually for the past twelve years, concentrating on spoken Cornish and giving an opportunity for students of the language to use it as a living tongue; records and tapes are available for Cornish learners.

There are two other organisations devoted to the culture of Cornwall. One is the Institute of Cornish Studies which since 1972 is based at Redruth and sponsored jointly by the University of Exeter and Cornwall County Council. Under its director Professor Charles Thomas, and with a staff of five research fellows, the Institute exists 'to promote and to co-ordinate all forms of research and study connected with any aspect of Cornwall, past, present and future;' it publishes a quarterly bulletin and a journal, *Cornish Studies*. Among the subjects which fall within the Institute's purview, defined as 'the study of Man in his regional setting', are the archaeology, topography, land-use, art, music, geography, geology, society and language of Cornwall. In 1972 the Institute published a selected hand-list of publications in or about the Cornish language comprising a total of over a hundred titles published since 1900.

The other organisation is the Cornish *Gorseth* founded in 1928. Its aims are 'to maintain the National Celtic Spirit of Cornwall and to give expression to such spirit; to encourage the study of Cornish History and the Cornish language; to foster Cornish literature, Art and Music; to link Cornwall with other Celtic countries and to promote a spirit of peace and co-operation among those who work for the honour of Cornwall'. Unlike its Welsh and Breton counterparts, the Cornish *Gorseth* has neither druids nor ovates: it confers the title of Bard only, either in recognition of work done for Cornwall or as evidence of proficiency in Cornish. Its ceremonies, held

on the first Saturday in September, and in which about half of
its 350 members usually take part, are held entirely in Cornish. Following the model of the Welsh *Gorsedd,* the Cornish
ceremonies feature the *Corn Gwlas* (Horn of the Nation),
Pysadow an Orseth (Prayer), *Garm Cres* (Cry of Peace), *Dons
an Blejyow* (Flower Dance), *Keskerdhes an Vyrth* (Procession
of Bards), and the songs *Kernow agan Mamvro* (Cornwall our
Motherland) and *Bro Goth agan Tasow* (Old Land of our
Fathers), adapted like the Breton *Bro Goz va Zadou* from the
Welsh national anthem *Hen Wlad fy Nhadau.* The Cornish
organisation differs from the Welsh in one major feature: the
significance it gives to the belief that *Nyns yu marow
Myghtern Arthur*—that King Arthur is not dead but that as
the symbol of the Celtic spirit he will return to restore the
nationhood of Cornwall.

   In conclusion, it must be said that not all prominent Cornishmen are in complete sympathy with attempts to revive
Cornish as a spoken language. Indeed, attitudes to the
language vary a great deal. From philologists abroad the comment by Chaim Rabin, Professor of Hebrew at the University
of Jerusalem, is often quoted: 'The rebirth of Cornish is the
only case which can be reasonably considered as a parallel to
that of Hebrew'. To the many English writers and artists who
have their homes or holidays in Cornwall or who, like John
Betjeman, have extolled its charms, the entire Cornish
Revival movement is one huge joke. Many Cornishmen would
agree: for example, the distinguished historian A. L. Rowse,
author of *A Cornish Childhood* and Fellow of All Souls
College, holds views which invite attack from language enthusiasts. On the other hand, some eminent figures like the
Reverend Richard Rutt, Assistant Bishop of Truro, have learned to read and speak the language. Even inside the Cornish
movement there are wide differences of opinion. Many bards
of the Cornish *Gorseth* do not take its ceremonies or their
oath very seriously and openly admit that they are not at all
interested in the language. Others within the ranks of *Mebyon
Kernow* put political objectives first, although its leaders like
Richard Jenkin and L. H. Truran have taken the trouble of
learning Cornish and encouraged their children to do the
same. According to *Mebyon Kernow,* 'It seems unlikely in
present circumstances that the language will ever regain the

status of a regular means of verbal communication. Its existence will continue to be a limited one, confined to literature, ceremony, scholarship and as a means of expressing Cornish patriotism'.

On the other hand, Charles Thomas confesses that he has little interest in attempts to revive Cornish, preferring to give his time to the study of Cornwall's archaeology and place-names, an interest he shares with P.A. S. Peel. In his inaugural lecture as Professor of Cornish Studies in the University of Exeter and Director of the Institute of Cornish Studies in 1973, he said, 'A long-held and cherished belief, namely that the Cornish language in its real Late stage possessed the same phonetic system, vowels, tone and pitch, as the present spoken English dialect heard in the voices of elderly natives in the Land's End area, is now under heavy fire. If true at all it would refer only to the very last stage of Cornish. The work of the Survey of English Dialects suggests that the various spoken English dialects in Cornwall derive most of their phonetic quality from the Middle English of Wessex; and that the influence upon the last two centuries of genuine spoken Cornish were almost wholly, one might say subjectively ruinously, those from English. It follows that the true pronunciation of Cornish in, say, A.D. 1600, cannot possibly be gleaned by hanging around the harbour mouth at Mousehole or from evenings in the Commercial Hotel at St Just. It may well have been (a) quite different from what has been taught in the last fifty years, (b) largely irrecoverable at this late date, and (c) if recoverable at all, to be sought in place-name forms or some other source . . . In other words, revived Cornish, as to its spelling, an increasing part of its vocabulary, and most of its pronunciation, cannot be regarded as genuine, and this is why it is viewed with such suspicion and reserve by almost all Celticists . . . This does not amount to failure: the major achievement of Henry Jenner, Robert Morton Nance and their contemporaries, was the establishment of a sense of Cornishness, of national consciousness. This was in itself a tremendous task and it was accomplished entirely by hard and devoted work with relatively little support. An obliquity of direction in the matter of Revived Cornish is unfortunate, perhaps rectifiable; it hardly detracts from the plain fact that, had this overall Cornish

Revival not been attempted, and accomplished, it would by now be quite impossible to construct the particular platform on which the linguistic, cultural, nationalistic, and environmental movements in Cornwall all perform'.

Finally, the view of those who are actively engaged in teaching Cornish is summed up by John Page, writing in the magazine *Cornish Life:* 'Cornwall is not an English county, though Whitehall likes to believe, and indeed insists, that it is. A crossing of the Tamar is as much the crossing of a border as is a journey into Scotland or Wales, and the Cornish want this fact recognised . . . We want road signs and public notices in our own language: we want that language used in official functions. But before we can have that—indeed before we deserve to have it—we must first win back that which we have lost partly, it must be admitted, through our own inertia: our language. In this generation there are no born speakers of Cornish: all those who have the language have deliberately acquired it. But each year more and more are doing this through attendance at the evening classes held, under Cornwall County Council auspices, from end to end of the land. There is no reason, *if the will is there,* why there should not be Cornish-speakers born to the next generation. But only an awareness on the part of the young parents of today can ensure this. We who love to teach the language are doing all that we can to bring this state of affairs about . . . That we regain our land it behoves us first to regain our language, for a man without a language has lost his land'.

THE CHANNEL ISLANDERS

Situated between Britain and France, the archipelago known in English as the Channel Islands, and in French as *Les Iles Anglo-Normandes,* consists of four main groups of islands. The most northerly is Alderney, some fifty miles from Britain and eight from France, with the islets of Burhou, the Casquets and Ortac. Sixteen miles to the south-west is Guernsey, together with the smaller islands of Sark, Lihou, Herm and Jethou. Jersey, with Les Ecrehou and the Minquiers Reef, is fifteen miles to the south-east of Guernsey. About twenty-eight miles to the south of Jersey, and fifty-two miles from Alderney, is the small group of Chausey Islands. Unlike the others, this latter froup, of which only one island is inhabited, is not under British jurisdiction but belongs to France. The largest of all the Islands is Jersey with an area of forty-five square miles; its chief town is St Hélier. Guernsey. the second largest, has an area of twenty-four square miles and St Peter Port is its chief town. Of the smaller islands, Alderney is the largest with an area of three square miles. The population of the Channel Islands in 1971 was 120,998, of whom 69,329 lived on Jersey, 49,399 on Guernsey, 1,686 on Alderney and 584 on Sark.

The language of the majority of the Channel Islands' population is English. But dialects of Norman French are still spoken in some parts. These *parlers* differ from the dialects spoken in Normandy, and from standard French, being much older than the latter. They are nevertheless comprehensible by the visitor from Normandy and, only with a little difficulty, to anyone with a command of standard French. While retaining many early characteristics of the languauge spoken by the Normans in 1066, the dialects have been enriched over the centuries by a sea-faring and farming people with an extensive communal life of their own. There are also variations between the dialects of the main islands and even between parishes in the same island. Nor are the dialects used to the same extent in all parts. On Alderney (French: *Aurigny)* they have almost completely died out and only a few are able to speak them on Sark *(Sercq)*. It is therefore only on Jersey (Norman French: *Jèrri)* and Guernsey *(Guernesey)* that they survive. About 10,000 people are estimated to have a knowledge of *le jèrriais,* the dialect of Jersey, and about 4,000 of *le dgernésiais*, that of Guernsey. They are, for the most part, the older natives of the Islands living outside the towns. The process of anglicization has proceeded rapidly during the present century and by now the majority of the Islands' population is no longer indigenous. About 76% of Jersey's inhabitants were born outside the Islands, mainly in the countries of Britain, attracted there by a milder climate and, as in the Isle of Man, by a lower rate of taxation.

It was Victor Hugo, the French writer who spent fifteen years in exile on Jersey and Guernsey, who described the Channel Islands as 'fragments of Europe dropped by France and picked up by England'. Given their close proximity to France—the Cotentin peninsula and the coast of Brittany are in full view from many points—this description may be acceptable in a geographical sense. But in historical terms it needs some qualification, for the Islands became the possession of the English Crown in the twelfth century, and have remained so ever since.

The Channel Islands were first inhabited by the Beaker Folk and during the Bronze Age, as the dolmens on Jersey such as the Hougue Bie and the menhirs like La Gran'mere du Chimquière on Guernsey remind us. The Iberians, the first permanent inhabitants of the Islands who left all these monuments, formed the most important element in the population until the arrival of a Gaullish tribe known to Caesar as the Unelli around the year 300 B.C. Over the next six centuries the Islands were ruled by Rome as part of Gaul. According to a Roman route list, Alderney, Guernsey and Jersey were known as Riduna, Sarnia and Caesarea. During this period a low Latin dialect took root as the speech of the inhabitants who were converted to Christianity at a much later date than the rest of Empire. In 486 the Romans occupying the territories between the Somme and the Loire were defeated by Clovis. During the Dark Ages the Islands were settled by Britons fleeing from the Anglo-Saxon invasion of England and, in the ninth century, after the death of Charlemagne, the Islands and the Cotentin peninsula fell under the control of Bretons. Although the lack of evidence in language and in archaeological remains suggests that there was no heavy settlement by Bretons, the legends which associated Breton saints with the Islands suggest that it was from this source that they first received Christianity. The Celtic Church's missionary zeal and adaptation to local conditions enabled it to become established in the area in the sixth and seventh centuries, although the more disciplined Roman Church was eventually to prevail there. The Islands were attacked by the Vikings throughout the ninth century and, by the Treaty of Claire-sur-Eptes in 911, their leader Rollo won from Charles the Simple, King of Francia, the grant of the area from Dieppe to Caen, which became known as Normandy. The duchy did not include the Islands which, together with the Cotentin, were still under Breton rule, never having been conquered by the Franks. They were therefore not part of Francia and so, it can be argued, never under the French Crown up to this time.

They were conquered by the Normans only in 933, under the leadership of Rollo's son, William Longsword, and after that date Normans crossed to the Islands in substantial numbers. Many of the rocks around the Islands such as Etac and Ecrehou were given Norse names which resemble those given to coastal landmarks in the Shetlands and Orkneys. But the new occupants of the Islands had been living among a population speaking Norman French for over a generation. The Norse language left little trace while Norman French soon established itself. It was only in law and government that the Norse influence was to survive. The 'custom' of Normandy, which was codified in 1199, just before the conquest of the region by the French Crown, remained in use until the French Revolution and, in a modified form, it remains in use in the Channel Islands today. The most unusual feature of the Norse legacy is the *Clameur de Haro,* a device by which those with a grievance can claim to have it considered in law. The name Jersey (usually spelt in early documents with a G) also dates from Norse times, from a charter of 1025. The final *ey* is the Norse word for island, while *gers* is either Old Frisian for 'grass' or a Norwegian personal name.

Up to 1066 the Channel Islands formed part of the Duchy of Normandy. When, in that year, William I of Normandy (the Conqueror) became William I of England, the Islands were united under the English Crown. It is therefore the Islanders' proud boast that they were never conquered by England, indeed, they sometimes claim that the opposite is true. The Battle of Hastings in 1066 had an enormous effect on the linguistic history of England and later on that of Wales, Scotland and Ireland. The Norman French language was imposed absolutely as the medium of government and administration, entirely supplanting the language of the conquered. The new circumstances were summed up in the lines *'Li reis amat mult ses Normanz; les Engleis enveia as chans'* (The king loves his Normans greatly; the English he sent to the dogs). By 1110 the Old English literary language had fallen into disuse and it was not to recover until Chaucer's time. Norman French expressed the dominance of the Conqueror and the prestige of France, the most advanced country in Europe at this time. England was a province on the periphery of the Angevin Empire. Only about 5% of the population acquired French, however, for the common people went on speaking English. But French continued as the language of education, literature, parliament and law for another three hundred years. It was in protest against this situation that John Trevisa, in his translation of Ranulph Higden's *Polychronicon* (1387), protested with the sarcastic assertion that 'Jack would be a gentilman if he coulde speke frensshe'.

Jersey was separated from England in 1087 when, on the Conqueror's death, his eldest son Robert succeeded to the Duchy and his brother William, surnamed Rufus, became King of England. Six years after the accession of Henry I, he invaded Normandy, defeated his brother Robert's army at the battle of Tinchebrai and took possession of Normandy and the Islands. In 1135, however, on the succession to the English throne of Stephen, the territory passed to Geoffrey of Anjou. On the succession of Henry II, England and the Duchy were re-united once more. Finally, in 1204, the French King defeated King John's army and took possession of Normandy. The Channel Islands remained faithful to the English Crown. Eleven years later King John visited Jersey and, as a reward for their loyalty, presented to the Islands what is known as 'The Constitutions of King John' which gave them a form of self-government which has continued up to the present time. These Constitutions have been disputed at various times but were accepted by the Royal Commissioners in 1860.

From being the scourge of Western civilisation the Normans, after three generations of settlement and assimilation, came to be among its greatest champions. During the second half of the twelfth century Norman kings in England and Sicily were establishing architectural styles, social customs, systems of justice and administration which were to last for centuries and, at the heart of this Plantagenet kingdom, were the Channel Islands. It was at this time that Wace, a Jerseyman who declared, *'En l'isle de Gersui fu nez'* (On the Isle of Jersey I was born), was chosen by Henry II to write the *Roman de Brut*, a legendary account of the early history of Britain. This work derives much of its material from the Welsh writer Geoffrey of Monmouth but some of it drew upon Breton legends which had survived in the Islands. Wace's other great work was the *Roman de Rou*, the history of the Dukes of Normandy from the first settlements of the Norsemen. With the assimilation of the nobility for whom Wace wrote, Norman French was replaced by English in England. The special historical interest of the Channel Islands today is that they alone represent the Normandy to which Europe in general, and England in particular, owe so much.

This survival is largely due to the fact that, only some twenty years after Wace's death around 1184, from being at the centre of the Norman kingdom they found themselves on the periphery of the English. For the next three hundred years England and France were at war, and during the whole period they fought one another over the Channel Islands. The Islands' many forts were built in this period. The French occupied Jersey on several occasions, only to lose them whenever the English armies arrived. At last, it was agreed by the Treaty of 1483, the Islands and the sea around them 'as far as the sight of man goes', were to be considered as neutral territory, so that the French should not attack them nor the English use them as a military base.

At the Reformation the Channel Islands, largely French-speaking, took their religious ideas from the Calvinism of continental Europe rather than from the Lollards of the Englishman John Wycliff. Moreover, the Reformation was generally associated with the use of the spoken language, instead of Latin, in church services. As a result, the French of the Channel Islands became the language of worship for the common people. The increasing bitterness of the religious conflicts in France after the Massacre of St Bartholomew in 1572 caused still more Huguenot refugees to seek shelter in the Islands. It was therefore a Presbyterian rather than an episcopal church which grew up in the Islands, after the final break with Rome. The first synod met on Guernsey in 1564 and representatives from all the Islands attended. To this period belongs the re-entry of Sark and Alderney to the full community of the Islands, the one in 1559 and the other in 1565. Up to now they had been occupied by the French, and by pirates, or had been left deserted. The Channel Islands remained under the Calvinists until 1662 and the Restoration of Charles II, but their influence lasted much longer. When, at the end of the eighteenth century, John Wesley came to preach Methodism in the Islands the new faith enjoyed immediate success. In Guernsey today the Methodists are the most numerous of all the denominations. Everywhere in the Islands the word for a church is not *église* but *temple*.

During the Civil War the Presbyterianism of the common people put the Islands on the side of Parliament, which was mainly Presbyterian, against the King. Charles I raised his standard at Nottingham in August 1642 and in the following year fighting spread to the Islands. Guernsey was virtually besieged by Parliamentary forces for the next nine years under the Royalist Lieutenant-Governor Sir Peter Osborne. Jersey also held out against Cromwell's forces under Sir Philippe de Carteret who, on being arrested, declared, 'This island has nothing to do with Parliament, but only with the King in Council'. For the next eight years his nephew Sir George Carteret ruled Jersey which, despite its Calvinist traditions, gave him its nominal allegiance. The Lieutenant-Governor based his right to resist Parliament on the grounds that 'our laws and liberties differ from theirs, and though subjects of the same King, we have never had dealings with the English Parliament, save when necessary to ask permission to export wool from their country. All our charters are authenticated solely with the name of the King as Duke. Party squabbles in the English Parliament are no concern of ours. Let us remain

true to our Duke and our own constitution'. Sir George Carteret was appointed Vice-Admiral of Jersey in 1644. Over the
next four years, as the King's armies were crushed one by one,
he began launching attacks on shipping in the Channel. Captured ships were converted into privateers and Carteret's fortunes grew from their exploits. By 1651 his fleet had become a
menace and a force of 3,000 English soldiers, assisted by 900
Guernseymen, was sent to remove him from office. Jersey was
bombarded and Carteret surrendered. Because of this defiance, Jersey suffered more from military rule than Guernsey
during the Commonwealth and the Protectorate. Decrees
were issued incorporating the Islands as counties into the
English administrative system; but these were never carried
out.

In 1660, with the Restoration of the Monarchy, life in the
Channel Islands continued as before. Sir George Carteret was
granted a province in America which he named New Jersey.
The Book of Common Prayer, as revised in 1662, was translated into French and Anglican worship was introduced into
both Jersey and Guernsey. The Protestant inclinations of the
Islanders were re-inforced by the arrival of Huguenot refugees
after the Edict of Nantes in 1685. For the next hundred years
Guernsey prospered on the wealth created by privateering.
The French made several attempts to put an end to this trade,
especially during the Maritine War of 1779-83. At the same
time Jersey's political life was marked by conflict between the
Charlots, or supporters of Charles Lemprière, and the
Magots, originally a term of abuse meaning cheese-maggots,
defiantly adopted by the followers of the reformer, Dumaresq,
who preached the ideas of Voltaire and Rousseau. Just as in
the sixteenth century the ideology of the religious reformation
had come from the Calvinists in France, so in the next century
the political reformers were influenced by the En-
cyclopaedists.

The French Revolution was at first welcomed in the Islands,
as it was in England. But reaction set in even before France
declared war on England in 1793, mainly as a result of the
excesses of the Revolutionary Government which drove hundreds of refugees to the safety of the Islands. The town of St
Hélier grew rapidly at this period as the new arrivals built
homes for themselves. In the War between France and

England which followed the Revolution the Islands once again assumed their strategic importance, both for English forces and French exiles. In 1795 3,500 exiles sailed from Jersey but were defeated at Quiberon Bay off southern Brittany.

The history of the Islands from 1815 can be briefly described as their gradual evolution into the communities which they are today. They received their first substantial influx of English settlers—some 15,000 by 1840—after the battle of Waterloo when officers were returned there on half-pay. The result of this immigration was predictable. Shop-keepers and servants had to learn English. Newspapers in English were launched. By the end of the century, in the towns at least, English had ousted French as the medium of everyday intercourse. In 1834 the old currency of *livres tournois* was changed to the British system. Over the next hundred years, as one Reform Bill after another in Britain brought the vote to wider sections of the populations, so in both Jersey and Guernsey elected deputies were added to the States, the Parliaments of the Islands.

By today their constitutions are as follows. The Lieutenant-Governor and Bailiff are appointed by the Crown, the latter acting as Prime Minister and Speaker. Twelve senators, elected for a nine-year term, sit in the States of Jersey, together with the twelve Constables of the twelve parishes and twenty-eight deputies elected every three years. In Guernsey the States consist of the Bailiff, twelve *Conseillers,* thirty-three Deputies, ten representatives of the *Douzaines* or parish councils, and two from the States of Alderney. Guernsey is responsible for police, education, taxation, social services, public health and the airport of Alderney, but that Island also has its States, with a President, nine elected members, and six *Jurats* appointed by the Crown. On Sark the Dame appoints the three officers of the Seigniorial Court, with the Crown's approval: the *Sénéchal* or Magistrate, the *Prévôt* or sheriff and the *Greffier* or Registrar. Twelve deputies on the Chief Pleas are elected by the people of Sark. Local government is based on the parish, the *Douzaine* in Guernsey and the Parish Assembly in Jersey. Politics are organised on non-party lines at all levels, except that the Jersey Communist Party has some support among agricultural workers.

The connection between the Channel Islands and Britain

has been severed only once during the present century: between 1940 and 1945 they were occupied by the Germans. The only part of the United Kingdom to suffer this fate, the Islands were prized by Hitler and defended with a force of over 30,000 men and 114,000 mines—the most highly fortified area for their size in Europe. The Germans arrived in Guernsey by air on 30 June 1940 and in Jersey the following day. Alderney, strategically the most important Island, was totally evacuated of its inhabitants and used as a camp for slave workers brought there by the infamous *Todt* organisation to build defences. Almost half the population of Guernsey, some 20,000 people including all the school-children, left the Island for England. Only about 10,000 people, or a fifth of the population, left Jersey. At first, the generals in charge of the Islands were, according to most accounts, firm but not vicious rulers, provided that their orders were obeyed in every detail. Food, fuel and clothing were in short supply, radios were prohibited, the economy was ruined by the introduction of worthless *Reichsmarks*. The principal figures in the Islands' public life remained at their posts: Alexander Coutanche, President of Jersey's Superior Council and Civil Governor, and in Guernsey Ambrose Sherwill, *Procureur* and President of the Island's Controlling Committee. Prayers for the British Royal Family were allowed in the churches, but *God Save the King* was banned. German lessons were made compulsory in the schools. Hitler made plans for turning the Islands into a 'Strength through Joy' camp after his victory. All vehicles had to drive on the right. In 1941 sweep-stakes on the Derby race were openly organised. A German soldier caught stealing was executed. During the closing stages of the War, however, especially after the failure of the bomb-plot against Hitler in July 1944, and as Soviet forces approached the German heartland, the commanders of the Islands were replaced by Nazis. Count von Schmettow, Commander-in-Chief of the Channel Islands since September 1940, was replaced in February 1945 by Rear-Admiral Hüffmeier, an extreme Nazi. The Islands' leaders, during the last months of the War, dreaded the possibility that this man might try to hold out after a German capitulation and so bring about an Allied bombardment and the destruction of the population they had worked so hard to save. But when the time for surrender came, Hüffmeier's representative signed readily on 9 May 1945.

The occupation was a traumatic experience for the Channel Islanders and there is not always agreement among them about the details of these five years. There was no sabotage and the Islanders were mostly passive. But although tempers ran high during 1945, good sense usually prevailed and there were few reprisals: no case was shown to have sufficient evidence to merit criminal prosecution. Profits made during the War were reclaimed by retrospective taxation and an orderly, hard-working people set about the task of restoring the Islands' economy.

Since 1945 the Channel Islands have returned to prosperity. Improved communications by air and sea have linked them even more closely to the mainland of the United Kingdom. Agriculture and horticulture have been greatly improved, particularly the growing of tomatoes and flowers. Tourism was also developed, however, with the result that life in the Islands has been transformed during the last thirty years. The number of English people settling in the Islands has increased rapidly, so that immigrants are now in a majority on all four Islands. Among the attractions are a milder climate, and a quieter life for those of pensionable age and a tax system favourable to investment and business.

The development of tourism and the arrival of wealthy residents have had predictable effects on the indigenous language and culture of the Islands. French was the official language of government up to 1946, but although some legal documents are in French only, English has replaced it almost everywhere else. The proceedings of the States, after their opening by the recitation of the Lord's Prayer in French are conducted in English. Commercial life is almost completely in the hands of English immigrants except in a few rural districts. The streets of St Hélier have signs in both French and English. Tombstones erected before 1900 are usually in French, while those erected after 1914 are in English. Norman-French personal names still abound. French is compulsory as a second language in the schools from the age of seven, but Norman-French is not taught at any level. A quarterly bulletin in Jersey-French carries news, verses and stories. Attempts to start classes for the teaching of Jersey-French under the auspices of the Evening Institute have met with little success in recent years.

Interest in local culture is confined to the *Société Jersiaise*, founded in 1873. Among its patrons are Sir John Davis, the Island's Lieutenant-Governor, and Sir Robert Le Masurier, the Bailiff; based at the museum in St Hélier, its aims are the study of Jersey's archaeology, history, natural history and folk-lore. The only organisation concerned with Norman-French is the *Assembliée d'Jèrriaise* which was founded in 1951. Its aim is *'la consèrvâtion dé l'usage dé la Langue Jèrriaise par touous les mouoyens pôssibl'yes* (the conservation of the use of the Jersey language by all means possible). But it has only a handful of members and is not active. Members of this society insist that the speech of Jersey is not a *patois* or dialect but a language in its own right. An annual festival is held under the society's auspices; it bears no relation to the Welsh institution but is called an *eisteddfod*, for what reason there seems to be no explanation. Guernsey also has both a *Société Guernesiaise* and an *Assembllaie Dguernesiaise* with similar aims to those of their Jersey equivalents. Public interest in Jersey French was shown in 1966 on the publication of a *Dictionaire Jersiais-Français* by Frank Le Maistre. There is not much literature written in Norman French, however. The Islands' most famous literary resident was undoubtedly Victor Hugo, exiled by Louis Bonaparte to Jersey and Guernsey between 1855 and 1870. It was here that Hugo wrote *Les Travailleurs de la Mer* (The Toilers of the Sea), which he dedicated 'to this corner of ancient Normandy', as well as two other major works, *L'Homme qui Rit,* and probably the greatest of all his novels, *Les Misérables.* Anthony Trollope was among the English writers who have lived in the Islands, and Elinor Glyn was born in Jersey.

The twelve parish churches of Jersey are all Anglican and belong to the diocese of Winchester; services are in English, except on special occasions when French is used. A few of the many Methodist chapels hold services in French and there are two Roman Catholic churches in St Hélier which use French regularly. There is a strong element of francophobia among Protestants in the Islands these days. The only French newspaper published in the Islands, *Les Chroniques de Jersey*, ceased publication in 1959. There is a weekly article in Norman-French by George Le Feuvre in the *Jersey Evening Post*. There is no French on Channel T.V., the local television service, but French stations are obtainable from all parts of the Islands, and French newspapers are on sale.

The Islands' proximity to France has little effect on their cultural life. Farm-workers from Normandy and Brittany arrive in fairly large numbers but only for the season. Social attitudes among the Islanders remain solidly 'British' and there is widespread pride in the saying that the Channel Islands are 'the jewels in the English Crown'. There is little hope among them that the Norman-French dialects, now spoken only by the older generation, will survive for more than a few more decades and little evidence to suggest that in this view they are not entirely realistic.

4 DENMARK

Constitution: Kingdom

Area: 16,614 square miles

Population: 5·051 million (1974)

Capital: Copenhagen

Administrative divisions: 14 counties

Present Government: The Social Democratic Party; elected 1975

Language of majority: Danish

THE GERMANS OF NORTH SLESVIG

North Slesvig is that part of Denmark on the border with West Germany where, in the *Amter* or counties of Tønder, Åbenrå, Sønderborg and Haderslev, but particularly in the four towns of those names, there live about 23,000 people whose first language is German. Known in Danish as *Sydjylland* (South Jutland), this part of the Zimbrian Peninsula became Danish territory in 1920 when the frontier between Denmark and Germany was fixed at Flensburg (Danish: *Flensborg*), leaving on the southern side of the river Koenigsau a Danish-speaking minority in South Schleswig.*

The area of North Slesvig (Danish: *Nord Slesvig)* where German-speakers are the autochthonous inhabitants is about 1,530 square miles, with a total population of approximately 255,000 (1971). It is the northernmost point of the entire German-language area, with the densest concentration of German-speakers in villages along the frontier. The reason for the inclusion in Denmark of such places as Tønder (German: *Tondern), Højer (Hoyer)* and Tingler *(Tingleff),* where the majorities in 1919 were German-speaking, is that in order to concede as much territory as possible to Denmark, in compensation for war-losses, the voting in the northern districts, described in the Treaty of Versailles as Zone 1, was carried out *en bloc* whereas in Zone 2, to the south, voting was by individual parishes. On 10 February 1920, 75,431 inhabitants of Zone 1 voted in favour of joining Denmark and 25,319—more or less the whole German-speaking population—voted for union with Germany with the result that the whole of Zone 1, forty-one parishes in all, was taken from Germany and given to the Danes. In Zone 2, on 14 March 1920, 51,724 voted in favour of Germany and only 12,859 of Denmark. On 15 June 1920 the southern limit of Zone 1, about forty-two miles long, was declared the new State border, and on 1 July King Christian of Denmark rode across the old frontier on a white horse, to the rapturous welcome of his new subjects.

*As the history of the Schleswig-Holstein question is described in Chapter 8, together with the Danish minority of South Schleswig, the present account deals mainly with the German-speaking majority of North Slesvig since 1920.

The German-speakers of North Slesvig, who had played a leading role in maintaining Prussia's rule in Schleswig-Holstein during the nineteenth century and who had enjoyed full linguistic equality with the Danish-speaking majority, now found themselves in a difficult position as a minority within the Danish State. They had no leaders, few civil servants and almost no teachers of their own because around 15,000 of their number had left for Germany between 1919 and 1921. Nevertheless, anxious to resist attempts at assimilation, they began immediately to organise themselves in a political movement, the *Schleswiger Wahlerverein* (Electoral Association of Schleswig). Their leader was Johannes Schmidt-Wodder, a pastor who had founded a Society for friendly relations between Danes and Germans in 1907. From 1920 to 1939 he represented the minority with intelligence and tact in the Danish Parliament. During those years the party's support, based mainly on its call for a new referendum, increased from 7,500 votes to over 15,000. Johannes Schmidt-Wodder was succeeded in 1939 by Jens Möller who represented the German-speakers in Copenhagen until 1953.

First among the aims of the *Wahlerverein* was the reopening of German schools and this was achieved almost immediately, in 1920. German newspapers were allowed and by 1930 the minority's cultural life was flourishing once more. On the other hand the Danish Government decided against special legislation for the minority, mainly because it was generally agreed that the régime was so liberal that such laws were considered unnecessary even by the German-speakers. But Danish now became the language of officialdom, as it continues to be today. The only exception is that street-names and place-names appear in both languages in *Tønder* and Åbenrå (German: *Apenrade).*

The minority's development suffered a set-back when Hitler's army invaded Denmark on 9 April 1940. There had been mounting tension in the years up to then, especially as the *Wahlerverein* began to be infiltrated by Nazis, but after 1940 open hostility was shown by the Danes. On Hitler's defeat there were recriminations and reprisals against the families of those who had been conscripted by the Third *Reich:* over 3,000 German-speakers were convicted of collaboration, their land and investments confiscated, pastors deported and all German schools promptly closed. But once again the Danish Government did its utmost to heal the wounds inflicted by the War. A new organisation, the *Bund Deutscher Nordschleswiger* (League of German North Schleswigers) was formed in November 1945 with a constitution which included a declaration of loyalty to the King of Denmark, and the following year German-language schools were allowed. The new spirit of reconciliation resulted in the Bonn-Copenhagan declarations, of 29 March 1955 which guaranteed the free development of the minorities on either side of the frontier. By 1968 there were twenty-eight German-language secondary schools and twenty-four primary schools. All the minority's schools are private but receive the larger part of their funds from the Danish Government. Their administration is co-ordinated by the school association, *Nordschleswiger Schulverein*. Certificates awarded to German-speakers in Denmark are recognised in West Germany and this arrangement is reciprocal.

In 1947 the *Bund* began constesting elections and in 1953 a farmer named Schmidt-Oxbull was elected with 9,721 votes to the *Folketing* in Copenhagen. The party lost its only seat in the Danish Parliament, however, when it failed in 1964 to win the necessary 2% of the votes cast. It has not regained a seat since then, but continues to win seats on local councils. In the Regional Council of North Slesvig, which has twenty-five members in all, the party has one representative. Like its counterpart in South Schleswig, the minority was compensated for the loss of its mandate by the establishment of an advisory committee, on which it has three seats, for good relations with both the Danish and German Governments.

The *Bund* is primarily concerned with problems of unemployment and migration. Mainly an agricultural area, about one-third of North Slesvig's German-speakers are farmers, one-fifth industrial workers and the rest employed in commerce and the professions. Because of the region's peripheral status it has not enjoyed the prosperity of areas further to the north and south. The exodus of workers goes on in the direction of Aarhus and Copenhagen where they become assimilated, usually losing the German language after one generation. Few Germans move into the area from south of the border. For this reason the German-speaking minority is decreasing slightly from year to year.

Despite this decline, the social and cultural life of the minority is well organised and vigorous. The *Bund* publishes a daily newspaper *Der Nordschleswiger*, founded in 1946. Although there are no radio or television programmes on the Danish networks for German-speakers, they listen regularly to transmissions from West Germany. Much depends on contacts with Germany, which are unhampered by the Danish authorities. The minority has its own libraries stocked with books published in Germany, its choirs and orchestras are led by German musicians, its evening classes organised by Kiel University, and many cross the frontier for theatre performances and other cultural events at Flensburg.

Even before Denmark's entry into the European Economic Community, the Danish-German frontier was always one of the easiest to cross in Western Europe. Taking full advantage of the just and generous terms of the inter-State declarations of 1955, the German-speakers of North Slesvig are in close contact with their neighbours in South Schleswig and have developed a wide variety of organisations through which their ethnic personality can be expressed. Unlike German-speakers in other areas, such as the Eastern Cantons of Belgium, they have successfully overcome the tragedy of the War years, and are now well established within the host-State of Denmark, of which the tolerance and goodwill towards its German-speakers have been in all respects exemplary.

THE FAROE ISLANDERS

The Faroe Islands lie in the North Atlantic, about mid-way between the Shetlands and Iceland, 824 miles from Denmark to which they belong, and 355 miles from the coast of Norway, the nearest mainland. The total population of the eighteen islands which are inhabited was 38,731 in 1972—0·8% of the population of Denmark with Greeland—the total land area is 540 square miles, and the capital Tórshavn. The biggest islands are Streymoy, Eysturoy, Vágoy and Suðuroy.

The people of the Faroe Islands (Faroese: *Føroyar*, Danish: *Faerøerne*, both meaning Sheep Islands) trace their ancestry to the Vikings who settled there between A.D. 800 and 1000, from Norway and the northern islands of Scotland, having first driven out communities of Gaelic monks. Tórshavn is named after the Nordic god Thor. Their language, Faroese *(Foroyskt)* is most closely related to Icelandic and rural Norwegian *(Landsmål)* but has developed separately as a language in its own right.

A province of Norway from 1035, the Faroes passed to the Danish Crown as a Norwegian dependency in 1380. When Denmark ceded Norway to Sweden under the Treaty of Kiel in 1814 the Faroes remained with Denmark, along with Iceland and Greenland. Like the other two former Norwegian territories, the Islands should have gone, at least in theory, to Sweden. That this did not happen was partly due to the ignorance of the Swedish representative at the Treaty conference who was, it is said, not sure of his historical facts, but also because Sweden was more interested in unifying the Scandinavian peninsula than in acquiring distant, impoverished provinces of no economic or strategic significance. Norway, however, never fully accepted the conditions of the 1814 Treaty and, as Norwegian law continued to operate in the Faroes, pressed for their recognition as Norwegian territory. The Danes responded by abolishing the *Løgting*, the Faroese Parliament, probably the oldest parliamentary institution in Europe, and the Faroes were demoted to the status of a Danish *Amt*, or county.

Although the Faroes were represented in the Danish Parliament from 1851, this decision to incorporate the Islands was fairly typical of Danish attitudes during the nineteenth century. Despite the fact that the Faroese are temperamentally more akin to Icelanders than to Danes, their individuality as an ethnic group was rarely recognised by the Danes who considered the Islands as a colony, or at best a province. Danish officials were known, for the most part, to be arrogant towards the Faroese, refusing to recognise their language at any level, although most were monoglots at this time, and generally despising them.

In the year 1844 the Faroese appealed for the establishment of schools in the Islands, there being none, only to boycott them the following year because, when established, they neither taught nor tolerated the Faroese language. Ten years later the Danish Government, exasperated, passed a law which allowed Faroese parents to decide for themselves whether or not their children should be sent to school. These early difficulties between the Faroese and the Danes took place shortly after the Danish State's bankruptcy and against a background of economic decline in both Denmark and the Faroes. Poverty was rife on the Islands, partly because Denmark was unable to provide subsidies and partly because the Faroese practice of *gavelkind* had reduced the little cultivable land to unviable units.

There was further trouble in 1850 when Denmark's new Constitution was extended to include the Faroes—without the consent of the Faroese people. Although their numbers had by now dwindled below the necessary minimum, the Faroese were nevertheless allowed to elect one member to the *Folketing*, the Danish Parliament, and another to the second chamber, the *Landsting*. The Danish administration was greatly shocked when its candidate was defeated and a radical, outspoken Faroese patriot was elected as one of two Islanders representing the Faroes in both chambers. Niels Winther (1822-92) immediately began a campaign for the recognition of the Faroes on the same basis as Iceland, which had successfully opposed closer union with Denmark.

Winther's first two objectives were the re-establishment of the *Løgting* with similar powers to those of the Icelandic Parliament *(Althing)* and the end of the Danish trade monopoly which was considered to have reduced the Islands to their economic plight. His first objective was achieved in 1852 when the *Løgting* was reconstituted, although only with consultative powers. The abolition of the trade monopoly followed four years later: free trade brought an almost immediate improvement in the Faroese economy for now the people left the land and took to the sea, where greater, quicker profits could be made. Soon, despite what was still an extremely hard life and a legislation far behind Denmark's (there was no unemployment benefit, for example) the Faroes were able to support a larger population. Only 8,922 in 1850, the population grew to 15,230 in 1901 and to 24,000 in 1930.

After the abolition of the trade monopoly, the Islanders' attention was again turned to education which was still suffering from the unpopularity of the earlier legislation. The first secondary school was opened, at Tórshavn, in 1861 and a teachers' training college in 1870. The language of instruction in all schools at this time was Danish, according to law, but in practice much of the teaching was done in Faroese—although this was not officially recognised until 1938. The interest of the great Danish scholar and patriot N. F. S. Grundtvig (1783-1872) in the Faroes as a source of genuine Nordic culture led to the establishment in 1899 of a Folk High School in the Islands. The Folk High Schools of Denmark had been founded, from around 1844 on, in response to the growth of democracy and the threat that Danish culture might be overwhelmed by German-speakers from the south. They aimed at giving the Danish peasantry a liberal education and awakening in it a love of its own cultural heritage. The Faroese, many of whose leaders had attended the Folk High Schools in Denmark, now formed their own cultural movement, the *Føringafelag*.

This revival of interest in the culture of the Faroes, particularly in their language, had its roots in the eighteenth century, with Jens Christian Svabo (1746-1824) the first philologist to have studied the ancient ballads and legends. Faroese had ceased to be a written language after the Reformation, when Danish was introduced in churches and law-courts. But it had lived on among the people and during the nineteenth century its oral literature began to be written down for the first time. The outstanding pioneer in this work was the clergyman V. U. Hammershaimb (1819-1909), Provost to the Faroes, who created a written form of the language on etymological principles which is the basis for modern Faroese.

Nevertheless, by the beginning of the twentieth century the Faroese language was still regarded by many in Denmark as a simple curiosity. It was spoken by only a few thousand Islanders, albeit the entire population, and was rarely believed to be an adequate means of communication outside the fishing and farming communities which were its home. Freedom of trade between the Islands and Denmark had opened up the archipelago for merchants from Copenhagen who had started businesses to exploit the fishing industry. The old patriarchal, self-sufficient, peasant society had begun to crumble, and with it the Faroese language. Danish was supreme not only in the church but in administration, law, business and soon, to some extent, even in the everyday speech of the people, especially around Tórshavn and the larger villages.

Alarmed at the prospect of imminent extinction for their language, and inspired by the achievement of Norway's independence in 1905, the Faroese people now began to organise themselves in a national movement with self-government as its aim. Denmark was puzzled and disappointed when, in 1906, a Home Rule Party calling itself the *Sjálvstýrisflokkurin* was founded by a farmer and poet Jóannes Patursson (1866-1946). With the preservation of Faroese at the top of its programme, this new party made slow progress at first. By 1914 the Unionist Party, the *Sambandsflokkurin*, formed in opposition to the nationalists by supporters of the Danish *Venstre* party, had the support of two-thirds of the *Løgting*. However, the Home Rulers had won the allegiance of younger people and by 1918 it had a majority. As it gained ground the national movement met increasing opposition from the unionists who—although they considered themselves to be as good Faroese as the nationalists—feared that the general introduction of the Faroese language into schools and churches would mean that, in time, Danish would be neglected and eventually forgotten.

In 1912 the *Sjálvstýri* acquired a martyr in the cause of Faroese in the schools when a young teacher, Louis Zachariasen (1890-1960) insisted on using the language in the classroom. When rebuked by the Danish *Amtmand*, he resigned his post. The controversy which followed took many a bitter turn in the pages of the Islands' two newspapers, the old-established *Dimmalaetting* supporting the unionist and the *Tingakrossur* siding with the nationalists. Between 1920 and 1938 the Faroese language continued to win ground in a number of minor official sectors. In 1920 the telephone directory was published in Faroese, in 1925 the language was accepted for postal purposes and from 1927 the proceedings of the *Løgting* were recorded in it. By the outbreak of the Second World War the language controversy had been virtually concluded in accordance with the aims of the *Sjálvstýri*. One of the most decisive of the *Løgting's* actions which commanded the support of all parties was the sponsorship of a major series of publications in Faroese which helped the language to reach maturity. The party-political dispute, often very bitter and exacerbated by the intervention of Danish officials, resulted—more by evolutionary than by revolutionary means—in victory for the language campaigners. Today, while Danish is still taught in all the schools as a second language, Faroese is the first language of all the Islanders and has the same full official status as Danish.

Following the success of the Home Rule Party, the *Løgting* was reformed in 1923 and given more powers. All its members were to be elected and the appointed members were removed. Although remaining as a county, the special position of the Faroes was to be respected in all matters. Many Danish laws were declared obsolete and all legislation affecting the Islands, whether specifically or generally, had to be approved by the *Løgting* first. However, although the Faroes now had wider powers for internal self-government, their attempts to express themselves as a nation in symbolic terms were thwarted by Denmark. Flags having much significance in the Scandinavian countries, the Faroese flag—a red cross with a blue border on a white ground—was for long a real cause of controversy. The Danes had acquiesced in its use when it was first designed in 1919 but protested when it was flown at the Icelandic *Althing* celebrations in 1930, so that it had to be lowered. The same year, during their celebration of the Faroese national day, St Olaf's Day (29 July), the *Danebrog*, the Danish flag, was cut down by Faroese nationalists and the Danish *Amtmand* walked out of the ceremony in protest.

It was not until the Second World War, under British occupation, that the Faroese flag was allowed and then, prosaically enough, only to distinguish Faroese ships from those of German-occupied Denmark. Throughout the War connections between German-occupied Denmark and the Faroese were completely severed and during five years of isolation the cause of Faroese nationalism flourished. The internal administration of the Islands was left in the hands of the Faroese and, under these conditions, a second nationalist party, the *Fólkaflokkurin* (People's Party), was formed, demanding independence from Denmark. In 1943 this party had a near-majority in the *Løgting*. Britain refused its demand, however, believing that the question of Faroese independence was a matter to be settled with Denmark after the War was over.

In the autumn of 1945 the strength of the parties in the *Løgting* was: People's Party eleven seats, Unionists six seats and Social Democrats *(Javnaðarflokkurin)* six seats. The Unionists were now in favour of the closest possible association with Denmark, while the Social Democrats and the old Home Rule Party (which had temporarily lost all its seats) wanted self-government with legislative powers for the *Løgting* and full recognition for the Faroese language. The People's Party advocated a common Crown and foreign policy but in all other matters the maximum independence. On the Danish side there was little interest in a very loose association: failing maintenance of 'national unity', which they would have preferred, the Danes declared themselves in favour of complete separation. After protracted negotiations between Faroese representatives and Copenhagen, a proposal was drafted in 1946 which was intended to provide limited self-government for the Islands. But none of the Faroese parties was satisfied: The Unionists thought it went too far and the others not far enough. A referendum was therefore held at which the Faroese were asked to express their preference for either limited self-government, as proposed, or complete independence. The voting was 5,660 (48·7% of the votes cast) in favour of independence and 5,499 (47·2%) in favour of the proposal; 481 votes were deliberately spoilt by people who wanted dominion status but not secession. On the strength of this result and when one member changed his mind in favour of independence, the People's Party, supported by one Social Democrat, declared an independent Faroese State. The Danish Government, on the other hand, considered the result inconclusive and, when it refused to endorse unilateral action by the *Løgting*, the King dissolved the chamber.

At the election which followed, the People's Party won eight seats, the Unionists six, the Social Democrats four and the Home Rule Party two. Renewed negotiations after this victory for the nationalists led to the Home Rule Act of 23 March, 1948, which granted the *Løgting* legislative powers in a number of fields, notably the Faroese economy. A governing council, the *Landsstýrid* was appointed by the *Løgting* as the executive body. The Home Rule Act consists of two schedules: List A and List B. The first includes such matters as education, public health, harbours, roads, power supplies and cultural institutions. List B includes matters of both local and general interest such as church affairs, police, radio and air transport. It was decided that responsibility for matters on List A would be transferred from the Danish Government to the *Løgting* as soon as either requested it. Those on List B would be transferred only after negotiation. In 1948 the Løgting took over a large number of matters on List A, including housing, taxation, communications, employment, agriculture and fishing. From List B, with the subsequent sanction of the Danish Government, it took charge of broadcasting. At the same time the Faroese language was recognised as the principal language of the Islands, the use of Danish being permissible in all public sectors, and both languages were to be taught in the schools. The new law also granted the Faroese the right to fly their own flag on all Government buildings and on ships registered in the Islands, and a year later they obtained their own currency notes.

The fundamental principle of the 1948 Act is that the Faroes, to the extent they so wish, can take over various responsibilities as 'special matters' relating to the Islands. This means that the *Løgting* and the *Landsstýrid*, as they acquire legislative and executive powers in these spheres, have to bear the costs incurred. The Act has been the subject of more or less permanent debate in the Faroes since the year it was passed. In recent years this debate has moved from the general to the particular and now revolves around the annual grants made by the Danish Exchequer to the *Løgting*, amounting to about £3·5 million in 1968, and in the growing realisation that if the Faroes are about to accept even more responsibility their administrative apparatus must be improved.

Opinion in the Islands is generally agreed that the Faroese community, with its own cultural background, should be developed into a self-governing unit with a comparatively high degree of economic independence from the outside world, including Denmark. Many of the necessary conditions, it is claimed, are already present, not the least of which is no doubt a high standard of education, as in the other Scandinavian countries. Faroese enterprise, moreover, is in all essentials a result of local decisions, leadership and manpower. Public investment in roads, power stations, harbours and so on, makes for a modern, highly efficient economy based on the fishing industry. But there are problems connected with this extensive and rapidly increasing public expenditure, since a large part of it is met by the Danish Exchequer. It is becoming vitally important that private investment should increase and, at the same time, that the current rise in revenue and wealth should be maintained because, in the last resort, the Faroes are dependent on being able to maintain their population.

In recent decades the population of the Islands has grown at roughly the same rate as that of Denmark; in fact the birthrate has been higher but net emigration has also been greater. It is estimated that, despite a drop in the birth-rate which is expected to follow urbanisation, the population will grow to around 47,000 by 1978, of whom 17,000 will be living in Tórshavn, a town with about 10,500 inhabitants at present. These figures take into account the emigration which has been a traditional aspect of life in the Islands. Between 1961 and 1965, for example, emigration was 26% of the national growth. Young Faroese leave in search of work and education; many marry and settle in Denmark. Few return to the Islands, especially those with professional qualifications, for it is not difficult for them to educate themselves to the point where they find it almost impossible to find employment at home.

The economy of the Faroes depends almost entirely on the deep-sea fishing industry: over 90% of Faroese exports consist of fish and fish products. Only about thirty-five square miles of land are cultivated and only 3·2% of the population are engaged in agriculture. The little land that is available is given over almost entirely to the native breed of Faroese sheep. Even so, the Islands cannot supply all their own mutton: they are net importers of all foods—except fish. This economic imbalance does not mean, however, that all Faroese are fishermen. The relatively high income level, thanks to efficient methods and government grants corresponding to about 15% of the gross national product, creates a large demand for housing, crafts and public services: the majority of the Islanders are engaged in these occupations. Fishing remains crucial to the whole economy, of course, for when the fishermen's wages are good, everyone benefits. Since 1968 fish prices have been going up and this trend has contributed to the renewed expansion that has marked the Faroese economy during the last five years. In 1970 a trade surplus was recorded for the first time, with exports totalling £18million as against imports of £16·25million. A quarter of these exports went to Denmark, another quarter to the countries of the European Economic Community and a half to other countries. Such figures explain why Faroese politicians, like Attli Dam, are united on the issue of protecting the fishing grounds in the North Atlantic: at stake is the very survival, in the case of the Faroes, of an entire people. Indeed, when Denmark applied to join the Common Market in 1967, retention of the fishing limits around the Islands was a minimal condition and the General Election of 1970 made this abundantly clear.

In that year the *Løgting* consisted of twenty-six members: six Unionists, five members of the People's Party, one each from the Progress Party and the Home Rule Party, seven Social Democrats and six from the Republican Party *(Tjódveldisflokkurin)*, founded in 1946. All had campaigned on platforms opposed to the threat of foreigners, especially boats from Britain, fishing inside Faroese territorial waters, and their success was in direct proportion to their respective policies on this question. When, in 1973, Denmark was admitted to the European Economic Community, it was agreed that the Faroese could postpone a decision on whether they wished to join for another three years, and the matter is currently under consideration by the *Løgting*. At the general election of 7 November 1974 there was little change in the political complexion of the Faroes, except that the Home Rule Party increased its representation to two seats (1,433 votes) at the expense of the Unionists who won five seats (4,067); the Social Democrats kept their seven (5,118), the Republicans their six (4,463) and the Progress Party its single seat (489).

The *Løgting* is unlike any other legislative assembly in Europe in that it has a variable number of members. Twenty are elected by constituencies and supplementary seats are then distributed to parties by a system of proportional representation. Up to ten supplementary seats can be allocated and so the *Løgting* can have from twenty to thirty members. In turn the *Løgting* appoints the five members of the *Landsstyrið*, the Executive Council, including its Chairman, the *Løgmadur* (Lawman) or Prime Minister, on a similar basis. The political pattern is complicated further by the fact that there are two fundamental criteria to which the parties can conform. In addition to the socio-political approach, where they divide in a manner not essentially different from their counterparts in other Scandinavian countries, there is the equally important question of how they regard the relationship between the Faroes and Denmark: 'the degree of separation'. In this second respect the *Løgting* is divided into six groups, as the result of the 1970 election showed, of which four have been more or less equal since 1956. From 1962 to 1966 the *Løgting* was formed by parties requiring changes in the Home Rule Act, but since then it has consisted of members less critical of the *status quo*. In the 'fifties a 'conservative ' Government held office; there has never been a Socialist Government, although the success of the Republican Party in 1970 caused speculation as to whether the Islands were moving towards the left. It is apparent too that while the party-political dispute, which originated in the first decade of this century, cannot be said to have ended, the basic assumptions have gradually evolved so that the Unionists, a generation or two later, now stand more or less where the first Home Rulers stood in 1906, while demands for a Faroese Republic seem to be growing. Nevertheless, the Islands still send two representatives to the Danish Parliament in Copenhagen.

Meanwhile, the cultural life of the Faroes has also developed at an astonishing pace since the Second World War. The Faroese language is now the natural medium for all teaching; it is used in the Island's legislature and on radio (there is no television), in the churches and in theatres. Children of Danish parents who live in the Faroes must learn the language in order to attend the official schools, just as all Faroese children are obliged to learn Danish. Six newspapers with editions of between 1,500 and 6,000 copies each and twenty magazines are published in Faroese, including the principal literary quarterly *Vardin*, as well as an average of forty books a year, of which about half are for educational purposes and the rest novels, stories, poetry and translations.

A good deal of Faroese literature has appeared during this century. Among the most important poets are J. H. O. Djurhuus (1881-1948), Hans A. Djurhuus (1883-1951), Christian Matras (born 1900), Karsten Hoydal (born 1921) and Regin Dahl (born 1920). The prose-writers, some of whose work is in Danish, include Jergen-Frantz Jacobsen (1900-38), William Heinesen (born 1900), and Heðin Brú, the pseudonym of H. J. Jacobsen (born 1900) whose novels and short stories have been translated into English and other languages. Among books now available in Faroese are the Bible, the *Iliad*, the Icelandic Sagas, the plays of Shakespeare, and a variety of contemporary works, both classical and popular, from many countries. Books in Faroese have to take their place in the libraries and shops with books in Danish, of course, and—given the inevitably small editions and sales—the Faroese press and publishing industry are heavily subsidised. The *Løgting* is responsible for all financial support to the arts, including the National Museum, Library and Art Gallery. Faroese artists, such as the painter S. J. Mikines (born 1907) and the sculptor Janus Kamban (born

1912) have produced work which is admired in the Faroes and has attracted favourable attention in Denmark and beyond. There is a new experimental theatre in Tórshavn which performs new plays in Faroese and classics in Danish.

Life in Tórshavn moves a little faster, and easier, than in the villages. Yet even there, especially among young people, the problems of the Faroes are as apparent as their achievements. Because the sale and public consumption of alcohol were banned in 1907 after a popular referendum intended to combat widespread abuse (the biggest sect on the Islands is still the Plymouth Brethren), the young people gather in the coffee bars or walk the kilometer of the town's main street. Many admit that, although they regard Denmark as a foreign country and would prefer to stay at home, they will probably have to leave, 'if only for a while', as soon as they have finished their education. Never having been at war with anyone, there is no military service in the Faroes. Like the *Løgting,* these young people are fully aware of the need for a more varied economy on the Islands, particularly in view of the real uncertainty about fish-stocks in the North Atlantic. Apart from fishing, and fish processing, a fully modern and efficient industry, the efforts to achieve a more versatile economy have resulted, so far, only in the building of a few small ship-yards. Unlike so many other numerically small peoples, the Faroese have no tourist industry, although the Islands are very beautiful and only three hours by air from Copenhagen. The greatest lack, of course, is a domestic market of sufficient size to maintain any industry. Nevertheless, determined efforts are being made to overcome this obstacle in the context of the debate on whether the Islands should follow Denmark into the European Economic Community. Apart from the difficulty over territorial fishing rights, the Faroese—who are well aware of the marketing advantages which Denmark believes would follow their membership—are uneasy about joining for another reason: they fear that if they become too involved in international cooperation they will have military responsibilities which they would prefer to avoid. They are also anxious that, if they decide to join, their existence as an ethnic minority with its own language and cultural traditions should be acknowledged.

It is a remarkable fact that these traditions, which form part of everyday life in the towns and villages of the Faroes, have thus taken on a new significance by serving both as a catalyst of a growing national consciousness and as a safeguard against the conformity threatening all societies which, since 1945, have come to terms with economic progress at home and new political alignments abroad.

THE GREENLANDERS

Although it is 2,500 miles away from Denmark, and about fifty times larger, Greenland has been an integral part of the Kingdom since 1953. In that year the colonial status of the Island was abolished and Greenland became a Danish *Amt*, with representation in the *Folketing* at Copenhagen. For this reason, despite the fact that Greenland is geographically nearer to the North American continent than it is to the European, and because the language of the autochthonous Eskimos is Greenlandic, it must be considered here.

Greenland (Danish: *Grønland)* is the world's biggest island, with a total area of 840,000 square miles, of which about 93% are covered to a depth of at least 10,000 feet by the Arctic ice-cap. The Island has magnificent scenery, air free from all forms of pollution, the longest and deepest fjord in the world, the fastest glacier which calves every five minutes and temperatures falling regularly to minus 70°C. The highest peak is Gunnbjørns Fjaeld (12,247 feet). The Island is also one of the most sparsely populated regions in the world. Its coastal fringe, which is about 24,000 miles in length from Julianehab to Thule on the western side and to Scoresbysund in King Christian X Land on the eastern, is inhabited by only 47,935 people (1972). They live in about 120 settlements and twenty small townships, including Frederikshåb, Sukker-toppen, Holsteinsborg and Godthåb (population 7,600) which is the captial.

All Greenlanders are Danish citizens, but only about 8,000 are of completely European stock. The rest are Eskimos who have mixed Danish, Norwegian and Viking blood but who are ethnically akin to the other Amerindian peoples of Northern Canada, Alaska and Siberia. Their language, known in Greenland as *Kalâtdlisut,* is a holophrastic or polysynthetic speech, rich in vocabulary for use in its own community but hardly adapted to the modern world. Greenland is called by the Eskimos *Kalâtdlit Nunât*—the Land of Men.

The Island was first visited, by Eric the Red, around the year A.D.960. Outlawed from Iceland, where he had heard rumours of a land to the west, he discovered a fertile area on the eastern coast and later travelled north as far as where

Godthåb (Greenlandic: *Nûk),* is now situated. Iceland at this time was over-populated and on his return Erik persuaded about 3,000 Norsemen to settle in Greenland, the name he invented for what remains one of the bleakest territories known to man. Erik's son, Lief, who subsequently sailed to America, brought a priest from Norway in the year 999 and a bishop was appointed in 1126. But it was not until 1270 that the Greenland Norsemen acknowledged the King of Norway.

By swearing loyalty to Norway and allowing Norwegians a trade monopoly, the Norsemen hoped to improve their economic situation which had declined after Europe lost interest in the narwhale tusks which they had provided. This event coincided with a move southwards by the Eskimos who up to then had had little contact with the settlers. Although the Eskimos learnt a good deal from the newcomers, there was hostility at first: in the fourteenth century the West Settlement was destroyed by Eskimos and in 1379 the East Settlement was attacked. Norway made attempts to relieve the settlers but was in decline at the time and could offer little assistance. By the year 1500 all contact had ceased and when, in 1721, the Norwegian missionary Hans Egede (1686-1758), backed by the Danish Government in return for promises of trade, went to preach the Lutheran faith in Greenland, isolated since before the Reformation, he found besides Eskimos only the ruins of the Norsemen's farms. Whether malnutrition, disease, the effects of constant inter-marriage, or attack by Eskimos had wiped them out is not known: their disappearance remains one of the great unsolved mysteries of the Middle Ages.

During the eighteenth and nineteenth centuries, Denmark competed with Holland in trading with Greenland, mainly for whales and for cryolite, a component of aluminium which the Island had in plentiful supply. This increase in trade brought profound changes in the life of the Eskimos. Up to this time they had enjoyed a natural economy based on seal-hunting which had provided them with all their needs. But now they began bartering far too much in exchange for the cargoes of Danish ships—sugar and coffee in particular—which called during the summer months. Soon there was a shortage of skins for both food and clothing. The dangers inherent in these early contacts were known to the Danes and the Greenland trade monopoly was maintained largely with a view to protecting the Eskimos from themselves. The Danish view was paternalistic but genuinely humanitarian: they saw it as their duty, as early as the eighteenth century, to preserve the Eskimos as an unique ethnic group.

The increase in wealth and the changed economy resulted in a rapid growth of Greenland's population: numerically it was small, from 7,000 in 1834 to 9,000 in 1855. This growth was accompanied by a decline in the seal-catch owing to the presence of European sealers off the coast of Newfoundland, and the Island now entered a period of stagnation and poverty. H. J. Rink (1819-93), Director of the Greenland Trade Organization from 1871 to 1882, was the man responsible for tackling the Island's problems in the face of diminishing interest on the part of the Danish Government. But after 1901 Greenland's problems were taken up again by a new organisation called the Danish Atlantic Islands.

Efforts to encourage Greenlanders to work for greater participation in their own affairs were now made, despite opposition from the Greenland Trade Organisation which wished to continue with its paternalistic methods. In 1908 a law for the government of Greenland was passed which introduced local councils and a National Council elected by all Greenlanders but under the jurisdiction of the Danish Government's Greenland Administration. By 1912 the Greenlanders were beginning to participate in the administration of the Island, mainly as a result of better education and an improved economy. From 1917, following an increase in temperatures, large quantities of cod appeared in Greenland's waters and there was a switch from sealing to fishing. Depots were built, with the aid of Government subsidies, for salting the catch. With the revival of trade, the Eskimos could now import European foods and sheep-farming was established for the provision of meat. Up to this time the Eskimos had prayed, 'Give us this day our daily fish', as Hans Egede had taught them in the eighteenth century. The fish and sheep were bought by the Greenland Trade Association, at inflated prices, in return for the export of cryolite.

The year 1925 saw a new law on Greenland's administration which was aimed at fostering co-operation between the Eskimos and the Danes by giving local rights to
Danish civil servants who had been resident on the Island for
a minimum of two years. In the following year an Education
Act gave Greenland the same schools as those in Denmark
proper, though they were virtually ignored by the Eskimos at
first. Danish jurisdiction over Greenland was almost universally accepted by the Eskimos. The only objections were made
by Norway, to which the Island had once belonged and which
still refrained from acknowledging Denmark's right to the entire territory. Denmark had aquired Greenland, together with
Norway, at the union of 1380 and when Norway was taken
from Denmark in 1814 many Norwegians believed that
Greenland should not have been dealt with separately. In
1931 a group of Norwegian fishermen landed on the eastern
coast and occupied it in the name of King Håkon VII. They
won the support of the Norwegian Government and it was
only by taking the case to the International Court of Justice in
The Hague that Denmark re-asserted its rights. The verdict
was accepted by Norway and since then Danish sovereignty
has been recognised by all.

In the years between the two World Wars Greenland was
treated by the Danish Government as a closed territory on the
grounds that a unique ethnic minority should not be exposed
to the impact of an industrial world. Outsiders, including
Danes, were not admitted except by special permission from
the Greenland Board in Copenhagen. Paternalism continued
to be the characteristic Danish attitude towards a colony
which was not expected to produce a surplus, but merely to
pay its way. Greenland was a world apart, heard about mostly
when Arctic expeditions—such as the Fifth Thule Expedition
of 1921-4 led by the polar explorer and folklorist Knud
Rasmussen (1879-1933)—set off or returned to base. The old
Eskimo sealing communities continued as before, settling
wherever the catch was within reach, the highly skilled prac-
tioners of the art of survival in the world's most hostile
climate. There are still those who live in this way in the north-
west and the east, perhaps a thousand families in all, depen-

ding on seal, whales, polar bears, foxes, reindeer and birds
and only to a small extent on the products of a new age.

Greenland entered a new era with the advent of the Second
World War. Up to 1939 the Island's tiny communities had
lived their quiet, monotonous life, presided over by Danish officials, for more than two hundred years. The ancient stillness
was broken by bull-dozers when the Americans built the air-
fields Blue West One and Blue West Eight as intermediate
stops on the way to the battle-fields of Europe. Although contact between Eskimos and Americans was at first sporadic,
the Greenlanders—cut off from occupied Denmark—soon
became dependent on food supplies from the United States
and familiar with a higher standard of living. As a result the
windows were swung open so wide they could no longer be
closed.

Once again the question of who owned Greenland was
raised. Because of the Island's strategic importance in the
event of a German attack on Canada or the United States, it
was expected that one of these countries might occupy the
Island, especially as it was still nominally under the control of
occupied Denmark. The Danish ambassador in Washington,
Henrik Kauffmann, therefore drafted a treaty with the United
States allowing American bases in Greenland for as long as
there was a threat to America. The two Governors of
Greenland agreed to this treaty and also decided not to
recognise the Government in Copenhagen, but to rule
Greenland themselves for as long as the War lasted. A commission was set up in the United States to take care of the
Island now that connections with Denmark had been severed.
The Danish Government protested and dismissed Kauffmann
but he was acknowledged as the representative of Denmark in
the United States and kept his post until 1945, when the
agreement he had signed was accepted by Denmark. There
are still American military bases on Greenland as part of the
joint defence system with Denmark.

After the War, prominent Greenlanders declared in the
United Nations that they wished to remain attached to Denmark but that the colonial period, the trade monopoly and the
isolation must end. Following the report of the Greenland
Commission in 1953 it was recommended that Greenland

should be made a Danish county, on equal terms with those of metropolitan Denmark. The colonial status of Greenland was thus brought to a close and its new status as an *Amt* incorporated in the Danish Constitution. The Island's two District Councils were merged into a single Provincial Council *(Landsrådet)* a body with up to twenty-one members elected by all Greenlanders over the age of twenty-three and headed by a *Landshøvding,* or Governor. The Council drafts local regulations and levies taxes while all legislation relating to Greenland passed in Denmark must be referred to it. There has been no instance of legislation by Copenhagen against the wishes of the Islanders. The Island is the special responsibility of the Ministry of Greenland in Copenhagen, which has three Departments: the Greenland Technical Organisation, the Royal Greenland Trade Department and the Greenland Geological Survey. The Minister for Greenland is advised by the Greenland Council, an independent body with eleven members who include one appointed by the Crown, three elected by the Provincial Council, the two Greenland members of the *Folketing* and five others nominated by the major political parties. The first Greenlandic Minister for Greenland, appointed in 1971, was Knud Hertling, a lawyer who became a member of the Danish *Folketing* in 1964 and founder of *Suqak,* a moderate left-wing party for Greenlandic workers and fishermen.

The present Governor of Greenland is H. J. Lassen. The Island's two representatives in the *Folketing* are Nikolaj Rosing and Lars Emil Johansen. Since the party stystem is undeveloped, these two are elected personally but while Rosing has no party affiliation, Johansen has been admitted as a member of the Socialist People's Party parliamentary group. Members of the Provincial Council are also elected on a personal basis. Local councils, nineteen in all, were also reorganised and given greater control over the Island's affairs. Church and education, which had been one up to now, were separated and the schools administered by a Board of Education. The health service was extended and modernised: the incidence of tuberculosis and infant mortality was lowered and life expectancy was raised from thirty-two years for males to fifty-six and, for females, from thirty-seven to sixty-three.

Tuberculosis, which used to be the most widespread disease in Greenland has now been almost completely wiped out, only to be replaced by gonorrhoea, of which there are about 8,000 cases a year. Group sex, which so horrified Hans Egede in the eighteenth century, is still practised in the more remote communities and half the children of Greenlanders are born to unmarried parents. The introduction of birth control methods is recent and still not popular, but the average number of children per family has dropped from seven to five. In 1951 a Justice Act brought legal practice in Greenland into line with that in Denmark.

Before long the Island suffered a population explosion, known as 'the race with mid-wives', which greatly taxed the existing housing facilities. By 1956 there were 21,000 Greenlanders, by 1960 there were 30,000, ten years before such numbers were expected, and in 1968 over 45,000. Construction in Greenland is difficult and costly, all materials having to be shipped from Denmark. The building season is short and sites are few and far between, so the authorities encouraged the Eskimos to abandon the small, inaccessible villages for the 'open towns' on the west coast where modern facilities were provided. Massive investment by Denmark brought houses, schools, hospitals, power-stations, waterworks, shopping centres and factories—in short, the entire infra-structure for sustaining a modern, urban community. This development, the most peaceful revolution that any former colony has ever experienced, led in the early 'sixties, to the arrival of Danish workers, technicians and administrators, with devastating effects on the hunting and fishing culture of the Eskimo settlements. Business and technology remain in Danish hands up to the present.

As half the native population of Greenland is under fifteen years old, the education system is a heavy tax burden on Denmark. There are 100 schools and all education is free, but thirty-four schools have less than twenty children each. Pupils may attend schools in Greenland or Denmark up to and including the tenth year (age fifteen), and about a thousand children are sent every year to Danish schools for supplementary education. There is no higher education available on the Island, but navigators, craftsmen and machine-operators are trained at the central technical school at Godthåb where there is also a college for the training of teachers.

When the connection between Denmark and Greenland was re-established in 1945 the pre-war policy of language teaching was replaced by new guidelines. Pride of place was given to Danish, as a subject and as the medium of instruction. Danish teachers were sent to Greenland in large numbers where they came to exert so strong an influence that Greenlandic was partly supplanted after 1950. A reaction against this Danicization has now occurred, however, and strong efforts are being exerted, especially by the well-educated young, to ensure that Greenlandic keeps its place in cultural development. The question is still under debate but it has caused a new lively interest in the Island's culture with a view not only to preservation but also to renewal.

The debate over the Greenlandic language (Danish: *Grønlandsk*) must be seen in the context of a growing national awareness and the younger generation's search for a new identity. These young people, the best educated of the entire Eskimo population, are the ones who have been able to cross the language barrier. At a time when they have to consider themselves representatives of a Danicized Greenland, in view of their bilingual status but not because they necessarily approve of Danicization, they feel compelled to give a warning against a trend which, in their opinion, may shake the very foundation of Greenlandic culture—the language. Uppermost in the language debate is the need for Eskimo children to be taught by Greenlandic-speaking teachers, who are in short supply, rather than by mololingual Danes, as at present. There is no wish, however, to oust the Danish language, only to warn that it should not be at the expense of the indigenous language. The debate has a rather sharp character, not least because of an extremely hard-headed lead from unofficial Danish quarters. The view of many Danes working in Greenland is that the language barrier is the most serious obstacle to the recovery of self-respect and inner security by the Greenlanders which is necessary if they are to escape from their dependent and subordinate relationship with the Danes. The price of breaking through this barrier is recognised on both sides to be an efficient knowledge of

Danish. It may mean a very uncertain future for Greenlandic
as a written language, but the spoken language—even where
Danish succeeds—is expected to survive as a cultural
inheritance, uniting Greenlanders in one nationality without
shutting them off from the world outside. These views, which
sparked off the language debate, were urged on the ground
that there is no going back to the traditional Eskimo
society—technological and economic factors alike exclude it.
Nor would it do to reduce the pace of modernisation for that
would mean a longer but no less painful period of transition.

An alternative policy has been mooted during the last five
years which would involve far more thorough training of the
Danes who are sent to fill jobs in Greenland. A Danish
sociologist and expert on the Eskimos, who introduced this
idea into the language debate, has written of the Greenland
Danes, 'An overwhelming number of them return home with
a painful awareness of their inadequacy in a Greenlandic
social and working environment. While serving there they
have a feeling of impotence because, in spite of all their personal expectations and endeavours, they did not come to
know the Greenlander at first hand, and failed to become true
members of the society their contract had formally admitted
them to. Although often deeply immersed in administrating
reforms, and in the major and minor problems associated
with them in day-to-day business, they in fact remained
merely outside observers of the process of adjustment. The
polar life of these Danes came to be an unhappy period of
frustration with respect to the Greenlander'. The consequence is that there is in Greenland today the problem of a
double lack of identity on the part of both the indigenous
population and those who arrive from Denmark.

Many efforts have been made to involve the Eskimos in the
work of reconstruction, but with only limited success. It was
here that the problems involved in helping them to adjust to
new conditions become apparent. More auspicious have been
the attempts to motivate them towards fishing as their main
occupation, even though a certain period of adjustment has
been allowed. Over a third of all Greenlanders have by today
turned to fishing as their means of livelihood and hunting the
seal has become a secondary occupation. The Eskimo, within

a few decades, has abandoned the kayak and harpoon for the
trawler, although the boats are skippered by Danes, Faroese
and Norwegians. They serve about sixty fish-processing factories, owned by the Danish State. The Greenland haul
remains only 10% of all fish taken from the Atlantic,
however, and the industry costs Denmark an annual loss of
about £1million. Since the Second World War the Danes have
paid prices for Greenland fish which were far above current
world prices in order to support the Island's economy. Three
factors among others have prevented its success. A
deterioration in the climate is on the way and is expected to
last until the year 2050. Enormous ice-bergs have formed
along the western coast in recent years, harassing the
trawlers, and the temperature of the sea has also fallen
slightly. As the difference between life and death for cod fry is
only half a degree, the fish stock has declined badly. The
second factor was the wave of protests from the United States,
Canada and Britain against heavy salmon-fishing in the
Atlantic. In order to preserve friendly relations with these
States, Denmark has set a limit to the number of salmon
which Greenlanders are permitted to catch. The third factor
is that of world competition: large shrimp beds have been
found off Alaska with serious consequences for the Greenland
industry which, until now, has been exporting 8,400 tons of
shrimps a year. For these reasons the Danish Government has
begun to look for alternative sources of wealth for Greenland.
Recent geological surveys have revealed widely diverse
mineral deposits, including the cryolite used by Eskimos for
centuries in the blending of tobacco, together with lead, zinc,
iron ore, uranium, chromium, nickel, platinum and molyb-
denum, which is used for tempering steel. At the same time
intensive prospecting for oil has begun, while more than a
score of the world's leading oil companies are waiting for the
Danish Government to allow them to begin drilling on the
continental shelf off the west of Greenland, in Davis Strait.
Already the prospect of wealth from oil has prompted the
Provincial Council of Greenland to claim that the Island's
mineral resources belongs exclusively to Greenlanders and to
press its growing demand for self-government.

With its natural grandeur, its distinctive population and a

variety of Arctic fauna, Greenland might be expected to attract a large number of tourists—not from Denmark, which is four hours away by Greenland Airlines—but from Canada and the United States. But this is by no means the case: tourists number less than two thousand a year. There is interest in the development of tourism but travel facilities on the Island are still very uncertain—Godthåb is served by only twenty miles of roads—and there are few hotels. There is a helicopter service from Søndre Strømfjord in central West Greenland carrying 32,000 passengers a year to every important town on the western coast but, in the north, travel has to be by sledge.

With changes in Greenland's economy has come a transformation of the Eskimos' way of life. Hans Egede, the first missionary, found in Greenland a distinctive and highly developed culture. But his successors believed the Eskimos to be without culture and from the first encounter between Danes and Eskimos little of the indigenous ways survived. The hunting culture and its artistic creativity, which had flourished for centuries, now disappeared. The legends preserved in oral tradition were replaced by Danish folk-tales, the traditional music by hymn-singing, and the composition of poetry came to an end.

But, far from being totally obliterated, Eskimo culture was to revive in the 1850s under the encouragement of the Danish official and scholar Hinrich Johannes Rink who realised that self-respect and self-reliance were what the Eskimos needed. Having dispensed his professional duties by establishing the first District Council of Greenland in 1862, he set about publishing the old legends in both Danish and Greenlandic, together with a monthly magazine in the native language which was to become the spearhead of an independent Greenlandic literature. Following Rink's example, it may be said that a growing interest and goodwill was shown by the Danish authorities towards the material and spiritual advancement of the Eskimos at this time, when they numbered about 10,000, but that efforts to rouse them from their torpor were nevertheless one-sided. It was believed that progress in Greenland could be based only on the Greenlandic language, and so the teaching of Danish was very poor up to about 1920.

Even when the Island's educational system was modernised in 1905 Danish was not included in the curriculum. When, in due course, the language was recognised in the schools, there were no Danish teachers to teach it. Between the two World Wars, however, Greenlanders began to realise that equality with the Danes could be achieved only through the medium of Danish. Demands were now made by the Eskimos for the effective teaching of Danish, even at the expense of Greenlandic.

By today both languages are taught well in the schools. Only the younger generation is bilingual, apart from a small number of Danes who learn Greenlandic. Teaching in Greenland's two languages starts in the first class, but the Education Act of 1967 allows local education committees to decide to what extent the language should be used in subsequent years and their decisions usually depend on the availability of qualified teachers and text-books. At present only about a third of teachers are able to speak Greenlandic and they are employed mainly at the smaller settlements.

There are books, magazines, newspapers and radio programmes in Greenlandic. The most outstanding living author and translator is Frederick Nielsen, whose works include the novel *Tumarse* (1944) and a volume of verse *Qilak nuna imaq* (1943), fairy-tales, essays and text-books. Nielsen, whose father was a sealer, was a member of the Greenland Provincial Council from 1951 to 1955, and head of Greenland Radio from 1957 to 1969. Other authors are Ole Brandt, Hans Lynge and Otto Sandgreen. At Godthåb there is a bilingual official newspaper, *Atuagagdliutit—Grønslandsposten*. This newspaper, founded by H. J. Rink in 1861, was entirely in Greenlandic until 1952. Despite huge distribution and literacy problems, it has a fortnightly circulation of 6,000 copies and it is subsidised by the Danish State and the Greenland Provincial Council. Many small communities have their own local news-sheets.

With the framework for future development now established, the Island's Council is tackling the many problems still not solved, such as housing and health where the need remains acute. A growing political consciousness has helped the Greenlanders to set about the task of rehabilitation. Although relations between the two groups remain good there is a certain uneasiness on the part of the Eskimos about continuing in a passive role, and an increasing ability to be critical about what has been done for them. Criticism is usually directed at the policy of urban concentration because it represents too sharp a break with much that was viable in the inherited social pattern. It is feared, especially by some young, educated and nationally aware Greenlanders, that the price of progress may prove too high. They quote J. K. Galbraith's warning about the sterility of economic monuments standing isolated in a sea of ignorance, and wonder whether it is possible to find alternatives so that those settlements which retain a sound economic basis should not only be preserved but encouraged to take a share in the benefits of urban life. The trend towards urbanization cannot be halted—indeed, most young people have already moved to the towns—but there is a growing realisation that some of the more vigorous settlements can be helped to survive.

Many young people, such as those organised under the leadership of Moses Olsen (born 1939) in the movement known as the Young Greenlanders' Council, take a lead in criticising Greenlandic society. Moses Olsen, who has played a prominent part in the language debate, was elected to the Danish *Folketing* as the member for South Greenland in 1971. As the voting strength in the Parliament at that time was equally divided between the Government and the opposition parties, he found himself a central and influential figure in Danish politics, succeeding in drawing a great deal of attention to the Island's problems. A hunter's son, he studied modern languages and later Eskimology at Copenhagen University, and as a qualified translator of Greenlandic and Icelandic, he is the only Greenlander who can read *The Saga of Erik the Red* and *The Greenlanders' Saga* in their original language. While recognising that wages and the standard of living have been raised and health services improved—that, in short, the dreams of the colonial period have in many ways been realised—he points out that the creation of a modern social pattern has not been accompanied by a regard for human well-being in the new environment. Evidence for such a view is the fact that more and more families are breaking up, crime, alcoholism and mental ill-health are on the increase, even among the very young, so that the social privation of the past seems to be replaced by human disintegration.

Voices have been raised during the last few years to suggest that it was a mistake to base Greenland's development on the Danish pattern, that Greenlanders cannot be expected to behave like Danes. But if the present system is to continue, say these young Greenlanders, the people must be given a bigger part in planning for the Island's future, the administration decentralised from Copenhagen and, finally, 'Greenland policy must be conducted according to Greenland realities—the integration with Denmark must be subordinated if the whole is to benefit the Greenlanders'.

The Danish Government is already responding to this point of view. In August 1975 it announced the creation of a Joint Commission which is to consider proposals for a new, self-governing status for Greenland providing the Island with a wider degree of autonomy on the model of the Faroe Islands.

The Chairman of the Commission, Isi Foighel, professor of international law at Copenhagen University, has described the wishes of young Greenlanders as 'a movement to find their identity and confirm their consciousness as a people.' The Commission is expected to report in 1977. L. E. Johansen, one of Greenland's two representatives in the Danish Parliament, believes that the Commission will recommend full self-government and that most Danish politicians will accept its proposals.

The Provincial Council has pursued a policy of accomodation to the new era, stressing native requirements and giving a good deal of attention to education, in the hope of raising a generation capable of taking over many of the positions so far unavoidably occupied by Danes. But now that a new social model, pre-fabricated from the Danish design, is being imposed on the Islanders, and enthusiasm at the glowing prospects has waned somewhat, the Danes are asking themselves not whether they have done enough but whether they have done the most appropriate things. Some believe that they have already done too much, in the sense that so much has been done so rapidly that the Eskimos have trouble in keeping pace with a way of life that is alien to their traditions. It is generally agreed that the Danes should pay more attention to the Eskimo's viewpoint than they did during the years of ceaseless re-construction. But of the Greenlanders it is expected that they come to terms with their new world and aquire the self-confidence to suppress the desire to be merely spectators, or to give up and run away. Only then will the assistance which Denmark provides for its northernmost county become a means of self-management. What is taking place in Greenland today is in every respect a break with the past. No one can say with certainty when and how the two cultures will find a way of living together. The question remains: how much 'progress' can a people take without suffering permanent injury, given that in Greenland the Danish Government has compressed into decades the evolution which for other peoples takes centuries?

All in all, Denmark has put more into Greenland than it has derived from it, in a regional development plan of unique dimensions and problems. There is no doubt that it has faced the task of modernising a large and primitive economy, almost Stone Age in character, putting the standard of living as far as possible on a European level. But what is not yet clear is whether a Europeanised community can be successfully established in extreme Arctic conditions among a people who are not European. That a few decades will not suffice for the task of reconstruction has been the common experience of both Danes and Greenlanders alike.

5 FINLAND

Constitution: Republic

Area: 139,119 square miles

Population: 4·598 million (1970)

Capital: Helsinki

Administrative divisions: 12 provinces

Present Government: The Centre Party *(K.E.P.U.)* in coalition with the Social Democratic Party *(S.K.P.L.),* the Swedish People's Party *(S.F.P.)* and the Liberal Party *(L.P.)*; elected 1975

Language of majority: Finnish

THE SWEDISH FINNLANDERS

Swedish is the language spoken by 6·6% of Finland's population—some 303,406 people (1970) who live on the coasts of the provinces of Vaasa, in Ostrobothnia (Finnish: *Pohjanmaa),* Turku-Pori in the south-west, and Uusimaa where Helsinki is situated. The language is also spoken in the capital and on the Åland Islands.

Finland's Constitution of 1919 recognised Swedish, with Finnish, as an official language of the State. But bilingualism has been a feature of life in Finland throughout its recorded history. From about the first century A.D. small bands of Finns migrated northwards from the Baltic countries, driving the Lapps further and further towards the Arctic Circle. By the year 1000 permanent settlements and a national culture—reflected in the Finnish epic the *Kalevala*—had been established. The *Kalevala* (published in 1835), the national epic of the Finns, a mythological poem of fifty cantos (22,795 lines) compiled by Elias Lönnrot (1802-84) from the folk-poetry of Karelia in the east of Finland, served as an important focus for Finnish nationalist feeling in the nineteenth century.

In 1155 the country was invaded by the Swedish King Eric the Good who secured the position of Christianity there. A hundred years later the western parts were incorporated into Sweden, while the eastern region of Karelia was ruled by Russia. That Finland was in alliance with Sweden, rather than conquered by her, is clearly demonstrated by the status of the Finnish provinces in the extended Swedish Kingdom. The Finns kept control of the land they cultivated and were allowed to hold office as burghers, sharing in the making of laws but also bearing the cost of Sweden's foreign wars. Alliance with Sweden was easily effected because throughout the Middle Ages Sweden was a loose union of more or less autonomous provinces and Finnish society was not unlike that of its neighbouring communities to the west.

Swedes had settled in the Åland Islands, off Finland's south-western coast, long before the alliance and now they came in large numbers to the uninhabited coastal areas of the

Gulfs of Finland and Bothnia, to ensure the defence of their new territory. The Swedish-speakers are therefore the autochthonous inhabitants of these areas. Finn and Swede learned to live together, for three hundred years, on Finnish soil. Either Finnish or Swedish was spoken in the country districts but in the towns both languages were in common use. The official language, however, was Swedish and this did not change even after the recognition of Finland's status as the equal of the Swedish provinces in 1362, when the Finns were granted the right to participate in the election of kings.

Until the nineteenth century Finland was governed as part of the united realm of Sweden. Government centralisation was minimal, however, and Finnish affairs were decided in Finland and discussed in Finnish. Although the Catholic Church had a dominating position in the country up to this time, the Reformation did much to strengthen the position of Finnish. A translation of the New Testament appeared in 1548 and in 1642 the Finnish Bible was published, together with a relatively large body of vernacular literature.

The situation changed suddenly during the reign of Gustavus Adolphus (1611-32) with the development of a strong movement towards central government and political uniformity. Finland began to lose her separate status and attempts were made to impose conformity with Sweden. The Finnish language was neglected more and more: first the nobility abandoned it in favour of Swedish, then the bourgeoisie.

The collapse of Sweden in the Great Northern War of 1700-21 led to a further weakening of Finnish. Although literacy had spread among the common people by this time, there was little for them to read in Finnish, except devotional works. The acquisition of Swedish and Swedish attitudes proceeded apace among all classes and the language factor became a token of social standing. It was no longer only Swedish officials who spoke Swedish but artisans, merchants and farmers. The only group which did not lose contact with Finnish entirely was the clergy, although even they used Swedish among themselves. Only Swedish was taught in the schools and universities and Swedish was the language used in government, the courts and business. This situation was not altered by the Russian conquest of Finland in 1808. Protected by its autonomous position as a Grand Duchy within the Russian Empire, Finland continued to be administered by Swedish-speaking officials.

The growing force of Romanticism in Europe and the threat of Pan-Slavism in Russia swelled during the nineteenth century, creating in Finland a Nationalist Movement. Beginning as a literary and philosophic movement among young intellectuals who were critical of the linguistic gulf between the upper classes and the bulk of the common people, the struggle was led by Adolf Ivar Arwidsson, a lecturer at the University of Turku (Swedish: *Åbo),* Johan Vilhelm Snellman (1806-81), and Elias Lönnrot (1802-84), under whom it gained political significance. Elias Lönnrot, compiler of the epic *Kalevala,* was Professor of Finnish Language and Literature at Helsinki University. The establishment of a standard literary form was due largely to his efforts and, by helping to win official recognition for the language, his work opened up the possibility of modern Finnish literature. The slogan of the day was, 'We are no longer Swedes, we cannot become Russians, let us then be Finns!' Pinioned between Swedish culture and Russian power, Finland now had to find its own cultural and political identity by a return to the sources of its nationhood in the Finnish language. The future of Finland depended on Finnish becoming the language of government, public life and education.

The overwhelming majority of the educated class and the nobility responded to Snellman's challenge with enthusiasm, proclaiming themselves—despite their language—to be Finns. Dissatisfaction among farmers at the continued use of Swedish in courts and Government offices led to the movement's first important victory with the Language Ordinance issued by Emperor Alexander II in 1863. Although Swedish was to remain the official language of Finland, 'Finnish is hereby declared to be on a footing of complete equality with Swedish in all matters which directly concern the Finnish-speaking part of the population'. Implementation of this decree was to be carried out over a period of twenty years and during the following two decades a series of reforms, passed

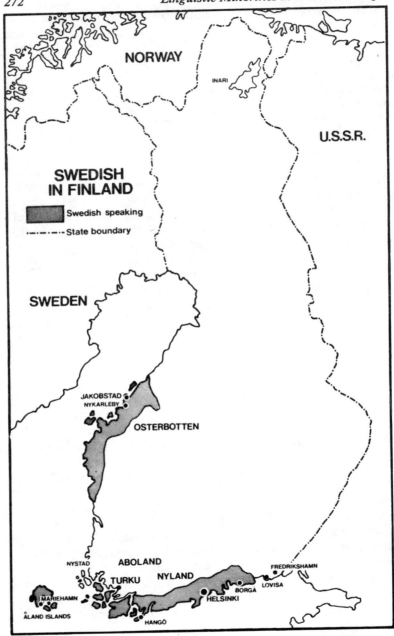

SWEDISH
IN FINLAND

Swedish speaking
State boundary

NORWAY

INARI

U.S.S.R.

SWEDEN

JAKOBSTAD
NYKARLEBY

OSTERBOTTEN

NYSTAD   ABOLAND
                TURKU   NYLAND   FREDRIKSHAMN
MARIEHAMN   BORGÅ   LOVISA
ÅLAND ISLANDS   HELSINKI
                 HANGÖ

by the re-constituted Diet of Finland, gradually improved the position of Finnish in administration.

The progress of Finnish did not take place without conflict, however. The Finnish language movement had found widespread support from among the more liberal elements of the Swedish-speaking upper classes, some 2% of the population. As long as pro-Finnish sentiments could be expressed in Swedish all was well, but now the law required that all documents be produced in Finnish and that the schools should teach in the language. Many Swedish-speakers began to change their minds and to suspect that perhaps they were Swedes after all. But the Swedish language was considered to be too deeply rooted in Finnish history and too valuable a link with the other Scandinavian countries to be ousted from Finnish public life. The existence of a considerable Swedish-speaking population on the western coast gave this opinion a necessary democratic validity.

So, while the protagonists of Finnish, known as the *Fennomen,* organised their own political party, the *Suecomen,* the defenders of Swedish—spoken by about 10% of the population at the time—also closed their ranks, under the leadership of a Swedish journalist August Sohlman (1824-74). There was a danger at this time that Finland, like Belgium, might be torn apart by the mounting tension, but this did not happen. Finns and Swedes had become so intermingled over the centuries that, in the end, the Swedish-speakers decided that they too belonged to the Finnish nation. United in their resistance to Russia, the Finns might be divided over the language question but were in no doubt, in the end, that they were all Finns.

Although the linguistic strife continued, with varying intensity, from 1880 up to the Second World War, it was never a major problem. The liberalisation of economic and social life brought rapid changes and by the turn of the century the Finnish-speaking educated classes outnumbered the educated Swedes. Many families were bilingual, with linguistically mixed marriages having little effect on the number who spoke Swedish at this time. One great advantage of the new *modus vivendi* was that the educational tradition—Finnish in content but Swedish in language—could be shared by both groups so that the Finns did not have to start building anew on the basis of a conservative, rural culture. By 1902, although the privileged position of the Swedish language had been finally abolished in favour of a system of equality between the two languages, Swedish had not disappeared but had maintained its position as Finland's second language.

A crucial moment in the fortunes of Swedish in Finland came after the Bolshevik Revolution in 1917 when the country declared its independence from Russia. After the Civil War and the peace concluded with the Soviet Union in 1919, the makers of the new Republic's Constitution of that year had to define the basic laws governing the official use of the two languages and the constitutional provisions on languages have remained unaltered since this date. The basic premiss in the legislation of 1919 was that, in spite of the tension which existed between Swedish-speakers and Finnish-speakers, they generally consider themselves not only as belonging to the same State but also as members of one nation. The Swedish-speaking group is thus not a national minority in Finland in the same way as, say, the Basques are in Spain. The only exception is the Swedish-speaking population of the Åland Islands.

The fundamental provisions regarding the position of the two languages are contained in Article 14 of Finland's 1919 Constitution: 'Finnish and Swedish are the national languages of the Republic. The rights of Finnish citizens to use their mother tongue, whether Finnish or Swedish, as parties before courts of law and administrative authorities, and to obtain from them documents in that language, shall be guaranteed by law, so as to provide for the rights of the Finnish-speaking and the Swedish-speaking population in accordance with equal principles. The cultural and economic needs of the Finnish-speaking and the Swedish-speaking populations shall be met by the State in accordance with equal principles'.

The first clause of this Article declaring Finnish and Swedish to be the national languages of the Republic was inspired by a similar declaration on the three languages of Switzerland. Although this statement was intended as a political and moral principle rather than as a legal rule capable of immediate application, it was meant to be the basis of the entire fabric of the State's language legislation. As Finnish and Swedish are 'national languages' on an equal footing, legislation providing for special protection of the Swedish-speaking minority was regarded as incompatible with this general declaration, and no such legislation exists—except in that concerning the autonomy of the Åland Islands. The second clause refers to implementation by the State of the principle of linguistic equality and all legislation since 1919 has been devoted to this end.

The third clause has caused more difficulty than the first two. Since 'the cultural and economic needs' of the two groups vary considerably and are not always easily calculated, the authorities must have a certain freedom of judgement in applying this clause. Nevertheless, the fact that education at all levels is provided in both languages can be regarded as a consequence of the principle that the State shall meet the cultural needs of both groups 'in accordance with equal principles'. It would also be against the spirit of this clause if a body dispensing public funds, for example, discriminated against any organisation or individual on linguistic grounds.

The fundamental principles of Article 14 are supported by a number of provisions set out elsewhere in the Constitution of 1919 and its subsequent amendments. For example, all acts and statutory orders, as well as bills submitted to Parliament, must be drawn up in both Finnish and Swedish. The 'Official Gazette' is also bilingual. Both Finnish and Swedish can be used in the transaction of parliamentary business: the citizen has a right to receive a written reply in the language of his choice. In practice, however, the use of Swedish is limited to the published reports of Parliament's affairs, Finnish being used in committees and debate. More importantly, perhaps, boundaries of the administrative districts must be drawn so as to make them unilingual or at least to render the linguistic minorities in them as small as possible. On result is that the language border is often very distinct, especially on the western coast, sometimes with one village speaking Swedish and the next Finnish. The Swedish of educated Finns imitates the standard usage of Sweden, but in the country areas the influence of Finnish and isolation from Sweden have resulted in a number of provincialisms in the Swedish spoken.

While this last Article has been successfully implemented, a complementary Article, which states that the same principle ought to be applied to the boundaries of administrative units larger than municipalities, has remained a *lex imperfecta*, no units of this kind (except Åland) ever having been created. Also, the increase in the number of linguistically mixed areas, a result of urbanisation, has made the implementation of this article more and more difficult. In ecclesiastical affairs, however, there has been more success: a separate bishopric consisting of the exclusively or predominantly Swedish-speaking parishes has existed since 1923. Finally, every conscript to the Finnish Army has the right to be placed 'whenever possible and unless he desires otherwise in a unit whose members speak his own mother tongue', although the language of command remains Finnish.

The core of the legislation on the official use of Finland's national languages is formed by two Acts passed in 1922—the Language Act, and the Knowledge of Languages Required of Civil Servants Act. The object of this complex body of laws is to work out in detail the content and spirit of the general rule set out in the second clause of Article 14 of the 1919 Constitution. Two conflicting aims have to be reconciled here. One is the citizen's right, recognised by the Constitution, to use his own language when dealing with the authorities. The other arises from the fact that the two languages are not evenly spread throughout the country, the Swedish-speaking population being concentrated in a small part of it, so that the uniform application of bilingualism to the whole country is often extremely difficult and sometimes impossible.

The search is for a working formula of compromise and this is usually between the territorial and the personal principles. The territorial principle is to be found in the country's division into administrative districts of homogenous linguistic character, the municipalities. According to the Language Act a municipality is unilingual if the minority which speaks the other national language does not amount to 10%; if the minority exceeds 10% the municipality is to be considered bilingual. In order to avoid the influence of temporary or occasional shifts in the linguistic composition of the population on this classification, it is also stated that a bilingual municipality shall not be declared uni-lingual before the minority has decreased to under 8%. In 1962 this law was amended thus: if the size of the minority exceeds 5,000 persons the municipality is to be considered bilingual irrespective of the percentage of the total population which the minority represents.

Up to 1939 the Language Act had declared that the cities of Helsinki, Turku and Vaasa (Swedish: *Helsingfors, Åbo* and *Vasa)* were to be permanently bilingual, irrespective of the percentage rule. The amendment of 1962 was made to meet a demand from Swedish-speakers faced by a rapid influx of Finnish-speakers into the cities which threatened to change traditionally bilingual areas into unilingual Finnish municipalities. The linguistic status of the municipalities is decided by the Government every ten years on the evidence of the latest Census. For the period from 1963 to 1972 they were grouped according to their official language as follows: 456 Finnish, thirteen bilingual with a Finnish majority, thirty-four bilingual with a Swedish majority and forty-four Swedish. The territorial subdivision according to linguistic criteria has important legal effects, especially on the 'internal official language'—the language to be used by the authorities in their internal work and in their correspondence. In Turku official signs are allowed in Swedish according to which language is spoken by the majority.

In relations between the State and individuals, important concessions are made to the personal principle. The main rule states that before law courts and other State or municipal authorities, the language of the district (in bilingual districts either language is permissible) is the one to be used. However, when a Finnish citizen appears before a court of law or some other State authority he is entitled to use his own language, irrespective of the linguistic character of the district concerned. In 1960 the percentage of Swedish-speakers in the principal towns was Närpes 96.5% (7,471), Sibbo 69.3% (7,236), Pietarsaari *(Jakobstad)* 63.8% (9,426), Porvoo

(Borga) 62% (9,652), Vaasa *(Vasa)* 32.6% (13,924), Esbo 23.5% (13,297) and Helsinki *(Helsingfors)* 14.4% (65,338).

The Language Act also states that officials must issue documents and make public announcements in the language or languages of the local population. That officials have an adequate knowledge of the language they will have to use is ensured by the Knowledge of Languages Required of Civil Servants Act, which was issued simultaneously with the Language Act. The requirements vary with the linguistic character of the district and the type of office, but all officials in bilingual areas are required to pass examinations in both Finnish and Swedish.

No specific provision for legislation in education is made in the Language Act, but from the start the language struggle in Finland was to a large extent centred around cultural problems. The success of the *Fennomen* was based on demands for adequate education in the majority language and for equal cultural opportunities. Yet it was only after the Second World War that the proportions of pupils from the two language groups in the secondary schools began to coincide with their shares of the total population. It is therefore not surprising that education has played a crucial role in the Finnish Government's legislation.

In accordance with the requirements of Article 14 of the Constitution, the Government maintains educational establishments of many kinds, from primary schools to adult education, in both national languages. There are seventeen people's colleges, fifty vocational schools and seventeen evening schools teaching in Swedish. There are about fifty schools at secondary level with 17,000 pupils and 575 primary schools with 34,000 pupils. The Swedish-language schools are the special responsibility of a department within the National Schools Board. At the primary level, the compulsory Education Act prescribes that if the number of children speaking a language other than that of the municipality's majority reaches eighteen the authorities have to provide for instruction in their own language. In Finnish and Swedish secondary schools the study of both languages is compulsory. In 1968 the Finnish Government passed an act by which the primary and middle schools would be amalgamated in 1970 into a comprehensive system of schools known as 'basic schools', but this has made no difference to the laws governing instruction in Swedish and, despite larger classes, Finnish-speaking children still receive Swedish lessons.

The position of the languages at the University of Helsinki is now regulated by the University Act and the University Language Act. During the years between the two World Wars the University stood at the centre of the political conflict engendered by the language question. In spite of successive gains by Finnish, public opinion found the amount of instruction given in Finnish entirely insufficient and pressed for complete Finnicization. In 1937 the wishes of Finnish-speakers were carried out and, after the War, the Swedish minority's view was also taken into consideration. Since then the University question has played almost no role in politics. According to the reformed University Language Act of 1937, instruction in all subjects and internal administration is in Finnish, but Swedish is the official language of about twenty-two departments out of a total of 180. The law also recognises the rights of teachers and students to use their respective language in examinations. While the University of Helsinki is thus, to some extent, bilingual, the other Universities of Finland are all unilingual. The *Akademi* situated in Turku is a private but Government-supported Swedish University with five faculties and 2,000 students, the centre of higher Swedish learning in Finland which has produced a number of eminent Finns such as sociologist Edvard Westermarck (1862-1939).

The presence of two linguistic groups in Finland has had a real effect on many aspects of the country's political and social life during the last hundred years and has resulted in an important body of legislation dealing with the two national languages. It should be noted, however, that present legislation contains no special guarantees for the maintenance of Swedish. For a few years after the First World War the idea of an autonomous administration for the coastal areas where Swedish is spoken was canvassed in some circles, but the concept of special legislation has not been at all popular with either linguistic group. One of the few examples of protective measures was a clause in the legislation on land reform after the Second World War: the south-west was exempted from receiving refugees from Karelia, on the border with the Soviet Union, in order to avoid the swamping of the Swedish-speaking areas by Finnish-speaking settlers.

During the years between the World Wars the language legislation of the Finnish Government was the target for a great deal of criticism from the Finnish-speaking majority. It was felt that the equal treatment which Swedish-speakers enjoyed, despite the numerical inequality of the two languages, was an obstacle to the free development of the majority's aspirations. The Finnish-speakers also pointed out that the status enjoyed by the Swedish minority in Finland contrasted sharply with that of Finnish-speakers in Sweden where a strict unilingual policy was carried out in the schools around the mining areas of Kiruna and Galliväre, and the border town of Haaparante, where about 40,000 Finns still live today. However, as a result of growing mutual understanding, especially during the ordeal of the Second World War, this mood changed and language legislation as a political problem lost much of its significance. The progress made in all fields of social activity during the post-war decades has guaranteed the Finnish language a clear dominance in public life and there has been a relaxation in relationships between the two linguistic groups, so that the special interest of the minority can be safeguarded without any threat to the majority.

That Finland is genuinely concerned for the maintenance of its Swedish-speaking community is to be seen in the establishment of a Popular Assembly, the *Svenska Finlands Folkting,* a Parliament elected by the Swedish-speaking population which exists for considering their grievances and problems. It is elected by the Swedish-speaking population every six years. Every voter claiming Swedish as his or her mother-tongue is entitled to vote, and in 1970 over 100,000 votes were cast. The *Folkting* has representatives from all the political parties in which Swedish-speakers are active: the Swedish People's Party, the Social Democrats and the Conservatives. The *Folkting* is charged with promoting and safeguarding the social and cultural interests of the Swedish-speaking population. Its sixty deputies meet once every three years and between the sessions a board of fifteen deputies and a permanent secretariat manage current business, but not on party political lines. The efforts of this body have resulted in many valuable reforms and it is generally considered to be sufficient for the proper administration of the Swedish-speaking areas.

Despite these facilities and official attitudes towards them, however, it is somewhat surprising to discover that the Swedish-speaking population continues to decline. In 1880, 14·3% of the population of Finland had Swedish as their first language, 12·9% in 1900, 11% in 1920, 9·6% in 1940 and 8·6% in 1950. By 1960 the corresponding figures were 7·4% and 6·6%—about 303,406 people—in 1970. Of these 290,000 live in the distinctly Swedish districts of Vaasa and Turku, but there are also 65,338 Swedish-speaking Finns in Helsinki, which is predominantly Finnish-speaking. All urban dwellers among the Swedish-speakers also speak Finnish, but about 160,000 in rural areas are said to be monolingual. About 8,000 Swedish-speakers live outside the main Swedish areas in other parts of Finland.

At the same time the Swedish speakers' representation in Parliament has decreased to the same extent: the *Svenska Folkparteit* (Swedish People's Party), a coalition organised on broad lines and founded in 1906, had fifteen members in 1945, twelve in 1970 and ten in 1972 (out of a total of 200), with a total of 138,079 votes (5·4%). About 75% of the Swedish-speaking population in Finland supports the Swedish People's Party, mainly for linguistic and cultural reasons, and its representatives have participated in the formation of cabinets during most of the post-war years. The province of Åland is not included in the area covered by the Party. Most Ålanders support a political league of their own but their member in the Finnish Parliament considers himself as belonging to the Swedish-speaking parliamentary group and its committees. There are also Swedish-speakers among the Social Democrats and fourteen out of 200 members in 1972 were known to be Swedish-speakers. The strength of the Swedish People's Party in the Finnish Parliament decreased to nine members in 1973 when one left, together with a member of the National Coalition Party, to form a new party called the Finnish Constitutional People's Party.

Despite the decline in their numbers, the Swedish Finnlanders, as they prefer to be known, continue to make an important contribution to the cultural life of Finland. Besides the major bilingual organisations, there are many smaller bodies representing the Swedish Finns, including those for the arts, sport, youth, students, women, the labour movement, religion and literature, all independent but co-operating with their Finnish-speaking counterparts. There are also a number of business firms, banks, insurance companies and co-operatives using Swedish as their main language. Many Swedish Finns have played leading roles in the political, industrial, financial, social and cultural life of the country, holding high office. Finland's greatest composer, Jean Sibelius (1865-1957) was a Swedish Finn, some of whose early compositions were based on the *Kalevala,* and they have produced several eminent artists and sportsmen. They also played an important role during the two World Wars. Gustav Mannerheim (1867-1951), Marshal and President of Finland from 1944 to 1946, was Swedish-speaking and so is K-A. Fagerholm, who has been on several occasions the country's Prime Minister.

Literature has been published in both languages since the nineteenth century, when many outstanding authors, including J. V. Snellman, champion of the Finnish language, and J. L. Runeberg (1804-77), Finland's national poet and author of the national anthem, wrote in Swedish. At the beginning of the present century almost 60% of the books published were in Swedish, but in 1970 the proportion had decreased to 7·5%, about 500 new titles, roughly equivalent to the proportion of the Swedish-speaking population. In absolute terms, on the other hand, the number of Swedish books has remained constant for decades, while the number of books in Finnish has increased rapidly. The Finnish State recognises the existence of Swedish literature, which has developed independently of literature in Finnish, with its subsidies to the publishing industry, the library service, its pensions to writers and its annual prizes. The two principal literary societies for Swedish writers, both subsidised by the State, are *Svenska Litteratursäll-skapet i Finland* (Society of Swedish Literature in Finland), established in 1885, and *Svenska Forfattareföreningen* (Society of Swedish Authors), founded in 1919, with a membership of 170 in 1971. Among the leading Swedish-language writers of this century are Runar Schildt, Edith Södergran, (1892-1923), Gunnar Björling (1887-1960), Elmer Diktonius (1896-1961), Tito Colliander (born 1904), Walentin Chorell (born 1912), Marianne Alopaeus and Christier Kihlman. But the Swedish-speaking population has had many other writers during the last hundred years, including Z. Topelius (1818-98), K. A. Tavaststjerna (1860-98), Mikael Lybeck (1864-1925), Arvid Mörne (1876-1946) and Jacob Tegengren (1875-1955).

Of the eighty-nine newspapers published in Finland, twenty are in Swedish with a total circulation of about 161,000, 7·3% of the total circulation of all newspapers. Although the number of Swedish-speakers has declined, the number of Swedish newspapers has not changed and their circulation remains almost constant. Most were established in the nineteenth century and, unlike many of their Finnish counterparts, the Swedish newspapers are not owned by political parties. The biggest Swedish-language daily is *Hufvudstadsbladet,* with a circulation of 70,000, published in Helsinki but widely read in all Swedish-speaking areas. Approximately 130 magazines including *Finsk Tidskrift,* founded in 1876, the oldest periodical in all the Scandinavian countries, and ten local newspapers, are also published in Swedish.

In broadcasting, Finland has two radio networks in Finnish covering the whole country and a third for the area inhabited by the Swedish-speaking population, which broadcasts about 3,700 hours in Swedish annually. There are also Swedish-language programmes on both television channels, four professional theatres working in Swedish and a travelling dramatic company which tours the rural districts. The principal theatre is *Svenska Teatern* in Helsinki, the National Theatre of the Swedish Finns, with 900 seats and thirty-six permanent actors.

Despite this remarkable cultural activity, there is no denying the fact that the Swedish-speaking population of Finland is steadily declining in comparison with the Finnish-speaking population. The chief factor in the decline is known to be the lower birth rate—17·9 per thousand for Swedish-speakers, 21·5 per thousand for the Finns. Also more

Swedish Finns emigrate, especially to Sweden where they feel at home, despite their accents. Mixed marriages usually result in homes where children are reared in Finnish, and the mass media have the usual effect on the minority. Nevertheless, the absolute number of Swedish Finnlanders has not declined.

For the Finns the Swedish-speaking community forms a very important bridge between Finland and the other Scandinavian countries. Speaking on Independence Day, 6 December 1944, President Paasikivi said, 'Our social organisation and our outlook on life have been determined by nearly seven hundred years of association with Sweden. This, and the fact that our nation includes a considerable Swedish-speaking population, have led to the establishment of close cultural and economic ties with our western neighbour'. The vast majority of Finns would agree with this view. It can be concluded that the Finnish Government has done a great deal to ensure that the Swedish-speakers enjoy most of the fundamental rights needed by linguistic minorities if they are to flourish. While there is certainly cause for concern at the decline in their numbers, the Swedish Finnlanders see no need for pessimism, at least for the present.

THE ÅLAND ISLANDERS

The Åland Islands, an archipelago of about 6,500 small islands—only eighty are inhabited—are situated in the Gulf of Bothnia. In this province Swedish, the mother-tongue of 96% of the population, is the only official language and Finnish a foreign language in all respects.

The principal island in the archipelago is Fest-Åland, where 80% of the inhabitants live; the islands of Eckerö and Lumparland are connected to it by bridges. Mariehamn (Finnish: *Maarianhamina*), the chief town, is situated on Fest-Åland; other important towns are Storby, Vardö and Foglö. The total land-area of Åland (Finnish: *Ahvenanmaa*) is approximately 475 square miles and the population in 1971 was 20,873.

About 40% of Ålanders live by agriculture and associated trades. The rest are employed in commerce, small industries and a merchant fleet of sixty trawlers (4000,000 tons) which makes up nearly a third of the entire Finnish fleet. The Islands are extremely beautiful in spring and summer, with rich flora and fauna, a major source of income being provided by the 450,000 tourists who visit them every year. Sea and air links with both Finland and Sweden are excellent: there is a daily car-ferry and a daily flight from Mariehamn since 1960. Although a demand for improved social services among the scattered communities has resulted in widespread desertion of the less accessible islands, the average income for the Åland islands is 10% higher than that in the rest of Finland. Nevertheless, the population has declined since the Second World War, mainly as the result of emigration to Sweden.

There is no doubt about the ethnic origins of the Åland Islanders: they have always been and still consider themselves to be of Swedish nationality, differing in this respect from the Swedish-speakers on the mainland of Finland. Settlement by Swedes began in the middle of the thirteenth century when Birger Jarl subjugated a large part of Finland under his rule. But the Islands had been visited by Swedes from heathen times on account of their favourable trading position for the countries of northern Europe. They were used at various periods as a base for the whale and seal industries, as a port between east and west after the Volga route was discovered around A.D. 800, and by the Vikings in their raids on the coastal towns of the Baltic.

By the year 1000 the Islands came under the influence of Christianity, more than a century earlier than Finland, as part of the bishopric of Uppsala and the territory of Gotland. At this time they had their own laws and Parliament. Sweden incorporated Åland in 1340, after which they lost their commercial importance to Stockholm where Germans had the monopoly of trade. The only Swedes among the rich merchants of Stockholm at this time were Peter Ålanding and Gunder Ålanding, their names betraying their origins. At the end of the sixteenth century the Islands came under the direct control of the Swedish Crown.

In 1634, however, Sweden decided to include Åland in the districts of Åbo *(Turku)* and Björneborg (present-day *Pori),* on the Finnish mainland. Although the Islands still sent representatives to the imperial Parliament, they were now exposed to attack from Russia. During the Great Nordic War, Åland was invaded by the Russians in 1714. The inhabitants immediately fled to Sweden, returning seven years later to find their villages destroyed. But when the Russians arrived for the second time, in 1808 during the Finnish War, the Islanders were prepared and defeated the invaders. Sweden, anxious to protect Stockholm, then sent 6,000 soldiers to Åland, only to recall them when a superior Russian force crossed the sea-ice in the following year for a third attack. Following unsuccessful attempts by Sweden to reclaim her lost territory, the Islands were given to Russia by a treaty of 7 September 1809. During the Crimea War of 1854-6, Sweden again asked for the return of Åland. Russia refused but recognised the Islands as neutral territory in the Åland Convention which was attached to the Paris Peace Treaty of 1856.

During the First World War Czarist Russia violated the terms of the Åland Convention by using Mariehamn as a base for its fleet. But after the February Revolution of 1917, Åland's leaders were able to resume work for re-union with Sweden. On 20 August 1917 the Islanders' representatives applied to the King of Sweden to join his Kingdom. Following the Bolshevik Revolution in October of that year, in which the

Council of Peoples' Commissars proclaimed the principle of self-determination for all peoples within Russia, an unofficial plebiscite was held in Åland at which re-union with Sweden was favoured by 96% of the inhabitants—virtually the entire Swedish-speaking population. Finland, however, after declaring its own independence on 6 December 1917, refused to grant Åland's request, claiming the Islands as part of the new state's territory. It was not until the Prime Minister of France, Georges Clemenceau, attracted the world's attention by declaring that the Islands should be returned to Sweden that Finland responded, passing autonomy laws for Åland on 30 April 1920. This move did not satisfy the Islanders, however, and they continued to press for separation from Finland and re-unification with Sweden. The Finnish Government re-acted by having the Åland leaders, Julius Sundblom and Carl Björkman, arrested and accused of high treason. A rapid exchange of diplomatic notes followed.

At the suggestion of the British Government, the problem was put in the hands of the League of Nations and its International Law Commission was asked to study it. The Commission's findings were that Russia had taken Åland from Sweden later than Finland, that the Islands had been an independent State before Finland, that the inhabitants of Åland had clearly demonstrated their will in favour of re-unification with Sweden and, furthermore, that they had good reason to fear annexation by Finland. The Commission's decision was greeted with joy in Åland. By this time, however, the Finnish Government had undertaken to introduce measures for the protection of the Island's Swedish character. A new body, known as the Rapporteur Commission, therefore recommended that Finland should have sovereignty of Åland, but that special guarantees on the Islands' language and culture should be provided, and that the archipelago should be demilitarised. This recommendation was accepted by the Council of the League of Nations on 24 June 1921 and three days later Finland and Sweden agreed to make Åland an autonomous Swedish region within the Finnish State. This agreement was accepted by the vast majority of the inhabitants of Åland and the Provincial Parliament met for the first time on 9 June 1922.

During the Second World War the Islands were occupied as a neutral territory by a Finnish garrison. Allegations that the Finns had not respected the agreements on nationality and language during the period of their occupation led to protests by Åland's Parliament and, after the War, to new autonomy laws, which were passed on 18 December 1951. As is clear from this brief account of Åland's history, the whole of this legislation has its *raison d'être* not only in the special linguistic and ethnic character of the Islands but also in their position as a link between Finland and Sweden, and thus with the other Scandinavian countries, including their strategical importance in the Baltic sea.

Nevertheless, the autonomy laws of 1951 also include a number of clauses which aim at maintaining the dominance of Swedish in the Islands. The self-Government of Åland Act prescribes, for instance, that in administration and education the only language permissible is Swedish. No person without full command of Swedish is allowed to hold public office in Åland. All State authorities in the Islands must deal with the local population, with one another and with the Finnish Government in Swedish. Place-names, street-signs, and commercial advertising are also exclusively in Swedish. Finnish is taught, as a foreign language, only in the few communities where it is requested, otherwise Swedish is the medium of instruction in all schools.

The right of domicile in Åland belongs only to those who are permanently resident in the Islands and is granted, on application, to other Finnish citizens only after a period of five years' uninterrupted residence; only those granted this right can vote or own property or be engaged in trade. As the Islands were de-militarised in 1947, the right of domicile includes exception from military service in the Finnish Army. The number of Finnish-speakers in Åland does not exceed 1,000 and most are assimilated by the Swedish majority after one generation.

The Provincial Parliament of Åland, the *Landsting*, is responsible for all internal legislation and for the administration of the Islands. Its powers to legislate are sovereign except in cases where the security of the Finnish

State is threatened. All laws passed by the Finnish Government must be approved by the *Landsting* before they can be implemented in Åland. The Parliament's powers include the supervision of schools, health and social services, trade, fishing and hunting, the police force, communications and cultural affairs. Administration is in the hands of a seven-member committee, the *Landskapsstyrelse,* which is elected every four years, and a civil service. The annual grant paid by the State, out of taxes raised in Åland, towards the cost of administration, is voted jointly by the *Landsting* and the Finnish Government. Any public expenditure in Åland which is not usual in the rest of Finland is met by the Islands. The *Landsting,* headed by a Speaker, consists of twenty-seven members representing the nine districts of Åland and is elected annually. The member for Åland in the Finnish Parliament, although not a member of the Swedish People's Party which represents the majority of Swedish-speakers on the mainland of Finland, is considered as belonging to the Party's parliamentary group and its committees. The Governor of Åland, who represents the interests of the Finnish State in the Islands, is appointed after consultation with the *Landsting*. Since 1954 the Islands have had their own flag, a golden cross bordered by a red cross on a light-blue background.

The cultural life of the Åland Islands is conducted entirely in Swedish and under the patronage of the *Landsting*. There are two daily newspapers, each with a circulation of approximately 8,000. Mariehamn has museums, libraries, a cultural foundation and cinemas showing only Swedish films. A local radio station broadcasts throughout the day in Swedish and, with the full approval of Finland, the Islanders receive television programmes from a transmitter at Väddö on the coast of Sweden. Clubs and societies for young people, housewives and sportsmen are as popular in Åland as they are among Swedish-speaking Finns. The Island's distinctive folk-culture is to be seen in the architecture of houses and wind-mills, in farm equipment and work-methods. The hey-day of the Åland clippers—as described in Elis Karlsson's novel *Mother Sea*—is commemorated everywhere, by the four-master in Mariehamn's harbour which is part of the town's

maritime museum and by the retired seamen who are to be
met in the villages. A more remote history is marked by the
ruins of many fortresses, the most impressive of which is the
medieval fort of Kastelholm, destroyed by the British and
French fleets in 1854.

Since the autonomy laws of 1951 the Ålanders have maintained a loyal attitude to the Finnish State. It is clearly the
degree of autonomy which they enjoy, as advanced as that of
any linguistic minority in Western Europe, with the possible
exception of the Faroe Islands, which makes for good
relations between Åland and Finland. The Finnish Government has been exemplary in its implementation of the
autonomy laws. Complaints about Åland are heard from time
to time, more especially because, like Finland's remote frontier territories, they require subsidy in the more inaccessible
islands. But, in general, the self-government of the Åland
Islands works so successfully that it has few critics.

THE LAPPS OF LAKE INARI

There are no official statistics for the number of Lapps, or people of Lappish descent, in Finland today—primarily because there is no reliable way of determining who is a Lapp. But according to the results of an enquiry by the Lapp Council in 1962, out of a total of 3,477 who had at least one grandparent for whom Lappish was the mother-tongue 3,112 considered themselves as belonging to the ethnic group, without necessarily speaking the language, while 253 were undecided and 112 did not. This figure confirms the total of 2,529 Lappish-speakers estimated by the State Commission for Lapp Affairs in 1949. Owing to improved health services and diet, it is unlikely that there have ever been more Lapps in Finland during the present century than there are today—perhaps 2,500 in all.

They are to be found in the northernmost part of the country, above the 68th degree of latitude, in an area of about 15,400 square miles between Lake Inari and the border with Norway. Only around the border town of Utsjoki, however, are they in a majority, being scattered for the most part in small settlements over the whole area. Originally the sole inhabitants of all northern Finland, the Lapps withdrew to north of the Arctic Circle during the seventeenth century, under pressure from Finns and Swedes. The retreat was peaceful, marriages between Lapps and Finns, whose languages belong to the same Finno-Ugrian group, being common. The Lapps declined in number for the next two hundred years, never developing any institutions beyond their *siida,* or village communes.

Today Finland's Lapps all know Finnish and speak it for all purposes outside their work as reindeer herdsmen. In the schools all instruction is in Finnish, there are few books in the Lappish language and almost no teachers qualified in it. Children whose mother-tongue is Lappish are among pupils at nineteen primary schools, in seven of which they are a majority. Finnish is the only official language except for place-names which nave kept their Lappish spelling. The speech of Lapps on the shores of Lake Inari is the East Lappish dialect, while those to the north-west speak Central Lappish and the Skolt dialect.

About half the Lappish population live from the breeding of reindeer but most also keep cows and small plots of cultivable land, and all have fixed dwellings; a few semi-nomadic families survive in the part of Finland which lies between Sweden and Norway but everywhere else hunting and fishing have been almost totally abandoned. Few are very poor except the Skolts who, having lost their homeland in the Pechenga (Petsamo) region, now in the U.S.S.R., after the Peace Treaty of 1945, have not settled well in the district of Inari. There is no conflict whatsoever between the Lapps and Finns at a social level.

Most Lapps in the region belong to the Laestadian sect of the Lutheran Church, except the Skolts who were influenced by the Russian Orthodox Church, and services in Lappish are frequent. Colourful traditional costumes, which vary from community to community, are worn on Sundays and other important occasions. Secular organisation in the modern sense is foreign to the Lapps. They have no political organisations of their own and there are no Lapps in the Finnish Parliament, although several have been elected to local councils in the towns of Utsjoki and Inari. At general elections the Lapps usually support the Agrarian and Socialist Parties. There are, however, small societies for fishermen, hunters and young people, none very active and all using Finnish. The Lapps of Finland have no flag or emblem but a national song by the Norwegian Lapp Isak Saba, *Sami Soga Lavla* (Song of the Lapp People) was adopted after the Second World War, as the anthem of all·the Lapps in Scandinavia.

Among Finnish Lapps who have written verse and short stories in Lappish are Pedar Jalvi, Aslak Guttorm and Pekka Lukkari. A group of young people recently published an anthology of world literature in Lappish translation. A leaflet entitled *Sabmelaš* (The Lapp), published bi-monthly, reaches about 800 families. There is news in Lappish for five minutes three times a week and a weekly ten-minute church service on radio from Studio Rovaniemi.

The problem of the Lapps in Finland has only recently begun to attract serious attention and with the Governments of Norway and Sweden which have larger Lappish populations, Finland is now attempting to find ways of supporting their culture. From the above facts it must be concluded that it is almost certainly too late to save them as an ethnic group in Finland. Given their small numbers, increasing industrialisation and the rapid rate of assimilation, the Lapps of Lake Inari are not likely to survive longer than a few more decades.

6   FRANCE

Constitution: Republic

Area: 212,209 square miles

Population: 52,674 million (1975)

Capital: Paris

Administrative divisions: 95 departments

Present Government: The Independent Republicans *(R.I.)* and the National Union of Republicans *(U.N.R.);* elected 1973

Language of majority: French

THE OCCITANS

Occitanie is that part of southern France where *la langue d'oc* is spoken. Northerners, who speak *la langue d'oil (oil* and *oc* are the equivalents of *oui),* usually refer to Occitanie as *le Midi* and to Occitans as *les Méridionaux.* The word Occitanie dates from the end of the thirteenth century but the region has also been known, inaccurately because it is only one province, as *Languedoc.* By today, largely as the result of the Deixonne Law of 1951 which made it 'official' and a growing autonomist movement, *Occitanie* and *occitan* are well established as the names by which the region and its language are known in French.

The region, about one third of metropolitan France, includes the provinces of Languedoc (Occitan: *Lengadoc),* Provence *(Provençal),* Limousin *(Lemosin),* Auvergne *(Auvernha),* Gascogne *(Gasconha),* Guyenne *(Guiana)* and Dauphiné *(Daufinat)*—about thirty departments in all, including the Principality of Monaco but excluding, of course, the northern Basque Country and the Roussillon and Cerdagne districts of Catalonia. The principal towns of Occitanie are Toulouse (Occitan: *Tolosa),* Pau, Bordeaux *(Bordèu),* Limoges *(Lemòtges),* Clermont-Ferrand *(Clarmont),* Nîmes, Avignon *(Avinhan),* Montpellier *(Montpelhièr),* Albi, Narbonne *(Narbona),* Marseille *(Marselha),* Aix-en-Provence *(Aïs),* Toulon *(Tolon),* Carcassonne *(Carcassona),* Cannes *(Canas)* and Nice *(Nica).*

About fifteen million people live in Occitanie (Occitan: *Occitània),* a quarter of France's population. Of these around ten million have some knowledge of Occitan, if we count also the 5,000 inhabitants of the Val d'Aran (the upper valley of the Garonne) in the Catalan province of Lerida, and the 200,000 who speak the Occitan dialect of Provençal in the Piedmont valleys of Italy. It is estimated that about two million people use Occitan in their daily lives. They live for the most part in rural areas and all are also able to speak *la langue d'oil,* the last monoglot speakers having died in the 1930s. So powerful an influence have the French educational and political systems had on the older generation that many people, when questioned about the language they speak, believe that Occitan is no more than a local, uneducated and corrupt form of French, and that it is incapable of being written down. This is certainly not the case but it is true that, owing to the existence of a variety of dialects, no standard literary form has been universally accepted. Occitan is still divided, as might be expected over such a large territory, between the northern dialects of Limousin and Auvergne, those of Languedoc and those of Gascogne. Their linguistic differences are complicated by ethnic and historical factors, so that local loyalties have sometimes prevented attempts to rouse the Occitans to concerted action. As Mistral, their greatest poet, once put it, 'Occitanie is not a country, it is an idea'.

Despite this variety, the language and literature of Occitanie have an illustrious history and have made an important contribution to the culture of Western Europe. Their origins are to be traced to those centuries up to the tenth when, with the triumph of Latin over the language of the Gauls, especially in their southern territories, and with the Frankish invasions in the north, the phonetic structure of Gallo-Roman began to develop differently until, as early as the eleventh century, there emerged two separate languages: *la langue d'oïl* around the Paris basin, from which modern French has developed, and *la langue d'oc,* another member of the Romance family, to the south of the *Massif Central.* The first poet to write verse in Occitan was Guillaume IX of Aquitaine (1071-1127). For three hundred years the Occitans maintained an independent civilisation of high sophistication, especially in the poetry of the troubadours and their ideals of courtly love. Through their influence on the *Minnesänger,* the poets of southern France and those of Italy, the troubadours were to take Occitan culture to all the courts of Europe. The tale of Tristan and Isolde, although it is of Celtic origin, we owe to the troubadours of Occitanie.

Defeated and invaded during the Albigencian Crusades of 1209-71, especially by Simon de Montfort, Occitanie lost its independence and was incorporated into the Kingdom of France. Simone Weil in her book *L'Enracinement* (The Need for Roots) described the French conquest of the territories below the Loire as one of the great atrocities of history: 'These territories, where a high level of culture, tolerance, liberty and spiritual life existed, were inspired by intense patriotism for what they called their 'language' *(langage)*, a word by which they meant their country. The French were for them foreigners and barbarian, as the Germans are to us. In order to establish their terror, the French began by exterminating the whole town of Béziers . . . Once the country was conquered they brought in the Inquisition . . . It can be seen how strongly those regions hated the central power by the religious fervour shown at Toulouse towards the remains of the Duke of Montmorency who had been beheaded for rebellion by Richelieu'. According to Simone Weil, it was for the same reasons that the Occitans embraced the Revolution of 1789 and, later, rallied to the cause of radical socialism and anti-clericalism just as the Cathares had resisted the Inquisition.

Under the Third Republic they were no longer the adversaries of the central Government because to a large extent they were exploiting it for their own ends. As with the Corsicans, there is a widespread prejudice among the northern French against the Occitans, whom they accuse of having grabbed power and influence at the centre. If it is true, it has rarely been in the interests of Occitanie that Occitans have ruled France, however. Georges Pompidou, the former Prime Minister of France, who was fond of pointing to his origins in the Auvergne while refusing to tackle its problems by introducing a policy of regionalisation, was among the most recent—but probably not the last—Occitan to hold high office in Paris.

From the end of the thirteenth century on, the history of Occitanie was the history of its language and its culture. Indeed, it is from this time that the very name Occitanie dates, the region having taken its name from the language spoken there, as if—deprived of all political status—the language was its only means of identity. For three centuries more the language survived both in the *Jocs Floraux,* founded in Toulouse in 1323, and among the common people. But in 1539 it was banned by the Edict of Villers-Cotterêts from administrative use, with the result that many Occitans such as Brantôme, Montaigne, La Boetie and Montesquieu, chose to write in the official northern form of French. Thus began an intellectual tradition which continued with Fénélon, De Sade, Pascal, Emile Zola, Alphonse Daudet, Francis Jammes and, in our day, with the writers Pierre Emmanuel, Jacques Reverdy, François Mauriac, Auguste Comte, Jean Giono, Antoine de Saint Exupéry, Teilhard de Chardin, André Chamson, Jean Giraudoux, Paul Valéry, Francis Ponge and René Char—these are a few of the many writers born in Occitanie and with some knowledge of its language but not enough education in it to use it for their literary work.

There followed a period of decline and decadence in Occitan literature and, under Louis XIV, an inevitable reaction against the language and its culture which continued during the Revolution of 1789 and afterwards. The Occitan language, once the vehicle of the most esteemed culture in Western Europe, was condemned as a *patois,* a regional dialect, a vulgar and provincial speech which hampered the new revolutionary ideals of centralisation and French nationalism. Yet, despite systematic discrimination at all levels, and mainly because education was not obligatory, the majority of the common people remained Occitan-speaking up to the middle of the nineteenth century. The language survived, and long enough to benefit from the Romanticism which, throughout Europe, saw merit in the Middle Ages, and admired all things picturesque such as ruins and vernaculars. Occitanie's past was 'discovered' through the work of writers like Augustin Thierry and Mary-Lafen, who wrote the first history of Occitanie in 1842. The Occitan language was now about to enter its second great period.

The poet Frédéric Mistral (1830-1914) was the man mainly responsible for the renaissance. At the age of twenty-one he decided that his aim as a writer would be 'to revive the historical sense of my people by writing in Provençal'. Around him gathered a group of young writers with similar ambitions including the six other founding members Joseph Roumanille. Théodore Aubanel, Anselme Mathieu, Jean Brunet, Alphonse Tavan and Paul Giera. On 25 May 1854 they founded the movement known as the *Félibrige.* Their intention, in the first place, was to create a standard, unified language based on the Provençal dialect which they spoke, and then to write in it. The pioneer in this respect was the *Abbé* Joseph Roux of Limousin who wrote the first Occitan poems in a unified orthography based on etymological principles; he was followed by Prosper Estieu and Antonin Perbosc. Saluted by Lamartine as 'the new Homer', Mistral's contribution to European literature was recognised in 1904 when he won the Nobel Prize for his poem *Mirèio* (1851).

The *Félibrige* was also intended to be a political organisation. Among its earliest members was the socialist Jean Jaurès who later became the first leading politician in France to call for the teaching of Occitan and other 'regional languages' in the Republic's schools. Another member was Charles Maurras who was responsible for drafting the movement's manifesto, in 1892, demanding cultural and political autonomy for Occitanie and Brittany in a federal France. The regionalist programme set out in this manifesto, however, proved too much for some members of the *Félibrige*, especially those whose interests were only linguistic and literary. From this moment on the movement and its founder became increasingly *passéiste,* and reactionary, out of touch and sympathy with the virile oral and popular tradition of Occitanie and soon acquiescing in the spread of tourism and folk-lore throughout the region. Above all they refused to take a political lead in the growing economic crisis and even suffered the Third Republic's suppression of the *'patois'*. Having failed to awaken the Occitan conscience in his own way, Mistral became a monarchist and a French nationalist and moved to the right, decrying in his elegy for Lamartine *'les chiens enragés de la démocratie'* (the angry dogs of democracy). While ordinary people moved more and more to the left between 1848 and 1914, the *Félibrige* fell under the influence of Maurras. During the controversy which followed, Maurras left the movement, although still claiming allegiance to *la petite patrie,* to found a new party, the royalist and right-wing *Action Française.* In 1907 Mistral joined him and Maurice Barrès in its ranks, but their proposal for a popular front of all the autonomist parties in France was never pursued.

The *Félibrige* continued as a cultural and linguistic organisation but even in this function it ran into serious difficulties. For it soon became clear that the reform intended for the Provençal dialect, with a view to elevating it to the status of a language for the whole of Occitanie, was not acceptable to those of its members who spoke the numerous other dialects.

The *Félibrige,* however, survived the death of its founder and most eminent member. It still has sections throughout Occitanie and is organised in a *Consistoire* comprising fifty life-members elected by ordinary members for their literary work or contribution to Occitan studies and under the presidency of a *Capoulié.* Among its activities are the award to its members of titles such as *Mèstre en Gai Sabé, Mèstre d'Obro* to activists and *Soci* to friends of the Occitan language in various parts of the world. But by today, except in matters of scholarship and esoteric ritual, the *Félibrige* has lost much of its authority and its former glory has been eclipsed by more militant organisations. The schism within the *Félibrige* ended in a total break in 1919 and the formation of a group calling itself *Escola Occitana.* The aim of this new group was to employ all the dialects of Occitan in the creation of a new, synthetic literary form based on the orthography of the *troubadours.*

During the German occupation of France under the Vichy régime, the Occitan movement was for the most part in support of Pétain. Many of the regionalist magazines carried articles and reviews which praised French nationalism, even in defeat, some changing their titles to reflect their new function. Only a small group of writers, including Aragon, Eluard, Simone Weil and René Nelli, met to discuss the older democratic tradition of Occitanie. On the defeat of Hitler and the liberation of France, both camps were persecuted, the followers of Maurras and those of De Gaulle who favoured regionalist solutions for France after the War.

In 1945 the *Societé d'Etudes Occitanes,* founded fifteen years previously, became the *Institut d'Estudis Occitans* under the leadership of Jean Cassou. Among its early members were Max Rouquette, René Nelli and Tristan Tzara who had formulated new regionalist principles for Occitanie, in *Cahiers du Sud,* during the War, and who now began publishing an important magazine entitled *Oc.* The *I.O.E.* did much valuable work in the linguistic field, publishing a large number of texts, dictionaries and grammars. It also gave a new direction to the Occitan movement by accusing the *Félibrige* of provincialism, conservatism, clericalism, folklore, defeatism and of associating the cause of the language with the cult of Mistral and reactionary politics. On the other hand, the *Félibrige* denounced the *I.O.E.* as Marxist and revolutionary. What is clear is that up to 1962 the Occitan movement consisted mainly of poets and novelists with little political experience or ambitions and, it sometimes appeared, who were more interested in internecine ideological feuds than in taking practical steps in the cause of the Occitan language and its culture. Nevertheless, the post-war years were not without their fruits for it is to this period that the beginning of regionalist ideas in Occitanie must be traced.

The renaissance of Occitan poetry has continued with the publication of the work of poets like Pierre Rouquette (born 1898), Pierre Bec (born 1921), Robert Lafont (born 1923), Yves Rouquette (born 1936) and his brother Jean (pseudonym of Jean Larzac, born 1938) and many others. One of the problems which these writers have had to face is the tradition of *'méridionalisme'* in which Occitan has often been used for comic purposes. Ever since Daudet and his Tartarin, through Marcel Pagnol's *Topaze* (1928) and Fernandel, the Occitans have been considered by Northerners as lazy, untrustworthy, cowardly, garrulous, boastful and emotional, usually caricatured as wearing the wide-brimmed hat and loosely-tied bow popularised by Mistral and the Republican students of 1848. This misrepresentation of *le type du Midi* has also been based on various Occitans such as Edouard Daladier and Paul Reynaud, who have held high political office, and on Philippe Pétain who, although a Northerner, was a disciple of Mistral's, was advised by Maurras and headed the collaborationist Vichy régime during the Second World War.

Meanwhile, the decline in the economic life of Occitanie has continued to an extent now generally regarded throughout France as serious in the extreme. In fact, the region has been neglected and exploited since the eighteenth century. Even under the Second Empire in the heyday of the *Félibrige,* there was widespread depression in both industry and agriculture, especially in the vineyards on which the economy depends. In 1907, faced with the likelihood of being ruined, the wine-growers revolted and Languedoc was put under military control by Clemenceau. During the crisis the *Félibrige* was asked to support the workers by their leader Ernest Ferroul, a former Communard, but Mistral—by now far to the right—refused and the rising came to an end with nothing gained for Occitans.

Occitanie's economic problems are familiar enough to anyone acquainted with the peripheral areas of France: foreign capital is invested in industry which is already near bankruptcy; depression and closures follow, the local population is forced to leave, companies go into liquidation and are replaced by military sites and arsenals which are controlled from Paris. As a result, regional enterprise and local capital have almost completely disappeared and many areas of Occitanie are completely deserted. The process of 'interior colonisation' is exacerbated by tourism and, in particular, by the existence of innumerable 'holiday homes' in all parts of the region. Like most other minorities in Western Europe, the Occitans are of the opinion that tourism, as it is administered by the centralist, capitalist State, is among the most pernicious influence on the region's economy and culture and on the personality of its people. The *Côte d'Argent,* for example, has been developed by purchase of land at low prices, the exclusion of regional companies, the clearing out of the local population or their employment in the seasonal trade at the most menial level, followed by massive immigration by wealthy families from Italy, Germany and the Netherlands. The continuing crisis in the wine-growing industry has led to many strikes and other disturbances during the last ten years, so that the growing cultural consciousness of Occitanie has been reinforced by workers who, although more concerned with wages, conditions and subventions, have made common cause with the Occitan movement. With the Basques and the Catalans, the Occitan autonomists are among the minorities who have succeeded most in uniting proletariat and middle-class in their opposition to the State.

It is little wonder that, during the last fifteen years, there

has been a crisis in the political and cultural conscience of Occitanie. On the cultural plane there has clearly been a growing
awareness of the need for the teaching of Occitan in the
schools and colleges and, among the young, a new interest in
the region's history, language and literature. But Occitan is
not taught at primary level, it is only an optional subject for
the oral examination at the *baccalauréat*. In 1972, the numbers of people choosing to take the oral examination in Occitan
were as follows: Aix 457, Bordeaux 1,038, Clermont 160,
Limoges 205, Montpellier 1,334, Nice 120 and Toulouse
1,217. An Occitan Summer School is held annually at Montpellier and Villeneuve-sur-Lot, with the aim of developing the
language in science, technology and education, and of
teaching the history, literature and music of Occitanie; a
Festival d'Oc is also held annually as part of the *Festival
d'Avignon*. But the language has not yet been accorded official recognition of any kind. There has been too a vigorous
revival in Occitan poetry and song—the singers Claude Mar-
ty, Mans de Breish and Patric have played a leading role
here—with the publication of many anthologies and records
by such companies as *Ventadorn*.

In political terms, however, Occitanie is in a state of flux at
the present time, with a bewildering proliferation of
groups and organisations, none of which has won the
substantial support of any section of the electorate. The
fact remains that the majority of Occitan activists choose
to work through the main French political parties,
especially those of the left.

The only group calling itself nationalist in the political
sense is the *Partit Nacionalista Occitan (P.N.O.)*, founded
in 1959 and led by François Fontan. The *P.N.O.* refuses all
commitment to either the left or right while working
for an independent Occitan Republic. Fontan, the
general secretary, owes more to Maurras then to Marx,
having belonged in his time to the *Action Française*. Some of
his theories about 'ethnism' are properly regarded as bogus
by other organisations in the region; certainly, many of his
more extreme declarations amount to racialism. The
P.N.O. has also attracted members of right-wing convictions

such as Pierre Maclouf, editor of *Lu Lugar,* and former members of *Languedoc* and *Auvergne Combat.* The party has not yet taken part in elections and has only a few dozen members; their activities are said to be confined to painting slogans on walls (a contribution taken seriously for its propaganda value in Occitanie) and to making press statements on various aspects of the region's situation. It was most in the news from 1959 up to the strikes in the mines at Décazeville in 1962. But by 1974 it had not developed beyond the status of being *'groupusculaire'.* Although it has attracted much attention to the Occitan problem the *P.N.O.* and its leader are mistrusted by most other groups, especially those on the left. A characteristic of almost all accounts by Occitan writers of the situation in Occitanie is that they attack with the most ferocious ideological bitterness not only the *P.N.O.* but all other groups in the spectrum of opinion throughout the region. A recent book by Robert Lafont, *La Revendication Occitane* (1975) appears to be among the most reasonable, if *engagés,* assessments to be published so far.

More worthy of serious consideration is the movement known as *Comitat Occitan d'Estudis e d'Accion* (Occitan Committee for Study and Action). This group, which includes all the most important figures in the Occitan movement, bases its activities on the principles of socialism, regionalism and support for Occitan culture in all its manifestations. Its director, who was formerly president of *I.O.E.,* is the distinguished philologist and author Robert Lafont whose contribution to the progress of regionalist and ethnic-political thinking in France has been of major importance. The term *'colonialisme intérieur',* which has gained widespread currency in France, was first popularised in a manifesto signed by Lafont and others in December 1961. The *C.O.E.A.* co-ordinates the work of a large number of its branches in association with local trade union councils and agricultural co-operatives. In 1968 it took part in the Sorbonne conference with *Jeunesse Étudiante Bretonne* and the *Front Régionaliste Corse,* of which the *Comité pour la Révolution Socialiste des Regions* (Committee for the Socialist Revolution in the Regions) was formed. From its formation the *C.O.E.A.* has demanded the abolition of the *département* as an administrative unit, more regional planning, more powers for the smaller unit of the commune, and the creation of three main Occitan regions: a Mediterranean region, the region of Aquitaine (Bordeaux—Toulouse) and the region of Auvergne—Limousin; included in its programme is autonomous status for Corsica, North Catalonia and the Northern Basque provinces. Each region would have its own Assembly. The organ of *C.O.E.A.* is the magazine *Viura* (To Live). Many of its members are involved in the organisation of folk-concerts and in street theatre which, since 1970, have enjoyed tremendous success in the villages of the region. In 1971 the *C.O.E.A.* was taken over by a small revolutionary group known as *Lutte Occitane* whose main aim is to create in Occitanie an autonomous region based on working-class solidarity in which the people will be able to realise their potential in cultural and political terms.

The function of *C.O.E.A.* has been largely that of a catalyst in the creation of *'la conscience Occitane'*. Many of its members were students and writers under the age of thirty who took part in 'the events of May 1968'. It was at this time that productions like *Mort et résurrection de M. Occitania* (The Death and Resurrection of Mr Occitanie) and *La Guerre du Vin* (The Wine War) had enormous popular success throughout the region. But the excitement was to last for only two years before the *C.O.E.A.* showed signs of schisms once more, particularly between the younger generation and the middle-aged. The ideological conflict came to a head at its conference of 1971 when, under pressure from younger members wishing to move to the left, *C.O.E.A.* changed its name to *Lutte Occitane*. This small revolutionary group aims to create in Occitanie an autonomous region based on working-class solidarity in which the people will be able to realise their potential in cultural and political terms.

Among the basic tenets of *Lutte Occitane (Lucha Occitana)*, which remains the principal political organisation with a regionalist commitment to Occitanie at the present time, are that the region has its own linguistic and cultural character and its own history of resistance to 'the French hegemony'; that it suffers from capitalist exploitation of a colonial type by means of which the French State is in the process of liquidating a national minority, especially its working-class; and that this situation calls for a regionalist rather than a nationalist ideology, making common cause with the working classes of the regions of France. The movement's aims are therefore defined as those of the class-struggle led by Occitan workers against both capitalist and national exploitation; it seeks to win for the Occitan working-class the right to live and work in its own districts and the power to resist 'interior colonialism' by which is understood the pillage of the region's material and human resources. 'The question', its manifesto states, 'is therefore not one of Occitan nationalism or of European federalism or of regionalism, but the destruction of the French capitalist State; the role of the popular Occitan movement in this destruction is . . . the abolition of the imperialist system by the Internationale of the proletariats and oppressed peoples'. That such declarations are not only youthful rhetoric is suggested by the fact that *Lutte Occitane* has won a wide measure of active support during the last five years and by now has become the flame-bearer of the Occitan movement. It was this organisation which led the famous campaign in 1971-2 against the use for military purposes of agricultural areas around Larzac. Its newspaper *Que Faire* sells 8,000 copies monthly and it is attracting members all over Occitanie, from the *I.O.E.* and other left-wing groups such as the *P.S.U.,* the *S.F.I.O.* and the *P.C.F.* Whether it can unite the Occitan movement, and the other *groupuscules* such as the *Parti Socialiste Occitan* founded in 1967, the *Fédération Anarchiste Communiste d'Occitanie (F.A.C.O.)* founded in 1969 and *Pòble d'Oc,* remains to be seen but such a *rapprochement* seems most unlikely, given the polarisation of the movement and the polemical nature of the debate.

It is more probable that, while the Occitan regionalists, the autonomists, the federalists, the nationalists and the revolutionaries continue to argue and thus to make their contribution to public discussion of the Occitan problem, the major French political parties—which the majority of the people still support—will be persuaded, or obliged, to introduce a greater measure of devolution into the government of France. That they have refused to do so up to the present says more about the Republic's Jacobin tradition than about the demands made upon it by the Occitans.

THE CATALANS OF ROUSSILLON

Like the Basques, their counterparts in the Western Pyrénées, the Catalans are to be found on both sides of the frontier between the French and Spanish States, but are more numerous to the south where, in the *Principat* of *Catalunya,* they number approximately eight and a half million.* There are however, about 260,000 Catalans on the northern side of the frontier who are citizens of France. They live in the districts of Roussillon and Cerdagne, in the department of *Pyrénées Orientales,* of which Perpignan (Catalan: *Perpinyà)* is the principal town and which has a total population of approximately 299,400 (1975). Although the State frontier lies between them, the Northern Catalans and their compatriots in Spain are ethnically one people speaking the same language, *català.* This language, which belongs to the Romance family, is also spoken in the Republic of Andorra (population: 22,000) where it is used for official purposes with French, and in the Balearic Islands.

French interest in the Roussillon *(Rosselló)* and Cerdagne *(Cerdanya)* began two hundred years before these districts were annexed to France by the Treaty of the Pyrénées in 1659. They were occupied by the army of Gaston IV, Count of Foix, in 1462, only to be ceded in 1475 by Juan II, King of Aragon, to Louis XI who put them under military control; twenty years later they were handed back to Spain by Charles VIII. The Castilian suppression of the area then began, mainly because the Catalans had become francophiles during the French occupation. So oppressive was the Spanish Crown's policy in Roussillon, particularly under Phillip II, that the district was strongly in favour of re-unification with France. In 1642 the town of Perpignan was besieged and finally fell to the French. Having failed to annex the whole of Catalonia, the French Army retreated to Roussillon, accompanied by many Catalans from Barcelona who had fought with it against the Castilians. Seven years later, however, as the Treaty of the Pyrénées was about to be signed, the greater part of the local aristocracy,

* As the history of the Catalan people is described in Chapter 14, the present account will deal mainly with the Northern Catalans since the Treaty of the Pyrénées in 1659.

the bourgeoisie and the priests, all by now bitterly anti-French, left for Barcelona. This double movement of population, in which the anti-French Catalans emigrated into Spain and the pro-French Catalans settled in Roussillon, ensured for France the enthusiastic support of the Northern Catalans for the new régime. Under Francese de Sagarra, a pro-French refugee, all attempts by guerrillas, known as the *Angelets* to assert the Catalan identity of the area were crushed and the policy of *francisation* began. In the year 1700 French was proclaimed the only legal language for official purposes. Despite this edict, the first hostile act of the French Government against Catalan, the language continued to be spoken by the common people and to show the resilience which has been one of its chief characteristics ever since. It was only the bourgeoisie and the upper classes who abandoned the Catalan language in favour of French. From 1662 the ancient University of Perpignan had been dominated by the Jesuits and to them were sent the sons of the upper classes for a French education. Unable to make their way without supporting the French Monarchy and cut off from their compatriots in Spain, these young Catalans were soon denationalised, abandoning the language and their ethnic identity.

With the revolution of 1789, the Roussillon became once again the subject of conflict between France and Spain. Designated as the department of *Pyrénées-Orientales* in 1790, it was invaded by the Spaniards in April 1793 but was restored to France in the same year. Following the school laws of Jules Ferry, Catalan was banished from the education system by teachers determined to wipe out all 'Spanish sentiment' in the region: *'Soyez propre, parlez français'* (Be clean, speak French) was the order of the day. Despite this oppression of the local culture, the Roussillon remained content with its status after the Revolution of 1848 and under the Second Empire, becoming and remaining to the present day one of the most Republican areas in the whole of France. It also accepted that its markets were to the north, where railways were built as early as 1848, long before those of Spain, so that even economic contacts between the Roussillon and the *Principat* were few. Unlike the Northern Basques, the Northern

Catalans were thus prevented from developing links with their countrymen to the south, preferring relations with the Occitans.

It is therefore surprising to discover that, although it was proscribed by the Revolution and allowed, at least theoretically, only in the schools under the Deixonne Law of 1951, the Catalan language is still spoken by as many as 260,000 people or 60% of the population of the Roussillon and Cerdagne—a rare and much-quoted example to demonstrate that the maintenance of a language does not always depend entirely on the political circumstances in which it is spoken.

In reality, however, the situation of the language in North Catalonia is not at all satisfactory. In the schools there is a deliberate policy of suppressing the pupil's interest in the language, literature and history of Catalonia. Even the local accent and Catalanisms are not accepted by teachers of French. The Deixonne Law has been resisted by the authorities ever since it was introduced in 1951. In the mass media there have been a few symbolic concessions: five minutes are broadcast daily in Catalan, very early in the morning, and a monthly half-hour on television has been promised. There is a column of about 300 words in the newspaper *L'Indépendant des Pyrénées Orientales* every other day, but the opinions expressed are always in support of the French Government's 'hexagonal' attitudes. Folk-lore, tourism and a simple local patriotism are the main subjects for official pronouncements. Since the Second World War the bilingualism of North Catalonia, always asymetrical, has turned heavily in favour of French, under pressure from the schools and mass media.

One of the most potent factors in this situation is the widespread prejudice that Catalan is a lower-class language spoken in rural districts and the poorer quarters of some towns. To some extent this is the case, of course, for it is mainly among the agricultural workers of Roussillon, who make up 32% of the region's population, the lower sections of *la petite bourgeoisie* and the urban proletariat, that Catalan still flourishes. It is the French-speaking upper middle-class, including the civil servants, who look down on the Catalan-speakers and prevent a just recognition of their language. As a result of this social degradation the Catalan language is most frequently heard on such occasions as after-dinner speeches, for jokes illustrating the gaucheries of peasants in the company of the *'moussious et madimouselles'*, in patriotic verses extolling the natural beauty of the Roussillon, and so on. But for 'serious' purposes the language is French.

Social attitudes towards the Catalan language have their origin, of course, in the economic problems of the Roussillon. Chronically under-developed, the region loses around 1,000 of its population annually. Few jobs are available for school-leavers and over 90% emigrate, mostly to the north of France. A large proportion of young Northern Catalans make their careers in the French Army or the police force or, as in Corsica, become administrators. At the same time, there is a high immigration rate into the area of retired French people which began with the resettlement of *les pieds-noirs* from North Africa in the early 1960s. In some districts Walloons own up to 80% of the land, while tourism has brought 'holiday homes' to the region, reducing the autochthonous population in some communes to 5% of the total. The Catalans are nowhere stronger than 60%. In North Catalonia as a whole the Catalans have been dispossessed of more than 10% of their land since 1960; in eleven communes 20% belongs to non-French foreigners, in five communes more than 50%. Unlike their compatriots in Spain, the Northern Catalans have lost almost all their powers of assimilation. There is widespread awareness among them that they are *'l'exili interior'* (interior exiles), a feeling expressed in the topical song: *'De quin país veniu? On aneu? Soc d' aqui, soc estranger'* (What country do you come from? Where are you going? I am from around here, I am a foreigner.) The extreme point of alienation among the Northern Catalans is the subject of the stories written by Albert Saisset, author of *Les Catalanades d'un Tal*.

The predicament of Northern Catalans, characterised by apathy and alienation from their cultural heritage and by an increasing inability to control their own affairs, contrasts with that of the Catalans of the *Principat* beyond the Pyrénées. There is still, nevertheless, a traditional attitude of superiority among the Catalans of Roussillon towards their southern

compatriots, whom they mock as the *espanyol*. The most orthodox of their leaders are fond of justifying the region's integration into the French State by claiming that the 'Spanish
Catalans' have a cruel step-mother, Spain, while the Catalans
of Roussillon have made a love-match with France. More
seriously, the poet Josep Sebastia Pons has written, 'Between
our neighbours and us there exists a line of literary demarcation which is one of sensibility, taste and culture'. But the
grounds for this superiority have been eroded in recent
decades. By today, while the Roussillon's economy has
deteriorated, the *Principat* has enjoyed an economic boom,
becoming synonymous with factories, motor-ways and
prosperity. Many middle-class Catalans in Perpignan have
already realised that their interests lie over the border; a
growing number have moved their businesses there and have
become integrated with the middle-class of Barcelona, only to
re-cross the border as week-end tourists, thus contributing
further to the Roussillon's cultural crisis.

For over twenty years the region's problems have grown
more and more apparent. Over 80% of the local enterprises,
making such goods as shoes, toys, chocolates and
confectionery, employ less than five salaried persons
each: the remainder of the work-force is badly paid
and suffers poor conditions. Lacking outlets to the south,
these businesses have been closing in rapid succession
and unemployment is higher than anywhere else in France.
There are frequent crises in agriculture, which employs a
third of the work-force, mainly the result of take-overs by
large companies such as the jam-makers, *Roussillon Alimen-
taire*. Family businesses are no longer viable and many sell up
before entering the tertiary sector which has been developed
by tourism controlled from outside the region. Land abandoned by farmers is bought up and used for tourist camps,
whole villages belonging to Parisians are occupied in summer
and deserted in winter, with the usual consequences for the
life of the community.

Attempts to save the language in North Catalonia have
been made during the last twenty years but usually without
reference to the economic decline of the region, the linguistic
problem tending to be considered in a vacuum. For example,

the *Grup Rossellones d' Estudis Catalans (G.R.E.C.),* founded in 1960, rallied several hundred members for 'the defence
and promotion of the Catalan language', but they were drawn
from both the left and the right wing and never agreed on a
practical policy or programme. After eight years the most extreme right-wingers left the group and founded the *Institut
Rossellonès d' Estudis Catalans* and its periodical *Revista
Catalana.* Neither group really defined what it meant by
bilingualism in the context of North Catalonia, preferring to
believe in the possibility of an indefinite, harmonious co-
existence for Catalan and French regardless of economic and
political development. Little research has been done into the
socio-linguistics of the region, except to draw attention to the
need for a unified standard for use by both intellectuals and
the working-class. The *Universitat Catalana d' Estiu* (Catalan
Summer University), an unofficial body, has striven to give
prestige to the language by demonstrating that it is capable of
technical, intellectual and scientific use. Other groups, such
as the youth organisation *Grup Cultural de la Joventut
Catalana,* founded in 1967, have studied the problem facing
the language, only to break up over ideological differences in
the same way as the *G.C.J.C.* did, becoming the *Front de la
Joventut Catalana* in 1970.

A number of individual writers such as Josep Sebastia Pons
(1886-1962) and Jordi Pere Cerda have made important
contributions to the progress of Catalan in Roussillon by
writing essays, journalism and poetry in it, while a younger
generation of poets have turned from the *'floretes, ocellets i
canigonetes'* (little flowers, little birds and hymns to Canigo,
Roussillon's sacred mountain) of their elders, the generation
of Albert Saisset, to more contemporary themes of engagement.
Among the clichés which these young writers attack is the French
caricature of the Catalan as a beefy, boozy, loud-mouthed
and simple-minded exhibitionist who lives on sausages and
snails. They are few in number but in such groups as *Grup
Guillem de Cabestany* and *Escola Popular Catalana* they have
introduced a new, serious note to discussion of the Catalan
problem by studying the political thought of their southern
compatriots, especially the national idea, the history of the
Gèneralitat during the Spanish Republic, the Pan-Catalan

periodical press and the problems shared by other minorities within the French State. One of their greatest obstacles is that the University of Perpignan is, in the words of the review *La Falç*, 'in the image of its region: under-developed and alienated', taking little interest in the national culture which remains, in Roussillon, without focus and without direction, 'a culture without a centre'. The cultural activities of Catalans from over the border reach only a few hundred intellectuals in Roussillon; few subscribe to the principal magazines published in Barcelona and theatrical performances in Catalan are infrequent save for special occasions organised by such groups as the *Universitat Catalana d' Estiu* at Prades. The major exception to this rule is the huge success enjoyed by the *'nova canço Catalana'* (the new Catalan song) by means of folk-concerts. This is one of the few ways in which the Roussillon is linked to the national Catalan culture and is able to express itself vigorously and often in political terms. It is only recently that intellectuals have begun to look to Barcelona and its cultural life.

The steady growth of an autonomist movement in North Catalonia dates only from about 1967. Three years later the first political organisation was formed, the *Comitat Rossellones d'Estudis i d'Animacio,* a left-wing group which was critical of the culturalist approach. The *C.R.E.A.* was joined in 1972 by the *Accio Regionalista Catalana,* a regionalist, federalist and European movement founded by Gilbert Grau which campaigned at the time of the French Government's regionalisation plans in 1969, and by *Esquerra Catalana dels Treballadors,* a Marxist-Leninist party which grew out of the *C.R.E.A.* in 1972. None of these parties has ever won more than 2% of the votes cast at elections. The cultural movement remains unaligned and the political organisations, although using Catalan in their electoral campaigns, have not yet outlined their cultural and linguistic programmes. There are various other *groupuscules* in the political spectrum of North Catalonia, to almost the same extent as in Occitanie.

It was Mistral who referred to the Catalans as *'nos fraires de Catalonha'* (our brothers of Catalonia) and it seems likely, as most Occitan organisations make provision in their programmes for the autonomy of the Catalan and Basque districts at present incorporated within the French State, that the future of the Northern Catalans depends as much on the success of the Occitan movement as on the restoration of democracy on the other side of the Pyrénées.

THE NORTHERN BASQUES

The three departments known collectively in French as *le pays basque* are Labourd (Basque: *Lapurdi*), Basse-Navarre *(Benapara)* and Soule *(Ciberoa)*. Separated since 1659 from the four Basque provinces under Spanish rule by the State border, the Northern Basque Country forms about one fifth of Euzkadi's total area (1,100 square miles) and has a population of approximately 200,000 (1970), about one tenth of the whole.* The principal towns of the region are Bayonne *(Baiona)*, Biarritz *(Biarritze)* and Saint-Jean-de-Luz on the coast, and inland Saint-Jean-Pied-de-Port *(Donibane Garazi)* and Mauléon *(Litzare)*.

Although, like Catalonia, the seven Basque provinces are divided between the French and Spanish States, the Basques living on both sides of the Pyrénées are one people speaking the same language. It is estimated that 90,000 Basques in the northern provinces have a knowledge of this language, *euskera;* about 90% of these are people in their sixties and seventies.

Despite the fact that the Northern Basques belong to the same ethnic group as their compatriots to the south, speaking dialects of the same language and sharing the same culture, their fate as citizens of France and their attitudes to Basque nationality have not always been the same. In the years before the Spanish Civil War, for example, while following the fortunes of the Basque Nationalist Party which culminated in the creation of the Basque Republic and subsequent defeat by Franco's forces, the Northern Basques made little attempt to prepare for re-unification within the new State. The reserve of the Northern Basques during those years is explained largely by the fact that, although deeply Catholic, the Southern Basques were in the Republican camp and this was known to disconcert the traditionalists in the north. Also, the Basques in Spain scrupulously avoided calling on their countrymen in France for fear of losing the French Government's support. The sympathy of Paris was important to the Basque

---

* As the history of the Basques is described in Chapter 14, the present account will deal mainly with the Northern Basques since the Spanish Civil War.

nationalists, especially after their defeat when the Basque Government in Exile moved there. The paradox was that, while helping the Basque cause against Franco, the French authorities consistently refrained from the slightest reference to the situation of the Basques within their own borders. Among prominent critics of the French Government's hypocrisy and the Vatican's acquiescence at this time were the writers François Mauriac, Jacques Maritain and Georges Bernanos in his books *Les Grands Cimetières sous la Lune* (1937) and *Nous Autres Français* (1939); but theirs were lone voices.

It is true that the Basque problem in France has not been posed in the same terms as in Spain. Far less numerous, 'the continental Basques' as they are sometimes known to distinguish them from 'the peninsular Basques', have only on rare occasions shown the national consciousness and militancy which have for long been characteristic of their southern brothers. The process of assimilation has been rapid since the Revolution of 1789. Napoleon consolidated the centralism of the Revolution and his régime saw the end of the ancient Basque liberties in the three northern provinces, whereas the four southern provinces continued to enjoy some autonomy until 1839. In 1789 the autonomous regions of Soule and Labourd were abolished, the French revolutionaries considering their desire for autonomy and their Catholicism as reactionary. Barrère's dictum, 'Fanaticism speaks Basque' was accepted everywhere in 1794 when 4,000 Basques were deported from frontier villages to a detention camp in the Landes where about 1,600 of them died. In 1808, at a conference in Bayonne at which Napoleon proposed discussing a new constitution for Spain, Mendiola the deputy for Viscaya and two French deputies, the Garat brothers of Ustaritz, spoke in favour of a unified Basque State within the Napoleonic Empire. Napoleon accepted this idea but because the Basques supported Spain in its war with France nothing more was heard.

Since then the Basque Country has been an economically poor region, one of France's depressed areas. During the *Ancien Régime* and the two World Wars, when there was a Basque regiment with the Allied forces, many Basques served and died *'pour la France'* and showed a certain French patriotism characteristic of the Republic's peripheral areas. About 150,000 are to be found in Paris today and many others in Latin America. Among these emigrants, who leave at the rate of over 1,000 every year, is a very high percentage of the young and educated who have had to leave home for lack of opportunities. About 80% of pupils leave the region annually in search of work. During the past decade the region's small industrial base has contracted and unemployment has grown; it depends now on small-scale farming, fishing and seasonal tourism. Despite this neglect, or perhaps because of the drain on the region's resources, very few Basques have any form of active political involvement. In Paris the region is represented mainly by conservative Gaullist deputies upon whom few local demands are made. There has been no nationalist deputy for over ten years. The Church is extremely conservative with little interest in mobilising the population for radical purposes. The only non-political organisation which has made a serious attempt to win recognition for the region's economic problems is the *Union pour le Développement et la Défense du Pays Basque* (Union for the Development and Defence of the Basque Country). The significant but dwindling numbers who speak the Basque language are to be found mostly among the older generation, and the region's culture consists mainly of *fiestas* and pelote tournaments which seem to be more tourist attractions than the expression of a living tradition.

For these reasons the Northern Basques have not developed a nationalist movement comparable with that on the Spanish side of the border, and are far less politically conscious. Nevertheless, the region has not been entirely inert. The growth of the separatist movement in the southern provinces since 1950 has encouraged some Northern Basques, especially the young, to examine their consciences. Exiles from the south have helped to awaken their political awareness and the deterioration in the region's economy has also contributed to a growing crisis.

The first and most important political movement in the northern Basque provinces was *Enbata*. It was founded in 1959 by Ximun Haran, a pelote champion and now a chemist in the border town of Hendaye. The group's first conference was held at Itxassou in Labourd in April 1963. Deputies, local councillors and senators as well as delegates from Brittany, Catalonia, Flanders, Wallonie and Occitanie were present. According to a report in *Le Monde*, three quarters of the 500 people present were under the age of thirty. The 'Charter of Itxassou' proclaimed on this occasion became the rallying point of *Enbata*: 'On this national day, 15 April 1963, the Basques who are present around the young oak-tree of Gernika planted at Itxassou declare that we Basques are one people, by land, by race, by language and by institutions; one nation by our will in the past and in the present, one democracy by our way of life and history. As one people, one nation and one democracy we claim our right to unity and to free individual and collective status . . .'. One of the leading speakers at this conference was Jacques Abeberry and he it was who defined the party's aims. Its first aim was the creation of a single department to be known in French as *Le Pays Basque* which would be 'the legal expression of an entity existing today only for the use of tourists', and the General Council of which would prefigure a Basque political authority. But the ultimate aim of *Enbata* was the re-unification of the northern with the southern provinces as an independent, democratic State within a confederal Europe. The confederal idea was accepted by the Northern Basques from the party's second conference in 1964 at which Jacques Abeberry was reported as saying, 'It is not France, Germany or Italy which we will have to face tomorrow, but Bavaria, Alsace, Wallonie, Sicily, Brittany, Luxembourg and Catalonia'. *Enbata* (the west wind which precedes a storm) was thus launched as a political party *'un mouvement fédéraliste de libération nationale'* (a federalist movement of national liberation).

The party's founder, Ximun Haran, was of the opinion, however, that its function should be to educate the Basques, particularly the young, in the history of their country. Against his advice, the party entered the political arena in 1967. Up to then the only Basque nationalist ever to contest an election in France had been Paul Legarralde who had won 7,000 votes in a municipal election at Hendaye in 1934. The new party now put up two candidates in a general election and polled 5% of the votes. A year later it won 2·8%, also in a general election.

In the election of 1973 the party did not participate, having decided that for the time being this was not its role. In January the following year *Enbata* was banned by the French Government, at the same time as the *F.L.B.* in Brittany, on the grounds that it was 'a subversive organisation inimical to the unity of the French State'.

Enbata did not have much power anywhere in the three provinces. Among the few local councillors elected on its ticket was Jean Etcheverry, a former deputy and a well-known personality, but that was in 1964, a year after the party's launching and before the emergence of a Marxist wing which later caused internal dissension and the departure of Ximun Haran from active leadership. A number of mayors in rural areas, farmers mostly, sympathised with the party but were opposed to the public demonstrations which *Enbata* organised and to the growing influence of *E.T.A.* refugees among the party's younger members. For them, while opposition to Spanish persecution demanded revolutionary techniques, the situation on the French side of the Pyrénées required different methods. The bodies in which these farmers are grouped, such as the wine co-operative at Baigorry, although patriotic in sentiment, took a more pragmatic approach and the activists of *Enbata* never really persuaded them that separatism was the answer to the region's economic problems.

Inevitably perhaps, the party found it had rivals and splinter-groups. Foremost among the new organisations were *Mende Berri* (New Century) which, starting as a publishing imprint and bookshop, broke away from *Amaya* because that body forbade any part in political activity to its members. Another organisation *Anai Artea* (Between Brothers) cares for Basques who are on the run from the Spanish police for nationalist activities; it is led by the famous *Abbé* Larzabal of Socoa, near Saint-Jean-de-Luz, who is also a distinguished writer.

Although the ordinary Basque people in France have not yet shown the resolve of their counterparts on the Spanish side, Basque nationalists can expect to find aid and refuge among them. When, during the Burgos trials of 1970, the West German Consul was kidnapped by *E.T.A.*, taken to a village in Soule and escaped, he was handed back to the nationalists by people from a local café who kept the secret until the end of the affair. The existence of a friendly, if reticent, population on the other side of the frontier facilitates the transport of persons, literature and arms. The huge summer traffic in the Pyrénées and the innumerable crossing points make it fairly easy to pass from one side to the other, except in states of emergency. In their efforts to prevent contacts between the two regions, the Spanish authorities can sometimes rely on co-operation from the French police who have been known to hand back Basque nationalists on the run. There is little evidence that the French Government disapproves of these local decisions. Indeed, after demonstrations following *Aberri Eguna,* the Basque National Day, celebrated on Easter Sunday, two prominent Basques Telesforo de Monzon and José-Luis Alvarez, known as Txillardegi, a highly esteemed writer and one of the founders of *E.T.A.,* were expelled from the northern provinces after promoting the nationalist cause there and compelled to live some 200 miles away. They were allowed to return to the northern Basque provinces on condition that they signed a declaration promising not to take part in any political activity and only after a hunger-strike had been held in the cathedral at Saint-Jean-de-Luz. The campaign to cancel the French Government's *interdiction de séjour* was led by Marc Legasse who, at the end of the Second World War, was imprisoned for calling on Basques to boycott the general elections.

On the other hand, the French Government has given hospitality to several groups of Southern Basques on the French side of the border. France is in fact obliged to treat Basque refugees as Spaniards under a convention agreed by Pétain and the Madrid Government which has never been rescinded. France is obliged to remove the refugees from its territories contiguous to Spain but is not allowed to banish them altogether nor to return them to the Spanish authorities. After the Second World War the French Government chose not to implement the Pétain agreement and to allow Basques from the Spanish side to settle north of the border. Spain, on the other hand, continues to arrest and imprison Basques from the northern provinces for nationalist activities in the south, as was demonstrated in 1965 when a young teacher from the north named Christine Etchalus, a member of *Enbata's* executive committee, was arrested on the way to Pamplona *(Iruna)*.

During the 'state of exception' in the southern provinces in the first half of 1975 violence also erupted on the northern side of the border. An attempt was made to blow up the Basque refugees' headquarters in Paris and a bomb exploded at the home of José Urrutikoetxea, an exiled nationalist in Biarritz. Commenting on these incidents in an editorial, *The Guardian* (London, 10 June 1975) said, 'Not since Mussolini sent hired assassins to Marseilles to murder the Rosselli brothers has a dictator shown such vindictiveness'. In retaliation, an armed uniformed Spanish policeman was shot in a square at Bayonne.

The exiled Basque Government which fled on the fall of the autonomous Republic in 1937 still has a delegation in Paris and an official representative in Bayonne. The majority Basque party at the time of the Republican defeat, the Basque National Party is also based in Bayonne. The reason why up to now these organisations have been tolerated by the French authorities is that they are officially concerned only with the Basques in Spain. The moment they turn their attention to the Basques in France they expect to be prohibited: for Paris is as centralist as ever in its attitudes and policies towards its Basque minority. The Pompidou régime, and its Ministers such as Michel Debré and Marcellin, was anxious to co-operate with the Spanish Government and to avoid offending it by showing leniency to the Basques. The sympathetic gestures it made towards the Basques on trial at Burgos in 1970 were the result of public opinion following the events of May 1968 rather than sincerely held convictions.

The history of the French Government's intransigence towards the Basques, as towards other minorities of the hexagon, is centuries old. Following the example set by the *Abbé* Grégoire in his hatred of 'rude idioms' and Talleyrand's proposal for the creation of primary schools in order to combat the growth of 'dialects', the municipal authorities of Bayonne recommended the immediate introduction of French into all the schools of the Basses-Pyrénées. In 1802 the region's *sous-préfet* had a college built at Mauléon 'in order to save from ignorance a people who because they have their own idiom can hardly communicate with the rest of the Nation and to frenchify the Basques who are backward in their customs, manners, civilisation and language'. By 1846 the official policy was 'to substitute the Basque language in our schools by the French language'. As in Brittany, the use of *le symbole,* the equivalent of the Welsh Not, was widespread in the State schools of the northern Basque provinces throughout the nineteenth century and the early years of the twentieth. The private, confessional schools had a slightly better record but were entirely ineffective in their teaching of Basque. Only in the *ikastolas,* the voluntary Basque-language schools, has any progress been made. At the same time, the French Government reacted to the growth of the *ikastolas* in 1971 with a ministerial circular which allowed the teaching of three hours of Basque, and other 'regional languages', per week. Since 1971 little has been done to implement this regulation, however. The main problem is an alleged lack of funds to pay teachers. Only during the last three years has Basque been accepted as a subject eligible for study at the *baccalauréat.*

A similar situation faces the Basque language in radio and television. The first radio station *'Radio Côte Basque Vacances',* opened at the Biarritz Casino in 1960, was intended exclusively for tourists, run voluntarily and its Basque content censored. After many petitions, the first Basque television programmes were broadcast in October 1971. They were mainly folkloric in content and were consistently censored. During the summer months, the radio station reverts to broadcasting a news programme for tourists in French. By today there is a monthly television programme of fifteen minutes in Basque, mainly cultural, five minutes of news daily and half an hour of radio in the language on Sundays. This provision for tourists at the expense of the local population is a particularly vicious aspect of the French authorities' policy. Tourism, while bringing prosperity to most areas of the region during the summer months, has also brought serious problems for Basque culture. It was calculated in 1970 that

41% of the land at Ciboure and 35% at Urragne belonged to Parisians.

The principal organisation representing Basque culture in the northern provinces has been, since its foundation by a priest in the nineteenth century, *Eskualtzaleen Biltzarra*. Although it is held in low esteem by the young activists of *Enbata*, this organisation has done much to represent, co-ordinate and develop the various forms of Basque culture, especially the language. It is nevertheless true that it became the preserve of its Paris section during the years between the two World Wars, attracting the non-political, 'professional Basques' to its cause. After 1945, under the leadership of André Ospital and Louis Dassance, the decline in membership continued. Under its present chief Michel Labéguerie it has not won back its former conviction that the Basque language can be saved only by radical policies. In the words of *Enbata*, 'an association having as its mission the saving of the Basque language cannot be content only with eating, dancing and singing . . . their consciences are in their stomachs'.

The growth of the voluntary schools known as *ikastolas* in the northern provinces is one of the few encouraging signs that the Basques in France have not given up all hope of keeping their identity. The first school was opened at Bayonne, under the impetus of *Enbata*, but moved shortly afterwards to Biarritz and then to Arcanques. The following year two more schools opened at Bayonne and Saint-Jean-de-Luz and in 1971 four more at Saint-Palais, Saint-Pée, Ciboure and Hendaye, with less than twenty children in each. At first hindered by the municipal authorities, the State schools, the Church and the police, by 1973 there were thirteen *ikastola*, organised by the society *Seaska*, and by today they are to be found in all three provinces, many having succeeded in winning the support of the municipal authorities. Apart from a financial contribution by the General Council of Pyrénées-Atlantiques, State aid to the schools is non-existent, however.

There has been little real change in the attitude of official French political circles towards the Basque problem during the last thirty years. The two Gaullist deputies in Pompidou's

Government who represent the majority of the Basque electorate, Bernard Marie and Michel Inchauspé, are widely considered to be using the growth of regionalist feeling for their
own ends. The majority of Basques support the centre parties
and their Independent allies who have, at least on paper,
adopted a policy of regionalisation including 'defence and
promotion' of the Basque language. Yet nothing has been
done to implement it. In 1964, the deputy Labéguerie refused
to intervene in the National Assembly in favour of a statute for
Basque and by 1966 he had publicly proclaimed his opposition to all further attempts to recognise it in the schools.
The region's leaders all discuss the Basque problem in terms
of the glory of the French State: the deputy Ybarnégaray has
spoken of France as *'la grande patrie',* the *U.D.R.* of 'a France
serene and dynamic', the Centre of 'a Nation with a glorious
past', the Socialists of 'national unity'.

A small number of Basques recognise in their plight the
problems facing all minorities within the French State. It
remains to be seen whether, since *Enbata* no longer legally
exists, a new political party will be able to win influence and
power. Already a Basque Socialist Party publishing its lively
newspaper *Euskaldunak/Le Peuple Basque* and modelling
itself on the *U.D.B.* in Brittany, has come into existence and
supports the French Socialist Party.

It seems unlikely, at least at the present time, that the first
aim of *Enbata*—the re-unification of the Basque nation in an
independent State—will be achieved in the near future.
Ideally, before autonomy for the northern provinces can be
won, the State border will have to be abolished. Given the
Spanish Government's repression of the Basques, such a move
is improbable. Nor would the Basques in France wish to join
their compatriots in the south if that meant living under
repressive Spain. Furthermore, as Spain is not a member of
the E.E.C. nor of the Council of Europe, and cannot be until
its system of government is made democratic, the idea of a
federal Europe holds little hope for the northern Basques.
The solution clearly lies in the hands of the French Government itself. A sensible regional policy which allowed for diver-
sity of culture and language and for local initiative in the
economic sphere would answer many of the demands first

made by *Enbata*.

Meanwhile, as Patricia Elton Mayo has concluded in her book *The Roots of Identity* (London 1974), 'If the lives of Basque patriots are not in danger in the French Basque provinces as they are in Spain, Basque identity is nevertheless threatened by the present policies of the French Government, both culturally and economically. In the Europe of tomorrow there must somehow be an answer which will equate economic viability with the survival of a people like the Basques who wish to retain their way of life in their own land'.

THE CORSICANS

Corsica, the third island of the Mediterranean after Sicily and Sardinia, has belonged to France since 1768. But it is nearer Italy—fifty-two miles from the peninsula of Piombino and only eight miles across the Strait of Bonifacio from Sardinia—than it is to France: Cannes and Nice, on the Côte d'Azur, are more than a hundred miles away.

The Island, the fifth largest department of France with a surface area of approximately 2,900 square miles, is very mountainous, Monte Cinto rising to 8,950 feet. It has a coast line of about 600 miles, equal to Portugal's and almost as long as France's Mediterranean shore. In 1948 two-thirds of Corsica were covered by *le maquis*, the famous scrub-land of Prosper Mérimée's stories after which the French Resistance of the Second World War was named, and by the forests which are the last remnants of the legendary Tyrrhenia. Even today, after attempts at re-afforestation and reclamation of cultivable land, one-fifth of the Island is still under *le maquis* and no more than half under cultivation or grass.

The language spoken over a large part of Corsica (Corsican: *Corsu),* north and east of a diagonal line which runs from Calvi on the western coast between Venaco and Vizzavona to Porto-Vecchio *(Portu-Vettiu)* on the eastern side, has generally been considered until recent times as a dialect of Italian resembling Tuscan. To the south and west of this line the dialect spoken has closer affinities with Sardinian. Elements from both these dialects were used by poets in the nineteenth century in an attempt to create a standard form of a new language. But it is only since the Second World War, largely as the result of a growing autonomist movement, that Corsican has been recognised and studied, at least in Corsica, as a language in its own right and belonging with Sardinian, Occitan and Catalan to the Romance family. It is not known exactly how many people are able to speak Corsican but the number is estimated at approximately 200,000 inhabitants of the Island and many more living elsewhere.

Corsica's population in 1975 was 220,000. It is known, however, that this total represented not the actual number of inhabitants but, more probably, the number listed on the electoral register. Many thousands are not resident in the Island but working, more or less permanently, in metropolitan France, particularly in Paris and Marseilles, typically in the police force or as civil servants. The Corsican diaspora, in the U.S.A. and in France's former colonies, is estimated as being greater than the present population of the Island.

In her book *L'Enracinement* (The Need for Roots), Simone Weil has this to say about Corsicans: 'Corsica is an example of the danger of infection which is involved in uprootedness. After having conquered, colonised, corrupted and debased the people of this island, we have had to put up with them as police chiefs, detectives, sergeant-majors, *pions* and in other roles of a similar nature, in pursuit of which they, in their turn, have treated the French as more or less conquered people. They have also contributed towards giving France, in the minds of many natives of the colonies, a reputation for cruelty and brutality'.

It is not only against their enterprise, clearly unfulfilled in a neglected economy at home, that the traditional French view of Corsicans complains but also, predictably enough, against their solidarity abroad. Paul Sérant, in *La France des Minorités* (1965) adds: 'The Corsican problem is, in certain respects, very different from that of other ethnic groups in France. Much fun has been made of the peculiarities of the Flemings, the Bretons, the Basques or the Alsatians: their stubbornness or their obscurantism has roused our indignation. But they have never been accused of systematically defying the law, or of having formed a *mafia* within the French administration. Corsica is without doubt the only ethnic group against whom the French have sometimes made allegations comparable with those which anti-Semites make against Jews'.

Despite this low reputation among those whom the Islanders call *'les continentaux'* or *pinzuti* (from a kind of hat) the Corsicans are also well-known for the French patriotism which they have always demonstrated from the time of their annexation by France up to the Second World War. Indeed, there was no serious separatist movement in Corsica throughout the nineteenth century and its people played a full part in the making of the Republic. Yet, in its long history, the Island suffered invasion and exploitation so often and to such an extent that the Corsican personality has been largely shaped by the military and economic ravages experienced by its people. From earliest times—like Sardinia it is dotted with megalithic monuments—through twenty-five centuries of war, insurrection and disaster, Corsica has been a peripheral, disputed and impoverished place—*'ce fichu pays'*.

The earliest population was of Iberian and Celto-Ligurian extraction. Invasions began in 564 B.C., by Phoenician traders, who knew the Island as *Kyrnos;* settlement by Phoceans, Etruscans, Carthaginians, Vandals and Saracens followed. With the Roman occupation, completed in 162 B.C., Latin civilisation was established.

In the Middle Ages, after suffering under the Byzantines in the sixth and seventh centuries, Corsica came under the influence of the Papacy, particularly in the time of Gregory the Great, who was elected Pope in the year 590. After the expulsion of the Saracens in the eleventh century, the Holy See entrusted the Island to the Archbishop of Pisa, in 1078, and it is to the Pisans that Corsica owes some of its splendid bridges and basilicas such as those at Nebbio and Murato. The year 1132 saw the first arrival of the Genoese who, despite resistance and efforts to unite the Corsicans against them, continued to plunder the Island for the next four centuries. In 1359 the north-eastern part, then known as *Terra del Commune,* reached an agreement with Genoa by which a Council of six Corsicans, under the leadership of Sambucuccio d'Alandu, was responsible for administration and justice in return for an annual tribute, whilst the south retained a feudal system. Today, quite unusually in the context of the highly centralised French State, Corsica's five *arrondissements,* sixty-two cantons and 365 communes are based on the ancient *pieve* of Sambucuccio's day.

Genoa's continuous difficulties with the Corsicans obliged her to call for French assistance. Marshal Boucicaut governed the Island in the name of Charles VI from 1396 to 1409. Then, in 1553, a commander of the Corsican Regiment founded by François I, Sampiero d'Ornano, won the Island from the Genoese, only to see it restored to Genoa six years later.

D'Ornano became so identified with the cause of Corsican independence that he was nick-named Sampiero Corso. After his death in 1567 the Island's control was resumed by Genoa, under the *Statuti Civili e Criminali,* until the beginning of the eighteenth century.

In 1729, however, the heavy taxes imposed by Genoa, the negligence of its representatives in Corsica who rarely attempted to implement the Government's plans for the Island, the general economic disorganisation and the refusal of the Genoese to allow the Corsicans a share in administration, led to an uprising which culminated the following year in a 'Manifesto to the Corsican Nation' addressed to the Assembly of San-Pancruziu-di-Biguglia. The Genoese turned for help to the Holy Roman Empire, and then to France. Forty years of bloodshed in victory and defeat, admired by many European thinkers such as Rousseau and Voltaire, began in 1735 when the National Assembly of Corsica proclaimed and implemented a constitution for the Island.

The leaders who chased the Genoese from Corsica and united the people under their command were Hyacinthe and Pascal Paoli. The first led the insurrections of 1734-9 but, after his offers of Corsica to the Pope and to Spain had been declined, he was beaten by the French. Pascal, his son, founded a legal system and a university at Corté, the traditional capital of independent Corsica, and made education compulsory. Under his rule, agriculture, commerce and the beginnings of industry were encouraged, and free elections based on universal suffrage took place.

But Genoa still considered that Corsica belonged to her and in 1768 the Island was sold to Louis XV of France. General Marbeuf's troops arrived immediately, meeting ferocious resistance from the Corsicans under the leadership of Pascal Paoli. At the battle of Borgo that October the French were routed and all their officers captured. When a further 30,000 French troops arrived, however, the Corsicans were crushed, on 9 May at Ponte-Novu. Paoli fled to London but was later recalled as Lieutenant General of Corsica, until once again he broke with France and offered the Island to England. There followed twenty years of 'pacification', a period which

featured new revolts, reprisals, public torture and deportation. Finally, although under Marbeuf from 1768 to 1786 it
preserved a certain autonomy based on its traditional institutions, Corsica was absorbed into the *Ancien Régime,* and
it was to be completely integrated into the French Republic
after the Revolution of 1789. Pascal Paoli, whom Nietzsche
called 'the most accomplished man of his century', died in
exile on 5 February 1807, in London, where he was buried in
Westminster Abbey. The plaque, which bears the name
Pasquale de Paoli, describes him as 'one of the most eminent
and most illustrious characters of the age in which he lived.
The early and better part of his life he devoted to the cause of
liberty; nobly maintaining it against the usurpation of
Genoese and French tyranny: by his many splendid
achievements, his useful and benevolent institutions, his
patriotic and public zeal manifested upon every occasion . . .'
More of a statesman than a general, Paoli is remembered
today as Corsica's Owain Glyn Dŵr.

The fame of the Paolis was soon to be eclipsed, however, by
the rise to power of Corsica's other great son. Napoleon
Buonaparte was born at Ajaccio in 1769, the year after Corsica had become French territory. The son of a spend-thrift
lawyer who had been a deputy in the Corsican Estates,
Napoleon was brought up by his mother, Letizia Ramolino.
Paoli's revolt, and the subsequent occupation of the Island by
the English, drove the Buonapartes from Corsica. Poverty and
austerity made the young Napoleon sympathetic towards the
new revolutionary ideas and during the civil strife in Corsica
he became a lieutenant-colonel in the National Guard. It took
him all his life to master the subtleties of the French language
and it is said that his pronunciation and spelling of French
were always poor.

It was not that Napoleon showed any special preference for
the Island of his birth. After leaving home he never returned
and, during the Empire, he placed Corsica under a military
occupation which was among the most vicious it had known.
But Corsicans, like many another peripheral people from
among whom a leader emerges to win power at the centre,
were filled with pride that one of their own was the master of a

mighty empire which extended as far as Moscow and whose brothers shared the thrones of Europe.

Under the Second Empire Corsica began to prosper, at least for a while. There was fiscal reform, an amnesty for exiles, the roads and the administration were improved. From this time on, and especially after the Empire's fall, the dream of Corsican independence began to fade. Its place was taken by nostalgia for the Napoleonic régime, the days when France dominated Europe and when Corsica, by the prestige of its most illustrious son, ruled both. By today, if in the rest of France the Buonapartist Party belongs to the past, in Corsica it is still not without power: in the municipal elections of 1963 there was a Buonapartist majority in the town of Ajaccio (Corsican: *Aiacciu*), the administrative capital.

Throughout the rest of the nineteenth century Corsica suffered an economic decline on a huge scale. Isolated, lacking industrial resources and the new agricultural techniques, it lost its population in increasing numbers. Yet it was now that the Corsican identity was re-awakened, in the cultural sphere. Under the influence of the *Félibrige* and the renaissance in Provençal poetry, magazines like *Cirnea, A Lingua Corsa, Revue de la Corse*, and *A Muvra* began publishing poetry in the Corsican language. A number of writers emerged, including Santu Casanova, 'the Mistral of Corsica', and D-A. Versini, Jean-Pierre Lucciardi and Carulu Giovini, members of a literary movement which by the end of the First World War had become more or less autonomist in character. Lucciardi was among those who appealed to President Clemenceau to allow the teaching of Corsican in the Island's schools, without the least success.

On the eve of the Second World War Mussolini tried to exploit the growing autonomist movement in Corsica for his own ends. Many young people were invited to follow university courses in Italy. As in the Romansh valleys of Switzerland and the Ladin districts of the Dolomites, efforts were made to demonstrate the Italian affinities of the Corsican dialects, together with claims that the Island should be 'given back' to Italy. The Italians were surprised, however, when they occupied Corsica—following the German invasion of the Free Zone of France in November 1942—that they were unable to raise a popular movement in their favour. The Corsican resistance against the Fascists was led by Fred Scamaroni. In September 1943 the Island was the first department of France to be liberated, by French troops from North Africa.

At the Allies' victory in 1944 the Corsican autonomist movement suffered a fate similar to that of other regionalist and nationalist parties in France: it was accused of wholesale collaboration with the enemy. The case of Petru Rocca is fairly typical. As editor of the weekly newspaper *A Muvra* before the War, he had been openly autonomist in his views. The French authorities had suspected him of having contacts in Italy, which could hardly be denied, and he had therefore been expelled from the *Légion d'Honneur*. Despite protests by a majority of editors and publishers in Corsica, the newspaper had been forced to close. But after the fall of France in 1940 Rocca resumed publication, for which in 1945 he was tried and imprisoned. Many other publications and organisations devoted to the language and culture of Corsica, against which no political reproach could be made, were suppressed and never re-appeared.

To understand the emotional climate of the day it must be remembered that about 200,000 French citizens had died in captivity in Germany during the War, mostly in concentration camps. Many had been betrayed by their neighbours and rounded up by the militia and officials of the Vichy régime. Rough justice was done in many parts of France, not only in those where regionalist movements existed: there were hasty trials, summary executions, public beatings and humiliating acts—such as the shaving of heads for women known to have consorted with Germans—and many old scores were settled which had little to do with the occupation. The number of people put to death in this process of '*épuration*' (purification) is not certain, but is estimated at between 30,000 and 120,000. In his *Mémoires d'Espoir*, Charles de Gaulle commented on this vicious time: 'To pass the sponge over so many crimes and abuses would have meant leaving a monstrous abcess to infect the country forever. Justice must be done'. It is nevertheless true that the most ferocious acts of the months following the liberation of France were often against those accused of regionalist views, whether political or not, as in Corsica.

Thirty years later, and over two hundred since Ponte-Novu, how does Corsica fare today? According to *Le Journal Officiel de la République Française* (Official Journal of the French Republic) for 2 April 1957, which published the text of the French Government's 'Regional Programme for Corsica', the population of the Island during the first half of this century fell from 320,000 permanent residents in 1900 to just under 200,000 in 1950. During the same period, the population of Sardinia, not exactly the most prosperous of Italian regions, increased from 680,000 to approximately 1,500,000.

Emigration in Corsica is, of course, an ancient phenomenon. But the revelation that the Island's population had decreased to such an extent in fifty years was greeted with alarm, even in Paris. It is now clear that technical progress had altered the basis of Corsica's economy, upsetting the precarious balance by which it was able to live on its own resources—cereals, chestnuts, edible oils, milk, meat, honey and homespun textiles. Agriculture had declined with the population, so that the Island was importing more than half the commodities which it had formerly been capable of producing for itself.

The Regional Programme, signed by six cabinet ministers, proposed the creation of two new bodies to be financed by public and private enterprise which would tackle the serious situation by implementing the government's plans in the spheres of agriculture and tourism respectively. These were *La Société pour la Mise en Valeur de la Corse (SOMIVAC)* and *La Société pour l'Equipement Touristique de la Corse (SETCO)*. The tasks of the first were to study the main factors governing agricultural improvement such as the nature of the Island's soil, climate and water resources, to put back under cultivation about 50,000 acres of *le maquis*, and to carry out the essential hydraulic schemes in the areas thus developed. The aims of the second body were to realise the Island's exceptional tourist potential by the improvement of air and sea links, the construction of hotels, private residential development and the provision of recreation facilities both on the coast and inland. The work of these two societies has begun to have an influence on the Island's economy by now. Between 1965 and 1970 tourist accommodation increased from 50,000 beds to 100,000 and the number of visitors rose from 240,000 to 360,000. During the same five years the gross agricultural product, mainly wine, increased by 10% annually.

But Corsica's progress was slow at first. Many aspects of the Government's plans met with apathy and sometimes with hostility from the local population, especially from farmers who wanted a bigger say in land clearance. Furthermore, since it was the Minister in Paris rather than any authority in Corsica who had over-all responsibility for the Programme, there was widespread resentment against decisions taken elsewhere. As a result, only a few of the proposals made have been implemented. Re-organisation of water resources and public transport has not taken place. The Island's traditional activities of stock-farming and olive-growing have been virtually ignored and newer ones like the production of citrus fruits, flowers and market gardening have not been attempted. Land continues to be bought by property investment firms from France and Italy. Industrial development is negligible and confined to a few small zones around some of the towns. Promises of a co-ordinated policy for the Island's economic progress have not been kept and complaints are heard that tourism, 'the gigolo industry', is no solution for a stagnant economy.

Local discontent at the Government's failure to implement the Programme's proposals was deepened in 1962 when 18,000 *pieds-noirs,* French settlers from the newly independent State of Algeria, were repatriated and settled in Corsica, buying land and taking over some businesses. The total population of Corsica at this time was approximately 176,000. Three years later, in 1965, in protest against the French Government's decision, there were bomb attacks on the property of some of the refugees. Also in that year mass demonstrations against an announcement that an underground nuclear research centre was to be built on a site near the holiday resort of Calvi ensured that the scheme was promptly abandoned. The Corsican problem had entered a new phase.

Meanwhile, the Island's economic troubles had been matched

since 1955 by a crisis in its cultural identity, centred on the Corsican language. The French Government has consistently refused to recognise Corsican as a language capable of being taught, not even within the parsimonious terms of the Deixonne Law of 1951. An attempt by the deputy for Bastia, Jean Zuccarelli, to win recognition for the language in the education system was vetoed by the National Assembly in 1965.

The growing demand for the teaching of Corsican has been led by the *Centre d'Etudes Régionales Corses* (Centre for Corsican Regional Studies), founded in 1957. The Centre (Corsican: *Centru di Studi Regiunali Corsi),* has campaigned for the re-opening of Pascal Paoli's University at Corté and has formed a teachers' organisation called *Scola e Universitá.* It also runs a correspondence course in Corsican and publishes books in the language. A new grammar was published in 1968 and a dictionary in 1974, together with the magazine *U Muntése,* published by the association *Lingua Corsa;* the bilingual series entitled *A lingua corsa e a so'scrittura* (The Corsican language and how to write it) has made an important contribution to the study of Corsican. By now the local edition of the daily newspaper *Nice-Matin,* the most widely read in the Island, carries articles and news in Corsican. A separatist magazine *Kyrn,* edited by Aimé Pietri, which sells around 40,000 copies monthly, supports the language campaigners. In 1972, when the French Minister of Education visited the Island, he promised to set up a commission to consider the problems involved in the teaching of Corsican at secondary level, but nothing has been announced up to the present time.

The Centre's President is Jean Albertini. He has played a paramount role in the cultural and political renaissance of Corsica during the last two decades. Since 1969, when a students' conference was held at Nice to commemorate the bi-centenary of the battle of Ponte-Novu, Jean Albertini has been largely responsible for the Centre's success in rallying the young people of the Island in an autonomist movement which is by now an important force in Corsica's political life.

In 1960 the Island was incorporated into a new region which included Provence and the Côte d'Azur, a ministerial decision generally recognised as a nonsense in economic and

administrative terms. The Centre for Regional Studies—
which had been opened to support the Regional Programme
of 1957—now moved away from co-operation with the
central Government towards a more hostile position and
open support of demands for autonomy. As a protest
against Government policy in the Island, the Centre organised
a mass abstention by the Corsican electorate in the presidential elections of 1965. Despite the influence of the mass media
reporting the contest between De Gaulle and François Mit-
terrand, leader of the French Socialist Party, 44% of the
population refused to vote in response to the Centre's campaign. In 150 of Corsica's 365 communes the abstention rate
surpassed 50%, in some it was as high as 85%, while in France
as a whole it was only 15%. Of the total population of Corsica, 21% came out in favour of De Gaulle and 14% of Mit-
terrand.

The Centre's manifesto, published in 1967 at Corté (Corsican: *Corti)* lists the many problems with which Corsica is
still beset at the present time. These include the closure of
schools and factories, the transference of railways to private
companies, the disrepair of roads and bridges, land
speculation, the lack of a university, emigration and a cost of
living about 35% higher than in the rest of France. The
manifesto calls on the Corsican people 'to resist colonialism
and state centralism' and to demand the full recognition of
Corsica's identity at the cultural, economic and political
levels. Among the Centre's aims are the abolition of the office
of Prefect, because the incumbents are always subservient to
Paris, the establishment of new institutions with both
executive and financial powers, local control of natural
resources, the recognition of Corsican as the Island's
language in education and public life, a proper degree of
regionalisation within the French Republic, the creation of a
Sénat des Régions to represent all the regions of France and,
eventually, a federal Europe. The public's response to these
objectives, overwhelmingly in favour of autonomy for Corsica,
was crystalised when in 1968 the *C.E.R.C.* campaigned
against the bi-centenary celebrations commemorating the
sale of Corsica to France in 1768: it met with complete success
and the plans were cancelled.

In the same year the General Council of Corsica, gathered to consider the French Government's enquiries as to how regionalisation was progressing on the Island, prior to a referendum to be held the following year, decided unanimously to seek autonomous status at the earliest opportunity. The majority of mayors and councillors agreed to vote *non*, with the result that in 1970 Corsica was detached from Provence-Côte d'Azur. This decision was a major victory for the *C.E.R.C.* which, with the Corsican Socialist Party, had led the debate. Again on 23 April 1972 the Centre led a campaign to vote against the referendum on President Pompidou's plans for regional reform in France, on the grounds that they were so limited as to be a caricature of true regionalism, failing to provide for an Assembly in Corsica and having the effect of increasing the central Government's power. The electors responded by an average abstention of 59%, in some districts as high as 77%.

The Centre is not alone in its campaign for Corsican autonomy. Four other organisations have been founded during the last few years: *Action pour la Renaissance de la Corse*, *Partitu di u Popula Corsu* (formerly the *Front Régionaliste Corse*), *Le Parti Corse pour le Progrès* and the Corsican branch of the European Federalist Movement led by Jean Albertini. At the presidential elections of 1974, Albertini secured the support of all these parties, and the votes of a majority of Corsicans for the candidature of François Mitterand against that of Giscard d'Estaing.

It was the *A.R.C.*, led by Dr Edmond Simeoni, which in August 1975 clashed with police at Aleria. During a twelve-hour siege of a wine depot two policemen were shot and about twenty others wounded. Fifty Corsican farmers were protesting against the ownership of land on the Island by outsiders and demanding the release of a comrade, Dominique Capretti, imprisoned for displaying autonomist posters. Two thousand riot police belonging to the *Compagnies Républicaines de Sécurité* were flown in from the mainland. There were pitched battles with armed separatists at Bastia, during which another policeman was shot. Simeoni, aged forty-one, together with his brother Roland and ten others, was arrested and sent to Fresnes prison. They were later accused of 'action against the State'. A general strike paralysed the Island on 1 September as a demonstration of solidarity against Michel Poniatowski, the Minister of the Interior. The Prefect of Corsica, Gabriel Gilly and the Sub-Prefect, Jacques Guerin, were dismissed and replaced by a Corsican, Jean Riolacci. The *A.R.C.*, which claims about 8,500 militants among its members, was banned after a leader of the Gaullist Party, Alexandre Sanguinetti, himself a Corsican, demanded that the Government should outlaw all 'regionalist movements' in France. Giscard d'Estaing, under attack from the left for the way in which he handled the crisis, could only declare, 'We must say to the Corsican population that it enjoys not only my affection but the understanding of the French Community to which it belongs. No one can forget the role which Corsica has played in our national history . . .' More pertinently, the newspaper *Le Monde* commented on the rising by pointing out that France, with its tradition of centralised rule, 'has shown less imagination in dealing with regional aspirations than several of its European neighbours. This attitude is now provoking resistance, passion and tragedy'.

More than any other region of France, Corsica today is perhaps the most politically conscious, especially among its young people, having developed in twenty-five years an autonomist movement which is both determined and effective. If the French Government, during the last quarter of the twentieth century, is to reorganise the Republic according to truly decentralist principles, Corsica will doubtless be among the first regions to benefit.

THE ALSATIANS

Of all the regions within the borders of the French State, Alsace has one of the most clearly defined personalities. It is here, in the department of *Bas-Rhin* and *Haut-Rhin* (Lower and Upper Rhine) between the Vosges Mountains and the border with Germany, that the majority of the population, some 1,300,000 out of a total of 1,515,200 (1975) speak dialects of German.

With the exceptions of a few valleys in the Vosges and some villages in the Belfort Gap, these dialects are to be heard all over the region, although to a lesser extent in the north where, as in the neighbouring but quite separate region of Lorraine, the language most widely spoken is dialect French. There is no single Alsatian dialect, only a variety of forms which differ from village to village. The standard written and cultivated form of these dialects is *Hochdeutsch*, (High German). Most Alsatians are bilingual, that is to say able to speak their own dialect of German as well as French, the language of the State which has grown more widespread in the region during the present century. Between 1931 and 1961 the number able to speak French, mostly as a second language, has increased from 50% to 79% in Lower Rhine, from 55% to 83% in Upper Rhine and from 65% to 90% in Moselle, the department in Lorraine where as far north as Thionville (German: *Diedenhofen)* German is still spoken today.

Although Alsace (German: *Elsass)* has been incorporated in the French State at various times in its history and was last claimed under the Treaty of Versailles in 1919, the region existed for centuries without any direct relationship with France. By its geography, religion, art, economy, language and culture, it was always a province of the Rhine Land, a corridor between north and south rather than east and west, from Roman times and throughout the Holy Roman Empire, an integral part of the Germanic world with its own psychological traits and social customs. Even today, despite the centralism of the French State over the last two hundred years, the Alsatian personality is expressed in a number of legislative and administrative peculiarities which do not exist elsewhere in France. The law of 1905, for example, which

separates Church from State, is not applicable in Alsace, nor
are the laws on secularisation of the schools, so that primary
education is denominational or, more frequently, interdenominational but religious.

The social and religious history of Alsace is inextricably
linked with that of Germany. In the Peasants' War, one of the
chief events to shape Germany, many of the leaders were from
Alsace. The town of Sélestat (German: *Schlettstadt)* was
among the cradles of German Humanism, Grunewald worked
at Strasbourg (German: *Strassburg)* and at Colmar, Alsatian
students were famous at the Universities of Basel, Heidelburg
and Freiburg. In its literature too, Alsace remained until the
sixteenth century one of the most fertile of all the German-
speaking territories. The oldest poem in the German language,
the *Evangelienbuch* was written in the year 868 by Otfried von
Weissenburg (c. 800-70) and such illustrious names as Gottfried von Strassburg (fl. 1210), author of the great epic about
Tristan and Isolde, Reinmar von Haguenau, Sebastian Brant
and the satirist Johann Fischart (1547-90) remind the world
that Alsace was undoubtedly one of the great cultural hearths
of the Germanic world. When Latin began to be abandoned
in favour of the vernaculars, the towns of Alsace were among
the first to adopt German as their official language and,
during the Reformation, the German Mass was first introduced in Strasbourg, where too the first German Bible was
published in 1466, sixty-eight years before Luther's.

The annexation of Alsace by France under the Treaty of
Westphalia in 1648 which seriously interrupted the rich intellectual life of the region, was neither complete nor easily
achieved, many towns such as Haguenau resisting bitterly until they were defeated by force of arms and then disen-
franchised. Only the town of Strasbourg held out against the
French Crown until 1681, by refusing to take the oath of
loyalty, and resistance in Mulhouse (German: *Mülhausen),*
which was allied to the Swiss Cantons, lasted until 1798. The
Government of Louis XIV, however, did not attempt to reverse
the old order. His policy was to respect the region's ancient
frontiers, its traditions and language, to avoid interfering
with its schools and imposing military service. As a result, the

new administration took root without much serious opposition while Alsace, enjoying the status of an occupied area, separate from France, continued to trade freely with other communities on the Rhine. The only classes to be affected by the French régime, excepting those Protestants who left Strasbourg in 1697 under religious persecution, were the aristocracy, the intelligentsia, and some sections of the upper middle-class. Elsewhere in Alsatian society the German language held its own. The University of Strasbourg continued to be a Lutheran institution like its counterparts in Germany, while family documents and legal papers were usually written in German. A few years before the Revolution of 1789 the Alsatian André Ulrich was able to declare, 'There are three hundred inhabitants of Alsace who do not know French for every one who does'.

By breaking Alsace's links with Germany, which had been maintained after the Treaty of Westphalia, and by introducing a common legislation for the whole Republic, the Revolution of 1789 deprived the region of a large measure of its individuality. Despite an appeal by the clergy, fearful for Church property, to the Diet of Ratisbonne, Alsace was now drawn into the orbit of the Revolution's Jacobin ideals, as much by the bourgeoisie's greed for new wealth as by the peasants' desire to be released from the last vestiges of feudalism. The enrolment of many Alsatians, including generals Kleber, Berckheim, Lefèbre and Kellermann, in the armies of the Revolution and the Empire, gave birth to a new French sentiment in Alsace which was to survive even the setbacks of 1814 and 1815. Even so, the Revolution and the subsequent Terror were as vicious in the region as anywhere in the Republic. In 1793, after an announcement that citizens unable to speak French were to be shot, as many were, or deported to the interior of France, about 30,000 nobles, priests and others from all classes fled from the new department of *Bas-Rhin* to take refuge in Germany. Napoleon's attempts to enforce the spiritual and political integration of Alsace were resumed after the restoration of order under the Consulate and the Empire. If the prefects were allowed to manage certain regional adaptations in the administrative and legislative spheres, the French attitude in linguistic matters was typified in the remark attributed to Napoleon: 'Let them speak German as long as they use their swords in French'!

This process of Alsace's integration and exploitation in foreign wars continued under the Restoration, the July Monarchy and the Second Empire, the growing industrialisation of the region providing favourable conditions for the spread of French. But however much, in political terms, the Alsatians came to be absorbed into the French State at this time, it was not so as far as their language was concerned. A knowledge of French had not penetrated to any wide extent lower than the bourgeoisie and even those who could speak French were also able to speak their native German. It is recorded that both Louis Philippe and Napoleon III, passing through Alsace in 1870, addressed the people in German. The Catholic Church was among the staunchest supporters of the Alsatian identity. The *Abbé* Cazeaux, writing in 1867, was typical: 'To declare war on the German language is to attack, in a certain sense, the religion, morals and civilisation of Alsace'. By this time French had become the medium of instruction at secondary and university level but not in the primary schools. In 1843 an inspector of schools complained that many parents were keeping their children from school, in an attempt to prevent them from learning French. But it was not until 1853 that French was officially introduced as the language of primary education, and then German was taught for at least one lesson every day. If, by the end of the Second Empire, French was more widely spoken in Alsace, especially among the young, German was still the language of the masses in their homes, churches and daily intercourse.

With the fall of Napoleon and Bismarck's annexation of Alsace by the Treaty of Frankfurt in 1871 the region—French in sentiment but German in speech—entered one of the most troubled periods of its history, changing hands four times in less than a hundred years. By 1874, after over 50,000 of its inhabitants had left for the interior of France, the only Alsatian representatives in the *Reichstag* were those who objected to re-unification with Germany and Bismarck's anti-clerical policies, although in the years which followed there was some progress towards improving the status of Alsace within the German State if only to use it as a barrier against any threat of French invasion. In 1879 two elected Councils were established in the region although the authority of the *Statthalter*, the Emperor's lieutenant, remained dictatorial. In 1877 an autonomist party led by August Schneegans, and such men as Charles Hauss, Ricklin and Blumenthal, demanding a more liberal deal for the region, within the context of Germany, won five seats in lower Alsace and paved the way for the granting of a Constitution in 1911 which provided for a federal parliament at Strasbourg. Alsace, economically flourishing and with a modern, progressive administration, was beginning to grow accustomed to its new situation.

Only a few, notably the novelist Maurice Barrès (1862-1923) expressed hostility to the process of Germanisation, as in his book *Au Service de l'Allemagne* (1906) which describes the predicament of a young Alsatian named Ehrmann, whose family was French in culture but who had to do his military service in the German Army. Tempted to desert but taught by his father that it was the duty of Alsatians to stay in Alsace, in order to resist Germany, when asked by a superior officer what he would do in the event of war with France, he replies only that he is a doctor, but leaves the army more convinced and prouder than ever that he is *'fils d'Alsace et fils de France'*. The French nationalism of Barrès particularly in his view of Lorraine, was described in other books such as *Les Déracinés* (1897), *Le Jardin de Bérénice* (1891) and *L'Appel au Soldat* (1900), and was later to have an influence on the thinking of Charles Maurras (1868-1952), founder of the right-wing, royalist party *Action Française*. The predicament of Alsace, both politically and culturally, has been experienced by many of its writers since Barrès. His view that the duty of Alsatians was to remain in Alsace was contested by René Bazin in his novel *Les Oberlé* which suggested that the best course for an Alsatian wanting to remain French was to leave for another part of France.

With Lorraine, Alsace has produced four other important writers. Growing up in frontier towns, they all aimed at producing a climate of mind which would be European rather than merely French or German. Hans Arp (1887-1966), poet and painter, was an Alsatian equally at home in German and French who began writing in German, went over to French but returned to German at the end of his life. Ernst Stadler (1883-1914) was killed in action during the first months of the war in 1914. Yvan Goll (1891-1950) was a Lorrainer and the language of his childhood was French. But because the language of culture and education in Lorraine before 1914 was German he wrote his early works in German. In fact, he mastered both languages and on both sides of the frontier, equally at home with the German Expressionists and the French Surrealists. His major novels were written in French but one novel and his plays are in German; he frequently translated his plays and essays (but rarely his poems) from one language to the other. His reputation as a lyric poet rests on his work in French, especially on the cycle *Jean Sans Terre* but in his last years, after returning from America and in hospital in Strasbourg, he returned to German to write the cycle *Traumkraut*. René Schickelé (1883-1940), who up to then had written in German, also left Alsace in 1933 and published his only French work *Le Retour,* the 'return' to the language of his childhood, just before his death.

The social nuances attached to German and the Alsatian dialects is illustrated well by the case of one of Alsace's greatest sons, Albert Schweitzer (1875-1965), who wrote in his *Aus Meinem Leben und Denken* (1931), 'It is true that ever since my childhood I have spoken French as freely as German; but I never feel French to be my mother-tongue, although in my letters to my parents I always used French because that was customary in the family. German is my mother-tongue, because the Alsatian dialect, which is my native language, is Germanic'. It was Schweitzer too who made the well-known distinction between reading or writing in French and German, comparing the one to 'strolling along the well-kept paths of a fine park' and the other to 'wandering at will in a magnificent forest.'

A further illustration of 'languages in contact' was noted by Leonard Forster and described in his study of multi-lingualism *The Poet's Tongues* (Cambridge, 1970). He recalls over-hearing a conversation in a café at Mulhouse during the 'thirties in which, for discussion of family news, three

Alsatians used the local dialect, but began using words like *mairie* and *préfecture* when they turned to local politics, and went on entirely in French when they reached national politics: there was, however, no indication that they were conscious of any change—they were simply using perfectly natural means of expression each suited to its subject.

Finally, the film *Kammeradschaft,* made by G. W. Pabst in 1931, deals with a mining disaster in Lorraine where the newly drawn frontier runs across the galleries of the mine. An explosion occurs on the French side but the German miners break down the steel bars across the gallery to rescue their French comrades: the film's message is the triumph of common humanity represented by the working-class over the barriers imposed by governments.

From 1913 on, international tension mounted and the prospect of conflict between France and Germany became imminent. As relations between the two States deteriorated rapidly, there were incidents involving Alsatians and Germans at Saverne and Schirmeck. Thousands of Alsatians suspected of pro-French sentiments were arrested. When war was declared in 1914, 250,000 men from Alsace were conscripted in the Kaiser's army while 20,000 volunteers went to serve with the French. There is a war memorial in Strasbourg which shows a woman holding in her arms the bodies of two soldiers, brothers perhaps, who had fought on opposing sides.

Following the Treaty of Versailles in 1919, the return of Alsace to a victorious France took place among scenes of tremendous enthusiasm, described by Paul Sérant in *La France des Minorités* thus: 'The joyful explosion of the Alsatian population was the most resounding of plebiscites. After long domination (under the German Empire), the Alsatians behaved as if they had never ceased to be French, they showed their French patriotism which the test of time had done nothing to impair'. But it soon became apparent, despite a promise by General Joffre in the town of Thann, captured as early as November 1914, that the German character of Alsace would not be respected after the area had been reclaimed by France, that there was no place for particularism in the new arrangements. Alsatians, while welcoming the return of their region to France, took it badly that German was now treated

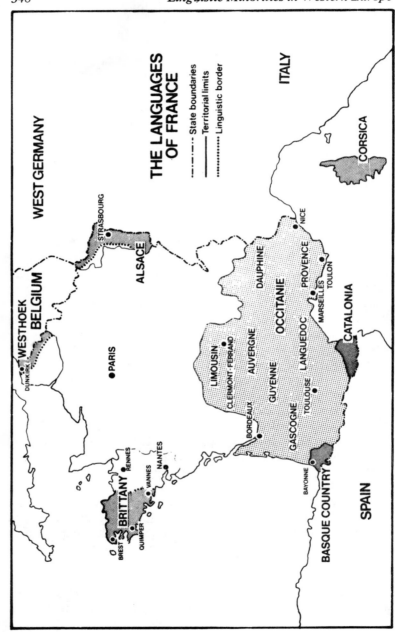

THE LANGUAGES
OF FRANCE

‑‑‑‑‑ State boundaries
——— Territorial limits
·········· Linguistic border

as the language of a foreign and recently hostile power. Having enjoyed a certain autonomy within the German Empire, they found difficulty in growing accustomed to the highly centralised institutions of the French Republic, especially when it became clear that there was to be no permanent administrative autonomy for Alsace. Whereas under the German Empire, there had been a French-language press in Alsace and French had been taught in the schools, the French Government now set about the prohibition of German in the three departments where it was the language of the majority, only to have many of its decisions reversed by President Poincaré who authorised the teaching of German at primary level after protests had been made. These misgivings came to a head with the arrival of Edouard Herriot as Prime Minister of France, when a strong current of regionalist feeling surged through large sections of the population after it was announced in June 1924 that the Republic's laws on the separation of Church and State were to be extended to Alsace, so that religious instruction would disappear from the syllabus. The force of Alsatian opinion, both Catholic and Protestant, prevented this move, however.

By now the French Government's mistakes in administrative, religious and linguistic matters had caused what in Parisian political circles was known as *'le malaise alsacien'.* Political parties began to emerge which were autonomist in their demands, such as the *Landespartei* and the *Elsässische Fortschrittpartei,* the latter founded by the radical George Wolf, and which began calling not for reunification with Germany, as the French claimed, but for legislative and administrative devolution for Alsace. Even the main party in the region, the Popular Republican Party, included the creation of regional institutions and the introduction of official bilingualism among its policies, while the Alsatian Communist Party denounced French imperialism and supported the movement for self-government. Although Maurice Thorez, leader of the French Communist Party, was to express approval of the Alsatian movement even if it meant complete separation from France, at the seventh Congress of the French Communist Party in 1932, the Communists later reversed their position; with the rise of Hitler

Thorez, in 1936, called for a France *'ferme et unie'*, after which the French press described the movement as being of fascist inspiration.

The year 1928 marked the high point in the progress of this movement. Three autonomists and a communist were elected to the French Assembly and eight leaders of the *Heimatbund*, the autonomist movement accused of 'plotting to harm the integrity of the national territory', were tried at Colmar between 1 May and 24 May 1928. When accused by the prosecution of using the slogan *'L'Alsace aux Alsaciens'* (Alsace for the Alsatians) the prisoner Schlaegel replied, 'This saying was popular in Alsatian politics before the War and the German State never felt obliged to see a plot in it. For us, Alsace for the Alsatians means that in Alsace we must feel at home, and also that we will be good French citizens'. Another, named Ricklin, pointed out that the extreme right-wing *Action Française* made it no secret that they wished to overthrow the State by force but that as soon as Alsatians showed a desire for change they were in danger of being executed. But largely owing to the contributions of distinguished figures of the time, including Jean de Pange of the Popular Democratic Party and Victor Basch, president of the League for the Rights of Man and one of the most important figures of the French left in his day, the eight accused—who also included Hauss, Paul Schall, Rossé, Baumann, Karl Roos and Robert Ernst—were sentenced to only one year's imprisonment each. Nevertheless, the verdict of guilty incensed public opinion in Alsace: in the local elections which followed, Ricklin and Rossé were elected. A few months later there was an attempt on the life of the prosecutor and the next year, Roos—who had escaped before the verdict—gave himself up, was tried and acquitted. In 1939 Roos was found guilty of treason and was executed at Nancy. Bicker and Schall went to Germany on the invasion of France in 1940, while Rossé worked for the Germans as liason officer between Alsace and the Vichy Government.

During the 'thirties the Alsatian movement lost much of its momentum as satisfaction was given on a number of issues but also after the deaths of the leaders Haegy and Ricklin and defeats at the elections of 1932. Also, with Hitler's rise to power, attention shifted from events at home to the mounting international tension of the time. Indeed, it may be said that Nazism did more for the French cause in Alsace than all the French patriots in Paris in the years up to 1939. After the German invasion of France, there was determined resistance against the occupying powers in the region. The first measure taken by the German authorities concerned the languages spoken in Alsace. On 23 November 1940 *Gauleiter* Wagner announced, 'All inhabitants of this area are of German origin, including those who speak French. From now on in German Alsace only German will be spoken: there will be no half-measures'. The French language was banned in a number of detailed edicts. All personal names had to be Germanised, to conform with specially prepared lists, French books were burned in public, the 'Basque beret' was prohibited because it was considered 'unflattering to the Aryan face', speakers of dialect were expected to learn standard German within two years, the land and property of French-speakers were confiscated, those found listening to the B.B.C. were sent to prison, German-speakers from Germany and the South Tyrol were brought in to fill key administrative posts, the abbey of Saint Odile, one of Alsace's holy places, was converted into a hostel for the Hitler Youth, and concentration camps were built at Schimerck and Struthof for those trying to avoid conscription in the armies of the *Reich*. Alsace lost three times as many of its population, killed at the front, than any other region of France, and many thousands of Alsatians died in the camps. In April 1943 there was an attempt on the life of *Gauleiter* Wagner when his car was blown up—the first attack on a high-ranking official in the whole of occupied France.

The brutality of the German occupation to which Alsace was subjected, the Nazi hostility to any manifestation of the region's individuality, and the yoke of totalitarian ideology, united the population against the invaders and, after Hitler's defeat in 1945, the Alsatian autonomist movement no longer existed. The collaboration of some, but not all the leaders, whether by conviction, opportunism or conscription, caused bitter hatred and, as in Brittany, many reprisals followed.

About 45,000 Alsatians suspected of collaboration were interviewed during the first months after the armistice. Two prominent autonomists, the *Abbé* Joseph Braumer and Joseph Rossé, died in camps without having been tried. But the most notorious incident following what was generally considered to be the most atrocious crime committed by the Germans in occupied France, was the trial at Bordeaux of the soldiers of the *Das Reich* regiment, among whom were many Alsatians, for their part in burning alive the 1,200 inhabitants —men, women and children—of the Limousin village of Oradour-sur-Glane. The recrimination which attended such atrocities ensured that even the most modest and reasonable claims on behalf of Alsace were suspect and resisted for many years after the War.

In 1945, the teaching of German in the schools of Alsace was prohibited—'temporarily, to allow French to regain lost ground'. Over the next two decades French gained at every level and in every sector of public life. The result was that by 1964 an estimated 80% of Alsatians, although they could and did speak their German dialects, were unable to write or read German. This is still the case despite the fact that in 1952, following the Deixonne Law and under pressure from local opinion, the teaching of German for three hours a week was re-introduced for children between eleven and fourteen years of age. The Alsatians were content with this concession until 1970 when a poll revealed that 80% of parents in the towns and 95% in rural areas were in favour of German instruction in the primary schools. The following year an experiment entitled 'Introducing German' was conducted with the approval of the Ministry of National Education among dialect-speaking pupils, at first in thirty-two classes and then throughout Alsace with encouraging results.

By 1970, the wounds inflicted on Alsace during the Second World War were beginning to heal as a new generation grew up for whom the War was an event of which they had no personal experience. Since then there has been a fairly wide measure of sympathy for a new autonomist movement, created not only in the face of the French State's intransigent centralism but also by the economic situation prevailing in the region since 1945. At a popular level, the cabaret artist Germain Müller is generally considered to have had a part in reviving Alsatian spirits with his satire of local customs and attitudes, especially towards their own culture. There has also been a new interest in the dialects of the region, and a growing number of poets using them. Town councils have opened *Volkshochschulen* (people's education colleges) which hold courses in the history and literature of Alsace. The newspaper *La Voix d'Alsace,* founded by the former deputy Camille Dahlet in 1953, at first alone in defending the region's cultural identity, has been joined by a number of groups outside the main political parties which, run by young people, are calling for a bigger measure of devolution and more effective bilingual education. The periodical *Elan,* for example, published for Catholic intellectuals, has declared itself in favour of decentralisation and the creation of a regional assembly with financial and legislative powers. Stating that 'the demands of the Alsatian economy as prescribed by the region's geographical position cannot be satisfied by the present system of teaching German', the periodical demands that German be introduced during the first year at the infants' school.

A second group, the *René Schickelé Kreis,* founded in 1969 by Pierre Gabriel, has as its function to rally all sections of Alsatian opinion in a popular front in favour of decentralisation and the safe-guarding of the region's cultural and economic life. Named after the poet René Schickelé who fled at the time of the German invasion because he was obsessed with the idea of reconciliation between Germany and France, the Circle is affiliated to the *Association pour la Défense et Promotion des Langues de France.* It has over 3,000 members, its most eminent supporter is the Alsatian physicist and Nobel Prize winner Alfred Kastler and its motto is *Zweisprachig: unsere Zukunft/Notre Avenir est bilingue* (Our future is bilingual). The Circle's aims are supported by two lively newspapers, *Klapperstei 68* and *Uss'm Follik.* Against much opposition from the Ministry of Education in Paris the Circle organises private German lessons and in 1972 addressed an open letter to the President of the French Republic asking for the recognition of German as an official language in Alsace. Meanwhile, the radio station Strasbourg One has begun broadcasting a few literary programmes in Alsatian dialect and Strasbourg Two interrupts the *R.T.F.* in German from time to time. The local press is French or bilingual, as are religious services; the biggest daily newspaper published in Alsace sells 67,800 copies in its French edition and 117,000 in its bilingual edition.

The return of Alsace to economic prosperity after 1945 was slow. The first steps towards recovery were taken under the leadership of an Alsatian, Robert Schumann. As a German citizen during the First World War, Schumann had served in the Kaiser's army and, during the Second, he had fought in the French Resistance. Now as France's Foreign Minister and later as Prime Minister, he was determined to end the Franco-German feud. With the help of Jean Monnet and Germany's Chancellor Konrad Adenauer, Schumann's solution was to internationalise the coal and steel industries on which the military power of both States had been based. The creation of the European Coal and Steel Community in 1953 was a preliminary stage on the way to the Treaty of Rome and the subsequent formation of the European Economic Community. Yet, despite its favourable geographical position and the nomination of Strasbourg as the seat of the European Parliament, largely owing to Schumann's influence, Alsace was still not among the first regions to benefit. The canalisation of the river Moselle linking the Ruhr with Lorraine was an early blow to the port of Strasbourg (population: 257,300).

Today, compared with neighbouring areas of Western Germany and Switzerland, Alsace—one of the most heavily populated regions of France—is among the poorest parts of the prosperous belt which runs from Switzerland to the Netherlands. One reason for this is that its industries are mainly small enterprises which are barely competitive in the context of the European Economic Community. Many textile works have fallen on hard times and not a few have had to close their doors. The rate of investment by the French Government, never sufficient, has had to be supplemented in recent years by foreign capital. Between 1955 and 1967, 46% of jobs in Lower Rhine were created by French companies, 42% by

German and 12% by Swiss, while in Upper Rhine 41% of new jobs were created by foreign firms and only 17% by companies based in Alsace. A large proportion of the region's industry is run from Paris or from towns across the borders such as Basel, Zurich and Frankfurt. The attraction of German and Swiss industry for the local work-force is considerable. Every morning 30,000 workers leave Alsace for Basel, Wissemburg, Baden and other areas, where wages are higher. In one *arrondissement* three out of every ten work in Germany. This daily exodus, (the traffic is one-way), continues despite the French Government's attempts—35,000 salaried jobs created between 1969 and 1972—to develop and diversify the region's economy. Alsace has an experienced, enthusiastic work-force, great mineral wealth, excellent roads and canals and stands at the cross-roads of European trade, but it is unable fully to control its economic and social destiny. The mining industry has declined since the War, despite the known existence of ample seams.

Autonomist feeling moved into a new dimension with the creation, in November 1970, of the *Mouvement Régionaliste d'Alsace-Lorraine,* (Regionalist Movement of Alsace-Lorraine). A Committee for the Promotion of Alsace was set up in 1971 which promised to recognise the linguistic character of the region and Pierre Messmer, Prime Minister of France in 1972, declared, 'To be bilingual is a good fortune and a strength on condition that both languages are known well and that one feels equally at home in both. That is what many Alsatians desire, without diminishing their patriotism in any way'.

According to its manifesto and newspaper *Elsa,* the aim of the *M.R.A.L.* is the official recognition of a territorial and administrative area which would include Alsace and the German-speaking parts of Lorraine, within a decentralised France and a federal Europe. It calls for a regional Parliament invested with all economic and cultural powers, on the model of the German *Länder,* or the Swiss cantons, and demands that German, in both its literary form and its local dialects, become with French one of the region's official languages. The movement, broadly based on socialist principles, has already met with considerable success. In May 1971 Dr Marcel Iffrig, its president, won 31% of the votes cast in the local elections at Lauterburg and later that year 12,000 autonomists gathered at the *Palais des Fêtes* in Strasbourg to support the new movement.

Following campaigns for the teaching of German, the municipal councils of Lower Rhine and Upper Rhine have voted in fabour of obligatory German lessons in primary schools, supported by ninety-two members of the academic staff of the three universities of Strasbourg. In 1972 the *U.D.R.* deputy for Sarreguemines (German: *Saargemünd)* M. Hinsberger—one of the thirteen members of this party representing the entire region at this time—introduced a law for the teaching of a second language including 'regional languages' in all the schools of France. For the moment, not much more can be expected of a movement which has been in existence for only five years.

The extreme caution with which the cultural re-awakening of Alsace has progressed since 1970 is explained, of course, by the traumas of the Second World War. The Alsatians, opposed to much that was German then and French now, are understandably anxious that defence of their heritage should not be mistaken as 'unpatriotic' sentiment within the context of the French State. There is a sense in which the region has shown its traditional face, by voting in the referenda of 1958, 1961 and 1962 in favour of De Gaulle's Republic. Unfortunately for Alsace, as for other regions of the hexagon, France still subscribes to the old German theory which defined nationality according to linguistic criteria and has followed a policy of assimilation by which Alsatians can be French citizens only when they abandon the German language and their traditions. Everything has been done to persuade Alsatians that their French citizenship justifies the complete Gallicization of the region's education system and public life, with the result that—despite its strong personality—Alsace has become in the last decade more and more like Burgundy or Normandy, with fifteen hundred years of its history denied. The region's linguistic character is also being destroyed, for the dialects these days are becoming impoverished and bastardized, while a knowledge of standard

German has regressed. Local culture has been reduced to a folklore for tourists and there is widespread ignorance of the region's history, literature and customs.

The autonomist voices raised in the last few years are calling on France for the recognition not only of Alsace as a European community in economic terms but also as a symbol of reconciliation between the States and a model for the integrated federal Europe of tomorrow. But the attitude of the French Government remains as expressed by Maurice Duhamel in a letter to the autonomists tried at Colmar in 1928: 'When you were under the Prussian boot you were able to be both Alsatian and German at the same time, because Germany was a Federal State. Under French rule you cannot be both Alsatian and French because France is a unitary State'.

THE FLEMINGS OF WESTHOEK

In the north-east corner of France, between the Artois hills and the border with Belgium, there is an area of about 580 square miles which is known to some of its inhabitants as Westhoek. Here, north of the river Lys and east of the Aa, live approximately 90,000 Flemings, speakers of Dutch. They form part of the rural population in the *arrondissements* of Dunkerque (Dutch: *Duinkerke)* and Hazebrouck *(Hazebroek),* but are also to be found in some of the towns such as Bailleul and Cassel. The total population of *Le Nord,* the department in which these Dutch-speakers live, was 2,514,300 in 1975.

The extent of the Dutch language in this part of France —like Belgian Flanders it is known in French as *La Flandre*—included during the Middle Ages the towns of Lille (Dutch: *Rijsel)* and Valenciennes *(Valencijn)* in the east and, to the west, a number of villages in the Pas-de-Calais where, around Saint-Omer, a few families still speak it among themselves. In 1926 the only cantons in this area which were entirely French-speaking were Gravelines, Merville, Nieppe and Steinwerk. But since then the French language has rapidly gained ground, especially along the coast and in the towns, so that—although no official figures are available—it is known that the concentration of Dutch-speakers (perhaps 200,000 in the whole of French Flanders) is high only in those villages along the border with Belgium.

The process of assimilation by the French State began for Westhoek, as for other regions where French was not the indigenous language, in the seventeenth century. Louis XIV banned the use of Dutch for official purposes throughout his territory in the Low Countries, including Ypres, in 1648. After the Revolution of 1789 the teaching and printing of Dutch were prohibited. Opposition to the highly centralist policies of the new régime was punished on a wide scale by imprisonment and, for priests, by dismissal from religious orders.

It was not until 1853, when the Baron Edmond de Coussemayer founded the *Comité Flamand de France* (Flemish Committee of France) that the Flemish movement, already well rooted to the north, began to be organised. In

1870 the famous petition for the teaching of 'provincial idioms' presented to the French Government by a group which included the Count Henri de Charencey, a Basque patriot, Henri Gaidoz, editor of *La Revue Celtique,* and Charles de Gaulle, from a Lille family which was later to give France a president, called for the use of Dutch in the region's schools, and the endowment of a chair of Dutch language and literature at the University of Douai. The petition was ignored, however, under both the Third Republic and the Second Empire. Napoleon III banned the use of Dutch in school and during the last years of the Concordat between France and the Catholic Church (1896-1902) the State forbade the clergy to teach or use the language.

The Flemish movement in France up to the First World War was more cultural than political but it was also in more or less regular contact with the Flemings of Belgium, who were politically more militant. For this reason the French authorities maintained close surveillance of their Flemings and, uneasy over the problem of Alsace, expected them to form a fifth column during the hostilities of 1914-18. However, contrary to what happened in Belgium and Alsace, the German occupation of the Dutch-speaking areas of France found few collaborators.

After 1923 and the foundation of the *Vlaamsch Verbond van Frankrijk* (Flemish League of France), the movement's influence spread with the publication of its newspapers and the creation of a chair of Dutch at the Catholic University of Lille. Nevertheless, the movement's demands were completely ignored by all French Governments during the years between the World Wars. There was a notable attack on it by President Edouard Herriot who, at Roubaix near the Belgian border, in 1924, bitterly accused the Flemings of being reactionary, right-wing and intent on destroying the Republic.

It is difficult to defend the League against such charges. That some members, inspired by the movement's newspaper, *De Vlaamse Leeuw* (The Lion of Flanders) and the *Vlaams National Verbond* (Flemish National Union) sympathised with the Germans during the occupation of France in the Second World War, mainly on racial grounds of 'Nordic superiority', is clear enough. There were certainly Nazi plans for the incorporation of the Dutch-speaking areas, as an autonomous part of a greater *Reich,* which were known to Flemings in both France and Belgium. With the Allies' victory, the Flemish movement was accused of treason by the Resistance, and reprisals followed. In 1946 five leaders of the League were found guilty of having expressed regionalist sentiments during the War. The sentences of hard labour and, in the case of the *Abbé* Gantois, of death, which were passed on the State prosecutor's demand, were eventually commuted to terms of imprisonment of up to five years. Many other Flemings were acquitted of similar charges, but two leading separatists, P. Visieux and P. F. Quesnoy, were found guilty of open collaboration with the Germans. The first was sentenced to twenty years' imprisonment and died in detention at Marseilles; the other was executed.

It is quite apparent that, unlike the nationalist movement in Brittany, where similar incidents took place during and after the Second World War, the Flemish movement has not yet begun to recover from the damage done during those years. Since 1951, when the Deixonne Law authorised the limited teaching of 'regional languages', the Flemings of Westhoek, although greatly reduced in numbers and influence, and despite the fact that their formerly vigorous cultural life has deteriorated, have concentrated their efforts on attempts to have Dutch included among the languages which can be taught in the State schools. But up to 1975 they had met with no success whatsoever. Dutch is not taught, not even as a foreign language, in any of the region's schools. The Catholic seminary at Hazebrouck is one of the few private institutions which provide lessons in Dutch, and the language is still studied at the Catholic University of Lille.

There is no Dutch on the *R.T.F.* although Flemings in France are known to listen regularly to radio and television broadcasts from Belgium. The campaign for a few minutes of Dutch on radio, for the application to the language of the Deixonne Law, and for inscriptions in Dutch on public buildings, is led by a cultural periodical entitled *Vlaamse Vrienden In Frankrijk (Flemish Friends in France)* and by a new society, the *Michael de Swaen Kring,* a circle named after a Dunkerque poet of the sixteenth century and founded in

1971, which claims among its 350 members a number of eminent political and cultural figures. The basic assumption of these two groups is doubtless correct: that, denied recognition in the schools and mass-media—and everywhere else for that matter—the Dutch language in Westhoek is doomed to imminent extinction.

THE BRETONS

Brittany, situated in the north-west of France, consists of the five departments of Ille-et-Vilaine, Côtes-du-Nord, Finistère, Morbihan and Loire-Atlantique—although for official administrative purposes the latter is not included. It is a largely agricultural country, with an important fishing industry; the principal towns are Rennes, the administrative capital, and the major ports of Nantes and Brest. With a total area of 13,460 square miles, Brittany (French: *Bretagne)* had a population of 2,598,000 at the Census of 1975, about 7% of the total population of France.

Like Welsh and Cornish, which it most closely resembles, Breton belongs to the Brythonic group of the Celtic languages; although it is also related to the Gaelic languages of Ireland, Scotland and Man, Breton shares fewer characteristics with the Goidelic group. The language *(brezhoneg)* is spoken, for the most part, to the west of a line from Plouha on the northern coast through Pontivy to Vannes *(Gwened)* on the southern coast, over a region known as *Basse-Bretagne* or Lower Brittany *(Breizh Izel)* which includes Finistère *(Penn ar Bed)* and the western parts of Côtes-du-Nord *(Aodau an Hanternoz)* and Morbihan, some 600 communes in all. To the east of this line, in *Haute-Bretagne* or Upper Brittany *(Breizh Uhel),* the language spoken is French and the Gallo dialects; since the ninth century the Breton language has lost about half of its territory, the linguistic border continuously moving west.

As there are no official figures for the Breton-speaking population, no Census ever having attempted to enumerate it, the statistical evidence is that provided by estimates based on information elicited by various individuals and organisations devoted to the language. According to Coquebert de Montbret, there were approximately 967,000 Breton-speakers in 1806 and, according to Sébillot, 1,300,000 eighty years later: their estimates were easily made because, except for a few French-speaking enclaves, Lower Brittany was wholly Breton-speaking. The decline in the numbers able to speak the language did not begin until the twentieth century. On the eve of the First World War there were about

1,300,000, 90% of the inhabitants of Lower Brittany, and no fewer than in 1886. In 1928 the magazine *Gwalarn* published the results of a survey which estimated that there were still around a million Bretons, some 75% of the population of Lower Brittany, having Breton as an everyday language. In 1952 Francis Gourvil believed there were around 700,000 Bretons who 'used French only in the case of necessity', to which he added a further 300,000 who were able to speak Breton 'if the need arose'.

It was after 1952 that a more rapid decline began, particularly after the advent of television and as the result of the French Government's intransigence towards repeated demands for the teaching of Breton in the State's schools. All estimates since that of Gourvil have confirmed the acceleration of the decline. The most recent, made by Jean-Claude Bozec in the magazine *Dihun* and subsequently published by Roger Laouénan in the newspaper *Le Télégramme de Brest* (21 February 1974), revealed that out of a total population of approximately 1,500,000 there were in Lower Brittany only 685,250 persons, or 44%, who were capable of speaking Breton; of these only 18,000 (out of 360,000) were children under fourteen years, while 56,250 (out of 225,000) were aged between fifteen and twenty-four, 423,000 (out of 705,000) between twenty-five and sixty-four, and 168,000 (out of 210,000) over sixty-five. Bozec's estimates of how many people speak Breton on a regular, day-to-day basis were as follows: about 8% of children under fourteen, 6% of young people between the ages of fifteen and twenty-four, 50% of adults aged twenty-five to sixty-four and 75% of old people aged sixty-five and over; that is to say, about 385,650 persons, or 25% of the population of Lower Brittany, speaking Breton during the course of their daily lives. To these figures must be added a further 300,000 who are believed to understand spoken Breton of an elementary kind, so that perhaps a million can claim to have some knowledge of the language. The vast majority of this total, however, probably as high as 75%, can neither read nor write the language. They are for the most part the peasants and artisans of the rural areas, fishermen and sailors, for the towns of Brittany have long been French-speaking.

The history of the Breton people began in Britain. Up to the fifth century the peninsula known today as Brittany was inhabited by Gaulish tribes united in a confederation which was destroyed by Caesar. The Bretons arrived in Armorica, as the land was called, in flight—'as from a ravaging flame', according to Saint Gildas—from invasion of Britain by Angles, Saxons and other Germanic peoples over the next two centuries. Under the leadership of their monks and chieftains, these Celts brought their language and customs to a new country which was known to Roman historians as *Brittania Minor* to distinguish it from the 'Great Britain' from whence they came. There were other reasons for this emigration, notably economic ones, but the flight of the insular Celts, mostly from Cornwall, *'pell diouz douar kuñv o c'havel'* (far from the gentle land of their cradle), as Frañsez Vallée described it, has never failed to inspire Breton poets in later centuries.

At about the same time as the Bretons were laying the foundations of their new country, by peaceful means at first, the Franks were streaming into Gaul. The Bretons established themselves to best advantage along the northern coast and in the districts around Quimper today known as *La Cornouaille*. Further east, the Gallo-Roman settlement was denser with the result that the Breton of the Vannes region was developed at a much later date, after the year 579, and later became one of the four main dialects of the modern language and the one most dissimilar to the rest.

From the time the two peoples found themselves as neighbours the Franks began attempts to subordinate the Bretons to their rule. Subdued for a short while by Charlemagne, the Bretons launched numerous campaigns against his successors and, under the leadership of Nominoe, they defeated the army of the Emperor Charles the Bald in the year 845. Brittany's independence was acknowledged and Nominoe proclaimed King. His successors, Erispoe and Salomon, extended the kingdom's territories during further wars against the Franks, including the Cotentin peninsula of Normandy and large parts of Anjou and Poitou. The Breton language, however, was never spoken to the east of what is now known as 'the Loth line' (after the eminent scholar Joseph Loth of the nineteenth century) which ran from the estuary of the river Couesnon, where Mont St Michel stands, to Pornic on the southern coast near the mouth of the river Loire; for this reason the towns of Rennes and Nantes have never been Breton-speaking.

The linguistic unity of the whole of Brittany might have been achieved were it not for events which had disastrous consequences for the kingdom. Beginning in the ninth century, the raids of the Vikings devastated the country during the tenth and reduced it to political chaos. The clergy and the aristocracy having fled to France and Britain, the people were left, as the Chronicle of Nantes records, to 'the domination of the barbarians, without leaders and without support'. In 938, however, the Breton prince Alan Barvek (Alain Barbetorte) drove out the Norsemen at the battle of Trans and, as Duke of Brittany, re-established the independence of his country, the boundaries of which (except for Cotentin and Western Normandy) have remained more or less the same down to the present time.

For the next six centuries Brittany was to enjoy and defend an independent, national existence. The interregnum of the Viking raids had a serious effect on the Breton language, however. When, on the country's liberation, the clergy and nobles returned from exile they brought with them the Gallo-Roman speech of their hosts which became the language of religion, law and administration in the districts of Rennes and Nantes, traditionally the non-Breton-speaking areas. Over the next two hundred years the Breton ruling class married into Norman families and took part in William's conquest of England in 1066, becoming all the more French in manners as their success grew. The last Breton-speaking sovereign of all Brittany, Hoël, died in 1084. From now on Breton was relegated to become the language of the peasants and the minor nobility of Lower Brittany.

During the next four hundred years the Bretons fought for their country's independence against the rival claims of England and France. The English influence in Brittany during the twelfth and thirteenth centuries changed little in the linguistic situation because the English aristocracy spoke Norman French and, like the French, used Latin and Old

French in administration, while Breton was pushed into a marginal position. Never again was Breton to be the language of the country's governing élite. Only among the minor clergy was it used with any vigour, a fact which became central to its survival into modern times. At the same time, the language began its retreat westwards, not at the same pace in all parts —it was spoken at Dol in the tenth century and at Dinan in the twelfth—but nevertheless its retreat away from the centres of power. Meanwhile, the rulers of Brittany were pre-occupied with the threat of annexation by France and England, playing each off against the other during the Hundred Years' War and managing to preserve the country's independence until the end of the fifteenth century. Under the government of the *États de Bretagne*, a representative Assembly meeting once a year, Brittany became a prosperous country in which not only commerce flourished but the arts and social laws also, while its merchant fleet was among the most powerful in Europe.

The defeat of the Duchy's army at the battle of Saint-Aubin-du-Cromier in 1488 marked the end of Brittany's independence. François II was obliged to accept the Treaty of Le Verger, the first step towards the total annexation of Brittany, and in 1491 his daughter Anne, a girl not yet twenty, to annul her marriage with the Emperor Maximilian of Austria and to marry the King of France, Charles VIII. After the death of her husband Anne de Bretagne married his successor Louis XII in 1498 and tried to secure in her marriage settlement the independence of her country by the betrothal of her daughter and heir, Claude, to the heir of France's enemy, the house of Austria. But after Anne's death in 1514, and years of intrigue and tortuous politics, Claude was given to François d'Angoulême, later King François I; Brittany was then linked to the French Crown. Before this could happen, however, the approval of the *États de Bretagne* had to be given, since the Duchess Anne had signed her marriage contract not in her own name but in that of the Breton people. Sums of money were therefore distributed to influential Bretons with the result that on 4 August 1532 the *États* requested an Act of Union. By the Treaty of the same year the Kings of France were to become the Dukes of Brittany, which was thus incorporated. The French agreed to respect the political and administrative rights to which the Bretons were deeply attached, leaving them responsibility for internal administration; no taxes were to be levied without the consent of the *États de Bretagne,* only Bretons were to hold public office and they were not to be conscripted for military service outside Brittany, which became an autonomous province within the French Kingdom.

At first France respected the Union and there was little alteration in the situation of the Breton language. The ordinance of Villers-Cotterêts in 1539 proclaimed by the Government of François I to secure the exclusive use of French in acts of justice, or in all other legal documents, abolished the conception of a bilingual Kingdom as far as *la langue d'oc* was concerned, but had no effect on Breton because this language was not used for official purposes. Latin became the language of law and French did not succeed it until forty years later in Upper Brittany and not until 1630-40 in Lower Brittany. The rule of the French King grew more and more powerful, however, increasingly antagonistic to Breton rights as defined in 1532 in which it saw a serious hindrance to the new order it was seeking to establish.

In 1675, when Louis XIV announced taxes on certain commodities including tobacco, revenue stamps and cooking utensils against the wishes of the *États,* the Bretons rose in the episode of *les Bonnets Rouges.* On 18 April 1675 the tax office in Rennes was sacked by a crowd of 2,000 and about fifty noble homes were burned in western and central Brittany. The local aristocrats and clergy came out in support of the Government against the people and the rising was brutally crushed, with many peasants hanged. 'The trees on the main road from Quimper to Quimperlé', wrote one witness, 'are beginning to bend under the weight upon them'.

Early in the next century, in 1720, the struggle was resumed when four Breton noblemen, Pontcallec, Montlouis, Talhouet and Couedic were beheaded in Nantes for trying to restore Breton independence. From then until the eve of the French Revolution the opposition of Brittany was expressed in the struggle of the Breton Parliament against the centralising policies of the French Crown. Led by La Chalotais, many members were imprisoned or went into exile.

The Revolution of 1789 was readily accepted in Brittany, where popular support for the French Crown had always been luke-warm. Many of the new laws and proclamations were translated into Breton such as the *Almanach du Père Gérard* which explained the Constitution to the people. Soon, however, the idea that French, and French alone could be the language of *'liberté, égalité, fraternité'* was widespread. A bill of 1792 proposing bilingual education for Lower Brittany, Corsica, Alsace and the northern Basque provinces was rejected. The following year the disastrous implications of this decision became apparent when the law of 21 October 1793 established a State school, recognising only French, in every commune. From this moment dates the implacable campaign waged by the French State towards all minority languages within its borders. As Jorj Gwegen describes it in *La Langue Bretonne face à ses Oppresseurs* (1975), 'The purging zeal unleashed was such that it still persists intact in our own time among all those who imagine that they hold in their hands the unifying torch of the great Revolutionary ancestors'.

The *États* and the Breton Parliament were abolished by the Revolution and Brittany divided into the five departments which survive to the present day (Loire-Atlantique was originally called Loire Inférieure but the name was changed in deference to the feelings that name aroused in its inhabitants). The *Procureur* of the *États,* the Count of Boterel, made a famous defence of the regional statute but to no avail. When it became clear that the French Government was intending to continue even more rigorously the centralist policy of the monarchy, a general rising took place in 1793 under the leadership of La Rouerie and Georges Cadoudal in defence of Brittany's threatened faith and suppressed liberties. On 26 May 1794 twenty-four members of the *Conseil Général* of Finistère were executed. French historians have usually presented this revolt of the Chouans as a purely royalist and clerical rising. But Brittany was warmly attached to its political freedom and even the Breton Republicans, who had supported the Revolutionaries in the early days, now joined the federalist cause and fought against the Jacobin Convention. In 1801 La Rouerie formed the first *Association Bretonne* which demanded that Breton rights be restored and three years later Cadoudal was beheaded in Paris for persisting in the demand. To this day the worst insult a good **French Republican can make to a Breton is to call him a**

Chouan—the word has become synonymous with a refusal of social change, but in fact *Chouannerie* began as a protest at the abolition of the Breton Assembly; only later was it infiltrated by royalists and even then its last strongholds were not in Brittany but in the Vendée.

The Revolutionaries saw in provincial traditions, and the aristocratic privileges and exploitation of workers which went with them, major obstacles to the reforms and progress they wished to achieve by the imposition of uniformity. From their point of view, all attempts to defend the Breton language after 1790 were politically reactionary, as indeed many of those aristocrats who were among the early enthusiasts for Breton culture undoubtedly were. It was in 1794 that Barrère declared that 'federalism and superstition speak Low Breton; emigration and hatred of the Republic speak German; the counter-revolution speaks Italian and fanaticism speaks Basque', concluding 'Among a free people, language must be one and the same for all'. He was supported by the infamous *Abbé* Grégoire, who declared his own war against 'regional jargons', adding in 1792 that in a Republic *'une et indivisible'* French was to be the only language of liberty.

Over the next hundred years Barrère and Grégoire were to have many disciples. In 1831 the Prefects of Finistère and Côtes du Nord expressed themselves in favour 'by all means possible, of the impoverishment and corruption of Breton to the extent that from one commune to the next it will no longer be understood. For the need for communication will oblige the peasant to learn French. The Breton speech must be absolutely destroyed'. Teachers, such as Guillaume Marzel at Saint Renan in 1837, were now fined and imprisoned for teaching Breton to their pupils. In 1845 teachers were told in a public address by a Sub-Prefect, 'Remember above all, gentlemen, that you have been set up only in order to kill the Breton language'.

Napoleon made peace with the Chouans and many were given Government posts—although not in Brittany. But under his Empire the French Government tightened rather than loosened the grip which Paris now had over the provinces. Furthermore, it was Napoleon, 'the ogre from Corsica' as he was known in Brittany, who created the office of Prefect, the official who was to rule the departments in the Government's name and who abolished primary schools in order to develop the *lyceé* and the *écoles normales* in which French was obligatory. As only one person in fifty spoke French in Brittany the prospects of secondary education for Bretons were small.

The series of school laws passed between 1880 and 1887 at the instigation of Jules Ferry, which introduced free, compulsory education for all through the medium of French, speeded up the process of *francisation* by now well under way. It was at this time that the notorious *symbole,* a heavy object such as a clog hung around the child's neck, was introduced. The *symbole* was worn by the child caught speaking Breton until he, in his turn, could find another of his class-mates speaking the language; the child wearing the badge of shame at the end of the school day was punished (c.f. the Welsh Not). According to some witnesses the *symbole* was still in regular use between the two World Wars and a few instances of its use were reported even as late as the 1950s and 1960s. To the French territories overseas colonised at this time—Congo, Tonkin, Sudan and Madagascar—was added the 'internal colony' of Brittany. During a speech in 1885 Jules Ferry said, 'If France wishes to remain a great country, it must take everywhere it can its language, its customs, its flag, its arms and its genius'. This was certainly the case in Brittany: defeated and ruled from Paris, the country's name had been removed from the maps and it was now known as 'the departments of the West'.

Despite the terrible persecution it had suffered, Breton nationality was not dead, however, and as part of the Romantic Revival of the early nineteenth century it revived and, in the manner of its time, began to flourish once again. The first manifestations of *Emsav* (Resurrection), as the whole of the Breton movement came to be known, were literary. In 1836 Hersart de la Villemarqué published a collection of folk-songs and ballads in Breton, entitled *Barzaz Breiz* (Songs of Brittany). Translated into other European languages, this work made a profound impression outside Brittany in those countries where interest in vernaculars and the medieval tradition was in vogue. Le Gonidec now united three out of the four Breton dialects and published a grammar, while La Tour d'Auvergne (the pseudonym of Malo Carret) extolled the language in his writings. As in other countries, the work of these pioneers was undertaken at a time when Brittany was entering a long period of economic decline, losing its industries and becoming a poor, rural and socially backward region. Yet their significance in the history of Breton is immense, for while on the one hand the language was being stamped out among the common people, on the other it was preserved by the intelligentsia in readiness for use by later generations.

The nineteenth century also saw the growth of a number of cultural societies and regionalist organisations. Relations with Wales were resumed in 1838 when a Breton delegation including Le Gonidec and Villemarqué was received at Abergavenny by *Cymdeithas y Cymreigyddion* under the direction of Carnhuanawc. The French poet Alphonse de Lamartine, who took part in this reunion, later wrote an ode about the bringing together of the two halves of Arthur's sword by the Welsh and the Bretons. The second *Association Bretonne* was founded in 1843 to promote the unity of Brittany—but was dissolved by Napoleon III in 1858. In 1867 the first meeting of the Inter-Celtic Congress was held at Saint-Brieuc as a result of which a petition calling for the teaching of Breton, and other 'provincial languages' was made to the French Government by Henri Gaidoz, editor of *La Revue Celtique*, the Count de Charencey and the poet Charles de Gaulle, great-uncle of the General. Nothing came of this petition, partly due to the imminence of the war with Prussia which began in 1870. During that war the Breton regiments were decimated by the Prussians at the battle of Le Mans.

Under the Third Republic, the Breton movement continued to gather momentum. La Borderie published his *Histoire de Bretagne*. Folklorists like Anatole Le Braz gathered popular songs, philologists like Loth, Vallée and Le Roux turned to the scientific study of Celtic languages. In 1898 the *Union Régionaliste Bretonne* was founded by Charles Le Goffic, Le Braz and the Marquis de l'Estourbeillon, the latter a deputy for Morbihan from 1902 to 1946. A numerous Breton delegation visited the National *Eisteddfod* of Wales at Cardiff in 1900 and a Breton branch of the *Gorsedd* of Bards was formed in the following year under the leadership of

Taldir (Jaffrenou) who composed the Breton words *'Bro Goz va Zadou'* (Old Land of my Fathers) on the model of the Welsh national anthem *'Hen Wlad fy Nhadau'*. Delegations from the *Gorsedd* of Brittany and the other Celtic countries have paid official visits to the National *Eisteddfod* of Wales in almost every year since 1900. In 1905 the Catholic association known as *Bleun Brug* was launched by the *Abbé* Perrot for the encouragement of Breton in religious and cultural life.

By the eve of the First World War, despite the gathering strength of the Breton movement, the language was still prohibited for all official purposes. It had been forbidden in church by a circular of 1903, although it was still in widespread use after that date, and in the same year attempts were made to oblige priests to give first communion only to French-speaking children. The village schools of Brittany at this time were run by *instituteurs* who were mostly left-wing and anti-clerical, the disciples of Jules Ferry who had created the system of State schools teaching exclusively through the medium of French. The opponent of uniformist French ideals in Brittany was the Church, which at its worst could be reactionary and traditionalist in the extreme, opposed to all social progress. Requests for the teaching of Breton by all Brittany's deputies in 1905 and again in 1911 were therefore ignored, the Minister of Education remarking in 1909 that 'the teaching of Breton would encourage Breton separatism'.

There were only a few signs that such fears were based on reality. After the Franco-Prussian War a movement in favour of regionalisation in France was begun but had been supported by the major political parties only when in opposition and abandoned whenever such ideas conflicted with the Government's policies as laid down by the Civil Service in Paris. The earliest organisation with a political, as distinct from a cultural aim, was the *Fédération Régionaliste de Bretagne,* founded in 1911, which put Breton autonomy at the head of its programme and published a newspaper *Breiz Dishual* (Free Brittany). In the same year Camille Le Mercier d'Erm, a young student, started the first Breton Nationalist Party. It was this party which staged a famous demonstration of whistling during the ceremony at which a statue symbolising the union of Brittany with France in 1532 was unveiled at Rennes. Both organisations ceased activity as the year 1914 approached.

The Great War opened in Brittany with the French Government, for the first time in centuries, using Breton for official purposes: to persuade peasants to exchange their gold coins for paper money, *'evit difenn ar vro'* (to defend the country). The poet Theodore de Botrel, up to then largely responsible for the popular image of the Breton in France as a *bécassine* (a snipe), followed the Government's appeal for Breton gold with exhortations for their blood: 'The Republic calls us, let us know how to live and die; a Frenchman must live for her and for her a Breton must die'. However much gold was collected, the Bretons shed their blood in enormous sacrifices: a total of 240,000 Breton soldiers were killed during the next four years—one out of every four who went to the front. The figure for the rest of France was one out of every eight, for Germany one out of nine, for Britain one out of sixteen. Among those killed were a large number who, because they could not speak the language of the French State, were believed to be spies or deserters, tried without interpreters and shot. They also included one of the best Breton poets, Yann-Ber Kalloc'h, who was killed on 10 April 1917. Kalloc'h died with the hope that Brittany's agony would be rewarded. In one of his last letters from the trenches, he wrote, 'As soon as the peace is signed, let there be circulated in Brittany a sort of petition to the government, asking for the teaching of Brittany's language and history . . . The signatories of this petition? Everyone, but above all the soldiers, those who will have spilled their blood for France . . . Examined in good faith the Breton question would soon be solved'.

Such a petition was made to the Peace Conference at Versailles in 1919, bearing some 800 signatures including that of Marshall Foch and many leading Breton politicians and the country's five bishops. But it met with no response and France vetoed any discussion of the Breton question. For the victors the fate of minorities in former enemy territory was more important than the clearly expressed aspirations of minorities at home. While the Czechs, the Slovenes and the

Hungarians, and others, gained their independence, Brittany was condemned to remain a province of the French State.

After the War, Breton nationalism was to gain ground rapidly. Before the year 1918 was out, a newspaper was published under the title *Breiz Atao* (Brittany Forever). There now gathered around this publication a number of young Bretons, many former combatants, who came together to form a new political party, the *Parti National Breton,* in 1919. The first leaders were M. Marchal, O. Mordel and F. Debeauvais. It was from the annual congress of the *P.N.B.* in 1928 that the idea of a federal Europe, designed to secure autonomy for minorities, emerged for the first time. The party was thus not concerned exclusively with Brittany, having helped to launch a Committee for National Minorities at Quimper in 1927 and having contributed to the review *Peuples et Frontières* from 1936. Indeed, during the trial, at Colmar in 1928, of a group of Alsatian autonomists, it was remarked that the wind blowing across the Vosges came from the Atlantic. But the *P.N.B.* brought a dynamism to the national movement which it had lacked for centuries.

Up to now the cultural movement had won the support of Breton opinion because its leaders had always kept the cause of the language above political strife; many who were involved in the linguistic campaign made no political claims. On the other hand, all who demanded some kind of political autonomy for Brittany were supporters of the language. The two main tendencies which had emerged by 1930 were the moderate wing who called themselves regionalists and the more radical but less numerous group inside the *P.N.B.* The regionalists did not oppose French rule in Brittany but advocated administrative reform which would give Brittany a degree of cultural autonomy: in this they were in the tradition of earlier organisations like the *Union Régionaliste Bretonne* and *Bleun Brug.* They demanded the creation of a Region and the restoration of the Breton liberties granted in 1532 and destroyed after 1789. The *P.N.B.* accused the regionalists of ineffectiveness, taking as its slogan 'With France if possible, without France if necessary!'

The growing strength of the *P.N.B.* during the 'twenties and 'thirties was supported by a cultural movement of great importance in the history of the Breton language. Before this time Breton literature had consisted mainly of fragments of texts from the tenth century, mystery plays and other works of a religious, didactory nature, a few grammars and dictionaries. After the publication of *Barzaz Breiz* in the nineteenth century the oral tradition and legends of Brittany had been revealed, and the first decades of the twentieth had seen the appearance of some lyrical poetry, much of it mediocre. The publication in 1925 of the review *Gwalarn* (North-west) edited by Roparz Hemon, marked the birth of modern Breton literature. The young writers who worked in the *Gwalarn* group, including Hemon, were Jakez Riou, Abeozen, Fant Meavenn, Maodez Glanndour, Langleiz, to name but a few. Yeun ar Gow, Tanguy Malmanche, Per-Jakez Helias, Youenn Olier, and Youenn Drezen declared war on provincialism in both politics and literature alike and allied themselves with European standards of the day. At first a supplement of *Breiz Atao, Gwalarn* became a monthly in 1927 and for the next twenty years it dominated the Breton literary scene. One of the features of the new literature thus created was a number of translations into Breton from other languages including the stories of Grimm and Hoffmann, the works of Aeschylus, Marlowe, Cervantes, Hans Christian Anderson, J. M. Synge, Shakespeare and Shelley as well as the masterpieces of the other Celtic languages such as the Welsh *Mabinogi* and the Irish sagas.

While the *Gwalarn* school led the agnostic wing of the Breton movement, the Catholic element was represented by the *Abbé* Yann-Vari Perrot (1877-1943) and his motto *'Ar Feiz hag ar Yez a zo breur ha c'hoar e Breiz'* (The Faith and the Language are brother and sister in Brittany). Around the magazine *Feiz ha Breiz*, which he edited for thirty-two years, there grew a festival known as *Bleun Brug* (Heather Flower), a name chosen to signify 'the tenacity of the Breton People', which played a vital part in creating a modern theatre in the language. Perrot's earliest play *Alanig al Louarn* was performed in 1905 and he wrote over thirty others for presentation at his festival. His *Buhez ar Zent*, a life of the saints, sold tens of thousands of copies in Lower Brittany, to become in many instances the only Breton book in the possession of the country people.

Another outstanding figure of the inter-war years was Loeiz Herrieu (1879-1953), editor of the review *Dihunamb!* (Let's wake up!) from 1905 to 1944 except for seven years after 1914. A total of 395 numbers of this magazine were published, in monthly editions of several thousand copies each, and all in the Vannes dialect of Breton which differs in its phonetic qualities and orthography from the other three main dialects. A small farmer, Herrieu also published a volume of his own short stories, a history of Breton literature, a collection of poems and a war diary in which he relates the horror and absurdity of the years 1914-18. Herrieu's work as a publisher is generally thought to have maintained the interest of the Vannes region in the Breton movement of the time.

The fourth name among the leaders of the Breton cultural movement between 1918 and 1939 was that of Yann Sohier. A member of the *P.N.B.*, Sohier was also a militant revolutionary inspired by the Bolshevik Revolution of October 1917 and by the Soviet Union's policies towards minority cultures within its borders. For him the Breton language was an instrument of social emancipation. Born at Lamballe in Upper Brittany, in 1901, he learned Breton as an adult, the first of many such people in the present century who have contributed to the Breton movement. He was also remarkable in that he was an *instituteur,* a profession traditionally hostile to Breton, but worked all his life for the teaching of the language in State schools. Known as *Yann Skolaer* (John the Schoolmaster), Sohier launched a monthly bulletin, *Ar Falz* (The Sickle) in 1933, but died two years later, worn out by the intensity of his efforts, at the age of thirty-four. His work was continued by his comrades A. Keravel and Kerlann who opened a private school, where all teaching was done in Breton, in the village of Plestin, thus becoming the pioneers in a field later entered by others, including the *Abbé* Armand Calvez who opened *Skol Sant Erwan* at Plouézec in 1957.

During the decade preceding the Second World War, relations between the *P.N.B.* now enjoying widespread support, and the French Government deteriorated. Acts of violence by the clandestine organisation *Gwenn ha Du* (Black and White, the colours of the Breton flag) began to occur. The most noteworthy was the blowing up, at Rennes on 6 August 1932, of the monument symbolising the union of Brittany with France, on the day President Edouard Herriot was celebrating the fourth centenary of the Union in Vannes. Later in the same year the train bringing Herriot to Nantes for a similar occasion was derailed at the Breton border. Then, in 1938, the French Government decided to take steps against the Breton movement. Active members were arrested for making propaganda 'likely to endanger the unity of France'. The two leaders of the *P.N.B.,* Debauvais and Mordrel, were sentenced to a year's imprisonment each but only the former served the sentence. The newspaper *Breiz Atao,* which had warned of the danger of Brittany becoming involved in another European war and had recommended pacifism, was closed down by the police. A few days before the declaration of war, Debauvais and Mordrel—judging their arrest to be imminent—left Brittany for Belgium, later travelling through Italy and Hungary to Germany.

The War put an end to every kind of Breton activity. Those periodicals not suppressed had to close as their editors were called up for service in the French Army. Raids were made on the homes of Breton nationalists, their books confiscated and burned. The Breton centre in Paris, *Ker Vreiz,* was ransacked by the police and closed down. It is clear that as early as 1939, long before the fall of France in June 1940 and the invasion of Brittany by German forces, the French Government was carrying out an extensive attack on the Breton movement as a whole, proscribing every manifestation of Breton life, whether political or cultural.

The accusations of fascism made against the whole Breton movement since 1939 are based on the events which followed the departure of Debauvais and Mordrel for Germany. The first moves towards an understanding between the Germans and what was always a very small number of Breton nationalists were made from the German side. In the early days of National Socialism there was a special section of the Secret Service which studied minorities in States which Hitler intended to occupy. Brittany was paid particular attention with a view to creating a fifth column in the west of France. It is true that in the 1930s, despite the left-wing convictions of the *P.N.B.*, the Breton movement had members whose views if not fascist or pro-German, were certainly anti-French and right-wing. Other small groups like *Gwenn ha Du,* presumed to be led by a man who favoured a return to druidism, Celestin Lainé, were openly fascist and anti-Christian. It was Lainé who, during the War, founded a Breton unit known as the *Kadervenn* and later led a Breton section of the *Feldwehr*. After their arrival in Germany, Debauvais and Mordrel tried to persuade the Germans to set up, in the event of France's defeat, an independent Breton State and on 20 May 1940 they were both condemned to death *in absentia* by a military tribunal at Rennes. The decision of the two leaders to leave Brittany for Germany had been repudiated by the vast majority of the *P.N.B.* and the whole of the regionalist movement bitterly criticised their activities. Unfortunately, Debauvais and Mordrel pursued a policy disastrous for themselves and for the future of the whole Breton movement. Now treated as enemies of France, they took France's plight as Brittany's opportunity. Like Roger Casement did for Ireland and Masaryk for Czechoslovakia in the First World War, they interceded on their country's behalf. They met with some success at first, for Goering declared at the Nuremberg trials that a Breton State was to have been created at the end of the War, and Flemish newspapers actually announced the constitution of a free Brittany as the Germans entered Rennes. The armistice between France and Germany in 1940, however, dealt a deadly blow to the hopes of Debauvais and Mordrel because from then on the Germans considered the cause of Breton independence as contrary to their interests and began a policy of co-operation with the authorities of occupied France.

Within eighteen months after the German occupation had begun the Breton movement entered a new phase. The Vichy Government, weakened by internal tensions and by the presence in London of De Gaulle's Free French forces, was compelled to take the Breton problem into account. In 1941 it authorised the teaching of Breton history and language and the following year a Consultative Committee for Brittany was set up. These were small gains but they were to have serious consequences. The Resistance, led in Brittany by the communists and socialists who had always been the enemies of Breton culture, now set out to destroy the Breton movement by forcing it to renounce its convictions and to take sides in the conflict. On 12 December 1943, as a move calculated to provoke, they murdered the *Abbé* Perrot, editor of *Feiz ha Breiz* and rector of Scrignac. The death of Yann-Vari Perrot at the age of sixty-six and in the foulest circumstances, the apostle of Breton culture venerated by all sections of the Breton movement including the left-wing, a pioneer of the Breton revival for over forty years, marked a major turning-point. Perrot was in no way political or pro-German and his murder meant a declaration of war on the Breton movement in its entirety. The tension which existed between the moderate majority led by R. Delaporte and the extreme right-wing minority within the *P.N.B.* was now crystalised. A second Nationalist Party was formed which recruited a military unit known as the *Benzenn Perrot* after th e martyr whose death it sought to avenge. Operating and armed as a section of the German Army under the command of Lainé, its first operations were against the *maquis* of central Brittany where the priest's killers were believed to live. In so doing it gave up the neutrality of the Breton movement and, as the Resistance had foreseen, condemned the cause of Breton nationalism to decades of the most bitter opposition.

Following the break-through of the Allies in July 1944, the entry of American troops into Rennes on 4 August and the German withdrawal from Brittany, accompanied by a few members of the *Bezenn Perrot,* the Resistance took immediate revenge on known Breton nationalists and sympathisers. The journalist Joseph Martray commented in 1948, 'the operation proceeded in fantastic confusion where comedy alternated with tragedy. Lists were drawn up on which the smallest bag-pipe player was promoted to be chief of the *Gwenn ha Du* or director of *Breiz Atao:* it was enough to have danced in a Celtic Society or to have followed a Breton language course to be considered as a dangerous extremist. Hundreds were arrested who had often combined their Breton activities with undeniable Resistance activities'. Among those killed by the *maquis* was Madame Du Guerny, author of a 'patriotic' history of Brittany, the poet Barz ar Yeodet and his brother, Yves de Cambourg and Louis Stephan, members of the editorial board of the newspaper *'La Bretagne'*, and the brothers Tattevin who sold the newspaper *'L'Heure Bretonne'*. A young artist named Philippon was shot while praying on the *Abbé* Perrot's grave and the old parish priest of Quinper-Guézennec, the *Abbé* Lec'hvien was also killed. The farm of Loeiz Herrieu, publisher of *Dihunamb,* was looted and his valuable library burned. Priests were shot in public and hundreds arrested. In all, over 2,000 were arrested, 1,000 sent to concentration camps in Rennes and Quimper, 300 arrested, sixty sentenced to death and fifteen executed. Over 1,000 others were killed in reprisals or mysterious circumstances. According to some reports, the Breton *maquis* tried to prevent the slaughter by their French comrades and rounded up the prominent collaborators themselves. Among those who died in camps were the *Abbé* Guivarc'h and James Bouillé. The French authorities now appointed a notorious anti-nationalist Breton, Le Gorgeu, a former mayor of Brest, to supervise the administration of Brittany. Arrest warrants were immediately issued for anyone connected with any Breton society, irrespective of political views. Taldir, president of the Breton *Gorsedd* and James Bouillé, President of *Bleun Brug,* were among those arrested, as well as B. de Guébriant, leader of the Breton agricultural unions. The wives of nationalists who could not be traced took their place in detention centres. The American authorities had to intervene several times to prevent French troops from raping these women. In September 1944 the writer Florian Le Roy and André Dézarrois, the curator of a museum, were among those arrested; both had been members of the *maquis* throughout the War but were also known to be interested in Breton culture.

The French authorities now admitted that the reason for arrest was 'the holding of Breton ideals' and not necessarily collaboration with the Germans. At a protest meeting held near Folgoët attended by around 10,000 people, local troops refused to intervene when the crowd threatened to storm the Sub-Prefect's offices at Lesneven. General Allard, military commander of Brittany, called in reinforcements from Rennes and the crowd dispersed only after the Bishop of Quimper personally intervened and negotiated the release of some of the people arrested.

Roparz Hemon, who had run a radio programme in Brittany during the occupation, and other members of the *Gwalarn* group, was tried for collaboration but was acquitted. It is believed that the efforts made on his behalf in Wales and Ireland saved Hemon from execution; he was nevertheless sentenced to be deprived of his civic rights for ten years, lost his university post and went into exile in Ireland. Yann Fouéré, sentenced to twenty years hard labour for his Breton sympathies, was also helped by friends in Wales where he found a post at University College, Swansea; he was subsequently 'pardoned' by the French Government. Debauvais died of natural causes in Germany in 1944 but Mordrel escaped to Argentina.

The brunt of the *épuration* was borne by the younger men who had belonged to the *Bezenn Perrot*. Many were captured and beaten mercilessly, tortured and starved; some came before the courts with broken limbs. Others like Jasson and Geoffroy died before firing squads, marching to their deaths singing patriotic songs and shouting *'Bevet Breizh!'* (Long live Brittany!). They were unrepentant, convinced that France was the enemy for as long as it refused to recognise Brittany's right to live its own national life and believing to the end that in the War between France and Germany they had simply joined the losing side. Such opinions and the neutrality professed by others were, of course, vehemently attacked in the France of 1944 and 1945.

The French Government attempted to make it clear that Breton nationalists were tried and sentenced because they had been found guilty of collaboration with Germany, claiming that Bretons were treated 'like all other Frenchmen'. But Brittany was not the only part of France where the Germans found collaborators, as the film *Le Chagrin et la Pitié* has since reminded the world. And there were as many members of the Resistance in Brittany both inside and outside the Breton movement as elsewhere. Yet the force and extent of the Government's action in Brittany were generally greater than in the other parts of France, mainly because behind these measures there lay the traditional French Jacobinism which sees in all minorities a threat to the Republic's political unity. From the widespread support which the Breton movement had won between 1920 and 1939 the French Government was probably correct in its assumption that Brittany was on the point of gaining some degree of autonomy. If the collaboration of other parts of France was to be gradually forgiven if not forgotten, it was to be another two decades before the Bretons were to be allowed to raise their voices again.

The irony of the War years was that, under the German occupation and the Vichy régime, the Breton language and culture had been accorded a degree of recognition greater than any wrung from the French Government as the result of repeated demands over the previous two decades. A Breton National Council had been set up at Pontivy in July 1940 and a weekly newspaper, *L'Heure Bretonne,* published a manifesto in favour of independence. Under the leadership of R. Delaporte the moderate *P.N.B.* won even greater support among the people. The old regionalist wing of the Breton Movement had resumed its activities, under Yann Fouéré, publishing its newspapers *'La Bretagne'* and *'La Dépêche'* from 1942 on. Almost all the Breton reviews which had stopped publication in 1939 now appeared once more: Roparz Hemon, now President of the Celtic Institute, launched the weekly *'Arvor'* in 1941 and another weekly for children was started by the brothers Caouissin in Landerneau. Many societies and Breton classes re-opened. The language was heard regularly on the radio for the first time; the teaching of Breton history was authorised in the schools and language classes permitted outside school hours. In 1942 the *Comité Consultatif de Bretagne* was set up, composed of twenty-five members chosen jointly by the Regional Prefect and by the main societies. Among this body's members had been the Marquis de l'Estourbeillon, the *Abbé* Perrot and Taldir as well as representatives of Brittany's agricultural and commercial life; Yann Fouéré was elected as its secretary at the beginning of 1944. For the first time since the *Etats de Bretagne* a body existed to advise the French Government in

Breton cultural affairs. From 1942 the Committee succeeded in winning for Breton the status of a subject for the *certificat d'études primaires* and hundreds of Breton classes were started. In July 1943 a summer-school for the teaching of Breton was inaugurated by the Regional Prefect and the Rector of the University of Rennes. Although not allowed to enter the political field, the Committee prepared a new constitution for Brittany; although this was rejected by the French authorities it was supported in 1944 by the councils of over 200 communes and over a thousand prominent personalities.

The fatal error of the Breton movement during the years of the Second World War was, of course, that it had made these substantial gains under the tutelage of the Vichy régime and therefore, it was clear in the eyes of liberated France, in collaboration with the Germans. In retrospect, it seems impossible that any régime so centralist, authoritarian and barbaric as that of Nazi Germany would have granted any real and lasting degree of autonomy in the event of the Allies' defeat; its record in other parts of Europe is now proof of that. Even in 1940, keen to have French support in the war with Britain, Hitler wanted nothing done to upset the French Government, as Otto Abetz, the German ambassador to France, subsequently confirmed in his memoirs. But equally, or so it seemed to some Bretons, there was no hope of winning autonomy for Brittany from the French Government which had turned a deaf ear to even their most modest requests for decades. The predicament of the Breton movement was that in its attempts to further the cause of autonomy its only choice was between the French and German States, both of which were by tradition opposed to its aspirations. The tragedy was that, expecting a German victory after the fall of France in 1940, it was led—out of opportunism and the obvious fascist convictions of Debauvais and Mordrel—to side with Germany. Whatever the motivation, the decision was taken and the damage was done. The final irony was that the extent and ferocity of the repression it suffered from the victorious French was second only to that carried out by the defeated dictators of modern Europe, Hitler and Mussolini, and by the Franco régime in Spain.

During the confusion of the years which followed the War

there was no shortage of pretexts for accusing the entire Breton movement of pro-German sympathies, despite the fact that only a few of its leaders had been found guilty of this charge. Clearly, not all the thousands involved in cultural work could have been pro-German and many of the most eminent figures of the day had unimpeachable records. In some instances the French Government ordered the arrest of Breton scholars who had already been executed by the Germans for their Resistance activities. It is even reported that Breton-speaking children were tormented at school because the Breton word for 'yes', *ya,* resembles the German *ja.* In such an atmosphere it is little wonder that for the next ten years there was an almost total absence of political activity in Brittany on the part of the nationalist movement.

The first signs that the political consciousness of Brittany was stirring again was when, in 1957, Yann Fouéré—whose sentence, with that of others had been quashed by the French Government in a belated recognition of injustice—returned to Brittany from Ireland to lead a group of federalists in the *Mouvement pour L'Organisation de la Bretagne.* By now the effects of centralised government on Brittany and other regions in the French State were becoming more and more clear. It is significant that despite the disasters of the War, Brittany was the first to react against them.

In the first place, Brittany had suffered depopulation on a vast scale: over the last hundred years the population of France has increased by 135%, while Brittany's has remained the same. Between 1831 and 1926 a total of 1,127,000 Bretons left Brittany and a further 17,000 left every year between 1946 and 1954. This loss has continued up to the present time. Between 1954 and 1962 about 100,000 people under thirty years of age left Brittany, while the number of people in their sixties increased by some 5,000. Agriculture and fishing declined after the War and transport was neglected. Small industries closed or were bought up by companies from Paris—and then run down. More and more young men took the traditional way out by joining the French navy and army, while young Breton women—as Simone Weil pointed out in *L'Enracinement* (The Need for Roots)—joined the other traditional profession as prostitutes in Paris. In the Paris region today, out of every thousand Breton immigrants, twenty belong to the upper class, 280 to the middle-class and 700 to the working class of the lower-paid bracket. A typical solution to the problem of decaying regions like Brittany was described in the report of a committee set up by Prime Minister Michel Debré in 1962 as 'the conversion of these deserted areas into national parks'. Prior to Debré, Pierre Mendes France during the Fourth Republic and his successor Pflimlin, an Alsatian and mayor of Strasbourg, had shown sympathy with the plight of Brittany. But with the advent of the Gaullists in the Fifth Republic, plans for limiting the growth of Paris were reversed and the Government's policy became to make it 'the European capital of the twentieth century'. Among other cities to be developed, Strasbourg and Rennes were conspicuous by their absence.

Following the visit by De Gaulle to Brittany early in 1969—during the course of which, at Quimper on 2 February, he quoted four lines of Breton verse written by his great-uncle—it seemed as if the French Government was about to release somewhat its hold on the regions. But no tangible plans were announced and the Gaullist régime proceeded as before.

It was against this background of vacillation and the eventual return of the old Jacobin insistence on central authority under De Gaulle that the political life of Brittany revived in 1957. Taking as its slogan that of the old *P.N.B.*, *'Na Ruz na Guenn'* (Neither Red nor White), the *M.O.B.* met with considerable success in its early years: its monthly newspaper *'L'Avenir de la Bretagne'* (Future of Brittany) sold thousands of copies and several of its candidates were elected as municipal councillors. It attracted in particular those who had supported the *Comité d'Étude et de Liaison des Interéts Bretons* (Committee for the Study and Co-ordination of Breton Interests), a consultative body since 1955 concerned primarily with the modernisation of agriculture in Brittany. The *Loi Programme* presented by *C.E.L.I.B.* had been rejected by the Government and the Committee's existence ignored by De Gaulle when he visited Brittany at the beginning of 1960. Following reforms of the same year which created regional committees but, in reality, gave even more power to Paris, *C.E.L.I.B.* was divided and began to lose influence. Demonstrations by peasants and trade unionists took place at Morlaix in June and September 1961, during which the leaders Alexis Gourvennec and Marcel Léon were arrested. The Committee won its last successes in securing certain improvements for Breton agriculture and the supply of electricity for industrial purposes; also as a result of its ultimata, colleges of further education were opened at Rennes and Brest.

Having won the support of the declining *C.E.L.I.B.*, the *M.O.B.* seemed about to rally all sections of the population when there occured the first of a series of quarrels and breakaways which have become characteristic of the Breton movement since 1962. At its conference in that year a motion supporting Algerian independence and condemning the *O.A.S.* was defeated and, in disgust, the younger left-wing element left the movement. Two years later, in January 1964, they formed the *Union Démocratique Bretonne* (Breton Democratic Union). Although it is true that this party, the *U.D.B.*, has led the left wing of the Breton movement up to the present time, that is not to say that it has yet had much electoral success. It is generally agreed that no more than 5% of Brittany's population are active in the autonomist or nationalist cause; out of some 280 mayors of communes in Finistère, about eleven are committed nationalists while many of the others would welcome a greater degree of autonomy. At the municipal elections in Brest of 1971 the *U.D.B.* won only 2,618 votes (4·8%), although its members had been elected on United Left Wing tickets at Auray where its candidates had polled 12% of the votes in the previous year. Since then there has been little evidence that Brittany does not continue to be in the grip of the right-wing and Gaullist parties. At the Brest elections of 1971 the moderate right-wing won 24,056 votes (45%), the Gaullists 12,767 (23·5%), the French Communist Party 8,059 (15%) and the French Socialist Party 6,198 (11.4%).

It is nevertheless true that *U.D.B* is the only Breton party which has made a mark on the political scene during the last decade. A party of militants for whom attendance at the annual conference is obligatory, its main organs are the monthly newspapers *Le Peuple Breton* and *Pobl Vreizh* (The Breton People) which sell about 5,000 and 2,000 copies each. Although its constitution recognises 'the national vocation of Brittany' the party is anti-capitalist, anti-militarist, socialist and believes in workers' control. It criticises the traditional nationalists for their nebulous position as expressed in the slogan *'Na Ruz na Guenn'*, (Neither Red nor White), the militancy of the *U.D.B.* being quite definitely *Ruz*. It co-operates with the main French parties of the left, such as the *P.C.F.* (French Communist Party), the *P.S.* (Socialist Party), and the *P.S.U.* (United Socialist Party) and is associated with the workers' unions like the *Conféderation Française Démocratique du Travail*, the most powerful in Brittany.

The party has not been without its schisms, however. Following 'the events of May 1968' there was a profound upheaval in the political life of France and Brittany was no exception in this respect. The first crisis in the *U.D.B.* was caused by the clandestine organisation known as the *Front de Libération de la Bretagne*. Rejecting a manifesto by the *F.L.B.* which called for 'an autonomous Socialist Brittany with or without France', the *U.D.B.* proceeded to expel some of its younger, more nationalist members and to move nearer to the French Communist Party. The second period of dissension followed in 1970 when the *U.D.B.*, which follows the Marxist-Leninist line on the dangers of excessive intellectualism, individualism and neglect of the proletariat, expelled another group of its members accused of *gauchisme* and of displaying 'the spirit of May 1968'.

Although the *U.D.B.* clearly fulfils the need for a left-wing, doctrinaire, political party in Brittany, it is by no means the only representative of Breton aspirations. Indeed, it owes much of its early strength to the publicity created by the *F.L.B.*'s campaign of violence which began in 1966. In 1968 the headquarters at Saint-Brieuc of the *Compagnies Républicaines de Securité*, the security police specialising in the use of gas and truncheons against demonstrators in France, were destroyed by the *F.L.B.* and, a year later, some fifty members—including a number of highly respectable citizens,

priests and professional people—were arrested. These activists were never tried, the French Government fearing
another confrontation with Breton nationalism in the courts,
and all were released under an amnesty of the new Government which came to power in 1969.

Besides the *F.L.B.* there are several other groups, such
as *Jeunesse Etudiante Bretonne* (Breton Student Youth)
who were expelled from the *U.D.B.* The *F.L.B.* has formed
the *Comité Révolutionnaire Breton* (Breton Revolutionary
Committee) which in turn created in 1970 a Breton
Communist Party, *Strollad Komunour Breizh*, a group
of non-violent intellectuals and workers without the
ideological rigidity of the *U.D.B.* and independent of the
French Communists; it publishes a newspaper, *Bretagne
Révolutionnaire*, and calls for 'the destruction of the
anachronistic Jacobin State and the building of a socialist and
internationalist Brittany'.

There are other *groupuscules* on the Breton Left,
notably the *Tribune des Jeunesses Progressistes de
Bretagne*, founded in 1970 and working mainly among
young workers and school pupils; like almost all the
others, the *T.J.P.B.* is politically immature and significant
only insofar as it serves as a training-ground for militants
who later join the *U.D.B.* More importantly, the *U.D.B.*,
the *J.E.B.* and *Ar Falz*, the society of non-Catholic Socialist
teachers founded by Yann Sohier, in 1933, came together in
1969 to create a movement known as *Galv* (Appeal) which
campaigns in favour of the Breton language.

Finally—although there seems no end to the creation and
demise of political parties in Brittany and the situation is
changing all the time as the Bretons emulate the French in the
complexities of their political life—there is on the non-
socialist wing of the Breton movement a number of groups in
existence at the present time. The principal one is *Strollad ar
Vro* (The Party of the Country), begun in 1972 by Yann
Fouéré, founder of the *M.O.B.* Federalist and embracing
most political views outside the Breton left, *S.A.V.* put up
candidates in the General Election of 1973 but with little success, and it seems to have its resources fully stretched in the
publication of its newspaper. Yann Fouéré was arrested in

October 1975, together with about forty other nationalists suspected of being involved in preparation for a bombing campaign against the Government's plan for the building of nuclear power stations in Brittany. Another right-wing group is *Bretagne Action*. Relations between 'pure nationalist' groups and the parties of the left are intermittent and they view one another with obvious distaste.

It is partly for this reason that none has been capable, up to the present, of uniting a majority of politically active Bretons in a single party comparable for instance, with the S.N.P. in Scotland, or *Plaid Cymru* in Wales. The bitterness of the Breton experience during the Second World War, together with what appears to be a typically French predeliction for ideological dissension, no doubt partly accounts for the internecine splits among the various groups. The French Government is quick to conclude that their lack of electoral support is evidence that the Breton movement's claims are 'groundless' and its objectives 'unrealistic'.

Yet it is abundantly clear that the Breton movement has real grievances and excellent cause to criticise the French Government's policies in Brittany, particularly from a cultural and economic point of view. Indeed, the growing political consciousness of Brittany is spurred to a large extent by the Government's continuing refusal to grant the country any real control over its own affairs in these two sectors.

The first initiatives to be taken after 1945 were in the field of folklore: the association of music and dance circles known as *Kendalc'h* was founded at Quimper on 15 October 1950. But the next important step towards the post-war revival of the Breton cultural movement was the Deixonne Law passed by the French Government on 11 January 1951. Yann Sohier had launched the movement *Ar Brezoneg er Skol* (Breton in School) in the 'thirties and by 1938 a total of 305 communes out of 634 in Lower Brittany, representing 710,000 out of 1,430,000 inhabitants (the total number of Breton-speakers at this time was around a million) had voted in favour of teaching the language in the schools on an official basis as part of the curriculum. But nothing had been done by the Government to secure a place for Breton in the State's schools. In 1925 the Minister of Education Anatole de Monzie had stated quite clearly, 'for the unity of France the Breton language must die'. When a delegation from the Council of the National *Eisteddfod* of Wales under the leadership of W. J. Gruffydd visited Brittany at the invitation of the French Government in April/May 1947, they were informed that the Minister of Education was 'irreducibly opposed' to the teaching of Breton, and that, in his opinion as there were several dialects of Breton it would be difficult to find a form capable of being written and taught. The Deixonne Law now allowed *in principle* the teaching of Breton and three other 'local languages' of France—Occitan, Basque and Catalan. The limits set up by the Government on this law, however, were so stringent that little was conceded in fact. Breton was to be taught as an optional subject for not more than an hour a week and was not to count in the pupil's final grading at the examination for the *baccalauréat*. There now began a campaign to improve the terms of the Deixonne Law and fifteen attempts to revise it were made during the Fifth Republic alone, all without success. A lone rebel against the Government's refusal to teach Breton on a proper basis was Dr Etienne of Chateaulin, who from 1963 challenged the authorities by having his five children educated at home through the medium of Breton. As a result he was deprived of all family allowances and informed that under the law of 1882 he had no right to have his children taught in any language but French. In 1967 *Emgleo Breiz* collected 150,000 signatures on a petition calling for Breton in the schools, to no avail. Up to 1971 this organisation had made over fifty approaches to the departmental authorities of Brittany and had canvassed all the Breton deputies, twenty-three of whom had approved the programme.

Since then little has changed in the status of Breton in the schools. Most of the major French parties support the principle of teaching the minority languages of France but do nothing when in power to implement it. Thus Georges Marchais, general secretary of the French Communist Party, said at Rennes in March 1974, 'Yes, the regional languages must live where they correspond to historical and social reality. And that is the case of Brittany'. François Mitterand, leader of the French Socialist Party, in a reply dated 30 April 1974 to the organisation *Défense et Promotion des Langues de France* (Defence and Promotion of the Languages of France) stated, 'I have written clearly and several times that I deplore the destruction of minority cultures. I believe that all forms of bilingualism are to be encouraged. That means in the event of my election to the Presidency of the Republic, I will support the efforts being made to preserve the diverse collective identities of French citizens . . . I believe that the presence of diverse cultures on French territory is an asset and that their uniformisation must be combated'. Giscard d'Estaing, now President of France, also declared himself in April 1974 to be in favour of 'the regional languages of France', adding that their promotion must never threaten 'national unity'. The vague nature of the President's statement to the *D.P.L.F.*, in which no promise was actually made, should be contrasted with that of his predecessor Georges Pompidou in 1969: 'If the will of the French carries me to the Presidency of the Republic, I will see to it that this defence of regional traditions and cultures benefits by real help from public authorities . . . As an Auvergnat, therefore an Occitan, I am particularly aware of all the efforts being made to safeguard the linguistic and cultural traditions of our provinces'. It was only three years later that President Pompidou was to say, on 14 April 1972, at Sarre-Union in Alsace, 'There is no room for regional languages in a France destined to mark Europe with its seal!'

Despite the impunity with which the major French political parties break their election promises on the Breton language, some progress has been made in recent years. On 10 July 1970 the language was admitted with fuller status to the *baccalauréat* examinations. This concession was widely believed to be a result of the campaigns conducted by *Emgleo Breiz* and *Galv* as well as of the public attention drawn to the situation of Breton outside France. Difficulties were still put in the way of pupils wishing to take Breton at *baccalauréat* level, however. In 1973, in reply to Le Pensec, deputy for Finistère, Fontanet the Minister of Education stated that 'it remains to be seen whether the study of a regional language during the whole of a school career is necessary and useful, bearing in mind the possible consequences on the general balance of lessons, the learning of modern languages and the correct practice of the French language'. In that year it was estimated that about 4,000 pupils were studying Breton in official classes at private and public schools. The numbers taking it as part of the *baccalauréat* have increased from 180 in 1969 to 761 in 1971, 886 in 1972 and over 1,000 in 1973 and 1974. To place these figures in perspective, however, they must be seen as part of the whole educational system in Brittany. The situation has not changed to any great extent since 1971 when in the area of Rennes only 3,662 pupils were studying Breton out of a total of 614, 391 pupils in elementary schools, that is 0·59%. Only in some primary schools are children taught in a bilingual manner but they are few. Although no reliable official figures are available, it is estimated by Gorj Gwegen in *La Langue Bretonne face à ses Oppresseurs* (1975) that the number of pupils at present following Breton courses either at school or in a cultural organisation or by correspondence is between 8,000 and 10,000. According to a survey carried out by *Kevredigezh an Deskadurezh Nevez* (The Society for New Education) in the school year 1970-1, 81% of all pupils studying Breton in school or in a cultural group were under the age of twenty, 40% in State schools (where the language is still largely taught as an optional extra outside school hours, 42% were in cultural groups outside school and 18% in private educational establishments; of these 74% were receiving only one hour of instruction a week, 22% two hours and 4% three hours; 63% were pupils for whom Breton was not the mother-tongue; 77% of the teachers were unpaid volunteers.

At university level Breton is taught in the Celtic Departments of the Faculty of Arts at the Universities of Brest and Rennes. Per Denez, the well-known writer, former editor of the magazine *Ar Vro* (The Country) and now editor of *Hor Yezh* (Our Language), *Skol* (School) and *Skrid* (Essays) and specialist in the teaching of modern Breton, is a lecturer in the Celtic Department at Rennes. Despite repeated requests by the two Departments, the Ministry of Education has refused them permission to offer degree courses, so that Breton is studied as part of a Diploma of Celtic Studies or a Diploma of Higher Celtic Studies, for the second of which a knowledge of another Celtic language is necessary. At Brest the Celtic Department has pioneered audio-visual techniques in the teaching of Breton. Both Departments have assumed a central role in the revival of interest in Breton culture during the last few years.

An important adjunct to their work is the teaching of Breton by correspondence. About 1,700 learners are currently following the three main courses offered by *Skol Ober,* started in 1932 by Marc'harid Gourlaouenn, *Ar Skol dre Lizer* founded by Visant Seïte in 1945, and *Skol dre Lizer ar Falz* run by the teachers' organisation. All report a rapid increase in the number of correspondents, especially among the young since 1967-9. Also, since 1970, Visant Seïte has run a Breton Course on the local radio at Kimerc'h in Finistère; the texts of these lessons are published the evening before transmission in the newspaper *'Le Télégramme de Brest'*. Another organisation, *Strollad an Deskadurezh Eil Derez* (Party for Secondary Education), teaches through the medium of a correspondence course in various subjects, including the natural sciences, geography, mathematics and history. The age-group and occupations of Breton learners show a marked preponderance of people under the age of thirty, which is typical of a situation in which the mother-tongue has not been taught in the schools for decades; the motivations of these learners is also classic—the desire to understand conversations between their parents, patriotism and the practical need to pass in the subject at school examinations.

Despite the fact that the wish to read Breton does not figure prominently among reasons given for learning it, there is a lively press in the language at the present time. In 1936 there were thirteen periodicals published partly or wholly in Breton. By today there are twenty exclusively in Breton and about ten which publish some Breton in every number; several of the newspapers published by political groups also carry articles and features in the language. Given the repression of the post-war years and the fact that Breton publishing receives no Government subsidy whatsoever, this revival is quite remarkable. *Al Liamm* is the most important literary review. Founded by Ronan Huon after the Second World War and still edited by him, it appears in an edition of about a thousand copies; in March 1974 it had 839 subscribers. Other literary or linguistic magazines are *Skrid, Hor Yezh* and *Skol,* all edited by Per Denez, and *Brud;* magazines devoted to sociological, political and economic studies are *Emsav* and *Imbourc'h. Studi hag Ober* is a Catholic review while *Yod Kerc'h* publishes cartoons and humorous texts. *Wanig ha Wenig* is a magazine for children. The only political newspaper in Breton is the *U.D.B.'s* newspaper *Pobl Vreizh.* Other periodicals concerned with the language are *Ar Gevnidenn* and *Evid ar Brezhoneg.* The latter is a popular magazine launched in 1973 by Claude Henry, a lecturer at the University of Upper Brittany, Rennes, and now selling over 6,000 copies a week. Published in Breton but with a glossary in French, the text is intended primarily for learners and those who have never read Breton (that is the vast majority of the population) consisting of transcriptions of spoken Breton, local news and humorous stories.

The problems involved in the publishing of Breton books are more serious. In the face of rising production costs over the last few years it is necessary to sell at least 800 copies of a book before even the printer's bill can be paid, and this is not easily achieved in a community where most are illiterate in Breton, and where only about 20,000 at the most are interested in Breton culture. Most books are published in editions of 1,500 to 2,000 copies. Among recent 'best-sellers' is *Kan an Douar* (Song of the Earth) by the poet Anjela Duval which sold a thousand copies in a year. Only the Breton-French Dictionary of Roparz Hemon sells in huge numbers: about 20,000 copies since 1964. The publishing imprint of *Al Liamm* directed by the indefatigable Ronan Huon now has a list of over eighty titles. The more important are the novels and plays of Youenn Drezenn, Roparz Hemon and Tangi Malmanche and the translations of parts of the Bible by Maodez Glandour. Other imprints, such as those of *Emgleo Breiz, Preder* and *Hor Yezh,* specialise in less literary works. Among the best known contemporary writers, besides those already mentioned, are Erwan Evenou, Sten Kidna, Maria Prat, Youenn Gwernig, Yann-Ber Piriou, Paol Keineg, Yvon Le Men, Jakez

Helias, to name but a few who have continued and developed the work of the *Gwalarn* group of the inter-war years.

Outside Brittany the Paris publisher P. J. Oswald has given prominence to Breton writers, as well as to Occitan poets, in bilingual editions such as the anthology which takes its title from public notices erected at the beginning of this century, *Défènse de cracher par terre et de parler Breton* (Spitting and the speaking of Breton are prohibited). Another book, published in Paris in 1970 which has had a deep and lasting impression on Breton consciousness is *Comment Peut-on Etre Breton?* by Morvan Lebesque, one of the most brilliant and perceptive books about minority cultures ever published.

Although, in comparison with other minority languages, Breton has a flourishing press and a contemporary literature of high standards, it is in its strength as an oral medium that it is most remarkable. Like Occitanie and Catalonia, Brittany now has a number of outstanding singers who have achieved phenomenal success in recent years. Alan Stivell, who acknowledges in his music 'my Celtic roots, my electric times', is the best known but there are other singers like Youenn Gwernig and Glenmor who have contributed to the renaissance of Breton singing. Absolutely modern and *contestataire,* their songs—far more advanced in both content and style than their counterparts in the other Celtic languages—have become the *porte-parole* of the younger generation, expressing a new confidence in their language and nationality. At the same time the more traditional but equally lively *'festoù-noz'* (traditional folk evenings) have continued to flourish, indeed to such an extent that the popularity of *Kan ha diskan* (song and dance) has attracted the attention of commercial firms more interested in quick profits from tourism and substantial sales of records than in the integrity of the art forms. This tendency was denounced by *Kendalc'h* in 1974, after which a society to defend the authentic character of Breton folk-lore against commercialism was formed.

In the theatre the most famous company is *Strollad Beilhadegou Treger* (The Trégor Traditional Entertainment Group), directed by Maria Prat; smaller companies have performed at Brest and other centres. As among the Gaels of

Scotland, another minority long denied a theatre in their language, the response of audiences to Breton plays at which they are 'released into their own culture' is invariably enthusiastic. There is no full-time, professional theatrical company working in Breton, however. The most striking success in the theatre of recent years has been the production, first in Paris and later in Brittany of the play written in French by Paol Keineg, *Le Printemps des Bonnets Rouges* which relates in the most memorable way the history of the Revenue Stamps Revolt of the seventeenth century. There has hardly been any cinema in Breton since Henri Caouissin made a film about the *pardon* of Folgoët in the 1950s.

Another sector in which the Breton language holds its own is the Catholic Church. Before the Second World War Roparz Hemon reported that 75% of parishes in Lower Brittany used Breton in preference to French in sermons and the catechism. For many years after 1945 the clergy of Lower Brittany followed the general trend towards *francisation* but, in the regions of Leon and Vannes in particular, the Breton Mass has been re-introduced. At the beginning of 1974 about eighty parishes in the bishopric of Quimper and Leon used the language at Mass. A considerable boost to the use of Breton and other vernaculars in Church affairs was the papal encyclical of 1963 *Pacem in Terris*. Other factors have been the unrelenting work of writers like Maodez Glanndour (the *Abbé* Le Floc'h), the *Abbé* Le Calvez, the *Abbé* Le Klerc and their magazines *Barr-Heol* and *Studi hag Ober,* together with countless other priests, have remained faithful to the language of their parishioners. They are gathered today in the society *Kenvreuriezh ar Brezhoneg.* The Church plays a part in the organisation of camps for Breton-speakers and learners of the language, especially young people. The principal camp, held annually, is *Kamp ar Vrezhonegerien* and the main groups responsible are *Al Leur Nevez, Skol an Emsav, Breuriezh Sant Erwan, Kuzul ar Brezhoneg,* and *Ar Brezhoneg er Ger.* Some of these groups co-operated in 1974 with *Emgleo Breiz* and *Ar Falz* in the organisation of a festival, hoped to be the embryo of an event comparable to the National *Eisteddfod* of Wales.

Although most of the work of the political parties in Brittany,even the nationalists, is done in French, there is no single group dedicated to winning official status for Breton in public life, but following the tactics of *Cymdeithas yr Iaith Gymraeg* (Welsh Language Society), some young Bretons have attempted in recent years to draw attention to this important matter. French road-signs and place-name signs have been obliterated with paint and Breton names inserted on signs in all parts of the country. Responsibility was claimed in October 1973 by a group calling itself *Brezhoneg Bev* (Living Breton) and in June 1974 five young people were found guilty at Brest of painting anti-military slogans. Only in a few instances has there been any response to such activities by municipal authorities. The commune of Plourin, near Morlaix, for example, has erected bilingual plaques on some of its streets and the authorities at Saint-Pol-de-Leon have decided to put up a sign bearing the town's Breton name, *Kastell-Paol*. The chief obstacle to this policy is the Department of Roads and Bridges of the French Government which up to now has ignored all representations made to it. Hopes of official status for the language were until recently centred on *Galv* which, at its numerous demonstrations, has succeeded in bringing the matter to the public's attention.

On radio and television the Breton language is very poorly served. Since 1969 there are seventeen minutes in Breton audible only in parts of Finistère, just before the one o'clock news on the radio channel *France-Inter*. On Sunday afternoons this transmission is replaced by the Breton features programme of Fanch Broudic which lasts for an hour and can be heard all over Brittany. According to *Emgleo Breiz* between 50,000 and 80,000 listeners hear the daily broadcasts in Breton, mainly because they are awaiting the news. During the winter months, the fortnightly magazine programme *Breiz o Veva* (Living Brittany), which began in 1971, lasts about twenty minutes on television. Twice a week two 'spots' of ninety seconds each are broadcast during the television news. Breton is therefore heard on radio for two hours and forty-two minutes a week and for thirteen minutes weekly for forty-six weeks of the year on television. There is no Breton-

speaker on the staff of the regional section of the State broadcasting corporation at Rennes; all programmes are edited by
free-lance journalists.

In its 'cultural charter' adopted on 18 December 1972
the *C.E.L.I.B.* (which none can accuse of extremism in
Breton affairs) demanded three news bulletins and two hours
of radio programmes in Breton plus two news bulletins and an
hour on television daily, together with the creation of a
Breton-language service by *O.R.T.F.-Rennes*. The President
of *C.E.L.I.B.* and the mayor of Brest, Georges Lombard,
reminded the Government, 'It is no longer a handful of
militants, it is the whole of Brittany and above all, led
passionately by its youth, which is rising to protect the old
Celtic language . . . We must make the Government of
tomorrow understand that the situation in which the Breton
language exists at present will no longer be tolerated'. Defending the corporation's policy (but ignoring the fact that it
broadcasts daily in sixteen foreign languages), the Director of
O.R.T.F.-Rennes Bernard Griveau pointed out in the
newspaper *Ouest France* (February 1974) that *'Télé-
Bretagne'* is the only news programme in France during which
'regional languages' are sometimes used—a reference to the
ninety second spots twice a week, saying 'I would like to
remind you of all that the *O.R.T.F.* has done for the Breton
language'. He was replying to the charge by Louis Le Pensec,
Socialist deputy for Finistère, in the Chamber of Deputies the
previous month: 'In the sector of radio and television transmissions, the French authorities should blush to know themselves to be behind the transmissions in Catalan and Basque
allowed in these languages by the Franco régime in Spain'.
Following this exchange, the *Groupe d'Etudes Politiques et
Economiques pour la Bretagne* (Political and Economic
Studies Group for Brittany) commented, 'We are well and
truly gagged. This situation is dangerous: he who cannot
speak can still strike'.

Not unexpectedly, there followed an explosion which
destroyed the television installation at Roc'h Trédudon,
in the Arrée Hills, on the night of 14 February 1974.
Responsibility was claimed by the *F.L.B.* and the *Armée
Républicaine Bretonne* (Breton Republican Army) who

signed the incident with the words *'Evit ar Brezhoneg'* (For the Breton language). As a result almost the whole of Lower Brittany was deprived of television for ten weeks, but nothing was done or said to suggest that the French broadcasting authorities might reconsider its attitude to Breton, and the situation therefore remains unchanged.

The monopoly exercised by the State Broadcasting service has created its own internal problems in recent years but it is difficult not to concur with the opinion expressed by the American magazine *Newsweek* (29 April 1974) in a review of television all over the world: 'With an annual budget of 500 million dollars, French television viewers are those who in Western Europe, have least for their money. In the absence of commercial competition, the French Government has transformed television into a simple instrument of propaganda'.

The Bretons have long been well aware of the propaganda value of television in both political and cultural terms. Most activists in the Breton movement are convinced that, together with the campaign for adequate teaching of the language in State schools, the need for more Breton programmes on radio and television, which have penetrated the majority of homes throughout the country, is the first priority in the cultural struggle. For by now the decline in the frequency with which Breton is spoken has become abundantly clear. Many districts which in 1940 were predominantly Breton-speaking have turned almost exclusively to French. According to research carried out by the sociologist Fanch Elegoët in 1971 the parish of Le Grouanec *(Ar Grouaneg)* near Plouguerneau *(Plouguerne)* in northern Finistère is fairly typical of this trend. Ten years ago Breton was the common language of the district and its children. Today Breton has been abandoned by all married couples under the age of thirty and none have reared their children to speak it: 'the child is the pole towards which one turns only in French', writes Elegoët. Even grand-parents, who until now had lived their lives mainly through Breton, have gone over to speaking French to the children. French is also used in shops, cafés and at recreation, even by native Breton-speakers. Only in the fields, at work, is the language still in regular use, and there even by young people from households where French is generally spoken. As soon as the country people go into Plouguerneau, a distance of only a few miles, they turn to French for all purposes, especially the women—who are particularly susceptible to the attractions of urban living. Breton is never heard in the public offices at Plouguerneau or in any other official context in the town. Writing in the magazine *Imbourc'h* (May 1974), Youenn Olier concluded that the general situation is one in which 'parents who speak Breton to their children today do so deliberately, and are therefore militants. There remain only the backward people who for routine reasons still speak Breton to their children in the country areas today'.

Apart from the influence of television, there are other factors militating against the Breton language and they too are mostly political and economic in character. Patricia Elton Mayo has put the matter succinctly in *The Roots of Identity* (1974): 'Brittany's economic life has run slowly downhill since her annexation by France'. Having had its artisan industries and merchant fleet ruined by the naval blockade during the Napoleonic Wars, when France was in conflict with Britain and Spain, Brittany's best customers, the country was to find itself outside the zone of industrial development which was created during the nineteenth century around Paris and in the east of France. After the First World War, when it lost an exceptionally high proportion of its male population, Breton agriculture was allowed to become archaic and emigration began on a huge scale. The town of Penmarc'h in Finistère, for example, had some 15,000 inhabitants in 1910 but has a population of only 4,000 today. For Paris, Brittany became a reservoir of cheap labour, a peripheral region doomed to the status of a park for tourists. Government attitudes were content to acquiesce in the popular view of Brittany in the rest of France, *'c'est belle mais c'est triste'* (it's beautiful but it's sad).

Tourism, as in other peripheral, undeveloped but scenically attractive areas, has a pernicious effect on the social life, language and economy of Brittany. While it brings in income during the summer months, mainly via property developments which are in French rather than Breton hands, it encourages the building of chalets and second homes for outsiders with whom local people, who earn on the whole about 30% less than the inhabitants of the Paris region, are not able to compete. In the usual pattern, holidays are followed by retirements into the country and coastal districts so that Brittany has an increasing retired, non-Breton population who contribute little to social life; in some areas whole villages are deserted for most of the year. The remaining Breton population of the resorts is mostly engaged in the tourist services, usually at a low level, or depend for their livelihood on renting their homes to visitors. The resulting effects on the mentality of Bretons, who are becoming more and more obliged to accept menial jobs and to sell anything the tourist demands, are reported to be as apparent as they are on that of most other minorities. Alienated from their own culture but not able to share fully in that of the French, these areas of rural decay tarted up in the crudest fashion are among the first to lose their language, and, with it, their social cohesion and personal self-esteem.

The legacy of poverty, under-nourishment, begging, prostitution, tuberculosis and alcoholism may have been combated by now but the general economic depression of Brittany has spread since 1945. Only the department of Ille-et-Vilaine in Upper Brittany around Rennes has made any real recovery, partly because it is nearest to Paris. The Côtes du Nord and Morbihan, in central Brittany, still have serious problems in agriculture and industry alike, while Finistère—which has been losing 2,500 young people annually—is still depressed. The basis of Breton agriculture is the small family farm but this unit is threatened by Government policies which suit the large cereal-producing farms like those of the Beauce.

It was René Pleven, ex-Prime Minister of France and later Minister of Justice in the Government of 1972 and President of *C.E.L.I.B.*, who wrote in his book *L'Avenir de la Bretagne* (1961), 'France is heading towards unsuspected trouble if it refuses Brittany the possibility of satisfactory growth and of playing a proper role in the general development of France'. Since then there has been a marked increase in the number of strikes, demonstrations and major incidents, beginning with the peasant manifestations of 1961. In 1972, to give but two examples, milk-tankers were upset in Finistère in the *Guerre du Lait* (Milk War) as a protest against low prices by the *Comité Departmental des Jeunes Agriculteurs* (Departmental Committee of Young Farmers). In the same year there was an eight-week strike, supported by the union *Conféderation Française du Travail* on specifically Breton grounds, at the factory known as the *Joint Français* at Saint-Brieuc. The actions of the *Compagnies Républicaines de Securité* on these occasions, their gratuitous use of violence and gas, have rallied a wide section of public opinion against the Government and in favour of many autonomist demands. Among those now openly sympathetic to the Breton movement are Senators, members of Chambers of Commerce and Agriculture, mayors and other local difnitaries.

On the other hand, with the possible exception of the socialist Louis Le Pensec, the representatives of Brittany in the Chamber of Deputies, the lower house of the French Government, and notably Raymond Marcellin who has served as Minister of the Interior in recent Governments, have shown little cause for belief that they are prepared to put the interests of Brittany before personal ambition and the dictates of the major parties to which they belong. The autonomists and nationalists have yet to challenge the position of these parties in any substantial way at elections. Before that can happen, they will no doubt have to reach a far greater degree of solidarity among themselves, even at the expense of some of their dearly held ideological convictions.

If, on the other hand, the French Government is persuaded or obliged to implement a policy of greater regionalisation over the next few years, it will largely be due to the pressure of public opinion which the smaller parties helped to create. But for that to happen Paris will have to concede that the Jacobin tradition's insistence on a centralised, unitary State has done irreparable harm to the economic and cultural life of its constituent parts. Over the next decades the French Government will have to yield to the demands of Brittany for, as Patricia Elton Mayo has said, 'When modern political protest finds roots and nourishment in the collective memories of an ancient nation its rulers ignore such a situation at their peril'. All that remains to be seen is how soon and to what extent the French Government will recognise this historical and contemporary fact.

7 GERMANY (EAST)

Constitution: Democratic Republic

Area: 41,573 square miles

Population: 16·979 million (1974)

Capital: East Berlin

Administrative divisions: 15 districts

Present Government: The Socialist Unity Party of Germany *(S.E.D.)*; elected 1974

Language of majority: German

THE SORBS

About fifty miles to the south-east of Berlin there is a region which has no precisely defined boundaries other than the German Democratic Republic's frontiers, to the east and south, with Poland and Czechoslovakia. At its widest point, measured from east to west, this region extends for about thirty miles while the river Spree, measuring its entire length, flows from south to north for nearly twice that distance. The principal towns are Bautzen and Cottbus.

Although it no longer belongs to Western Europe in the political sense, for it was incorporated into the German Democratic Republic in 1945, Lusatia (German: *Lausitz*) is historically part of Germany as a whole, having acquired its identity centuries before that country was partitioned, and as such it requires attention in this book. The people who live here have been known, in English, as Lusatians, as Wends and as Sorbs. Speaking their own unique language, one of the eleven Slavonic languages, they are a national minority of West Slavonic origins. But, although their existence as an ethnic group is officially recognised by the Government and they enjoy certain important rights, they do not form a separate political entity within the German Democratic Republic. Nor are they part of a larger ethnic unit based in another State: they live entirely in their own territory and do not look beyond the East German border to any spiritual homeland elsewhere. They are, in the words of the Slavist W. R. Morfill (1834-1909) quoted by Gerald Stone, the English authority on the Sorbs, 'a Slavonic island in a Germanic sea'.*

The name Lusatia (Sorb: *Luzica*) is comparatively recent as the region's official designation. In German the word *Lausitz* used to refer not only to that part of Lusatia inhabited by the Sorbs, mainly Upper Lusatia (*Oberlausitz*) in the south, but to the whole of the territory including Lower Lusatia (*Niederlausitz*). The German words for Sorb and Sorbian,

*There is very little information available in non-Slavonic languages on the Sorbs. Dr Gerald Stone, Lecturer in Slavonic Studies at Hertford College, Oxford, has written the only full-length study of the Sorbs in English: *The Smallest Slavonic Nation* (The Athlone Press, University of London, 1972). The present account of the Sorbs draws heavily, with his permission, on information published in Dr Stone's book.

until recent times, were *Wende* and *Wendisch*. These have
been replaced by *Sorbe* and *Sorbisch* for the reasons that they
were imprecise, since they could be applied to other Slavonic
peoples (such as the Windisch of Carinthia in Austria) and
because they had pejorative connotations as the result of puns
based on the verb *wenden* (to turn) and on the plural noun
die Wände (walls). Nor can confusion be entirely avoided by
use of the word Lusatian, in English, for it is not clear
whether is meant a Sorb-speaking or a German-speaking
citizen of what is today a region of mixed populations. In both
forms of the Sorbian language, however, that is to say the forms
spoken in Lower Lusatia and in Upper Lusatia, the word
for Sorb is *Serb* and the adjective *serbski*. It therefore seems
preferable, in English, to call the Slavonic inhabitants of
Lusatia Sorbs, not only to avoid further confusion with the
Serbs of Ygoslavia, but because this name is used in all official documents and also the one preferred by the Sorbs
themselves.

Varying opinions have been expressed on the question of
whether there is one Sorbian language or two. It is clear that
there are two standard languages, one used in Upper Lusatia
and the other in Lower Lusatia. But the question is are there
two variants, that is to say two separate standard forms of one
language, as there are in other countries such as Norway,
Switzerland and Greece, whose separate evolution comes
from their having been based on different dialects of one and
the same language, or have two separate languages each
produced a standard literary form? There is no definitive answer to this question, but the extent to which the singular is
deliberately and consistently used in works on Sorbian subjects suggests that the most common view is that there is only
one Sorbian language.

The Sorbs have lived in their present homeland since the
beginning of recorded history, although because writing was
brought to all the Western Slavs with Christianity there are no
records of their own which describe their history in the centuries before Christ. They are, in fact, the survivors of the
Slavonic tribes who once occupied most of the territory between the rivers Elbe and Oder. The Sorbs are therefore
related to their nearest neighbours, the Poles and the Czechs.

But there is no doubt about their separate identity: they have their own history, traditions and sense of nationhood, which are expressed in their own language. Despite their small numbers, never more than a few hundred thousands, and despite their inferior political status, or lack of it altogether, they have been a clearly recognisable ethnic group throughout their history.

The survival of the Sorbian nation up to the present day is more astonishing when considered in the context of the ancient conflict between the German and Slavonic peoples which began with the decline of the Roman Empire and reached its climax during the Second World War in the Battle of Stalingrad. Defeated by the Germans towards the end of the eleventh century, the Sorbs never regained their political independence. For centuries their land was invaded and occupied, in turns, by Germans, Poles and Czechs. Converted to Christianity as late as the twelfth century, they survived the Middle Ages and the religious conflicts of the Reformation without their existence having once been recognised in any adjustment of boundaries.

In 1815, however, the Congress of Vienna obliged Saxony, to which Lusatia had been ceded two hundred years before, to give up all claims to Lower Lusatia and part of Upper Lusatia in favour of Prussia. This division of the region between Saxony and Prussia, together with the Napoleonic Wars which had ravaged the population, was the main reason why the Sorbs failed to develop the same degree of national consciousness, at this point in their history, as the other Slavonic peoples. The Sorbs remained an overwhelmingly rural people throughout the first half of the nineteenth century. But with the abolition of serfdom in 1819, the growth of capitalism, the advent of railways, the opening of the iron, brown coal and glass industries on which Lusatia's economy still depends, there emerged an urban proletariat, a bourgeoisie and even an intelligentsia of sufficient numbers to enable all three classes to withstand the process of Germanisation which had previously gone unchecked. The Sorbs, like many another people before and after them, began to aquire the habit of keeping their language while changing their social status.

Typical of the new middle-class was Jan Ernst Smoler,

born in 1816, who founded the major cultural organisation of Lusatia, the *Maćica Serbska*. It was among his contemporaries, at first a tiny proportion of the total population, that the idea of a Sorbian nationality in a modern sense began to grow. When, in 1842, there appeared the first newspapers not to be banned on account of their nationalism they were full of a new spirit of pride in the Sorbian language. Smoler's generation had learned the lessons of German Romanticism and of Pan-Slavism, especially Herder's emphasis on language as the determining factor of nationality and his sympathy for the Slavs. Pan-Slavism with its message that peoples with linguistic affinities had a common cultural destiny, appealed strongly to the Sorbian intellectuals, just as Pan-Celticism sometimes appeals to the Bretons, another people isolated for centuries from the rest of their linguistic group. 'And although my nation is small, I have brothers numbering millions', wrote the poet J. Lisec in 1868. Under the stimulus of the Pan-Slav Movement and re-inforced by the new ideas of social justice born in the French Revolution of 1789, the Sorbs began attempts to achieve cultural emancipation, including official status for the language and its instruction in the schools. At first, the numbers involved in the *Maćica Serbska* were small and the movement met with little success.

However, in the year 1849 there was a turning-point in its fortunes. Following a Republican plot in Dresden and the King's escape under the protection of his Sorbian troops, Friedrich August of Saxony decided that his son, Albert, should study the Sorbian language. This gesture, which was regarded as patronising by the intelligentsia, had a considerable effect on the common people who were led to conclude that their language could not be as worthless as many Germans said it was. Only Smoler welcomed the move, foreseeing what its effect might be, and when the Crown Prince came to Lusatia for this purpose Smoler was appointed as his tutor. Smoler's belief that the Sorbian language would receive a fillip as a result of royal interest in it proved to be well founded; its social status was improved almost overnight and the national movement won many adherents to its cause. The national ideals of the Sorbian middle-class were thus transmitted to the common people, but only for a short while, however, the long-term effects of the Prince's attempts to learn the language being negligible.

The cultural renaissance of Lusatia was now underway. Prominent among the organisations which led it were the student societies which sprang up at the Universities of Leipzig and Prague and of which the underground newspapers were the first to carry news of events in the other Slavonic countries. These societies were not directly political, at first, for their declared aim was to spread knowledge of the Sorbian language. But the cultural activities of the writers and scholars who grew up in their ranks inevitably assumed a political aspect, just as it was the philologists, poets and historians of Czechoslovakia and Yugoslavia who prepared the way for the eventual emergence of free nations in those countries.

The national heroes of the Sorbs in the nineteenth century were to be found among the writers who belonged to the *Maćica Serbska*. In 1847 this Academy had sixty-four members, 220 in 1854 and 413 in 1923, and among the subjects studied by its specialist departments were linguistics, natural history, economics, literature, education and music. It also published a magazine, and many texts and works of imaginative literature which did much to create a standardised and sophisticated literary language. Poetry in Upper Sorbian dates from the late seventeenth century, beginning with the work of Jurij Mjen (1727-85). He was followed by his son Rudolf Mjen (1767-1841), Handrij Zejlier (1804-83), Jan Radyserb-Wjela (1822-1907), Jan Mućink (1821-1904) and Jacob Bart-Cisinski (1856-1909) and many others who contributed to a literature which grew in imaginative vigour throughout the nineteenth century.

For the first time in their history the Sorbs now had an opportunity of expressing their national identity, symbolised in the *Serbski Dom* (Sorbian House), the headquarters and library of the *Maćica*. The task of collecting money to pay for this building occupied Smoler and his movement over a period of many years. At first they had to rely on Slavophiles in Russia because the Sorbs would not or could not contribute. Indeed, the efforts of the *Maćica* soon became a powerful new factor in uniting the movement and it began to succeed in strengthening the solidarity of the common people. Long before the House was opened, in 1904, it had become the principal symbol of Sorbian national pride.

By this time, of course, the Sorbs were part of the newly united Germany, and as such their position was not expected to improve much. The year 1871 had seen the culmination of the Pan-German Movement and the extension of the Prussian spirit. The process of Germanisation of the Sorbs was part of the wider policy of Prussia throughout the territories under its power. The fierce resistance of the Poles made the Prussians keep an even more watchful eye on the Sorbs. To the German ruling classes the very existence of the Sorbian minority was a potential threat to the *Reich*. Although the Sorbs had a reputation for loyalty to the State, especially after the events of 1849, they were regarded with increasing suspicion during the first years of the twentieth century.

After the First World War, during which Sorbs had served and died in great numbers, many believed that the defeat of Germany meant the prospect of independence for the minorities under Prussian control and in this they were supported by Czech demands for Sorbian independence. In 1918 a National Committee argued the case for Sorbian representation at the Peace Conference in Paris, and the right to national self-determination. The Sorbs were given assurances that they would be granted a certain degree of cultural, educational and religious autonomy but, in the event, their case was ignored and there was no mention of Lusatia in the Treaty of Versailles. On their return to Lusatia, several leaders of the National Movement, including Arnost Bart, were arrested and imprisoned for 'preparing to commit treason'.

Under the Weimar Republic the situation of the Sorbs did not improve. In 1926 the Communists in the *Landtag* of Saxony pressed for the implementation of the Constitution, in so far as they affected the Sorbs, calling for the training of teachers, the appointment of Sorbian judges and the abolition of social and political discrimination against the Sorbs, but without success. In 1925, in an attempt to hold out against the **Germanising policies of Weimar, the minorities of Germany—**

Sorbs, Poles, Danes, Frisians and Lithuanians—formed a defence organisation known as the *Verband der nationalen Minderheiten Deutschlands* (Union of the National Minorities of Germany). The Sorbs also had their own organisation, the *Domowina* (Homeland), founded in 1912, which had been suppressed during the World War. In 1920 this organisation resumed its activities, mainly in Upper Lusatia, together with *Sokot* (Falcon), originally a sporting organisation but then strongly opposed to fascism. The existence of these two bodies, and the intervention of the Communist Party on the Sorbs' behalf, led to increasing hostility on the part of the German authorities. In 1923 a special department, the *Wendenabteilung,* was formed to consider 'further appropriate measures in keeping watch on the Wendish question'. Its aims were to strengthen the German element in the 'Wendish territory' by every possible means, to oppose the threat of 'Wendish irredentism' in public and private life, and to report on 'the treasonable nature' of all Sorbian activities, including surveillance of the press, public meetings and leading figures. At the same time the existence of the *Wendenabteilung* was kept a secret and care taken to ensure that official attitudes were not seen to be hardening by the granting of occasional support for the more innocuous aspects of Sorbian folk-culture.

With the rise of the Nazis the official aim was to play down 'the Wendish question' and to accelerate the process of Germanisation as quietly but as effectively as possible. At Hitler's request, in 1935, a new organisation known as the *Bund Deutscher Osten* joined forces with the *Wendenabteilung* in its work against the Sorbs. Soon, one by one, the national organisations and institutions of Lusatia were closed, begining with the *Sokol* and the *Lausitzer Bauernbund* (Lusatian Peasants' Union) in 1933 and then, two years later, with the banning of all publications in the Sorbian language. Only Catholic publications were allowed, for these were protected by the Nazi Concordat with the Vatican, but even they were suppressed with the outbreak of war in 1939. The contents of the library and museum of the *Maćica Serbska* were confiscated, Sorbian books in private homes were seized and destroyed. Many intellectuals and public figures were arrested and some sent to concentration camps. During the War, while Sorbs were deported or enlisted or went underground, there were plans for the deportation of the entire Sorbian population. Before they could be implemented, however, the Germans were defeated at Stalingrad.

In April 1945, after fierce resistance from the retreating Germans, the forces of the Second Polish Army fighting under Soviet command as part of the First Ukrainian Front, liberated Lusatia. Parts of the region changed hands twice during the fighting, which destroyed the Sorbian House, but on 8 May Bautzen was finally captured by Soviet forces. Unlike the German population, the Sorbs had not fled before the Soviet advances and now they gave a rapturous welcome to their liberators. The *Domowina* was re-constituted and a Sorbian National Council set up in Prague. The Council demanded political independence for Lusatia, a seat in the United Nations, the establishment of Sorbian schools and land reform. But these demands were considered unrealistic by the *Domowina* which severed its connections with the Council. Nevertheless, many of the demands were implemented: the wealthy land-owners and war-profiteers were dispossessed and the economic circumstances of the entire region were transformed when 10,000 Sorbian families benefited from the re-distribution. With the permission of the Soviet authorities, newspapers began to be published again and in 1947 the first Sorb-language secondary school was opened. The Socialist Unity Party *(S.E.D.)* called on the *Landtag* of Saxony to insert a clause in the Constitution ensuring the use of Sorb as an official language and the employment of Sorbs in the public sector. This statute, passed in 1948, was later superseded, but not revoked, by others confirming the special position of the Sorbs in the Soviet Occupation Zone, and then in the German Democratic Republic. In the *Länder* election of 20 October 1946, 75% of the inhabitants of Lusatia voted for the German Christian Democratic Party.

It is clear that the German Democratic Republic has done a great deal to ensure, since 1948, the identity of its Sorbian minority. The principle of the Law for the Protection of the Sorbian Population's Right, passed on 23 March in that year and providing *inter alia* instruction in Sorb in the schools of

Saxony, has not been fundamentally changed. Indeed, the East German Government has made determined attempts to emulate the policies of the Soviet Union in its attitudes to national minorities within its borders. Its Constitution's decrees (Article 11, 7 October 1949, and Article 40, 6 April 1968) state that the Sorbs' development as an ethnic group must not be hindered but encouraged in every possible way; these guarantees do not exist merely on paper, they are *de juro* and *de facto*. The use of the Sorbian language is specifically authorised in local government, in law and all official pronouncements must be made in Sorb as well as in German, while Sorbs once again have the right to use the original forms of their names which were banned under the Nazis. These guarantees entail the appointment of Sorbs to official posts with the result that the number of Sorbs taking part in public life has grown enormously. The State Council of the German Democratic Republic has one Sorbian member, there are four Sorbian deputies in the *Volkskammer,* nine Sorbian deputies in the Council of Dresden and eighteen in Cottbus. Membership of the Socialist Unity Party is obligatory for all public offices, of course. The Ministry of the Interior has a special department for Sorbian affairs with committees dealing with problems specifically pertaining to the region. The Sorbian language is allowed in law-courts and in all correspondence with the authorities.

In education parents still have the right to send their children to schools (type A) where the language of instruction is Sorb, or to schools (type B) where it is taught as a subject. In the areas where the German population is in a minority parents have the choice of learning Sorb and it is significant, as an indication of the remarkable change in the attitude of many German-speakers living in the region to this formerly despised language, that parents quite frequently choose lessons in Sorb for their children. On the other hand, some Sorbs choose not to send their children to type A schools, although they speak Sorb at home. The usual reason is that Sorb is considered to be of no practical value outside Lusatia, and that it is somehow intrinsically inferior as the result of its status for centuries as the language of the poor and the under-privileged. There are other problems, including the fact that although there are colleges which train teachers through the Sorbian language there is no university in the region. There is, however, a course in Sorbian Language and Literature at the Karl Marx University in Leipzig.

Literature in the Sorbian language has continued to flourish up to the present time. Several writers who first appeared on the literary scene during the Weimar and Nazi periods lived to produce more good work after 1945. These include Ota Wićaz (1874-1952), editor of *Luzica* from 1926-37, Marja Kubasec (born 1890), Merćin Nowak (born 1900) and Michal Nawka (1885-1968). The position of the Sorbian writer today bears little resemblance to that before the Second World War and still less to that of those writing in the nineteenth century. Only a few are able to earn their living as writers and then only, like Jurij Brezan (born 1916), if their works are translated into German. Brezan is the most successful Sorbian writer of this century and has twice been awarded the National Prize of the German Democratic Republic. His readiness to write in German occasionally has contributed to his success but it has also provoked criticism from other Sorbian writers. While the number of books published since 1960 (1,800 titles) is greater than the number published before that date taken together, the range and themes and *genres* of Sorbian literature have expanded also. Novels have left the village and the last century for their settings and now deal with all aspects of contemporary life in Lusatia. A recurring subject in Sorbian fiction is their fate under the *Third Reich,* involving their resistance to the Nazis and the problem of those who, being German citizens, were obliged to serve in the German armed forces. Among the best known contemporary Sorbian poets are Kito Lorenc, Jurij Mlyńk and Jurij Koch, most of whose verse—unlike the novels written in Sorb—is firmly rooted in the village communities.

While they are not uncritical of certain aspects of official State policy towards the Sorbian language and its culture, there are few Sorbian writers who are not genuinely committed to the support of communism and the German Democratic Republic. This does not mean, however, that the literary scene has been without ideological controversy. At the

Fourth Union Congress of the *Domowina,* for example, held in 1957, the question of 'pessimistic nationalism' was discussed and the Circle of Young Sorbian Authors *(Kruzka mrodych serbskich awtolow)* was taken to task for the unacceptable view that the Sorbian nation was dying. Representatives of the Circle renounced this heresy at the Congress but the debate continued in literary circles. At the root of this affair lay the apparent conflict between the demands of communism and those of patriotism, and opinions as to their relative priority still differ, of course.

Despite these efforts to maintain the Sorbian language, the number of speakers has declined from 166,000 in 1868 to about 70,000 at the present time. The German Democratic Republic authorities estimate that there are about 70,000 Sorb-speakers but this figure is contested by the Federal Republic who claim that there are no more than 50,000. The population of Lusatia is by now thoroughly bilingual, as most Sorbs have to use German for some purposes. Only the very young know no German and the number of Sorbian monoglots has dwindled since the Second World War to insignificant proportions. The Sorbian language is much better preserved in the country areas than in the town, mainly because agriculture has always been mainly in the hands of Sorbs whereas the industrial workers have a large German element in their midst, which by now is larger than the Sorbian element, as the result of immigration during the Nazi period and unprecedented influxes of German workers into new industries since 1945. Bautzen (Sorb: *Budysin),* a town of about 45,000 inhabitants, now has only a thousand Sorbs althought it is considered the capital of Upper Lusatia and has several important national institutions. Most of the other towns, such as Lubbenau *(Lubnjow)* and Cottbus *(Chosebuz)* were German from their foundation. Up to 1945 there were some villages with almost completely Sorbian populations, the only Germans being the police, but all are now in areas of mixed populations together with approximately 500,000 Germans. Many of the Germans expelled from territories beyond the Oder-Neisse line and from the Sudetenland were re-settled in Lusatia, with profound effects on the linguistic compostion of the region.

Economic changes have also affected the Sorbs, hastening the process of Germanisation. A key factor in the economic planning of the German Democratic Republic is the exploitation of the brown coal resources which it possesses in abundance. The *Schwarze Pumpe* (Black Pump Combine) which processes brown coal from the biggest deposits in Europe and produces gas and electricity, is situated in the middle of Lusatia between Spremberg (Sorb: *Grodk)* and Hoyerswerda *(Wojerecy).* A new town has been built especially to house the German workers and their families in what was once a predominantly Sorb-speaking area. The highest concentration of Sorbs is to be found in the district of Kamenz *(Kamjenc),* a village which is still predominantly Catholic. In the central areas between Lower and Upper Lusatia the process of Germanisation is complete: where the language survives in these parts, it is usually spoken only by the middle-aged and old. One of the distinguishing features of the position of the Sorbian language in Lusatian society is its almost total identification with Sorbian nationality: few who know no Sorb claim to be members of the Sorbian minority, so that once a person loses the language he is automatically considered to be a member of the German ethnic group.

Despite this decline in the numbers of those who can and do speak Sorb, now reaching serious proportions, there is no indication of a change in the German Democratic Republic's support for the language and culture of Lusatia. The number of newspapers, periodicals and books has increased during the last ten years and all are subsidised by the State. Most are published by the *Ludowe Nakladnistwo Domowina* (Domowina People's Press), founded at Bautzen in 1947, a national publishing house which is responsible for all aspects of book production and distribution in the region. Among the eighty or so new titles published every year in editions of between one thousand and two thousand copies there is a wide variety, including translations of classics and contemporary writers, as well as textbooks and imaginative literature. There is also a professional theatre company and a daily newspaper in Sorb, *Nowa Doba* (New Times) as well as political, folklore and youth magazines, including one for learners of the language. The first radio programmes in Sorb were broadcast from Dresden in 1949 and there has been a Sorbian section of the State Radio since 1953. The weekly transmitting times in the language have been gradually increased from a hundred minutes in 1957 to 290 minutes since 1964; there are no regular television programmes in Sorb. The central role of the *Domowina* in the region's cultural life is crucial. organised under the direction of the Socialist Unity Party, it sponsors concerts, films, plays and folk evenings, sporting events, exhibitions and festivals. There is a House of Sorbian Folk Art at Bautzen which belongs to the Ministry of Culture, an Association for Sorbian Folk Culture, founded in 1952 and a Folk Theatre which includes a company of puppeteers. Among the musical instruments popular among the Sorbs are the *tarakawa* (a wooden wind instrument), the bagpipes and the *huslicki,* a three-stringed violin. Many folk-customs still survive, such as the lighting of Easter fires and dancing around the may-pole.

It is clear that the Germanising processes of today on the Sorbian minority are quite different from what they were in Nazi times and previously. There is no longer a deliberate, official policy aimed at the destruction of the Sorbian language; on the contrary, substantial State aid is given to help the Sorbs maintain and develop their language, culture and institutions. Nevertheless, the Sorbs are a minority constantly subjected to all the usual assimilatory pressures from the majority in whose midst they live. How long they can preserve their identity without a degree of political autonomy is obviously a matter for speculation and there is much discussion of the problem in Lusatia. In favour of their survival is the fact that the position of the Sorbian people in Lusatian society, and hence the social functions of the language they speak, have improved greatly in the last twenty-five years, albeit within the context of Marxist-Leninist ideology as practised by the German Democratic Republic. Also, the old contempt among Germans living in the region has now almost completely disappeared—which may, of course, hasten the incidence of inter-marriage between Sorbs and Germans. Again, the Sorbs have seized their new opportunities with real enthusiasm; the Catholics, in particular, cling to their language, as to their religion, with special determination. The cultural vitality of Sorbian society, at least in Upper Lusatia, the renewed interest among students and young people, and more than all the number of children who learn the language in school: these are signs that the Sorbs of Lusatia, unlike the other Slavonic peoples of Germany, all now extinct, are likely to survive as an ethnic minority for many more decades.

8 GERMANY (WEST)

Constitution: Federal Republic

Area: 95,520 square miles

Population: 61·991 million (1974)

Capital: Bonn

Administrative divisions: 10 provinces (and West Berlin)

Present Government: The Social Democratic Party *(S.P.D.)* in coalition with the Free Democratic Party *(F.D.P.)*; elected 1974

Language of majority: German

THE DANES OF SOUTH SCHLESWIG

A region which was disputed for centuries by Germany and Denmark, Schleswig has been divided between the two States since 1920. North of the frontier, which runs from Flensburg across the Jutland or Zimbrian Peninsula at its narrowest point, is the area known to the Danes as *Sydjylland* (South Jutland) or *Nord Slesvig* (North Schleswig) and where a German-speaking minority lives. South Schleswig, the area on the other side of the frontier, to the south of the river Koenigsau, is part of West Germany's northernmost *Land* of Schleswig-Holstein. The population of Schleswig-Holstein is approximately 2,543,000 (1975). Although there are no precise, official statistics for the Danish-speaking population of South Schleswig, for reasons mentioned below, it is estimated that there are about 50,000 who have a knowledge of the language at the present time.

Since the local government reforms of 1970 the *Land* of Schleswig-Holstein has been divided into twelve *Kreise,* or districts, and four municipalities or *Kreisfreie Städte,* which include the town of Flensburg. The Danish-speakers of South Schleswig live mostly in the villages along the frontier with Denmark in the *Kreise* of *Flensburg-Land* and *Nordfriesland* but to a lesser extent in the *Kreis* of Schleswig, a much smaller area than the historic region of the same name. On the western coast of *Nordfriesland,* and on the North Frisian Islands, there are also small numbers who speak North Frisian.

Further inland, as far as the river Eider (Danish: *Ejder),* Danish is replaced by Low Saxon, a German dialect, as the language of educated speech. Low Saxon is, in fact, a number of dialects which were spoken, at least until recent times, over an area from Groningen in the Netherlands as far south as Aachen, on the Belgian border, and north of a line from there through Dessau to Guben, on East Germany's border with Poland. These dialects are different from that other group of Low German dialects *(Niederdeutsch)* which went to form the Dutch dialects *(Niederfränkisch)* and from the dialects of Middle and High German *(Mitteldeutsch* and *Oberdeutsch),* for while the latter developed written forms in the sixteenth century under the influence of Luther's Bible—literary Dutch and German *(Hochdeutsch)*—the speech of Low Germany remained fragmented in four unwritten dialects: Low Saxon, Westphalian, Schleswig and Eastern Low Saxon. By today only 12% of the population of Schleswig speak Low Saxon, but the dialect is still to be heard in country districts north of the Eider and has influenced the accent and vocabulary of the German spoken in the region.

Schleswig-Holstein is the most sparsely populated of all West Germany's *Länder*, after Lower Saxony and Bavaria, with only 460 inhabitants per square mile (1969). It is a flat, largely agricultural region but there are important food factories near Flensburg. The seat of the Provincial Government is Kiel.

If the Jutes, Angles and Frisians are excepted, the Danes were the autochthonous population of Schleswig from the ninth century until 1864, with the river Eider the historic frontier between the King's domains and his Empire. Since the Middle Ages, however, Schleswig has been infiltrated by Germans from the south, beginning with Knud Laward in the twelfth century and, two centuries later, ending with the Holstein dynasty of the Schauenburgers which, when it became extinct, passed to the Kings of Denmark. The process of Germanisation continued for a further five hundred years, under administration from Holstein after 1460, with the influx of noble families, merchants, artisans and the ministers of the Reformation. Whereas in 1825 the Germans to the north of the traditional frontier of the Eider were no more than an influential minority, by 1848 the zone of compact German settlement had reached the present-day frontier, transforming the Danish communities in its wake into a residual minority.

For the next fifty years Germans and Danes clashed over the disputed region. The Germans were organised in the Schleswig-Holstein Party, whose members—drawn mainly from the towns, having strong links with the Liberals of Germany itself, and supported by the wealthy German landowners of the region—wanted a separate Constitution for a united Schleswig-Holstein. The Danes were mainly farmers from north and central Slesvig who, alarmed by the spread of German from the south, wanted a closer union with the

Danish Crown and less contact with German-speaking Holstein. Although the Danish King Christian VIII was opposed to the more extreme claims made by both sides, he worked hard to restore harmony between them, but the task of reconciliation became harder as the century drew to its end. The Schleswig-Holstein Question, largely a product of Grundtvig's National Romantic Movement, was to bedevil Denmark's political life and its relations with Germany for over half a century.

In 1848, stirred by a series of Liberal revolts in Germany following the Revolution which had created the short-lived Second French Republic, the German-speakers of Schleswig-Holstein demanded not only a Constitution for the region but its entry, as a State, into the united Germany which seemed likely to be created. The Danes, led by a fiery young lawyer named Orla Lehmann, responded by demanding the establishment of an autonomous Danish State in the region, according to the Eider Programme named after the river. In the crisis which followed King Frederick of Denmark, who had succeeded his father in 1848, met a deputation of two thousand Danes and announced that a Constitution would be drawn up immediately.

Meanwhile, however, the Germans of Schleswig-Holstein took the law into their own hands by proclaiming a Government of their own and seizing the fortress of Flensburg for the defence of their interests, calling upon the states of Germany to support them. In an upsurge of Danish feeling, thousands of young Danes flocked to defend Denmark against what they considered to be German oppression. They were joined by many Norwegians and Swedes who, under the influence of the Scandinavian Movement and resenting the recent loss of Finland to Russia, sought closer links and eventually political union between Denmark, Norway and Sweden. The civil war of Schleswig-Holstein thus became an international one, with Prussian troops occupying the province before Russia succeeded in negotiating a temporary peace, during which Denmark approved its Constitution of 1849. After a pause of only a few months, fighting broke out again in Schleswig-Holstein. The following year Denmark defeated the Prussian regiments and agreed to an armistice, leaving the isolated Germans of

Schleswig-Holstein to be over-run at the battle of Isted. The rebel Army and Government were dissolved but while the Danes were re-establishing themselves in Schleswig, Austrian and Prussian troops, backed by the German Confederation, re-occupied Holstein in 1850, intending to stay there until the *status quo* was restored. On the fall from power of the Liberals in Copenhagen, the Danes finally agreed that the Constitution of 1849 would apply only to Denmark and that separate provision would be made for Schleswig. At this news the German forces withdrew from the province.

But the situation in Schleswig-Holstein did not improve. By 1865 the conflict had escalated to involve not only Denmark and Germany but Prussia, Austria, the Scandinavian countries, France, Britain and Russia, all of which were represented at the various conferences which discussed the problem. Prussia, with Bismarck its Chancellor, was bent on war to deprive Denmark of the whole region and German troops now entered Holstein, crossing the river Eider into Schleswig. The Danish Army, seriously outnumbered, hoped for intervention but Sweden would not act without France. During a brief truce, but after bitter fighting, a conference of European powers was held in London at which Britain proposed the division of Schleswig along the language boundary with Holstein. But no agreement could be reached as to where the line should be drawn: the conference ended and the fighting broke out again. Eventually it became clear that Denmark, defeated by the Prussians, could not hope to hold Schleswig and losing Britain's support, it conceded the three Duchies to the victors. The region was ruled by the Prussians until after the Austro-Prussian War of 1866 when it was again incorporated with Prussia. The loss of Schleswig-Holstein, representing nearly a half of the Danish Crown's territory, was a shattering experience for the Danes and it was to have a divisive effect on their internal politics for the rest of the century.

On the defeat of Germany in 1918 many Danes were of the opinion that as Schleswig had been seized by force it should be returned to Denmark in its entirety. But all the political parties of the day supported the Government's decision to hold a referendum, as happened in other States after the First

World War. Voting took place on 10 February and 14 March 1920 under the eyes of international observers and the results were as follows. The northern part of Schleswig, described in the Treaty of Versailles as Zone I, was in favour of a return to Denmark: 75,431 inhabitants voted in this way and 25,319 voted in favour of Germany. In Zone 2, that is the central part including Flensburg together with the North Frisian Islands, chose by 51,724 votes against 12,859 to remain with Germany. The plebiscite did not include the rest of the region, Zone 3, as this area was thoroughly Germanised by then. Not one district in Zone 2 voted in favour of Denmark and so the Danish-speakers of South Schleswig became a linguistic minority and German citizens.

During the inter-war years and the rise of fascism in Germany, the Danes were particularly sensitive about the fate of the Danish-speaking minority in South Schleswig who were increasingly subjected to the process of Germanisation which the Nazis had inflicted on Austria and Czechoslovakia. By the end of the War there had grown up among both the Danish and German-speaking communities a strong movement in favour of reunion with Denmark. Although their view was supported by left-wing parties in Denmark, the majority in Parliament was fearful of the complications which might follow any changes in the Danish province's southern frontier at this stage, especially because large numbers of East Germans fleeing the Russian advance had settled on the German side and would take generations before becoming naturalised. When, in 1946, Britain—within whose zone South Schleswig lay—proposed an adjustment of the frontier or an exchange of population, both solutions were rejected by Denmark.

An important factor in the peaceful conditions prevailing throughout the entire region since 1945 has been, no doubt, the conciliatory spirit of the local German authorities and their Government after the rise of national socialism in 1933 and the horrors of the World War. The reciprocal nature of the situation, in that there exists a German-speaking minority in Denmark, has also been taken into account. Nevertheless, the Federal Republic of Germany assures its Danish minority of favourable conditions for its development to such an extent that it enjoys a cultural situation and faster economic growth than many other minorities in Western Europe.

Flensburg (Danish: *Flensborg*), on the frontier but actually in Germany, has become again what it ceased to be in 1920—the economic centre of the whole region—largely as the result of initiatives taken with a view to overcoming the problems arising from the region's peripheral status, before Denmark joined the Common Market, when North Schleswig was in the E.F.T.A. Zone and South Schleswig was part of the European Economic Community, and when custom duties between the two were often as high as 32%. Danish industrialists, taking advantage of these tariffs, established many branch factories near the frontier, with Government aid, so that by today—with Denmark in the Common Market and the tariffs abolished—there is a steadily increasing density of industralisation on both sides.

It is therefore surprising to discover that, from time to time, claims are made for the revision of this eminently successful arrangement from among the Danish minority in South Schleswig. Such sentiments are usually expressed in general terms, however, which hardly threaten the continued existence of the *status quo*. 'The frontier exists', said the deputy Berthold Behnsen in 1966, 'but the right of self-determination remains unaltered. We look forward to the dissolution of the frontier and the creation of a region in which the two Slesvigs *(sic)* will be re-united'. And Herman Tychsen, president of the *Sydslevigske Forening*, an umbrella organisation representing the Danish community of West Germany in all its aspects, said in 1964, 'Today, as in former times, reunification with Denmark is the aim of all our efforts in South Slesvig'. More recently, in 1968, the deputy Ernst Meyer, has commented, 'Cultural frontiers are not forged once and for all time'.

These views are difficult to reconcile with the policies of the organisations and institutions to which the speakers belong, and it must be concluded that the minority character of the Danes in South Schleswig is a highly personal matter. It certainly does not depend entirely on language because the majority of Danes in Germany, although considering themselves to be of Danish nationality, also speak German, just as most Germans in Denmark speak Danish or its Jutland dialect. Nor can it depend on religion, which is the same, Lutheranism, for all three ethnic groups in Schleswig-Holstein.

The exact number of Danes in Germany cannot be calculated precisely; it can only be inferred, with all the usual risks of extrapolation, from electoral statistics and membership of the minority's organisations. To complicate matters further, many families after the Second World War declared themselves as Danish in order to receive relief from the privations they had suffered. The effect of these *Speckdanen* (bacon Danes) on the life of the region gradually decreased, however, as the electoral results of the *Sudschleswiger Wählerverband*, the party of the Danish minority, illustrate. Winning 75,388 votes (5·4% of the electorate of the *Land* of Schleswig-Holstein) at the first Federal elections in 1949, this party received only 44,585 votes (3·5%) in 1953, 32,262 (2·8%) in 1957 and 23,600 (1·9%) in the Federal Diet of Kiel elections of 1967. This vote, subsequently fairly stable, corresponds to a total population of about 35,000 of which Flensburg, with a population which is about 23% Danish-speaking, serves as administrative centre.

After the end of hostilities in 1945 the three ethnic groups of Schleswig began to re-constitute themselves, encouraged by the two Governments directly concerned. The first initiatives were taken on the German side when, in September 1949, the authorities announced the *Gesetz und Verordnungsblatt für Schleswig-Holstein*—a declaration on the situation of the Danish minority under their jurisdiction. At the same time about 340,000 refugees from other parts of Germany moved into the area, creating serious problems of housing and social unrest and thus making the implementation of the new laws more difficult but not impossible. Most of these refugees subsequently settled in other areas until by 1960 only 128,000 were still in Schleswig. The Kiel Declaration of 1949 was replaced under Adenauer's Government by the Bonn Declaration of 6 July 1955. The latter is not a law but represents rather a moral obligation on the part of the host-State to respect the linguistic minority, and it is on the scrupulous implementation of this understanding that the

present situation has been founded, especially after the
Danish Government responded with the *Kopenhager Ver-
merk* of October 1944 offering similar guarantees for the German-speakers of North Slesvig. Among the first steps which
the Bonn Declaration allowed were the re-opening of Danish-
language schools and cultural organisations in Schleswig.
Relaxation of tension between Danish-speakers and German-
speakers dates from this time. Schleswig thus became one of
the four regions in Western Europe to achieve this special
status, the others being the South Tyrol, the Italian zone of
the free city of Trieste and the Croatian and Slovenian
minorities of Austria.

The Bonn Declaration of 1955 is the statute by which the
three minorities of Schleswig are governed today. The
historical background and the dispersion of the minorities
having ruled out the constitution of autonomous territories,
the Declaration does not attempt to invest the ethnic groups
with the protection of public law but is, rather, a system of
protection for the individual buttressed by public recognition
and assistance for minority organisations. Definition of
minorities is made according to the private, subjective principle as it applies in Schleswig: membership of an ethnic
group, whether Danish, German or Frisian, is free and cannot be contested or investigated by the authorities. The principles upon which the statute depends are thus non-
discrimination against persons and promotion of ethnic
groups.

The Declaration guarantees the minorities, as individuals,
equality of civil rights. By this is meant not only the normal
rights of democracies but also those appertaining to the individual's, or the family's, dealings with the authorities and in
this respect it is highly unusual. Each citizen has the right to be
administered in his own language or to use it before all
tribunals, while all public announcements must be published
also in the press of the minorities. An important clause which,
in other countries, might be openly or surreptitiously ignored,
concerns the right of minorities to maintain relations with
their country of origin. Finally, the Declaration of 1949
stipulates that all Danish pastors, schoolteachers and officials
must avoid discrimination in such matters which concern

them and must refrain from political activity in the parishes where they work.

Also guaranteed the right to form political parties and to contest elections, the Danish minority is encouraged in this respect by the obvious and abundant goodwill of both Governments. The Federal Government at Bonn in 1955, for example, suspended the electoral law which prevented parties with less than 5% of the total suffrage from sitting in Parliament, while the Government of Schleswig-Holstein has done the same. As a result the *Sudschleswiger Wählerverband* (Electoral Association of South Schlesvig) won two seats in the Diet of Kiel in 1958 with only 2·8% of the local votes cast. In the regional elections of 25 April 1971, the *S.S.W.* won one of the seventy-three seats, the remainder being shared by the Christian Democrats *(Christlich Demokratische Union)* with forty and the Social Democrats *(Sozialdemokratische Partei Deutschlands)* with thirty-two. At the Federal level, however, the Danish minority—as a result of its decreasing numerical strength (44,585 in 1954)—lost the deputy Herman Clausen who had represented it from 1949 to 1953. To compensate for the absence of a deputy, a mixed advisory commission of minority and Government representatives was immediately set up. From 1962 the *S.S.V.* was granted advisory status in the Regional Parliament at Kiel and representation on important committees and it won 27,577 votes (9%) of the votes cast in Schleswig in the election of 1967. In the seven districts of South Schleswig the *S.S.W.* has at present fourteen local councillors out of a total of forty-two, and 179 parish councillors.

In the State elections which took place in Schleswig-Holstein on 13 April 1975 the Christian Democrats maintained their absolute majority, winning 50·3% of the votes cast, while the Social Democrats won 40·3% and the Free Democrats 7%. In the light of this victory for the *C.D.U.* its leader Mr Stoltenberg, Prime Minister of Schleswig-Holstein, is regarded as one of the candidates who will fight the federal elections, and thus put himself forward for the Chancellorship of West Germany, in the autumn of 1976.

It is evident that the very favourable conditions guaranteed to the Danish minority of Schleswig have allowed it to develop as rapidly and as satisfactorily as if it lived in the State of its ethnic origin. The chief cultural organisation which co-ordinates the work of a large number of other bodies is the *Sydslesvigsk Forening,* founded in 1920 and claiming a membership in 1971 of 24,000. The Danes of South Schleswig are among the smallest minorities in Europe to support their own daily newspaper in their own language, *Flensborg Avis.* The Danish Church has about 6,400 members, twenty-three pastors in fifty-nine parishes. They have also publishing houses, theatres, libraries, choirs, orchestras, youth and sports clubs, housing associations, credit schemes and banks, academies and museums, all operating in Danish and financed from public funds. The cultural life of the Danish-speakers, organised at high professional standards, is in direct and unrestricted contact with Denmark's. There exists no official legislation, however, according legal status to the use of Danish for official purposes. Nevertheless, it is generally agreed that Danish can be used, when the citizen chooses, in law-courts and for communicating with the Regional Government. There is no television or radio in Danish produced in the region but the Danish broadcasting authorities transmit daily programmes, which can be seen and heard in South Schleswig. Danish films are shown regularly in the cinemas of Flensburg.

It is in the field of education that the Danish minority has made most progress. In the years between the Wars, a complete educational system was devised for and by the minorities. Although not obliged to do so under any treaty, Denmark and Germany doubled the number of German and Danish schools within their borders during these years. Schools in towns and villages had both German and Danish classes and monolingual schools could be opened in the rural areas on request by a minimum of 20% of the inhabitants. Today, the educational system of the Danish minority is based on the principle of private schools which are maintained by 'school associations', principally the *Dansk Skoleforening for Sydslesvig* (Danish School Association). The *Dansk Skole* of Niebull has also introduced obligatory teaching of Frisian while the school at Risum was converted into an officially bilingual school in 1961. Admission to all minority schools is strictly by choice, cannot be contested by the school or by the education authorities and there is reciprocal recognition of certificates between Germany and Denmark. The schools, although officially designated 'private', receive 80% of their finances, including salaries and the cost of equipment, from Government funds which is provided by both States, the remainder being contributed by voluntary organisations such as the *Graensforening* (Association for the Frontier) which has about 150,000 members. The total number of schools maintained in this way is sixty-nine Danish schools, including a secondary school at Flensburg (4,599 pupils) and fifty infants' schools (1,790 pupils). There is also an adult education centre at Jarplund. The number of entrants to secondary schools has remained constant during the last ten years—an average of 425 annually.

Finally, it must be noted that another important factor in the harmony which characterises the situation of the German minority in North Slesvig and the Danish in South Schleswig is that Germans and Danes living in the region co-operate with one another in all possible ways. This co-operation exists not only among similar institutions, not only with equivalent organisations on the majorities' side and not only with the country of origin but also among themselves: from ethnic group to ethnic group, they share experiences and resources. There is hardly a public meeting for example, where delegates from the other language group are not present.

Clearly, the linguistic situation in Schleswig is without parallel anywhere in Western Europe. The minorities' rights are respected here as essential for the well-being of the community as a whole rather than as a last resort. The remark by Gustav Heinemann, President of the Federal Republic of Germany, at the fiftieth anniversary celebrations of the plebiscite on South Schleswig in 1970 seems fully justified, 'The time has passed when frontiers could be considered as lines of separation: today the frontier territories are becoming, rather, places of contact and reconciliation between peoples'.

THE NORTH FRISIANS

The North Frisians live in the *Land* of Schleswig-Holstein, on the coastal strip between the rivers Eider in the south and the Wiedau in the north. They also inhabit the adjacent islands of Föhr, Amrum, Sylt, Norstrand, Pellworm, the ten islands which form the Halligen group, and the island of Helgoland. This area of about 800 square miles corresponds to the administrative units of Eiderstedt, Husum and Südtorndern, amalgamated in 1970 and now known as the *Kreis* of *Nordfriesland*. It had a total population of 154,302 in 1970, about 6% of Schleswig Holstein's, and 13% of its area.

Although about 60,000 inhabitants of North Friesland consider themselves to be of Frisian origin, only about 10,000 still have a knowledge of the language. They speak dialects which belong with West and East Frisian to the Anglo-Frisian branch of the West Germanic languages but which are unintelligible, outside their own communities, to all but a few educated speakers of West Frisian, the language spoken in the province of the Netherlands. Unlike the language of West Friesland, the North Frisian dialects have no clearly defined and officially recognised standard forms, so that the Frisians who live on the islands usually have to converse with those on the mainland in Low Saxon. Their numbers are dwindling rapidly. On the island of Sylt, for example, where 150 years ago the entire population spoke Frisian, only one third spoke it in 1927 and no more than a thousand out of 25,000 in 1970.

Little is known about the early history of the North Frisians except that the first settlers arrived peacefully between the eighth and eleventh centuries. In 1362 they were followed by others after storms had submerged the marshy areas of the North Sea to the south. On the 'dry islands' (German: *Geestinseln)* of Föhr, Amrum and Sylt they met a very sparse population of Jutes, with whom they mixed. Although subjects of the Kings of Denmark and later of the Dukes of Schleswig, the Frisians kept their own laws based on *Jyske Lov,* the Jute Law-books, throughout the Middle Ages. But their attempts to win independence—they had won a battle at Oldenswort in 1252—were thwarted after their defeat at Langsundtoft in 1344.

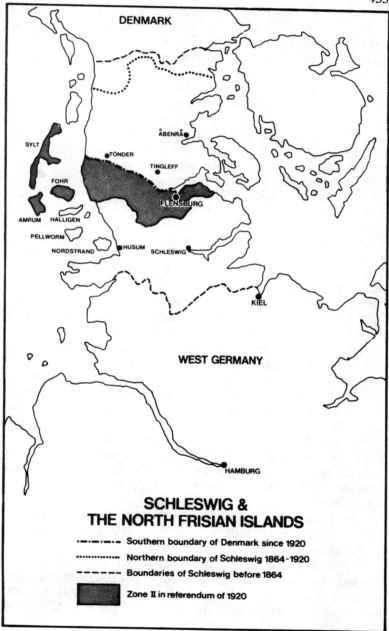

**SCHLESWIG &
THE NORTH FRISIAN ISLANDS**

–·–·–·– Southern boundary of Denmark since 1920

·············· Northern boundary of Schleswig 1864-1920

– – – – – Boundaries of Schleswig before 1864

Zone II in referendum of 1920

From then on the fate of the North Frisians was that of Schleswig up to the year 1864 and of Prussia after the area's annexation in 1867. In 1807 Helgoland was taken over from the Danes by the English and in 1890 was exchanged by the Germans for the East African State of Zanzibar. Since 1867 the North Frisian area has belonged to the province—and since 1946 to the State of Schleswig-Holstein. Helgoland was joined to the *Kreis* of Süderdithmarshen until 1922; up to 1932 it was an independent district and since then it has belonged to the rural district of Pinneberg, near Hamburg.

The North Frisian cultural area does not coincide with the administrative boundaries, however. In the east of the districts of Husum and Südtondern it extends outside the islands only in a few places such as the district between Rantrum and Horstedt, Bohmstedt, Högel and Lütjenholm, Stadum and Leck. Linguistically, North Friesland is even more restricted. On the other hand, the town of Friedrichstadt, founded in 1621 by West Frisians but now belonging to the *Kreis* of Schleswig, is counted as part of North Friesland because of its historical and economic ties. A good deal of qualification is therefore necessary if North Friesland is to be described as the districts of Eiderstedt, Husum and Südtondern.

Nevertheless, the awareness of being a distinct geographical area has gown since the Second World War, even among the inhabitants of North Friesland who are not of Frisian descent. Since 1964 regional planning authorities in the *Land* of Schleswig-Holstein have regarded the three districts as a single unit, known as *Planungsraum 5,* and local politicians worked for more co-operation between them in readiness for local government reform when, in 1970, they became the *Kreis* of *Nordfriesland.* The principal towns are Husum (24,690), Westerland (10,272), Niebüll the administrative centre of Südtondern (6,352), Wyk on the island of Föhr (4,980), Tönning the administrative centre of Eiderstedt (4,507), Bredstedt (4,178), Friedrichstadt (3,092) and Garding (1,877).

The economic structure of North Friesland is reflected in the fact that the average gross product per inhabitant in 1961 was the lowest in Schleswig-Holstein which itself has the lowest product per inhabitant in the Federal Republic. This weakness in the economic structure is also reflected in that farming and fishing employ 24% of North Friesland's population, 12% of Schleswig-Holstein's but only 6% of West Germany's. Many North Frisians have had to emigrate, mostly to America, and to work on ships from the Netherlands, whaling and sealing in the North Atlantic. From Föhr, for example, half the school-leavers have left for America in every decade since 1920. Measures taken by the Government of Schleswig-Holstein under the scheme known as *Programm Nord* have done much, since 1953, to improve agricultural conditions in North Friesland by water-control and land-reclamation, but there has been comparatively little commercial or industrial development. Only tourism, which weakens still further the Frisian character of the coast and islands, has been developed.

It is very questionable whether the North Frisians can be regarded as a national minority in the same way as the West Frisians undoubtedly are in the Netherlands. The Frisian language has been virtually abandoned by the North Frisians. As with the Cornish language in Cornwall, for example, family and place-names are all that remain over most of the area, and there has been continuous inter-mixture between Frisians, Danes and Germans over the centuries. By today it is extremely difficult to assess the numerical strength of the North Frisians for there is no way of knowing who is a Frisian and the Census does not ask for information about the language. Private estimates indicate that there are about 60,000 people of Frisian origin in North Friesland. But they have always lacked the ethnic awareness of the West Frisians, mainly owing to the region's topography and German influences on their language and way of life. Hardly ever has their consciousness developed beyond the realisation that they are the last descendants of a once flourishing poeple and then only in times of oppression and disaster as when, in 1634, the coast sank and two-thirds of the population were drowned.

The historical and linguistic interests of Romanticism were not without their effect in North Friesland, however. Men like Christian Fedderson (1786-1874), Bende Bendsen (1787-1875), Lorenz Friedrich Mechlenburg (1799-1875), Knut

Jungbohn Clement (1803-73), Christian Peter Hansen (1803-79), Moritz Momme Nissen (1822-1902) were among the writers who were aware of Frisian traditions. But the conflict between Denmark and Germany over Schleswig-Holstein prevented the development of a national movement. The North Frisians were compelled to take sides and all societies founded in the region until after the Second World War showed signs of the tension which resulted from their decision.

The first North Frisian Society was founded in 1879, followed by another in 1902 led by Lorenz Conrad Peters (1885-1949). The Frisian-Schleswig Society founded in 1923 protested against the process of Prussianization begun in 1867, demanding political and legal protection for the minority culture by recognition of the North Frisian group as a member of the European Minorities' Congress. The Society joined the *Verband der nationalen Minderheiten Deutschlands* (Society for the National Minorities of Germany) in 1926, but only against opposition from many of its members who declared, 'We North Frisians feel ourselves to be German. We feel ourselves bound together with Schleswig-Holstein and the German culture and have been so for centuries. Within this culture we want to retain our distinctions. We want our language to be used in school and church. We do not wish to be regarded as a national minority'. Under powerful German influence, the European Minorities' Congress rejected the North Frisians in 1928 on the grounds that 'the national characteristics of this group are not sufficiently marked'. In 1935 the North Frisian Society was turned into the folk-group known as *Nordfriesland* which was a section of the Nazi organisation *Abteilung Volkstum und Heimat* (Cultural Group for Folk Culture and the Love of Home) and the Frisian-Schleswig Society was banned.

In 1945 the Frisian-Schleswig Society reformed and since 1948 has been known as *Forüning for nationale Frashe* (Association of National Frisians). Closely related in its activities to the organisations of the Danish minority in Schleswig, particularly those of the *Sudschleswigschen Wählerverband*, its aims are 'to promote the Frisian language, to revive its folk-culture and to develop cultural contacts with the East and West Frisians'. Since 1950 the

Association has belonged to the Federal Union of European Nationalities (F.U.E.N.). Another society founded in 1946, the *Nordfriesische Verein für Heimatkunde und Heimatliebe*, (North Frisian Society for Knowledge and Love of Home) works not only for Frisian culture but also for the Low German dialects to be found in the region. Among prominent Frisian activists who did not agree with the aims of the Frisian-Schleswig Society during the National Socialist period were L. C. Peters and Albrecht Johannsen. These two founded the *Nord-friesisches Institut* (North Frisian Institute) in 1949, but this body was accused of pro-Danish sympathies. The relationship between the two main North Frisian Societies did not begin to change until the sixth Frisian Congress held at Aurich, in East Friesland, in 1955, at which the West Frisians attempted to reconcile them. Both now agreed to support the Frisian Manifesto, a statement of common views and objectives, and the North Frisian Institute. This body (Frisian: *Nordfriisk Instituut*) has also attempted to awaken interest among the East Frisians of *Ostfriesland*, the area around the towns of Emden and Oldenburg in Lower Saxony (German: *Niedersachen*) to the south, and those in the small, scattered communities of Saterland, Jeverland and Butjadingen where East Frisian dialects are still spoken by about 11,000 people, mostly the older generation. However, the East Frisians do not consider themselves as an ethnic minority and have shown little response so far except in that they send representatives to the Frisian Congress held every three years in one of the three regions where Frisians live.

The North Frisians have no special legal position as a minority in West Germany. The Declaration of Kiel in 1949 referred to them as a minority but in that of Bonn in 1955 their existence was no longer mentioned. Cultural activity receives financial support from the Governments at Kiel and Copenhagen and from local councils, but is confined mainly to the maintenance of museums and historic buildings. Local customs include horse-riding and the lighting of bonfires on the evening before St Peter's Day (22 February). The North Frisians have no official emblem or flag, but the song *Gölj, rüüdj, ween* (Gold, red, blue—the national colours) is often sung by the more nationally aware, who also wear a pin in their lapels to denote that they wish to speak their language to others.

The North Frisian dialects are today spoken only on the mainland north of Husum, on the *Geestinseln* of Fohr (Frisian: *Fering*), Amrum *(Ömring)* and Sylt *(Söl'ring)*, on some of the Halligen islands and on Helgoland *(Deät Lun)*. The retreat of the language has been caused mainly by the acceptance of an increasing number of loan-words from High German and the attraction of Low German dialects. In 1890 there were 19,300 speakers of North Frisian, in 1928 about 15,500 and in 1968 about 10,000. It is estimated that no more than 35,000 people ever spoke North Frisian at any one time. Nevertheless, the language has not been without its writers who include Jap Peter Hansen (1767-1855), Jääns Mungard (1866-1944), Gondel Wielandt (1894-1964), Hermann Schmidt (born 1901), Nis Albrecht Johansen (1855-1935) and his son Albrecht Johanssen, Katherine Ingwersen (1879-1968) and Herrlich Jannsen (1906-63). There are, however, few writers in North Frisian nowadays.

The language of instruction in the schools of North Friesland has been German ever since the introduction of the State education system in the nineteenth century. A directive of the Prussian authorities in 1925 allowed lessons in Frisian for a few hours a week but during the National Socialist period the use of the language was completely forbidden. It was allowed again by the Provincial Government of Schleswig-Holstein in 1947, for two to three hours a week at primary and secondary level. Frisian is also taught as a special subject in some of the German schools while at the Danish school at Niebüll it is obligatory. Since 1961 the Danish minority's primary school at Risum has taught in Frisian for the first two years and later in Danish and German. Private lessons for adults are given by the *Frasch Följkehuuchschöljferiining* (Frisian Evening School Association), founded in 1968.

In public life the Frisian language has no role to play. Only a few villages around Risum and Lindholm, and on Helgoland, have bilingual road-signs. There is no Frisian press but the German daily newspapers occasionally publish articles in the language. Periodicals include *Fuar Söl' ring Lir* (For the People of Sylt), *Üüsen äine wäi* (Our own way), and since 1926—except for the Nazi period—there has been a Frisian supplement to the German newspaper *Sylter Rundschau*.

Institutions concerned with academic research into the North Frisian dialects are the *Nordfriisk Instituut* (North Frisian Institute) and, in Kiel, the *Nordfriesische Wörterbuchstelle* (North Frisian Dictionary Office) which has published the work of Julius Tedsen (1880-1939), now under the supervision of Hans Kuhn of the North Frisian Institute at the University of Kiel. The North Frisian Institute is a private body supported by donations from both Germany and Denmark and it cooperates with the *Fryske Akademy* at Leeuwarden in the Netherlands.

The North Frisians have no political organisations of their own and not all support the *Sudschleswigscher Wählerverband*, the body which represents a large section of the Danish minority in South Schleswig. Nor do they appear to be concerned in any significant numbers that the Frisian dialects spoken in their area are probably now entering the final stages of decay. Nevertheless, there have been a few attempts during the last two years to win recognition for the language. In December 1974 a group of forty students at Christian Albrecht University in Kiel, led by Folkert Faltings, met representative of Schleswig Holstein's Ministry of Culture to present a petition demanding the teaching of Frisian at university, secondary and elementary level. They were told that the *Land* authorities did not have the financial resources to carry out these demands and that the money would have to be raised by the Frisian community. At the present time the students are collecting signatures in protest against the authorities of Schleswig-Holstein and preparing a campaign for the awakening of the North Frisians to the fate of their language.

9 IRELAND

Constitution: Republic

Area: 27,136 square miles

Population: 2·978 million (1971)

Capital: Dublin

Administrative divisions: 26 counties

Present Government: Fine Gael in coalition with the Irish Labour Party; elected 1973

Language of majority: English

THE GAELS

Although Ireland is unique among the countries of the Celtic group in having established its own State, it is nevertheless not without a linguistic minority—those 789,429 of its inhabitants who, at the 1971 Census, were enumerated as being able to speak the Irish language. This figure, 28·3% of the total population of the Republic, may appear to be low when it is remembered that, according to Article 8 of the Constitution, 'the Irish language as the national language is the first official language'. At the same time, as the following account will attempt to suggest, a good deal of progress, in certain sectors at least, has been made by Irish since the beginning of the present century and especially since the creation of the State in 1922. Indeed, since 1946, there has been a remarkable increase in the numbers able to speak the language, for in that year only 588,727 (21.2%) were enumerated as Irish-speakers.

The important fact which has to be borne in mind when considering the present situation of the Irish language is that while between a quarter and a third of Ireland's population have a knowledge of Irish, largely as a result of the education system in which the language is extensively taught, the number who have it as their first language and who use it for everyday purposes is generally believed to be no more than 120,000. Precise information on this point is not available but almost all adult Irish-speakers are also able to speak English, which the vast majority do during most of their daily lives. While Irish-speakers are therefore to be found in all parts of the Republic's twenty-six counties, including Dublin (Irish: *Baile Atha Cliath*) and the principal towns, it is only in the extreme west of Ireland that Irish is substantially the medium of daily life for the majority of the population.

The areas where Irish is still spoken as an everyday language were officially designated as *Gaeltacht* areas by the Government's orders of 1956 and 1967. They are now seven in number and lie mainly on the north-west and south-west coasts, comprising parts of Counties Donegal (Irish: *Dún na nGall)*, Mayo *(Maigh Eo)* and Galway *(Gaillimh)*, and smaller districts of Counties Kerry *(Ciarrai)*, Cork *(Corcaigh)*,

Waterford *(Port Láirge)* and Meath *(Mí)*. The total population of the *Gaeltacht* in 1971 was 66,840, of whom 54,940 were Irish-speakers. Excluding the 500 Irish-speakers enumerated in Meath by the 1971 Census (because figures for this area were not available in 1961), this total shows a decrease of 9,335 (3·3%) in the Irish-speaking population of the *Gaeltacht* between 1961 and 1971. During the same decade the number of non-Irish speakers increased from 9,986 to 11,042.

The *Gaeltacht,* now reduced to small, peripheral, poor and isolated communities in the far west of the country, are the last vestiges of a time, twelve centuries ago, when Irish *(Gaeilge)* was the language of the whole of Ireland and when all Irishmen were Gaels.

There is no agreement among scholars about the precise date at which the Irish language, or Gaelic, arrived in Ireland but recent archaeological surveys suggest that the first Irish historians, writing in the eighth century, were fairly accurate in their belief that the coming of the Gaels, a Celtic people, took place in the same period as the conquests of Alexander the Great in 331 B.C. They found another Celtic culture known as the Ivernic, already there, but brought their own oral traditions and language. The word 'Celtic' in this context is only a linguistic term, of course, referring to that Indo-European family of languages which spread over Europe and parts of Asia during the two thousand years before Christ. It is therefore known that many different ethnic strains must have been amalgamated in the solidly Irish-speaking population which existed in Ireland when written records began in the fifth century A.D., and when the Latin alphabet was introduced with Christianity. Up to then the Irish had developed an alphabet of their own, the Ogham script, which was written mainly on stone. As most of these inscriptions consist mostly of proper names in the genitive case they are of little historical value, although they reveal a certain amount about the language used. These forms are to later Irish what Latin is to French and belong to a period before the arrival of Christian missionaries but also to one when Latin grammar had reached as far as Ireland. They were abandoned in the seventh century, together with

BALLYCASTLE

CREESLOUGH

LIMAVADY

LETTERKENNY DERRY

DONEGAL STRABANE

BELFAST

KILLYBEGS

ARMAGH

ENNISKILLEN KEADY

NEWRY

KILLALA

MALLARANY

MAYO

CONG

GALWAY

GALWAY

MEATH

TRIM

DUBLIN

KERRY

WATERFORD

ANASCAUL

DUNGARVAN

CORK

SNEEM

MACROOM

CLEAR ISLAND

THE GAELTACHTA
OF IRELAND & RELIGIONS OF
NORTHERN IRELAND

Areas where over 25% of
population speak Gaelic

Catholic areas
of Northern Ireland

Border with Northern
Ireland

County boundaries

paganism, and replaced by Irish, the language of the people by that time, and were written in Roman letters. This form, the earliest which is thoroughly known, is called Old Irish and it remained fairly uniform from about the year 600 to 900. A considerable body of literature survives from this period.

A little before the year 600 Irish colonists had taken their language to Scotland, to the Isle of Man and to Wales. It did not last very long in Wales, although a few Ogham stones are to be found there. In the Isle of Man, Irish survived even the Scandinavian invasions and has been displaced by English only in the last two hundred years. In Scotland it became the language of almost the entire country but was soon challenged by the spread of English from the south. The Lowland Scots were well aware of this language's origins, calling it *Erse*, which is the Scots form of the word *Irish*. By today the Celtic languages of Scotland and Man are known as Gaelic, a name also applicable to Irish insofar as all these languages are known by names deriving from the Old Irish *Goídelg* which, with the noun *Goídel*, was borrowed from the Welsh *Gwyddel* (Irishman) and *Gwyddeleg* (the Irish language). Both the Irish words may be derived from the Welsh word *gwydd* (wild, uncultivated) as applied to early Irish settlers in Wales. The modern Irish word *Gael* came to mean those who maintained the native language and culture, in contrast to the *Gall* (originally a Gaul), which was used to refer to Scandinavian, Norman and English invaders. The present account will sometimes use 'Gaels' to refer to the speakers of Irish. But as the normal usage in Ireland today is to describe the national language as Irish not Gaelic, this is the word which will be employed here. Gaelic is therefore reserved for the language of the Highlands and Islands of Scotland.

The Old Irish period came to an end around the year 900 with the destruction by the Vikings of the monasteries where the standard language had been upheld. The Middle Irish period, from 900 to 1200, represents the struggle between the speech of the common people and older forms defended by scholars who no longer had the authority to impose them. By now, and during the Norman invasions of Ireland, the education of Irishmen was in the hands of the Bardic Schools which had replaced the monastic system of the previous period and which continued to use Irish. For the next four and a half centuries the Irish language flourished, in its Early Modern or Classical Period, as the great powers of the land maintained with their patronage the poets and scholars who made Ireland's name famous throughout Europe.

The political collapse of Gaelic Ireland is usually dated from the battle of Kinsale in 1601. Up to then Irish had been the language of the whole country outside Dublin and a few other English-speaking settlements. Educated people had used it as a rich and versatile language with centuries of cultivation behind it and there had been a vigorous popular tradition, both literary and oral. But after Kinsale the aristocracy was ruined and with it the scholars who had maintained the classical language. From then on it began not only to decay as the dialects of the common people took their place, but to fail in all parts of Ireland under pressure from English. Also at this time Scottish Gaelic and Manx began to develop in their own ways, to become in time independent languages. Over the next two centuries the language receded further and further towards the west, to the narrow valleys, rocky peninsulas and small islands of the western and southern coasts which are the *Gaeltacht* today.

The fate of Ireland and the Irish language from the first arrival of the Gaels is well illustrated by the poetry written in it up to the seventeenth century. The beginnings of the Gaelic tradition are to be seen in *Leabhar Gabhala* (The Book of Invasions) which records how the relations of Noah, 'great primitive princes of our line', refused places in the Ark just before the Flood, 'watched the soft edge of Ireland draw near'. Irish patriotism became a theme of this poetry at an early date: Amergin, presumed to be the first known Gaelic poet or *file*, was followed through five centuries by many a poet who sang of his devotion to Ireland in victory and defeat with the sixth-century Colmcille the representative saint: 'I have loved the land of Ireland almost beyond speech'. The same tenacious attachment to people and territory is clearly discernible in the famous epic *Táin Bó Cuailnge* (The Cattle Raid of Cooley) and the Fenian Cycle.

The bard's central role in Gaelic life continued into the Middle Ages. In a predominantly oral culture he had been a mixture of historian, politician and priest, a repository of learning and magic, especially when a monk. By the thirteenth century the bards had become members of a professional caste who had to learn how to praise patrons by mastering and practising the traditional Gaelic metres. Theirs was an aristocratic poetry in poems of *amour courtois* whose principal exponents, Gerald Fitzgerald (died 1398) and Pierce Ferriter (died 1653) were Normans who adopted the bardic tradition and contributed greatly to it. If by their wit, passion and elegance these medieval Gaelic poets remind the reader of such English Elizabethans as Surrey, Raleigh and John Davies, contemporaries of Fitzgerald, it should be noted that several of the English poets of the time had a leading hand in the destruction of a society which produced poetry quite similar to their own. For by the time Edmund Spenser (c. 1552-99) had began to write, the systematic annihilation of Gaelic culture was well under way. Had circumstances been more favourable than the English Crown allowed, Ireland seemed capable of achieving as much in literature as its neighbour. But a unique culture now went down under Henry VIII's system of political suppression which was both vicious and thorough. The last of the bards, like Tadgh Dall O Huiginn (died 1591) and David O'Bruadair, (1625-98) sang of their country's defeat and the prohibition of its language: 'The pride of my country I sang through forty long years of good rhyme without any avail . . . So I'll sing no more songs for the men who care nothing for me'. Even then Gaelic tradition was not quite dead: there were poets like Egan O'Rahilly (1670-1835), Anthony Raftery (1784-1835) and Brian Merriman (1747-1805), whose *Cúirt an Mheán Oíche* (The Midnight Court, 1850) remains a classic. But the end was drawing near and the wish of the poet Sir John Davies in 1612 seemed about to be granted: 'We may conceive and hope that the next generation will in tongue and heart, and every way else, become English; so that there will be no difference or distinction but the Irish sea between us'.

One of the ironic consequences of the English Government's policies in Ireland, however, was that when—over a century later—the Irish language had ceased to be a medium for major writing, it was replaced by verse in English which was staunchly nationalist in tone and thus more able to reach wider audiences in Ireland. Although under the influence of London as the literary capital of the British Isles the verse of Thomas Moore (1779-1852) was famous for its cloying charm, it was in his work and that of his contemporaries, James Clarence Mangan (1803-44) and Samuel Ferguson (1810-86), that the idea of a specifically Irish literature in English began to emerge. In turning to folk-song and ballads these poets were writing in English the kind of poetry that Owen Roe O'Sullivan (1748-84) had composed in Irish in a last, desperate attempt to reach his dwindling audiences in the west of Ireland. As Irish declined as a spoken language it came to be sung more and more and many of the songs were based on anonymous Gaelic originals, the last remains of the country tradition. Thus began an Irish literature in English which was later to have its outstanding exemplars in W. B. Yeats, J. M. Synge, Sean O'Casey and James Joyce.

From the end of the seventeenth century, and from the Treaty of Limerick in 1691, right up to the Great Famine of 1845-50, that Irish continued to be the language of the rural areas of Ireland, although not of the middle-class and aristocracy, was largely attributable to the poets and priests who strove to defend it for their own purposes. The poets sought new patrons among the common people by promising that Catholicism and Irish would one day be restored to favour, while the priests were well aware that the language provided an effective barrier to the progress of Protestantism. In 1773, for example, the Pope was informed that the bishops of Ireland believed it essential that the students at the Irish College in Rome should be trained in both English and Irish. Catechisms and works of poetry were already published in Irish, first on the continent and later at home. In 1768 an Irish dictionary was published in Paris for the express purpose of helping priests in Irish-speaking parishes and in 1798 the clergy of Kerry prevented the appointment of a Corkman as bishop of the diocese because he knew no Irish. After 1782, however, when Catholic colleges became legal, the language which became the medium of higher education was English. Abroad too, the great schools like those of St Omer and Douai, where many sons of wealthy Irish families were educated in penal times, provided what was known as 'a good English and classical education'. The Catholic middle-classes who aspired to higher education now took advantage of the repeal of the penal laws by demanding similar institutions in Ireland. Maynooth College, founded in 1795, went 'with the English tide' and from it many English-speaking priests left to serve in Irish-speaking parishes. It could hardly have been otherwise for there was, at this time, a severe lack of printing facilities; Irish was far from being standardised, few scholars and no university were interested in it as a living language.

By the year 1800* the pressure of six centuries of foreign occupation but particularly the political, religious and economic pressures exerted by English government in Ireland during the previous two hundred years, had killed Irish at the top of the social scale and had seriously weakened its position everywhere else. The language had been excluded from Parliament, the law-courts, local government, the civil service and commercial life in the towns. Yet, around 1840, before the Famine, there were more Irish-speakers in Ireland than at any time in its history and there seemed to be few who were perturbed that it might disappear, at least among the lower classes. When the first Census to include questions about Irish was taken in 1851, the language was still spoken by about a million and a half people, or 23% of Ireland's population. But by now Irish had come to be quite definitely associated with the poor and uneducated, for all but a few Irish-speakers at this time were unable to read and write their language. The hedge-schools run by barely literate peasants, in the years up to the Famine, taught the three Rs in English and from 1760, when the struggle against soaring rents and tithes began in earnest, a knowledge of English was essential for survival. Unlike the Gaels of Scotland whose lack of English often led to their exploitation by English landlords, the Irish acquired at least a rudimentary knowledge of their masters' language between 1745 and 1845.

Typical of his time was the case of the Archbishop of

---

*The present account draws heavily on the essays edited by B. Ó Cuiv: *A View of the Irish Language* (Dublin, 1969).

Tuam, John MacHale, one of the few enthusiasts for spoken Irish during the first half of the nineteenth century. Born in County Mayo in 1791, the son of monoglot Irish-speakers, he recalled in later years how his father, determined that he should speak nothing but English, instructed the hedge-schoolmaster to hang a 'screen' or tally around the boy's neck and to notch it every time he spoke Irish so that when the notches reached a certain number the child would be flogged. Commenting on this practice in *The Gaelic League Idea* (Cork, 1972), David Greene writes: 'No British government prescribed these brutalities, anymore than did the landlords or the priests, though the representatives of authority no doubt turned a blind eye to them; it is clear that the system of policing and flogging was planned and carried out by the parents and school-masters working in co-operation. Over a quarter of the Irish people was bent on linguistic suicide'. So began the custom which, whether as 'the Welsh Not' or *le symbole* in Brittany, was to spread throughout the countries where the Celtic languages were spoken, and elsewhere, during the nineteenth century.

The aims of the National Schools which followed the hedge-schools after 1831 was to raise their pupils as law-abiding, British citizens, but—although they had a huge success in stamping out the Irish language—in their first aim they failed. Soon there was a great increase in the number of schools and children, the knowledge of English spread as Irish continued to decline—and a new generation was preparing to overthrow British rule in Ireland. The process usually went something like this: a clever child of poor parents might, with some sacrifice by his family, become a teacher in the National Schools, or join the Royal Irish Constabulary, or even the Post Office or the Civil Service. So it was, from around 1878 when secondary education was brought within the reach of the poor classes, that many of the workers in the national revival of the late nineteenth century sprang from the people who had been intended as the products and champions of the British Government in Ireland. The decline of Irish and the growth of a nationalist movement cannot be attributed to the National Schools alone, however. Equally devastating in its effects was the Great Famine during which about one million and a half people died, and another million emigrated. As they were usually from poor, rural areas they can be presumed to be, for the most part, Irish-speaking. Those who survived the failure of the potato crop went mostly to America where, as poor immigrants with little of value except their *fáinne* (rings) they gave a new word, *phoney*, to the language of that continent, lost their own language after a generation or so, became policemen or politicians in New York and where, still inexplicably proud of their origins but good American citizens, their descendants wear shamrocks and drink green beer on Saint Patrick's Day.

At the same time as the Irish began to lose their language on a massive scale, they entered politics for the first time. Their complete isolation from political life, which had helped to keep them Irish-speaking, came to an end with the emergence of the movement known as the United Irishmen in the 1790s. After 1798, when the Fenian rising led by Wolfe Tone was crushed, a new type of Irish nationalism began to gain ground, and it was propagated almost entirely in English. Irish words were used in nationalist circles, then as now, but often by people whose vocabulary was limited to such phrases as *Erin go Bragh* (Ireland Forever). Long before the Famine the harp and shamrock had been used by Daniel O'Connell (1775-1847) and the Home Rulers and now, particularly among the emigrants, the sentimental aspect of Irish nationality came to the fore. It was a critical moment in the nation's history for, if only the language had been given a more important place in the political movement, it might have been saved and restored as the principal language of Ireland. Instead, Ireland and the world warmed to the melodies of Thomas Moore while Irish was relegated to the cabins of the far west where for the majority of Gaels, republicanism had always been largely incomprehensible and therefore ignored. There the people continued to speak Irish not because they were in love with the Dark Rosaleen or Cathleen ni Houlihan, as Ireland came to be popularly known, or because they were consumed by revolutionary fervour, but because it was, quite simply but incontrovertibly, their own language and because they were essentially a conservative people. Meanwhile, over the larger part of the country, more and more people learned to read English in order to follow in newspapers the fortunes of their political leaders. Beginning with O'Connell in 1823 and continuing with the Repeal Movement, the Tenant League, the Home Rule Movement and the Land League, English replaced Irish as the language required by Irishmen in their efforts to throw off the English yoke.

By 1891 the decline of Irish was self-evident: only 14·5% of the population could speak it, fewer than 1% were monoglot Irish-speakers, and only a handful of people were able to read and write it. One of the first problems facing those who wished to see a revival of the language towards the end of the nineteenth century was that it was necessary to reach agreement on how Irish was to be written. Some traditionalists argued in favour of resurrecting the classical language, pointing to the example of Wales where the sixteenth century Bible still provided the basis of literary Welsh. The tradition had remained unbroken in Wales, however, whereas in Ireland all contact with the classical standards of Irish had been lost. The initial argument over what constituted written Irish was eventually won by those who claimed that the speech of the people, that is whatever a 'native speaker' of Irish said, was correct. Thus began the habit of giving to the Irish of the *Gaeltacht* an importance which has persisted to the present time. In a strictly linguistic sense, this was an informed attitude for its day, as David Greene has shown, but it was faulty in that it ignored the need for a standardised language to be used in education and administration. All attempts to impose one dialect on the speakers of other dialects, or the vague hope of revivalists like Osborn Bergin that one day one dialect, perhaps that of West Munster, would emerge supreme, came to nothing. For the next fifty years the only semblance of a standard was an orthography based on classical Irish which, although used by nearly all writers, was inadequate to represent the sounds of the various dialects spoken by the people. Dineen's *Irish-English Dictionary*, first published in 1904, followed this example and, re-appearing in an enlarged edition in 1927, it remains the fullest lexicographical work on the modern language.

When the Irish language revival movement began in the closing decades of the nineteenth century, the first lesson learned from a study of Ireland's history was that it was not a question of one language receding before the advance of another, but of a society which used one language being overthrown and subjugated in a political struggle. Two nations, two languages, two civilisations, had been competing with one another for supremacy and Irish had lost. In the year 1541, when Henry VIII had been proclaimed King of Ireland by his Parliament in Dublin, his speech had to be translated into Irish for the benefit of his court. Yet it was that same Parliament which took the first steps towards the Tudor conquest: 'Be it enacted that every person or persons, the King's true subjects, inhabiting this land of Ireland . . . shall bring up children in such places, where they shall or may have occasion to learn the English tongue, language, order and condition'. This measure, the Act of 1537, was enforced only as far as the writ of Parliament ran, but from being confined to the Pale, or eastern Ireland, the King's authority was in force all over the country by the end of Elizabeth I's reign. The political advance of the Tudors and their suppression of the Irish language went hand in hand: for the English Government the extermination of Irish was the *sine qua non* for giving permanence to what was being achieved politically. It is necessary to emphasise this close connection between Ireland's political defeat and the demise of its language in order to appreciate why, over four centuries later, some political leaders strove to strengthen the language in their efforts to win back for Ireland its own political institutions.

The beginnings of a new interest in the revival of Irish can be traced to the end of the eighteenth century. They were partly antiquarian and partly the result of Romanticism which was sweeping Europe in the wake of McPherson's Ossian. Some of the leaders of the United Irishmen, such as Lord Edward Fitzgerald and Robert Emmett, had made attempts to learn Irish. They were exceptions, however: in a century during which very few political leaders bothered about the language, what interest there was came from Young Irelanders like Thomas Davis (1814-45), and Smith O'Brien (1852-1928), and from Fenians like O'Donovan Rossa (1831-1915) rather than from constitutional leaders like O'Connell and Charles Parnell.

The contrast between the attitudes of O'Connell and Davis—the first of Gaelic and Catholic stock with a fluent knowledge of Irish but happy to promote the use of English, the other of an Anglo-Irish and Protestant family with only a little Irish at his command but devoted to its restoration—is one of the many apparent paradoxes of Ireland's history. While O'Connell's view was shared by the majority of his contemporaries, Davis was a pioneer in this respect whose influence on later generations was more than that on his own. Where the scholars ignored the existence of the living language, Thomas Davis advocated its cultivation and restoration: 'Irish should be cherished, taught and esteemed, it could be preserved and gradually extended', he wrote in his newspaper, *The Nation.*

Many of his famous utterances, such as 'A people without a language of its own is only half a nation' and 'To have lost entirely the national language is death: the fetter has worn through' were to be re-echoed by patriots of the next generation, and not only in Ireland. Before Thomas Davis the many societies interested in Irish had been scholarly and defensive, more devoted to manuscripts than in the language's survival. Neither the Gaelic Society of Dublin (1806), nor the Iberno-Celtic Society (1818), nor the Irish Archeological Society (1840), for example, had any interest in contemporary literature. The usual attitude towards Irish-speakers was expressed in a pamphlet published in 1822: 'The barbarous tongue in which they converse operates as an effectual bar to any literary attainment'. It is known that two of the most eminent Irish scholars of the day, O'Curry and O'Donovan, both native speakers of Irish, invariably spoke English to one another and brought up their children without a knowledge of Irish. O'Donovan referred to the language spoken by over a million of his countrymen as 'local jargon' and believed that the proper duty of scholars was to collect as much as possible of the ancient lore of Ireland before the death of the language made it impossible. The only exception to this general rule was the Ulster Gaelic Society (1830) which concerned itself not only with 'the venerable remains of ancient Irish literature' but with the teaching and publishing of the language. Thomas Davis's work, his poems and ballads, his journalism, his progressive social views and his attractive personality, marked a new beginning in Ireland's history. Like many another language, Irish owes to one for whom it was not the mother-tongue an immeasurable debt.

The population of Ireland in 1891 was not much greater than it is at present but it had a different distribution and was largely rural. Emigration, having begun at the Great Famine, was still in full spate and poverty was rampant both in the towns and countryside. The entire island was part of the British Empire and the split brought about by the fall of Parnell had broken the political spirit of the people. Irish, spoken by some 700,000 people, was still regarded as a symbol of poverty and illiteracy, especially by the townsfolk of the English-speaking east.

Without the example set by Thomas Davis it is unlikely that the society which was to lead the Irish language revival into the twentieth century could have been founded as early as 1893. The Gaelic League *(Conradh na Gaeilge)* grew out of the Gaelic Union, publisher of the first periodical *Irisleabhar na Gaeilge* (1882) and earlier societies like the Society for the Preservation of the Irish Language founded by David Comyn in 1876, which had campaigned for the teaching of Irish in the intermediate schools. Comyn's society had brought about a small concession on the part of the Government: Irish was recognised as an additional subject to be taught outside school hours, the 'screen' and attendant flogging for speaking Irish had been abolished. Yet in 1888 the language was being taught in only about fifty-one National Schools and there only as an extra, optional subject. Nothing further had been done to preserve the language in the *Gaeltacht*. Different from all its predecessors, the Gaelic League was exclusively concerned with the revival of the Irish language and its culture. It set out, with men like Douglas Hyde, Eoin McNeill and Father Eugene O'Growney among its members, to provide leadership and to change the attitude of the Irish people to their own language. The

League's principal aims were the revival of Irish as the vernacular of the entire Irish people and the creation of a new literature in Irish. 'The moment Ireland broke with her Gaelic past', wrote Douglas Hyde, the League's founder, 'she fell away hopelessly from all intellectual and artistic effort'.

The Gaelic League grew very slowly but surely. At first money was scarce and the public apparently apathetic. By 1897 it had only forty-three branches, although by 1902 there were 227 and by 1904 nearly 600 with a total membership of about 50,000. It is difficult to say precisely why the League, founded by 'a half-dozen nonentities' as Douglas Hyde described himself and his colleagues, met with its success. In part it was because the leaders had served in the earlier societies and saw the need for a more dynamic approach, but also because their zeal had a direct appeal to ordinary people, especially the young. But the main reason was that in the political field Ireland was becoming more and more ripe for such a movement. Two events were to prove decisive for its progress: the publication of Father O'Growney's *Simple Lessons in Irish* and the appointment of organisers whose task it was to set up branches in all parts of the country. As so few were able to read and write in Irish, colleges for the training of teachers had to be opened, beginning with *Coláiste na Mumhan* at Ballingeary in 1904, at which students also learned the traditional arts of instrumental music, dancing, storytelling and singing. In time the League began to publish *The Gaelic Journal* as well as books in Irish and soon there was well over a hundred pamphlets to explain its aims and on subjects related to the language's revival. Within two years it could claim that, thanks to its efforts, the position of Irish in both intermediate and primary schools had been improved and that a growing number of county councils supported its aims. At the same time, however, it is true that about one third of all secondary school pupils and almost three-quarters of primary pupils were still not being taught in Irish at school by 1921. In 1913 a place for Irish as a compulsory subject in matriculation for the National University was secured, and much of the League's doctrines became incorporated into the programme of *Sinn Fein* (Ourselves Alone), the Nationalist Party of Ireland. As an early Leaguer had said, 'Every speech we make throughout the country makes bullets to fire at the enemy'. Patrick Pearse was to write in 1914: 'I have said again and again that when the Gaelic League was formed in 1893 the Irish revolution began'.

Only in one respect did the Gaelic League fail, at least in part: despite the creation of a new literature, the achievement of those who learned Irish under the League's auspices and the many more who sympathised with its aims, the primary aim of 'preserving and extending the use of the spoken tongue' proved much more difficult to realise. Hyde's dream of an Irish-speaking Ireland meant that the entire movement should have been based and built on the *Gaeltacht*. But the economic and social rehabilitation of the *Gaeltacht* could not be carried out because it involved political organisation and agitation which the Gaelic League was not prepared to consider. The *Gaeltacht* therefore continued to decay while the new political parties of the day used the League as a recruiting ground and paid only lip-service to its policies. They had little choice for it was by now clear that Hyde's vision of an Irish-speaking Ireland was more inspiring than anything yet offered to the Irish people and they were responding with enthusiasm. It thus became evident early in the League's history that no voluntary organisation unsupported by the Government would hope to achieve this status for Irish.

Douglas Hyde, the first President of the Gaelic League, had been the quickest to realise the dangers involved in introducing political and religious views to the constitution of the new movement. It was to be twenty-one years before the *Ard Fheis,* the League's Council, was to admit political freedom as one of its aims. Yet many of those already entirely engaged in such organisations as the Irish Republican Brotherhood, a secret society, the army known as the Irish Volunteers and the party *Sinn Fein,* were members also of the Gaelic League and, although officially 'non-political' this society proved to be the greatest force in the Nationalist ranks. Most of the leaders of the Easter Rising of 1916, including Patrick Pearse, were members of the League and if, during the years that followed, it was military struggle which won independence, it was certainly 'the Gaelic League idea' of rebuilding an Irish-speaking Ireland which inspired the Nationalist Movement. Pearse's definition of an Ireland 'not free merely, but Gaelic as well; not Gaelic merely, but free as well', was the aim from the start. Even during the height of the Civil War, Michael Collins was to declare, 'We only succeeded after we had begun to get back our Irish ways, after we had made a serious effort to speak our own language, after we had striven again to govern ourselves. How can we express our most subtle thought and finest feelings in a foreign tongue? Irish will scarcely be our language in this generation, not even perhaps in the next. But until we have it again on our tongues and in our minds, we are not free'.

With the establishment of the Irish Free State in 1919 the restoration of the language was among the first priorities of the Government. The first session of the Irish Parliament in 1919 was held largely in Irish and the first *Dail* created a Ministry of the Irish Language with Douglas Hyde at its head. But by this time the Gaelic League was no longer the force it had been at the turn of the century. In one sense, it had been infiltrated and transformed by activists like Pearse who had seen the connection between the language and Statehood. By its identification of cultural and political aims, the League had brought about its own downfall, at least as an influential cultural organisation. Many felt, now that Ireland was free, it would soon become Gaelic as well and there was no longer need for voluntary organisations. Furthermore, the advent of partition and the loss of the six northern counties, and the disastrous Civil War, had caused bitterness and disillusion. Some of the League's leaders had died, some shot by the British in 1916 or by their compatriots in the Civil War, or they had emigrated. Also, it must be added, the ham-handed and hyprocritical way in which the new State carried out its language policies during the years between the two World Wars made it difficult for the League to function properly. New organisations now arose—*Glún na Bua* and *An Comhchaidreamh* were two of many—all rebelling against the League's failure to achieve its aims.

The Census of 1926 gave some indication of what had been happening to the Irish language over the previous thirty years, despite all the efforts of the Gaelic League: the total number of Irish-speakers had declined by over 120,000 (18%). Connacht and Munster had lost about 100,000, the position of the language in Ulster had remained much the same, while Leinster recorded an increase from 14,000 to 101,000. In the western countries it was the native speakers who had disappeared whereas in Leinster the increase was among learners of the language. Of those who claimed to know Irish in 1926, it is estimated by Brendán S. Mac Aodha in *The Gaelic League Idea* that only between 5% and 10% had really mastered it. In other words the League, after thirty years of activity, had failed to prevent the contraction of the *Gaeltacht* and had transformed, either directly or through the schools, some 5,000 to 10,00 English-speakers into fluent speakers of Irish.

On the other hand, some real progress had been made in other directions. Whereas in 1891 the ability to write Irish was almost non-existent and only a few hundred could read it, the Gaelic League had not only spread literacy among its members, both in the *Gaeltacht* and elsewhere, but had provided books and periodicals in the language—about 400 works between 1900 and 1925. Nevertheless, it is true to say that, although the Gaelic League had made an important contribution to the establishment of the Irish State, its first aim of restoring Irish as the language of the people was far from realisation.

What had gone wrong? Brendán S. Mac Aodha suggests a number of reasons for the League's failure. In the first place, it did not fully appreciate the scale or the difficulty of the problems involved in the task of cultural revival. It could not exercise any real control over the economic destiny of the *Gaeltacht*. It made the mistake of becoming directly involved in politics thereby identifying the nation with the State and, once the State was established it virtually opted out of responsibility for the language's promotion. This is reflected in the sudden decrease in the number of its branches: after the Treaty, of the 819 branches in 1922 only 139 remained in 1924. Fifthly, both the League and its successor, the State, lacked clearly defined objectives and tried to solve problems by *ad hoc* measures rather than by long-term policies backed by research and hard work. By presuming that the establishment of an Irish State ensured the preservation of Irish culture the League left the Government and its 'gombeen men' with no effective critics. The *Gaeltacht* was allowed to wither away and the Government's dedication to it became more and more a dead letter. Finally, the League is indicted for failing to mould, according to its own principles, the State which more than any other body it had called into being.

However limited the success of the Gaelic League in its heyday, what happened subsequently reflects little credit on its successor, the Irish State. By 1966, fifty years after Pearse had proclaimed *Poblacht na hEireann*, the Provisional Government of the Irish Republic, from the steps of the General Post Office in Dublin, the number of people for whom Irish was their mother-tongue had dropped to less than 70,000 or much less than 20% of what it had been at the foundation of the State. This decrease in the number of native-speakers was more than counter-balanced by a steady increase in the numbers of those who had studied the language at school and could claim to speak it. According to the 1961 Census over 7000,000 people, or almost a quarter of the Republic's population, knew some Irish. How much they knew it is difficult to say, but it seems likely that only 5 to 10%, or 35,000 to 70,000 people had become fluent Irish-speakers. When this figure is added to the figure for native-speakers, the total number of Irish-speakers therefore stood at about 140,000, or one-fifth of what had existed in 1891.

It is therefore not surprising that the *Gaeltacht* has assumed a special significance in any consideration of the Irish language's future. For the majority of those who are able to speak Irish, with varying degrees of accuracy and fluency, it is a second language acquired at school or in some other way. As a spoken language, Irish is still confined to a comparatively small number of people, mostly farmers and fishermen, on the western and southern coasts. Although it now has a population of less than 1% of the Republic's, the *Gaeltacht* contains not only the sole surviving communities where Irish has never ceased to be spoken, but it is also the source from which the majority of Irish-speakers, those who have learned the language, can learn to speak it fluently. In 1866 there were nearly a million Gaels in the coastal areas between Waterford and Donegal, in 1891 there were 580,000 or about

90% of all Irish-speakers in Ireland, so that native-speakers outnumbered learners by about nine to one. In 1922 the number was halved again, to about 200,000, again by 1939 to 100,000, and again by 1963, leaving less than 50,000. Thus in every generation during the last century the Gaelic population has fallen to one half of what it was in the previous generation, so that by now there are ten Irish-speakers who have learned the language to every native-speaker. Should a decrease similar to that which occurred between 1926 and 1956 take place again within the next thirty years or so, it seems likely, as the Commission on the Restoration of the Irish language has stated, that the *Gaeltacht* will be wiped out during the next generation, by about 1995. It is widely believed that if the *Gaeltacht* disappears the will to maintain Irish as a spoken tongue in the rest of Ireland will probably die with it.

The fate of the Irish language therefore depends on the seven districts officially designated as *Gaeltacht* areas by the Government in 1956 and 1967. The largest is in County Donegal where, out of a total population of about 23,000 in 1971, 18,321 were Irish-speaking. It is divided into four parts: in the south-west, the villages of *Cill Charthaigh, Teileann* and *Ard an Latha:* in *Lar Thir Chonaill* the five communities of Fintown, Edenfinfreagh, Dochary, Lettermacaward and Letterbrick: in *Gaoth Dobhair* the villages of *Anagaire, Bun Beag, Gort a'Choirce* and *Fol Carrach;* the fourth part is a number of scattered Irish-speaking pockets along the Fanad Peninsula and around *Ros Goill*. Also belonging to the Donegal *Gaeltacht* are Aran Island *(Arainn Mhor)* with a population of 773 and *Toraigh* (Tory Island) with 273. The second largest *Gaeltacht* is in County Galway and includes *Cois Fharraige,* the area around *Caethru Rua,* north Connemara, *Carna-Rosmuc,* Claregalway and the Aran Islands. This *Gaeltacht* has a population of 20,400 of whom 17,698 are Irish-speaking. In County Mayo the *Gaeltacht* includes *Achill, An Corran, Gob an Choire, Dumha Eige,* the Erris peninsula, *Ceathru Thaidhg, Ros Dumbach,* the area around *Tuar Mhic Eadaigh,* with 9,270 Irish-speakers. The *Gaeltacht* of County Kerry consists of *Corca Dhuibhne,* which takes in the Dingle peninsula including the villages of *Baile an*

Fheirtearaigh, Dun Chaoin, Baile na nGall and *An Clochan*, with a population of 6,200, and to the south *Uibh Rathach*, which includes the villages of *An Caladh, Baile an Sceilig, Cathar Donall* and Waterville (population 2,300). The total number of Irish-speakers in this *Gaeltacht* is 6,200. In County Meath, the villages of *Baile Gib* and *Rath cairn*, about forty miles from Dublin, where Irish-speaking familes from Galway, Mayo and Kerry were re-settled in the 1930s, about 900 persons in all, were designated as *Gaeltacht* areas in 1967. The population of the only *Gaeltacht* in County Water-ford, at *An Rinn*, was enlarged in 1971 from 866 to 1,073, of whom 730 are Irish-speakers, when the adjacent district of *An Sean a'Phobal* was added to it. The *Gaeltacht* of County Cork, with 2,700 Irish-speakers out of a total population of 3,700, comprises *Cuil Aodh, Baile Bhuirne* and *Beal Atha an Ghaorthaidh*, while off the coast *Oilean Cleire* has 192 Irish-speakers.

The decline in the Irish-speaking population of the *Gaeltacht* has come about in two ways: the geographical area in which Irish is spoken has contracted: there are portions in all seven counties of the *Gaeltacht* where the language is now spoken only by people over sixty, while other portions have gone entirely English-speaking since 1940. Secondly, the population of the *Gaeltacht* has not increased at the same rate as that in the rest of the country. Although the total number of Irish-speakers in the Republic of Ireland increased between 1961 and 1971 from 716,420 (27·2%) to 789,429 (28·3%), and from 588,725 (21·2%) in 1946, the Irish-speaking population of the *Gaeltacht* decreased during the decade 1961-71 from 64,275 (86.6%) to 54,940 (83.3%). The population of the Dingle peninsula, for example, was 8,300 in 1891. By 1901 it had fallen to 4,342 and to 2,156 in 1961.

The numerical decline of the *Gaeltacht* has gone hand in hand with a deterioration in the quality of the Irish spoken there. The last monoglots have died and the Irish-speaker today has lost if not the fluency then the vocabulary of his parents and grand-parents. This trend has serious con-sequences for the continuance of writing in the language. Throughout the revival period the writers have been either native-speakers of Irish or they have spent prolonged periods in the *Gaeltacht*. The total collapse of the *Gaeltacht* will mean, or so it is believed, not only the end of creative writing in Irish but that those who are not native-speakers will find it impossible to acquire fluency in the language. The problem is exacerbated by the fact that Irish exists in a number of dialects from which it draws much of its strength. Since 1945 there has been some standardisation, conservative enough but preferable to the chaos which reigned before that date, when enthusiastic amateurs had tried to create a synthetic form for Irish which was completely divorced from the living language. Even up to recent years primary school-books had to be published in three dialect versions based on the Irish of Connacht, Munster and Ulster and people from these provinces took it in turns to read the news on radio. The authorities and scholars were reluctant to intervene because it was feared that the small number of native-speakers, on whose continuing interest the survival of the language depended, would resent linguistic standards which appeared to be imposed from outside the *Gaeltacht*.

A further problem has been whether or not to use the Gaelic script in preference to the Roman. The decision to abandon the Gaelic script was taken in 1952 but was not implemented until 1963 when it was dropped in the infant classes of primary schools: it appeared for the last time in examination papers for the School Leaving Certificate in 1972. The Roman script was already in use during the 1930s and has now replaced the Gaelic script in printing and for official purposes.

The plight of the *Gaeltacht* is that most of its land is not productive enough to give the people a standard of living as high as that which is now common in the rest of Ireland. The Government's efforts during the past fifty years to improve the economic condition of these areas have almost invariably led to further weakening of the language traditionally spoken there. Relief of congestion on the land, for example, has meant loss of population, while the establishment of small industries and the improvement of communications has often led to the arrival of English-speakers. This trend is usually followed by the training of Gaels in English, who after mastering English leave to work elsewhere. Comparison between the depressed *Gaeltacht* and the more prosperous world outside, whether in America, England or Ireland, produces a psychological reaction against the traditional way of life, which comes to be seen as old-fashioned and unworthy, while the modern, affluent society elsewhere seems more desirable. It is still true, despite the coming of cars, telephones, television and other facilities to the *Gaeltacht* in recent years, that the Irish language for many of its native-speakers is associated with poverty, drudgery and backwardness. Abandonment of Irish and the adoption of English has seemed a necessary step on the road to social advancement. The first attempts to reverse this trend which are now under way have to take into account the *Gaeltacht's* present desperate situation.

There are signs that the Irish Government has woken up to face reality. In 1975 it passed an estimate of £6 million for the Department of the *Gaeltacht* to be spent through a new body known as *Gaeltarra Eireann,* the equivalent of the Industrial Development Authority in the rest of Ireland. This money is intended to be used for the purpose of attracting new industries and developing industrial schemes on housing, the promotion of tourism, marine projects, electricity installations, grants to education, cultural activities, and as subventions to organisations engaged in promoting Irish in the *Gaeltacht.*

A number of bodies already exist with the development of the *Gaeltacht* as their primary aim. In Donegal, for example, there are several co-operative societies like the one at Glencolumbkille *(Gleann Cholm Cille),* marketing crafts and holiday cottages, organising land reclamation schemes; small factories making tweeds and potato crisps have been opened, and there are others canning fish, and cutting Achill quartz. Among the organisations set up in Galway are *Comharchumann Chois Farraige* while in Mayo the co-operative society *Comhar Iorrais* has recently joined with *Gaeltarra Eireann* in develop-ing several thousand acres in the north of the county. And in Kerry the co-operative known as *Comharchumann Forbartha Chorca Dhuibhne* organises agricultural schemes and promotes Irish-language summer schools. There are about twenty-five co-operatives in various parts of the *Gaeltacht* and they were supported by Government grants totalling £75,000 during 1974.

The Minister for the *Gaeltacht* since 1973 is Mr Tom O'Donnell, a member of the political party *Fine Gael*. There is speculation that Mr O'Donnell may become the first Minister for Regional Development in the present coalition Government *(Fine Gael* and Labour). If he does, it is clear that he believes the *Gaeltacht*, 'the least developed area in Europe', should have a special claim on the E.E.C.'s regional fund. Meanwhile, he is confident that his Department will have created 6,000 jobs in the *Gaeltacht* by the end of the 1970s. Already, since April 1973, more than a hundred industrial projects and about 2,000 new jobs have been created. Mr O'Donnell was quoted in *The Irish Times*, (2 April 1975) as saying, 'No jobs, no people, no people, no *Gaeltacht*, no *Gaeltacht*, no language'. Furthermore, a special national resources division has been set up by *Gaeltarra Eireann* and the Minister speculates on the chances of oil or gas being found in the *Gaeltacht* or off its coast. A severe problem is the lack of an infrastructure of skilled industrial labour in the *Gaeltacht*. The Minister hopes to recruit key personnel from Gaels who have migrated to Dublin for this purpose. He is also planning a land bank, and a scheme for training business executives in Irish. Emigration from the *Gaeltacht* is not stopped yet, says Mr O'Donnell, 'but I hope that by the end of the present decade it will be totally stopped. That is my whole motivation'. The task before him and his Department is enormous. Over 50% of the *Gaeltacht's* inhabitants are still engaged in agriculture, mainly of a subsistence nature, 11% of the work-force is unemployed and the average income *per capita* is less than 50% of that in Dublin.

Although tourism has declined somewhat in the west of Ireland in recent years, it is making steady progress in the *Gaeltacht*. Small air-ports are being built on the islands of Inishmore and Inishmaan, Ballinskelligs, Inishere and at Gweedore. About a thousand homes with accommodation for some 3,500 visitors are registered with *Roinn na Gaeltachta*. Young people attending Irish-language summer courses in the

Gaeltacht have long been a source of revenue for local families. In 1974 about 17,000 students attended these courses and the Department of the *Gaeltacht* paid out grants of over £378,000. Critics of *Bord Failte* (Irish Tourist Board) are convinced that tourism is doing irreparable damage to the Irish language in the *Gaeltacht* and has contributed over the years to a situation described by the poet W. B. Yeats as 'fumbling in a greasy till'—that the traditional Gaelic hospitality of the areas has been exploited and replaced by the subservient outlook which will sell anything, including land, property and culture, that the visitor demands.

Among the facilities won largely as the result of a campaign led by *Gluaiseacht Cearta Sibialta na Gaeltachta* (Civil Rights Movement of the *Gaeltacht*), an organisation launched in 1970, is the Irish-language radio station *Radio na Gaeltachta*. Set up with Government subsidy of some £344,000, the station first went on the air in 1972 and now has studios in Donegal and Kerry and its headquarters at Costello *(Casta)* in Connemara. It broadcasts on both medium wave and VHF from 6 p.m. to 9.15 p.m. every evening, carrying not only national and world news but items of local interest, and its VHF transmissions are heard all over Ireland. The movement, whose members are mainly students from the universities of Galway and Cork, continues to exist and campaigns for full implementation of official status for the Irish language, following the example of *Cymdeithas yr Iaith Gymraeg* (The Welsh Language Society) by painting out English road signs in the *Gaeltacht*.

There are several other signs that the Irish Government is at last beginning to tackle the *Gaeltacht's* problems. The Minister for the *Gaeltacht* announced in 1975 that a new authority, 'an authority without parallel in Europe', to be known as *Udaras na Gaeltachta* (Local Government Authority of the *Gaeltacht)* was to be set up as a body with wide-ranging powers to involve the Irish-speaking communities in a comprehensive plan of action for their own areas. It was also expected that, based at Furbo like the Department of the *Gaeltacht,* by the end of 1975 it would have assumed the development functions of *Roinn na Gaeltachta*

and *Gaeltarra Eireann* and be given new, broader responsibilities for the economic, social, linguistic and cultural
development of the *Gaeltacht*. It is therefore apparent that
the Government is aware that in order for the *Gaeltacht* to be
saved, planning and investment will have to be priorities and
that, before it can grow, proper financial provision has to be
made for higher education through Irish, for the publication
of a daily newspaper and for the production of television
programmes in the language. Above all, the hyprocisy characteristic of the Government's attitudes towards Irish will have
to be admitted and eliminated. Otherwise, the *Gaeltacht* will
never become the well-spring for the restoration of Irish
throughout the country and, in the words of Sean Ó Tuama in
The Gaelic League Idea, 'if the *Gaeltacht* goes we will have
lost our last chance of continuing and developing as a distinct
cultural community'.

Meanwhile, what is the situation of the Irish language in
the rest of the Republic? There was a time, up to about 1939,
when it seemed that Irish might soon become the spoken
language of the people. Both the main parties, *Fine Gael* and
Fianna Fail, supported this aim, the latter also calling for
national unity in a thirty-two-county State. This was the
period when a writer like Brendan Behan, from Dublin's
working-class, could speak the language fluently, and even
write in it. Under the Presidency of Eamonn de Valera, a keen
enthusiast for the language who always wore the *fainne* in his
lapel to show that he was an Irish-speaker, many of the most
distinguished statesmen of the day were genuinely concerned
about the language's fate. But even then it soon became apparent that Irish was to be reserved for a symbolic or
ceremonial role, especially in such spheres as Parliament, the
Army, the Police and the various political organisations,
while English remained for all practical purposes. One of the
few exceptions was the Gaelic Athletic Association which insisted on the language's use in all its activities and which thus
became a bastion of Irish among the ordinary people. It was
not until the Second World War that the growing realisation
that the narrow base of the *Gaeltacht* needed to be widened
was accepted and seriously considered.

By 1960 it was clear that Irish was about to lose further

ground because there was no adequate provision for it on television. The campaign for a full television service in Irish, preferably an all-Irish second channel, has been led by the Gaelic League which still exists and has regained some of its former influence in the last four years. The society is opposed to the 'open broadcasting' plan of the Minister for Posts and Telegraphs, Dr Conor Cruise O'Brien, by which British television programmes would be shown in Ireland. It has the support of many professional bodies, including that of journalists employed in broadcasting. But the Broadcasting Bill went before the Senate during 1975. Dr O'Brien argues that as 40% of the population already has a choice of channels, it is not reasonable to exclude those who do not live in areas where B.B.C. Ulster Television programmes cannot be seen at the present time. He also believes that the State Broadcasting corporation, *Radio Telefis Eireann,* ought to respond to the challenge of a second channel by a greater emphasis on home-produced programmes. At the moment *Radio Eireann*— broadcasting from 7.30 a.m. to midnight—transmits four short news periods daily and thirty to sixty minutes of material in Irish, although not while *Radio na Gaeltatcha* (which can be heard on V.H.F. all over Ireland) is on the air. *Telefis Eireann,* beginning every day at 5.30 p.m. and finishing around midnight, devotes 2·2% of its time to Irish-language programmes. According to official ratings for 23 March 1975 the current affairs programme *Teach* had 600,000 viewers, while its English-language counterpart 'Seven Days' had 742,000. A late-night discussion programme *Gairm* had an audience of 288,000 and *Nuacht,* the news in Irish, had 456,000. On 8 December 1974, when *Nuacht* was screened at the more favourable time of 7.15 p.m. it had 694,000 viewers—only about a 100,000 fewer than the total number who claimed to know Irish at the 1971 Census. In protest against the absence of a full Irish-language television service, eighteen members of the Gaelic League refused to pay their television licences in April 1975 and the campaign, again following the example of *Cymdeithas yr Iaith Gymraeg* (The Welsh Language Society) continued throughout that year.

There have been a number of other developments affecting

the status of Irish during recent years. When the present coalition Government came to power in February 1973 it announced that Irish would no longer be necessary to obtain a school-leaving certificate but that the language would continue to be studied and would count as a subject for matriculation at the National University. Among other measures announced at the same time were extra grants for young people, summer courses in *Gaeltacht* areas and a new plan for the provision of Irish textbooks. At primary level Irish continues to be taught to all pupils but since 1940 the number of primary and secondary schools outside the *Gaeltacht* which teach all subjects through Irish has declined to about twenty in 1970. Anxious about the ineffectiveness of the State schools in giving pupils a command of the spoken language, some parents have opened their own schools, seven in all, where Irish is the only medium of instruction. The parents of Ballymun, an area of high-rise flats in Dublin, have defied the Government on several occasions in their demand for an all-Irish school.

In a statement during the autumn of 1974 the Minister for Public Services, Mr Richie Ryan, announced that Irish was no longer necessary for entry to the Civil Service. This decision was widely and bitterly criticised by Irish-language organisations and met with strong opposition from a wide spectrum of opinion. Mr Ryan added that Irish would still be counted as a factor in promotion. The measure was defended by Dr Conor Cruise O'Brien when he claimed that, while it was reasonable for anyone wishing to use Irish in dealing with public bodies to be able to do so, this was not really the case even when Irish was compulsory.

Conor Cruise O'Brien, a member of the Irish Labour Party, is a distinguished journalist, diplomat, administrator and writer, 'a kind of Irish Malraux', and his wife Maire Mhac an tSaoi is one of the best poets writing in Irish today. His views on the Irish language are well-known and may be taken as fairly representative of what, in some quarters, have become a new approach to the problem. 'I would like to see more people know Irish, more people interested in Irish literature, music and history', says Dr O'Brien, 'Their lives would be richer for that; I would agree 100 per cent. But I think people are put off this kind of modest use of Irish by the hyperbolical objectives they are presented with. For people to take seriously the idea that we should all be Irish-speaking and to find, at the same time, that we are not getting anywhere, leads them to feel guilty, and that is dangerous'. It is the stridency as well as the clarity of O'Brien's criticism, especially of *Fianna Fail,* which has marked his contribution to Ireland's political life. 'I have great respect for the Irish language', he said at Waterford in 1974 ('You'd better,' said a voice at the back of the hall) and went on, 'But I have very little respect for what is called "the first official language". I believe that "the first official language" and the narrow concept of the national culture go hand in dreary hand'. What, in his view, is the future of Irish? Says Dr O'Brien, 'I see signs that the dimunition of compulsion and hypocrisy in this area is leading not to less but to more interest in the Irish language'.

It is too early to say whether there is any substance to Dr O'Brien's view. The position of the language continues to be much the same as it was thirty years ago. In the *Dail,* the Irish Parliament, simultaneous facilities are provided to deputies wishing to speak Irish in debates. Many are able to do so, and five or six are native-speakers, but the language is used mainly in a ceremonial way or on certain occasions such as when the estimates for education and the *Gaeltacht* are discussed. The use of Irish in law-courts is never questioned but in practice an interpreter must be requested. Only in the *Gaeltacht* are the entire proceedings in Irish, although the *Gárda* (police) in Galway give their evidence in it, even when the accused knows only English. The language has the same official status in several other fields. Road-tax and driving licences, insurance policies and cheque-books are available in Irish. A high percentage of Government documents are provided in Irish, although they are not always displayed and provided when requested. The Government subsidises the weekly newspaper *Inniu* and there is a review or article in Irish in every edition of the daily newspaper *The Irish Times,* (to which the writer Flann O'Brien contributed under the pseudonym of Myles na Gopaleen until his death in 1966), and a half-page review of political events every week. The theatre *An Peacog* (The Peacock) performs regularly in Irish as part of the Abbey Theatre. The Government's publishing department *An Gúm*, founded in 1926, is active and has recently taken on more staff, but it publishes only about thirty titles a year. The seminary at Maynooth publishes an important critical journal *Irisleabhar Mhá Nuat*. There is, however, a serious lack of shops selling Irish books—only four or five outside Dublin stock them regularly. *Sáirséal agus Dill*, the principal Irish-language publisher, sold around 23,000 copies of their books during 1973 half of which were school text-books. One of the few writers who was able to live on a professional basis was Seán Ó Riordáin (1917-72).

Telephone operators accept calls in Irish. In about half of Dublin's parishes there is an Irish-language Mass every Sunday and the Protestant Church of Ireland also has a weekly Irish service in the capital. In country dioceses the Irish Mass is rarer, except in the *Gaeltacht*, but their number has increased during the last two years. Reaction against the Government's support for Irish over the last two decades has been expressed by the so-called Language Freedom Movement, a very small group of individuals disgruntled by their own experience of learning Irish at school.

Among the many organisations devoted to the cause of Irish the Gaelic League is still active, with branches all over Ireland and abroad. It publishes a number of periodicals in Irish, including a monthly review of the arts *Feasta*, the quarterly *Nasc* for teenagers, *An tUltach* which is published in Belfast, and the monthly bilingual newspaper *Rosc*. A publishing company *Glodhanna Tea* is controlled by the League and the annual national festival *An t'Oireachtas* is organised under its auspices; similar services are provided for *An Chomhairle Náisiúnta Dramaíochta*, the body which co-ordinates the Irish-language amateur drama movement. At local level League members are involved in promoting the language in public and commercial life. They encourage the wearing of *An Fáinne Nua*, the badge which distinguishes Irish-speakers, and they promote the Irish-language book-clubs. Some branches organise the annual *Glór na nGael* competition to discover the town, village or parish which has done most to promote the language during the year. The League also holds folk-concerts and language classes. Apart from its routine work, the League has also defended Irish-medium schools, it has demonstrated about the position of Irish in broadcasting and has helped to set up the Civil Rights Movement in the *Gaeltacht*. It has about 4,000 members in 200 branches and a full-time staff of twenty. In a re-statement of its aims at its *Ardfheis* in 1972, a new constitution was adopted in which its aim was defined as 'to promote a free Irish national community . . . principally through making Irish the normal language of all the people of Ireland'.

Contact with other organisations such as *Comhaltas Ceoltosírí Eireann* (Irish Music Society) and *Cumann Lúithchleas* (Gaelic Athletic Association) is maintained through *Comhdail Naisiunta na Gaeilge* (National Council of the Irish Language). Irish-speakers in the professions are also linked to this co-ordinating body in such organisations as *An Comhchaidreamh*, which publishes a monthly review for university graduates; *Comhar na Múinteoirí*, a teachers' society; *Na Teaghlaigh Ghaelacha*, an association of Irish-speaking families; *Cumann na Sagart* for priests in *Gaeltacht* areas; and *Scéim na gCeardchumann* for trade unionists. One of the most remarkable of all organisations devoted to Irish is *Gael Linn*, a limited company which runs football pools (based on Gaelic football) and which uses its profits in a variety of ways with great success. *Gael Linn* sponsors radio programmes in Irish, scholarships for young people, the annual youth festival *An Slogah*, the theatre *An Damea*, records and debating competitions, films such as the famous *Mise Eire* which have won awards at festivals in Moscow and Berlin. Its chairman is Donal Ó Morain, a barrister and publisher who is also chairman of the *R.T.E.* authority. During 1975 the first meeting of a new body called *Bord na Gaeilge* was held in Dublin. Under the chairmanship of Kenneth Whitaker, ex-chief of the Civil Service and head of the Central Bank of Ireland, it has statutory and executive powers and a brief to promote Irish 'as a living language' in all parts of the Republic.

The crisis of the Irish language at the present time is shared by many kinds of people—politicians, broadcasters and journalists, administrators, teachers and students—but perhaps it is most keenly felt by the writers whose creative work is done in the language. Over the last eighty years, since the foundation of the Gaelic League, Irish has slowly been made into a medium suitable for communication in the modern world. This process has been supervised by the State which has encouraged the acceptance of simplified spelling, standardised grammar and modernised vocabulary. Progress in the writing of creative literature has been quite impressive. Very little of what was published during the League's hey-day has withstood the test of time, except for the two plays, a few short stories and lyrics by Patrick Pearse (1879-1916) and the works of Padraic Ó Conaire (1883-1928), the first writer to handle city life convincingly in Irish. The introduction of Irish as a compulsory subject in 1909 and the establishment of the Irish Free State in 1922, served to open up great prospects for the language and its writers. But the lack of a standardised form was not the only problem facing Irish writers. There was, of course, no great audience for books written in the language and most had to be subsidised by *An Gúm*, the Government's publishing section. Before a book could be accepted for publication, however, it had to pass the fierce puritanism and prejudices of official bodies. The Censorship of Publications Act, passed in 1928, resulted in the banning of most contemporary Anglo-Irish writers; sexual themes were untouchable, politics were almost as dangerous, recent Irish history was too hot to handle, religion could be treated only in a conventional way. Only a few writers like Séamus Ó Grianna and his brother Seosamh Mac Grianna (they chose different official versions of their surname) managed to live under these conditions; in the end, the latter ruined his health and died as a result of translating 'miserable rubbish at a pound per thousand words' for *An Gúm*.

Outside the treadmill of official publishing, the first Irish classic of modern times was written by an old Blasketman, Tomas Ó Crimhthain (1856-1937)—*An tOileánach*. This book, which was published in 1929, and translated as *The Islandman* (1937), inspired other islanders like Peig Sayers and Muiris Ó Súilleabháin to try their hand at setting down, in a way quite alien to the oral tradition to which they belonged, something of the way of life they had known, and of which 'the likes will never be there again'. Ó Súilleabháin's book *Fiche Bliàn ag Fás* (1933), translated as *Twenty Years a'Growing*, was described by E. M. Forster as 'an account of neolithic civilisation from the inside'. The whole genre of 'Blasket literature' was satirised in a hilarious but also serious account of the *Gaeltacht*'s problems by Flann O'Brien (Brian O'Nolan) in *An Béal Bocht* (1941), translated as *The Poor Mouth* (1973).

Irish prose was developed during the 'twenties not only by writers of 'Blasket literature', but by a number of intellectuals such as Pádraig de Brún, George Thomson and Liam Ó Rinn who translated from literatures other than that of English, so that by the end of the 'thirties Irish prose was becoming a medium in which any theme of modern life could be handled. In poetry, however, very little has been done, and perhaps deliberately, for as David Greene reminds us in *Writing in Irish Today* (1972), 'Those who have studied minority literatures know how easy it is for a handful of poets to exploit the neglected resources of their native tongue, without thereby making any impact on the linguistic situation; Mistral did not save Provençal, nor did the Lallans poets avert the steady anglicisation of Scottish speech. Prose is the foundation of all modern literatures and the only form readily accessible to all speakers of a language.'

The Irish literature of today begins with the emergence of two Connacht writers, Máirtín Ó Diréain (born 1910) and Máirtín Ó Cadhain (1906-70). The first published a book of lyrics in 1942, *Coinnle Geala,* which—uninfluenced by traditional forms such as folk-songs but using their rhythms —announced a new beginning and was to prove very influential on the subsequent course of Irish poetry. O Cadhain, a native of Cois Fharraige in Connemara, published his first book of short stories in 1939 which, while using ordinary speech, brought a fresh style and new richness to the language, an obscurity even, based on a highly organised system of metaphor and simile. Interned by the Irish Government during the Second World War, or 'the European hostilities' as that event is known in Ireland, because he belonged to the Irish Republican Army, Ó Cadhain's next book did not appear until 1948, followed by his only but outstanding novel *Cré na Cille* (Cemetery Land) in 1949. Among his other works was a translation of the lecture by Saunders Lewis, *Tynged yr Iaith* (The Fate of the Language), published as *Bás nó Beatha* in 1963.

The magazines which became platforms for the new

literature were *Comhar,* launched in 1942 by *An Comh-chaidreamh* (Association of University Graduates), and the Gaelic League's *Feasta,* both of which are still in existence. Pioneers of publishing in Irish were Seán Ó hÉigeartaigh and his wife who founded the firm *Sáirséal agus Dill.* They started a book club in 1948 and were soon able to sell around 3,000 copies of their books. In 1952 the Government agreed to offer subsidy to publishers without censorship thus enabling them to compete on more equal terms with *An Gúm,* where censorship was still in force. Among writers already well-known in English but who now turned to Irish were Liam O'Flaherty (born 1897), Brian O'Nolan, alias Flann O'Brien and Myles na Gopaleen (1911-66) who wrote *At Swim-Two-Birds* (1939) and Brendan Behan (1923-69) whose *The Hostage* was first written and produced in Irish as *An Giall.*

In poetry the most distinguished writer of the 'fifties was still Máirtin Ó Direáin but he was joined by Seán Ó Tuama, Seán Ó Ríordáin and Máire Mhac an tSaoi. The critic Valentin Iremonger, in an essay published in 1955, summed up the Irish poetry of these years as follows: 'By and large the poetry that appears today in Irish magazines is as good as that which appears in contemporary English and French magazines, and one should beware of looking for more than that'. After Ó Cadhain there were few outstanding prose-writers, but Diarmuid Ó Súilleabháin is a notable exception. Apart from poetry and creative prose, the amount of historical, biographical and academic writing in Irish has increased steadily over the last twenty years. Younger writers under thirty, mostly poets, include Seán A. Ó Briain, Daithi Ó hÓgáin, Finín Ó Tuama, Seán Ó Leocháin, Padraig Mac Suibhne, Micheál Ó hUanancháin, Máire Nic Gearailt, Aogán Ó Muircheartaigh and Liam Ó Muirthile.

The reading public for contemporary Irish literature, as David Greene has pointed out, is a largely urban intelligentsia, some of whom are native-speakers living in towns but most of whom have learned the language. But the vast majority of Irishmen would say with W. B. Yeats, 'Gaelic is my national language but not my native tongue', or even with the younger poet Michael Hartnett, who in his collection of poems entitled *A Farewell to English* (1975) announced his intention of abandoning English in favour of Irish, 'She was a language seldom spoken / She was a child's purse, full of useless things'. The potential size of the writer's audience is therefore estimated to be about 400,000—more readers than at any time in the country's history but a public, nevertheless, for which Irish is for the most part a second language learned at school.

The implications of this imbalance for the future of writing in Irish, and for the language's future, are abundantly clear. The new literature's achievement is that it grew out of the speech of the people. But the continual shrinking of the Irish-speaking areas and the real possibility that they will disappear in another generation or so has caused a division in the minds of writers: while working to develop the range of their language they are deeply aware that it may soon become little more than a subject for academic study and that 'a new England called Ireland' will be the result. Máirtín Ó Cadhain expressed this dilemma in a lecture about a year before his death: 'A dark cloud hangs over Irish again. A worse thing than lack of recognition at home and abroad weighs on the writer. It is hard for a man to give of his best in a language which seems likely to die before himself, if he lives a few years more: this despair engenders a desire to fight fiercely for the language. Neither despair or fighting is good for him as a writer'.

10 ITALY

Constitution: Republic

Area: 116,290 square miles

Population: 54.4 million (1974)

Capital: Rome

Administrative divisions: 19 regions

Present Government: The Democratic Christian Party *(P.D.C.)* in coalition with the Republican Party *(P.R.)*; elected 1974

Language of majority: Italian

THE PIEDMONTESE

Piedmont (Italian: *Piemonte),* since 1970 one of Italy's Regions, is situated on the frontier with France and has a population of about 5 million. The capital is Turin *(Torino),* one of the largest and most heavily populated cities of Italy which depends on the huge Fiat plant making cars, ball-bearings, rolling-stock and agricultural machinery. Other industries are textiles at Biella, food and confectionery, wine-growing and the rearing of livestock. The provincial capitals of Piedmont are Asti, Cuneo, Novara and Vercelli.

Like Romagnol, Piedmontese belongs to the Gallo-Italic group of dialects which, with Ligurian, make up the northern branch of Italy's dialects. The Gallo-Italic group, which also includes Lombard and Emilian (to which Romagnol belongs), is the largest of the northern dialects, accounting for about two thirds of the area and roughly corresponding to the ancient seat of the Celts. The chief features of Gallo-Italic are the voicing of intervocalic breathed occlusives, the loss of final vowels, the simplification of double consonants, the loss of atonic syllables, the nasalisation of vowels before final *n* and *m,* the use of the third person singular after a plural subject and consequent loss of third-plural forms, and the growth of the perfect tense at the expense of the preterite. Special features of Piedmontese are that it palatalises infinitives *(canté, parlé,* etc) and the intervocalic *n* is pronounced as in the English *sing (lunng'a* for *luna);* furthermore, the dialect has not absorbed the speech-habits of Milan so that its inhabitants say *pioré* for *piangere* (to weep), *bòsch* for *legna* (wood), *mare granda* for *nonna* (grandmother) and so on; they also use a large number of words borrowed from French.

First recognised as a separate dialect by Dante Alighieri in his *De Vulgari Eloquentia* (1303), Piedmontese was established as having developed independently of modern Italian by the Romance scholar G. I. Ascoli in his major work *L'Italia Dialettale* in 1873. The Swiss philologist Heinrich Schmid, supporting Ascoli's view, has stated that if the Gallo-Italic group is denied an existence independent of Italian's, then one might as well accept the Italian nature of French.

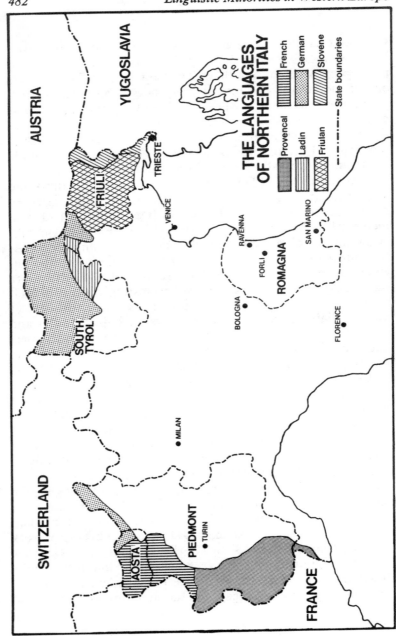

THE LANGUAGES
OF NORTHERN ITALY

French
German
Slovene

Provencal
Ladin
Friulan

State boundaries

AUSTRIA

YUGOSLAVIA

FRIULI

TRIESTE

VENICE

RAVENNA

FORLI

ROMAGNA

SAN MARINO

BOLOGNA

FLORENCE

SOUTH
TYROL

SWITZERLAND

MILAN

PIEDMONT

TURIN

AOSTA

FRANCE

More recently the Catalan ethnologist Guiu Sobeila-Caanitz has suggested in *Le Peuple Piedmontais* that the area in which the Gallo-Italic dialects are spoken should be given the name *Médiolanie* in recognition of the distinct ethnic character of its inhabitants, and after the Latin name for Milan, *Mediolanum*. The name *Médiolanie* has been accepted by several ethnologists in Italy and France, including Guy Héraud. Of this group, while Lombards, Emilians and Ligurians have expressed their cultural identities through Italian, the Piedmontese (with the Romagnols) have developed their own literature in a modest but uninterrupted way since the twelfth century.

The area in which Piedmontese is spoken has a population of approximately 3 million. Its northern limit is near Monte Rosa on the border with Switzerland where, apart from the German-speaking village of Land, the upper basin of the Sesia as far as Grignasch speaks Piedmontese. Further south, towards the river Po, the towns of Lissandria, Aqui, Mondovi, Cuneo, Suluzzo Pinerola, Ivrea and Biella are all included in the linguistic area. Although not corresponding to the new administrative boundaries of Piedmont, being smaller, this area has always been a natural geographical unit which served as a corridor, from the thirteenth century, between Rome and Paris, between Milan and Barcelona, and has prospered as a commercial centre accordingly.

United under the Holy Roman Empire by Count Amadeo VI (1343-83), Piedmont was given a university at Turin and its own autonomy which, despite continuous attacks by the French throughout the next two centuries, was developed by the Dukes of Savoy until it was virtually an independent State. During the eighteenth century under Duke Vittorio Amadeo, the region's independence was again defended against French and Spanish invasions, notably in 1747 when the Piedmontese won a famous victory at Assieta in the Susa Valley. From this time dates the beginning of a sophisticated literature in Piedmontese, including a dictionary and grammar, and the first stirrings of the region's social conscience as illustrated in the writings of the reformer Vittorio Alfieri. That Piedmont had its own character and status is suggested by the saying, still to be heard these days, that the traveller from Turin passing

Casale is 'going into Italy'. At this time too the Piedmontese gained a reputation for being more dour and serious
than their neighbours in Lombardy and Genoa, and more like
the German-Swiss or the Catalans in their outlook and personality.

Under Napoleon from 1800 to 1814, Piedmont was heavily
taxed and drained of its resources to such an extent that the
bourgeoisie began clamouring for the establishment of a
modern legislative and administrative system on liberal
lines. A new anti-French mood was created by poets like
Edoardo Calvo who wrote satires against *ij gaj* (the cockerels)
and by other intellectuals critical of the extreme conservatism
of the French régime up to 1848. Elsewhere in Italy the same
process was taking place and soon the Piedmontese liberals
were making common cause with their newly discovered compatriots in Emilia and Liguria. Foremost among the Piedmontese patriots of the *Risorgimento* were the aristocrat
Cesare Balbo and the poet Angel Brofferio who edited an influential magazine in the regional language.

The call for Italian unity had been stifled but the years between
1849 and 1859 saw great progress to this end. Under King Victor
Emanuel II of Savoy, Count Camillo di Cavour (1810-61),
described by Lord Palmerston as 'one of the greatest patriots
that have ever adorned the history of any nation', succeeded
in breaking the isolated position of Piedmont by inserting 'the
Italian question' in all important international discussions.
As Prime Minister of Piedmont from 1852, Cavour's plans
bore fruit in 1859 and agreements were reached with France
for a war against Austria. The Second War of Independence
ended in victory for the forces of France and Piedmont. Lombardy was united to Piedmont and so were the Grand Duchy
of Tuscany, the Duchies of Parma and Modena, Emilia and
Romagna and the Kingdom of Sardinia. Following
Garibaldi's Expedition of the Thousand in May 1860 they
were joined by Naples, Sicily, Marches and Umbria. With the
unification of Italy, except for Latium and Venetia, Victor
Emanuel II was proclaimed King of Italy in March 1861.

Despite the strong regionalist sentiments of those who
worked for Italian unity on federalist lines at this time, it was

the followers of Cavour who triumphed in founding a centralist Italian State on the French model. The immediate impetus for the revolution had come from Piedmont and Turin now became the capital of the Italian Kingdom and the seat of its Parliament, while the Piedmontese Constitution was extended to the whole country. Among the Government's first acts was 'a declaration of war against dialects': in 1864 the use of Piedmontese was banned in the schools while teachers and administrators from outside the region were appointed in large numbers. Piedmont, which had led the struggle for Italian unity, found itself incorporated in the unitary State which had little regard for its particularism.

Fascism caused a crisis in the Piedmontese conscience. As early as 1927 the poet Pinin Pacòt (1899-1964) and his friends known as *'Companìa dij Brandé'* had begun formulating new orthographical standards according to principles enunciated by the *Institut d'Estudis Occitans* and the Catalan grammarian Pompeu Fabra. But it was their traditional distrust of rhetoric and demagogy and their regard for law which ensured that fascism was to be unacceptable among the majority of Piedmontese. Throughout the Second World War there was a deeply rooted resistance movement in Piedmont, despite Allied bombing and famine; in 1943 there were two massive strikes in Turin against Mussolini's intransigence and up to 1945 partisans based in the Alps fought courageously against his forces. Nevertheless, unlike the Aosta Valley, there was no autonomist movement in Piedmont during these years: the only aim of the resistance was to win back 'a free and united Italy'.

It was left to the post-war generation to define the case for Piedmontese autonomy. Once again the revival of regionalism was led by a cultural movement, the *Companìa dij Brandé* which had survived the fascist years. The work began with new editions of Piedmontese classics, a dictionary and a grammar. They also organised a *Festa dël Piemont* to commemorate the victory at Assieta. In May 1970 the group asked for the teaching of Piedmontese in local schools, but without success. The movement, which is strongly federalist in its thinking and has regular contact with similar organisations in

Italy and France, comprises about twenty associations including the newspaper *Assion Piemontèisa,* the political
group *Associassion Liber Piemont* and the cultural *Ca dë
Studi Piemontèis.*

The *Regione Piemontese* was created in 1970 under the
Constitution of 1947 which provided for the introduction of
Regional Parliaments in Italy. In the elections of June 1975
the Communist Party took control of the Regional Council of
Piedmont winning twenty-two out of the sixty seats and made
much progress at municipal level. The old administration was
criticised by federalists of the *Companìa dij Brandé* because,
from the outset, it made no provision for Piedmontese in any
sphere, least of all education. It is pointed out that the Italian
Government's concept of regionalism excludes all possibility
of federalism. The Republic, *'una ed indivisible'* (Article 5 of
the Constitution), delegates certain administrative and legal
powers to the Region which are clearly defined and therefore
severely limited by Article 117 which puts 'national interests'
above all. In depriving the Region of the right to discuss its
own affairs by sending all important matters for the attention
of the central Government in Rome, Piedmont is prevented
from nurturing its own administrators and political representatives. Despite the efforts of the *Companìa dij Brandé,*
the ethnic conscience of the majority of the Piedmontese, who support the major Italian parties, remains
weak. In November 1970 the Regional Parliament refused to
include a reference to the Piedmontese language in its Constitution. Meanwhile, an influx of workers from the poor and
neglected areas of Italy's *Mezzogiorno* into Piedmont's industrial area continued to threaten the linguistic personality
of the Region and to lessen the likelihood that its language
and culture will ever win the recognition they require for survival. It remains true, however, that the *Compania dij Brandé,* with its brave motto *Fiama che as dëstissa nen* (A flame
which is never extinguished) is alone in its concern for the
future of the Piedmontese cultural identity.

THE OCCITANS OF PIEDMONT

The Region of Piedmont includes, besides areas where the Gallo-Italic dialects are spoken, about a dozen valleys which belong from a linguistic point of view to Occitanie, their speech having been Provençal for centuries. According to François Fontan, the leader of the Occitan Autonomist Movement *(M.A.O.)*, Provençal can be traced from the Province of Cuneo as far as the valley of Frabosa, south of Mondovi, and even to small enclaves in Calabria which were founded by emigrants from the Vaudois Valleys at the time of the Counter-Reformation. But the area where Provençal is still spoken to a considerable extent today takes in only the high valleys of Piedmont, between Limone Piemonte in the Province of Cuneo and Chiomonte in the Province of Turin. It is extremely difficult to say precisely how many inhabitants of Piedmont speak Provençal because there has never been a Census which asked this question. Almost all also speak Piedmontese. But it is probable that at least 200,000 people, 'according to the estimate of Robert Lafont, have a knowledge of the dialect. In the valleys of Varaita, Maira and Grana the dialect is widely spoken, even by children. Elsewhere it tends to be the speech of older folk. The valleys of Piedmont where the dialect survives can be divided into three: the Valle di Susa (French: *Vallée de la Doire de Suse)* and the left bank of the Chisone valley; the Vaudois valleys; and the valleys in the Province of Cuneo.

In the Susa Valley, on the Dora Riparia river above Chiomante *(Chaumont)* there was an official French-language culture, as in the Aosta Valley, until the nineteenth century. Place-names and family names remind the visitor of this francophone past. But from the establishment of the Kingdom of Italy in 1861 anti-French feeling spread throughout these valleys. Only the Aosta Valley was able to defend itself against the policy of Italianisation. In the Susa and Chisone Valleys, for example, Cézanne became Cesana, Chaumont Chiomante and Prégelas Pregelato. What was not attempted by the Italian Governments of 1861-1922 was accomplished by fascism in the years up to 1945. Only a few villages such as Loux, Pourrières and Mentoulles escaped this process and after the Second World War one or two, like Oulx and Sauze, reverted to their original Provençal forms. The majority accepted the Italian names forced on them by Mussolini.

For centuries before then the Cluson Valley had been a part of the Dauphiné; the Vaudois way of life had flourished there until 1700 when, following a ducal edict obliging them to renounce the Protestant faith, about 3,000 inhabitants left the district for new homes in Wurttemburg, Baden and Hesse. The Provençal dialect which they took to southern Germany was preserved there through seven or eight generations and died out only during the Second World War. Since 1861 the schools have used only Italian in the Cluson and Susa Valleys, so that the education system, allied with tourism, the Church and the mass media, has ensured that by today the Provençal dialect is heard only among the older generation.

The valleys known as the Vaudois Valleys are to the west of Pinerola and include the Germanasca Valley, the Pellice Valley and the smaller Angrogna Valley. The principal town of this district is Torrè Pellice *(La Tour)*. The Provençal dialect was helped in the Vaudois Valleys, as was Romansch in the Graubünden, by the efforts of Protestant reformers to reach the common people in their own language rather than in Latin. They thus developed an Occitan culture as early as the thirteenth century, with *la langue d'oc* the official language up to the time of the Reformation. Church services were held in the language and throughout the fifteenth century there was a modest ecclesiastical literature. The Bible was translated into Provençal in 1532. But by the Edict of Villers-Cotterêts of 1539 *la langue d'oïl* replaced *la langue d'oc* as the official language of the whole of France and Provençal lost its status in the Vaudois Valleys.

There were other reasons why Provençal was replaced by French: the need to maintain close relations between the Vaudois subjects of the Duke of Savoy and those under French rule, the use of the French Bible of Olivetan, the numerous contacts with the Protestant Academies of Switzerland and France, and above all the plague of 1630 which killed ten out of thirteen priests who served the valleys through the medium of Provençal.

The language was relegated to the status of a dialect and became associated with the uneducated and the poor. French became the language of officialdom and culture, a process reinforced in 1911 when the Italian Government passed the Credaro Law which made it obligatory in all schools of the Vaudois Valleys as well as in Aosta. Under fascism the Provençal dialect was discriminated against by decrees of 1925 and it was expressly banned in 1935. It is significant that among the six signatories of the Charter of Chivasso of 1943, which later became the basis of Valdotain autonomy, there were four from the Vaudois Valleys.

On the collapse of fascism in Italy a committee for the introduction of French in schools was formed in 1944 which, after a campaign of ten years, won permission to teach French at the elementary level wherever the local authorities were willing to pay the cost, whereas up to 1911 this teaching had been financed by the State. Since then little progress has been made towards recognition of either French or Provençal in public life. Few priests are committed to any language other than Italian, there are no newspapers in French and the language is not used for any official purpose. Provençal survives only as an everyday speech in small villages, mostly in the Germanasca Valley.

The general impression that Provençal in Piedmont is in the last stages of decay is relieved only in the third area, the Valleys of Cuneo. From north to south these are the Valleys of the Po, Varaita, Maira, Grana, Stura di Demonte, Gesso and Vermenagna. But only the upper part of the Varaita (Provençal: *Varacho),* known as Castellata and comprising the three valleys of Casteldelfino *(Chasteldelfin),* Bellino *(Blin)* and Chianale *(La Chanal)* have preserved their Provençal character, mainly because they were part of France until the Treaty of Aix-la-Chapelle in 1748. All the other valleys have had an Italian administration for centuries.

Until 1961 there were no attempts to assert the old Provençal character of these valleys. The dialect was held in low regard and seemed destined for imminent extinction. But in that year a group of poets writing in Piedmontese founded the *Escolo dóu Po* in association with the *Félibrige Mistralien,* a Provençal poets' society, in Crissolo. Their aim was to awaken the conscience of the Occitans in Piedmont and to promote their language. Since then the *Escolo dóu Po* has organised Piedmontese-Provençal meetings on every Sunday in August at villages where the languages are still remembered. It has had most encouraging responses in the Valleys of Cuneo. At Santo Lucio in the Val Garna the teacher Sergio Arneoda has introduced Provençal in the village school and his pupils, many now prominent in the Occitan renaissance, publish a newspaper, *Coumboscuro,* which has become the official organ of the Provençal minority in Italy. They also perform folk-plays in village squares and Christmas plays in the churches, organising themselves as a co-operative actors' studio. In the church of Santo Lucio preaching is regularly in Provençal and there are several public inscriptions in the dialect.

From such small beginnings a considerable regionalist movement has begun to grow but without much success in the linguistic sphere to date. In Monterosso Grana on 30 August 1964, the *Escolo dóu Po* organised a petition bearing the signatures of thousands of writers, teachers, former resistance-fighters and country people, which was addressed to the Minister of Education of the Italian Government and asking for Provençal to be taught in the Occitan Valleys of Piedmont. It remains unacknowledged to the present day. Nevertheless, under the auspices of the *Muviment Autunumisto Utsitan (M.A.O.)* and its organ *Utsitonye Libro,* and other organisations based on the other side of the border with France, such as *Comitato d'azione Occitana* and *Unione Autonomisti Valli Occitaniche,* some progress has been made in political terms. In the Variata Valley, for example, Toni Boudriè (Antonio Bodrero), deputy mayor of Melle *(Mèel),* has supported autonomist candidates who have won seats at local elections in Sampeyere *(San Peire),* Frassino *(Fraisse)* and in his home village.

THE ROMAGNOLS

Romagna is not itself one of Italy's Regions but only part of Emilia-Romagna, the Region in the Po Valley which includes the towns of Parma, Modena and Bologna. It is situated on the peninsula's Adriatic coast and is divided into two parts, mountain and plain, by the *Via Emilia* and the *autostrada* which run from Bologna to Rimini. Among the principal towns are Cesana, Faenza, Forlì, Imola and Lugo. The Republic of San Marino is situated on the border between Romagna and the Marches. It is essentially an agricultural area, with vineyards and market-towns, one of the most highly cultivated areas in Europe and where dairy cattle are raised on a huge scale. The population of Romagna is a little over 1,200,000 (1971) and that of Emilia-Romagna about 4 million. The capital of Romagna is Ravenna, the cradle of Byzantine civilisation in Italy and now an important industrial town.

Always a disputed area, Romagna was claimed by the Pope in 1278 and enjoyed a brief period of unity under Cesare Borgia up to the beginning of the sixteenth century. For the next 250 years the area was rent by faction and ravaged by war as the Venetians and French competed for it. Between 1796 and 1815 it changed its name and status seven times: it was known as Cispadane, the Cisalpine Republic, as an Austrian province, as part of the Italian Republic, then of the Italian Kingdom, as an Austrian-Neapolitan province and finally it was restored to Papal sovereignty. Byron's letters record that the Austrians were called in twice by a besieged papacy, once in 1831 and again in 1849, when Romagna rallied to Garibaldi's cause. It was to Romagna that Garibaldi escaped, pursued by the armies of the Papacy, and the men of Ravenna who smuggled him into neighbouring Tuscany. Ten years later the Papal authority was over-thrown and in 1860 Romagna joined a united Italy.

Romagnol, the speech of Romagna, is not a language but a dialect belonging to the Emilian group of dialects which, with Piedmontese and Lombard, make up the Gallo-Italic family which in turn belongs with Ligurian to the northern dialects of Italy. Although it has features in common with the other

Gallo-Italic dialects, especially with Emilian, Romagnol has some which are peculiar to itself alone: these include the masculine definitive article *e'*, the personal pronoun *u*, the lengthening and closing of open vowels in open syllables (e.g. *brev, nov)* and resistance to the infiltration of the Lombardian *ö* and *ü*; it also has a large number of words which do not occur in other dialects, and other distinguishing features.* Apart from the mainly phonological variations the syntax of Romagnol hardly differs from that of Italian. Like most dialects, Romagnol divides further into various groups, each important town of the area having its own form; there are also differences between the speech of the town and the countryside, although since the Second World War a greater mobility of population has resulted in a blurring of these differences. If there is a *koine* it is the speech of Ravenna, the *'glauca notte rutilante d'oro'* described by the poet D'Annunzio. It is generally regarded as being harsh on the ear, rough or uneven, full of staccato, syncopated sounds uttered in an impetuous manner; consonants are close-packed, elisions frequent and words often mutilated. The *Romagnoli* are fond of jesting about their dialect's peculiarities, quoting the sentence *La l'à lì la lon?* (Have you the light?). To the foreign ear accustomed to the Italian of Rome or Florence the Romagnol dialect is certainly a new experience. It is the everyday speech of the vast majority of Romagna's inhabitants, except those who have moved into the area in recent times.

There is no significant autonomist movement basing its claims partly on the fact that Romagna has its own linguistic identity, and no regionalist movement which seeks to improve its economic or political fortunes. The only time at which the Romagnols expressed themselves politically was in the 1920s when peasants began to organise occupation of the land under the leadership of the Maximalist Socialists who controlled large parts of the area. The strikes which occurred throughout Emilia in these years were the culminating point of the crisis which led to the rise of Benito Mussolini who, like his wife,

---

*For a description of the features common to all three dialects see D. G. B. Gregor: *Romagnol Language and Literature* (1971) on which the present account draws heavily.

was himself a *Romagnolo,* born in 1883 at Predappio, a village near Forlì. It is said that the Duce's hostility to Catholicism was typical of the Romagna's tradition of chafing against papal rule and that his early socialism was born of the area's rebellious and freedom-loving instincts. Few *Romagnoli* were among his active supporters, however.

Today, the city of nearby Bologna, in Emilia, is famous throughout Italy for the efficiency, honesty and popularity of its Communist administration. A countryman of Mussolini's was the Socialist Pietro Nenni. But the region has had no corporate political identity since the Second World War and is represented by members of most of the parties in Italy today, particularly the Republican Party which has its stronghold there. Emilia-Romagna was one of the Regions in which the Communists made substantial gains in the elections of June 1975, winning twenty-six out of fifty seats, the remainder shared by the Christian Democrats, who won thirteen seats, and six other parties.

Nevertheless, Romagna's cultural personality is quite distinct, for it has its own literature written in the dialect of the people. Dante Alighieri, in his *De Vulgari Eloquentia,* was of the opinion that Romagnol should be chosen from among the fourteen main dialects of Italy to be the country's new vernacular, praising its softness which he preferred to the harsh speeches further north. This is surprising in that modern Romagnol is distinguished not by its mellifluous sounds but by its monosyllables and truncated words. It must therefore be assumed that the dialect has evolved since Dante's day: there is no proof because no legal or ecclesiastical documents have survived in Romagnol to show what it was like. The first time it was used for literary purposes was in the *Commedia Nuova* of Pier Francesco da Faenzia in 1545 and it was employed then as the ancient comic device of contrasting the uncouth rustic with the more refined townsman. But in the second earliest instance of written Romagnol, it was used to demonstrate that it was as versatile as any other Italian dialect as the vehicle of literary creation—*Pulon Matt* (1591) by an anonymous author is an imitation of Ariosto's *Orlando Furioso.*

Over two hundred years were to pass before the dialect was

used again for literary purposes and as part of the Romantic Movement's interest in vernacular languages. Foremost among the poets of the early decades of the century were Don Pietro Santoni (1766-1823) and Giuseppe Acquisti (1801-81), the first of many poets who were imprisoned for their revolutionary patriotism. Most of the poets of the day were liberals and patriots, opposed to Austria and the conservative Catholic Church. Their work, when not dealing with political and anti-clerical matters, is full of humour and in the poems of Olindo Guerrini (1845-1916)—who also wrote in Italian under the pseudonym of Lorenzo Stecchetti—a Rabelasian bawdiness. At the same time there was a vigorous body of popular and religious songs in the dialect, as well as narrative poems intended for recitation.

In his esteem for the Romagnols (he is buried at Ravenna), Dante was followed by many Italians. They have praised the people's sincerity, their intolerance of injustice and their love of liberty. The Romagnols are certainly aware that these are the qualities for which they are famous and have blended them in an intense local patriotism. They are proud of Romagna's connections with Garibaldi and of its past in the *Risorgimento,* and choose their heroes from among the bandits and partisans of their history. All these matters are considered in the poetry of Romagna, as well as more general themes.

There was a moment when it seemed possible that the Italian poet Giovanni Pascoli (1855-1912), one of the greatest Italian poets of the nineteenth century, would choose to write in Romagnol. Many of his poems contain phrases which are based on the dialect. However, Pascoli settled in Tuscany and the absence of any elevated poetry in Romagnol at that time convinced him that he should write in Italian. So it was left to Aldo Spallicci (born 1886) to establish the dialect as a medium for lyrical expression of high standards. 'I have chosen to sing in my mother-dialect', he wrote, 'because in it I have felt myself closer to the soul of things, to the heart of man and to God'. Spallicci has had a most distinguished career as both man of action and poet. He fought in Greece with the Red Shirts of Garibaldi's son and, a Republican, became a Senator after the Second World War. It is said that he was so attached to the Romagnol countryside that he could write a poem after every walk. Among his volumes of verse, thirteen in all, are *E' canon dri dla seva* (1926), *Sciarpa Nigra* (1956) and *Adess ch' l'ha smess ad piovar* (1960), all of which were included in a volume of collected poems in 1961. His magazine *La Piê* (Bread) has been since 1920 a focus not only for Romagna's literary life but for artists, musicians, historians and folklorists. Like Hugh MacDiarmid in Scotland, throughout his life Spallicci argued that the use of dialect should not be confined to satire and humour but could be used to express the other side of the Romagnol personality—its delicacy, melancholy and capacity for deep feeling. He is regarded as the creator of Romagnol literature, as Romagna's Mistral, crystallising the sense of regional identity and writing poems, which have not been rivalled, to prove his point.

This strong attachment to Romagna, the precondition for a literary revival, was nothing new but was already apparent in the novels of Italian writers of Romagnol background such as Alfredo Oriani (1852-1909), Antonio Beltramelli (1879-1930), Marino Moretti (born 1885), Francesco Serantini (born 1889). There is, however little prose written in the dialect except for a few fairy-tales and comedies. Only the poets have used Romagnol. With the philosopher Benedetto Croce they affirm that 'much of our soul is dialect'.

THE FRIULANS

The autonomous region of Friuli-Venezia-Giulia, created by the Statute of 1947 but not fully established until 1963, includes in its northern parts, on the borders with the Austrian province of Carinthia and the Yugoslav Republic of Slovenia, an area where Friulan is spoken. A dialect belonging with Romansch and Ladin to the Rhaeto-Romance family, Friulan is the speech of Friuli (Friulan: *Furlan)*, the province of which lies between the rivers Livenza and Timavo. Friuli-Venezia-Giulia has an area of 3,055 square miles and a population of 1,232,439 (1971) distributed among 900 villages and a few small towns which include, beside the capital Udine (Friulan: *Udin)*, Gorizia *(Gurizze)*, Pordenone, Grado, Aquileia *(Aquileé)*, Tolmezzo *(Tumiec)*, Cividale *(Cividât)* and Monfalcone. The capital of the Region is Trieste, which is not in the Friulan-speaking area.

Friuli-Venezia-Giulia lies within the natural boundaries of the Dolomite Alps on the west, the Carnic Alps on the north, the Julian Alps on the east and the Adriatic on the south. The Friulan language is not spoken over all this area, however. Linguistically, Friuli is an area of less than 3,000 square miles with a population of approximately 800,000 of whom about 600,000 are believed to be speakers of Friulan. There is argument about the precise numbers able to speak the language because at the 1971 Census Friulan-speakers were not given the opportunity of registering themselves as such. Certainly within Friuli there are districts where the language is replaced by Venetian, such as Sacile, Monfalcone and Portogruaro, and there are also wedges of Slovene in the Julian Alps north of Tarvisio and islands of German in the Carnic Alps. On the other hand, more Friulan is spoken in the town of Gorizia than in Udine because all the Slovenes of the area are able to speak it.

The historical Friuli was known in Roman times, when it was the homeland of the Tenth Legion, as *Patria Fori Julii,* which was later abbreviated to give its present name. Attacked and settled by the armies of Attila the Hun, Charlemagne, the Lombards and the Magyars, Friuli became a sovereign state with its own Parliament in 942 under the German King Heinrich IV. But dissension among its rulers during the Middle Ages resulted, in 1751, in the dissolution of Friuli, known then as Aquilia, and occupation by Napoleon in 1797. The Friulan Parliament met for the last time in 1805. With the fall of Napoleon in 1814 Lombardy and the former Venetian provinces reverted to Austria, under whom they remained until 1866. In that year Friuli voted for union with the newly proclaimed kingdom of Italy. The eastern frontier of Italy was now on the river Judri, not far enough east for Italian sentiment. It was only after Friuli had again suffered Austria for its master during one terrible year (October 1917 to October 1918) that the frontier was pushed back beyond the Julian Alps. After the collapse of the Habsburg Monarchy and the Treaty of St Germain in 1919, it was returned to Italy. When the Trieste Question was resolved after the Second World War, parts of the Gorizia area went to Yugoslavia but the greater part of Friuli remained with Italy.

The Friulan language emerged from vulgar Latin after the demise of the Roman Empire, the commentary on the New Testament composed in the fifth century in *lingua rustica* suggesting that Friuli had began to develop its own speech before other parts of what are today northern Italy. Friulan has been recognised by philologists as akin to the other Rhaeto-Romansch dialects since 1870, when C. Schneller and F. Rausch both came independently to the conclusion that the speech of Friuli was related to the Ladin of the South Tyrol and the Dolomites and to the Romansch of the Graubünden. Schneller called the Romansch family *Churwälsch* after the town of Chur; *wälsch,* following the Roman invasion, had shifted its Germanic meaning from *Celts* (cf. Caesar's *Volcae)* to *Roman*. Three years later this conclusion was accepted by G. Ascoli who gave the name Ladin to this family, a term first used in 1560 in the Engadine to describe the language of their New Testament, and used there ever since. Carlo Battisti, on the other hand, whose theories were used by Mussolini to justify Italian irredentism between the two World Wars, considered Ladin to be an abstraction and all the Rhaeto-Romansch forms as the archaic speech of neighbouring plains, so that for him Romansch was archaic Lombardian, like the Ladin of the South Tyrol, and Friulan archaic Venetian.

Subsequent research has shown that the Germanised zone north and south of the watershed of the Central Alps covers an old Romance area linking the Ladins of the Graubünden with those of the Dolomites, and where Romance is known to have been spoken down to the close of the seventeenth century. The whole area is mountainous and mountain people often develop a phonetic system of their own. Never having been welded into a political unity and lacking a literary language which could give one patois the upper hand, the area was exposed to infiltration both from the south and the north. Under such circumstances disintegration was inevitable. By the tenth century a unique form of Romance had evolved in Friuli.

There never was a simple homogenous Ladin language. If Friulan is akin to the Rhaeto-Romansch family it is because, like them, it was spoken by formerly Latin-speaking Celtic mountain-dwellers; if it is independent it is because its parents were earlier forms of Latin*. Friulan is not a dialect of Italian, any more than Romagnol, but a dialect of Latin in the same way as Tuscan which as the result of historical and literary factors became the language of the Italian State. This is the political distinction between dialect and language, of course; there is also linguistic evidence for considering Friulan as a separate language but related to the Rhaeto-Romance family, or in the words of Gianfranco Contini in *Letteratura dell' Italia unita* (1968), *'una lingua minore, che d'un dialetto'* (a minor language, not a dialect). The language was consolidated under the Christianised Lombards and held its own into the Middle Ages, as numerous documents show, although it was influenced by Germanic and Venetian dialects. The earliest books in Friulan date from 1150.

From the beginning of the fourteenth century it was used in law and government; in the next three centuries a vigorous literature quite unlike the artificial Italian style of the period was written in it. In the eighteenth century, however, the prestige of Venice relegated Friulan to the status of a peasant dialect. But the language showed remarkable resilience and in the

---

*For a fuller description of Friulan see D. B. Gregor: *Friulan Language and Literature* (1975), to which the present brief account is indebted.

nineteenth century Friulan benefited from the Romantic interest in vernaculars. The work of poets like Graziadio Ascoli, Giulio Andrea Pirona and Vincenzo Joppi was rediscovered and that of Pietro Zorutti admired. This renaissance continued into the twentieth century, with works written for the theatre and a substantial body of poetry. Among writers who have used Friulan was Pier Paolo Pasolini, the film-maker murdered in 1975, who published his early work in the volume *La Nuova Gioventù*.

After the First World War there were a number of societies dedicated to Friulan such as *Scuele Libare Furlane* and the publishing house *Int Furlane* which still publishes a lively monthly newspaper with the same title. Enthusiasts for Friulan point to the Swiss Government's attitude and support for Romansch in the Graubünden and complain that Friulan has to rely on the efforts of voluntary organisations like the *Società Filologica Friulans* and private groups such as the young writers who since 1948 have co-operated in a movement known as *La Cortesele di Furlan,* publishing their magazine *Risultive* at their own expense. One of the few signs of official recognition for the language was the introduction in 1973 of Friulan language and culture into the Theological Seminary at Udine as a subject in the curriculum.

Today, Friulan is beginning to lose ground to the Venetian dialects of Italian, especially in the towns and the south of the province. Although the illiteracy rate among children, in Italian, is among the lowest for the whole of Italy, the form they speak is heavily influenced by Friulan, as are the Friulan place-names of the area. The local language was abandoned by the Church after the Second World War. It no longer has any kind of official status and is not taught in the schools at any level, despite provisions allowing instruction in local languages by Article 3 of the 1947 Regional Statute. Voluntary classes, started by Guiseppe Marchetti, the author of an esteemed Friulan grammar, are well attended, especially by students and teachers. Nevertheless, the old inferiority of communities which speak minority languages persists. Writing in the newspaper *Patrie dal Friûl* (July-August 1950), a Friulan author commented: 'Certainly ignorance of our unwillingness to speak Friulan is not ethically a sin, but it is the

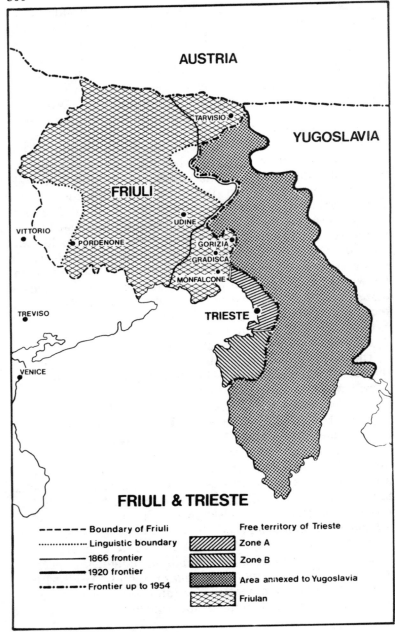

FRIULI & TRIESTE

– – – – – Boundary of Friuli	Free territory of Trieste
·············· Linguistic boundary	Zone A
——— 1866 frontier	Zone B
——— 1920 frontier	Area annexed to Yugoslavia
·—·—·—· Frontier up to 1954	Friulan

AUSTRIA

YUGOSLAVIA

FRIULI

TARVISIO

UDINE

VITTORIO

PORDENONE

GORIZIA

GRADISCA

MONFALCONE

TREVISO

TRIESTE

VENICE

unambiguous symptom of a whole complex of pitiable qualities, lack of principle, spiritual weakness, servility, mental inconsistency and so on. It is the clear index of that widespread evil which makes men ashamed to be what they are . . . It is the index of our gradual bastardization, our moral decadence, our perversity as a people ethnically distinct and autonomous. If we fail to apply a brake to this subtle form of cowardice we may as well give up hope of a Friulan renaissance'.

There is no university in the province. Two daily newspapers are published, each of which carries a page in Friulan. Radio programmes in the language are occasionally broadcast from Trieste and there is regional news on television in Italian. The theatre continues to flourish in Friulan. Local culture now consists mainly of a rich heritage of songs, the poetic form known as the *villotte*, dances and customs which include the Mass of Spadone, celebrated at Epiphany and followed by fires on the hills, and the bird festival of Sacile.

Friuli has never been economically prosperous. The textile industry of Udine, the docks at Monfalcone and the breeding of silk-worms have not been sufficient to absorb the local labour-force, which is famous for its diligence. On the other hand, the region is not poor, and the high rainfall and greenness of the countryside give it a mild, fertile aspect. Farming and stock-rearing are the principal occupations in rural areas, but there are also lead and tin mines, marble quarries and marl-pits which supply the province's cement and ceramic factories. The hydro-electricity industry, delayed after the War, is now fully operational and there is a major wharf for ships at Monfalcone, as well as important paper, clock, sweets, beer, clothes and chemical factories. Saw mills and furniture workshops are numerous, while in the higher villages, such as Manigo, Pesaris and Gamporosso the toys, cutlery and baskets made during the winter months are famous in Italy. The presence of large tracts of woodland has supported some of these industries since medieval times.

Relations between Friulans and the Slovenes and German-speaking minorities, established in the area since the twelfth century, are good, mainly because the latter, who live in the

Kanal and Resia valleys, are numerically very weak. But there is a growing hostility towards the influx of Italians from the south as to the 25,000 refugees from Istria, now part of Yugoslavia, who have settled in the province during the last two decades.

By the end of the Second World War, Friuli was a united area of Italy and before long its old spirit of independence stirred again in the form of demands for regional autonomy. This demand was finally satisfied on 31 January 1963 when Friuli-Venezia-Giulia was established as the fourth Region of Italy. The only detail to mar the joy of Friulan autonomists was the decision to make Trieste, the regional capital, rather than Udine. The creation of the new Region was the work of a centre-left Government, in response to the fact that Friuli is predominantly Christian Democrat. The joy of the Triestines was also marred because they found themselves in the minority on the Regional Council (24% of the seats against Udine's 65%). Furthermore, for socialist Trieste, Friuli is a reactionary, priest-ridden area which makes unreasonable demands for such institutions as its own University.

With Trieste and Venezia-Giulia, Friuli forms one of the five autonomous regions of Italy and is divided into three administrative units: Udine, Gorizia and Pordenone. Since 1963, however, when the Regional Statute began belatedly to take effect, there has been a substantial feeling in Friuli that it should not have been incorporated in the new region. The problem is that Trieste has become a symbol of the Italian spirit and is being continually held up as a model of what the Republic believes it has achieved for the peoples of this peripheral area since the Second World War. Growing criticism of the non-implementation of the Regional Statute, as far as Friuli's language and culture are concerned, has crystallised since 1963 in a new political party known as the *Movimento Friuli (Moviment Friûl)* which is associated with a number of cultural organisations and students' societies such as the *Union Furlane dai Universitaris*, founded in 1971. This movement has campaigned against the inclusion of Friuli in the Region by calling for an adjustment in the

Regional Statute which would make Friuli an autonomous administrative unit, and for the creation of a University at Udine and the teaching of Friulan in the schools. Contacts with the other Rhaeto-Romance language communities, in neighbouring South Tyrol and the Swiss canton of Graubüden, have grown in recent years. Candidates representing the Movement stood in local elections for the first time in 1968 but they have yet to contest general elections. Nevertheless, it is clear that the movement is winning support among young people and workers who, throughout the Region, are exhorted by slogans painted on walls such as *'Furlans'o sejs un Popul, clamajt la vesta Libertât!'* (Friulans, you are a People, demand your Freedom!').

One of the more interesting German-speaking islands in north-east Italy is situated in Friuli: the parish of Sauris (German: *Zahre),* high in the Carnian Alps at an altitude of 3,000 to 4,400 feet. It has been separated for over seven centuries by intervening Romance territory from Sappada *(Pladen),* its nearest German-speaking neighbour. The German dialect of Sauris has preserved a number of archaic features of Southern Bavarian and has developed other features of its own. These two factors combine to make it relatively difficult to understand for other German-speakers. As part of Friuli, Sauris—which was first settled in the thirteenth century—was separated from the Austrian Empire and entered the Italian State in 1866; its history has therefore been different from the South Tyrol's, from which it is separated by some thirty miles of mountains. The population of Sauris is about 800 and has probably never been much more than a thousand.

The area is remarkable from a socio-linguistic point of view in that, as well as their German dialect, its inhabitants use two other languages in the course of their everyday lives—Italian and a dialect of Friulian. Nowadays most children acquire Italian either as a first language from their parents or at school from the age of two. On the other hand, adult males learn some standard German while working in Austria or Germany. The use of the three languages is described as *diatypal,* in that language selection among adult Saurians shows a high degree of correlation with situational

factors. Italian tends to be used for 'high' situations such as
in church and school: most of the villagers can read and write
no other language. Italian is also used for speaking to outsiders and, more significantly, among Saurians in the presence
of outsiders and, increasingly, to children at home so that a
generation is now growing up for whom Italian is the only
language. But adult Saurians speaking to their fellows still
use the German dialect even in the hearing of their children,
so that most children have at least an acquaintance with the
dialect, especially those in Lateis and Sauris di Sotto. Friulan,
on the other hand, or perhaps the Carnian variety of it, is
spoken for 'middle' purposes, such as when Saurians address
acquaintances from the surrounding Friulan-speaking area
and also, in their preserve, by Saurians to each other. For
example, villagers hailing one another from a distance use
Friulan and then switch to German when within conversation
range. Most males in their twenties and thirties who have
been to secondary school at Ampezzo use Friulan for conversation. For most Saurians Friulan has the degree of integrity which goes with a modest station in life—less than they
see in Italian but far more than in the German dialect which is
kept for 'low' purposes. It is said that middle-class visitors
from Udine use Friulan in Sauris in a rather patronising way
when speaking to the rural population. The Saurians are
aware of this and often reply in Italian, thus restoring a
degree of dignity to the relationship. Thus the villagers are
able to deal with the affairs of the parish (in German dialect),
of the region (in Friulan) and of the outside world (in Italian).

THE LADINS OF THE DOLOMITES

Many of the characteristics of the South Tyrol's German-speaking population are shared by the 15,456 inhabitants (1971) who also speak Ladin, a dialect with Romansch and Friulan of the Rhaeto-Romance family.

The Ladins live in several valleys of the South Tyrol but principally in the Valle Gardena (German: *Grödnertal*) and the Valle Badia *(Gadertal)* in the autonomous province of Bolzano *(Bozen)* where they form about 3·7% of the population. There are also Ladin-speakers in the contiguous provinces of Trento and Belluno, in the seven parishes of the Valle Moena *(Fassatal)* and in the parishes of Cortina d'Ampezzo, Pieve-di-Livinallongo and Colle-Santa-Lucia *(Buchenstein)*. The total number of Ladins in the Dolomite Alps is not officially known but is variously estimated as between 30,000 and 35,000 of whom 23,577 lived in the three provinces in 1971.

Despite their linguistic individuality, the political allegiance of the Ladins who live in these high valleys has never been in doubt. Since the Venician Wars of the fifteenth century when they drove out the Italians and then the French, the Ladins have always made common cause with the German-speakers of the South Tyrol. In 1810 they appealed to the King of Bavaria to prevent their annexation by Italy and throughout the nineteenth century they united against Napoleon's armies in defence of their South Tyrolean traditions and liberties. Again in 1848 they resisted Mazzini by force of arms and, under the *Risorgimento*, all attempts at assimilation.

Although the language was not written until 1700 and is still divided into seven dialects, it was Ladin and the work of poets like Tita Alton in the eighteenth century which first gave a communal identity to its speakers, especially by the knowledge that it was a member of the Rhaeto-Romance family and thus related to the more illustrious Romansch of the Graubünden in Switzerland. But it was the rise of Italian nationalism in the nineteenth century which fostered their political consciousness, the conviction that as an ethnic group they were strongly attached to Austria and the South Tyrolean way of life which they shared with the German-speaking majority.

Shortly before the collapse of Austria in October 1918, the South Tyrol having been invaded by Italy three years previously, the parishioners of Gröden, Enneberg, Buchenstein and Fassa made their famous appeal to the German-speakers among whom they lived, ending: 'We are not Italians and have never wanted to be numbered among them. Nor do we wish to become Italians in the future. The fate of the German Tyroleans must be our fate too, their future ours. With them we and our fathers have always lived in the closest union and harmony. May it always remain so!' The following year the same parishes made a similar appeal to President Wilson at the Peace Conference of Versailles, but to no avail. With their German-speaking neighbours the Ladins of the Dolomites were obliged to become citizens of Italy.

The Italianisation of the schools, which up to now had given some instruction in Ladin, began under the fascist régime in 1921 when Mussolini's policies of political and linguistic coercion were implemented in all sectors of the South Tyrol's public life. Like his predecessor Ettore Tolomei (1865-1952), the philologist Carlo Battisti supported the fascists by attempting to prove with pseudo-scientific theories that Ladin was not related to the Rhaeto-Romance language but a dialect of Italian and that the Ladins were therefore Italians. When it became clear that the South Tyroleans remained unconvinced, the use of the word Ladin was promptly banned. In 1939, under the terms of the agreement on evacuation between the Italian and German Governments, about 2,000 Ladins (3·6%) left the South Tyrol for Austria in preference to being deported to places all over Italy.

After the Second World War, the Statute of Autonomy (Article 87) passed for the region of Trentino-Alto Adige in 1948 allowed the teaching of Ladin during the first year at primary school. But in Trento and Belluno no such provision was made and the language is still not taught there today. In 1967 a delegation led by Alois Pupp, the Ladin representative on the Regional Council of Bolzano at that time, called for the creation of an electoral district for the Ladin areas, equal status for German and Ladin, and more teaching through the medium of Ladin in the primary schools. Rome's refusal to grant these demands was criticised in the Ladin-speaking valleys, especially by Guido Jori, editor of the news bulletin *Postiglione della Dolomiti*. Also under attack was the Regional Council's failure to include the Ladins of Trento and Belluno, some 12,700, in the total enumerated at the 1961 Census. Since 1967 there has been growing support for Guido Jori's campaign.

Among the achievements of the *Union di Ladins*, founded in that year, was the introduction of a weekly programme and twelve minutes a day in Ladin on radio. This society, which publishes a bi-monthly journal *Nos Ladins*, joined a students' organisation called *Union Generala de la Dolomites*, founded in 1962, in leading what appears to be the first phase of a cultural renaissance of the Ladins in Italy. Meanwhile, in 1974 they had one out of thirty-four representatives in the Regional Council of the South Tyrol, a member of the *Süd-tiroler Volkspartei*.

The first task of these organisations is to unite the Ladins of the three areas in which they are scattered. For although they now have their own flag—an edelweiss on a blue, white and green background—they are not without their divisions. In 1972 five of the seven Ladin parishes in Fassatal, increasingly disappointed by the Regional Council of Trento, voted in favour of joining the South Tyrol. Their ambition was thwarted not only by the local authorities but by the Ladins of the South Tyrol who saw in such an extension of their territory the danger of further dilution of their numbers by the Italian-speaking majority of Trento. A similar proposal by the *Movimento Ladini* for the reunion of all the Ladins in the Dolomite Alps within a single administrative unit is likely to remain theoretical. Not only do the Ladins of the South Tyrol—the only group with even minimal linguistic rights—find it unacceptable but the regional experiment in Italy, already in serious difficulty, seems incapable at the present time of such development.

THE AOSTANS

The Aosta Valley (Italian: *Valle d'Aosta)* is a region of high valleys which form the upper reaches of the river Dora Baltea, a tributary of the Po, in the north-west of Italy on the borders with Switzerland and France. With an area of 1,260 square miles, it is bounded on three sides by the giants of the Western Alps: Monte Rosa (15,203 feet), the Matterhorn or Cervino (14,679 feet) and Monte Bianco or Mont Blanc (15,772 feet). The river Dora Baltea, formed by two streams which meet under Mont Blanc, flows east for about fifty-four miles as far as the town of Pont Saint Martin, thus defining the region, before it reaches the Piedmont plain to the north of Turin.

From the central valley rise thirteen lateral valleys: on the right bank, the Val Veni, Val de la Thuile, Val Grisanche, Val de Rhêmes, Val Savaranche, Val de Cogne and Val de Champorcher; on the left bank, the Val Ferret, Val du Grand Saint Bernard, Val Pelline, Val Tournanche, Val d'Ayas and Val de Grassoney. All the important towns such as Pont Saint Martin, Bard, Saint Vincent, Avise and the capital Aosta (population 36,961), are situated in the main valley of the Dora Baltea (French: *Doire Baltée).* At the 1971 Census the population of the Aosta Valley was 109,252, of whom about 70,000 gave French or its dialects as their mother-tongue.

The construction of the Grand Saint Bernard and the Mont Blanc tunnels, opened to traffic in 1964 and 1965, provided the first direct road-link between the Aosta Valley and the canton of Valais in Switzerland and Savoy in France. De Gaulle, as President of France, was present on both occasions and was greeted with great enthusiasm by the inhabitants of the Aosta Valley when he declared, 'I thank the dear *Valdôtains* for their moving welcome. There is no doubt that contacts between our two countries will multiply from now on, especially with this beautiful valley whose blood, language and sentiment link it so closely with France'.

The President of France was referring to the fact that from the Middle Ages until the eighteenth century the Aosta Valley, the ancient *Vallis Augustana* of Roman times, formed part of the *États de Savoie.* The region is the last remnant of an area which once extended the entire length of the Alps and where French or its dialects were widely spoken until recent times. The French language also survives within Italy's borders in the province of Turin, the upper Valle Canavais and times. When in 1860 Savoy became part of France, the Aosta Valley lost its old freedoms and was joined to Italy. The plebiscite of that year by which the Savoyards were able to vote in favour or against unification with France was not granted to the *Valdôtains* (Italian: *Valdostani)* on the other side of the water-shed.

From 1860 to 1914 the Aosta Valley was in an almost permanent state of economic crisis and was sometimes described as 'the Siberia of Italy', a cul-de-sac notorious for the incidence of inbreeding and mental illness among its inhabitants. During those years there was a continuous exodus from the Valley into France which continued even after the First World War, reaching a peak between 1922 and 1931. Deprived of the autonomy which it had previously enjoyed, the region suffered not only in economic terms but also linguistically from the Italian State's policies which made no provision for the existence of minorities within its borders. Following the example of France, Italy was opposed from the beginning to all claims on behalf of the Aosta Valley's individuality: the new Republic was to be *'una ed indivisible'*. Despite resistance from the clergy and the upper classes, sometimes violent, the Italian language gained more and more ground during the second half ot the nineteenth century. French was banned from the schools in 1879 and from the law-courts in 1880.

Nevertheless, there has always been a strong spirit of independence and local pride in the Aosta Valley, *'la petite patrie'* of the Aostans' songs. In 1919 they sent a delegation to Bern to plead for acceptance into the Swiss Confederation, but without success. The fate of a petition organised in 1923 by the *Ligue Valdôtaine pour la Défense de la Langue Française* (Aostan League for the Defence of the French Language) which has been founded by Anselmo Réan in 1909, asking the Peace Conference in Paris to protect the French language in the Valley, was similar. French was specifically prohibited in the schools by Mussolini in 1925. Again in 1926 the *Ligue Valdôtaine* appealed to the King of Italy for his intervention in the Government's policies towards French culture in the region, but in vain. During the years from 1923 to 1934 the fascist and francophobe régime persisted in attempts to destroy all French feeling in the Valley, banning the French language's use from all sectors of public life, including place-names and personal names, newspapers and speeches. The *Ligue Valdôtaine* was closed down in 1925. At the same time the Valley was industrialised, Italians brought in as workers and a new province comprising Aosta and the Italian-speaking area of Ivrea was created. The town of Aoste, for centuries French-speaking, became Aosta and predominantly Italian-speaking soon afterwards; only about 7,000 French-speakers live there today.

During the Second World War there followed a brief but heroic phase of active resistance by the Aostans to the fascist powers, led by two groups. The first of these, *La Jeune Vallée d'Aoste,* had been founded by a priest, Joseph Trèves, in 1925 as a movement for young people. Its aim was 'to come to the rescue of the homeland in its agony' by creating in every parish a centre where French was taught and the Valley's traditions upheld. The movement also stood for the abolition of the Italian monarchy, the foundation of a federal Aostan Parliament and the restoration of 'the region's rights, traditions and customs, its strength and honour'.

The *Abbé* Trèves died in 1941 but among his disciples was Emile Chanoux, a lawyer born in 1906, who led a second group (which was named after him) against the policies of Mussolini by organising armed resistance in the Valley during the last three years of the Second World War. Chanoux's own ambition as expressed in the Chivasso Manifesto of 1953, *'Déclaration des représentants des populations alpines',* which was supported by Piedmontese resistance fighters, was the complete separation of Aosta from Italy and the establishment of an independent State. He was arrested by the fascist police in 1944, tortured and executed without trial on 18 May.

The death of Émile Chanoux had a major effect on separatist feeling in the Aosta Valley and a third group, the *Union Valdôtaine,* was to make rapid progress in the years after the War with its demand, if not for the independence with Chanoux wanted, at least for federal status within the French or Swiss State. Switzerland, however, made it clear that it had no interest in the Aosta Valley. So during 1945 and 1946 the *Union Valdôtaine,* now representing 80% of the population, looked to France. In April and May of 1945 French troops entered the Valley, only to be withdrawn under pressure from Churchill and Truman, masters of Italy at the time, and to the chagrin of De Gaulle whose personal concern about the region's fate dates from this time. With the departure of the French troops the Italian Government made a number of small concessions in favour of the French language in the Aosta Valley, appointed 'safe' Aostans to key posts and set up an autonomous régime, separated from the province of Turin, to be formed in September 1945.

At the same time it was announced that France must relinquish its interest in the region and that the Aosta Valley was now expected to deal exclusively with Rome. The *Union Valdôtaine* greeted this announcement with defiance and attempted to persuade the Allies to recognise 'the Aostan people' by including bi-lateral guarantees for the region in the Peace Treaty with Italy, as had happened in the Treaty between Austria and Italy over the South Tyrol. In 1946 a telegram was sent to all foreign ambassadors at Bern seeking their support in the creation of an international commission on the Aostan problem. When both moves failed British troops were engaged by Aostan guerrillas during March 1946.

From 1948 to 1970 the Aosta Valley was governed under the Statute of 1945, with Frederico Chabod who had led the *Comité de Libération Nationale* against the fascists as the first President of the Regional Council. This period saw the restoration of Aostan rights, at least in theory, in the fields of administration, economy, language and culture. For the first time since becoming part of the Italian State the Aosta Valley—together with the South Tyrol, Sicily and Sardinia—was now an officially recognised region. Under the constitutional law of 26 February 1948 the Regional Council was given the rights of primary legislation in twenty-one sectors including agriculture, roads, water resources, tourism and cultural affairs and secondary legislation in thirteen including industry, commerce, hydro-electricity and education.

Article 14 established a duty-free zone for the Valley and Article 38 accorded equal status for the French and Italian languages. All administrative posts were to be filled by bilingual persons and school-lessons in both languages were to be equal in number and duration.

It was thus possible, following the Statute of 1948, to speak in a general way of a comparatively large measure of decentralisation in the Aosta Valley, to an extent not granted anywhere in France, for example, and to say that this region, the smallest in Italy, was to some extent an experiment in local democracy. But in practice the measure of effective autonomy remained below the prescribed standard, mainly as the result of resistance by the Christian Democrats who, more recently with Liberals and the neo-fascist *Movimento Sociale Italiano,* have set their face against any effective devolution for the Valley. It is therefore more accurate to claim that the Statute of 1948, which was conceded by the Italian Government rather than negotiated and wholeheartedly agreed, allowed a degree of autonomy more apparent than real and remained unapplied in several important aspects. For example, following State nationalisation of water supplies in 1962, the Aostans were not able to use or sell all the water collected in their Valley; the duty-free zone was not created; the teaching of French was not introduced and Italian remained the sole language of administation. The minority's rights as defined in 1948 were continuously denied by the political parties' ditortion of constitutional texts and by administrative practice.

Whether or not the second Regional Statute of 1970 will secure the implementation of the Government's policies in the Aosta Valley remains to be seen. Under this Statute the *Consiglio Regionale* (Regional Council), the legislative body, is composed of thirty-five members who are elected every five years and who, in their turn, elect the Regional Junta or executive body. The Council's President, at the present time Guiseppe Montesano of the Social Democratic Party, and seven assessors for education, finance, agriculture, industry, tourism, public works, health and social security, sit on the Junta, under the chairman César Dujany of the Popular Democratic Party. The region is represented in Rome by a deputy and a senator who are elected every five years. From 1958 to 1963 the representatives in the lower house were René Chabod and from 1963 to 1968 Severin Caveri, and in the upper house Caveri from 1958 to 1963 and from 1963 to his death in 1966 Conrad Gex, all of whom were members of the *Union Valdôtaine.*

The political life of the Aosta Valley is characterised by clashes of personality and a large number of parties, both local and national, with many of the schisms, plots, scandals, blunders, coalitions, dissidence and defections which have been typical of Italy's politics during the last three decades. From 1946 to 1949 the Regional Council had twenty-five members, five from each of the following: the Action Party, the Christian Democrats, the Communists, the Socialists and the Liberals. But in 1949 a coalition of the Christian Democrats and the *Union Valdôtaine* was formed, with twenty-eight seats and opposed to the left-wing parties who held seven. In the elections of 1954 the Christian Democrats split from the autonomists with the result that the *Union Valdôtaine,* fighting on its own, won 29·2% of the votes and one seat, the Christian Democrats and their allies 40·7% and twenty-five seats, and the left-wing parties nine seats with 30·1% of the votes. This election was famous for the passions it aroused and the intervention of the Church which denounced the alliance between the *Union Valdôtaine* and the Communist Party.

The year 1963, when the *Union Valdôtaine* had forty-five out of seventy-four mayors among its members, saw the introduction of a new electoral system based on proportional representation and the birth of a second autonomist party, the *Rassemblement Valdôtain*. In the elections of 1968 this party, in alliance with the Christian Democrats, won nineteen seats in the Regional Council. Four years later (at elections in which it was agreed to vote for two Christian Democrats and *Union Valdôtaine* candidates who had been killed in a road accident) the two autonomist parties won an over-all majority. But later in 1972 victory went to a coalition of left-wing groups, also autonomists, led by the son of Émile Chanoux. There was a similar result in the elections of 1973. The Popular Democrats and their left-wing allies won twenty out of the thirty-five seats, the Christian Democrats and the autonomists eleven. A new feature of the Regional Council's composition was that, mainly as a result of strife between the autonomists and socialists, the neo-fascist *Movimento Sociale Italiano* now holds a seat in the Council.

It is clear that, as autonomy functions today in the Aosta Valley, it provides a battle-ground for all the political parties of Italy, with excellent opportunities for intrigue and internecine strife. Although the regional parties such as the *Union Valdôtaine* and the *Rassemblement Valdôtain* sometimes win power overnight and can thus influence the course of events for a while, politics in the Aosta Valley are mostly the preserve of the national parties. The partisan ideologies of the Social Democrats, the Popular Democrats and the Communists, who are supported by about 60% of the population, inevitably reflect the politics of Milan, Turin and Rome, while the divisions of the autonomists into at least three camps do little to focus attention on regional affairs.

Among the first casualities of the Aosta Valley's political instability was the region's linguistic identity, now under serious threat from encroachment by the Italian language in all spheres and in most districts. In 1901, of 83,500 inhabitants only 6,700 were Italian-speakers. In 1921 Italian was confined to five out of the Valley's seventy-four parishes: Aosta, Bard, Verres, Chatillon and La Thuile. By 1965 only twenty-six parishes had less than 5% Italian-speakers, while twelve had up to 10%, fifteen up to 20%, eleven up to 30%, eight up to 50% and two over 50%. By today about a half of the population speak only Italian. The degree of assimilation of Italian-speakers is negligible for, with a high rate of mixed marriages, Italian tends to be the language of the younger generation. Italians also take the best jobs, especially in commerce and industry; tourism, which has developed rapidly in recent years since the opening of the tunnels—there is a winter and a summer season in the Alps—is almost completely in the hands of Italians, people from '*ba per lé*' as the Aostans say. While the population of the region's towns, especially Aosta's, increases, the mountain communes lose theirs and agriculture declines. Farmers, almost all French-speaking, now constitute only 12% of the total population—5,683 as against 11,756 in 1961. Between 1955 and 1964 nearly 20,000 Italians settled in the Valley. Unemployment is still a permanent problem, while the introduction of industry, mostly steel-works, mining, construction and water-works, has contributed substantially to the process of Italianisation since 1956.

The Regional Council, far from tackling the economic problems of the Aosta Valley, has also failed to implement the Article of the Statute of 1948 which accords equal status to the French and Italian languages, for nowhere in the public life of the region is French in regular, official use. The Church has shown no inclination to use both languages at any level, despite the example set in an earlier generation by the *Abbé* Trèves. In March 1975, however, there was a wedding in the church of Valle Maria which was the first to be celebrated in Occitan; the young couple were both members of the *Mouvement pour l'Autonomie Occitane* and the priest was a Friulan. It is only since 1969 that some but not all street-names and place-names signs have been erected bilingually. Inscriptions on State offices are in Italian, while those of the regional authorities are bilingual.

The last bastion of the French language in the Aosta Valley is now the school. Despite the fact that it leaves much room for improvement, the education system—which is the responsibility of the Region and not the State's—gives something like a proper place to French. The teaching of French, as a foreign language, is obligatory at both primary and secondary level, although the right to be examined in it at the *maturità* is often contested and it is the only language studied through the medium of the language itself. A survey of the home language of 7,657 pupils in primary schools carried out in 1967 revealed that just over half spoke Italian and the rest the Franco-Provençal dialect of Occitan; less than 10% spoke standard French. There is no University in the Aosta Valley and 92% of students go to Turin for their higher education.

The erosion of standard French and Occitan as everyday languages which has taken place in the Valley since the Second World War has been accelerated by the mass media which use Italian almost exclusively. Twenty years of protest by the *Union Valdôtaine,* backed by innumerable petitions and demonstrations demanding the installation of masts which would relay television programmes from France and Switzerland have met with no response from the authorities in Rome. In 1973, following *R.T.F.'s* installation of a television mast on the Hellbronner Mountain in the Mont Blanc massif, the Regional Council agreed unanimously to finance its own station for the reception of programmes from across the border, with the French Government's permission, but the Government in Rome over-ruled this decision. As television reaches three out of every four families, even in the remotest districts, the process of Italianisation by this medium continues apace. In the cinemas only Italian films are shown.

There is is a French-language press in the Aosta Valley. The Regional Studies Centre at Aosta and the Franco-Provençal Centre at Saint Nicholas publish anthologies, books and periodicals. Books in French still sell almost not all, however, and the region has produced no writer of any note. Newspapers arrive from France two or three days after publication, but there are a number of local papers, mostly published by the various political parties, which appear either in French or in bilingual editions. The *Union Valdôtaine's* organs are the fortnightly *Le Peuple Valdôtain* and the monthly *Le Drapeau Rouge et Noir* (the region's flag is red and black). The *Comité des Traditions Valdôtaines* publishes a cultural magazine *Le Flambeau* and since 1969 there is an important review entitled *Augusta* in French, Italian and the Walser dialect of German. The attitude of the French-speakers to the small Walser community of about 800 people in the upper Lys valley which constitutes less than 1% of the region's population is extremely sympathetic and every effort is made to guarantee education for them in their dialect and in German.

It must be concluded that, whereas fascism failed to stamp out all traces of the French past in the Aosta Valley, the Italian Government since 1945 has very nearly succeeded. Although the French language has regained some of its former strength, at least in theory, it has not won back the place it held before the rise of Mussolini. To many commentators on life in the Valley today its revival in part during the years immediately after the Second World War now appears illusory and, if present circumstances continue, its decay is regarded as likely to be irreversible. Far from having undergone a revolution in its political, social and economic life, Italy has continued to rely on traditional reflexes, on its own outmoded nationalism, in its attitude towards linguistic minorities within its borders. In the Aosta Valley, given the incompetence of the regional authorities and the pernicious influence of the national political parties, autonomy has proved to be a very effective instrument for the implementation of decisions by the central Government.

The Italian Constitution of 1948 provided for the creation of the Region as an autonomous unit for the purposes of local administration. Designed with the laudable aim of combating the over-centralisation which had been a feature of the fascist régime, the new Law divided the country into nineteen such Regions. It was first implemented in Sicily, Sardinia, the Aosta Valley and the South Tyrol, all peripheral areas with special problems. In Sicily, where a degree of autonomy had been granted as early as 1946, the Government's aim was to counter demands for separatism. After 1948 the nineteen Regions were given control over their legislative and financial affairs, as well as urban development, tourism, agriculture, roads and public works. They could raise their own taxes and elect a Council, and an executive Junta, or cabinet, with its own President.

That the regional experiment in Italy has not met with much success is due to several factors. Many Italians are of the opinion that the country already has far too many bureaucrats and they cannot see the need for adding to the provincial and communal councils. Secondly, there is a widespread fear—confirmed in the Regional elections of 1975—that communists and socialists would be bound to win control in their traditional strongholds of Emilia-Romagna, Umbria and Tuscany, thus forming 'a red belt' across the centre of Italy. Again, party attitudes have fluctuated according to the tactical situation: the Socialists, once in power, have exerted pressure on their more enthusiastic Christian Democratic colleagues to abandon all attempts to develop regional autonomy. They also point to the failure of the regional experiment in Sicily where preposterous alliances between the most incompatible of parties have been forged in order to allow their leaders to stay in power.

THE SOUTH TYROLEANS

The South Tyrol, known to the Italian State as the province of *Bolzano* and to its German-speaking inhabitants as *Südtirol*, is situated in Italy's northernmost region of Trentino-Alto Adige, on the border with Austria to which it is linked by the Brenner Pass. Here, among a total population of 433,215 (1971), live—together with 15,456 Ladins—approximately 26,000 people whose mother-tongue is German.

An Alpine region which shares the geography of the neighbouring Austrian province of Tyrol and the Swiss canton of Graubünden, the South Tyrol is clearly distinguished from the Lombardian plain to the south. The Alps, forming a natural barrier between Austria and Italy which is particularly wide at this point, are penetrated by narrow gaps but, once entered, road communications become relatively easy over low passes and along the deep, fluvial valleys of the river Adige and its affluents the Isarco (German: *Eisack)* and the Rienza *(Rienz).* In this area of 2,815 square miles, the principal towns are the administrative capital Bolzano *(Bozon)* and Merano *(Meran).*

The South Tyrol, which became the Italian State's territory after the Treaty of St. Germain in 1919, was for the previous fourteen centuries a part of the German-speaking world, situated as it is to the north of the Salorno Pass which marked the beginning of the Latin world and which is the province's southernmost point today. Under the Holy Roman Empire, the entire Tyrol—including the part which is now in Austria—was entrusted to the bishops of Trient (Italian: *Trento),* in an attempt to protect this strategically important area from the ravages of the local nobility. The bishops' powers were later transferred to bailiffs from among whom there eventually emerged, after merciless pillage, the Counts of Tyrol (Italian: *Tirolo),* they became the rulers of the entire region and gave it their name.

It was from about this time that the Tyroleans began to develop a strong independence of character based on local customs and liberties, and their own system of democratic government. In 1363 the Tyrol, under Rudolf of Austria, became one of the brightest jewels in the Habsburg crown, assured for centuries of a prosperous, peaceful existence and totally loyal to its rulers. As part of the Austrian Empire the Tyrol's history as a German-speaking area was illustrious, symbolised by the revolt in 1809 against the threat of Franco-Bavarian domination. Andreas Hofer, who led this revolt, was a native of Val Passiria *(Passeiertal);* he was captured and shot in 1810 but his exploits and end made him the national hero of the Tyroleans.

On the eve of the First World War the population of the South Tyrol consisted of approximately 232,700 German-speakers and Ladin-speakers, 7,100 Italian-speakers and 11,700 people of other language groups. It was essentially a rural region, dependent on the cultivation of vines and fruit in the valleys and, in the mountains, on stock-rearing, forestry and farming. The population, mostly farmers, were of sturdy peasant stock, highly literate in German and deeply Catholic, an ethnically homogenous community passionately attached to their way of life and their land, conservative and naturally suspicious of the south's *italinatà*. Mazzini had claimed the region for Italy during the previous century and, during the Risorgimento, Ettore Tolomei (1865-1952) led the cause of the South Tyrol's annexation by Italy, but the South Tyroleans had stoutly resisted all arguments based on Italy's 'natural frontiers on the Alps'.

When Austria declared war on Serbia in 1914, thus unleashing the First World War, Italy at first maintained its neutrality, although public excitement was soon fanned into open hostility. The Italian leaders sought to exploit the situation to the utmost; while Austria tried to persuade Italy to maintain its neutrality and the countries of the *Entente* strove to engage Italy on their side, for Rome the highest bidder was always the most convincing. Austria was prepared to relinquish Trentino and Trieste but refused all discussion on the future of the South Tyrol. On the other hand, the *Entente* not only promised the South Tyrol to Italy but also the Istria peninsula, now part of the Yugoslav Republic of Slovenia, and a large slice of the Dalmatian coast. This treaty, signed in London on 26 April 1915 between France, Britain, Russia and Italy, contained all these promises. It was thus that Italy entered the War, after deliberately and carefully weighing the advantages of neutrality against those of intervention.

Although the War was fought for the rights of small nations and although the ninth of the Fourteen Points enunciated by President Wilson recognised that 'the adjustment of the frontiers of Italy should be effected according to lines of separation between clearly recognisable nationalities', the Peace Conference of September 1919 decided to recognise Italy's claim to the South Tyrol. With the collapse of the Austro-Hungarian Empire, Italian troops were installed on the Brenner Pass where, for the first time, they were able to deal with resistance from Austrian units which, for decades, had been sent there by the people's militia of the Tyrol, the *Schützen.*

The annexation of the South Tyrol by Italy was widely resented as an injustice to Austria and contributed, according to some observers, towards the crisis of national identity in that country between the Wars. But the division of the Tyrol was most bitterly felt by the Tyroleans themselves. In May 1919 the Tyrolean Diet, adopted a resolution proposing the creation of an independent, neutral republic which was to include the South Tyrol, but no progress was made towards its establishment. The consequences of the annexation were dramatic. Not protected by any minority treaty, the South Tyroleans quickly learned how much the promises of the Government in Rome to respect their individuality were worth. To the subtle process of cultural assimilation was added outright oppression by the increasingly fascist authorities based on the programme previously advocated by Tolomei: proscription of the German language from all sectors of public life, replacement of South Tyrolean officials by Italians, substitution of the name *Südtirol* by Alto Adige, liquidation of German political parties and unions, complete Italianisation of the schools and personal names, repression of everything which might remind the people of their German past, and prosecution of all defaulters.

For several years the cohesion of the South Tyroleans enabled them to resist these measures intended to implement Mussolini's oath that he would achieve the complete Italianisation of the region over-night. Even more stringent

measures were therefore taken. The organisation known as
Ente Nazionale per le Tre Venezie began to evict South
Tyroleans from their land and to install Italians, to take over
agricultural enterprises and disenfranchise land-owners, to
open factories near Bolzano in which only Italians were
eligible for employment. Within a few years the South
Tyroleans were relegated to a position of economic and social
inferiority. Obliged to withdraw from the towns and to fall
back on the mountains for their livelihood, the South
Tyroleans reverted to being a principally peasant people. By
1939 a total of 85,600 Italians were living in the South Tyrol,
some 25% of the total population, of whom 48,300 were settled in the town of Bolzano. From the serious consequences of
the inbalance between the rural and urban nature of the
South Tyrolean population the region has not yet recovered.

Major blows had been struck against the economic
prosperity and the cultural identity of the South Tyrol. But
the 'Pact of Steel' between Hitler and Mussolini required even
greater acceleration in the process of assimilation. On 26 June
1939 an agreement was signed in Berlin providing for the
transference of the South Tyrol's population from Italy to the
German *Reich:* the region was to be sacrificed on the altar of
friendship between the Fascist States. It now became clear
that the population had a clear choice between complete
denationalisation, with the prospect of deportation to the
south of Italy, or transference to the *Reich* with their identity
preserved, at least according to the terms of the agreement.
Faced with such an alternative and under the most crude
pressure from the German authorities, as well as from the
Italians, the South Tyroleans opted *en masse* (183,365 out of
266,885) for transference to the *Reich.* The transference of
population was slowed down owing to wartime conditions but
by the end of 1943 some 75,000 had migrated to the *Reich.*
Most were townspeople or officials, for with the farmers' attachment to their land proved a stronger factor. Although a
decree of 1948 offered repatriation only a third took advantage of it. About one third of these, however, managed to
emigrate before German troops entered the South Tyrol and
many of those who remained later took part in resistance activities.

The defeat of fascism in 1944 provided the Allied Powers with the opportunity of correcting the errors and injustices committed in the South Tyrol as a result of the agreement reached in 1919. But for various reasons none was prepared to take advantage of the new situation in the region's interests. Vienna protested in vain against the decision by the Conference of Ministers for Foreign Affairs, on 30 April 1946, which handed back the South Tyrol to Italy and the South Tyroleans' demand to decide their own fate, supported by many popular demonstrations, was not conceded. At the Peace Conference in Paris on 29 July 1946 Austria failed to revoke the decision of the Ministers' Conference, between Alcide De Gasperi and Karl Gruber, although the intervention of some representatives allowed the signature on 5 September 1946, of an agreement between Italy and Austria which guaranteed the South Tyroleans a certain number of rights; these were to be added to the Peace Treaty of 10 February 1947.

The Paris Agreement was meant to close the controversy over to whom the South Tyrol was to belong. Placing the region under an international régime, with Austria entrusted with the responsibility of supervising the treatment accorded to the minority, the South Tyrol found itself in a new situation. According to the Agreement's first Article, primary and secondary education in German was to be guaranteed, parity between the German and Italian languages was to be restored, the German forms of surnames (which had been Italianised under Mussolini) was to be allowed, the equality of eligibility for public officials was recognised and other measures were to be taken in an attempt to achieve a more satisfactory balance between the three ethnic groups. The second Article conceded the South Tyrol's demand for regional autonomy with the exercise of legislative and executive powers. In the third Article Italy undertook to revise the option on nationality set out in the Hitler-Mussolini pact of 1939, to reach agreement with Austria on the reciprocal recognition of university degrees, and to permit the free transit of goods via the South Tyrol between the North Tyrol and the East Tyrol with special arrangements for frontier exchanges.

The aim of the signatories of this Agreement was to assure the inhabitants of the South Tyrol, in the words of Article 1, of 'a complete equality of rights with those of the Italian-speaking inhabitants, within the context of special dispensations designed to safeguard the ethnic quality and the economic and cultural development of the German-speaking group'. In practice, however, the situation was often quite different. The implementation of the third Article raised few problems but the same cannot be said, unfortunately, for Articles 1 and 2. For it seems clear that during the years 1946 to 1969 the actual degree of autonomy enjoyed by the South Tyrol was less than that described in the Paris Agreement, so that full recognition of the German and Ladin-speakers' rights has not, in fact, been achieved.

The attempt at granting the South Tyroleans their political autonomy was made in response to their desire for full control over their own affairs and was meant to compensate for their fundamental inequality with the Italian-speaking majority who run the Italian State. But what happened, over the decade up to 1969, is that regional autonomy was granted, not to the South Tyrol as a well defined unit, but to the Region of Trentino-Alto Adige, a much larger area in which the Italians were in a majority. The South Tyroleans claimed that the creation of this Region did not correspond with the spirit of the Paris Agreement and, furthermore, that it constituted a serious violation of it.

It is true that, in the regional context, the province of Bolzano and the province of Trento have considerable legislative powers and more or less autonomous executives. But this kind of autonomy was limited in scope and was beset with many problems. The matters under provincial supervision concerned, for the most part, folklore, culture and education, while responsibility for economic development (agriculture, commerce and tourism etc) belonged to the Region. The Article in the Statute of Autonomy which compelled the Region to exercise its administrative functions by delegating them to the province, was only minimally applied. What was even more serious, the decrees provided by the Statute, which were indispensable if the Province was to exercise its powers in an effective manner, were implemented in only a fragmentary way, slowly and in a spirit increasingly antagonistic to real autonomy. The meddlesome control of the Government in Rome and the centralist spirit of the administration there, together with the jurisprudence of the constitutional court, did the rest: autonomy in the South Tyrol shrank like a *peau de chagrin,* everywhere subordinate to the activities of the State and nowhere approaching the terms of the Paris Agreement.

The only exception, an important one, to the Government's failure to implement the Paris Agreement was that of Article 1 concerning education. In the province of Bolzano teaching was carried out in the infant schools, as well as in the primary and secondary schools, in the mother-tongue of the pupils, whether German or Italian, and by teachers who spoke the same language. Indeed, it is evident that the baneful effects of the fascist period on education in the South Tyrol, as in other regions of the Italian State, have been largely overcome—except for an inevitable lack of qualified teachers—and the South Tyroleans enjoy, in this respect, a situation which other European minorities might well envy.

Much more ominous was the question, also dealt with under Article 1, of employment. Nearly thirty years after the signing of the Paris Agreement, a satisfactory balance between employment of the two ethnic groups was far from being achieved by 1969. In all sectors the Italians were in a majority. The measures taken by the Government to 'prefer' South Tyrolean applicants for jobs had been so few that they had had little effect. The Italian language was still essential for administrative posts, and as a result, only the few who were bilingual succeeded in filling them. Furthermore, those parts of the Paris Agreement which provided for parity between the two principal languages of the South Tyrol in public administration were interpreted by the Government in a typically singular way. Distinguishing between external and internal usage, it obliged public bodies to use only Italian, both within the service and between services. The mayors of rural communes, almost entirely German-speaking, therefore had to correspond in Italian. It is not surprising that in daily life, except perhaps in the home, Italian began to be the usual language of communication in the South Tyrol.

The Government's failure to implement, in practice, the Paris Agreement caused the German-speaking population of the South Tyrol, after years of delay, to feel itself threatened as a linguistic community. The immigration of Italians on an increasing scale, a phenomenon encouraged by industrialists and by systematic discrimination in the allocation of homes, exacerbated the situation. The regional authorities, prevented by the Government from exercising their powers, have done little to stem this immigration. The consequence was that the South Tyroleans have not found the opportunities which the industrialisation of their region should have provided and its largely rural character remains unaffected. As the small farm cannot maintain the typically large family of the South Tyrol, many thousands have emigrated to Switzerland, Austria and Germany (especially to the industrial conurbations of the Ruhr) in pursuit of work and homes. If there has been an improvement in the region's standard of living during recent years it is at the cost of almost complete Italianisation of the principal towns and valleys, to an extent which many German-speakers consider to be irreversible.

Whereas in 1910 about 97% of the South Tyrol's population had been German-speaking, at the restoration of democratic conditions in 1945 only 66% were. Furthermore, over 70% of the German-speakers now lived by agriculture, while Italian-speakers were employed mostly in trade and administration. The linguistic division had become a social one, with serious consequences for the German-speakers' cultural life. By 1961 their numbers had dropped again to 232,717 (62%) while Italian-speakers had increased to 128,271 (34%); in that year, 79% (109,000) of the Italian-speakers were living in the principal centres of Bolzano and Merano, where only 23% (61,430) of the German-speakers lived; by 1971, 77% of the inhabitants of Bolzano were Italian-speakers and 55% of Merano's.

It is no wonder that after years of dispute and compromise, a profound feeling of resentment grew among the German-speaking community. This dissatisfaction has been expressed principally through the *Südtiroler Volkspartei* (South Tyrol

People's Party). In 1954 the *S. V.P.* handed a memorandum to the Italian Government asking for full application of the autonomy statute in accordance with the spirit of the Paris Treaty, but received no reply. This snub by the central Government caused a number of incidents during the next few years, both symbolic and pragmatic. A lady of seventy-eight years, Julie Grabner, was imprisoned for painting the shutters of her house in red and white—the Austrian colours banned in 1927. In 1957 a demonstration of 35,000 South Tyroleans moved into Austria after being prevented from entering Bolzano. The following year all the *S. V.P.* members of the Regional Assembly resigned in protest against continuing delays in implementing the statute. Then, in 1961, the first attacks on Government property, usually frontier posts or pylons occurred. On *Herz Jesu Nacht* (11-12 June) of that year there were no less than forty-seven explosions in various parts of the province, killing several people.

The dispute caused by the situation in the South Tyrol, between Italy on the one hand which always claims to have applied the Paris Agreement in the strictest way, and on the other the South Tyrolean minority and Austria, developed in complexity and intensity over the next five years. The emphasis in this highly litiginous dispute shifts from time to time, from wrangling over internal laws to appeals to international law. Negotiations between Rome and Vienna have been made tortuous by the refusals and dilatory procedures of the Italian Government, especially since the State came to the brink of economic and political chaos, but also by the halfhearted attempts of the Austrians at an international level which include representations to the United Nations, the Council of Europe and the European Commission for Human Rights. Meanwhile, terrorism increased, Italy vetoed commercial negotiations between Austria and the E.E.C.—and the South Tyrolean problem remained as far from a solution as ever.

The next important initiative was an agreement reached, after the most laborious of negotiations, and sealed at a meeting of the Austrian and Italian Ministers for Foreign Affairs, Waldheim and Moro, at Copenhagen in November 1969. Once again the agreement was a compromise, with the two Governments refusing to budge, in essence, from their fundamental positions of 1946. Italy agreed to add to the statute of the German-speaking minority a large number of improvements, commonly known as 'The Packet', which although they had no formal or legal status were to be applied through a 'calendar' over many years, supported by declarations by the two States that they intended abiding by the Paris Agreement. In taking part in this compromise the Austrian Government, more clearly than ever, abandoned its intention of using 'The Packet' to create a new document of international value out of which real and permanent guarantees for the South Tyrol might be negotiated, a step noted by the region's autonomists and those who advocated the use of violence against both Austria and Italy. They maintained that if 'The Packet' were properly administered it would satisfy most of their needs: the fundamental recognition of the South Tyrolean minority within the Italian State rather than as a troublesome group to be placated with promises that are rarely kept, the teaching of German at all levels of education and the training of qualified teachers, the wide and free use of German in public administration, the development of the German (and Ladin) cultures, and the extension of political autonomy to the extent agreed in Paris. The autonomists pointed out, however, that the sole effect of the 1969 Agreement was to preserve the context of the Trentino-Alto Adige province. Within this context there were, nevertheless, South Tyroleans who were prepared to advance the interests of their region as far as possible. Relations between the State and the Province have improved somewhat since 1970, notably as the result of the work of a permanent consultative commission, including both Italian and German-speakers, which exists to study and report on problems peculiar to the South Tyrol, and especially since 1972 when a new Autonomy Statute was finally agreed.

The majority of the German-speakers, 87% in 1974, still support the main political party of the South Tyrolese people, the *S. V.P.* In its ranks there was a minority which was hostile to the acceptance of 'The Packet', arguing that certain clauses assigned to autonomy not the function of ensuring the protection of the German-speakers but that of making possible the peaceful existence of the two groups—a situation in which the Italian-speakers were seen to have the upper hand. They claimed that the Italians, who enjoyed certain rights to 'protect' them from the German-speakers, were thus a privileged minority. Disputes between the two were frequent and vociferous. They were referred either to the constitutional Court or to the administrative Tribunal. There, according to a minority within the *S.V.P.*, the organs of the State were always more anxious about the defence of its interests than about the development of the South Tyroleans. They also complained that the Italians were able, at this level, to obstruct the South Tyrolean representatives and that, especially in the provincial assembly of Bolzano, the main political parties of Italy were thus able to interfere with business which is more properly the responsibility of the South Tyroleans themselves. This process has continued so blatantly that it was generally believed up to 1972 that the German-speakers, disillusioned by the new measure of autonomy, were about to turn on the Italian-speakers in more hostile ways. It seems paradoxical, but inevitable in such a situation, that the 'peaceful co-existence' attempted in 1969 should be seriously threatened in this way, but this was certainly the case.

At the same time, it was claimed by the Italian Government that the 1969 Agreement was rapidly implemented, at both internal and international levels, according to 'the operational calendar', and this view was shared by the Austrians. That they believed the South Tyrolean problem to have been solved was illustrated spectacularly by the official visit of Franz Jonas, President of the Austrian Republic, to Rome in November 1971. It is difficult to criticise the good intentions of the Italian Government's declarations, but the delays and muddle which followed can only be deplored. The doubts and impatience of the South Tyroleans grew with every year.

This cynicism seems to be as legitimate as that of the other Regions of Italy which, as a result of recent reforms, have in some respects more rights and powers than the South Tyrol. The danger was that it would have a disruptive effect on the *S.V.P.*, the only organisation in which the German-speakers are effectively organised. At the Party's 1971 conference, despite the re-election of its president Dr Silvius Magnago, there emerged two distinct camps, about equal in numbers, the one following the President in his moderate conciliatory attitude towards the Government in Rome, the other adopting a much more critical attitude. One deputy who had maintained his complete opposition to the 1969 agreement was expelled from the party. It appeared that there were tensions within the *S.V.P.*, and among the South Tyroleans in general which may have been caused by the complications arising from the attempts at implementing 'The Packet'. For the first time ever, the political unity of the people was shattered in the elections of May 1972. Their votes were cast in favour not only of the *S.V.P.*, but for an independent list led by Dietl, and in response to Dr Jenny's Progressive Party calling for support for the *P.S.I.*, (Socialist Party of Italy). The *S.V.P.* retained its seats, however, and Dietl was not elected. The trend towards internecine strife in the South Tyrolean movement continued with the creation, in October 1972, of a Social Democratic party. Nevertheless, the *S.V.P.* has achieved a great deal for the Region and its demise is not likely at the present time.

The Autonomy Statute of 1972 contained a large number of clauses designed to safeguard the three linguistic groups of the South Tyrol in such spheres as finance, law and local government. The matters, mainly economic, for which the province of Bolzano *(Südtirol)* now has primary responsibility within the region of Trentino-Alto Adige have been increased from fourteen to nineteen, and its secondary powers from three to eleven, including school administration, water resources, industrial development and the use of German in the civil service, all of which are intended to protect the economic, social and cultural rights of the two minorities. The province already had, before 1972, responsibility for agriculture, forestry, mines, tourism, roads, housing, employment and health.

Among the Statute's new provisions are several affecting the use of German in the province. Judges and civil servants must be appointed among all these linguistic groups according to their numerical strength: about 5,000 posts are thus reserved for German-speakers. The German language has been accorded official status with Italian and all documents and signs must be published in both. Each group has its own primary schools where instruction is given in the mother-tongue, but at secondary level parents have to choose whether or not to send their children to schools where German is the language of instruction. In 1973, of all the children in primary and secondary schools 31,200 and 6,600 were German-speakers, 11,300 and 5,450 Italian-speakers and 2,000 and 130 Ladin-speakers. The Statute also provides for provincial control of radio and television, formerly run by Italians from Trento, and of cultural affairs including libraries and museums.

Within the context of the Italian State the autonomy now granted to the South Tyrol, at least in theory, is extensive for—apart from such matters as currency, taxes, foreign affairs, jurisdiction and defence—the province of Bolzano has been granted full powers. There is, however, a very real danger that this degree of autonomy will remain a dead letter if it is not implemented soon and fully, and then if it is not used by the German-speaking population. The *S. V. P.*, which can claim almost exclusive responsibility for having created a new situation in the province, now sees as its next task to ensure that this happens. It is, after all, still the majority party within the Provincial Assembly. At the elections of November 1973 the *S. V. P.* won twenty seats (132,186 votes), the Christian Democrats five (32,990); the Communists, the Italian Socialist Party and the South Tyrol Social Democratic Party two seats each (13,343, 13,214 and 12,037); the Italian Social Movement, the Italian Social Democratic Party and the Social Progress Party won one seat each (9,431, 8,059 and 4,012). A total of 9,030 votes were cast for four other parties, including the Italian Republican and Liberal Parties, none of which won a seat. Among the thirty-four representatives there are now twenty-three German-speakers (mainly *S. V. P.*). The present *Landeshauptmann* (Provincial President) is Dr Silvius Magnago *(S. V. P.)*, the most distinguished figure produced by the South Tyrol question in this century who, as leader of his party since its formation, is highly esteemed throughout the German-speaking community. The *S. V. P.* is

still divided between those who wish to see full implementation of the regional statute and the separatists who fear 'the
historic compromise' between Social Democrats and
Communists in the Italian Government. In March 1975
Senator Peter Brugger of the *S.V.P.* said he was convinced
that if the communists won power in Rome the South
Tyroleans would hold a referendum demanding the creation
of a separate state.

The South Tyrol is in many ways typical of minorities which
are separated from their ethnic homeland and incorporated in
another State. Its German-speakers, obliged to accept Italian
citizenship in 1919 and again in 1945, learned from bitter experience that they were politically weak within the region
where they lived and possessed no institutions capable of
bringing pressure on the Government. They therefore had to
find ways of solving their problems within the host State. For-
tunately, this situation found its leaders in the *S.V.P.*, but it
will continue to call for men and women with new political
skills if the Autonomy Statute of 1972 is to become effective
and maintained. When this has been accomplished, Italy's
fears that Alto Adige is in danger of being exploited by
Austria should be laid to rest and the multi-lingual community of the province come to enjoy the economic and
cultural stability necessary to form a bridge between the German and Italian worlds, as a new and integrated but federal
Europe requires.

THE SLOVENES OF TRIESTE

Trieste, in the Region of Friuli-Venezia-Giulia on the border with the Yugoslav Republic of Slovenia, has throughout its history suffered the vicissitudes typical of frontier territories with mixed populations. Up to the First World War the town, and the whole peninsula of Istria in which it lies, belonged to the Austro-Hungarian Empire and had developed in the eighteenth century as the main port of the Adriatic. The town's population was largely Venetian, while the rural population was predominantly Slovene. With the unification of Italy in 1870 all the Italian-speaking territories, except for Trieste and the South Tyrol, were incorporated into the new Kingdom. After 1919 Italy gained both the South Tyrol and Trieste, and five years later the town of Fiume (Slovene: *Rijeka),* now in Yugoslavia. The Treaties of St. Germain and Rapallo required Italy to respect the Slovene and Croat minorities in the area, but during the two decades of fascist rule between the World Wars the Government's policy of Italianisation caused resentment against the new rulers.

After the Second World War the whole of Venezia-Giulia, including Trieste, was claimed by Yugoslavia in recompense for having been invaded by German and Italian troops. The claim was supported by the fact that Tito's partisans had resisted the invaders for three years and by April 1945 had captured all of Istria and were in control of Trieste. British and Yugoslav generals then reached an agreement to draw a line behind which the Yugoslavs withdrew: the area around Trieste was divided into two zones, Zone A including the city and a coastal strip to the north under British/American oc-cupation and a larger Zone B, south of Trieste, under the Yugoslavs. The Peace Treaty which was signed on 10 February 1947 provided for the cession to Yugoslavia of the rest of Istria and most of the northern parts of Venezia-Giulia. Italy was allowed to keep only the lower Isonzo area with the towns of Gorizia and Monfalcone. Zones A and B were to form an autonomous Free Territory of Trieste under a Governor appointed by the United Nations. This Free Territory was to be of some 285 square miles in all, of which Zone A would make up 86 square miles. Zone A had an estimated population in 1952 of 280,000 in Trieste itself (230,000 Italians and 50,000 Slovenes) and 22,200 in other communes (9,200 Italians and 13,000 Slovenes). The population of Zone B was estimated as half Italian and half Slovene but by 1945 the Slovene population was thought to have exceeded the Italian as the result of infiltration from Yugoslavia.

This solution satisfied neither the Italian nor the Yugoslav Government, however. In fact, it was the result of disagreement among the Allies whose boundary commission had failed to propose a solution acceptable to Britain, the U.S.A., France and the Soviet Union. The line suggested was meant to coincide with the ethnic frontier but such a concept was unrealistic in this area of patchily distributed populations. The Italians had hoped for a line further to the east while the Yugoslavs still claimed the entire area. While they continued to argue over the plan, and while the Allies failed to chose a Governor, the international political scene changed and the occupation of the two Zones, intended to be only an interim agreement, lasted for the next seven years.

Up to 1948 the Soviets, wishing to find a Governor sympathetic to Yugoslavia, systematically vetoed all the Western Powers' proposals who in turn rejected all names put up by the U.S.S.R. When, in June 1948, Yugoslavia went its own way and left the Comintern, the Soviet Union announced that it would adhere to the terms of the Peace Treaty and support the immediate establishment of the Free Territory. By this time, however, the Western Powers had come to consider that the solution of two Zones was impracticable. In Zone A, Italian laws remained in force but in Zone B the Yugoslavs had introduced a number of administrative, legal and economic amendments, all of which had the effect of absorbing the Zone into Yugoslavia. On 20 March 1948 the Governments of Britain, the U.S.A. and France issued a joint declaration recommending that the Free Territory should be returned to Italy. This proposal was immediately rejected by the U.S.S.R. and Yugoslavia but in Italy it was greeted with enthusiasm and given almost legal significance.

By now Trieste had become an obstacle in Mediterranean strategy but the deadlock continued for another three years.

Riots occurred in the city on the fourth anniversary of the Tripartite Declaration in March 1952. Sharp exchanges between Italy and Yugoslavia took place in September 1953 after Marshall Tito had declared that the only acceptable solution would be to internationalise Trieste city and incorporate its hinterland into Yugoslavia. The Italian Premier Giuseppe Pella replied with a proposal that a plebiscite should be held in both Zones, but this was not acceptable to Belgrade. On 8 October 1953 the British and American Governments announced that 'viewing with concern the recent deterioration of Italo-Yugoslav relations', they had agreed to end their occupation of Zone A and to hand it over to Italy. Tito warned that Yugoslavia would regard Italian entry into Trieste as an act of aggression. Tension increased on both sides of the border and on 5 November there were anti-British demonstrations in the city during which six Triestines were killed and many injured by British troops under the command of General Sir John Winterton, the military commander of Trieste. Pella moved two Italian divisions up to the Yugoslav border and Tito made a similar move. A new approach to the impasse now had to be found.

Early in 1954 the British and American Governments called meetings in London between Italian and Yugoslav representatives and, at last, on 5 October, both Governments agreed on a Memorandum of Understanding. The new plan was that the Free Territory would be partitioned, Zone A being handed to the Italians and Zone B to the Yugoslavs. The agreement was described as provisional because it needed the signature of the Soviet Union. Both Italy and Yugoslavia were prepared to accept this solution, unlike the Peace Treaty, because it had not been imposed from above but was negotiated by their own representatives. In Italy the settlement was generally thought to be the Government Plan for abandoning Zone B to the communists. In the city itself the ceremonial granting of the Territory to Italian administration took place amid scenes of great rejoicing.

But not all its inhabitants had unmixed feelings about the event. Some older people still remembered the gay and prosperous times of the Austro-Hungarian Empire. For them Italian rule was synonymous with the fascist régime and business people now feared that return to Italy would mean return to Italian bureaucracy. A few regretted that Trieste was not, after all, to become part of an autonomous Free Territory. They were aware that Trieste was not the city it had been in the nineteenth and early twentieth centuries when its wealth depended on its position as a centre for a vast mercantile Empire. The collapse of that Empire in 1918 had come near to ruining Trieste and during the inter-War years little had been done to improve its changing fortunes. New industries, including oil refineries, had been opened but the port faced stagnation under competition from Fiume and its old rivals, Genoa and Naples. Only in the last decade or so has the relaxation in Italo-Yugoslav relations brought better times for Trieste. After the years of dispute had ended, Italy established trading links with Yugoslavia and other States in Eastern Europe during the 1960s which helped to restore it to something like its former affluence.

Today the city of Trieste is the capital of the province of the same name which, with the provinces of Udine, Pordenone and Gorizia, form the Region of Friuli-Venezia-Giulia (Slovene: *Furlanija-Julijska-Krajina).* Since 1919 the province of Trieste, together with Gorizia, has been the home of a Slovene minority, while Udine has a minority of Friulan-speakers. The Slovenes of Trieste (Slovene: *Trst)* and Gorizia *(Gorica)* enjoyed many rights as a minority under the comparatively liberal Austrian régime up to 1918, were suppressed by Mussolini and under the German occupation, encouraged by the British-American administration and officially recognised at the restoration of Italian sovereignty. In all these periods they were an important element in Italo-Yugoslav relations and their interests have always demanded attention.

It is impossible to say precisely how many Slovene-speakers there were in Trieste and Gorizia during the first half of the present century, or previously. The first fairly reliable Language Census was held only in 1961. In that year, out of a total population of 298,645 in the province of Trieste alone, 25,582 gave Slovene as their everyday language (838 belonged to other linguistic groups). Of these Slovene-speakers, 15,819 lived in Trieste, 2,992 in Duino-Aurisina *(Devin-Nabrezina),*

4,137 in San Dorligo della Valle *(Dolina)* and 1,148 in Sgonico *(Zgonik)*, only in the last two towns were they in a majority. It was nevertheless believed that the actual number of Slovenes in Trieste province in 1961 was around 40,000, many of whom were fearful that the Trieste question was not finally solved and that they would suffer discrimination. In the province of Gorizia the number of Slovene-speakers in 1961 was approximately 15,000 out of a total of 140,200 and in Udine there were perhaps 21,000, although no accurate figures are available. According to the *Atlas Naradov Mera* (Moscow 1934) there were approximately 80,000 Slovene-speakers in Italy before the Second World War. It is generally agreed that the loss of Zone B to Yugoslavia was compensated by a natural increase in the Slovene population of Zone A and that this figure is more or less acceptable for the present time.

The Slovenian minority in Trieste is protected by laws based on the London Memorandum of 5 October 1954 which was signed by Italy, Yugoslavia, Britain and the U.S.A. The agreement is reciprocal in that it also applies to the 45,000 Italian-speakers who as inhabitants of Zone B are now citizens of the Republic of Slovenia and where its provisions have been incorporated into the Constitution. By a special statute added as an appendix to the Memorandum the Slovenes of Trieste were guaranteed equality with all other Italian citizens and their ethnic identity was also to be fully respected. Foremost among its clauses was the provision of elementary, secondary and further education through the medium of Slovene. Others included legislation for place-name signs to be erected in both Slovene and Italian. A mixed Commission was to meet every two years to consider the progress of this policy on both sides of the State border. The London Memorandum was subsequently rein-forced by three further agreements reached on 21 January, 20 June 1965 and 15 March 1967. The umbrella organisations instructed to see that these joint agreements are carried out are the *Union degli Italiani dell' Istria e di Fiume* (Union of Italians of Istria and Fiume) and the *Slovensko Kulturno Gospodarska Zveza;* both are communist-led.

According to Yugoslav observers, the clauses of the Memorandum have been only partially implemented by the

Italian Government. They quote, for example, the fact that Slovenes have been fined and imprisoned for refusing to use Italian in law-courts, contrasting it with a declaration by the Italian Government on 11 July 1945 that 'the democratic renewal of the State demands a body of special guarantees to citizens of non-Italian language groups. Free use of the language shall be allowed and guaranteed, not only in private and commercial affairs, in public meetings, in liturgy and in the press, but in relations with political, administrative and judical authorities as well. In areas inhabited by a considerable number of citizens of non-Italian tongue, instruction in the mother-language shall be ensured in State schools. The special requirements of these areas shall be met and protection granted to the free exercise of special forms of local self-government'.

The Italian view at this time was represented by the Prime Minister Alcide de Gasperi who said at the Council of Ministers for Foreign Affairs in London on 18 September 1945, 'If Italian democracy were able to put into practice all the principles which inspired it, it would grant to minorities protection of their own ethnic existence through a series of linguistic guarantees and regional autonomies. But the wave of nationalistic reaction has overpowered democracy . . . Yugoslavs are complaining with justice of repression of their minority . . . and they are right'. The Government's intention of treating the Slovenes in the same way as the German-speakers of the South Tyrol was not fulfilled. When the Peace Treaty came into force on 15 September 1947 and the Italian administration returned to Gorizia, serious attacks took place on Slovene persons and property which were not prevented by the authorities. A petition asking for protection of the Slovene minority was ignored.

Since the establishment of the Region of Friuli-Venezia-Giulia in 1963 a number of further concessions have been won by the Slovene minority in Italy. The Regional authorities decide whether the Italian or Slovene forms of place-names, or both, are to be used for official purposes, for example. Article 3 of the Regional Constitution affords the individual the right, at least in theory, to choose between Italian and Slovene in courts of law and before the municipal authorities. The Slovene forms of family names, banned in fascist times, have also been officially allowed since 1963.

The Slovenes enjoy the benefits of their own schools, without hindrance from the Italian State. In the province of Trieste, formerly Zone B, there were in 1970 twenty-eight primary schools and twelve private schools, with a total of 592 children being educated through the medium of Slovene by forty-seven qualified teachers. In the same year the Italian schools of the area had a total of 5,507 pupils and 309 teachers. There were also thirty-eight Slovene high schools (6-14 years), fifteen of which are in Trieste city, with a total of 1,058 pupils and 144 teachers. In higher education there were a teachers' training college with thirty-three students and five vocational/technical colleges, all teaching in Slovene. Since 1964 the number of Slovene-speaking children in primary schools has risen slightly. The minority language is not taught at the University of Trieste, but the University of Padua offers courses in Slovene and trains teachers. Although the Slovene schools of Gorizia *(Gorz)* are not protected by the London Memorandum they are nevertheless guaranteed by the Constitution of 1961 and are said to be sufficient for the numbers of Slovene-speakers living in that province. No provision is made for the Slovene minority in Udine.

Whereas in education the Slovene language has been given a prominent place, it enjoys no such status for other official purposes. With the exception of those parishes around Trieste where the Slovenes are in a numerical majority and which have a Slovene mayor, the language is nowhere recognised as having equal status with Italian. All attempts by the Regional authorities to secure official status for Slovene have been defeated in the law-courts which carry out the central Government's instructions. The language is not even allowed at meetings of the Regional Council. No bilingual or Slovene road-signs have been erected in Trieste, although a few have been introduced recently in Duino. Despite the guarantees, which exist only in theory, all administration is carried out in Italian.

The Slovenes of Trieste and Gorizia are, for the most part, supporters of the political left, although with the growth in recent years in the number of Social Democrats among them their effectiveness has been reduced. Since 1968 there has been only one Slovene-speaker in the Rome Parliament—the former mayor of Duino, A. Skerk. At the Regional elections of 1973 only two Slovenes were elected among the sixty-one members: Dusan Lovriha, a communist, and Drago Stoka from the *Slovenska Skupnost (Unione Slovena)* a Catholic and Christian Conservative Party, the only one specifically for Slovenes. Following the departure of one of its leaders for the Communist Party in 1969, the *Skupnost* has lost much support and most politically active Slovenes are now to be found in the Italian Communist Party, or support the Socialist Party of Italy *(P.S.I.)*. The Christian Democrats won 39·7% of the votes at the Regional elections of 1973, the Communists 20·9%, the Socialists 12·2%, the Social Democrats 8·2%, the Neo-Fascists 7·5%, the *Movimento Friuli* 3% and the *Slovenska Skupnost* 1.3%.

There are several political and cultural organisations representing the Italian Slovenes. They include the *Slovenska Kulturno Gospodarska Zveza/Unione Culturale Economica Slovena* (Slovene Society for Culture and Economy) which publishes the only daily Slovene newspaper in Italy, *Primorski Dnevnik,* the *Demokratska Slovenska Zveza/Lega Democratica Slovena* (Democratic Slovene League), as well as Christian Democrat, Independent and Catholic groups publishing weekly newspapers like *Katoliski Glas* (Catholic Voice) and *Novi List.* The *Goriska Mohorjeva Druzba* (Co-operative Society of Gorizia) is a Catholic organisation which, until fascist times, published the majority of Slovene periodicals. Today it has close contacts with the Slovenes of Carinthia. The periodical press in Slovene is particularly flourishing: there are about a dozen student news-sheets and family and parish magazines published fortnightly and monthly and two quarterly reviews *Zaliv* (moderate Left) and *'Most'* (moderate Right).

At the *Kulturni Dom* (House of Culture) the *Slovensko Gledalisce v Trstu* (Slovene Theatre of Trieste) has performed regularly in Slovene since 1890 and since the London Memorandum with the Italian Government's financial support. It works in association with a number of other cultural organisations including folk-groups, libraries and publishing groups. Farmers and workers belonging to the Slovene minority have their own unions, banks, co-operative and sporting organisations. The religious life of the minority, which is overwhelmingly Catholic, is conducted mainly in the Slovene language, especially since the appointment of a Slovene, Monsignor Skerl as Vicar General of Trieste. Whereas ninety-five priests preached regularly in Slovene in 1931, only thirty do so today. The radio station Trieste A broadcasts exclusively in Slovene, mainly cultural and news programmes, which are intended to be heard across the border in Yugoslavia.

From time to time there are disturbances, the heaviest in recent years those of 14-19 October 1963, in Trieste city. Apart from their failure to win full official status for their language, the main complaint of the Slovene minority in Trieste is that their parishes are suffering depopulation and, in some cases, have been obliged to accept Italian-speaking refugees from Istria and Dalmatia or have been compulsorily cleared in order to make room for industrial development. Such moves have seriously affected the Slovene character of many parishes in Trieste province since 1960, although their situation in education, church and cultural affairs is generally as good as can be expected in the circumstances. That of the Slovenes in Gorizia and Udine, where their small numbers mean that they can be virtually ignored, is less satisfactory.

Hope for settlement of the Trieste Question was raised in October 1975 when, in speeches to the Senate and Chamber of Deputies of the Italian Government, the Prime Minister Aldo Moro said that Italy should give up its 'academic claims' to Zone B of the former Free Territory, admit that the 1954 partition was final and recognise Yugoslav sovereignty over it. Moro's move was one of the first results of the Helsinki Conference of 1975 which eased East-West tension and affirmed the principle that post-War borders cannot be altered by force. He sought the Italian Parliament's authorisation to sign an agreement recognising the demarcation line between Zones A and B as a State frontier. Italy is anxious to have the problem settled while President Tito is still alive. The President of Yugoslavia is reported to be so annoyed at the prolonged delay that he has threatened to cut the city of Trieste's water supply which comes from over the border. In Belgrade, the Yugoslav Foreign Minister, Milos Minic told Parliament that Italy and Yugoslavia had now come to an agreement finally to settle the problem which has caused so much friction between them since 1945. The agreement, signed on 10 November 1975 at Ancona, included a series of co-operative ventures in the border areas and the creation of a free industrial zone with capital from both Italy and Yugoslavia. Minor adjustments of the border were to be made to take account of ethnic considerations. Both sides also agreed to inform the United Nations Security Council and the Governments of Britain and the U.S.A. that the 1954 London Memorandum is henceforth to be considered void.

THE SARDS

Whereas Sicily, separated from the mainland only by the narrow Straits of Messina, has always been closely linked in cultural and political terms with southern Italy, the Island of Sardinia—180 miles away across the Tyrrhenian Sea—had its own identity and history up to the beginning of the eighteenth century.

Never conquered by force of arms, not even by the Romans, Sardinia (Italian: *Sardegna)* was invaded in turn by the Phoenicians, the Carthaginians and the Vandals in the fifth and sixth centuries, like its neighbour Corsica. The structures known as *nuraghi,* half-forts and half-dwellings, of which about 3,000 are to be found in all parts of the Island, were built in the pre-Carthaginian period by the Iliensis, an African people. One of the earliest references to Sardinia in Christian times was when in 594 A.D. Gregory the Great, writing to the shepherd-king Hospito, advised him to baptize as many of his subjects as possible, describing them as *'sicut insensata animalia'.* During its long subjugation under the Byzantine Empire, from the reign of Justinian to the eleventh century, the Island was frequently attacked by Saracens who were expelled around 1025 by the republican armies of Genoa and Pisa. For the next two hundred years Sardinia enjoyed a brief period of independence, although under continuous attack from both Genoa and Pisa because of its favourable position as a trading post for North Africa. In 1297 Pope Bonifacio VIII handed the Island to the Kings of Aragon, together with Sicily. It was not until 1327 that Alfonso IV of Aragon, having fought his way to Calgiari against the Pisans, was able to exercise his rights over the Island. He immediately formed a government on the model of Barcelona's and thus, for the first time in history, the Sards gained some control over their own affairs.

Sardinia's heroine in the fourteenth century was Eleanora of Arborea. After the Aragonese over-ran the Island and disposed of the other three independent kingdoms— Cagliari, Gallura and Logudoro—Arborea with Oristano as its capital fought a long, bitter war which culminated in victory in 1395. The struggle was led by Eleanora,

renowned as a general, law-maker and wise ruler. The
Carta di Logu (Code of Laws) framed by her father were
now revised and implemented in legislation far in advance of
their time, eventually becoming the basis of law for the whole
of Sardinia. When Aragon and Castile were united in 1479
Sardinia was administered as a Spanish dominion and enjoyed the privileges concomitant with that status; the native
princes were deprived of their independence, however. In
1714 the Island was surrendered by the treaty of Utrecht to
the Elector of Bavaria who, in turn, handed it as a kingdom to
Vittorio Amadeo II, Duke of Savoy, in exchange for Sicily. In
1720 Vittorio Amadeo was proclaimed King of Sardinia at
Cagliari.

The eighteenth and early nineteenth centuries, during
which Vittorio Amadeo's descendants ruled the Island, saw
Sardinia conciliated and neglected by turns. Vittorio's son,
Carlo Emanuele III, rounded up most of the professional
malviventi, organised commerce and agriculture, and opened
schools; had there been trains, it is said that he would doubtless have made them run on time! In 1794 there was a revolt
against Vittorio Amadeo III, Carlo Emanuele's son, and the
Piedmontese officials installed under his aegis. At last, in
1847, after a hundred years of dismal rule by its own kings,
Sardinia's autonomy was abolished in 1847 and with the
elevation of Vittorio Emanuele III to the Italian throne in
1861, the Island was united with Italy.

It is evident from this brief sketch of Sardinia's history that
the Islanders had little opportunity of expressing their
national identity. Yet throughout these centuries of invasion,
annexation and exploitation the Sards acquired a resilience
not often found among Italians. They have an immunity to
bad fortune and seem inured to the fact that almost every
Mediterranean power has quarrelled over their Island, with the
result that they appear more reserved, more dignified and
more independent than many other Latin peoples.

They have also kept their ethnic character and their language.
The Sardinian language, or Sard, belongs to the Romance family
of languages. It is generally regarded as the most primitive, or
conservative, of all the Romance group in that it has most

faithfully preserved the original Latin, especially in the mountainous interior where the inhabitants fled under threat of invasion. Words now extinct in other Romance languages are used in Sard, which has also been influenced by Castilian and Catalan. The latter is still spoken by about 12,000 inhabitants of the town of Alghero, *(Alguer)* which has always had close links with Spain.

The Sardinian language is spoken by approximately 1,200,000 people out of the Island's total population of about 1,450,000 (1970). There are three main dialects of *sardu* (Italian: *sardo)*, as well as hybrid zones. In the south, *terra di sotto,* the dialect is Campidanese which is strongly influenced by the Tuscan dialect of Italian, while in the north, *terra di sopra,* the dialects are Logudorese and Nuorese. There are also enclaves at Sassari *(Tàtari)* and Gallura where the nature of the Sardo-Corsican speech in common use is the subject of debate by philologists, and Genoese dialects on the islands of San Pietro and Calasetta. No standard form of Sard exists, despite attempts by poets and scholars in the nineteenth century to fashion one in imitation of the *Félibrige* in Occitanie and Corsica. The three dialects of Sard are regarded as being unusually difficult for foreigners, including Italians, to learn. a common feature is that the letter *u* takes the place of Italian *o* at the end of nouns. Much of the vocabulary is quite different from modern Italian: *domus* (house), *diar bonas* (good day). But the vocabulary is mostly limited to words for concrete objects, the few abstractions being usually borrowed from Italian, with abstract nouns like *labor* meaning not 'work' but that on which labour is expended, that is to say 'wheat'. Like other peasant languages, Sard is strong on physical attributes and expletives.

Sardinia (Sard: *Sardigna),* is about 170 miles long from north to south and has an area of 8,030 square miles. The capital is Cagliari (*Casteddu,* population 200,000) situated at the southern end of the Island. Other towns are Sassari (100,000), Alghero (30,000), Iglesias (*Is Cresias* 30,000) and Nuoro *(Nùgoro* 25,000). The interior of the Island is wild and mountainous, rising in the Monti del Gennargentu to around 5,500 feet; the hillsides are covered with ilex, cork-forest and scrub. At least half the cultivable land is given to permanent

pasture, the rearing of cattle and pigs being the main occupation. Some 80% of the land is in private hands, and
belonging to large landowners and their tenants, the rest to
small agricultural firms which lease pasture to shepherds on
exorbitant terms. The Island also has mineral resources,
mainly coal, lead and iron, all of poor quality but in fairly
large quantities. There is also a power-station at Porto Vesine
near the Sulcis mines and petro-chemical and textile plants in
the north and south. Up to 1950 the Island's development was
hampered by malaria, the scourge of Sards since ancient
times, but massive American aid has cleared the marshes and
the disease is no longer a widespread problem.

Communications between various parts of Sardinia are difficult. The only good road links Cagliari with Oristano and
Sassari to the north. A well known proverb is: *Ki no iskit an-
dare a kaddu non podet esser sardu* (He who cannot ride a
horse cannot be a Sard). Few outsiders penetrated the interior
until the early years of the present century. D. H. Lawrence
was among the first to visit the Island—which he compared to
Malta, 'lost between Europe and Africa and belonging
nowhere', when he went there in 1921 and wrote *Sea and Sardinia* after a brief journey lasting six days from Cagliari into
the Gennargentu mountains. But in the 1960s, in addition to
the Aga Khan's luxury development of the Costa Smeralda,
Sardinia began competing with Corsica by building hotels
along its coast. When tourists visit the interior, it is often under the guidance of armed *caribineri* who have to protect
them from bandits. Together with witch-craft and the ven-
detta, a tradition which it shares with Corsica, banditry has
survived in Sardinia to the present day but it has avoided the
political nuances of the Sicilian *mafia,* being more akin to the
black-mail and cattle-stealing of the old days of lawlessness.

That the Italian State recognised the cultural identity and
economic problems of Sardinia was shown in 1948 when a
Statute of Autonomy was passed for the Island. According to
Article 116 of this Statute a Regional Assembly was
established in Sardinia which took its place, with the South
Tyrol and the Aosta Valley, as an autonomous region of the
Italian Republic. But the measure has been far less succesful
in Sardinia than in other regions. The first problem is that the

composition of the seventy-two seat Parliament at Cagliari is similar to that in other regions of southern Italy. There is no autonomist organisation of any influence as in the South Tyrol and the interests of the Island have been badly neglected in the party warfare, intrigue and scandal which have been marked features of political life in Italy since the Second World War. The second problem is that the work of the Regional Assembly has been continually obstructed by direct and indirect interference from the central Government in Rome. The guarantees set out in the Statute of 1948 have been virtually ignored and most of the disputes over what is Caligari's responsibility and what Rome's are usually settled in favour of the central authorities.

Autonomist feeling in Sardinia has rarely been much more than the expression of local pride and the only party dedicated to the solution of the Island's problems is the *Partito Sardo d'Azione* (Sard Action Party), founded in 1921 after growing out of the Sassari Brigade which had distinguished itself during the First World War. Under Emilio Lussu, Sardinia's foremost figure in the resistance against fascism and in Italian politics after the Second World War, the Party played a leading role in the Island's life from 1945 on. It is not that Sards are non-political by nature—Antonio Segni, the Italian Minister of Agriculture in the 1950s, and the early Communist leaders Antonio Gramsci and Palmiro Togliatti were among eminent politicians who were of Sardinian background—but that they have produced no equivalent of Corsica's Pascal Paoli or, in recent times, Jean Albertini. One of the most eminent Sards of the present time is Enrico Berlinguer, Chairman of the Italian Communist Party since 1972, who was born at Sassari of Catalan extraction; a protégé of Togliatti, he led the *P.C.I.* to its success in the Regional elections of June 1975. At present there are two autonomist groups in the Island, the Sard Revolutionary Movement, founded as recently as 1969, calls for 'a popular struggle against the dominance of post-fascist, reactionary and authoritarian Italy', declaring itself in favour of 'political and economic independence' for Sardinia as a region within a federal Europe, while *Sardigna Libera* is a second federalist

movement. Neither has any significant representation or support. The only member of the Italian Parliament known to
belong to the Sard Action Party is Michele Columbu who was
involved, during December 1975, in a rumour that Libya had
offered £1.3 million to the Sardinian separatist movement 'in
exchange for future pledges'. He was elected as an Independent on the Communist Party ticket.

The ineffectiveness of Sardinia's Regional Assembly is
nowhere more clearly demonstrated than in the economic
sphere. About 45,000 Sards are permanently unemployed and
180,000 young people have left the Island in the last ten years
for lack of jobs. Over half the population's income is derived
from cattle-rising yet poverty is extreme and the standard of
living is one third less than that of regions in northern Italy.
The central Government has shown extreme reluctance in
helping the Regional Assembly to tackle the Island's
economic problems by provision of capital investment.
Lacking a coherent policy, the regional authorities have
become more and more fractious while relations with Rome
have steadily deteriorated since 1948.

Not surprisingly, the Island's cultural life has also been
neglected. There used to be a very high rate of illiteracy, but
by today most Sards can read Italian. Only a few hundred are
literate in Sardinian. There is hardly any modern literature in
the language, except folk-songs and some minor verse. But
Sardinia has produced at least two writers in the past who are
worthy of attention: the poet Sebastiano Satto and Grazia
Deledda (1871-1936) whose novels, including *Conne al Ven-
to, La Madre* and *Cenere,* are well-known in Italy. The novels
of Grazia Deledda, in particular, who won the Nobel Prize in
1926, have done for Sardinia what Merimée's did for Corsica.
They deal, in Italian, with contemporary issues in backward
local settings: they are in a sense, old-fashioned but only in
the sense that Sardinia remains a traditional island torn between Church and Progress and the desperate urge of the
younger generation to escape to the towns of the mainland.
Compared by the English poet Alan Ross in his book *South to
Sardinia* (1960) with Thomas Hardy, the novels of Grazia
Deledda present the most authentic flavour of Sardinia's lan-
dscape and society. Apart from her achievement, however,

the Island's literature has decayed to become little more than folklore. Even the regional costumes have all but died out and *festas*, once the expression of a vigorous and colourful folk-culture, are held only in the tourist season.

As for the Sardinian language, only the older generation speak it in their daily lives and it is giving way everywhere to Italian. Cagliari and Sassari have Universities where the Island's history and folklore are studied, but Sard is virtually ignored. It is not taught in the schools either, for the language has no place in either public life or in education. There are two local daily newspapers one of which, *La Nuova Sardegna*, sometimes carries a few columns in Sard and *Radio Cagliari* occasionally broadcasts for a few minutes in the language. All attempts by the various folkloric and cultural societies to win a measure of recognition by the Regional Assembly for Sard have been fruitless. Despite Article 6 of the Autonomy Statute which recognises Sard as the second official language of the Island, nothing has been done to secure this status for it. As a result, the language is generally considered to be doomed. It has no prestige in the towns and no resistance to Italian even in the remotest villages.

Clearly, for Sardinia the autonomy described in the Statute of 1948 had little more than a formal meaning. Politically, the Island provides yet another arena for the political parties, large and small, which are to be found in other parts of Italy, while the Sards have been all but completely severed from their language and culture. Whether their failure to develop in social and economic terms, under the negative influence of the traditional Italian parties and their own representatives, will give rise to widespread dissatisfaction and eventually the birth of a united autonomist movement remains to be seen. At the present time there is little indication that such progress may be imminent.

THE GREEKS, CROATS AND ALBANIANS
OF THE MEZZOGIORNO

Apart from the linguistic communities already described, there are in the *Mezzogiorno* or southern regions of Italy a number of smaller, vestigial groups, often no more than a few villages, where languages other than Italian are spoken to a limited extent by parts of the indigenous population. It is difficult to state their numbers because the official Census makes no provision for the languages spoken in these enclaves. Nor are they formally recognised in any special way, either politically or culturally, for the Italian State ignores their existence as ethnic entities. When not Italian, the language spoken by these groups are usually confined to the older generation and, for all purposes other than conversation at home they must be considered in these districts as languages in the last stages of decay. They are, in Sergio Salvi's phrase, among *le lingua tagliate*, 'the severed tongues', of Italy.

According to the Census of 1921, the last to enumerate them, there were 19,672 Italians whose mother-tongue was the Italiot dialect of Greek, of whom 16,033 lived in Apulia and 3,639 in Calabria, in the extreme south of the peninsula. Private estimates in 1930 put the total at approximately 36,000, however. In the absence of official statistics, it is believed that between 10,000 and 15,000 Greek-speakers live in these areas today. They are to be found in two enclaves: around Salento, especially Calimera, and to the east of Reggio. These people are the last remnants of a population which had its origins in the Byzantine invasions of southern Italy between the sixth and tenth centuries. Their cultural life has declined in modern times but their awareness of their contribution to Greek civilisation in the Middle Ages has not been entirely lost. The poet Vito Domenico Palumbo (1854-1918), patron of the Greek renaissance, was born in Calimera. Cultural contacts with Greece have been renewed since 1955 and three magazines are now published for the promotion of Greek culture in Italy. It is nevertheless true that despite the enthusiasm of Dr Giovanni Aprile, mayor of Calimera, Italiot Greek is no longer used in the churches and is still not taught in the schools.

In the Molise there are, beside Albanian-speakers, about 4,000 inhabitants (1954) whose first language is Croat. They are the descendants of refugees who fled from their homes in what is today the Yugoslav Republic of Croatia to escape from Turkish invasions in the fifteenth and sixteenth centuries. The language they speak is an archaic form of that spoken along the Croatian border with Bosnia. It survives in only three villages: Montemitro (1,469 Slavophones out of a population of 1,669), San Felice del Molise (831 out of 908), Acquaviva-Collecroce (1,736 out of 1,927). The Census of 1954 was privately organised but is considered accurate. These villages were obliged to use Italian for all purposes in the years between the two World Wars and the number of Croat-speakers dropped considerably at this time. But during the last fifteen years there has been a revival of interest in their culture, encouraged by Gustavo Buratti, general Secretary of the Italian section of the International Association for the Defence of Threatened Languages and Cultures. Contacts with Croatia have been renewed and several students have been sent to finish their Slavonic studies there. A Croatian-Italian grammar has been distributed free to every home in the three villages and lessons in Croatian are given on a voluntary basis. Since 1967 the bilingual periodical *Nas Jesik/La Nostra Lingua* (Our Language) has been published as a medium for local news. In September of that year the villages were visited by Cardinal Franjo Seper, Bishop of Zagreb and primate of the Catholic Church in Yugoslavia. He celebrated mass in the Croatian language and received a rapturous welcome from the parishioners.

The population of Albanian origin in Italy is estimated at 260,000, of whom approximately a third use the language occasionally in their daily lives. They live, for the most part, in a hundred or so districts in the south of Italy, in the regions of Calabria, Apulia, Basilicate, Molise and Sicily. The districts inhabited by Albanian-speakers, who are usually farmers or shepherds, are poor and lack any natural centre. The most important communities are Bronte in Sicily and Galatina in Apulia, but in both these towns Albanian has been replaced by Italian. The Albanian-speakers are the descendants of mercenaries who helped King Alfonso of Naples to put down a series of rebellions by the barons of Calabria in the fifteenth century. They have expressed their cultural identity in literature written in the Albanian language. Constantino Bellucci (1796-1867) was a patriotic poet who sang of the lost homeland and his hope of returning there, while Jeronim di Rada (1814-1903) devoted his verse to the liberation of Albania from the Osman yoke. The latter also published books and periodicals, at his own cost, in the Albanian language and died in penury as a result. His poems were admired by the French Romantic poet Alphonse de Lamartine and by Fredéric Mistral. Among other Albanian writers born in Italy are Guiseppe Schiro (1864-1927) and Salvatore Braila (1872-1961), both of whom enjoy literary reputations in Albania. A number of Albanian-speakers have also held prominent positions in Italy's political and religious life. These include Luigo Giuro, a member of Garibaldi's Provisional Government, Rosalino Petrotta, a representative at the present time in Sicily's Regional Assembly, and Giovanni Stamati, Bishop of the Albanians in Southern Italy. The Albanian language is studied at the Universities of Rome and Naples and, since 1945, at the Institute of Albanian Studies at Palermo. But it is not taught in the schools and, despite its comparatively strong position in a few dozen districts, it has no official status whatsoever. All attempts to implement Article 6 of the Italian Republic's Constitution, which states 'Every national minority must be protected by special laws', have failed.

LUXEMBOURG

Constitution: Grand Duchy

Area: 999 square miles

Population: 352·7 thousand (1973)

Capital: Luxembourg

Administrative divisions: 12 cantons

Present Government: The Socialist Party *(P.O.S.L.)* in coalition with the Democratic Party *(P.D.)*; elected 1974

Language of majority: Letzeburgesch

THE LETZEBURGERS

Situated at the heart of Western Europe between Belgium, France and the Federal Republic of Germany, the Grand Duchy of Luxembourg has been an independent State since 1839, when the first Treaty of London guaranteed its territorial integrity and political autonomy. About half the size of a French department, which can be crossed by car in an hour, Luxembourg is a prosperous and highly industrialised country with close economic and political connections with its neighbours.

For administrative purposes Luxembourg is divided into the districts of Diekirch in the north, a region of the Ardennes between the Walloon province of Luxembourg and the German Rhineland; the district of Grevenmacher where the vineyards of the Moselle Valley are situated; and the district of Luxembourg in the south, a region of rolling farmlands and industry. The twelve cantons of Chervaux, Wiltz, Vianden, Diekirch, Redange, Mersch, Capellen, Esch, Luxembourg, Remich, Grevenmacher and Echternach are the basic administrative units. Each canton is made up of communes which have their own councils with wide powers based on the principle of territorial decentralisation.

The history of Luxembourg (German: *Luxemburg*) began in A.D. 963 when Siegfried, Count of the Ardennes, had a castle built where Luxembourg, the Grand Duchy's capital, stands today. During the Middle Ages this dynasty, one of the most illustrious of its day, gave four Emperors to Germany, four Kings to Bohemia and one to Hungary. In its heyday, the territories of the House of Luxembourg were five hundred times their present size, extending from the North Sea to the borders of Russia. With Sigismund (1368-1437), Emperor after Wenceslas, the great epoch of Luxembourg's imperial glory came to an end, however. For the next four hundred years the fortress of Luxembourg, 'the Gibraltar of the North', was besieged and devastated no less than twenty times by Burgundians in the fifteenth century, by Spaniards up to 1714, by the French in Louis XIV's time, by Austrians from 1714 to 1795 and by Prussians.

In 1815 a period of national independence began for

Luxembourg. The Congress of Vienna raised the former Duchy to the status of Grand Duchy and, after giving the eastern part to the Duchy of Prussia and the rest to William of Orange, handed it as personal property to the Dutch King. The personal union between Luxembourg and the Netherlands lasted until 1890, by which time its political autonomy had been strengthened and its institutions developed. In 1890, after the death of King William III, who left no male descendant, the crown of the Grand Duchy passed to the elder branch of the House of Nassau and since that date Luxembourg has had its own dynasty. In 1964 the present Grand Duke Jean, who is married to Princess Josephine Charlotte of Belgium, succeeded his mother, the Grand Duchess Charlotte who, after having reigned for forty-five years, abdicated in favour of her son.

Luxembourg, despite its declared neutrality, was invaded by the Germans on 10 May 1940. The royal family and Government escaped but resistance by the people was fierce, despite many reprisals and deportations. When military service in the *Wehrmacht* was imposed, workers ran up the national flag on their factories and went on strike. Thousands of young men and women escaped Hitler's *Festung Europa* to enlist with the British, Free French, Free Belgian and American Armies. The suffering of the civilian population was widespread. By 1945, over 45% of the cultivable land could no longer be tilled, 6,000 homes and almost all roads had been destroyed and the steel plants burnt out from forced over-production. Yet despite the devastation caused by the War, Luxembourg's recovery was resolute and rapid. In 1948 the Grand Duchy began to follow a policy of integration into the economic, political and military community of Western Europe. The second Treaty of London, signed on 11 May 1967, became one of the most important dates in Luxembourg's history when its territorial integrity and political autonomy were re-affairmed.

Since 1948 the Grand Duchy has known political and social peace as well as steadily increasing economic prosperity. Having regained its independence in 1839, its foreign policy since then has been dominated, on the one hand, by the desire to maintain its own security and, on the other, by its wish to become integrated into a larger economic system. It had felt the need for larger markets as early as the beginning of the nineteenth century and it joined the German *Zollverein* in 1842. At the end of the First World War, however, it withdrew from this economic union and turned towards Belgium with which it formed a close economic union in 1921. In 1958 this union was extended when the Netherlands joined Luxembourg and Belgium in the creation of Benelux. The Grand Duchy is also a founder-member of the European Coal and Steel Community, the European Economic Community, which it joined in 1957, and the European Atomic Energy Community.

This participation in European collaboration has set many a problem for Luxembourg and its Government has had to introduce a number of economic and social reforms as a result. Agriculture, the iron and steel industries have been modernised. Great efforts were made to extend the economic infrastructure of the towns and to increase the production of electrical energy. Dams have been built in Esch and Rosport, while the hydro-electric plant in Vianden is the largest pumping-station in Europe. The airport at Luxembourg was enlarged, the railway system electrified, the river Moselle was canalized to link the Grand Duchy directly to the large European waterways. In addition to its programme of public investment the Government had followed a policy of economic re-adjustment, diversification and expansion, trying to bring greater variety to the formerly monolithic iron industry by attracting foreign firms to the Grand Duchy.

Although it has neither coal-mines nor coke-ovens and no abundant mineral deposits, Luxembourg has a modern iron industry which is the basis of its economy. Huge public investment in the steel company Arbed has been made since 1969. This industry has a decisive influence on the national life not only because of the large number of people it employs and the capital it uses but also because it is a vital stimulus to the Grand Duchy's economic development. Annual steel-production, after reaching the record figure of 5·5 million tons in 1970, was 5·2 million tons in 1971, or about sixteen tons of steel per inhabitant (c.f. 1·3 tons per inhabitant in Belgium, 0·8 tons in Germany, 0·5 tons in France, 0·4 tons

in the Netherlands). Steel constitutes about 67% of the value
of Luxembourg's export trade.

The Grand Duchy now occupies the first trade-place in the
Common Market, as its foreign trade represents about 85%
of its national gross product. This means that Luxembourg,
despite its geographical and demographical size, is for
Belgium as important a trade-partner as Switzerland and
twice as important as are Denmark and France. Luxembourg's prosperity depends to a large extent on its ability to
recruit foreign workers, particularly in the steel and building
industries. The number of foreigners resident in Luxembourg
in recent years exceeds 22% of the total population—the
highest proportion in the Common Market. Of the 77,800
aliens working in Luxembourg, 8% came from Germany,
7·2% from Belgium, 9·4% from France, 23% from Italy,
3% from Spain and 15% from Portugal (1973).

The Grand Duchy also plays a prominent part as an international financial centre. Numerous banks and investment
trusts have settled there as a result of fiscal legislation, dating
from 1929, which favours holding companies. In 1952 the city
of Luxembourg was chosen as the provisional seat of the
European Coal and Steel Community, and Luxembourg has
now become 'the capital of Europe' with plenary sessions of
the European Community's Council of Ministers taking
place there for three months of each year. The city is also the
seat of the Court of Justice of the European Community and
the Secretariat of the European Parliament.

In Luxembourg's own Parliament, the Chamber of
Deputies, there are at present fifty-nine seats. The Government, elected on 26 May 1974, is a coalition of Socialists and
Democrats. The Christian Social Party has eighteen members, the Workers' Socialist Party seventeen, the Democrats
fourteen, the Social Democrats and Communists five seats.
The Minister of State, who is also President of the Government, is Gaston Thorn (Democrat), and the Vice-President
Raymond Vouel (Socialist). Each parliamentarian represents
not only his constituency (about 5,500 votes) but the whole
nation. The executive and legislative powers belong exclusively to the Grand Duke, who is Head of State, assisted by
the Government.

There is a sense in which Luxembourg, not counting the large number of foreign workers resident in the country, has no linguistic minority. For the entire indigenous population speakes a dialect of German known as *Letzeburgesch*. But the Grand Duchy's linguistic situation demands attention because this dialect, which is as different from High German as is Dutch, is replaced by French and German in certain sectors of the nation's life: that is to say, the everyday speech of Letzeburgers is not the official language of their State. Although it is not the only State in western Europe where three languages are spoken, Luxembourg differs from all others, even from Switzerland, in that—instead of being confined to their own territories—its languages are superimposed in an almost hierarchical manner.

This situation also differs from that of Norway, where schizoglossia prevails, in that *Letzebuergesch* or *Letzeburgisch* is not a second, standard form of German but a dialect of it. It is a Moselle dialect of Frankish-German origin (German: *Westmoselfrankish)* which is related to the dialects of *Mitteldeutsch,* the speech of that part of Belgium which became the Grand Duchy in 1839. Letzeburgesch is spoken not only in what is today the Grand Duchy but also by a dwindling number of people in the adjacent district of Arlon in Belgium, in the Bitburg area of Germany and in the district of Thionville in France: by about 300,000 people in all.

Although it is regarded as Luxembourg's national idiom, without a knowledge of which a person is not considered to be a Letzeburger, the dialect is limited in its vocabulary and not endowed with the means of expression for the purpose of a full, modern life in politics, science, economics and culture. It cannot be written with accuracy and few Letzeburgers can read it easily. Nevertheless, the dialect is a practical and vigorous means of communication at an oral level for all everyday purposes. But because it is also such a poor culture-bearer, as soon as a conversation reaches out into the higher levels of abstraction or refined sentiment, the limits of its vocabulary and grammar, together with its inability to conceptualise and its increasing lack of the imperfect tense, become all too apparent and it is then necessary to borrow from other languages. There was a brief, patriotic attempt after the Second World War to establish the dialect as a written language on models provided by poets in the nineteenth century, but the artificial creation of an official orthography has not been able to displace German and French. All attempts to make the dialect a written language for everyday use, as in newspapers, have failed.

While the dialect is still spoken everywhere in the Moselle Valley, as well as in Oesling *(Osleck)* and along the frontier with Germany, the growth of the French substratum is particularly noticeable in the capital, Luxembourg—mainly for reasons to do with social prestige—in the mining areas, where Walloons have settled, and along the border with France. The linguistic map is extremely complicated, particularly as the dialect differs in pronunciation from village to village. Like any other dialect, Letzeburgesch has many local variants but since the beginning of the twentieth century a national *koine* has gradually taken shape. This form is the product of a levelling process, an amalgamation of local variants and the exclusion of rare regional features, a kind of average language spoken by all those whose work brings them into daily contact with people from all over the country. The local forms are thus pushed back towards the periphery while the *koine,* the national spoken standard language, has made a rapid progress over a wide area in the centre. At the same time, modern technology and education have made inroads into the purity of Letzeburgesch: hundreds of loan-words and expressions from French and German have invaded the dialect, which was formerly the means of expression of a rural community.

Because Letzeburgesch is more clearly related to German than to French, German is favoured by industrial workers and the rural population, but French is the medium of expression mostly chosen by intellectuals and professional people. This choice is reflected whenever the use of language exceeds the requirements of daily conversation. The working rule employed by official bodies is that French is to be used as widely and as frequently as possible and German when it is indispensable, such as when the less well-educated public has to be reached. French therefore tends to be the first official language employed by the authorities. Both French and German are more or less foreign to the Letzeburger, who is by birth monolingual in his native dialect, and bilingual or trilingual only through education.

This rather unusual situation has its roots in the fact that the Dukes of Luxembourg had strong attachments with the French Crown, Universities and Army during the centuries when French culture enjoyed great prestige in Europe. The intellectual is therefore still orientated towards French cultural values by his education, the more so as he is most often educated at a university either in France or in Wallonie. Up to the First World War the pendulum swung in favour of German but since then French has returned to favour. With tradition and education, natural sympathy puts Luxembourg's élite within the French cultural orbit: French books, newspapers and magazines are widely read. Government texts are also published in French, and all contacts with foreign States are made in that language. German is used exclusively when it is necessary to bring announcements to the attention of all classes of people. Parliamentary documents and bills, for example, together with legal procedures, are published and held in French while the accounts for parliamentary debates (themselves carried out in dialect or in French) are printed in German because they are distributed to all households in the country. Speeches at political rallies, local council meetings and on other public occasions are in dialect. In the Chamber of Deputies French and Letzeburgesch are used, German having been dropped after the Second World War. Police reports are in German, road-signs, names of streets, shops, hotels, currency, tickets and so on, are in French. Newspapers printed in Luxembourg are in German, such as the Catholic *Luxemburger Wort* and the Socialist *Tageblatt*. Social accouncements and advertising are mostly in French, but German is predominant in the churches, which are mostly Catholic.

Since 1912 Letzeburgesch has been taught in the elementary schools and in the lower forms at secondary level since 1945. From the second year of primary education onwards, French is added to the syllabus which, at this stage, is still taught through the medium of German and dialect. Later on,

French gradually replaces German as the language of instruction, German being limited to courses in German language and literature. Those pupils who do not proceed to university are said to forget much of the German and French acquired in this way, especially the latter, because they lack the opportunity of speaking them regularly, and few can write either correctly. Luxembourg has no university of its own.

Although the Grand Duchy's size and geographical position hardly allow for a rich and complete national cultural life of the highest standards, the Letzeburgers show a strong desire to avoid the fate which would no doubt befall them if their country became a peripheral region of any one of its three neighbours. This awareness has resulted in an intense, diverse and unique cultural life. The theatre season regularly brings outstanding performances by the major companies of France, Germany and Belgium. Radio and television programmes produced in France and Germany are also heard and seen in Luxembourg, together with those produced at home, while the cinemas—of all the mass media usually the least affected by regional considerations—regularly show films in both French and German.

The opportunity of learning and using two European languages, other than his own dialect, is no doubt an advantage for the Letzeburger, but there are also disadvantages. Lacking his own linguistic roots, he is seldom able to make his own a language learned at school and spoken only on certain occasions. A critical consciousness of a foreign language is thus more common in Luxembourg than a partaking in its proper and peculiar genius of imagination and sentiment. Writers in the Grand Duchy are well aware that, despite many brilliant exceptions, for most people only the mother-tongue is the true instrument of creativity. Some have succeeded, within the relatively poor limits of the dialect, in writing poetry and popular theatre, but there are no sustained works of prose. Literature in the dialect continues to flourish at a modest level. Between 1948 and 1957 there appeared ninety-two books in Letzeburgesch, mainly poetry and plays. The only masterpiece produced in it is the poem *De Renert* by Michel Rodange (1827-76), a classic of wit and satire on the rival claims of France and Germany on the Grand Duchy during the Franco-Prussian War, which was based on Goethe's recreation of the medieval legend about Reynard the Fox. Novelists are obliged to use a standard or High German (*Hochdeutsch*) although they are fond of using figures of speech and dialect words, to give their writing a local flavour. The writer in French is less favoured, for he faces the refinements of a completely foreign language learned and cultivated in what is, after all, Germanic territory. He seldom reaches the higher realms of creativity, unless he emigrates to completely French surroundings, and even then he is at his best as a critic, philosopher, essayist or scientific writer where he can take full advantage of his unique participation in two cultural worlds of more or less equally high standards.

Before 1948 the Constitution of Luxembourg stated that French and German should have equal validity for all official purposes, with French being considered predominant in cases of dispute. Since then an amendment to the Constitutional text states that the use of the languages is to be decided by a law which, up to the present time, has not been passed. There has been no quarrel between those who favour one or other of the two languages, except during the Second World War when resistance to the German invaders included hostility towards their language, especially after Hitler justified the invasion by reference to the fact that 95% of Luxembourg's population spoke a German dialect. By today, however, there is little or no irritation on either side. As there is no exterior compulsion to use French or German, most Letzeburgers are content to speak whichever language they choose in the particular circumstances prevailing at any one time, accepting the situation with all its advantages and disadvantages. They are also fond of reminding outsiders that it takes time before a full appreciation of the nuances of the situation can be gained.

Meanwhile, the national motto of Luxembourg is often to be seen painted on porches of homes and public buildings: *Mir woelle bleiwe wat mir sin* (We want to remain what we are). A former Foreign Minister of Luxembourg, Joseph Bech, noted some years ago, 'It has often been said that the Grand Duchy is only an artificial creation of European diplomacy. This is not true. From the fifteenth century onwards Luxembourg was a distinct Principality, enjoying its privileges as such, whether under the domination of Burgundy, Spain or Austria. Surrounded by France, Germany and Belgium, this little country is neither French, Belgian nor German, nor a mixture of the three, but has an entirely distinctive physical, social and ethnic character of its own'.

12 THE NETHERLANDS

Constitution: Kingdom

Area: 13,967 square miles

Population: 13·6 million (1975)

Capital: Amsterdam (seat of Government: The Hague)

Administrative divisions: 11 provinces

Present Government: The Labour Party *(P.v.d.A.)* in coalition with the Catholic People's Party *(K.V.P.)*, the Anti-Revolutionary Party *(A.R.P.)*, the Radical Political Party *(P.P.R.)* and the Democrats '66; elected 1973.

Language of majority: Dutch

THE WEST FRISIANS

Friesland, a province of the Netherlands, is one of the three remnants of the ancient territories known as *Frisia Magna* which once extended from the river Scheldt, now in Flanders, to the Weser in Germany. Today the Frisian people are scattered in these three areas: while the West Frisians are citizens of the Netherlands, the East Frisians of Saterland, south of the town of Emden, and the North Frisians of the western coast and adjacent islands of Schleswig, live in West Germany.

By far the largest of these three areas is West Friesland, or *Westerlauwers* as it is called in Dutch in order to distinguish it from the northernmost part of the province of *Noord Holland*, which is also known as *Westfriesland*. The province has a land-area of 1,277 square miles, of which just over a third has been reclaimed from sea-marshes. It is protected from the North Sea (once known as *Mare Frisicum*) and the Zuider Zee (now called the *IJsselmeer*) by dykes which are nearly two hundred miles long. Although it is the fourth largest province of the Netherlands, Friesland's population is only eighth in size: 547,223 in 1974—about 4% of the total population. The provincial capital is Leeuwarden (Frisian: *Ljouwert*); other towns are Sneek *(Snits)*, Harlingen *(Harns)*, Drachten and Heerenveen *(Hearrenfean)*. The province also includes the islands of Vlieland *(Flylân)*, Terschelling *(Skylge)*, Ameland *(It Amelân)* and Schiermonnikoog *(Skiermûntseach)*.

Friesland is unique among the eleven provinces of the Netherlands in having its own language, which belongs to the West Germanic family and is more like English than Dutch in some respects. The number of Frisian-speakers in Friesland is estimated to be approximately 400,000. There are probably a further 300,000 living in other parts of the Netherlands but the language is not officially recognised outside the province and the precise numbers are not known.

From the time of Tacitus, with his *'Clarum Frisium nomen est'*, the name of Friesland has always been renowned. Down the centuries the concept of *patria* changed for many of the peoples of the Low Countries but for the Frisian, whether the

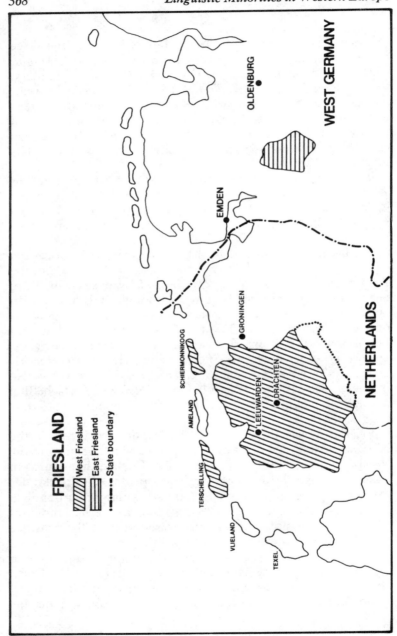

Renaissance humanists called him *Frisius* or *Friso,* it was always the same: he may have lost part of his territory, but never his national identity. He was in imperial Rome, paying tribute to Caesar in oxen skins; in the ninth century he invaded England with the Danes and throughout the Middle Ages he traded in wool and livestock all over Europe—his coins have been found in France and in Russia. By the twelfth century Friesland was one of the most prosperous countries in Western Europe and its people famous as a pugnacious, justice-loving, yet a most unwarlike breed.

The reputation of Friesland as 'a bulwark of freedom' dates from this time. Under the threat of invasion by feudal lords whose system was spreading across the whole continent, the Frisians of the northern coastal areas, trusting in the natural sanctuaries of the marshlands there, successfully resisted all attempts by princes, counts, bishops and even the Holy Roman Emperor, to subjugate them. These stock-men, who sent their sons to sea on mercantile adventures, were reputed to be completely free from servility, unlike their compatriots to the south, who were tied to their land and thus particularly vulnerable in times of war or economic crisis. This spirit of independence is still considered by the Dutch as one of the most prominent characteristics of the Frisian people.

Friesland maintained its status as a loosely associated group of Free Republics until 1498 when it was taken into the Habsburg Empire. Through the even greater opportunities for commerce which followed, and under the influence of Benedictine and Cistercian abbeys which fostered the national culture and developed agricultural methods, Friesland went on prospering and its common people speaking their own language. By this time, however, German and Dutch had begun to replace Frisian as the language of law, government, the church and learning. Although Friesland's fortunes began to deteriorate after 1648, when it joined the United Republic of the Netherlands, the Frisians persisted in considering themselves as a free people within what was a strongly federal State. The beginnings of the modern Frisian Movement can be traced to this period. Among the pioneers who spread a new interest in the Frisian language and its literature, notably in the works of the poet Gysbert Japicx (1603-66), who is now regarded as Friesland's national poet, were the scholars, Everwijn Wassenbergh (1742-1826) and the Dane Rasmus Rask (1787-1832).

The revival of interest in Friesland's past was a manifestation of Romanticism. For the Frisians of the nineteenth century the discovery that their country had a separate history and its own literature re-awakened in them the ancient concept of freedom which they had begun to lose in 1498. These sentiments were fostered by such organisations as the *Selskip foar Fryske Tael en Skriftekennisse* (Society for the Frisian Language and Literature), founded in 1844, and supported by many young Liberals in the towns, which revived knowledge of the Old Frisian Laws, defined the place of Frisian within the family of Germanic languages and stimulated recognition of the fact that, in former times, the province of West Friesland had been part of a much larger and more illustrious area. All this scholarly activity took place against a background of economic stagnation and widespread poverty. Many thousands were obliged to emigrate, mostly to America, and there was a continuous exodus of young people to other parts of the Netherlands. The modern Frisian reputation for taking a radical lead in religious, political and humanitarian causes began at this time, with the poet Pieter Jelles Troelstra (1860-1930) leading the new Dutch working-class movement of his day.

But the Frisian Movement of the nineteenth century was, for the most part, primarily a language movement. Only in North Friesland, long disputed by both Denmark and Germany, was there any attempt at political action of a specifically Frisian kind. The painter Harro Harring (1798-1870), for example, who became a professional soldier and a friend of Mazzini, appealed to the King of Denmark for his help in establishing a Scandinavian Republic in which Frisians could participate, but without success. In East Friesland too there were similar initiatives and for similar reasons. Occupied for a while by troops of the United Republic of the Netherlands, the region had been in turns a province of the Kingdom of Prussia in 1744, then a French *département*, then a part of the Hanoverian Kingdom governed by English kings and, in 1866, once more a part of Prussia. Then, in 1899, the Prussian Prince Edzard zu Innhausen und Knyphausen (1827-1908)—a relative of the royal house of Denmark, von Bismarck and the Krupp family—declared himself the King of all the Frisians. This attempt at German imperialism, under the guidance of Kaiser Wilhelm II, caused a stiffening in the national consciousness of the North Frisians which was led by Lolle Piers de Boer (1881-1970) and his clandestine movement *De Wrâldfries*. Nevertheless, the position of West Friesland as a province of the Netherlands during the nineteenth century was never seriously contested.

When, at the beginning of the twentieth century, the Frisian Movement began to gather momentum, it was again in predominantly literary terms that the Frisians expressed their national identity, at least in the early years. Modelling themselves on the Amsterdam Movement of the 'eighties, in which a group of Dutch writers had revolted against provincial and traditional literary forms, a number of young Frisian poets formed a new group. Of the many small societies which met under this umbrella, the most influential was the *Jongfryske Mienskip* (Young Frisian Fellowship) which was founded in 1915 by the poet Douwe Kalma (1896-1953). Kalma's ideas were revolutionary for his time: he wanted not only an end to provincialism, to folkloric and second-rate literature, but also to submission under 'foreign rule' from The Hague: he wanted, in short, not only the emancipation of Friesland's literature from the conservative standards which characterised it, but also a culturally independent Friesland, free of all ties with the Netherlands yet maintaining contacts with other countries such as England and Scandinavia. The slogan of the Fellowship was *Fryslân en de Wrald!* (Friesland and the World!).

Kalma's challenge caused a great stir among the Frisian Movement's older generation and out of the controversy which followed few ideas emerged intact. His views were generally considered to be completely unrealistic, but there was much in his position which came to be accepted as capable of development. Friesland needed his clarion call for his cultural programme included demands which were clearly necessary but which earlier leaders had failed to formulate. His advocacy of the teaching of Frisian on a more thorough and professional basis, for example, helped to create a situation which resulted in the establishment, in 1928, of a

Provincial Education Board and, in 1938, of the *Fryske Akademy*. Kalma's leadership lasted only a few years, however, and the members of the Fellowship subsequently joined other societies. For a time the various groups competed with one another but, after Kalma's demise, co-operation began over a wide area, especially between the Frisian Movement and the Dutch Social Democrats led by P. J. Troelstra. Kalma is still remembered in Friesland for his inspiration and the fresh insights he brought to his country's situation, many of which have since then borne fruit.

The years of the Second World War were a period of quiescence for the Frisian Movement, a tragic but useful time for reflecting on Friesland's position in the occupied Netherlands, to the fate of which the vast majority of Frisians felt inextricably bound. As in Brittany, there were attempts by the Germans to manipulate the Frisian question to fascist ends which caused schisms in the national movement after a small number of members were attracted by Nazi offers. But soon all contact between the Frisian Movement and the invaders ceased. It was only in East Friesland, a part of the Third *Reich,* that the stigma of collaboration was based on fact. One very vague Nazi proposal for a Frisian Council, to administer an autonomous province within the German Empire after the War, was never taken seriously by the West Frisians.

In the United States of America the exiled Berend Joukes Fridsma's appeal to Queen Wilhelmina for the establishment of an autonomous Frisian Parliament was ignored, after the victory of the Allies in 1944, and with their consent. At the defeat of Hitler, new violence broke out in East Friesland as Denmark and Germany quarrelled over the territory. After 1945 many West Frisians refused to have contact with East or North Friesland, suspecting them of complicity with the Nazis. The lack of close, regular contact between the three communities dates from this period. Today relations between West Friesland and the other two areas where dialects of Frisian are spoken are more friendly but officially confined to the work of the *Fryske Rie* (Frisian Council) which holds occasional conferences, publishes a year-book and organises exchanges of a cultural or economic nature.

It is in West Friesland that the Frisian language is most

widely spoken. That the number of Frisian-speakers has not declined as rapidly as might be expected since the Second World War, but has remained more or less constant during the last decade, is largely due to the Frisian Movement's progress in implementing the programme which it formulated between 1938 and 1945. This progress has been faciliated by a new climate of opinion, both in Friesland and in central government circles, which affords fairly wide recognition of the Frisian language and its culture. Although the old organisations have paled in significance they are still represented in the *Ried fan de Fryske Biweging* (Council of the Frisian Movement). Although not numerous, the members of this organisation have considerable influence on the cultural life of the province. The present situation is maintained and developed by two bodies, based at Leeuwarden *(Ljouwert)*, which are responsible between them for the Frisian culture in almost all its aspects. The *Fryske Akademy,* founded before the War, has assumed a central role since 1945, when it was joined by the *Fryske Kultuerrie* (Frisian Cultural Council). Both are financed from The Hague through the Provincial Council of Friesland but are autonomous bodies with their own secretariats and programmes.

The first aspect of Frisian culture to claim the attention of the *Akademy* and the *Kultuerrie* in 1945 was the language, particularly in the schools. Frisian had been admitted to education in 1937 when the Government of the Netherlands allowed the teaching of 'local dialects' during school hours. Strenuous attempts were now made to introduce the language as a subject in the curriculum. In 1955 it was recognised as a medium for instruction in the first two years at primary level and as a subject in later years. By today seventy-three of the 520 primary schools in Friesland use the lanaguage as the principal medium of instruction in the lower classes. In 1975 the Dutch Government accepted a proposal for the introduction of Frisian as the teaching medium in all classes at primary level and made it a compulsory subject. At secondary level, however, no schools use Frisian as the teaching language, and very few have Frisian as a subject. On the other hand, most colleges of education offer courses in Frisian. Friesland has no university but five in other parts of the

Netherlands, including Groningen and Amsterdam, study the Frisian language and its literature. The great deal of research now undertaken as an aid to the teaching of Frisian is carried out in association with the *Pedagogysk Advysburo* of the *Fryske Akademy*.

While real progress continues to be made in the teaching of Frisian, social factors in the speaking and use of the language remain a serious obstacle to its advancement. The Dutch Government has recognised Frisian as the second language for official use in certain situations. The Provincial Council of Friesland regularly publishes a report and other documents relating to cultural matters in Frisian. Nevertheless, the old readiness of bilingual Frisians (none is monolingual in Frisian alone) to speak Dutch before officialdom persists. Even in predominantly Frisian-speaking villages the presence of a few tourists, immigrants or officials is usually enough to turn committees and meetings into Dutch. Frisian, it is explained, is 'the jacket worn about the house', while Dutch is 'the best suit' kept for public occasions. According to a survey carried out in 1969, 71% of the 800 people questioned spoke Frisian at home, 62% in the shops and 42% to 'the notables'—doctors, ministers, and officials. About one third are unable to read the language but 60% cannot write it. These habits are gradually changing but are expected to disappear only with the death of the older generation and the growth of teaching in the language. They are particularly apparent in the towns where Frisian has for long been eclipsed by Dutch and 'town-Frisian', a mixed dialect of Dutch and Frisian dating from the seventeenth century. In recent years, however, 'town-Frisian' has begun to give way, sometimes to Frisian and sometimes to Dutch, while the status of Frisian has improved rapidly throughout Friesland as a result of the progress made on the language's behalf by the *Fryske Akademy* and other institutions.

The *Fryske Akademy* functions as a Permanent Commission with responsibility for the Frisian language's welfare. It collects information about the language and co-ordinates the work of other bodies concerned with the language. Its research has shown *inter alia* that there exists in Friesland a system of language ideology about Frisian—a number of opinions, norms and expectations with regard to the language which refer to group values from which Frisian-speakers assess their own attitude towards the language, and that of others. Analysis of this information reveals that, while there is no difference between the attitudes of male and female speakers of Frisian, older people appear to be more involved with language ideology than younger people, country dwellers more than townspeople, church-goers more than those who do not attend places of worship, farmers more than trades-people and professionals. Much valuable data about the reading habits and buying of Frisian books has been elicited in this way, which provides a basis for language planning in the schools, in administrative and cultural matters. Few linguistic minorities in Western Europe have established in-stitutions with the same substantial resources and important functions as those of the *Fryske Akademy*.

On the other hand, Friesland has no organisation directly responsible for control of its economic life and little progress has been made in tackling the province's problems in this respect. The influx of population into the towns from the traditionally Frisian-speaking rural areas, and from the other provinces of the Netherlands, constitutes a major problem for those who are active on the language's behalf. Agriculture has dominated Friesland's economy for centuries: over 90% of the cultivable land is used for grazing, there are more cattle than people, and the cow—to which a statue known as *Us Mem* (Our Mother) has been erected in Leeuwarden—is one of the traditional symbols of the province. The current problem is that agriculture is no longer able to provide suf-ficient work for the increasing agrarian population. The cause is two-fold: the area of agricultural land cannot be extended except in a limited way by reclamation from the sea, while modernisation of machinery and methods has reduced the number of jobs available in agriculture.

In 1947, 60,000 people (34%) were employed on the land, 37,000 (23%) in 1960 and in 1970, 21,000. Most of these are families working on about 15,000 farms: the number of em-ployees is as low as 6,000, of whom nearly a half work for less than six months a year. This trend is not limited to Friesland, of course, but the province is particularly vulnerable to its effects because alternative employment is provided not in Friesland but in the more favourably situated western areas of the Netherlands. Frisian industry, based mainly on farming, dairy products and agricultural machinery, has not grown quickly enough in compensation. The province's remoteness from the centres of Dutch economic wealth is another major factor which, it is feared, is now being increased as a result of that country's membership of the European Economic Community, in which market centres are even further away.

The lack of adequate employment at home has obliged many Frisians to seek work elsewhere or to remain and swell the already high unemployment statistics. Between 1950 and 1960 the number of people who left Friesland exceeded that of those coming in by about 50,000 and this trend has continued during the last decade. This net emigration has largely cancelled out the natural increase in the population's growth. While the population of the Netherlands as a whole has increased by 20% since 1950, Friesland's has increased by only 5%. The province's population density, about 470 people to the square mile, is less than half that of the Netherlands and about one-sixth of the coastal connurbations between Amsterdam and Rotterdam. Furthermore, residents of the densely populated urban centres are being attracted by the comparative peace of Friesland, where they come for holidays and to settle after retirement. As most of the emigrant Frisians are between twenty and forty years old, their departure has a profound economic and psychological effect on the communities left behind, where about 12% are aged sixty-five or over. It was expected that by the year 2000 the population of Friesland would reach a million, but that the Frisian-speaking population would not increase to the same extent.

In 1950 the Netherlands Government turned its attention to Friesland's economic problems. As agriculture offered few solutions and service industries do not grow of their own accord, the promotion of industry was seen as the only means of improving the province's situation. Roads and canals were built and improved, communications with the more prosperous areas to the west were speeded up, industrial sites prepared for building and workers trained in new technologies. Pending results from the Government's massive investment in the province, a system of direct incentives was devised so that industries wishing to move into certain development areas could receive subsidies towards their construction costs and reductions of up to 50% on land prices. Friesland already had a large labour force, so these measures soon began to pay handsomely. Between 1954 and 1964 the number of industrial employees rose from 19,000 to 33,000; the unemployment figures fell from over 5,000 in 1955 to 2,200 in 1964—but were still twice as high as in the rest of the Netherlands. The rate of emigration also slowed down, from 6,058 in 1955 to 1,576 in 1964. At the same time, the continuous decline in agriculture has compelled Friesland to go on industrialising: the aim now is to create job opportunities in diversified industries, for both skilled and unskilled labour, as well as for administrative and managerial personnel.

With agriculture no longer the major employer, Friesland's economic success has brought with it very serious problems for the province's language and culture. Much effort is being spent on trying to foster a proper understanding, especially among mixed Frisian and Dutch-speaking communities in the towns, of the Frisian language's importance for the province's identity. A crucial sector in which the Frisian Movement finds it difficult to make an impression is that of the mass media, which are almost entirely controlled from outside. There is no Frisian television service and only half an hour on the radio is filled daily by Frisian-language programmes. Both daily newspapers published in Friesland are in Dutch, although they usually carry some Frisian, and there is a modest weekly and monthly press in Frisian.

Since 1951, following riots on a day remembered as 'Friday of the Truncheons' after a Frisian defendant was refused the right to use his own language in court, and a magazine editor, Fedde Schurer, denounced the judge and was tried for libel, the Dutch Government has allowed the restricted use of Frisian before the law. Towns and villages are permitted to use bilingual signs on their boundaries and a few have Frisian street-names, but opposition—often from Frisian-speakers themselves—has prevented the full implementation of this regulation. The province is mainly Protestant with the majority belonging to the Reformed Church and its sects. Although there is a Bible and hymnal in the language, preaching in Frisian is not common. Nor is there any official Frisian anthem although *'Frysk bloed, tsjoch op . . .'* (Frisian blood will rise . . .) and *'It Heitelân'* (The Fatherland) are popular at most patriotic gatherings. The Frisian flag bears seven red water-lily leaves, representing the old territories of Friesland, on white between blue stripes.

Among the cultural activities which receive Provincial Government subsidies is the Frisian publishing industry, organised by *It Fryske Boek* (The Frisian Book), which continues to flourish, despite the problems faced by the language and the general economic climate at the present time. In 1970 a total of 159 books were published in Frisian including twenty-one novels, twenty-two books for children and thirty-six plays. After the Second World War, Frisian as a literary language was as vigorous as ever. The literary scene was exciting, led by Fedde Schurer, editor of the magazine *De Tsjerne* and later by *Quatrebras.* An important feature of Frisian literature today is not only its Modernism, as introduced by poets like Anne Wadman (born 1919) after the Second World War, but its bold experimentalism with form and content, especially in sexual ethics. This break with the past, as advocated by Kalma fifty years ago, is most clearly seen in poetry, even in the work of older poets, but also in the novel where specifically Frisian backgrounds have been replaced by analysis of the whole spiritual and intellectual crisis of the twentieth century. Frisian writers are able to read world literature in Dutch, of course, into which a large number of foreign works are translated, but also in their own language of which the same is true. It is here, in contemporary Frisian literature, that the new influences which are penetrating Friesland today, transforming the province's economic and social life, are reflected and discussed. At the same time Frisian literature has lost much of its national character and is merging, in theme and technique but without turning to Dutch, with the general trends of literature in other European countries.

Frisian is used to some extent in the Provincial Council. Headed by a Queen's Governor, the Council's thirty-five members are drawn from among the main Dutch political parties, the Christian Democrats with twnty-two, the

Labour Party *(Partij van de Arbeid)* with nineteen, *Liberals (Volkspartij voor Vrijheid en Democratie)* with seven, but also the Frisian National Party with four and smaller groups which include a Communist. The Council is responsible for a limited range of matters such as the maintenance of dykes, roads, bridges and canals, but also for cultural affairs. Friesland has no special representation in the Parliament at The Hague. The Frisian National Party *(Frysk Nasjonale Partÿ)*, which wins about 10% of the votes cast at provincial level, does not contest general elections. There is, however, a growing awareness of Frisian problems, especially among the young, and a good deal of public discussion in recent years of the need for greater decentralisation from The Hague, to which the provincial authorities often show themselves ready to respond. But the autonomist movement is still comparatively weak and it is likely that the comment by one of its leaders—'The Frisian people must be ploughed up and harrowed again and again'—is near enough to the truth. In linguistic matters the old pride of Friesland's democratic traditions has been eroded, giving way on the one hand to what appears to be a perverse arrogance and, on the other, to the usual inferiority complexes of linguistic minorities, with the result that the opinions of non-experts usually find a hearing in official quarters.

There are only a small number of signs which augur well for the future of the Frisian language and its culture. It is generally agreed that, unless the progress made in education is soon matched by a more substantial provision of broadcasting facilities, not even the efforts of such bodies as the *Fryske Akademy* will be sufficient to combat what some fear likely to be an inevitable decline, over the next decade, in the numbers who speak and use the language.

13 NORWAY

Constitution: Kingdom

Area: 125,181 square miles

Population: 3·948 million (1973)

Capital: Oslo

Administrative divisions: 19 counties

Present Government: The Labour Party; elected 1973

Language of majority: Norwegian *(Bokmål)*

BOKMAL AND NYNORSK

Despite the fact that only one language is spoken by all Norwegians, it does not follow that the country is without its linguistic problems. They do not arise from the existence of the small number of Lapps, perhaps 10,000, who live in the county of Finnmark, nor—unlike Denmark with the Faroe Islands and Greenland—does Norway have any overseas territories where another language is spoken. The problems are caused, rather, by the existence of two standard forms of the same language, Norwegian, and the advocation of a third which is a compromise between the other two. Since 1814, Norwegians have been trying to establish a modern, national language of their own and their efforts have been marked by a sharp conflict involving not only philologists and spelling reforms, but the press, writers, schools, universities, the Church, political parties and the national Government.

By today *Riksmål*, or *Bokmål*, has equal status in schools and official circles with *Landsmål*, or *Nynorsk*, but there is still great disagreement as to whether the two should be amalgamated at an early date or whether they should be allowed to develop naturally towards a common form known as *Samnorsk*. There are therefore important reservations to be made to Professor Higgins's statement, in *My Fair Lady*, that 'Norwegians learn Norwegian', if only to quote the saying well-known in Norway, 'When a man says he knows six languages, you can be sure that five of them are Norwegian'.

More seriously, the linguistic situation in Norway has been described by Einar Haugen* thus: 'The result of the language movement so far has been to create an image of schizoglossia, a personality split which leaves many persons linguistically divided and uncertain. It is not to be identified with the situation described (by Ferguson) as diglossia, the existence of a 'high' and a 'low' form of the same language within a political unit, as in Greece or German-speaking Switzerland.'

*The present account draws substantially on Einar Haugen's book *Language Conflict and Language Planning: the case of Modern Norwegian* (Cambridge, Massachusetts 1966).

The oldest written documents in Norway are runic inscriptions dating from the third century A.D., but the literary language (sometimes called Old Norse) was formed in the eleventh century with the introduction of Christianity from England and Ireland. When, in the thirteenth century, Bergen became the royal residence, the literary language adopted characteristics of the western part of the country but, in the following century, it was more influenced by eastern characteristics after the King's move to Oslo in 1314. The written forms used at this time, in official documents and in literary works, exhibited a strongly traditional and archaic character and soon became quite different from the less conservative vernacular, which underwent a continuous development.

When, in the year 1319, the ancient line of Norwegian kings became extinct and the throne passed to Sweden and later to Denmark, almost all literary work in Norway ceased. The Black Death of 1349-50 wiped out half the population, including almost all the clerics who had been responsible for maintenance of the literary standard. The linguistic structure of the few documents dating from this period is fractured, showing the influence of both Swedish and Danish forms. From 1380, when Norway was united to Denmark and Sweden, Danish influence became predominant. The country having no cultural centre and the old literary language having grown away from current speech, the influence of the language of the Danish administration spread, as a language not radically different from spoken Norwegian. Throughout the fifteenth century Danish was used more and more for official purposes. Then, in 1536, with the Lutheran Reformation, the introduction of the Bible and other books in Danish, the Danish language's position became firmly established. The reason was not only that Norway had no printing press but that the old language had become unintelligible to all but a few. Iceland, on the other hand, which had been colonized from Norway and had become its dependency in 1261, obtained its Bible in Old Norse because the language there had not undergone the same fundamental changes as in Norway.

In the sixteenth century the Norwegians began writing once

more, but now in Danish, taking as their models the language of the early Danish reformers. Their language was not, however, 'pure Danish' or the Danish of Denmark: it contained an admixture of Norwegian forms and expressions, as well as many elements of both Low and High German which had entered Norwegian speech, especially in the towns, under the influence of the Hanseatic settlers and with the advent of the Reformation. The same happened in the other Scandinavian languages, of course, which therefore possess many words in common with Dutch, historically one of the Low German dialects. During this period, with the revival of literary activity in Norway, Norwegian authors played a prominent part in shaping the literary language common to both Denmark and Norway. The language of Ludvig Holberg (1684-1754), for example, shows several Norwegian traits and he is regarded as the founder of the Danish and Norwegian literary idiom.

However, Danish did not become the spoken language of Norway. The literary language was used only on official occasions and even then was pronounced according to Norwegian articulation which differed from the Danish. The spoken language remained the various dialects which had survived from Old Norse up to the sixteenth century. But with the establishment of towns the situation began to grow more complicated. The common townspeople spoke the old town-vernacular, 'the vulgar language' of a purely Norwegian type but with many foreign loan-words, whereas the bourgeoisie spoke a vernacular influenced by 'the solemn language'—literary and ecclesiastical Danish pronounced in the Norwegian manner according to region and containing many Danish, German and, later on, French loan-words.

It was not until the eighteenth century that a more uniform Norwegian appeared, based on the middle-class, administrative and upper-class language of the towns in south-eastern Norway. The language was a mixture of spoken Norwegian and literary Danish forms: the proportions of these two elements have varied during different periods but, in general, the sounds were Norwegian and the vocabulary contained many specifically Norwegian words. When education was made compulsory, in the nineteenth century, the Danish element was increased through the use of Danish text-books. But all who used this common language also used the vernacular on more informal occasions. The new standard now led to a new way of reading the written language—Norwegian forms were read into the Danish orthography: e.g. _kage_ (cake) was read _kake, ud_ (out) pronounced _ut;_ in the southwest of the country, the old inter-vocalic _p, t, k,_ were voiced _b, d, g,_ as in written Danish, whereas in the south-east they were pronounced as such.

In 1814, as a result of the Napoleonic Wars in which the Dano-Norwegian King had sided with France, the union between Norway and Denmark was dissolved. Norway declared itself independent but was obliged to accept union with Sweden. The two countries had a common foreign policy under the Swedish Crown but were in all other matters independent of each other. Swedish at this time had no influence on the linguistic situation in Norway: however, the writers continued to use as a literary language the Danish written standard with a number of Norwegian words included. The Norwegians called this mixed, compromise language _Norsk._

After the severance of the union between Norway and Denmark, the influence of Danish did not diminish but increased rapidly, at first mainly because instruction in the schools imposed the Danish written forms. But with time there was a reaction against the Danish influence, led by the poet Henrik Wergeland (1808-45). He strongly advocated the need for rendering the written language more Norwegian by the adoption of words and forms from the spoken language and dialects of the common people. Danish tends to have simple vowels as in _sten_ (stone) and _løb_ (box) where Norwegian dialects have dipthongs as in _stein_ and _laup._ Wergeland wanted to be able to write the words as they were spoken, claiming that the vulgar language would enrich the grammar.

Wergeland was not only a poet but one of the leading nationalist figures in the first generation of Norway's independence. He believed that political independence, such as Norway had achieved in 1814, would of itself bring about linguistic independence. But he also believed that it would have to be worked for and that controversy, 'a literary civil war', would be necessary to bring it about. To him the problem was primarily the poet's need for a language rich in concrete, vivid terms, with symbolic and emotional force. But he concluded all his essays with appeal to national pride: 'Norway must no longer remain a cultural province of Denmark; if Norwegians should be persuaded to lose confidence in themselves and their future in the cultural sphere, then Norway will not long enjoy the benefits of political independence'.

The reality which faced Norwegians after 1814 was that four centuries of dynastic union with Denmark had left the country without a language of its own. The tradition of Norway as a sovereign nation had never died but there was little in the present to support it. Norwegians found themselves with an apparatus for democratic self-governmnt plus a set of institutions inherited from Denmark, but with little else that could contribute to the growth of a truly national consciousness based on language. Their first job was to define what was meant by Norwegian and to implement its use in their national life, as part of their search for individual and national identity. Poets like Wergeland were in the vanguard of this quest.

Wergeland had many followers including P. C. Asbjørnsen (1812-85) and Jørgen Moe (1813-82) who collected and published a large number of folk-tales. Although these tales were written in the traditional Dano-Norwegian language, the authors adopted and freely used many Norwegian words, thus giving their medium a distinct Norwegian flavour. In fact, discarding the heavy Latin-German models hitherto in vogue, they created a new prose, inspired by the style of the old folk-tales and akin to that of the Norse Sagas. These three men, who were responsible for inaugurating the Norwegianisation of the written language, were followed during the second half of the nineteenth century by the philologist Knud Knudsen (1812-95) who was untiringly engaged throughout his life in proposing orthographic changes based on the spoken language and in trying to replace foreign words by genuine Norwegian ones. He had a strong influence on the dramatist Henrik Ibsen (1828-1906), whose *Per Gynt* is considered to be the most Norwegian of all literary works, and on the nationalist poet and playwright Bjørnstjerne Bjørnson (1832-1910). Apart from his literary work, Bjørnson was actively engaged in political affairs throughout his life. He was famous as an orator and like Henrik Wergeland before him, he was often described as 'the uncrowned king of Norway'. He was also the author of the words of the Norwegian national anthem *Ja, vi elsker dette landet* and many other poems published in his collection *Digte og Sange* (1870) which have become a permanent part of Norway's poetic heritage. Yet, despite the efforts of these scholars and writers, the official orthography remained unchanged throughout the century.

The movement towards the creation of an entirely Norwegian written standard, based on the dialects, took a decisive turn with the work of the poet and philologist Ivar Aasen (1813-96). He believed that no satisfactory result could be achieved by merely changing the written language in a Norwegian direction. Since the grammatical basis of this language was Danish, it was impossible in Aasen's opinion to transform it into Norwegian simply by correcting the orthography according to Norwegian pronounciation and by adopting Norwegian words. These views were determined by the linguistic theories of his time which denied the existence and the possibility of mixed grammatical systems. Of peasant stock, Aasen travelled all over Norway in his study of the regional dialects, collecting material for a dictionary and a grammar. His *Det norske Folkesprogs Grammatikk* (A Norwegian Grammar) was published in 1848 and *Ordbog over det norske Folkesprog* (A Norwegian Dictionary) in 1850. The claim of these pioneer works was that it was possible to construct a written language which would be wholly Norwegian, demonstrated successfully by Aasen in his collection of poems entitled *Symra* (1863).

Aasen's language was named *Landsmål* or *Nynorsk* (Neo-Norwegian) in contra-distinction to the written language which originated in Denmark and which was spoken generally by the bourgeoisie of the towns, called *Riksmål* or, more officially, *Bokmål*. The expression *Riksmål* has often been used in reference to a linguistically more conservative tendency than that represented by the official language, *Bokmål*, its adherents usually being in strong opposition to the official language policy of the Norwegian Government. The term *Landsmål* too is ambiguous. Because *Land*, like 'country' in English, can mean countryside or country, one meaning for Aasen's language was 'rural language' but he always maintained that it was 'the proper language of Norway' since ancient times. For him and his supporters *Landsmål* came to mean a generalised norm based on the rural dialects as the spoken descendants of Old Norse. This conception was revolutionary, flying in the face of common opinion and prejudice, and it needed extraordinary effort for its practical realisation.

About the middle of the nineteenth century, there arose what is now known in Norway as 'the language conflict'. Ranged against the disciples of Aasen were those taking written Dano-Norwegian as a basis with the intention of changing the orthography gradually, in accordance with Norwegian pronunciation, adopting words from the different dialects and, where possible, giving access to other specially Norwegian word-forms and syntax, such as the diphthongs *ei, au, øy* and a separate gender for nouns. Between these two camps has been waged a battle, at times vehement, which has lasted to the present day.

At first the controversy was linguistic and literary. *Landsmål* had the advantage, especially for writers, of being new and fresh with exciting potential. Many lyric poets, born and bred in the towns, have preferred it to *Riksmål*, 'the language of the realm'. But the struggle also bore a marked social character. As *Landsmål* had no administrative or cultural centre, the literature produced in it had a strong regional character determined by the writer's origins. The new language fought its way into the nation's cultural life against considerable opposition. Being nearer to the western dialects than *Bokmål*, it gained its first footing in western Norway. Its adherents used mainly nationalist arguments in their campaign against *Riksmål*, accusing its speakers of using a foreign, imported idiom, an accusation resented by the supporters of *Riksmål* who felt that their language was Norwegian and quite distinct from Danish. In the towns *Landsmål* was supported by people from country districts who found themselves *dépaysés* among townspeople. All over the country the elementary school teachers have played an important role in the controversy, most of them being ardent supporters of *Landsmål*. Yet, as late as 1880 *Landsmål* was little more than a plaything of idealistic linguists and poets, one of the many cultural novelties in an era when Norway's cultural life was becoming rich and exciting. *Landsmål* took its place with the music of Edvard Grieg (1834-1907), the paintings of Adolf Tidemand (1814-76), the novels of Bjørnson and the dramas of Ibsen. Each in its way bore witness to an era of fruitful experimentation with forms and ideas in a population which since 1814 had progressed from poverty and semi-literacy to modest prosperity and general enlightenment. Norway had ceased to be a cultural province of Denmark and was exporting culture to its former partner.

Nevertheless, most of the writers whose work was read abroad still wrote in Dano-Norwegian, while the writers of *Landsmål* remained a small and comparatively unread group. They realised that in spite of the strong appeal their language had in poetry, its future depended on the recognition it could achieve in government and education. This required political action which was only possible through the growing left-wing opposition party, the *Venstre*. This party fought its campaigns on nationalist and democratic grounds: opposition to the Swedish King and extension of suffrage to all the people. By supporting the cause of *Landsmål* the *Venstre* party attacked one of the privileges of the official class, its linguistic superiority, and struck a blow for national sovereignty by helping Norwegian elements to enter the language. In 1884 it overthrew the King's cabinet in a bloodless parliamentary revolution. One of the new Government's first acts was to fulfil its pledge to the language reformers. In 1885 *Landsmål* gained official recognition as an official language.

The 1890s saw a revival of intense interest in Norway's folk traditions, music, dances and dialects. Youth and student societies which supported *Landsmål* were now formed. The response in the schools was slow but sure: by 1905 over 400 school districts had voted to make *Landsmål* their first language and by 1909 another 760, about 20% of all school districts. A chair in *Landsmål* was established at the University of Oslo in 1899 and students were given the right to use it at their final examinations from 1908. It was clear that by now *Landsmål* had come to stay. Young rural Norwegians who were flocking to the schools in increasing numbers felt a special sympathy for *Landsmål* in which they could write poems, find pride in their background and country's past and a political weapon with which to beat the ruling class.

There was soon, however, a reaction in the ranks of the *Landsmål* movement by a group which considered that Aasen's principles needed revision, in order to make it less dignified, more based on everyday usage. Many wanted to make it less of a western speech. The Government responded by appointing a series of committees, the reports of which showed that their members were as hopelessly divided as the people themselves, and nothing was resolved. But in 1892 the schoolboards were authorised to decide which of the two languages was to be the language of the elementary schools. Although under constant attack from its opponents *Landsmål* continued to spread, helped on its way by the wave of national feeling which took Norway out of the union with Sweden in 1905.

Two years later the supporters of *Riksmål* gathered their forces. The reaction on behalf of *Riksmål* was led by the writer Bjørnson. A supporter of *Landsmål* in his early days, and a lifelong agitator on behalf of national independence, he now declared that *Landsmål* was unsuited as a language of culture: it was 'artificial, regional, culturally underdeveloped, fit only for peasants. We are now living in an age when by means of our present *Rigsmaal (sic)* and the literature in this language, we have produced the greatest works of the spirit and have won recognition beside the greatest nations in Europe'. Within a month of Bjørnson's speech a public meeting was held in November 1899 to form a society for the defence of *Riksmål* against the supporters of *Landsmål*, the *Riksmåls forbundet*.

The Norwegian features of the spoken *Riksmål* were given expression in a recognized spelling. Minor alterations had been introduced from time to time but now the voiceless consonants *p*, *t*, and *k* were admitted according to the rules of the spoken language. Ten years later a new and very important step was taken in the direction of conforming the spelling to Norwegian tradition and of bringing the rendering of sounds and grammar nearer to the Norwegian features of the spoken *Riksmål*. At the same time a number of alterations were also introduced into *Nynorsk* whereby many words which had been pronounced alike in the two written languages were also given the same form in spelling.

Since then there has been a movement in favour of bringing the two languages still closer to one another with the ultimate aim of a complete fusion, by adapting the grammar and word-forms of *Nynorsk* to the dialects of eastern Norway and by ousting the last Danish forms from *Riksmål*. These reforms have raised protests, however. Many of the new forms, especially the introduction of the feminine of the noun in a number of words, were branded as 'vulgar'. The written standard had only a distinction between the common gender and the neuter as in the Danish and Swedish standards, but the feminine was in use in the dialects, except in the town of Bergen, and also in the familiar speech of the educated classes. This difficulty gave the language conflict, which had hitherto been mainly an opposition between town and country, a more general social character. Most Labour Party members sympathised with the 'radical' form of *Riksmål*, but the new names of *Nynorsk* and *Bokmål* which were adopted by decision of Parliament in 1929 were decided by the nationalists.

Gradually the agitation against the reform of 1917 died down, at least temporarily. *Landsmål* was adopted by a great number of schoolboards, mainly in the west, south-west and the central areas, mostly regions with small populations. The east, the north and the towns stuck to *Riksmål*. Then, in 1934 the Government appointed a committee of scholars, teachers and writers who were to work out new orthographic and grammatical rules for both languages. The recommendations of this committee were published in 1936, accepted by the *Storting*, the Norwegian Parliament, and introduced into public administration in 1939. Diphthongs were admitted to a large number of words in *Bokmål* in order to make them identical with *Nynorsk*. The grammar of *Bokmål* also underwent considerable changes such as the introduction of the feminine gender into many nouns. On the other hand, word-forms and grammar in *Nynorsk* were altered to make them correspond with the eastern dialects. Once again, there was disagreement. This time resistance from the partisans of *Nynorsk* was particularly determined. Most daily newspapers and all the younger writers adopted the orthography of 1917 or 1938, whereas several of the older writers, notably the great realistic novelist Sigred Undset (1882-1949) wrote according to the rules of 1907.

During the years between the World Wars the language question was taken up by the Socialists. The prosperity of the period 1914-18, when Norway's neutrality had remained intact, was followed by economic depression and the emergence of new class-conscious parties in the wake of the Bolshevik Revolution of 1917. In the elections of 1921 two new parties representing farmers and workers, the *Bondeparteit* (Agrarian Party) and the *Arbeiderparteit* (Labour Party) won a substantial number of seats in the *Storting*, the latter establishing itself as the major party in 1927 and as the party of Government from 1935. Before this period the Socialists had been indifferent to the language debate. As one of their leaders put it, 'What does it matter if one says *grøten i gryten* or *grauten i gryta* (porridge in the pot) as long as the worker gets enough of it?'

However, under the influence of Halvdan Koht, a young left-wing nationalist, the Labour Party altered its position with regard to linguistic reform. In his voluminous writings Kolst reinterpreted the national struggle of Norway as a class conflict between the native farmer and the foreign bureaucrat, and the worker's class struggle as part of the national liberation movement. The main contention of his pamphlet *The Labour Movement and the Language Problem* (1920) was that Labour must have not only an economic programme but a cultural one as well. Language was an important issue for the workers, he wrote, because the cleavage between their speech and the writing of officialdom was a serious hindrance to their educational progress. He had heard labourers who were uncertain of themselves in public discussion as long as they had to use *Riksmål* but when they became angry and forgot their inhibitions they reverted to their dialect and became linguistically effective. Koht's work for the establishment of *Nynorsk (Samnorsk),* a common

Norwegian written language based on the folk language, contributed to the victory of the Labour Party in 1933. The prospect of unification which would put an end to the language controversy and thus eliminate this troublesome issue from politics was particularly appealing. Koht's other contribution was that he persuaded the Labour Party to accept the idea that the Welfare State had a responsibility for providing its citizens with linguistic as well as economic well-being. The Norwegian Government's support for 'language planning', unknown in most States of Western Europe, dates from this time.

The debate ceased abruptly in 1940, with the German invasion of Norway, although even then the Quisling administration introduced a number of orthographic changes in an attempt to reverse the legislation of the previous Socialist Government. These were abolished at the liberation in May 1945. The Second World War made brothers of all loyal Norwegians—while it lasted and for a short while afterwards. In the election of 1945 the parties were returned in about the same proportions as before the War, with the Labour Party forming the Government. For four years there was political stability while the Norwegians set about rebuilding their country. But soon the unresolved problems of language posed by the reforms of 1938 once more became acute.

Since the new names of the languages were by this time firmly established in official usage and had crept into the press, the Dano-Norwegian languages were from now on called *Bokmal*, with *Riksmål* reserved for that special, conservative version of it, while the language created by Aasen, *Landsmål*, was called *Nynorsk*. There is no difference in meaning between these terms, only in attitude, the former is preferred by users of *Bokmål*, the latter by users of *Nynorsk*.

By this time *Landsmål* had lost ground, mainly because it had no administrative or cultural centre and no press of any importance. Many of those who had *Landsmål* as their first language before the War had given it up. A poll in 1946 showed that only 30% of the population wanted it; in the west 49% were for *Riksmål*, 48% for *Landsmål*, whereas the proportion in the east and north was 75% for *Riksmål* to 24% for *Landsmål*. Four out of five Norwegians of all ages, classes, regions and parties were in favour of fusing the two languages into one. Of 18,000 military recruits called up in 1947, of whom 78% came from rural areas, only 23% preferred *Landsmål*. In 1948 only 41% of the children in the country schools had *Landsmål*. This trend was the result of rapid industrialisation after the War and immigration from rural areas to the towns. A new situation had arisen which called for new measures.

The confusion caused by changes in the language's orthography and the many optional forms had serious effects on the schools. In Oslo and other towns parents started correcting the forms used in their children's text-books and exercise books and complained against the crude way in which poems and other texts had been transposed in the third form known as *Nynorsk*. As a result the ability to write a 'correct' form of Norwegian was reduced among school children and students. In an attempt to elaborate a more fixed standard and to work towards an acceptable compromise, the Government appointed in 1951 a permanent Language Commission, *Norsk Spraknemnd*, consisting of thirty experts in linguistics, school work, literary and journalistic activities and broadcasting, fifteen for each language. Many adherents of *Riksmål*, however, have been strongly suspicious of all Government action in linguistic matters declaring that politicians are not often properly qualified to pronounce on linguistic matters. When a majority of the Norwegian Writers' Association decided to elect representatives to serve on the Commission the minority who were against participation left the Association and formed their own. In 1966, after much ink had flowed between them, the two groups were again united after a slight change in the rules governing the representation of authors on the Commission. Some of the members of the Writers' Association, founded in 1953, an Academy whose main object is the defence of *Riksmål*. The *Riksmåls forbundet* has continued to elaborate its own orthographic standard which differs yet again from that of 1938 and this has been adopted by some of the most influential newspapers.

The rules for a fixed standard to be used in the schools, 'the textbook Norm' *(Laereboknormalen)*, elaborated by the Permanent Language Commission, were published in 1958. The Commission recommended that some of the forms introduced in 1938 should be discarded, but at the same time it went further in the direction of *Landsmål*. The new school standard thus created and approved by the Minister of Education is known, unofficially, as *Samnorsk* or Common Norwegian and it is bitterly criticised by the *Riksmålsforbundet*. Nevertheless, both *Bokmål* and *Nynorsk* continue to be taught in the schools and are recognised as having equal status. Pupils learn to read both, while the local school boards have to decide which is to be the chief language of each school. In the year 1964 79·5% of pupils used *Riksmål* as their main language and 20·5% used *Nynorsk*. In 1971 17·5% used *Nynorsk* as their chief language.

In 1964 a committee of nine members, led by the philologist Hans Vogt, was appointed by the Ministry of Church and Education to study the language situation in Norway and to suggest new ways of reducing the conflict between the various groups. The committee's report was completed in 1966. Among its proposals were new rules for the use of language in State administration, in schools and broadcasting, a revision of the principles for official spelling of place-names and the replacement of the Norwegian Language Commission by a new body. Among the most important measures implemented so far is the establishment in 1972 of the Norwegian Language Council, which is now studying the development of the language. The Council is to be an advisory body under the supervision of the Ministry of Church and Education. It will examine all books used in schools, regularise orthography, co-operate with public and private bodies in the standardisation of terminology in various fields and co-operate with the other Scandinavian language commissions. It has twenty-four members, divided equally between protagonists of the two rival forms and the Parliament appoints a further eight members. The unification of the two forms with one standard, which was official policy during most of the present century, has now been abandoned, or at least postponed for the distant future. Those language associations which refused to co-operate with the Language Commission are represented in the Language Council. A final worry for the language planners is that a serious problem these days is the increasing use by Norwegians of anglicisms, especially in technology and science, and under the influence of American and English films.

Finally, in conclusion, it must be noted that, whatever their effect on the education system Norway's linguistic problems have not prevented its writers from producing a rich modern literature. After Wergeland, Bjørnson and Ibsen came other important realistic writers like Jonas Lie (1833-1908), Alexander Kielland (1849-1906) and Arne Garborg (1851-1924). Towards the end of the last century Hans Kinck (1865-1926) and Knut Hamsun (1859-1952) created a new lyrical style in Norwegian prose. The great realistic novelists of this century, Sigrid Undset (1882-1944), Olav Dunn (1876-1939) and Johan Folkberget (1879-1967) have been particularly occupied with ethical issues, often against a historical background. A lyrical revolution around 1910 was led by Olaf Bull (1883-1933), Herman Wildenvey, Arnulf Øverland (1889-1968) and Olav Aukrust (1883-1929). The prose writers of the pre-war generation include Nordahl Grieg (1902-43), Sigurd Hoel (1890-1960), Cora Sandel (born 1880), Aksel Sandemose (1899-1965), Tarjei Vesaas (1897-1970) and Johan Borgen (born 1902). With Bjørnson, Hamsun and Undset were awarded the Nobel Prize in Literature.

It was not until 1827 in Oslo and 1850 in Bergen that the country's first permanent theatres were opened and during the period 1860 to 1870 Norwegian theatres became fully national and independent. The building of the National Theatre in Oslo in 1899 was of the greatest significance while the theatre at Bergen has had a major influence on the development of Norwegian drama since Ibsen and Bjørsnen. Seven of these theatres and six others including the State Travelling Theatre, are subsidised by the Government and the municipal authorities.

Although Norway is one of the world's smallest language communities, it is also one of the countries which has the greatest number of books published per inhabitant. About 2,500 titles are published every year, of which two thirds are usually of Norwegian origin, in editions totalling twenty

million copies. Norway's first periodical was founded in 1763
and the first newspapers in Bergen, Trondheim and Oslo
(then called Kristiansand) a few years later. Of these, the
Adresseavisen of Trondheim still exists and is the oldest
newspaper in Norway. But it was not until the freedom of the
press was recognised in the Constitution of 1814 that
newspapers became an important factor in the formation of
public opinion. The first daily, *Morgenbladet*, was issued in
1819 and Norway's largest newspaper, *Aftenposten*, which
appears twice daily, was launched in 1860. In recent years Norway has lost fewer newspapers than many other Western
European countries, despite the fact that television now
reaches 95% of the population: the total number declined
from 191 in 1950 to 159 in 1973, but total circulation increased by about 23%, from 1,513,000 in 1950 to 1,870,000
in 1973. Local newspapers are still a very important part of
the Norwegian press. In addition to eight dailies in Oslo,
there are seventy-two published in other parts of the country.
Of the eight dailies only three have a net circulation of more
than 100,000 copies. The *Aftenposten* (Conservative) sells
200,992 copies of its morning edition; the *Verdens Gang* (Independent) 114,487 copies, the *Dagbladet* (Liberal) 114,432
copies. Almost all newspapers are politically engaged,
although their political affiliation and circulations are seldom
comparable. The Labour Party, for example with 43% of the
votes in the 1969 general election, had only 23% of the daily
newspaper circulation.

The controversies over the language question in Norway
may seem to the outsider to be a wasteful squabble over very
little. It is nevertheless difficult to see how it could have been
avoided, given the historical background and the upsurge of
national feeling in the nineteenth century. At the same time,
the language battle has not been without its more positive
aspects. The spelling of Norwegian has become much more
phonetic than it was at the beginning of the present century
and this has assisted in the growth of a natural norm of
cultivated pronunciation, having removed the spoken
language from the influences which the printed word was able
to exercise on it. Yet still the differences of pronunciation between different parts of the country have meant that

there is no equivalent in Norwegian to Standard Received English, although the prestige of town norms with the increase of urbanization has grown in recent years, especially in the more densely populated parts of the south-east. Another major factor in the spread of *Nynorsk* as a literary language has been its use by many of the leading contemporary writers, although this has not led to a wider use in other fields. Whereas, in 1946, 32% of primary schools used *Nynorsk* as their principal language, only 18% used it in 1970. Only 10% of all books published in Norway are in *Nynorsk*. In the spoken language it seems probable that the town norms, especially those of the Oslo area, will continue to make progress at the expense of *Nynorsk* and the dialects, while in the written language—though this is still very much an open question—it is likely that some modified form of *Bokmål* will eventually become the sole speech of all Norwegians.

THE LAPPS OF FINNMARK

The Lapps of Finnmark, Norway's northernmost county, together with those in the Kola peninsula, were ruled for five hundred years by Russia, Sweden and Norway, from the Treaty of Novgorod in 1326 when the three countries agreed to share the taxes collected in these areas. The border between Norway and Sweden was established in 1751 and with Russia in 1826, after which Finnmark became part of Norway.

Of the 20,000 inhabitants of Finnmark who belong to the Lappish ethnic group today, only about 2,000 depend for their livelihood on reindeer, although perhaps 10,000 have a knowledge of the language. Their numbers have been halved since 1920. Most live in Finnmark but some have settled in the counties of Troms and Nordland, where they are to be found dispersed among the majority in a variety of occupations.

The greatest toll on the Lappish population was taken at the beginning of the present century when there was unconcealed discrimination against them by the Norwegian Government. A decree of 1902 forbidding the sale of land except to those who could speak, read and write one of the forms of Norwegian, very few at that time, was not abolished until 1965. Norwegian and its dialects became the only language to be used in schools under a law of 1898, also abolished as late as 1955. In other respects the Lapps were tricked and exploited by land-owners and local officials.

At present, however, the Lappish language is encouraged in the schools. It is the language of instruction, when parents request this, in the first year at primary level and subsequently if the child is to pursue his education at one of the Lapp secondary schools. The Government has published a small number of books for the teaching of Lappish and teachers are given special training for use in the Lapp districts under the supervision of an inspector whose responsibility this is.

The greatest difficulties of the Norwegian Lapps are economic. They are the least prosperous community in the whole of Norway. Poverty is caused by a lack of grazing land for those who herd reindeer and by large families who cannot live off herding alone. Government grants are available to young Lapps who wish to follow full-time courses of education but few do so. Training in animal husbandry is not widely provided as there are already too many herds for the pastures to support. Slaughter-houses have been established at Karasjok and Kantokeino in an attempt to improve the meat industry. Most educated Lapps are employed as lawyers, veterinary surgeons, dentists or nurses, often in communities where only a few hundred Lapps live among the Norwegian-speaking majority, and here they are to be found playing an important social role. The incidence of linguistically mixed marriages is high, of which the children invariably lose the ability to speak Lappish.

For these reasons, the Lapps of Finnmark are not expected to survive as a linguistic group for much longer, except perhaps in the most remote areas and there only in impoverished and precarious circumstances.

14 SPAIN

Constitution: Kingdom

Area: 194,883 square miles

Population: 34·130 million (1971)

Capital: Madrid

Administrative divisions: 50 provinces

Present Government: The National Movement

Language of majority: Spanish (Castilian)

THE CATALANS

Excepting the inhabitants of the comparatively small districts of Roussillon and Cerdagne, which belong to France, and those of the Principality of Andorra, the Catalans live on Spain's eastern coast between Alicante and the Pyrénées, but also on the Balearic Islands of Mallorca (Catalan: *Maiorca*), Menorca *(Minorca)*, Ibiza *(Eivissa)* and Formentera; there is too a community of about 12,000 Catalan-speakers in the town of Alghero *(Alguero)* in Sardinia. The seven provinces of mainland Catalonia (Spanish: *Cataluña*, Catalan: *Catalunya)* are Gerona, Lèrida *(Lleida)*, Barcelona *(Barcellona)* and Tarragona; these form the *Principat* of *Catalunya Vella* (Old Catalonia); to the south, Castellón *(Castello)*, Valencia and Alicante *(Alacant)* make up *Catalunya Nova* (New Catalonia). A number of small districts which are ethnically Catalan but where the language is no longer spoken have been incorporated into the neighbouring region of Aragon. With the Balearic Islands and Andorra, the *Països Catalans* have a population of approximately eight and a half million and an area of 26,980 square miles, about 26% of the total population of the Spanish State and 12% of its territory. About six million of the total population of Catalonia live in the four provinces of the *Principat* and, in all, it is estimated that about five million inhabitants speak *català,* the national language. The capital of Catalonia is Barcelona, with a population of over two million and textile industries which make it the most important industrial city in the Iberian peninsula.

Like Occitan, Sard, the Rhaeto-Romance group and Portuguese, Catalan is a Romance language which has remained close to its Latin roots and is consequently more archaic in appearance. As its geographical distribution suggests, it forms a bridge between the Ibero-Romance group of languages, which includes Castilian, and the Gallo-Romance languages north of the Pyrénées, sharing features of both but never absorbed by either. Catalan, although intelligible to Occitans from Provence, is therefore not an extension of the Provençal dialect, nor is it a dialect of Castilian. Portuguese and Castilian have more in common with one another than either

FRANCE

ANDORRA

ROUSSILLON

ARAGON

PRINCIPAT

LERIDA

BARCELONA

SPAIN

REUS

TORTOSA

MINORCA

MAJORCA

VALENCIA

VALENCIA

ALCIRA

BALEARIC ISLANDS

IBIZA

FORMENTERA

ALCOY

MURCIA

CATALONIA

– – – – – Linguistic frontier

———— Administrative frontier

·—·—·— State frontier

has with Catalan. Catalan is described by W. J. Entwhistle in *The Spanish Language* (London, 1936) as 'a separate language, the expression of a community which enjoys a culture with some pretension to permanence and possessing equipoise with reference to a cultural centre (i.e. Barcelona) independent of any other'.

The reason why Catalan belongs to the Gallo-Romance group is that, having an early cultural link with the south of France which was not broken until about 1250, the language began to take on a separate identity during the eleventh century. Linked politically with the town of Béziers in Languedoc, and with Narbonne for ecclesiastical purposes, Catalan was pulled away from the Ibero-Romance group to the south and west in the direction of its Gallo-Romance neighbours. The speech of Aragon, Catalonia's neighbouring province, is a zone of transition between Castilian Spanish and the western dialect of Catalan.

Compared with French or Spanish, Catalan has a strong consonantal quality and sounds, in W. J. Entwhistle's word, more 'abrupt' than either. It sounds rough, even at its most sophisticated, mainly because it has lost post-tonic vowels other than *a* and the spontaeneous dipthongs so characteristic of Spanish (e.g. *cielo*) do not occur in Catalan (cf. *cel*). This roughness is regarded by Catalan writers not as a primitive feature of their language but as a source of vitality, so that any attempt to eradicate it would seriously impair the literary form. Catalan has been more conservative than Provençal in its sound-changes but has borrowed many words from Occitan. Contact between Occitanie and Catalonia has been frequent but sporadic since the medieval period and were particularly fruitful in the hey-day of Mistral and the *Félibrige*.

The political history of Catalonia adds another dimension to the development of its language. A little after A.D. 800, after the Moorish invasion of the Iberian peninsula, the country was recognised by the Turks and divided into administrative units. In the year 864 these were re-grouped to form the *Marca Hispanica*, (the Spanish March), which was intended to be a buffer-state between France and Spain. By 900 the Frankish influence had declined and a strong native

dynasty became established around Barcelona. Throughout
the early Middle Ages the Catalans and the Occitans
established a feudal system more comprehensive than that in
the rest of the peninsula. By the time Catalan interests moved
beyond the river Ebro, towards the end of the twelfth century,
it was too late for the basic features of the language to be affected. Between 900 and 1300 the Catalan language developed
fairly quickly, as the territory over which it was spoken expanded. The earliest recorded use of *Catalunya*, which is of
unknown origin, as the country's name was in the year 1114.

In 1137 the Houses of Barcelona and Aragon were united
by the marriage of Ramon Berenguer IV to Princess
Petronila, an event which postponed the union of Aragon with
Castile for a few more centuries. Early in the thirteenth century contacts between Catalonia and Occitanie suffered a permanent blow when Pere I (Pedro II of Aragon) was killed at
the battle of Muret in 1213 while supporting the Albigensians
against Simon de Montfort. Pere I died in defence of his own
subjects, inhabitants of almost all Occitanie, for the counts of
Toulouse, Foix and Comminges had sworn allegiance to him
seven months previously. By this defeat Catalan dominion
north of Pyrénées was restricted to Roussillon and Cerdagne. In 1238, El Cid having established a base south of the
Ebro, the Catalan James the Conqueror took Valencia in
1238, pressed on to Alicante and Murcia, only to restore it to
Castile later, so that these areas, together with inland Valencia and Castellon, were to lose the Catalan language and
never regain it.

After the Treaty of Corbeil in 1258, Catalan expansion in
the Mediterranean began. Mallorca had been conquered in
1229, the other Balearic Islands shortly afterwards, and eventually Corsica, Sardinia, Naples and the Aegean also fell under their rule. Only in Sardinia, in the town of Alghero, was
there linguistic conquest by the Catalans, mainly because
their régime was liberal for its time. But the Borgias were a
Catalan family and in their day Catalan was the language of
the Vatican. The Catalan presence in the Mediterranean was
commercial rather than military during the thirteenth and
fourteenth centuries and their reputation was that of an active, enterprising but non-belligerent people very different

from their neighbours on the interior plateaux of the Iberian peninsula.

It was not until the discovery of America and the ruin of Mediterranean trade by the Turks that the Catalans suffered a decline and not until the seventeenth century, over a hundred years after its union with Castile, by when the prestige of the Aragonese Crown had been lost, was there any concerted attempt to regain their former brilliance. By now, in a Spain which was still the same confederation of loosely connected states which it had been in 1500, while the Basques, the Asturians and the Galicians retained their privileges, the provinces of Castile had been united in a single Kingdom. Of the four kindgoms and one country under the Crown of Aragon—Valencia, Mallorca, Aragon and Barcelona—each had its own laws and Parliament independent of Castile's. So foreign was Valencia that the poet Lope de Vega could find refuge there from Castilian law; the Catalans kept consuls in Andalusia and the King could neither raise taxes nor send his troops into Aragon without permission.

The Catalans were the first to realise that Spain's wars in Holland and Germany, waged for religious reasons, were responsible for its economic decline in the seventeenth century. When asked by Olivares, the chief minister of Castile in 1623, how the economic problems of Spain could be solved, the Catalans replied, 'Stay at home'. Their advice was ignored, however, and Olivares—fearful that France, as a more centralised State would prove more powerful than Spain—began to draw up plans for amending the privileges of the Catalans and the other autonomous regions. When news of his intentions reached the Catalans, on Corpus Christi Day 1640, they rose, in the middle of a war between France and Castile, and placed themselves under the command of the French King. At the same time there was a successful rising in Portugal and unsuccessful risings in Andalusia and Aragon. Barcelona did not surrender until 1652 and the war continued in the mountains for another seven years. By the Treaty of the Pyrénées in 1659 by which Spain ceded Roussillon and Cerdagne to France, the first major Catalan rebellion was ended. But forty years later, during the War of the Spanish Succession, the Catalans rose against Madrid once more and

offered their support to the Allies. Barcelona was besieged
and ransacked by the Castilians—this time not the descendants of Phillip II but of Bourbon princes who had learned
autocracy at the court of Louis XIV. The six Catalan universities were abolished and the Catalans deprived of their
traditional privileges. The centralising policies of the Bourbons were continued into the next century by their political
heirs, the liberals. The main source of controversy between the Catalans and Madrid was now the need for tariffs
and manufactured articles to keep out English and French
competitors. Organised in the *Institut Industrial de Cataluña*
and later as the famous *Fomento de Trabajo Nacional,* the
Catalan manufacturers were resolutely opposed to Madrid
and to every commercial treaty between Spain and France or
England. Thus began the tension which has existed between
Barcelona and Madrid up to the present time.

The next stage in the revival of Catalan national feeling
was, at first, primarily literary. Between 1822 and 1837
Catalonia had lost its own legal and monetary systems, and its
right to use Catalan in the schools, without a great deal of
protest. But in the 1850s, after the re-establishment of the
medieval festivals known as the *Jocs Florals* (Floral Games)
and over the next twenty years, the language—which was no
longer widely spoken in the towns—began to gain ground.
The first daily Catalan newspaper and a theatre were
established in 1862. The growing federal movement of the
years 1868-73 was supported by Barcelona intellectuals and
three of the most prominent figures of this revolutionary
period were Catalans: Franciso Pi y Margall, Juan Prim y
Prats and Figueras.

On the final defeat of the Carlists in 1876 the Catalan
national movement made rapid and substantial progress.
The Church took up the cause of Catalan autonomy,
attracting under the leadership of the Bishop of Vich
almost the whole of the upper classes in Barcelona. Up
to 1900, and even as late as 1923, Catalan nationalism was
thus a predominantly right-wing affair. The movement was
not without a left-wing, but it was less numerous and less influential because it appealed only to intellectuals, heirs of Pi y
Margall. The aims and history of Catalan nationalism were

summed up by the leader of the movement, Valentin Almirall, in 1886, when he published his book *Lo Catalanisme*, an important document on which the movement's programme was later based.

With the loss of Cuba, which the Catalan manufacturers had tried to resist, the scandals of administration from Madrid, the Government's indifference to trade and commerce, Catalonia's grievances multiplied and the national movement, fired by the persistent Carlism of the rural areas, became for the first time a powerful force in Spanish politics. The year 1906 is usually regarded as a watershed in the history of Catalonia because it brought a new sense of the relations between politics and culture. A new party, the *Lliga Regionalista* (Regional League) also known as the *Lliga Catalana*, had been formed under the leadership of Francisco Cambó, President of the *Fomento de Trabajo Nacional*, and the popular front *Solidaritat Catalona* five years later. Rallying all the right-wing but peaceful elements of Catalonia who were resentful of the country's neglect by Madrid, the *Lliga* won a sudden victory at the polls in 1901 and the struggle for Catalan autonomy was launched. Under the leadership of Enric Prat de la Riba (1870-1917), cultural life now came to be regarded for the first time as an essential component in Catalonia's political future. The year 1906 was not only the year of Prat's own manifesto, *La Nacionalitat Catalana*, but also of the first International Congress of the Catalan Language, followed in 1907 by the foundation of the *Institut d'Estudis Catalans*. Also in 1906 was published the work of Eugeni d'Ors (1882-1954) and Josep Carner (1884-1970), the leading figures in the literary and political movement which came to be known as *noucentisme* (twentieth century).

The next twenty years were to be among the most violent and corrupt that Catalonia had ever known. The immediate reaction to the success of of the *Lliga Regionalista* was the rapid spread of a left-wing republican party known as the Radicals. Its leader was a young journalist named Alejandro Lerroux who was thoroughly anti-clerical, anti-capitalist and anti-Catalan. His speeches inciting people to kill priests, burn churches and loot the homes of the rich, guaranteed him huge

audiences in Barcelona while the Governor of Catalonia, the
Duke of Bivona, and the police stood aside, in the knowledge
that while Lerroux was hailed as the Emperor of the Paralelo
(the slum and brothel quarter of the city) the Catalan
nationalists could make little headway. The radicals defeated
the nationalists at the election of 1903, but two years later and
again in 1907, the united front known as *Solidaritat Catalana*
won an overwhelming victory under Cambó. The Central
Government did everything in its power to prevent the
nationalists' progress: republicans contested elections with
the secret support of conservative Madrid, gangsters and
anarchists and the police were provoked or paid to explode
bombs in public places so that constitutional guarantees
could be suspended and Catalans imprisoned. Elections were
rigged by the personal intervention of the Prime Minister Antonio Maura and the Home Secretary, Juan de La Cierva, the
most notorious and corrupt politician of his day. In the
prophetic words of Francisco Cambó, 'In order to fight
against a Catalonia which was beginning to lift its head, the
Spanish Government set on foot every kind of demagogic
agitation. But, as was only to be expected, the bacillus which
scattered through the country did not keep to the field allotted
to it . . .'

In 1909, following a call-up by the Army which needed
troops to send to Morocco for the protection of iron-
mines said to belong to the Jesuits, the city of Barcelona was
engulfed by violence of unprecedented proportions. The
followers of Lerroux, the *Jóvenes Bárbaros* (Young Barbarians) filled the streets and led five days of mob rule during
which the unions lost control of their members, twenty-two
churches and thirty-four convents were burned, many monks
killed and tombs desecrated. In *The Spanish Labyrinth*
(1943) Gerald Brenan records that during these incidents
workmen danced in the streets of Barcelona with the disin-
terred corpses of nuns. The riot, known as 'the tragic week of
Barcelona' was put down by La Cierva in an equally brutal
way: 175 workers were shot and many executed later. Among
the victims was Francisco Ferrer, an anarchist who, although
not involved in the riots, had earlier founded a school,
Escuela Moderna where non-religious instruction was given

and who, it was claimed, had plotted the assassination of the King three years before. Ferrer's death and the riots were widely reported in the foreign press and Maura's Government fell as a result; it was ten years before he and La Cierva were able to return to public life. Another consequence of the riots was the ruin of the Radicals. The followers of Lerroux, who—despite his exhortations—had not himself joined in the burning and killing, now accused him of being bought off by Madrid, and they abandoned his Party in favour of the anarchists. As for the Catalan nationalists, they had been scared by the riots and for the next few years they chose to lie low. The *Solidaritat Catalana* broke up over the religious question, as the Government had hoped, and the *Lliga Regionalista* became once again the only body representing Catalan national aspirations. In 1913 a moderate measure of autonomy was restored in Catalonia.

The First World War divided opinion in Spain along the predictable lines: the Government, the Army, the Church, the aristocracy and the landowners were with few exceptions pro-German while the liberals, the intellectuals, the left-wing and the big industrialists of Barcelona and Bilbao supported the Allies. At the head of the anti-Government campaign was the Catalan banker Cambó. By now his demands were no longer only for an autonomous Catalonia, but backed by the large land-owners and industrialists, for 'a new Spain' run by a modern and efficient Government, either within a monarchy or a federal republic. The *Lliga* lost much of its support, however, when in 1917, it failed to support a general strike of railway-workers.

Up to the dictatorship of General Miguel Prima de Rivera, the *Lliga* had been the only Catalan party of any consequence but it became more and more reactionary and clerical. It now lost members to a new coalition party, the *Esquerra Catalana* (Party of Catalonia). It comprised several groups: the *Estat Catalá* of Maciá, the *Acció Catalá*, the *Unió de Rabassaires* and for a while the *Unió Socialistá Catalunya*. It was this party, with the Republican Action Party, the Radical Socialists and the Republicans of Galicia, which made up the group known as the Left Republicans, the largest group in the *Cortes* of 1918. They represented the more progressive members of the middle and lower-middle classes and a large proportion of the intellectuals, 'the generation of '98' whose ambition was to conclude the liberal revolution begun in 1812. Meanwhile, the *Lliga* was drawn further and further to the right by the syndicalist struggle in Barcelona in the years 1919 to 1923, its nationalism counting for less than its class feeling. It ended in an alliance with the Army, the most anti-Catalan force in Spain and welcomed the *coup d'état* which introduced the Dictatorship.

Primo de Rivera destroyed the *Mancomunitat,* as the moderate form of Catalan home rule established by Prat de la Riba was known, and with it every form of Catalan culture. His Government's repressive measures had the effect of re-inforcing national feeling, however, especially among the lower middle-classes and, with the *Lliga* discredited, young Catalans now joined the *Esquerra Republicana de Catalunya,* a coalition of left-wing groups with nationalist ambitions under Colonel Francese Macià. At the municipal and general elections of 1931 the *Esquerra* won a huge victory—its vote was five times that of the *Lliga* and in Barcelona all fourteen of its candidates were elected whereas only one *Lliga* candidate was successful. Cambó, who had become extremely unpopular through his support of the King, fled the country. Macià was triumphant and immediately proclaimed an independent Catalan Republic with himself as its first President. This act was not legal but when the question was put to the electorate in a referendum a few months after the election, 99% voted in favour of autonomy.

The Catalan Statute of Autonomy was put before the *Cortes* in the following May. It referred to Catalonia as a State entitled to its own flag but conceding to Madrid responsibility for management of customs, tariffs and foreign affairs, including relations with the Vatican. Catalan was to be the official language and the language of education. Catalans would serve in the Spanish armed forces but would be used only in defence of Catalonia. Laws passed by the central Government would operate in Catalonia only with the consent of the *Generalitat* (Commonwealth) which would alone be responsible for public order. The Statute, now regarded in Madrid as granting almost complete independence to Catalonia, was bitterly opposed, especially by the right-wing factions, led by Royo Villanovo, Madrid newspapers talked of 'the dissolution of Spain and over four centuries of history'. Above all, the Statute was seen as depriving the central Government of a major source of man-power and war materials. The Spanish Treasury would lose 25% of its revenue and the most advanced industrial and agricultural region of the State. Socialists in other parts of Spain joined with right-wing politicians in attacking the Statute becaue it would leave the Catalan socialists in difficulties and Catalonia, a stronghold of the *Confederación Nacional del Trabajo* but not of the *Union General de Trabajadores*, would be lost either to the anarchists or to the middle-class industrialists who were in favour of autonomy. And if an autonomous Catalonia, the centralists argued, why not the same for the Basque provinces, for Andalusia and for Galicia? Opposition to the Statute thus cut across all frontiers of class and politics, although in Catalonia itself a plebiscite the previous year had resulted in 592,961 votes in favour of Home Rule and only 3,276 votes against.

On 6 May the Statute came under heated discussion in the *Cortes*. Mass meetings to oppose it were held in Castile and Aragon. It was thanks to the determination of Azaña, who had promised Companys a measure of autonomy for Catalonia, that the Statute was piloted through the *Cortes* and finally passed in September 1932. The powers of the *Generalitat* were confirmed, except that Catalan was to share equal status with Spanish and the Catalan Government would not be in sole control of the education system. Azaña, his prestige increased for having put down the monarchist *coup d'état* of Sanjurjo on 10 August 1932, now won the support of the socialists who withdrew their opposition to the Statute. Catalonia was given control of local finances, radio, railways, roads, harbours, public works, civil law and Companys was re-instated as President. Castilian prejudice had been overcome by the diplomacy of Azaña who saw that the Republic would henceforth have in the Catalan people its staunchest supporters. Although he had expected more, Macià told a cheering crowd from the balcony of the Plaza de San Jaime, 'I have every confidence in the goodwill with which you will receive this Statute. But it is not the Statute for which we voted'. Thus began the brief, tumultuous and tragic history of the Catalan Republic.

By 1934, on the eve of the Spanish Civil War, the *Generalitat* or Autonomous Catalan Government, was controlled by the *Esquerra*, the *Lliga* having walked out in protest. Colonel Macià had died the previous year and the leader of the *Esquerra* was now Lluís Companys. It comprised four separate groups: the Republican middle-class, a separatist group known as the *Estat Català* led by Dencás and Badiá, the Catalan Socialist Party and the *Rabassaires* or Peasants' Party. Although opposed to a rising, under pressure from the *Estat Català*, a right-wing nationalist group with its own para-military wing, and reacting to what seemed to announce a Fascist Government in Madrid, Companys proclaimed the independence of *'L'Estat Català dintre la Republica federal espanyola'* ('The Catalan State within the Federal Spanish Republic') on the evening of 5 October. By the next morning, however, the rising was over with a minimum of bloodshed: the Catalan in charge of the division stationed at Barcelona had not ordered the intervention of his soldiers on the Catalan State's behalf. Companys broadcast a dignified appeal for his followers to lay down their arms and was then arrested. Later the chief of *Confederación Espanola de Derechas Autonomas* (Spanish Confederation of Autonomous Right Parties), Gil Robles, admitted in the *Cortes* that he had deliberately provoked the rising in order to discredit the Catalan left wing. The fact that the Asturian miners, in the name of anti-fascism, resorted to arms during the spring and summer of 1934, gave the Government an opportunity of discrediting the entire Spanish left. With their counterparts in the Basque provinces, the municipal Government of Catalonia and the Catalan Parliament were suspended on the grounds that their conflicts with Madrid amounted to direct attack on the Spanish State's sovereignty. The flag of Catalonia and the national anthem were banned and use of the country's name was declared illegal.

The Civil War, during which the Catalans took a heroic part in the defence of the Republic against the insurgent forces of General Franco, ended with the defeat of the Ebro front in July-December 1938 and the fall of Barcelona in February 1939. The complete collapse of Catalonia's political institutions was followed by savage repression of its cultural identity. Catalan resistance to the insurgents was national in character, many workers who had been previously indifferent to the national cause became 'Catalanised' during the struggle. But internal strife between communists and anarchists, and between the *C.N.T.* and *P.O.U.M.* *(Partido Obrero de Unificación Marxista)* during 1937, had led to the loss of Barcelona, then 'capital of Spain', and the occupation of all Catalonia by 10 February 1939. The first act of the victorious insurgents was to ban the Catalan language in the territories they held.

In his *Homage to Catalonia* (1938), George Orwell gives a vivid account of the brief life of the Catalan Republic and the fighting in Barcelona: 'It was the first time that I had ever been in a town where the working-class was in the saddle. Practically every building of any size had been seized by the workers and was draped with red flags or with the red and black flag of the Anarchists, every wall was scrawled with the hammer and sickle and with the initials of the revolutionary parties; almost every church had been gutted and its images burnt . . . There was much in it that I did not understand, in some ways I did not even like it, but I recognised it immediately as a state of affairs worth fighting for'. Of his experiences while fighting with the *P.O.U.M.*, Orwell wrote: 'The revolutionary atmosphere remained as I had first known it. General and private, peasant and militiaman, still met as equals, everyone drew the same pay, wore the same clothes, ate the same food, and called everyone else 'thou' and 'comrade'; there was no boss-class, no beggars, no menial-class, no prostitutes, no lawyers, no priests, no boot-licking, no cap-touching. I was breathing the air of equality, and I was simple enough to imagine that it existed all over Spain. I did not realise that more or less by chance I was isolated among the most revolutionary section of the Spanish working-class'.

For an account of the last days of the Catalan Republic, we must turn to Hugh Thomas in *The Spanish Civil War:* 'Attempts were now being made by the Republic to meet the situation . . . The streets and squares of Barcelona were filled with refugees from the country—numbered at over a million. The whole great city wore a desperate air of defeat. Soldiers, bourgeoisie, and anarchists alike thought only of how they could escape to France. Air raids were continuous, especially on the port . . . The Government, preoccupied first with the question of evacuating children, did not decide to move until the last moment. After a brief pause, following the fall of Tarragona, the battle drew nearer to Barcelona with very little fighting. Negrin, the Government, the communist leaders, the chiefs of the Army and of the Civil Service now hastily moved from Barcelona to Gerona, along with the Catalan and emigré Basque Governments. In the Catalan capital, there was no spirit of resistance . . . The Central Government's long feud with the *Generalidad* (sic) had its toll since it evidently greatly weakened Catalonia's desire and capacity to resist the Nationalist Armies . . . Meantime the streets were silent and empty. Almost a million persons had left the city for the north by all means possible. By four o'clock the main administrative buildings were occupied, untouched by incendiaries. In the evening, those citizens of Barcelona who had all the time secretly supported the Nationalists came into the streets to rejoice . . . After the fall of Catalonia, the world concluded that the Spanish war was over'.

It is estimated that over 250,000 Catalans went into exile during the last days of the Republic, including all the most prominent politicians and writers. As they fled towards France they were bombed by Franco's air-force, in scenes described by Hugh Thomas in *The Spanish Civil War* as follows: 'The flights from Irún, Málaga, Bilbao—all those terrible movements of a terrified population—paled into insignificance when compared with the flight from Catalonia along what Stohrer named 'this road of suffering'. This was a movement of hysterical panic, for only a small percentage of those who fled would have been in mortal danger if they had remained in Catalonia. But the whole of Catalonia now seemed to be on the move . . . All the towns on the way to the French border were crammed to over-flowing'. On 28 January 19,000 refugees crossed into France and on the following days this figure was far exceeded. To the

10,000 wounded, the 170,000 women and children, and the 60,000 male civilians who crossed at this time, there were added about 250,000 men of the Republican Army in the five days after 5 February. Hugh Thomas goes on: 'The frontier was a scene of consummate tragedy. The fugitives were worn out by hunger and fatigue. Their clothes were damp from rain and snow. Yet there were few complaints. Crushed by disaster, the Spanish Republicans walked on upright, erect and dignified'.

Up to 1938 the Catalan language had been official and used for all purposes in public life, including radio, administration and commerce. But after his victory Franco banned it in the schools and censored all books and periodicals discussing the Civil War and the Catalan heritage. Several aged Catalan writers were murdered by the police, whole libraries of Catalan books burned. All the political institutions of the Republican era and of the socialist and anarchist trade unions were proscribed and all legislation on regional autonomy, separation of Church and State, land reform and divorce, was dismantled.

As Gabriel Jackson says in his *Concise History of the Spanish Civil War* (1974), 'For five years prior to the Civil War, Spain had been a mildly reformist, unstable, parliamentary Republic. After the Civil War it was a conservative military dictatorship and that dictatorship became, through the cruelty, the skill and the longevity of General Franco, the most powerful Spanish Government since the reign of Philip II in the sixteenth century. The régime was consolidated by roughly eight years of political proscription (1936-44) positively awe-inspiring in its lack of pity and lack of imagination. It was as if the victors had deliberately set themselves not to reconcile the defeated majority of their compatriots'.

Among the victims was Luís Companys, President of the *Generalitat,* who had done his utmost in 1936 to reduce terrorism and to help even his political opponents to escape Franco's troops. Having escaped to France, he was caught by the Gestapo in Brittany, returned to Spain and on 15 October 1940 he was shot. Tens of thousands of veterans were court-martialled and either shot or given prison sentences of twenty and thirty years. It is estimated that executions and reprisals were far and away the largest single category of deaths during the Civil War. The Republicans killed about 20,000 people in this way, mostly during the first three months of the struggle. Franco's Nationalists, from July 1936 to 1944, killed about 300,000, on a scale of violence comparable to the repression of the Paris Commune in 1871 or the Nazi repression in Eastern Europe. About 400,000 people had left Spain up to mid-1939 as political refugees. About 100,000 died of disease or malnutrition. The population of Spain in 1936 had been approximately 25 million. It is therefore more or less true that, as Franco was fond of pointing out on 1 April each year, the anniversary of the victory in what the Spanish Government calls 'the Crusade', Spain lost *un millón de muertos* as a result of the Civil War. What is not stated is that the *Caudillo* was responsible for about 80% of these deaths. Executions ended only in 1944 with the approaching defeat of the Fascist powers in the Second World War and no amnesties were granted until the 1950s.

Franco took these savage measures not only out of personal revenge against individual Catalans who had opposed him but in a deliberate attempt to put an end to the cultural tradition which had flourished in Catalonia from medieval times and which had always provided a rallying-point for national feeling. Catalan literature, in particular, had been among the most illustrious in Europe from the time of Ramón Llull (1233-1316). He was the first writer to break with the literary Provençal used by the Catalan troubadours. He it was who created Catalan as a literary medium in an *oeuvre* which runs to thirty volumes in the modern critical edition; he was also the first writer to apply any Romance vernacular in a systematic way to every branch of medieval learning except music. Catalan literature was then established by such writers as Jaume I in his epic *Libre dels Feyts,* and Bernat Desclot and Ramon Muntaner, Bernat Metge and Ausias March. After these distinguished medieval beginnings, Catalan literature fell into decay between the sixteenth and nineteenth centuries, a period of decadence caused by the domination of Castile in culture and politics.

From the death of the poet Joannof Martorell in 1468 to the second half of the nineteenth century, there were no major writers in Catalan. The decline was one of standards, not of numbers, and Catalonia continued to produce painters, musicians and intellectuals who wrote in Castilian. Nor did it reflect a change in the status of Catalan for the language remained official up to 1714 and the teaching of Catalan was not prohibited until 1768. The main reason for decadence was the fact that after 1412 the country was ruled by the Castilian dynasty of the Trastámaras. Castilian became the language of the Court and after the union of Castile and Aragon in 1474 the Catalan aristocracy lost contact with the indigenous culture. Almost every writer before 1500 was connected in some way with the Court and most turned to Castilian. Forbidden to write plays exclusively in Catalan, it was at this time that some playwrights began a tradition of introducing Castilian characters for comic effect. Many writers in the sixteenth century continued to defend the use of Catalan for sophisticated literary purposes but there was no major talent. Popular and religious poetry, including ballads, on the other hand, kept their vitality throughout the whole period.

With the eighteenth century the character of Catalan culture changed as the intellectual life of the country moved under the influence of the Enlightenment. At first, the reprisals taken against Catalonia after the War of the Spanish Succession (1700-14) came near to destroying the national identity altogether: the suppression of the autonomous Government and the Catalan universities, together with the *Decreto de Nueva Planta* of 1716 which restricted the use of the Catalan, were severe blows. By 1750, however, there were signs that the revival of Catalan culture was imminent. A growing concern with the country's traditions led to the creation of new institutions such as the *Real Academia de Buenas Letras* in 1752, the *Junta de Comericeo de Barcelona* in 1758 and the *Academia de Ciencias* in 1764. There was also a new confidence in the commercial society of Barcelona after the opening up of trade with Spain's South American colonies in 1778. Interest in the Catalan language culminated in 1815 in the first modern grammar, Josep Pau Ballot's *Gramatica i apologia de la llengua Catalana.*

Like other countries in Western Europe at this time, Catalonia shared the growing interest in the remote and the exotic. The traditionalist reaction provoked by the Napoleonic Wars brought a heightened sense of the national past which was easily assimilated into the ideology of the time. Paramount among the major trends of the day were the aesthetics of Friedrich Schlegel, the vogue of Madame de Staël and Chateaubriand, the revaluation of Shakespeare and the achievement of writers like Goethe, Schiller and Scott. The problem facing Catalan writers of the Romantic period was largely a matter of audience: the first successful plays in Catalan were not staged until the 1860s and the first works of any significance were published even later. The *Renaixença* (Revival) was therefore concerned almost exclusively with poetry, and with poetry of a fairly conservative kind. The movement was dominated not by radical ideology, as in other countries, but by middle-class ideals and the nostalgic evocation of a legendary past.

Many poets referred to their language as *llemosí*, a name full of overtones from the troubadour days, and among the first manifestations of the Revival was the restoration of the interrupted tradition of the *Jocs Florals* in 1859. The word *llemosí* (limousin) was given to one of the areas closely associated with medieval Provençal poetry and for a time it was wrongly regarded as being synonymous with 'Catalan'. The title *Jocs Florals* (Floral Games) was originally given to the literary contests organised in the fourteenth century by the *Sobregaia Companhia dels set trobadors* in which the winners were awarded jewels in the form of flowers. The *Jocs Florals* are still celebrated but since the Civil War it has not been possible to hold them in Catalonia. It is difficult to speak of a school of Catalan poetry before the restoration of the *Jocs Florals* but from now on there was a much greater sense of collective enterprise as well as an assured audience. On the other hand the *Jocs Florals*, with their motto *Patria, Fe, Amor* (Homeland, Faith, Love), encouraged countless poets to express themselves in naive and conventional terms which confirmed the basic conservatism of the *Renaixença*.

Above all the *Jocs Florals* provided a context and platform for the three poets whose achievement were to render their further existence more or less superfluous. In 1877 the first prize was awarded to an epic poem entitled *Atlàntida* by Jacint Verdaguer (1845-1902). A young priest, Verdaguer was immediately established as the first major Catalan poet of the nineteenth century, and went on to write several master-pieces, including *Canigo* which deals with the legendary origins of Catalonia, and by his work to establish beyond doubt the possibilities of Catalan as a modern literary language. The success of the *Renaixença* was confined almost entirely to poetry, the *Jocs Florals* having little effect on the writing of prose.

The one gifted Catalan novelist of the period was Narcís Oller (1845-1930). Hearing Verdaguer read his *Atlàntida* in 1877, Oller became convinced of the value of Catalan as a literary medium; two years later he published his first collection of stories *Croquis del natural* and, in 1882, the first of his four novels *La Papallona* which established him as the leading prose-writer of his day. The third writer was a dramatist, Angel Guimerà (1845-1924). Up to now Catalonia had no theatre in its own language, but with the growing af-fluence of the urban middle-classes attempts were made to bridge the gap between the professional theatre and the traditionalist world of the *Jocs Florals*. With plays like *Mar i Cel* (1888), *Maria Rosa* (1894) and *Terra Baixa* (1897), Guimera proved that he was a dramatist of European stature and virtually created the modern Catalan theatre. Like Ver-daguer and Oller, Guimera extended the range of literary Catalan and by the end of the nineteenth century the European modernist qualities of their work had spread to other sectors of literature and the arts.

Among the major poets to emerge in the early years of the present century was Joan Maragall (1860-1911). The leading theorist of this time was the painter, novelist and playwright Santiago Rusiñol (1861-1931). At the same time there was a literary school on the island of Mallorca led by Joan Alcover (1854-1926) and Miguel Costa i Llobera (1854-1922), in whose work there is a sense of belonging to a Mediterranean world embracing both the pagan and the Christian traditions. Among personal accounts of the Civil War is the work of Carles Riba (1893-1959) whose remarkable *Elegies de Bier-*

ville (1943), poems about exile and return to Catalonia, are considered the finest to have emerged from that tragic struggle, and the fiction of Josep Carner (1884-1969), who as a Catalan diplomat became an exile in 1939. Also driven into exile, but by the Communists in 1936, was the most outstanding Catalan playwright and novelist of the period Josep Maria de Sagarra (born 1894); he has since returned to Barcelona but, although not all his writings have been approved by the Franco régime, he has translated the whole of Dante and Shakespeare into Catalan.

The national consciousness of Catalonia was understandably slow to recover from the havoc caused by the Civil War and the brutal policies of the Spanish Government after 1945. As a protest against repression of the language which he had done so much to develop for all modern purposes, the philologist and former Rector of the autonomous University of Barcelona, Pompeu Fabra, founder of the *Institut d'Estudis Catalans*, chose to leave Spain, dying at the age of 80 in 1948.

It was not until 1961 that the Government felt secure enough to allow the publication of books in Catalan on a wide scale and the existence of such organisations as *Omnium Cultural de Catalunya*. Up to 1938 there had been around 400 Catalan periodicals and twenty-three daily newspapers. Since 1961 only about 400 books a year have appeared; whereas Catalan books represented 20% of all books produced in Spain up to 1939, by now they amount to only 2% of the total. No book was published in Catalan between 1939 and 1946, but in 1950 a total of forty-nine appeared, 200 in 1960 and 650 in 1967. In 1933, 740 new titles had been published. There is a wide variety of Catalan books, from James Bond to Dostoyevski and including translations of Teilhard de Chardin, Graham Greene, Dickens and Marcuse. Paradoxically, while many books such as *La Condition Humaine* by André Malraux or *La Nausée* by Jean-Paul Sartre, are banned by the Spanish Government, they enjoy huge sales when published in Catalan.

The main bastion of Catalan resistance to Franco has been the Church, particularly the monastery at Montserrat, about sixty miles from Barcelona, traditionally the spiritual centre of Catalonia, and now the stronghold of a movement supporting Catalan autonomy in cultural, economic and political fields. From the publication of the papal encyclicals *Mater Magista* and *Pacem in Terris* in 1963, (two highly significant documents for all linguistic minorities in Catholic countries), the Benedictines of Montserrat have played a leading role in the national movement. The first breach in the Government's intransigence towards Catalan was made by Montserrat's magazine *Serra d'Or* which continues to be regarded as the leading review for Catalan intellectuals. It was joined in the 1960s by other periodicals all of which had to suffer constant supervision by the authorities and most of which have not survived. The principal magazines, however, enjoy a wide readership; *Serra d'Or*, for example, sells 30,000 copies monthly and *Tele-Estel* sold about 90,000 weekly before its demise in 1969. Periodicals for children, such as *Infantil, Oriflama, Patufet* and *Recull,* sell about 35,000 copies each.

Against Franco's policy of removing Catalan bishops and priests and replacing them with Castilians (the clergy are appointed by the Vatican after nomination by the State), the Church has taken an unequivocal stand. Cardinal Vidal i Barraquer, Archbishop of Tarragona and Primate of Spain, did his utmost to reconcile Church and State in Catalonia in a more democratic relationship, but was exiled for his pains. The Abbot of Montserrat Dom Aureli-Maria Escarré was also exiled for criticising the Franco régime in public, and he died in Italy in 1968. Like their Basque counterparts, many Catalan priests and monks have joined the opposition to Franco's régime; they too are persecuted, imprisoned, and tortured. There has been a significant drop in Church attendances throughout Catalonia since 1939 and there is already a shortage of priests. It is sometimes claimed that the Catalans as a people are less religious, or at any rate attend church less frequently, than the Basques. Certainly, many sections of the Church have been brought into disrepute by their acquiescence in the Government's policies in Catalonia. Montserrat represents the upper intellectual echelons of the Church and its influence does not always extend to the village priest, as in the Basque provinces. For this reason, among others, the situation in the Basque provinces is generally regarded as being potentially more explosive than in Catalonia.

There are other reasons why Basque and Catalan nationalism should not be considered as identical phenomena. In the first place, these movements grew out of societies which have different social structures and the Catalans are superior in number to the Basques. Furthermore, while Catalan nationalism tended to be of the forward-looking kind, the political aspirations of a modern-minded community, that of the Basques was more romantic and backward-looking, at least in the beginning. Basque nationalism was expressed mainly through one political party, the *P.N.V.*, whereas the Catalans divided on class lines and supported several parties. On the other hand, by now the national movements of both Catalonia and Euzkadi are predominantly left-wing and, in their opposition to Franco, have many characteristics in common. To begin with, the growth of industry in both Catalonia and the Basque provinces took place at an early date and there is a tendency for the industrial welath of the Spanish State to be concentrated there.

As Spain's principal industrial regions and the ones with the fastest growing population, the Basque provinces and Catalonia have long had to accept a large-scale immigration from other parts of the peninsula. A large proportion of Barcelona's working-class before 1936 was drawn from Andalusia. Over 40% of Catalonia's population at the present time was born elsewhere. Between 1961 and 1965 a total of 414,062 immigrants settled in Catalonia. Catalan nationalists see this high rate of immigration as the Government's official policy, begun deliberately in 1939. Up to now, however, the culture of Catalonia has shown resilience to the influence of new-comers to an extent greater than is the case in the Basque provinces. According to a survey of 3,500 people carried out by Antonio Badia i Margarit in 1964, about 30% of those born outside the Catalan-speaking areas had Catalan as their everyday language.

Among reasons for Catalan success at assimilation is the fact that the Basque language, not belonging to the Romance family, presents greater difficulties to foreigners than does Catalan. Also, immigrants to Catalonia usually come from backward areas with under-developed cultures and less political awareness. It is therefore a well-known phenomenon in Catalonia that people with no family roots in the area come to identify with their hosts, learn to speak Catalan, because they have to, and take part in Catalan organisations, especially the unofficial *Commissiones Obreres* (Workers' Commissions).

The aims of these bodies, which have sprung up throughout Spain since 1964, are to obtain higher wages and better conditions, to destroy the present system of State-controlled unions and to rally working-class opposition to the Falange. As a result of their growth in Catalonia the nationalist cause has been re-inforced by industrial and class interests which have become even more significant. The Workers' Commissions have been joined in recent years by middle-class and professional organisations such as the Barcelona College of Lawyers which has been prominent in organising anti-Government protests. Individual lawyers, writers and university teachers have also been imprisoned for their activities, notably after the Burgos trials of the Basque nationalists in 1970, and coinciding with widespread sympathy strikes throughout Catalonia. In dealing with offences of a political nature, the Spanish State usually employs special courts and their use for dealing with opposition to the régime in Catalonia, as in the Basque provinces, has attracted much attention. In the Balearic Islands the various political and cultural groups come together in *Taula Democratica de les Illes,* founded in 1965.

There is no co-ordinated, political, separatist resistance to the régime in Catalonia at the present time. The *Conseil Nacional Català,* based in London, attempted this but no lasting impression was made and that body was dissolved in 1945. Among political parties in Catalonia at the moment are *Moviment Socialista de Catalunya,* founded in 1943, the *Front Obrer de Catalunya,* founded in 1969, the *Partit Socialista Unificat de Catalunya,* the *Partit Socialista d'Alliberament Nacional dels Països Catalans,* and *Accio Regionalista Catalana,* launched in 1972. The main declaration agreed by all these parties in recent years called for a general amnesty for political prisoners and exiles, the right of association and free speech, guarantees for the unions, the re-establishment of the Catalan Statute of Autonomy of 1932 and the co-ordination of all the peoples of the peninsula in a democratic struggle against Franco. About 300 delegates from all these illegal organisations met in a clandestine Assembly of Catalonia on 7 November 1971 and again on 13 March 1972. There is also said to be a terrorist group known as *Front d'Alliberament Català*, directed from the Roussillon in France, which claimed responsibility for explosions in 1971 and 1972, including the spectacular demolition of a monument to Falangists in the centre of Barcelona, which was followed by the arrest and alleged torture of its members.

In December 1975 the creation of a new organisation called the National Council of Political Forces in Catalonia was announced. It comprises eleven groups representing the complete spectrum of political opinion in the country but united in their opposition to Madrid and their desire for Catalan autonomy. The national Assembly of Catalonia already exists, illegally of course, and has the formal support of all the political parties.

There is a great deal of political activity in Catalonia, but it is almost all clandestine and anonymous in nature. Typical of the country's attitude to Franco was the high rate of abstention in the referendum organised in 1966 for the purpose of eliciting support for his régime. There have been many other similar incidents. In 1959 the editor of *La Vanguardia*, a personal friend of Franco and bitterly anti-Catalan, publicly insulted a priest who had preached in Catalan. So thorough was the public's boycott of the newspaper that its editor had to be sacked. The following year, the centenary of the birth of Joan Maragall, celebrations were held at which Franco was present. In a spontaneous protest, the crowd sang Maragall's 'Hymn to the Catalan Flag', which Franco had banned. During the reprisals which followed Jordi Pugol was imprisoned and tortured for his part in organising the singing. In 1962 the image of the virgin of Núria, a deeply venerated symbol for Catalan Catholics, was removed from its church on the eve of its enthronement by a bishop appointed by Franco. Those responsible demanded the appointment of a Catalan bishop, the return of the exiled abbot, the dismissal of the Castilian Archbishop of Barcelona and an end to persecution of Catalonia's language and culture. Franco's response was to re-organise the administration of Catalonia by separating parts of Lerida *(Lleida)* and reducing the country to 'the three provinces' of Barcelona, Tarragona and Girona, to be known officially as 'the north-east region'.

The principal strength and symbol of Catalan nationhood or *catalanitat* is, of course, the language. It must be noted that the vast majority of Catalans are natural speakers of the national language, not only in the countryside but in the bigger towns, even in Barcelona, where it is the normal vehicle for social life among all classes, from labourers to the professions. There are therefore few inferiority complexes attached to the language's use for all purposes, and the majority are deeply attached to it. According to an enquiry in 1970 over 80% of the inhabitants of Barcelona were in favour of the compulsory teaching of Catalan in the schools, while 90% favoured it in the *Principat,* 91% in the Balearic Islands and 78% in Valencia. Castilian, by contrast, is clearly regarded as a foreign language by Catalans: it is recognised as being useful for relations with other countries and its rich culture is respected if not much admired, but it is not regarded as being integral to the Catalan experience. Always referred to as Castilian, even by Castilians themselves, and described as *español* only by foreigners, Castilian is often imperfectly understood and spoken in Catalonia. There is too a great deal of deep-rooted anti-Catalan feeling among Castilians not resident in the country. The language is still generally associated with revolution, with a 'progressive' Church, student unrest, workers' strikes—the living legacy of the bitter experience of the Civil War, when it was dubbed by Franco as 'the language of dogs'.

The only territory where Catalan enjoys official status at the present time is the Principality of Andorra where, out of a total population of about 22,000, perhaps 6,000 are indigenous Andorrans and the majority of the rest Catalans. All inscriptions in Andorra La Vella, the only town, are in Catalan and, since 1968, the language is used exclusively in public administration. The history, geography and language of Catalonia are also obligatory, following a law passed in 1972.

It is small wonder that, despite their numbers, the Catalans have been slow to re-assert their identity in cultural terms or to re-build the institutions which flourished before the Civil War. Nevertheless, it is true—since the beginning of liberalisation in the 1960s—that there has been a growing awareness of the Catalan language as a unifying factor of great potency. Topical songs, often sung and circulated clandestinely, have had a certain influence in this respect, and the singers Ramon, Joan Manuel Serrat, Lluís Llach, Antoni Ortega, Francesc Pi de la Serra are famous. The language is still not taught in the schools or at the University of Barcelona, but there is a course of Catalan studies in the University of Madrid. Thousands of young people have enrolled since 1968 in language courses organised by private groups and there has been a resurgence of interest among all age-groups. Many of the theatrical companies and societies which proliferated before 1939 have been re-formed, but with no official support of any kind. Translations of world classics are beginning to appear again in Catalan. There is still no daily or weekly newspaper in the language but the magazine *Terres Catalanes*, launched in 1971, has a readership of several thousands.

There is a fortnightly television programme of forty-five minutes in Catalan and a few radio programmes. Mass is now permitted in Catalan. Choirs, folklore and dancing, especially the *sardana*, Catalonia's national dance, are taken seriously and not merely as tourist attractions, although traditional costumes are now seen only on festive occasions. The central cult, that of the Virgin of Montserrat, is observed without interruption. The national flag of Catalonia (four vertical red bars on a golden background) is now more or less tolerated but the national anthem, *Els Segadors* is still banned altogether. Despite all the obstacles put in its way, and occasional savage repression, it is a remarkable fact that the Catalan language has held its own during the past fifteen years. The absence of formal instruction in languages other than Castilian seriously reduces literacy rates and the number of people who buy and read Catalan books. But according to the result of a survey published in 1970, 90% of housewives understood Catalan, 77% spoke it, 62% could read it and

38% were able to write it. Deprived of education in their own language, many students and intellectuals choose French rather than Castilian as their second language.

Just as the *Renaixença* of the nineteenth century and the *noucentisme* of the early twentieth were attempts to create a new Catalan national identity, the best contemporary artists are involved in their country's present situation. In the last half-century an impressive number of Catalan painters, architects and musicians, including Salvador Dalí and Pablo Casals, have been recognised as major artists outside their country. Among foreign artists influenced by Catalonia was Pablo Picasso who spent several years in Barcelona during the late 1890s. The leading poets of Catalonia are Joan Perucho (born 1920), Salvador Espriu (born 1914) and Josep Palau (born 1917), the last still in exile. The novelists of this century were Joaquim Ruyra (1858-1939) and Josep Pla (born 1897) whose *Spring Nocturne* (1935) is accepted as one of the finest novels ever published about Catalonia. Among novelists writing in Catalan today are Joan Sales (born 1912), Manuel Pedrolo (born 1918), Maria Aurèlia Capmany (born 1918), Jordi Sarsanedas (born 1924), Blai Bonet (born 1926) and Baltasar Porcel (born 1937). They lead a field in which, of all the *genres*, it is the novel which at the moment shows the greatest variety and originality.

The situation of the post-war theatre in Catalonia is more precarious, mainly because there is no official State support and all works are censored. There are, nevertheless, several professional groups such as *Agrupació Dramàtica de Barcelona, Escola d'Art Dramàtic Adria Gual* and the *Theatre Experimental Català*. It seems appropriate that the most influential play of recent years has been Espriu's *Primera Historia d'Esther* (1948), 'an improvisation for puppets' which relates the story of Esther in the small Catalan town of Sinera. It was originally conceived not for performance but as an epitaph for the Catalan language. Instead, it has become a symbol of renewal, a text which in its universality and its sense of having roots in a particular language and society, stands for the best qualities in modern Catalan literature, certainly the most vigorous being produced in the Iberian peninsula today.

In its political history and present predicament, Catalonia is in many ways a microcosm of modern Spain. For three years it was engulfed in a bitter and violent contest between the forces of the Republican Government and the insurgent troops of Franco. For the Spanish Nationalists who rose in military rebellion against the democratically elected Republic, the Civil War was against communism, atheism and liberalism. For the mass of peasants and the working classes who rushed to defend the young Republic in 1931 it was a long-awaited chance to create a decentralised, egalitarian, collectivist society based on a combination of Marxist and anarchist principles. For the Republicans and socialists, as for the greater part of world opinion, it was a crusade to save Spain and Europe from fascism and a grisly prelude to the Second World War. It was all of these for the Catalans, but it was also for them—as it was for the Basques—a matter of whether their country was to keep or lose its national identity, its institutions and its culture, all dearly won and stoutly defended.

Forty years have now elapsed since Franco destroyed the Republic but there have been few signs that the dictator's régime has lost any of its vindictiveness against those he conquered by force of arms and whom he ruled with the terrible machinery of a modern, totalitarian State. For the Catalans, Manuel Azaña's hope, as he put it at the height of the Civil War in 1938, of 'Peace, Pity and Pardon' has not yet been realised. Nevertheless, their sense of nationhood has survived, in the words of J. Vicens i Vives, 'four centuries under the Minotaur. The reality of our existence is thus proved. The life of the Catalans is an act of continuous affirmation . . . Ancient peoples have tough and deep roots. Many years may pass without any flowers appearing on branches broken by wind and frost. But under the ground, like a plant, they continue to work and accumulate reserves. Despite the appearance of death, they are alive and one day their vital force will begin to flow again'.

THE BASQUES

Euzkadi, the homeland of the Basques, is situated on both sides of the western Pyrénées, divided by the frontier between the French and Spanish States. Four-fifths of its total area of 8,076 square miles lie on the southern side, where about 2,184,000 people live (1970) in the provinces of Alava (Basque: *Araba*), Vizcaya *(Bizkaia)*, Guipuzcoa *(Gipuzkoa)* and Navarra *(Nafarra)*. The three provinces on the northern side of the frontier, which have a population of about 200,000 (1970) and are known in French as *le pays basque,* are the departments of Labourd (Basque: *Lapurdi)*, Basse-Navarre *(Benapara)* and Soule *(Ciberoa)*. Saint-Sebastian *(Donostia)* is the tourist and cultural centre on the southern side while Pamplona *(Iruña)* is the historic capital and Bilbao *(Bilbo)* in the province of Vizcaya, with its banks, ports, iron and electricity industries, the economic centre. Vizcaya is the province with the biggest population, 971,029 in 1967, followed by Guipuzcoa with 598,224 inhabitants, Navarra with 432,439 and Alava with 182,916.

Although the seven provinces of Euzkadi are thus incorporated into the two Western European States least sympathetic to the linguistic minorities within their borders, the Basques' defiance of political fact and their determination that their country shall one day be united and free are centuries old. They are summarised by the ancient motto *Zazpiak Bat* (seven in one) and, more recently, by a slogan which is surely among the most striking to be painted on walls anywhere in Western Europe: *3 + 4 = 1.*

The origins of the Basque people and *Eskuara,* their language, have often been disputed and much of the mystery surrounding them remains. But it is now generally agreed that they are the autochthonous inhabitants of the western Pyrénées whose territories once extended as far north as Bordeaux, as far east as Toulouse and as far south as the river Ebro, including what are today Catalonia and the Asturias—that they are, in short, the last remnant of a people from Cro-Magnon times whose language survived the Aryan invasions as they retreated into the Pyrénées under threat of invasion from all directions. Research into the blood-groups of

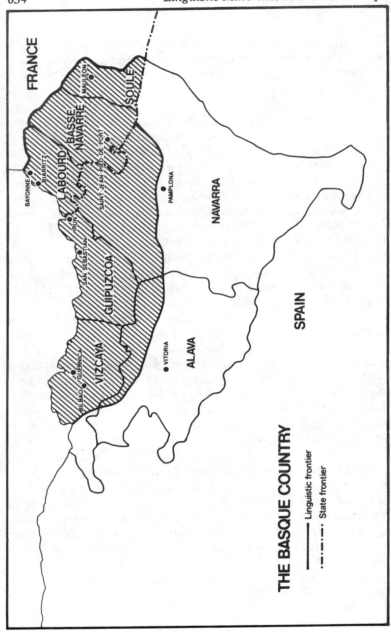

THE BASQUE COUNTRY

——— Linguistic frontier

–·–·–· State frontier

the Basque population, especially the preponderance of type O and the Rhesus negative factor over all others, supports the archeological and philological evidence that the Basques are not only ethnically different from their neighbours but they are, in fact, unique among the peoples of Europe, the direct descendants of the cave-dwellers whose art was discovered at Altamira and Lascaux. The Basque language is unrelated to the Indo-European family: it is believed to be a pre-Aryan or paleolithic language which, everywhere else, has become extinct. Similarities of vocabulary with certain Caucasian languages suggest that it is descended from a pre-historic family of languages which was spoken as far east as Tibet.

The history of the Basques dates from the seventh century B.C. when the Vascon tribes gave their name Vasconia to the inhabitants of the upper Ebro valley, today's Navarra. The area became the cradle of Basque culture, although Navarra was to lose its language before the other six provinces. In the first century B.C. Vasconia extended from Bordeaux to Saragossa, from Santander to Toulouse. When the Romans conquered Aquitaine they did not penetrate the mountains so that the region of Pau and Oloron-Sainte-Marie, under their command and known today as the Béarn, became separated culturally from the Basques to the west. Then in the fifth century A.D., as the Visigoths over-ran Spain, the Vascons moved to the northern slopes of the Pyrénées, as far as the Garonne. Vasconia adopted a Latin speech which was later to become Occitan while those who settled in the mountains continued to speak Basque.

While it is known that the Basques defended themselves against Normans, Franks, Carthaginians, Romans and Visigoths, their first recorded exploit in historic times was when, in the year 778, they were reputed to have crushed the rear-guard of Charlemagne at Roncesvalles on the slopes of Altabizcar: they were said to be the *Sarrasins,* or foreigners, described in *La Chanson de Roland.* For the next five hundred years, however, little was heard of them, except insofar as the French and Spanish Kings took an interest in their territories. In 1306 King Philippe-le-Bel, who had married the Queen of Navarre in 1284, annexed Soule. Labourd was conquered by Henry Plantagenet who, as Henry II of

England, owned it from 1154 until the end of the Hundred
Years' War. Labourd and Soule went to the French Crown in
1451 and Basse-Navarre was annexed to France by Louis XIII
in 1620. To the south, the Basques had rallied within the
Kingdom of Navarre but they became more and more
dominated by the Castilians, losing Guipuzcoa in 1200, Alava
in 1332 and Vizcaya in 1379, although they managed to retain
a degree of autonomy until as late as 1841. When, during the
Carlist Wars of 1833-4 and 1837-9, Don Carlos—who had
allowed the Basques certain administrative privileges known
as *fueros* in return for their support for his arch-conservative,
dynastic movement more interested in the religious
regeneration of Spai   than in regional autonomy—was
defeated, the national   pirit of the south was directed into
folklore and Catholicism.

The restoration of these *fueros*, or special charters, was
among the principal aims of the Basque Nationalist
Movement when it revived towards the end of the nineteenth
century. But the major factor in the national awakening was
the Basque language. In 1890, the son of a Bilbao industrialist, Sabino de Arana y Goiri (1865-1903) founded the *Partido Nacionalista Vasco (P.N.V.)*. It was he, 'the father of
Basque nationalism', who learned Basque at the age of 25,
who also gave the name Euzkadi to the Basque lands in 1893
and who designed the national flag—a white cross and a green
diagonal on a red background. Had the new nationalism,
based on claims for the restoration of foral rights and the
Catholic faith, not included Sabino Arana's insistence on the
value of Basque and its culture, it would have been hardly
distinguishable from the Carlism of the nineteenth century.
But the *P.N.V.*'s appeal to all Basques—*Euzkaldunak* and
Euzkotarak, those who speak the language and those who do
not—clearly made it the first specifically autonomist party
and it was supported by all Basque nationalists. Nevertheless,
its conservative, fervent Catholicism and the middle-class
origins of its founder, brought to the *P.N.V.* the hostility of
the Basque proletariat, most of whom supported the Spanish
Socialist Workers' Party (*P.S.O.E.*) at this time.

It also met opposition from the big industrialists, and from some leading Basque intellectuals such as the philosopher Unamuno and the novelist Pio Baroja, both of whom were Basque-speaking. Like many Spanish intellectuals, politicians and aristocrats, Unamuno was Basque in origin. In early life he was interested in the Basque language but he was later of the opinion that it ought to die and became bitterly opposed to everything Basque. He was a Spanish liberal and therefore anti-clerical and centralist who, probably because the *P.N.V.* of his day was reactionary and pro-clerical, was pushed to dramatic and ambivalent declarations about the country of his birth.

The new party's appeal to nationhood and Basque unity, its emphasis on race and religion which almost completely ignored any social analysis, found most response among peasants, small farmers and the business classes of the towns. Mutual hostility between the *P.N.V.* and the *P.S.O.E.* remained bitter up to the Spanish Civil War of 1936 and, even today, the principal argument within the left-wing and nationalist Basque movement continues to be whether class or nationality should be of first importance. Only the Basque communists, led by Astigarrabia and Dolores Ibarruri (*'La Pasionara'*), recognised the depth and extent of the problem in the early years of this century, founding a *Partido Communista Vasco (P.C.V.)*.

There is little doubt that Basque nationalism (together with its counterpart in Catalonia) contributed to the social and religious tensions within the Spanish State during the 'twenties and 'thirties and thus formed an element in the conflict of the Civil War of 1936-9. After the First World War both movements, having abandoned the monarchist cause, made rapid progress, at local level and in the *Cortes* at Madrid, in their demand for greater autonomy from the highly centralised State which Spain's rulers in the eighteenth and nineteenth centuries had created. Because the aspirations of the Catalans were largely satisfied in 1931, when the newly-born Spanish Republic recognised the autonomous region of Catalonia, most Catalans saw that their fate depended on the Republic and rallied to the Republican cause in 1936. But Basque demands were not met until three months after the outbreak of the war when on 7 October 1936, the Republican Government formally recognised an autonomous Basque

Government with its own monies, flag, constitution and army, in return for its military support. The Republic of Euskadi was proclaimed at Guernica, traditional centre of Basque liberty, the following day. Autonomy was granted to the Basque Country in 'el *Estatuto Vasco*' (The Basque Statute) and a coalition Government was formed by the *P.N.V.*, which by this time had become a Social Democratic party, three small liberal groups (including two branches of Spanish Republican parties), an autonomous branch of the *P.S.O.E.*, and local communists.

The leader of the Basque nationalists from about 1930 was a young lawyer named José Antonio Aguirre. He was of a middle-class Carlist family and owed much to his good looks and his fame as a pelota-player. His movement had been considered so far to the right in 1931 that he had been approached by a representative of King Alfonso to join the military plot against the Republic in return for autonomy and for the restoration of Basque *fueros*. Aguirre rejected this proposal and from then on the Castilian Monarchists and Generals reserved a special hatred for his party. By 1936 the leader and his movement were firmly on the Republican side. At a meeting of the *Cortes*, or what was left of it, on 1 October of that year, called to approve the Statute of Basque autonomy, Aguirre proclaimed that the Basques, though Catholic, were not fearful of the motives of the workers' movement 'for we know how much justice there is in them' and pledged the new Basque Republic, to stand by the Government 'until the defeat of Fascism'.

Whereas the Catalan Statute was adopted by the Constituent Assembly in Madrid as early as 1931, the Basque Statute was passed only three months after Franco's rebellion had begun. The Republican Government was in dire need of Basque support and could not afford to ignore their demands for much longer. But there were reasons for the delay. Navarra, no longer Basque-speaking, had not joined in the petition for Home Rule in 1932, mainly because that province, although in favour of autonomy, was strongly Catholic, anti-democratic and right-wing, having led its own separate existence as the Kingdom of Navarre up to the sixteenth century. Furthermore, there had been since 1932 a marked coolness between the *P.N.V.* and the left-wing of the Government in Madrid, especially regarding the anti-clerical convictions of the Spaniards. There is little doubt that Madrid's attitude to the Church and religious questions encouraged the growth of the Home Rule Movement. Nevertheless the autonomous Basque Government never betrayed the Republic. On 7 October all the municipal councillors of the three Basque provinces (i.e. excluding Navarra) met in the sacred village of Guernica and elected Aguirre, almost unanimously, as the President of 'the Provisional Government of Euzkadi' to govern during the Civil War. The Government named by Aguirre was sworn-in under the famous oak-tree and the Civil Governor of Bilbao handed over his authority. The first Basque Government, which included five Nationalists, three Socialists, one Communist (Astigarrabia, who was later in trouble with his party for his Basque sympathies) and one member from each of the two Spanish Republican Parties.

Then began the only Basque offensive of the Civil War—the attack on 30 November on Villareal de Alava, a position held by 600 of Franco's troops. The Basques were driven back by superior artillery and aeroplanes, 400 dying of gangrene in a single night because, so confident of victory, they had not provided for medical supplies. Aguirre rallied his soldiers, however, and they continued to fight with their Republican comrades throughout the War, although often—as during the retreat after the Santander campaign—losing some of their resolve when fighting for territory outside Euzkadi. In August, Aguirre having escaped by air to France, a leader of the Basque Nationalist Party, Juan Axuriaguerra, went to Santoña to negotiate the Basque surrender, choosing to meet an Italian rather than a representative of Franco. It was agreed that the Basques, after surrender, would deliver their armies to the Italians and maintain order in the areas they still held. The Italians would guarantee the lives of all Basque soldiers and they would not be obliged to fight on Franco's side; all Basque politicians and civil servants would be free to go abroad and the Italians gave assurances that the Basque civilian population would not be persecuted. The Italians then entered Santander and Santoña, and the Basques awaited the fulfilment of the Italian part of the armistice. On 27 August the Basques were told to board the British vessels in Santoña harbour. On doing so, they found themselves surrounded by Italian soldiers with machine-guns and ordered to disembark. The terms of the agreement negotiated by an Italian colonel had been betrayed by his superior, a Colonel Fragosi. The ships left the harbour empty (except for a few hiding in the machinery) and the Basques were marched off as prisoners. Summary trials and executions followed. Aguirre died in 1960, to be succeeded as President of the Basque Government in Exile by Jesús Maria de Leizaola. This Government continues to exist in exile with delegations in several cities where there are large Basque colonies such as New York, Bogota, and Buenos Aires, but it has grown increasingly irrelevant to the present situation in the Basque Country.

Although the Basque Government was in office only for a few months, from October 1936 to August 1937, its record under the President José Antonio de Aguirre was quite remarkable. Surrounded by Franco's troops and navy, bombed by the German Condor Legion, blockaded and short of food, it carried out a brave programme of social reform by introducing social insurance and childrens' allowances and by measures to ensure equal representation of workers and employers in industry and the banks. It also founded a university and supported State education, minted its own money and organised its own army.

During the Civil War, Basque Nationalists were supported by the majority of the Basque clergy, who had always been in sympathy with their cause. This fact is explained by the traditional loyalty of the Basque people to the Catholic Church and by the influence the Church has exercised on Basque society. It is not entirely coincidental, for example, that Ignatius Loyola, the founder of the Jesuits, was a Basque. The clergy, in both rural and urban areas, have maintained close, regular contact with their parishoners to an extent unknown in most other parts of Spain, where large sections of the working class are hostile to religion, or indifferent, playing a leading role in social and political life. The Basque Country, where in 1967 there was one priest for every 535 persons (one for every 1,528 in the province of Barcelona) and where church attendances are high, supplies a disproportionately large number of Spain's monks and nuns. This bond between priest and people helps to explain why, while a large proportion of the Spanish clergy were in Franco's camp, and claiming to be fighting a crusade, Basque priests were frequently to be found in the Republican ranks.

With the fall of the Republic before Franco and his German and Italian allies in 1939, and military victory for the Fascists, the Basque Church was not spared in Franco's reprisals against the Basque nationalist movement. Nowhere was the débacle of the legal Government more spectacular than in the destruction of the Basque Government which followed. Aguirre and three of his ministers who were not executed were obliged to flee abroad. According to Hugh Thomas in his monumental book *The Spanish Civil War,* about 278 Basque priests and 125 monks were imprisoned and deported and at least sixteen executed. Many more were dismissed from their parishes.

Having already bombed Guernica *(Gernika)* with German Stukkas on 26 April 1937, killing 1,600 inhabitants of that town in a trial run for Nazi air-attacks during the Second World War, and then crushing the Basque Republic which disappeared in October of the same year, Franco now unleashed the full force of his régime against all manifestations of Basque particularism. The 'New Spain', like its predecessors in the eighteenth and nineteenth centuries, was authoritarian and rigidly centralised. All local political arrangements were to be abolished and separatist parties, in common with other opposition groups, were banned. It is known that many thousands of Basques were shot for resisting these measures. The Basque Government, like the Catalan, was scrapped and its leaders imprisoned, exiled or evacuated. Those Basque provinces such as Guipuzcoa and Vizcaya, the so-called *Provincias Traidoras* (Traitor Provinces), which had recognised the authority of the Basque Republic, lost even the small administrative privileges, remnants of the *fueros,* which earlier Spanish Governments had been ready to allow. Only Navarra and Alava were allowed to keep their assemblies; these exist today but have little power.

Castilians were brought in to fill important administrative posts, and only Basques of middle-class, Carlist background could expect promotion. There were also determined, sometimes vicious efforts to stamp out Basque culture in all its aspects. There was a strict ban on the use of Basque for educational purposes which lasted until the 1950s. The language could not be used for public meetings or in public worship nor for street or shop signs and was ordered to be removed even from grave-stones. School-teachers were dismissed unless they could give evidence of their political 'reliability' and their places filled by teachers from other parts of Spain. Publishing in Basque was declared illegal and there was no question of broadcasting in it. Pupils speaking Basque were punished and *'hablo Cristiano!'* (Speak the language of Christians!) became the slogan of the day. The long-standing feeling among Basques that they were an oppressed national minority received confirmation. Opposition to the unitary State re-created by Franco was driven underground, becoming all the more bitter in some instances by its failure to find adequate expression.

By the 1950s, however, it had become apparent that, while the Spanish Government's measures would no doubt provide various obstacles to the spread of non-Castilian languages, they could not wipe them out altogether. At the same time, Franco's régime began to feel more secure and to rely less on the brutal methods for which it had become notorious. Small concessions, such as permission for folkloric festivals, were made and the everyday use of Basque was once again tolerated. A chair of Basque was created at the University of Salamanca and the *Euzkalzaindia* (Academy of the Basque language) was re-opened at Bilbao and allowed to function as a private institution, but without the right to co-operate with Basques on the northern side of the Pyrénées. Of course, by 1950 such sops to local and international opinion could not possibly undo the harm already done to the Basque language and culture since 1939. The proscription of Basque by the Franco régime not only silenced the cultural life of Euzkadi during the 'forties and 'fifties but ensured that the post-war generation would be unable to speak their language, as much out of fear of their parents and neighbours as for the reason that by this time the majority were now monoglot Castilian-speakers, anyway. Immigration from other parts of Spain, actively encouraged by the authorities, also contributed against the speaking of Basque.

As a result of Franco's policies against the Basque language, the number able to speak it in the south of Euzkadi declined from approximately 700,000 in 1936 to 525,000 in 1954. By today, out of a total population of 2,100,000 about 500,000 are believed to be able to speak the language in the four southern provinces. The language as an everyday medium has almost completely died out in Navarra and is in retreat in Alava. Bilbao, the chief town of Vizcaya, is on the linguistic border but outside the Basque language's domain. The strongholds of Basque are therefore in Guipuzcoa and Vizcaya, mainly in rural areas but also in some towns. Of the eight dialects into which Basque is divided that of Guipuzcoa tends to be the most frequently used as a common standard. There are then perhaps 615,000 Basque-speakers in the seven provinces of Euzkadi today, certainly not more. Nor is there, of course, any way of knowing how many of the countless thousands scattered in the major cities of Spain, France, Europe and the Americas still know their language. What is clear is that the language, with no official status whatsoever, has retreated almost completely from the provinces of Navarre and Alava, and from the city of Bilbao, surviving only in Guipuzcoa and the eastern part of Viscaya. Immigration into the Basque provinces from economically poorer regions of Spain has increased the non-Basque population, especially the working-classes, to over 50% in most industrial areas. On the other hand, these workers come mostly from economically neglected areas in the south of Spain, where they were familiar with the labour problems caused by the Franco régime's suppression of trade unions.

The crisis of the Basque language since 1939 is serious enough. That the decline has not been as rapid as might have been expected in such harsh circumstances is largely due to the efforts made on behalf of the language and its culture by various groups and individuals, but only minimally by the State or its local agents. Basque culture has always existed at a high level and Basques have made remarkable contributions (often in Spanish or French) to European culture: they include F. de Vitoria, precursor of international law, the religious thinkers Ignatius Loyola and Francois-Xavier, the adventurer Simon de Bolivar, the musicians Guridi, Donostia, Sarasate and Maurice Ravel whose mother was a Basque, the architects and sculptors Juan de Anchieta, Oteiza and Chillida, the painters Iriarte and Zuluoga, the poets Etxahun Iparraguirre and (despite their anti-Basque views) the writers and philosophers Unamuno and Baroja.

Even today, the cultural life of the Basques is quite intense given the circumstances in which it has to exist. About 200 books are published in Basque every year, including books on religion, sociology, philology, economics, poetry, novels, art-books in editions of up to 4,000, and twenty magazines, by ten publishing houses, including *Lur*, which publishes the work of perhaps fifty writers and journalists who are organised in their own association *Idazlen elkartea*. There are also six newspapers, some weekly and some monthly such as *Argia, Herria, Anaitasuna* and *Agur*. None of these publications receives subsidy from public funds. As all publications are subjected to the usual censorship of the Spanish State there is a vigorous underground press. There is very little theatre in Basque but, as well as many good poets and novelists, a lively number of song-writers has come to the fore in recent years despite the constant vigilance of the censor to whom their work has to be submitted before it can be sung in public. The language continues to enjoy no status, however, for legal and administrative purposes. The Spanish Government's refusal to allow the use of the Basque form of personal names is characteristic of all European fascist régimes in their persecution of linguistic minorities.

Among other cultural activities are a very popular folk-song movement, including new topical songs and many records, which holds festivals in a different town every Sunday; musicians and dancers are organised in their own associations. The theatre too has begun to flourish, with over a hundred modern plays at the disposition of *Antzerkilarien Biltzarra*, the actors' organisation which comprises about a dozen amateur groups. The national sport is *pelota* which is played almost everywhere through the medium of the Basque language.

Primarily responsible for the survival of the Basque language in recent years are the schools known as the *ikastolas* (halls of teaching) which began in private homes and church halls during the late 'fifties. At first they were clandestine but by now they are known to the authorities and tolerated. At the present time there are about 25,000 children (out of 450,000) under the age of fourteen who attend, in their spare time, perhaps 400 *ikastolas* throughout the seven provinces, but mainly in Guipuzcoa and Vizcaya. The 200 schools are financed entirely by the parents and organised with the help of the Church and national organisations. The official view of these schools is that to educate children in Basque is an act potentially hostile to the Spanish State. Clearly, the parents' decision to send their children to the *ikastolas* which distinguish between 'our country' and Spain is, if not a political act, one which calls for a certain intrepidness. The schools come under regular police surveillance on the grounds that they sometimes become centres for more overt forms of resistance. Lists of pupils, teachers and backers have to be submitted to the police. The State also makes it difficult to acquire a licence for their establishment. Since 1971 the State has found a way of causing schisms in the *ikastolas* movement by offering some—usually those organised by middle-class parents which teach the archaic form of the language and tend to avoid politics—a small amount of grant-aid. While some schools accept this subsidy many refuse them because they are always accompanied by police surveillance and bureaucratic interference, and so find their resources and influence diminished. It seems likely therefore that most of the schools will remain outside the official system. That they operate in unusually difficult circumstances and have had a major role in fostering the Basque language during the last decade is evident. As a result of their initiative the Spanish State provided in 1973 no less than 300 nursery schools in Guipuzoca where the occasional Basque lesson, but nothing through the medium of Basque, is given in an attempt to attract parents away from the *ikastolas*. Similar efforts to open private secondary schools teaching in Basque have met with difficulties, including a lack of teachers and textbooks and hostility from the education authorities; only about a thousand pupils are at present in the five schools established so far. The language is also taught by volunteers at night-classes in the towns and in the countryside, where the majority of Basque-speakers are illiterate in their mother-tongue. Attempts have been made to run summer schools through the medium of Basque. There is no Basque university but the language and literature are taught at Salamanca and Bordeaux from which certificates are now recognised as part of a degree course.

The Basque language has three dialects. Prior to the Civil War it was also an archaic language not always able to express the full range of life in a modern urban society. The archaic form is still widely spoken but determined efforts are being made, notably by the Academy of the Basque Language, to standardise its grammar and modernise its vocabulary.

Nevertheless, the damage done to the Basque language by decades of neglect and oppression has been heavy. The evidence is that married couples brought up before, during or just after the Civil War usually communicate with their children either in Spanish or by using both languages, but rarely in Basque alone. A survey of housewives published in 1970 shows that more people could understand Basque than could speak it and that the numbers able to read and write Basque were even smaller: about 50% understood Basque, 46% could speak it, 25% could read it and only 12% wrote it. The comparable figures of Catalonia were 90%, 77%, 62% and 38%. In other words, the absence of formal instruction in Basque has seriously reduced literacy rates since 1936. Such problems have been exacerbated by the mass media. Whereas some daily newspapers published in the south occasionally carry a page in Basque, the State-controlled television authority provides no programmes in the language and only a few minutes daily on the radio.

Since the Civil War the Basque Church has continued to play an important part in the defence and propagation of the national language and culture. It has, however, experienced grave internal troubles which have not always been the result of the world-wide upheaval taking place within the Catholic Church. A major difficulty in the Basque Country has been the traditional alliance between the Spanish Church and the State. Franco's régime gained in authority thanks to Church support and has had a hand in many episcopal appointments, appointing bishops known to be loyal to the State. Basque nationalists have therefore tended to regard Church spokesmen with suspicion.

At the same time, the clergy have continued to work with their parishioners. They are of three types: the small minority of older men who are fervently pro-Franco and who detest Basque nationalism in all its forms; the vast majority, mainly social democrats or moderate socialists, who sympathise with demands for local autonomy and who favour a democratic political system for Spain; another small minority who take a radical socialist position and are strongly committed to the cause of Basque nationalism, even to violence. The third group, who are usually of the post-Civil War generation, are organised in an organisation known as the *Gogortasuna* which has led a variety of political activities. In 1960 400 Basque priests sent a letter to their bishops protesting against the Government's suppression of the national language: 'We Basque priests love our people with the same natural and Christian devotion as the priests of Castile love the human society which is in their care. We have a duty to draw attention to the wanton or accidental attacks made upon the natural rights of our people. We accuse, before Spaniards and the world, the policy, disregard and naked persecution of the ethnic, linguistic and social characteristics which God has given us'. They have staged 'sit-ins' and hunger strikes to put pressure on their bishops, demanding less equivocal denunciations of official policy and police methods. Many of the members have been exiled or imprisoned: according to Amnesty International, there were twenty-six Basque priests in gaol for political reasons in late 1970. Two of the sixteen nationalists tried at Burgos in that year were priests. At the end of 1971, 196 Basque priests protested when the conservative, non-Basque Monsignor Antonio Añoveros was appointed Bishop of Bilbao in place of Monsignor José Circarda who had been identified with Basque aspirations. Since 1971 M. Anoveros had joined the ranks of those who criticise the State's policies in the Basque Country. Clergy have helped in the distribution of underground literature, made Church premises available for political meetings, arranged the escape to France of wanted men, organised demonstrations and advised nationalist organisations in the use of violence. Some have denounced the Government and the police from their pulpits.

Pressure from radical priests has put the Church in a delicate position, particularly over the use of torture. In April 1971, the Bishop of Pamplona denounced the methods of the police, thus demonstrating that by now the Basque Church at official level has become a real thorn in the flesh of the Spanish Government. In April 1972, 352 Basque priests protested to the Vatican about the conditions under which detainees are held. In 1973 Father Felix Vergara, of Eibar near Bilbao, was fined 250,000 pesetas (£1,880) after being beaten up by the police and found guilty without trial under the Public Order Law, for delivering three sermons which the Government considered politically objectionable. Two sermons dealt with a revolt and hunger-strike by priests who were held in the special prison at Zamora and the other with the trial of a group of labour leaders in Madrid. Father Vergara served a fifty-day sentence, in lieu of payment, during the autumn of 1974, in a monastery rather than jail, under the terms of the Concordat between Spain and the Vatican. On 27 October 1974 a pastoral letter entitled 'Freedom of holy preaching' by Mgr. Jacinto Argaya, Bishop of San Sebastian, was read in churches throughout Guipuzcoa which pointed out that the fine had been imposed without trial. The dispute between bishops and the Government continues. Indeed, Basque churches have given a lead to the clergy in the rest of Spain in this denunciation of police methods and State policies in the social and economic sectors. On the other hand, Basque militants among the clergy have caused a backlash in that the ultra-conservative Catholic organisation known as the *Guerrilleros del Christo Rei* (Guerrillas of Christ the King) have been responsible for acts of vandalism and terrorism against Basque nationalist leaders and the radical clergy.

As in Catalonia, the national question in the Basque Country is inextricably linked with social and economic problems, especially class conflict and the control of industry. Indeed, while it is true that the Basque movement finds inspiration in its national identity, the majority of Basques are more directly concerned with economic issues than with the national cause. The growth of industry in the Basque Country began earlier than in the rest of Spain and a great deal of Spanish investment is to be found in this area. In 1967, for example, the income *per capita* in the province of Vizcaya, where most industry is concentrated, was more than any other province in Spain except Madrid. At first sight this rather privileged and prosperous economic situation may seem an unusual basis for local grievances. But resentment is caused by the feeling that the Spanish State, especially its more backward regions, are being subsidised at the expense of the Basque Country, and that the region pays more in taxes than it receives in benefit from central government. The central Government, on the other hand, fails to see why economic prosperity should carry political privileges, and claims that the Basque Country must remain an integral part of Spain if only to provide labour for workers from the poorer areas. Furthermore, many Basques—traditionally more progressive than their neighbours in Castile—adopt a superior attitude towards the inhabitants of other areas and they, in turn, are accused of materialism and betrayal of Spain's 'traditional values'.

The workers of the Basque Country are organised most effectively by socialist, communist and left-wing Catholic groups which co-operate, since 1964, within the unofficial Workers' Commissions. Though the members of these Commissions may disagree over their long-term aims, they have achieved a temporary tactical unity by agreeing on their two aims: higher wages and better conditions, and the replacement of the present system of State-controlled unions by independent organisations. The tendency during the 'sixties for industrial conflict to increase is some indication of the extent of working-class opposition to Franco's régime. A series of strikes which brought to a halt large sections of industry had, as their primary aim, the weakening of the Government's authority and a number of economic demands. But even then, particularly at the time of the Burgos trials, there was a real and profound solidarity between Basque workers and nationalists. Strikes occurred all over Spain but stoppages were most complete in the Basque Country. It is clear that harsh official measures have resulted in communal solidarity among groups which have divergent interests; they are united only in their revulsion against the State's attitudes and methods.

Apart from the Church and the workers' organisations Basque nationalist opposition to the Spanish Government funds support from a third group—the professional and intellectual sections of society, from among whom the *P.N.V.* found its first members. Many Basques from this influential middle-class, especially lawyers and doctors, have played prominent roles in public protests against the dominance of non-Basques in the local administration and judiciary, against such outrages as the torturing of political prisoners and the arbitrary nature of many trials. Such individuals represent various shades of opinion: they include members of the Communist Party, the Christian Marxists, Socialists and Social Democrats, Christian Democrats and Nationalists. In some cases their organisations are not associated with the national question and most are unsympathetic to the use of violence. They demonstrate how moderately middle-class opinion in the Basque Country has consolidated in opposition to the Spanish State. The Basque middle-classes are also critical of what they see as the State's discrimination against Basques in many of its major public institutions. Since the Civil War a disproportionately small number of judges, civil servants, policemen and military personnel have been recruited from among Basques. Between 1960 and 1964, for example, the Basque provinces supplied only 2·7% of the students at the State's military Academies, although they had 6·2% of Spain's total population. The only Basques to be found at a high level in the civilian administration are either of Carlist background or come from the small social élite of the Basque Country which has close links with Madrid. A predominance of Castilians in official posts has helped to feed an already strong sense of grievance, with local leaders in business and the professions feeling remote from the centre of political power and often obstructed by officials with no real commitment to solving Basque problems.

Conflicts between the citizen and State in the Basque Country, particularly bitter in a dictatorship where the central Government is responsible for administrating most local services, are made worse by the relatively high level of political awareness among Basques, as among the Catalans. Not only are these the most economically developed but they are also the most politically sophisticated, having a deep-rooted tradition of popular involvement in civic affairs without parallel elsewhere in Spain. Another aspect of the Basque's involvement in community affairs is his propensity for joining specialist groups, clubs and voluntary organisations such as the long-established savings organisations. Opposition to the State is, in turn, fairly sophisticated: for example, the rate of abstention in elections. In September 1971 at elections held to elect the one-sixth of the *Cortes* deputies who are chosen by the people, the turn-out in the province of Viscaya (only heads of families can vote) was 33% and in the city of San Sebastian only 26%—despite the legal obligation to vote. Such figures are usually taken to signify not apathy but a deliberate repudiation by a politically conscious and well-organised population of the political system as it exists in Spain today. Meanwhile, since there are restrictions on opposition parties and on the free expression of political opinion, Franco's nominated representatives are in a majority everywhere at municipal and regional level and in the *Cortes*.

That opposition in the Basque Country to the Franco régime has hardened since 1960 is largely due to the activities of a nationalist organisation, founded in 1952, known as *E.T.A.* The initials stand for *Euzkadi ta Azkatasuna* (Basque Homeland and Liberty). This is the organisation which, after the Burgos trials of December 1970, focussed world attention on the Basque problem and has continued to attract publicity by its acts of sabotage against the symbols and agents of the Spanish State such as the assassination of Luis Carrero Blanco, Franco's Prime Minister, in 1973.

After the Civil War the *P.N.V.* attempted to direct Basque opposition to the new régime from its headquarters at Bayonne. The socialists and communists remained active, but clandestinely, among the proletariat in the south but were more or less unsympathetic to the nationalist cause. The *P.N.V.*

hoped that the victory of the Allies in the Second World War might lead to intervention in Spain and the collapse of the Franco régime. But their efforts to unite other opposition groups like the Catalan nationalists in 1946 came to nothing and Franco's power remained unshaken. The following year the *E.L.A.*, the trade union wing of the *P.N.V.*, organised a general strike of about 100,000 workers as an act of defiance against the government and the official trade unions, but little was gained. From this time its dynamism and influence began to decline. Its leaders lost much of their authority and younger men decided that the time had come for a less moderate approach.

Dissatisfaction with the *P.N.V.*'s inactivity and impatience with its leadership led, in 1952, to the emergence of a splinter-group composed mainly of technical college students in Bilbao calling for more militant methods. This group was known as *Ekin* (Action), after its magazine. After attempts by militants to infiltrate and influence the leadership of the *P.N.V.*, *Ekin* changed its name to *Euzkadi ta Azkatasuna*. A description of *E.T.A.*'s early years is quoted from an interview with one of its founders in Patricia Elton Mayo's *The Roots of Identity* (1974): 'To begin with, we called ourselves Socialist Humanists or Socialist Federalists. We accepted much of Socialist ideology, but we were not Marxist because we were violently against centralisation. We started educational groups, reading newspapers, learning whatever information we could from all over the world . . . Then we went out and worked in the villages and towns from which we had originally come, explaining what had been Basque law until the nineteenth century and the importance of the Basque language and culture . . . The Movement has now been largely taken over by Marxists. They are trained more for violent action and less for peaceful penetration of the community . . .'

This view was confirmed by several of the speeches made by defendants at the Burgos trials. One of the most famous declarations from the dock was that of Onaindia who, when asked by a lawyer what the final objectives of *E.T.A.* were, replied: 'I am not a separatist. I am a Marxist Leninist. I am internationalist . . . To obtain the national liberation of the Basque people, that is to say to create a national united State, comprising North Euskadi and South Euskadi, then to build Socialism, that is to say a classless society in which the means of production will be the people's.' After delivering his speech Onaindia, leader of *E. T. A.*'s Western Front shouted *'Gora Euskadi Azkatuta'* (Long live the free Basque Country) and led his fellow-prisoners in singing the marching song of the Basque regiment in the Civil War, *Eusko guadariak gera* (We are Basque soldiers). He was sentenced to death, but the sentence was commuted to fifty-one years of imprisonment.

In July 1960 the *E. T. A.* attempted unsuccessfully to de-rail a train carrying Falangists to San Sebastian for their annual celebrations. The police arrested over a hundred members of the clandestine movement; after torture some were found guilty and sentenced to periods of up to twenty years in prison, others escaped into exile while on parole and the organisation suffered badly as a result. At its first annual assembly in 1962 the *E. T. A.* described itself as a revolutionary Basque movement of national liberation and up to 1966 many socialists, workers and peasants joined its ranks.

However, at the Fifth Assembly in December 1966 the first serious schism occurred when critics of the new revolutionary, international Socialist line were expelled. From this moment on there has been division over whether the struggle of the working-class should come before that for the Basque nation and whether the methods used in opposing the Spanish State should be direct and violent or long-term and peaceful. In 1968 the *E.T.A.* killed a Chief of Police for Guipuzcoa, Meliton Manzanas, himself a Basque, who was notorious for the savagery of his interrogation methods and as a direct reprisal for the killing of Javier Etxevarrieta, a member of *E. T. A.*'s executive. Most policemen and other officials of Franco's régime in the Basque province come from other parts of Spain, according to the Government's deliberate policy. That Manzanas was a Basque, one of the few openly to side with the Spanish Government in its repression, increased the hatred he aroused with his methods. During the state of emergency which followed, a thousand Basque militants were arrested, 500 accused, 250 imprisoned and 250 exiled. Nevertheless, the movement survived, although increasingly plagued by factionalism.

In 1969 there emerged two groups: *E.T.A. Quinta* and *E.T.A. Sexta.* The former seeks alliance with the bourgeois and other non-proletarian sections of the population in a popular revolution which is to be essentially nationalist, while the latter is prepared to consider tactical, short-term alliances on the understanding that the final objective is the freedom of the working classes. At the Seventh Assembly in July 1970 the militarist wing of the *E.T.A.*, opposed to the leftward trend in the leadership and adhering to the programme agreed at the Fifth Assembly, were expelled. During the last five years there have been further ideological splits, but to chart them is beyond the scope of this account.

It is impossible to estimate the membership of *E.T.A.* The movement is organised in cells and no member knows more than a handful of his comrades. Also, other groups such as trade unions use its name for activities in opposition to the Spanish State. It seems unlikely that at most it has little more than 2,000 committed adherents. Membership of the *P.N.V.* is far more numerous. But *E.T.A.*, quoting Mao, explains that its members circulate among the Basque population 'like fish in water'. Apart from the military wing, there are fronts responsible for fund-raising, the promotion of Basque language and culture, and the spread of propaganda. There are two major groups. The first consists of those who are primarily nationalists prepared to use violence in order to win autonomy if not independence for the Basques; they subscribe to a socialist ideology but their socialism is secondary to their nationalism. Others see nationalism merely as a means towards the creation of a socialist society—for them independence is the pre-condition for a Basque Socialist Republic which will inspire similar republics on the Iberian peninsula. While the first group tends to regard all Spaniards as their enemies, the second argues that the Basque working-classes should join with workers throughout Spain against the common enemy whom they identify as the capitalist ruling class and the State which is its instrument. Until 1975 the second concept was in the ascendancy, with priority given less to guerrilla campaigns and more to political education of the masses.

Despite its internecine quarrels, the *E.T.A.* has never ceased to be active since 1968. The increasing number of incidents such as bank-robberies, explosions, and the kidnapping in 1971 of the West German Consul and in January 1972 of a prominent Spanish industrialist have emphasised the challenge which the movement presents to the Government. The most famous instance was when in December 1970 the world's press focussed its attention on a military court room in the Spanish town of Burgos when sixteen Basque nationalists were tried for a variety of offences, including an alleged assassination. Six were sentenced to death and their sentences commuted only after the exertion of great international pressure on the Spanish Government and following a heated political debate within Spain itself. The trial had been arranged by aggressively authoritarian elements within Franco's régime and was intended to deal a mortal blow to *E.T.A.* In the event, the trial proved to be highly embarrasing to the Spanish Government, demonstrating to the world the way it deals with its political opponents.

The Spanish Government's response to the Basque nationalist movement has been immediate and fierce. As a result, *E.T.A.* has worked on a theory that action will provoke repression which will provide further resistance and so on in a continuing upward spiral, and in some measure they have been proved correct. So far repression has been more than sufficient to contain the opposition but there has been a hardening of opinion in the Basque Country and a heightening of political tension throughout the rest of Spain. It is likely that the Spanish Government's reaction will continue as before.

There is on the Spanish right-wing, and in the Army, a strong commitment to a unitary State which can provoke irrational response to the appearance of centrifugal forces as in the huge pro-Government demonstration by Falangists and army officers at the time of the Burgos trials. Basque militancy produces an angry response because it has a rougher edge than its counterpart in Catalonia and the Spanish Government fears that concessions to one would encourage the other. In the maintenance of this view the Spanish Government

relies on the Army and the police—both the armed police force
in the urban areas and the para-military Civil Guard in rural,
coastal and frontier areas, and the political police or *Brigada
Social*. Since 1968 large numbers of extra police of all kinds
have been moved into the Basque Country—Civil Guards
were estimated at 15,000 in 1970. The incidence of arbitrary
arrest, illegal detention and the mistreatment of prisoners is a
frequent phenomenon. Lengthy beatings, deprivation of food
and sleep, near-suffocation by drowning, threats against
relatives, along with other forms of brutality, all have become
commonplace. Most of the defendants at Burgos, for example, were undoubtedly the victims of such treatment. In
dealing with offences of a political nature the State generally
employs special courts which date from the punitive
legislation of the post-Civil War period aimied at rooting out
all opponents of the victors. Lawyers representing Basque
nationalists have been harrassed, their offices systematically
searched and their telephones tapped. In December 1971 over
1,000 Basque political prisoners in all parts of Spain went on
hunger-strike to mark the first anniversary of the Burgos
trials and to protest against harsh conditions in the gaols. In
1972 four young *guadari* of *E.T.A.* were shot by *Guardia Civil*
while on nationalist missions. Most *E.T.A.* militants are
young men. The list of Basque nationalists killed since 1965
include Etxebarrieta (killed 1968), Asurmendi and Artajo
(1969), Murueta, Fernandez, Sanchez and Perez-Jaurequi
(1969); Yon Goikoetxea (22 years old), Benito Mugika (22),
Yon Miguel Martinez (27) and Arranguren (21) were the four
shot by police during 1972. In October 1973 there were over
150 Basque nationalists still in prison, mainly at San
Sebastian, Carabanchel, Bilbao and Segovia, but also in thirteen other towns, many of them serving sentences of between
thirty and a hundred years each.

The Spanish Government's repressive measures have succeeded in removing a significant proportion of Euzkadi's
most active nationalists and working-class leaders either by
sending them to prison or into exile. But hostility to Franco's
régime remains deep and widespread. During the crisis
caused by the Burgos trials, the closure of shops and factories
and the Government's failure to organise counter-

demonstrations on the same scale as those in the rest of Spain revealed the real state of public opinion in the Basque Country.

The most recent crisis in the Basque Country was in 1975 when on 25 April a 90-day state of emergency was declared by the Prime Minister, Carlos Arias Navarro, in Guipuzcoa and Viscaya. This move followed the *Aberri Eguna* (Basque National Day) celebrations at Guernica (population 13,000) at which some 20,000 people were prevented by armed police from entering the town on 30 March, the shooting of a police inspector, the fourteenth to die in eight years, at San Sebastian, and the blowing up of four television stations by *E.T.A.* units. Hundreds of Basques were arrested during the next twenty-four hours. The decree, the fifth in the last eight years and only one step short of martial law, stripped Basques of their constitutional rights: it allowed police to search houses without warrant, to arrest without charge, and banned the rights of assembly, *habeus corpus,* free speech and free choice of place of residence.

During the clashes between police and *E.T.A.* which followed daily, six policemen were killed and a separatist leader Migul Goiburu Mendizabel wounded. Arrested in Guernica were two Flemish members of parliament, Walter Luten and Willieb Kuijpers, accused of unfurling a Basque flag outside a church. Meanwhile, the *Guerrilleros del Christo Rey* (Guerrillas of Christ the King) ran wild in the Basque Country. Over sixty terrorist acts were claimed by them during the months of May and June, including machine-gun attacks on shops selling Basque books, on libraries, art-galleries, and the homes of Basque language teachers and priests. Lawyers and priests were beaten up and a number of young people who refused to give the fascist salute were also attacked in public. Up to 26 May at least 2,300 Basques had been arrested, including not only nationalists but communists, socialists and priests; many were tortured and severely beaten under interrogation.

The police were also active in Alava and Navarra, not included in the Government's decree. Local observers and lawyers described the situation as the worst since Franco's purges of the Basque provinces at the end of the Civil War. The violence was then followed by a period of demonstrations by Basque nationalists and their allies among the proletarian movement. On 11 June the nationalists joined with the illegal socialist organisation *Junta Democratica,* in declaring 'a day of struggle' in Guipuzcoa and Viscaya. About 20,000 workers came out in San Sebastian, 4,000 in Bilbao and about 1,000 in Pamplona. At the same time, students and workers were arrested for distributing leaflets as were priests for denouncing the authorities from their pulpits. The Bishop of Bilbao, Mgr. Anoveros, refused permission for clergymen to be brought to trial and the police broke the terms of the Concordat between the Vatican and Madrid by violating Church property in order to carry out arrests. A group of seventy-five Madrid intellectuals and politicians, not all Basques, sent a letter to the Prime Minister asking that the flying of the Basque flag be legalised as a gesture of peace and reconciliation during the emergency. The arrests, trials and violence continued however. By 10 June, the correspondent of *The Guardian* (London) in Bilbao reported that nearly 4,000 Basques had been detained since 25 April, although many of them for only short periods. Seven young *E.T.A.* members were tried by court martial at Burgos on 21 June and sentenced to terms of imprisonment of up to twenty-eight years each for raiding an explosives store in January 1973. Commenting on the torture to which prisoners were subjected *The Guardian* went on, 'This is the sort of legacy of cruelty, oppression and injustice by which General Franco will now be remembered'.

The Basque resistance came to a head once more during the summer and autumn of 1975. One of the leaders of *E.T.A.*, Pedro Ignacio Beotegui, was arrested in August. There were widespread strikes by about 26,000 workers against the trial planned at Burgos of two nationalists accused of complicity in the killing of a policeman: José Antonio Garmendia, aged twenty-three, and Angel Otaegui, aged thirty-three. There was a hunger-strike by 300 political prisoners. Magazines and newspapers were seized by the police. The outlawed Christian Democratic Party and the Socialist Parties called on all other democratic groups 'to hasten the end of the Franco dictatorship'. Shops and bars owned by Basque patriots, priests and nationalists were blown up and attacked by machine-guns.

Franco responded by denouncing his opponents as 'dogs that bark'; he added, 'They are tiny minorities who merely serve to show our own vitality and to prove the strength of our fatherland. We need not worry what the excited minorities think or say as long as we have on our side all that is sane in the Spanish provinces'. The judge and jury at the trial of Garmendia and Oteagui, on 28 August, consisted of five regular army officers. Only a few journalists were allowed to attend and the defence lawyers were ejected from the court-room before the trial was over. Liberal opinion in Spain was shocked to discover that Garmendia, who had been shot through the head by the police at the time of his arrest, had become a mental defective incapable of conducting his own defence, while Oteagui was clearly involved only in a secondary role. On orders from the Government, however, the two Basques were found guilty and sentenced to death; Garmendia's sentence was later commuted.

Franco's decision, at a meeting of the Spanish Cabinet on 26 September, to confirm the death-sentences was met with a wave of protest from all over the world. Among those who asked for clemency were the Pope, the United Nations, the European Parliament of the E.E.C. and Amnesty International. A delegation of leading figures from France headed by the Marxist Regis Debray, the actor Yves Montand, the writer André Malraux, the politician Pierre Mendes-France, the poet Louis Aragon and the philosopher Jean-Paul Sartre, delivered a protest in Madrid. But the only concession to world opinion was the decision not to use the garrotte—an iron collar which pierces and snaps the spinal cord—the traditional method used by the Spanish State to execute prisoners. Otaegui was shot by a firing squad on 27 September, together with Juan Peredes Manot, another member of the E.T.A., and three members of F.R.A.P. (The Anti-Fascist Patriotic Revolutionary Front) also found guilty of killing policemen: they were José Luis Sanchez Bravo, José Baena Alonso and Ramon Gracia Sanz, all aged under twenty-seven. Six other death sentences were commuted.

Widespread criticism of the Spanish Government from

abroad and at home followed the announcement of the executions. Norway, the Netherlands, Britain, East Germany and West Germany immediately recalled their envoys from Madrid. Spanish embassies in London, Lisbon, Strasbourg, Marseilles, Perpignan, Toulouse, Nantes, Paris, Utrecht, Brussels, Rome, Copenhagen and Geneva were attacked by demonstrators. The Pope expressed 'vehement disapproval' of the executions. The *Observer* (London) described them as 'an act of totalitarian barbarism'. Not only was world opinion flouted and offended but large sections of Spanish society emerged as hostile to the Government. Appeals were made by religious leaders, the professional bodies and even some Army officers, members of the clandestine *U.D.M.* (Democratic Military Union). The Cabinet, which split over the sentences with a majority of only three in favour of executions, grew more and more outspoken. There were sit-ins by lawyers at Madrid and Barcelona. More violence occurred in the Basque provinces and three policement were shot in Madrid. Priests were arrested for denouncing the Government and 832 signed a pastoral letter by Mgr. Alberto Iniesta, Madrid's Auxiliary Bishop, calling for the restoration of civil rights. Franco, at a mass rally on the anniversary of his becoming Head of State, told the crowd that Spain was 'unmoved by the international protest'.

Franco's refusal to call off the executions were to be his final public act. Throughout October 1975 there were reports that he was seriously ill with Parkinson's disease and a heart condition. On 31 October temporary power was transferred to Juan Carlos, the Prince nominated as Franco's political heir in 1969. At last, on 20 November 1975, aged eighty-two, Franco died. In a message to the peoples of Spain from his death-bed he said: 'Because of the love I feel for our fatherland, I urge you to persevere in unity and peace, and to give the future King of Spain, Don Juan Carlos de Bourbon, the affection and total loyalty that you offered me, and to lend him, at all times, the same co-operation that I received from you . . . Do not flinch in attaining social and cultural justice for all Spaniards and make this your first business. Maintain the unity of the lands of Spain, enabling the rich variety of its regions to be a source of the strength of the fatherland's unity'.

Juan Carlos was crowned King of Spain on 22 November 1975, the first since 1931 when his father was removed. In a speech to the *Cortes* he promised 'progress, change, understanding for the regional aspirations of the Basques', but took care to emphasise the key role of the armed forces in controlling Spain's political life. In the week after the King's succession a pardon was announced for political prisoners gaoled for non-violent crimes such as illegal propaganda or association and the death penalty for crimes committed before 22 November was abolished. Among the first prisoners to be released, about 6,370 in all, was the communist leader of the Workers' Commissions, Marcelino Camacho. Demands by the left-wing that Juan Carlos should announce a general amnesty for all prisoners were refused. Camacho, who had been in prison for eight years, was re-arrested on 7 December 1975 and accused of organising a demonstration outside the Carabanchel Prison where political prisoners were held.

Among the first duties of Juan Carlos, the very day that power was transferred to him, was to sign a decree allowing the public use of languages other than Castilian. This move followed a decree of 30 May 1975 by which 'it was deemed expedient to authorise the teaching of Spanish native languages, on an experimental basis, from the beginning of the 1975/6 academic year as a voluntary subject for pupils at primary schools and centres of general basic education, to safeguard Spain's cultural heritage'. The new decree of 31 October 1975 stated, 'it is now considered opportune, as a further step in the policy relating to early educational levels, to regulate the use of Spanish regional languages by the Central Administration and State Organisations, companies and private persons. The aim of this regulation is to protect the development of regional languages, whilst maintaining the use of Castilian as the official language'. The articles of the decree included the following: 'all regional languages are part of Spain's cultural heritage and must be accorded national status while a knowledge and the usage of these languages will be protected by the State and other national institutions;

regional languages may be used by all means of diffusion whether oral or written, particularly at meetings and events of a cultural nature; Castilian, the nation's official language and the means of communication of all Spaniards, will be used by all State organisations and public administration of justice, local authorities and all other official institutions; no Spaniard shall be the object of discrimination for not knowing, or not making use of, a regional language; municipal corporations and local administrations may make oral use of regional languages for internal matters, except at plenary meetings when the subject matter will result in agreements or other formal acts to be included in the official minutes, which must be recorded in the official language'.

On 28 December 1975 there was a meeting in Guernica, attended by over 2,000 people, at which a Democratic Assembly of Euzkadi was proclaimed.

What are the prospects for a more just future for the Basques within a democratic Spain? As *The Guardian* (London) commented in August 1975, 'All that can be said with certainty about the demand for political liberty in Spain is that it is strong, widespread and justified. Franco's dictatorship has satisfied none of this demand. He has only succeeded in containing it, with difficulty and with many policemen. His Government has also suppressed other nations, the Basques and the Catalans, in what would be a campaign of colonial oppression if it were not being waged in Europe. If the Basques resort to violence, the Government cannot really complain. In a police State democratic protest is impossible. There is nothing else the Basques can do to state their case. In a country in which politics have been frozen for twenty-six years, change is inevitable. The uncertainty in Spain is whether the change will be violent or peaceful'.

It is obviously very difficult, so soon after the King's succession, to say with any confidence what is likely to happen next. Franco personified Spain for so long that it will take time for the other elements of the State's political character to re-emerge. Over the next few years it seems likely that socialism, anti-clericalism and the nationalism of the Basques, Catalans and Galicians will clash with Falangism, Monarchism and Catholicism. For much of the past two decades Spain has been in the hands of the *Opus Dei*, right-wing Catholic technocrats who imposed an economic system which might, at best, be described as Christian Democratic. Spain today is therefore very different from the under-developed country in which the Civil War was fought. The apparent permanence of the Franco régime disguised this change; the question now is whether a political system will be created to reflect the new circumstances. Franco's legacy to Spain was a political void, the result of what seemed to be his indifference towards his country's future. Throughout his long and dark career he refused to allow the people even to rehearse the democratic processes, so that there is no machinery by which change can be brought about in a peaceful way. Franco died admired by many because he provided the sort of stability which allows the prosperity which, in turn, needs stability. But he died still at odds with the Basques, the Catalans, the Galicans and socialists in all the other provinces.

Juan Carlos, generally considered an amiable but weak young man, is not universally popular and has no mandate from anyone except his dead master. Already he is known in some circles as 'Juan the Brief'. By the end of the year 1975 he had done little to show what kind of ruler he intended to be. Faced in the Spanish Sahara with the gravest foreign crisis Spain had known for many years, he ordered his troops to stand firm behind a minefield designed to stop the advance of Moroccan marchers. Whether the right of self-determination for the Saharwis implies the same for the Basques remains to be seen. At least he knows that any attempt to fill the void between the Falange and the Army on the one hand and the socialists and liberals on the other, will be encouraged by the rest of Western Europe. But the entrenched right is sure to oppose any moves which threaten its decades of privilege. What Franco did to his people in the last years was often brutal and systematic: hatred on both sides is widespread.

During the summer of 1974, before the state of exception decreed the following April, it seemed as if Spain was about to transform itself from an absolute dictatorship to a more liberal system of government. The outlook at the end of 1975 was no less propitious. The Basques and other opposition groups have been given a small taste of liberty, enough to awaken their appetites and to secure concessions for their demands. Recent events in the Basque Country and Catalonia have compelled re-thinking and there now seems to be a more general readiness to consider the possibility of Basque autonomy within the context of a federal union. Some Carlists would now support this view, which is gaining ground in Navarra. The Spanish Communist Party, although centralist in outlook for tactical reasons, has also associated itself with regional demands. Such a solution would probably satisfy the majority of the Basque and Catalan population. *E.T.A.*'s views are not shared by all Basques but this movement has pushed the population towards more radical standpoints. When a more open political situation is created, the *P.N.V.*—but with changed leadership and a more radical approach to socio-political questions—will probably re-emerge as the chief mouthpiece for Basque demands. Such a party would certainly settle for something much less than complete independence from Spain and might be in a position to open a dialogue with centre and moderate left-wing parties in Madrid.

It is clear that there can be no solution to the Basque problem until Spain signs the Convention on Human Rights and joins the European Community. Meanwhile, the State has to make a firm choice between two kinds of authority—a stiffening of repression, which will further radicalise the opposition, or some degree of liberalisation which might get out of Government control and so provoke a reaction such as a military coup. Any serious secessionist tendency by Basques or Catalans would provoke strong resistance and perhaps induce the Army back into the political arena. But the outcome need not be violent or oppressive, of course. In this respect, Spain represents *par exellence* the predicament of several States in Western Europe at the present time; for over two centuries it has been the arena for a struggle between those who want a naturally diversified society and those who are in favour of a uniform culture in a unitary State.

THE GALICIANS

With the Asturias and the Basque provinces of Vizcaya and Guipuzcoa, Galicia forms Spain's northern seaboard. It is the province in the north-western corner of the Iberian peninsula which, with Portugal to the south, also faces the Atlantic. Much of it is over 3,000 feet in altitude and in the east there are peaks more than 6,000 feet high. Galicia's climate is very different from that of the rest of Spain. The moist, cool summers and mild winters bear comparison with Ireland's and references to the province as the Spanish Switzerland, or as a warmer and wetter Brittany, or even more accurately as a greener Portugal, abound. Galicia's topography is different too: deep gorges, fast rivers and drowned estuaries known as *rias* carve the granite and schist plateau, reaching far inland. The principal towns are Santiago de Compostela, Vigo, Corunna (Spanish: *La Coruña)* and Lugo, the last two of which with Orense and Pontevedra give their names to Galicia's four regions. The total population at the last Census in 1970 was 2,619,615, but is now around 3,000,000.

The first inhabitants of Galicia were not Iberians but *Gallatae,* as the Romans called them when invading the region in the second century B.C. It has been suggested that the Latin name derives from a Brythonic source and was meant to describe those Celts who, in the fifth and sixth centuries, were to leave southern Britain for Brittany. Only this much is clear: the *Gallatae* of this period were more likely to have been the inhabitants of small scattered communities who settled in the area after the exodus from Britain rather than any ancient or indigenous Brythonic population.

Whether or not it can be proved that the Galicians are of Celtic stock in the sense that they may be related to the Bretons, Welsh or Irish, they persist in the belief that they are a Celtic people. It must be admitted that the evidence on which this claim is based is far from convincing. Apart from a number of Brythonic word-roots in the Galician language, there is little except a few elements of folk-lore to support their view. Dances such as the *muneira* show some kinship with Breton dances and traditional Galician motifs rely to a limited extent on circular and spiral designs reminiscent of

Irish decorative forms. The *gaita,* a single-drone bagpipe, has survived in Galicia as it has in Brittany, Ireland and Scotland, but also among the Sorbs of Lusatia. The word *Celta* is popular as the name of many cafés, football teams and small businesses. Little can be said with certainty, except perhaps that—Celtic or not—Galicia's identity was cast during the post-Roman period when for a century or so, the region enjoyed a large measure of autonomy. Although the same is true of Wales, none of the facts were sufficient to persuade the Celtic League in the early 1960s to approve an application by the *Centro Gallego de Paris* for Galician membership.

Galicia did not keep its autonomy for long. Conquered by the Visigoths in the year 585, for the next two centuries it suffered from Arabic invasions like all the northern parts of the peninsula until, as a semi-autonomous statelet within the Kingdom of Castile, it became inextricably linked with the rest of Spain. This process of absorption was completed in the ninth century when the shrine of Saint James, the mighty leader of Arthurian stature who had led Spain's armies against the Arab invaders in the Christian Reconquest, was discovered in the region. Saint James became the patron saint of Spain and the cathedral of Santiago de Compostela the centre of his cult. Pilgrims flocked to the shrine from all over Europe, but especially from Provence, bringing the rich traditions of the troubadours to Galicia, which was now in direct contact for the first time with the Christendom of France and Italy.

With the unification of Spain under King Ferdinand and Queen Isabella in the fifteenth century, Galicia grew content with its status as a province of the new kingdom. The major events which took place within its borders during this period were those relating to the history of Castile as that province came to impose its will and personality upon its neighbours. The Spanish Armada, for example, set sail from La Coruña in 1588 and in the same city during the Napoleonic Wars, Sir John Moore was buried 'darkly at dead of night.'

For another three hundred years Galicia remained a quiet, under-privileged, conservative province of Spain, remote from the Castilian centre to the south. What events of any political significance there were had to do more with agrarian conditions under feudalism than with the expression of the province's communal identity. In the fifteenth century the society known as the *Irmandiños* (Brothers of the Same Country), believed to be about 80,000 in number, were led by Alonso de Lanzos in an insurrection against their feudal rulers and later established a Galician Council. The only resistance against the process of Castilanisation was from the followers of Pardo de Cela who, betrayed by the local clergy, was beheaded with his son in 1483. Not even the Carlist Wars which ravaged the Basque province of Navarra could change the character of Galicia. In 1815 there was a liberal uprising in La Coruña against the *foros,* the tithes which the Church extorted from tenant farmers, but it was violently suppressed and its leader, Sinforiano Lopez executed. Again, more successfully, on 6 March 1856 the 'Banquet of Conxo' at Santiago de Compostela rallied a large number of intellectuals, workers and peasants with the aim of re-establishing Galician autonomy which was to inspire the patriots of later generations. But there was none of the fierce and determined spirit of the Catalans and Basques in Galicia and the province's status remained unchanged.

For this reason, when the Galician cultural revival of the nineteenth century eventually got underway it was all the more surprising. Without a recent history of resistance to Castilian centralism, the Galician movement found its roots only in the language spoken by the people of the province. This language, called *galego* in Galician, is more closely related to Portuguese than to Castilian Spanish for it has a phonetic structure different from Castilian's and a less limited phonology. On the printed page, however, it is difficult to distinguish Galician from Portuguese, apart from a small number of consonantal variations and some differences in vocabulary; in their syntax they are identical. To the Portuguese Galician is an archaic but attractive form of his own language.

Although the Galician language has no official status in the province today, owing to the intransigent attitudes of the Castilian-dominated Spanish State towards all other languages spoken within its borders, the literature written in the language has enjoyed a certain prestige among Spanish writers over the centuries. The work of Galician writers also finds a place in anthologies and histories of Portuguese literature, as might be expected. But for the Galicians themselves their literature has an even more important role: it is the very core of their consciousness as a separate people.

Galician literature has several special characteristics which serve to illustrate some aspects of this people's history and its present situation. First, whereas the literature of Castile is mostly epic and religious, a product of the Arab invasions and the campaigns of the Christian Reconquest, Galicia's was developed during the Middle Ages under the influence of the troubadours as a literature of lyrical poetry and the ideals of courtly love. It has kept these qualities ever since, in the work of the Galicians and of Castilians like King Alfonso the Wise in the tenth century, 'the father of Castilian prose', who wrote in Galician and composed verses to be chanted in perpetuity over his tomb.

A serious blow was dealt to the Galician language and its literature when in the fifteenth century the frontier between Spain and Portugal was fixed on the river Minho. The standard speech of Lisbon (Portuguese: *Lisboa)* and Coimbra spread northwards as far as the border, leaving the Galicians stranded and unresponsive beyond the Minho, their language unacknowledged by the State to which they now belonged. The practice of writing lyrics in Galician died out among Castilian poets at this time. From now on, while Portuguese was to flourish and develop separately so that by today it is the language of the 8,124,019 (1970) inhabitants of Portugal, its close relative Galician was deprived of all status in law and the schools and thus literary prestige. It became more and more a patois and its literature degenerated into folk-song, the preserve of a small, educated upper class.

It was to be another three hundred years before Galician literature was re-discovered. Like Occitanie with its *Jocs* and Wales with the *Eisteddfod,* Galicia had the *Irmandades da Fala* (Brotherhoods of the Language) under the patronage of which a number of writers emerged who by the quality of their work were worthy of wider recognition than the peripheral status of their province had previously allowed. Rosalía de

Castro (1837-85), for example, although famous throughout Spain for a single volume written in Castilian, wrote her early poems in Galician and they are regarded as among the masterpieces of the language. She was admired by Frederico Garcia Lorca, the Spanish poet murdered by members of Catholic Action and the Falange during the Civil War, who wrote a number of poems in Galician in tribute to her, including an elegy.

Up to Rosalía de Castro's time Galician had been largely an oral literature for over four hundred years. The nobility had spoken Castilian and Galicia's language had enjoyed no official status of any kind. A rebirth of regional consciousness, from which a democratic national movement emerged, was the result of the Napoleonic invasion of Galicia in 1808. The revival was supported by such journals as *Revista de Galicia* (Galician Review), *Situacion de Galicia* (The Galician Position) and *El Emancipado Gallego* (Galicia Liberated). National feeling came to a head in 1846 with the Galician rising against the absolute centralism of the dictator Narvaéz. This movement was crushed and all its leaders shot but it coincided with a literary renaissance in which the work of writers like Pastor Diaz, Alberto Camino, Eduardo Poudal, Curros Enriquez and Manuel Pintos reached large, new audiences. Galician was thus restored to its former status as a literary language.

Curros Enriquez (1851-1908) was fairly typical of the new generation of writers. Exiled to London in 1870 for his political activities, he returned to Galicia under an amnesty and welcomed the proclamation of the short-lived First Spanish Republic in 1873 when Galicia's regionalism was recognised in political terms. Prosecuted by the Church for his anti-clericalism and by the State for his Galician nationalism, Curros Enriquez enjoyed great fame during his lifetime as a people's poet. He was made Poet Laureate of Galicia on two occasions and he is still among the most widely read of Galician writers. His collection of poems *Airiños da miña terra* (1880) took a determined stand against feudal oppression on behalf of the rural population and in favour of the regionalist spirit of Galicia. Above all, his feat was to lift up Galician from its lowly position as a peasant language and to restore its prestige as a language capable of expressing the full range of human experience.

Today there is a Galician Academy and an Institute of the Galician language at the University of Santiago de Compostela and a good deal of contemporary writing in the language. Among the most important Galician poets of this century are Manuel Antonio (1901-28) and Noriega Varela (1869-1947) while writers like R. Otero Pedravo and Alfonso R. Castelao, Maria and Celso Emilio Ferreiro have continued the Galician tradition. About 600 books are published in Galician every year, including many works of contemporary philosophy, literature and politics. There is, of course, no subsidy from the State for any cultural activity in Galician and all publishing houses are under the constant scrutiny of the censor.

The exact number who speak Galician at the present time is not known as the Census makes no provision for statistics regarding the language. But it is estimated that there are about 2,500,000 who speak Galician in the four regions. They are to be found mainly in the villages but also to some extent in the towns. The vast majority, with the exception of the intelligentsia, are unable to read or write Galician, the language not having been taught in the schools for over two centuries. There has been in recent years, however, a new pride among younger people in their ability to speak Galician and there are about fifty primary schools where the language is taught. There is no Galician on radio or television and the language has no official status whatsoever.

The linguistic dichotomy between the rural and urban areas, increasing since the Second World War, has been maintained by the economic problems which Galicia has suffered in this century. The province is dotted with little farms, each with just enough land to support one family. But the soil is more suited to grazing than to crops and sub-divided into unviable units. Until recently the controversy over the *foros* collected for *foristas,* the land-owners, dominated every other political question in Galicia. At the beginning of this century the tenants, the *foreros,* formed two organisations to defend their rights: the *Solidaridad Gallega* believed in redeeming the *foros* by compensation and the *Union Campesina* which originated under Anarchist influences in La Coruña, demanded their cancellation. The first was Republican and Liberal, believing in political action, while the second had a policy of boycotts and violence.

As Gerald Brenan points out in his account of the social and political background of the Spanish Civil War, *The Spanish Labyrinth* (1943), what made the Galician agrarian question unique in Spain was the attitude of the Church. Generally speaking, when the rural population is concentrated in large villages or towns the clergy are on the side of the middle-class against the people, whereas when the peasantry are scattered in hamlets and small farms the clergy usually supports them. This was the case in Galicia where the rural clergy were fanatically against the *foristas*. Only the town clergy, often sons of the middle-class, preached submission to the landlords. With the advent of the Republic, although socialist doctrine spread among the peasants, the political situation was therefore not the same as in the rest of Spain. Politics, centring on the question of the *foros* and confused by the split attitude of the Church, remained largely a local issue. In 1926 Primo de Rivera decreed compulsory redemption of the *foros* and this was completed shortly before the Civil War.

The general aspect of rural Galicia, green and cultivated, contrasts sharply with the sun-scorched wastes of Spain's interior and southern regions. The province, in fact, is not without its natural resources: it has good ports, it lands a quarter of Spain's fish and produces half of its wolfram and tin, the climate and soil are favourable to a wider variety of crops than those traditionally grown elsewhere. However, the small-holdings which are the basic unit of agriculture are usually of only about twelve acres. Denied subsidy from the central Government, they become more and more uneconomical until families have to sell up and move to the coast. New industries such as petro-chemical and motor-car factories have been opened only in a few areas and they have little effect on the over-all prosperity of the province except to drain the rural population into the towns where they tend to lose the Galician language within a generation.

The land is then bought by the Government, often for afforestation, with the result that the old communities of proud, hard-working peasants, on whom the Galician culture largely depends, are giving way to the easier attitudes and life-styles of an affluent, urban working-class. As in Corsica, emigration is the traditional way of keeping the province's problems within manageable proportions. Galicians played a major part in the settlement of Argentina and Cuba (Castro is a Galician name and Fidel Castro's father was Galician) and there are Galician communities in all the big towns of Spain, France, Germany and Switzerland, as well as many thousands among the *Gastarbeiter* of present-day Europe.

Like the Basque provinces and Catalonia, Galicia has suffered both culturally and economically from the centralist policies of the unitary Spanish State. But the Galicians, by nature less militant than the Basques and Catalans, have been slow to adopt the consistent methods of the separatist movements in other parts of the peninsula. It is true that when offered the opportunity during the last months of the Republic, they voted overwhelmingly on 28 June 1936 in favour of autonomy. The Galician movement at this time was led by the *Partido Galeguista* (Galician Party), a republican party founded in 1931 which was the first independent and homogenous separatist movement to be established in Galicia during the twentieth century. Its leader was Santiago Quiroga (1884-1950) who spent most of his life working for Galician Home Rule and became Minister of the Interior in Azana's Government of 1933. From 1931 his movement had sixteen members in the *Cortes* and they usually supported the Spanish republican parties, the republican left and the Republican Union, together with the autonomists from Catalonia and the Basque provinces. There was an armed revolt in the four regions in June 1936 but it was brutally crushed by Franco's forces. Bitter street-fighting occurred in many Galician towns during July 1936 when hundreds of poor peasants came in from the country on carts and on foot to defend the Republic, 'as if to a fiesta, resolved to fight to the death', in the words of Hugh Thomas in *The Spanish Civil War*. Alexander Boveda, secretary of the *Partido Galeguista,* was shot without trial and with him hundreds of autonomists and members of the main Republican parties. After Franco's victory there were guerrillas in the Galician mountains led by Ponte, and Raul, until 1950. By then the *Partido Galeguista* had moved its headquarters to Buenos Aires under the leadership of Alfonso Castelao, the most brilliant of Galician patriots, and there the *Concello de Galicia* (Galician Council), comprising all the Galician members who had sat in the *Cortes* in 1936, was formed. Brave as it was, the Galician autonomist movement died with the Republic.

Today the political situation in Galicia is similar to that of other peripheral regions of Spain. The spectrum of opinion ranges from the right-wing and traditionalist through the liberal and socialist to the Marxist and revolutionary. It is difficult to decide which of the several small, often clandestine and exiled groups, all claiming to lead anti-Franco opinion has the most influence, for few have any substantial popular support. But perhaps the most significant is the *Unión do Pobo Galego* (Galician People's Party). According to its publications, this group attempts to synthesise Galician identity with Marxist theory, cultural nationalism with economic policy, and aims at creating—by armed force when necessary—a viable base for the realisation of the province's potential by the common people. To it are ascribed many of the noteworthy events which have occurred in Galicia during recent years, such as the peasants' riots in Castelo do Miño and the *'Concentración Nacional'*, a rally held at Santiago de Compostela in July 1968, both of which were put down by the army in a typically brutal manner. Many of the *U.P.G.*'s members are in prison or in exile, so that its organisation is badly disrupted at the present time. But in 1974 it made a 'Declaration on the struggle against colonialism in western Europe' which included a clause, unspecific and apocalyptic like the entire document, calling for the official recognition of minority languages as part of the international, revolutionary, Marxist movement.

The *U.P.G.* is also associated with a number of organisations founded during the last ten years. These include the *Partido Socialista Galego* (Galician Socialist Party), the *Partido Communista Galego* (Galician Communist Party) and the *Vangardas Acratas Galegas* (Anarchist Galician

Vanguard). None of these has any power and their progress, obstructed by law and the army, is expected to be slow even if, as so often happens to such groups, they are able to survive their own internecine ideological divisions. But, more optimistically perhaps, their creation suggests how the Galician movement is thinking and preparing for the years ahead. Significantly, there is a committee based in Galicia known as *Galeuzka* which has attempted to co-ordinate the separatist movements of Galicia, the Basque provinces and Catalonia in their opposition to the Franco régime.

There were, however, no incidents in Galicia to match the events in the Basque provinces during 1975, but about twenty militants were arrested and one, José Ramon Reboiras, a member of the *U.P.G.*, was shot by police on 13 August. Like its counterparts elsewhere in Spain, the Galician movement looked forward to the death of Franco and the end of the régime which he symbolised. Franco was a Galician by birth and was generally admired in Galicia; the town where he was born in 1892 is officially known as Ferrol del Caudillo. But at the time of the dictator's death, in November 1975, this fact seemed irrelevant to the Galicians' aspirations. They find more assurance in the hope that the rigidity of the régime, with its intransigent attitudes to all Franco's opponents and all minority cultures, will surely change under his successors, and that when the time comes for Spain's re-organisation on democratic principles, the identity of Galicia will be acknowledged.

15   SWEDEN

Constitution: Kingdom

Area: 173,654 square miles

Population: 8·129 million (1972)

Capital: Stockholm

Administrative divisions: 24 counties

Present Government: The Social Democratic Party *(S.D.P.);* elected 1973

Language of majority: Swedish

THE LAPPS

Although the Lapps are not confined to any one State—they are, almost by definition, a migrant people who follow their reindeer across the northernmost parts of Norway, Sweden, Finland and the Kola peninsula of Russia—they can be considered most appropriately in the context of Sweden because they are distributed more widely here than in any other country and it is the Swedish Government which has done most for their status as an ethnic minority.

The number of people who have Lappish origins is currently estimated at between 30,000 and 40,000, of whom about a half are in Norway, a quarter in Sweden and the rest in Finland and Russia. It is difficult to assess their numbers with greater accuracy because, in the first instance, there is no single criterion for deciding who is a Lapp. Among possible criteria are reindeer-breeding, kinship and language, but each of these yields a different total. Of the approximately 10,000 Lapps in Sweden (1973), only about 3,000 or 700 households are directly engaged in the breeding of reindeer or dependent on the trade for their livelihood. Most Lapps therefore earn their living by other means: they are found within a variety of professions—as railway workers, miners, nurses, clerks and teachers—in the Lapp territories of Norrbotten where they have settled and are usually absorbed by the Swedish-speaking majority. Their ties with Lappish culture vary from strong identification with the language of their ethnic group to total assimilation in towns like Kiruna and Gällivare. Of the four kinds of Lapps—River, Sea, Mountain and Forest Lapps—only the last two are to be found in Sweden. The Mountain Lapps and the Forest Lapps are still more or less nomadic, while the River Lapps and the Sea Lapps are by now settled, the latter group having no reindeer and hardly differing from the fishermen and farmers of the Norwegian coast among whom they live.

The Lapp people call themselves *Samit*. The name *Lapp*, which comes from the Finnish *Lappalainen*, is the one by which they are usually known in Swedish, although *Same* is almost equally common. The Lappish language is closely related to Finnish and both belong to the Finno-Ugrian

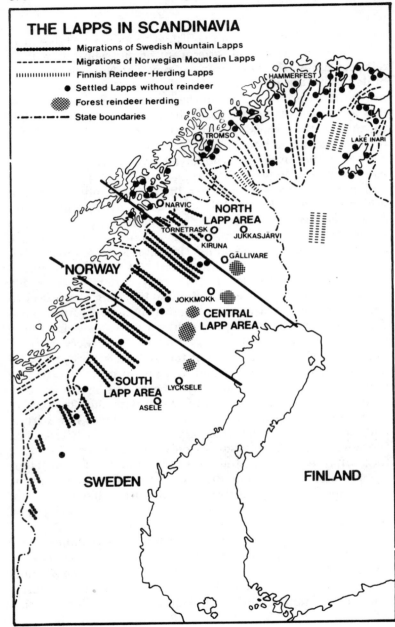

THE LAPPS IN SCANDINAVIA

- ●●●●●●●●● Migrations of Swedish Mountain Lapps
- - - - - - - - Migrations of Norwegian Mountain Lapps
- ⅰⅼⅼⅼⅼⅼⅼⅼⅼ Finnish Reindeer-Herding Lapps
- ● Settled Lapps without reindeer
- ▨ Forest reindeer herding
- -·-·-·- State boundaries

HAMMERFEST

LAKE INARI

TROMSO

NARVIC

NORTH
LAPP AREA

TORNETRASK

KIRUNA

JUKKASJÄRVI

GÄLLIVARE

NORWAY

JOKKMOKK

CENTRAL
LAPP AREA

SOUTH
LAPP AREA

LYCKSELE

ASELE

SWEDEN

FINLAND

family. Although the pre-history of the Lapps is shrouded in mystery, it is clear that a number of loan-words in Lappish prove that they must have lived in close contact with the ancestors of the Baltic-Finns during the latter part of the Bronze Age, and that they were therefore living much further east and south than in modern times. Numerous place-names around the north of the Gulf of Bothnia in Finland also suggest that at some early date the Lapps must have occupied large parts of that country. Indeed there is no doubt that the Lapps were not only the original inhabitants of Finland but that they were probably the autochthonous population of the whole of northern Scandinavia.

The Lapps are mentioned for the first time in history by the Roman historian Cornelius Tacitus, in the first century A.D., who called them *fenni,* just as Norwegians call them *Finne* to the present day. With the expansion of the Baltic Finns, the southern limits of the area inhabited by the Lapps had been pushed steadily northwards and now they came into contact, for the first time, with other peoples of Swedish, Finnish, Norwegian and Russian stock, as hunters and fishermen, and later as farmers and stock-men. In Viking times King Alfred of England heard an account of the Lapps when Ohthere, a wealthy farmer from Helgeland, told how 'of all Norwegians he dwelt the furthest north', explaining how he collected tributes—skins, down, walrus tusks and ship's ropes made of whale or seal hide—from the inhabitants of the northernmost parts of Norway. Gradually trade with the Lapps was taken over by Finns, the *bircarls,* who formed companies in the various territories, known as *Lappmarks,* such as the Kemi, Torne, Lule, Pite and Ume *Lappmarks* of modern Sweden.

During the reign of Gustav Vasa in the sixteenth century the Swedish Crown began to lay claim to the *Lappmarks,* even those in Finland and Russia, in an attempt to win the fur trade of the *bircarls.* Gustav's son, Karl IX, also wished to extend Sweden's dominion over the entire Lapp territories as far as the Arctic Ocean and the White Sea, calling himself 'King of the Lapps in the Northern Lands'. One of the causes of the Kalmar War between Sweden-Finland and Denmark-Norway, from 1611 to 1613, was the rivalry of these countries over the Lapps. The son of Karl IX, Gustavus Adolphus

(Gustav II Adolf), supported the churches founded by his father in the *Lappmarks* and opened a special school for Lapps, the *Skytteanska Lappskolan,* at Lycksele, which taught many students who later studied at Uppsala University and became ministers of religion and teachers among their own people. But throughout the seventeenth century the Lapps, who have never had any national political institutions, were exploited economically—they were forced to use their reindeer for transporting ore from the Nasa silver mine—and persecuted by Christian priests for their old shamanistic religion with its worship of the bear, rocks and celestial bodies.

Missionary work among the Lapps had begun in the thirteenth century: many of those in Sweden were converted to Christianity a century later and those in Russia in the sixteenth century. But the earliest missionaries had left no profound influence and it was not until the eighteenth century, with the rise of Pietism, that more intense efforts were made. The pioneer missionaries were Thomas von Westen, 'the Apostle of the Lapps', in Norway, and Per Fjellström in Sweden, who translated the New Testament into Lappish. Schools were founded in all the church communities of the *Lappmarks* and soon a new revivalistic religion was established. Laestadianism derived its name from the Swedish clergyman Lars Levi Laestadius (1800-61) who spent most of his life in the northernmost districts where, at the beginning of his career, social conditions were extremely poor and alcoholism rife. After Laestadius had experienced a spiritual crisis in 1844, he began preaching for the spiritual revival of the Lapps and his influence spread not only in Swedish Lapland but to the *Lappmarks* of Norway and Finland. Laestadianism is a very strict religion, a branch of Lutheranism which preaches a very rigorous code of morality and condemns everything that is not Biblical. Confession, and the ecstasy of weeping associated with it,plays a central role in its practice. Some observers see in it a development of the earlier shamanistic beliefs of the Lapps. It has had, however, a beneficial effect on social conditions both among the Lapps and the other inhabitants of the far north among whom it is equally widespread, particularly in Finland, and it has spread to the south of Sweden and to America.

The eighteenth century also saw the fixing of the border between Sweden and Norway-Denmark, along the water-shed which runs down the Scandinavian peninsula. Attached to the Strömstad Treaty of 1751 was an appendix which decreed that the Lapps should be allowed to move freely across the border with their reindeer and use the land and water of both Sweden and Norway for their herds; subsequent agreements between the two countries concerning the nomadic Lapps have been based on this Treaty. At the same time the boundaries of the *Lappmarks* were also drawn and the Lapps' right to fish and hunt within these areas were firmly established.

On the other hand, the *Lappmark* proclamation of 1751 made it plain, for the first time, that the Swedish State had an interest in establishing farming lands with a permanent population in the Lapp territories. The degree of consideration it showed to the original inhabitants varied considerably. During the first half of the nineteenth century very little regard was paid to the Lapps and their ancient rights, but later special legislation was introduced to protect them. However, this legislation often had an ambiguity which made it possible for the Lapps to lose large areas of land without any appeal to the courts, a process which has continued into the present century. The Crown's purpose in colonising the *Lappmarks* was that reindeer breeding and the agriculture of the new settlers should exist side by side without infringing upon each other, but they proved, in practice, to be mutually exclusive. Disputes between settlers and Lapps were to be settled at the district assizes. At first the rule was that the tax-paying Lapp could vindicate his hereditary rights before the law but when these clashed with the State's policy of colonization the assizes were ignored or over-ruled by the county administration. The result was that the Lapps lost access to their water-supplies, large parts of their pasturage and their hunting and fishing grounds.

By the end of the nineteenth century the colonisation of Lapland had gone so far that thousands of Lapps had been dispossessed. After grave concern had been expressed for their survival, the Swedish Crown finally ordained that a cultivation limit should be drawn between the Lapp territories and that of the peasants. This was done in all three of the northern provinces, Jämtland, Västerbotten and Norrbotten. The Lapps could be anywhere above this line all the year round and below it only during the winter months. This law was the beginning of special legislation designed to protect the Lapps and their reindeer husbandry which continued, under the pasturage laws of 1883, 1896 and 1928. Characteristic of all these laws was a highly ambivalent social attitude according to which the Lapps were to be 'protected' without having any say in their own affairs.

Another prominent feature of the pasturage legislation up to 1928 was its static and conservative character. It was intended to keep reindeer breeding within its traditional forms and thereby to conserve the distinctive mountain nomadism of Lapp culture. The structure which the Lapp communities acquired as a result, together with their attitude to Swedish authority, are undoubtedly among the reasons why their capacity for co-operation is still under-developed. In the classic system of reindeer-breeding, encouraged by the legislators, individualism was the principal feature: co-operation, when it existed, took the form of spontaneous helpfulness and solidarity among neighbours. A change-over to a regulated, co-operative means of earning a living has been extremely difficult to achieve. Two different systems of reindeer breeding have evolved in Sweden as a result. One is a stationary system in which the herds are allowed limited freedom within a forest region, often combined with other types of agriculture and livestock breeding. The other, practised to a much smaller extent, is more nomadic and characterised by long migrations of the *siida,* or villages, between summer grazing lands in the mountains and winter pastures in the forests or along the coasts. The type of nomadism in which whole families moved from one place to another has therefore largely ceased. Instead, only those who are actively engaged in herding the reindeer will follow the herds. Until the 1920s reindeer were used for milking and as beasts of burden but today the breeding of reindeer is entirely geared towards meat production. Among the modern methods now employed in reindeer herding are the use of air-craft, cars and snow-scooters.

About 3,000 Lapps in Sweden live by breeding reindeer. The total number of beasts varies around an average of 225,000, of which about 60,000 are slaughtered annually to a meat value of £230,000 (1972) marketed mostly in the south of the country. The meat is sold through the National Union of Swedish Lapps and the Swedish Farmers' Meat Marketing Association. Business structure is, however, still under-developed and ownership of reindeer is unevenly divided. The Forest Lapps have solved this problem by forming herding associations on the Finnish model. Wages are paid to the associations by the reindeer owners and the associations pay a daily wage to the herdsmen. Since 1945 reindeer-breeding has developed best among the Forest Lapps as a result of this initiative.

During recent years the Lapps have been the object of ex-tensive research by commissions appointed by the Swedish Government. The chief concern of this research has been to find ways in which reindeer-breeding can be re-organised into a more efficient source of livelihood. The most important event in the lives of reindeer-breeding Swedish Lapps for decades was the Reindeer Husbandry Law approved by Parliament in 1973. The basic motivation for this law was the low productivity level of reindeer-breeding in many areas. To yield a gross income of £3,000 a year it is necessary to own about five hundred reindeer. But a large number of Lapp families own fewer than two hundred animals which means that they cannot live on reindeer-breeding alone. The new law offers State subsidies and aims at making reindeer-breeding more profitable in a number of ways, and at protecting the Lapps' rights in this respect. It also grants the reindeer-breeding Lapps a greater measure of self-determination than they enjoyed under earlier laws. The Lapp village will become a kind of co-operative society, responsible for reindeer-breeding within its own grazing area. It will plan, construct and maintain common facilities including better housing—badly needed in many areas—as well as share the costs among its members. The power of jurisdiction over specific Lapp matters which public authorities exercised under the law of 1928 has now been removed.

Nevertheless, there is still a number of questions connected with reindeer-breeding, especially land and water rights, which have yet to be solved. Since 1966 most of the Lapp villages in Sweden have been involved in a suit against the Government in order to establish in principle that their right to the grazing areas of the county of Jämtland supersedes that of the Swedish Crown. The National Union of Swedish Lapps (Swedish: *Svenska Samernas Riksförbund*), which represents the bargaining interests of the Lapp villages, insists that the Lapps have the rights of joint ownership and permanent possession based on ancient prescriptive claims and that these rights should be recognised. Such legal controversies, most of which involve the problem of guaranteeing the Lapps a voice in deciding their relationship with the non-Lapp population, are kept in the limelight by continued encroachments on the reindeer-breeding areas. Increased traffic on the roads, extensive water-control projects, heavy tourism, intensive afforestation, the legal protection of certain predatory animals, all place demands on the reindeer-breeding Lapps to adjust to new conditions.

The steady reduction in the number of Lapps engaged in reindeer-breeding—and thus, according to one definition, of the total Lapp population—has stimulated interest in other aspects of their problems. Most important of these is the attempt to give the Lapps an opportunity of preserving their language and adapting their culture to a new environment. In 1973, at the same time as the Swedish Cabinet presented its bill for a new Reindeer Husbandry Law, it also appointed a special Commission for the investigation and study of Lapp affairs. The new Commission has as its main task to examine and solve the problems confronting the Lapps in Swedish society, particularly those who have left reindeer husbandry and moved away to other areas. It also attempts to ascertain their degree of identification with their fellow-Lapps and their attitudes towards their own culture and the various forms of assistance which the Swedish State is able to provide. Educational problems occupy a prominent place in the Commission's work. Among other matters it has investigated is to what extent the Lapps are able to take advantage of vocational training and adult education, as well as the opportunities which exist for the study of the Lappish language and culture at university level. The Commission has presented two preliminary reports, one dealing with college education for the Lapps and the second with research and adult training in the Lappish language. It has proposed *inter alia* that a chair in the language should be founded at the University of Umeå.

Education among the Lapps dates from the early seventeenth century when it began as part of a campaign to convert them to Christianity. Fourteen Lapp students were enrolled at Uppsala University between 1633 and 1722. After 1842, when compulsory education was introduced in Sweden, the Lapps continued to enjoy an education of good quality, mainly in permanent schools. But in 1913, after complaints had been made that these schools were keeping children from the reindeer herds, a new law made the ambulatory schools the chief type of school for the Lapps. The aim of the new schools was 'to order the tuition in such a way that it does not make the children unused to nomad life'. But in practice they were severely criticised, notably at the National Congress of Lapps in 1918, for their inferior standards. The effects of these schools can still be traced on the older generation, for while they taught the material culture of reindeer-breeding, they neglected the Lappish language and taught children to speak and write Swedish from the outset. Only through strenuous efforts after the Second World War was Lapp education able to regain its former standards.

Although the Lapp language has no legal status in Sweden, there is now complete equality between the nomad schools and the permanent schools. The former rigid association of education with the nomadic life has given way to the idea that tuition should not be too closely bound to certain vocations at too early a stage. Nomad culture has been developed and combined with Lappish into a subject that is compulsory in all schools. The report of the Government Committee on which the nomad school reform of 1962 is based, states: 'The Lapps are entitled to tuition which in all respects is the equal of—but need not be identical with—that available to the majority of the population. As an ethnic minority they have certain special tuition requirements which the community should not overlook. They have the right to receive instruction in the development of their culture and its situation at the present time, instruction which is intended not only to give information but also to awaken respect for the heritage from earlier generations and to imbue them with a feeling of solidarity with their own people'.

According to a parliamentary decision which followed the acceptance of this report, the system of nomad schools can be defended on pedagogical and psychological grounds and will be retained for as long as the Lapps favour their continuation. Lapp children can complete their nine-year compulsory schooling either in the ordinary schools in their home districts or at one of the eight State-run nomad schools, according to their parents' choice. The goals of the nomad schools are generally the same as those of the other primary schools except that the Lappish language and culture are also taught there. All schools in the Lapp areas teach subjects of special interest to the Lapps, as part of regional geography, folklore, history, sociology and nature study, and also give one or two lessons a week in the Lappish language. A Lappish grammar and a small number of text-books, including dictionaries, have been recently published mainly in the North Lappish dialect, which is spoken by about 75% of all Lapps. Lappish is taught at the University of Oslo, at the teachers' training college at Tromsø in Norway and at Uppsala University in Sweden. Although the Lapps are fully the intellectual equals of the majority populations, few complete courses of higher education or win positions in cultural and social life. Indeed many Lapps have lost faith in their own cultural heritage and wish to see speedy and complete assimilation with the majority population. These Lapps have started speaking Swedish, Norwegian or Finnish to their children.

Since 1944 there has been a special residential Folk High School at Jokkmokk, in Sweden, which has given those who went to school between the World Wars some compensation for their previous inadequate schooling which resulted from the reform of 1913. This school has also given a large number of younger people a training in civic affairs. Practical courses in conference leadership and organisational techniques have been of great help to the Lapps and almost all the leaders of the various Lapp organisations were trained there. An organisation known as *Ciegus Samii Vuoigna* (Secret Spirit of the Lapps) has been formed in recent years, mostly by young people, but it has no political aims.

The first Lapp Society in Sweden was formed in 1904, the Vilhelmina-Åsele Lapp Society, the aims of which were to improve the position of the Lapps socially, economically and politically. At the National Congress of Lapps held at Ostersund in 1918, the first of its kind, the Central Union of Lapps was founded but this body was dissolved five years later for lack of funds. Local societies were then formed in all parishes where reindeer-herding Lapps lived and out of these grew a series of national conferences, the main purpose of which was to discuss developments in the meat trade, in the years between the World Wars. The principal Lapp organisation, the National Union of Swedish Lapps (Lappish: *Ruota Sámiid Rii'kasaer'vi*) was founded by the Reverend Gustav Park, a champion of the Lapps, at a national meeting at Jokkmokk in 1958 and it now represents all the Lapp communities. It is financed by the Swedish Government's State Lapp Fund, from which the main cultural society, *Sallskapet Same-Ätnam*, also receives financial aid. This society, formed in 1944, consists of Lapps and others interested in their culture. Its committees work to organise Lapp handicrafts on a proper basis and to raise the standard of Lappish education.

Handicrafts play an important economic role for many Lapps as a source of supplementary income, but they are also noteworthy from an artistic point of view. Several Lapp homecraft designers have developed new forms of creative art which have brought about a revival in the Lapp handicraft tradition and kept it from the complete vulgarisation that is common in the souvenir industries of so many other minorities. *Same-Ätnam* lists as one of its most important tasks the preservation of this tradition by such means as public exhibitions and publications. Among the most outstanding craftsmen at the present time are Esaias Poggats, Lars Pirak, Sune Enoksson and Rose-Mari Huvva. The pictorial art of the Lapp is dominated by Nils Nilsson Skum whose original and powerful pictures depicit nomad life during the first decades of this century.

The Lapps do not have an extensive written literature. One of the reasons for this lack is that Lappish is divided into three dialects: North Lappish, numerically the strongest, is spoken in all the Mountain Lapp communities in the province of Norrbotten and all the Forest Lapp communities north of Jokkmokk; Lule Lappish is spoken to the south of the river Kalix; and Pite Lappish in the south of Norrbotten. Each has its own local forms and while the Lapps from, say, Jukkasjarvi and adjacent parts of Gällivare in the south to Utsjoki in the north-east can make themselves understood fairly easily in their North Lappish, those who speak the other two dialects have much greater difficulty. The language spoken at Lapp meetings in Sweden is usually Swedish. However, a common orthography has been adopted since 1945 for all three dialects and for the Lappish language as spoken in Norway.

Although the use of Lappish for literature has been restricted, the written language has been used to some extent ever since the seventeenth century and in the eighteenth century a small number of religious books appeared in the language. The New Testament was published in Lappish in 1755 and in 1811 the complete Bible. During the present century there have always been one or two writers in Lappish, including Johan Turi (1854-1936) whose *Mui'talus samiid bira* (Story of the Lapps) and *Från fjället*(From the Mountains) are classics of the language. The tale by Andreas Labba, *Anta,* published in 1969, is, also expected to become a classic.Other contemporary prose-writers are E. N. Mankok and Margareta Sarri, and Paulus Utsi is one of the best living poets. Among Norwegian Lapps Mattio Aikio (1872-1929) has expressed in his novels something of the loneliness of the Lapps in an alien cultural milieu. It remains true, however, that whereas the Lappish language is unusually well endowed with expressions for natural situations it is, like other peasant languages, poor in words for abstract concepts—a serious lack for the creation of written literature.

The oral literature of the Lapps, on the other hand, is extremely rich. After occasional periods of suppression, the oral tradition has recently undergone a period of revival, in particular the ancient practice of yoiking, a primitive way of singing. Yoiking, perhaps the most original of Lapp art-forms, has its origins in magic and consists, as a rule, of a brief text repeated over and over again until it is suddenly cut short. There are also longer yoikes with narrative content although most are of an impressionistic, lyrical character often with a satirical or erotic element. Among some groups, as in the Pite Lappmark, each person has a yoike of his own: through its words, rhythm and melody, the yoike characterises the man, often alluding to some special event in his life. Yoiking is also the art of recalling other people, whether in hatred, love or grief, and usually relies for its emotional depth on repetition of key words and phrases. One of the most famous yoikes is *The Reindeer of Oulavuolie* by Mattias Anderson which ends with the words, 'Our memory, the memory of us vanishes: We forget and we are forgotten'. The Lapps also have a rich store of fairy tales and legends which reflect, for the most part, their history and ancient ideology, with an undertone of eeriness and fear which expresses something of their hard struggle against a severe natural world. The central figure is the *stallo,* a cannibalistic monster which has borrowed features from the Arctic ghost world, from heathen Scandinavian fertility symbols, from Christian tax collectors and other dangerous intruders. The legends also refer to the Lapps' battles with other peoples such as the Karelians and the Russians, from which—mostly by cunning—the Lapps usually emerge victorious.

Since 1919 the Lapps in Sweden have had a newspaper of their own: *Samefolket* (The Lapp People). Its principal language is Swedish but it has a substantial section in Lappish. The newspaper deals in Swedish with such matters of special Lapp interest as the problems of livelihood, particularly those connected with reindeer-breeding, water regulations and animal husbandry. There are also reviews and articles on all aspects of Lapp society and news from the other Scandinavian Lapp communities. The section in Lappish contains mostly stories and poems. The Lapps of Norway have a newspaper, *Ságat,* published in Norwegian and Lappish and another, *Nuorttanaste* entirely in their own language, while in Finland *Sabmelas* appears in Lappish only. News and cultural programmes in the Lappish language are broadcast throughout the Lapp territory, sometimes in association with the Norwegian Broadcasting Company. Recent proposals for the creation of a common Scandinavian production centre for broadcasts in Lappish have been favourably received and are being planned at present. There has been a marked change in recent years from exotic reportage of the Lapps to a factual treatment of their way of life. No television programmes are broadcast in Lappish.

The growing interest which the mass media have taken in the Lapps is a direct result of the numerous national congresses held in Scandinavian countries during the last twenty years. At the 1956 conference, held in Norway, the *Nordiska Samerådet* (Nordic Lapp Council) was founded 'to guard the Lapps' interest, economic, social and cultural, in a manner compatible with their respective citizenships'. Three years later the Nordic Lapp Council and the Nordic Council organised a conference at Parliament House in Stockholm to formulate common rules concerning the Lapps' rights in Finland, Norway and Sweden. In the same year a third Nordic Lapp conference was held in Finnish Lapland to discuss elementary and higher education at which it was resolved 'that the Governments of Finland, Norway and Sweden, on the basis of the material produced by the Council, should jointly study the problems of the Lapp population with the aim of making clear what measures should be taken to develop this people's culture and to improve their living conditions'. In 1962 the fourth conference, taking as its theme 'Democracy and the minorities', made the following recommendations: that damages caused by natural disaster to reindeer husbandry should be paid for out of Government funds; that Nordic co-operatives should be created for research on the reindeer breeding industry; that the Governments of Finland, Norway and Sweden should appoint legal experts to examine the Lapps' land and water rights; and that the Governments should allow Lapps to take a greater part in all Nordic Lapp conferences. At the fifth conference in 1965 progress in the setting up of a joint Government Committee on Lapp questions was reported, and a call was made for the

Lapps to take a greater part in community work and to express their opinion on matters concerning their own affairs, especially in youth organisations. The conference also appealed to the Governments of Norway and Sweden to enumerate the Lapp population both inside and outside the Lapp areas, as had already been done in Finland.

Most of these recommendations have been accepted by the Governments and many of them implemented. An institute for research, public information and educational work among the Lapps throughout the Scandinavian countries is in the planning stages which will allow the Lapps to have a voice in determining the use of research grants of about £50,000 a year. The establishment of a Scandinavian Lapp Institute was also approved by the seventh Nordic Lapp Conference in 1971. The Nordic Lapp Council and its conferences are financed by State grants. Through the initiatives of the Nordic Council a joint State Committee was formed in 1965 which arranges congresses and training-courses for teachers of Lappish in all three countries. As a result, a new self-awareness has grown among the Lapps, especially among the younger generation.

The changes which have taken place during recent years in the Lapps' economic, social and cultural situation, mostly as a result of expanding industrial development in their areas, are the results of the way they have adapted themselves, actively or passively, to modern technology and to the society it has produced. The kind of adjustment to the society of the majority populations, whether Finnish, Norwegian or Swedish, is of the utmost importance. Passive adjustment usually means extinction for the Lapps, active adjustment a chance of survival. The invitation to the Nordic Lapp Conference at Jokkmokk in 1953 put the problem like this: 'Active adjustment is understood to mean that the Lapps do not adopt modern culture in a prejudiced and uncritical way and discard irreplaceable values in their own culture, but that in their new situation they keep in touch with the Lapp cultural heritage. Active adjustment also implies that the Lapps watch closely every change in the present position and themselves contribute to both research and care of the Lapp culture and the natural features on which it is based'.

THE FINNS OF THE TORNE VALLEY

Among the 411,000 foreigners living in Sweden who were enumerated in 1971 there were approximately 197,000 Finns, that is to say citizens of Finland. It is not with these but with the indigenous Finnish-speaking population, who are citizens of Sweden, that we must deal here. In the absence of official statistics, because the Swedish State makes no provision for the Finnish language on its Census forms, it is estimated that between 20,000 and 30,000 people with a knowledge of the language inhabit the northernmost, Arctic region of Sweden which is known as Norrbotten. The last Census at which Finnish-speakers in Sweden were enumerated was in 1930 when 30,000 had Finnish as their mother-tongue and 10,000 claimed a knowledge of the language. About 4,000 inhabitants of Norrbotten spoke Swedish only. Since 1955, however, the numbers of Finnish-speakers have decreased as a result of emigration and a lower birth-rate.

The area of their settlement, larger than Denmark but sparsley populated, lies between the border with Finland and a line about twenty miles to the west which runs north and then north-west before petering out in a linguistically mixed area around the lake of Torneträsk, on the border with Norway. As the Torne Valley (Swedish: *Tornedalen)*, which meets the Gulf of Bothnia at Haparanda and coincides with part of the border between Sweden and Finland, runs almost the entire length of this area, the Finnish-speakers of Norrbotten are sometimes known as *Tornefinnen*, or Finns of the Torne Valley. The most important small towns are Kiruna (17,000 inhabitants), the twin mining villages of Gällivare and Malmberget (18,000) and Haparanda (4,000). Owing to its situation on the Finnish border and its schools, the latter is the centre for the region. The everyday speech in these places is a dialect of Finnish which differs somewhat from the standard language. But the official language is Swedish, except in the names of the villages, such as Jukkasjärvi, Vittomgi and Korpilombolo, most of which have kept their original Finnish names even on road-signs.

When, in 1809, Finland was separated from Sweden, the establishment of the border along the Könkämä, Muonio and

Torne rivers left a Finnish-speaking population on the Swedish side. At first the language of the autochthonous inhabitants was respected by the Swedish State but after 1880 Swedish became the only officially recognised language of the region. This decision was upheld until 1930 with the full approval of the Finnish-speakers who, while keeping Finnish as an everyday language, pressed for more and more teaching through the medium of Swedish. During the 'thirties both the Finnish and Swedish Governments repeated their claims on the Finnish-speaking inhabitants but there was no change in the border or the language's status. Since 1950 there have been no further exchanges between them over the linguistic situation in the region. Finnish-speakers do not enjoy any special legal rights and the only provision made for them is that in the appointment of civil servants, lawyers and clergy in the Norrbotten region, at least in those districts where Finnish is spoken, a knowledge of the language is considered an advantage.

All instruction in the primary schools is in Swedish, exclusively. Finnish can be taken as an optional subject at secondary level in the schools of Haparanda and Kiruna, where about half the pupils are of Finnish families and in which teachers may use Finnish to the extent they wish. Most of the Finnish-speakers belong to the Laestadian sect of the Swedish Established Church. Nearly all clergy in Norrbotten are able to speak Finnish and the language is used regularly in church services.

The only bilingual daily newspaper in Sweden is published in Haparanda, the *Haparandabladet*, known in Finnish as *Haaparannanlehti*. This small, Conservative publication promotes the scenic and economic characteristics of the region but does nothing for the recognition of the Finnish language at any level. The matter of language in Norrbotten has been aired in recent years by the Swedish newspaper *Norrländska Socialdemokraten*, a Social Democrat organ published from Luleå. Since 1957 there are transmissions in Finnish on the State ratio, including news and the weekly programme *Pohjoiskalotti* which is also popular in Finland. By an agreement between the Swedish and Finnish Governments, a television station in north-western Finland is equipped to transmit Finnish programmes to large areas of Norrbotten. The local Finnish culture of the region is based largely on its peasant origins and is strongly influenced by the strict Laestadian religion.

The Torne Valley is one of the best agricultural areas in northern Sweden, while the towns of Kiruna, Gällivare and Malmberget have grown rapidly since the First World War as important mining centres. Nevertheless, farming in the region is only marginally profitable and an increasing number of farms have been deserted during the last thirty years. Attempts to specialise in the growing of fruit and vegetables have not compensated for the high rate of emigration, especially into Finland where, with the aid of Government subsidies, new settlements and small industries are being established along the border.

The situation and attitude of the Finnish-speakers of Norrbotten is unusual, if not unique, among the linguistic minorities of Western Europe in that it has been perfectly clear for nearly two hundred years that the majority of this ethnic group are quite content with the *status quo*. They have made almost no attempt to secure protection for their language in any sector of public life, content to speak it at home and nowhere else. Suggestions by Liberal and Social Democratic politicians in Stockholm that Finnish in Norrbotten should perhaps be granted a measure of recognition in the schools have been ignored by the Finnish-speakers themselves. They have no political or cultural movements of their own, preferring to support the main Swedish parties. While in the rest of Sweden, the existence of the Finnish minority is virtually unknown, in Norrbotten the attitude of Swedes to the Finnish language is generally disparaging, a view shared by the majority of Finnish-speakers as far as education, legal status and culture are concerned. There have been numerous articles in the Swedish press during the last six years about the presence of Finnish-speakers in Norrbotten, mostly prompted by the occasional hostile remark in Finland about the Swedish-speakers who live in that country. But there is little evidence that traditional attitudes in the region are beginning to change. It is therefore probable that, content to speak their language at home but nowhere else, and not insisting on education in it, the Finnish-speakers of the Torne Valley, already reduced to small numbers, will after one or two more generations become extinct.

16 SWITZERLAND

Constitution: Confederation

Area: 15,941 square miles

Population: 6.350 million (1974)

Capital: Bern

Administrative divisions: 26 cantons

Present Government: The Socialist Party in coalition with the Liberal Party, Christian Democratic Party and the Democratic Centre Party; elected 1975

Language of majority: Swiss German

THE TICINESE

Ticino, one of the largest cantons in Switzerland with an area of 1,084 square miles, is situated in the far south of the country beyond the Gotthard Pass in the Lepontine Alps and on the border with Italy. It is a largely agricultural area and the principal towns are Bellinzona, Locarno and Lugano; within its boundaries are the northern end of Lake Maggiore and the Leventina Valley along which run the road and railway linking Milan with Zürich. At the Census of 1970 Ticino (German: *Tessin*) had a population of 245,458, the majority of whom, 210,268, had Italian as their mother-tongue.*

The *italianità* of Switzerland dates from the fourteenth century. The region of Uri, now a canton, extended to the summit of the Gotthard during the first Confederation and soon joined in an alliance with the Valle Levintina which lay at that time on the southern side of the border between the Swiss states and the Italian. During the next century the Leventina nearly became a canton in its own right but in 1422 it fell under rule from Milan. Re-united with Uri about twenty years later it retained much of its liberty but, following a revolt against the administration to the north, it was subjected and incorporated into the German-speaking canton. The linguistic frontier between the Leventina did not shift, however, and the southern area remained solidly Italian-speaking.

The next extension of Swiss territory was into the region around the fortress of Bellinzona in 1500 and, over the next sixteen years, up to the line which marks the present frontier between Switzerland and Italy. The Confederate administration of Ticino by bailiffs known as *Landvögte* was by no means completely just but after the collapse of the old régime the Italian-speakers were content with their citizenship within the new Confederation and chose not to join the Cisalpine Republic. The 'bailiwicks beyond the mountains' were included in Swiss neutrality and therefore protected

*The total number of Italian-speakers in Switzerland at the 1970 Census was 743,760. There are Italian-speaking communities in three areas of Graubünden: in the Mesolcina (Mesocco) district between Ticino and the border with Italy, and in two districts to the south of St Moritz. But the present account will deal mainly with the Italian-speakers of the canton of Ticino.

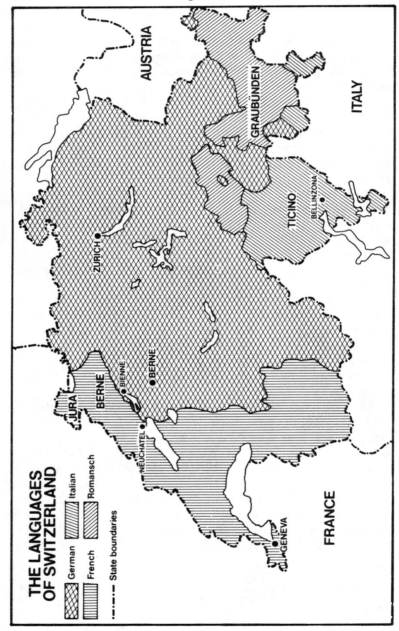

THE LANGUAGES
OF SWITZERLAND

German   Italian
French   Romansch

— · · — State boundaries

from invasion. The Ticinese thus survived the first major crisis in their history, keeping their language and their Roman Catholic religion.

The Swiss desire for transalpine expansion showed, to some extent, a return to their Confederate origin. The birth-place of Confederate thought was in Ticino: the idea of communal independence on the part of democratic farming communities and the growth of the *Schwarveband,* the basis of political organisation, were first pioneered in the region. As early as 1182 the Leventina had joined with Blenio in the Oath of Tarre to prevent the building of any more fortresses by the native aristocracy, most of whom had been driven away by this time. The new laws which were then agreed formed the embryo of the first Swiss Confederation and the communal idea continued to exert its influence even after that society's collapse in 1213. There were risings in the Leventina between 1290 and 1292 against foreign judges and for six months the Valley was ruled by the people as an independent Republic. Even the Visconti who, as Dukes of Milan, set up a powerful state in Upper Italy, had to respect the Ticinese love of independence, which they lost only in 1422 after the battle of Arbedo. This was the first heavy defeat of the Confederates who were thrown back onto the heights of the Gotthard. Twenty years later they won back the Leventina after 'the surrender of Milan', at which the Valley was taken under the protection of Uri. Still their autonomy was respected: they had complete internal self-government, went to battle under their own officers and elected their own representatives. There was no German-speaking administration in the Valley apart from the Governor, and the Ticinese were always addressed by the authorities in Uri as *'cari fedeli apparenti compatrioti'.*

Thus in the course of two decades, the Maggio Valley and Locarno having fallen to the Confederates in 1513 and the Blenio Valley in 1496, the whole of Ticino had become Swiss, partly through voluntary union and partly by conquest. It was not yet united, however, into a single canton: the eight provinces remained isolated from each other, each with its own statute, and under the protectorate of different sovereigns. As a result of this annexation, for that is what it was except in the case of the Leventina, there was to some extent a betrayal of the 'federal idea' which the Confederates had adopted two centuries earlier from the Ticinese themselves. It is true that Livinen, although gradually bound to the power of Uri, did not forfeit its privileges until 1755 when it rebelled, that Blenio had its own parliament, that the Maggia Valley was ruled by the Governor only at the express wish of its inhabitants and enjoyed wide privileges, that the old aristocratic Republic of Locarno kept its traditions and constitution up to 1798, and that Mendrisiotto enjoyed its freedom from taxes for even longer. But that does not mean the Confederates came as liberators. Most of these rights had existed under rule from Milan and they were not extended now. The twelve Cantons (Appenzell had not yet been admitted to full membership) were annexed territory—and not always administered in the most impeccable manner.

All in all, the Ticinese continued to live under their new masters as under the old, no more oppressed and no less independent than before. Nevertheless, from the reports which have come down to us, it is clear that the Confederate administration was not perfect. The Saxon writer Küttner commented on the Ticinese in 1785: 'I have never seen such a suffering people as these, nowhere found so many traces of the bitterest poverty as in the huts, clothes and general aspect of these provinces . . . He who has no strength seeks to keep his subordinate thin and weak and it thus never occurs to the latter to match his strength against his master's'. Because Ticino was neglected the Confederate idea as a whole came under attack. The Bernese administrator Karl Viktor von Bonstetten reached the conclusion that no more miserable and clumsy a form of government could be devised than that of the Twelve Cantons: 'A common meadow is not properly tended, so how much more would a land commonly ruled?' Chief among abuses singled out for attack was the fact that, as the Governors were almost wholly dependent on legal fees, there was a plethora of lawyers—thirty-three in Locarno out of a population of about a thousand. The litigious character of the Ticinese, noticed by many observers, dates from this period when, in Von Bonstetten's words, 'this most shameful administration never had money for useful things'.

Yet, after the catastrophe of the old Confederation and despite the corruption of their rulers, the Ticinese chose to remain Swiss. Why? Fritz-René Allemann in *25 Mal die Schweiz* (Munich 1965) suggests that in being subjected to the Confederate authority they had at least preserved their traditions and not lost their ancient privileges, unlike the Italians to the south. The administration achieved little but it did not oppress the people with fiscal burdens as did the more 'progressive' rulers of Lombardy under the Spanish or Austrian régimes. The Confederation required only a minimum of interference in the Ticinese way of life and the valley communities were as proud of their self-government as of the right to bear arms which was always allowed. Even the undeniable despotism and corruption left little resentement—there is hardly a reference to the tyranny of their masters among the wealth of folk-literature from this period. Rather, there grew up a reputation that the Ticinese regarded the Confederation more as their servants than as their masters.

The final judgement on whether the Ticinese were to remain within the Swiss Confederation was delivered by the people themselves. When the Confederate Alliance collapsed in 1798 under attack by the French Revolutionary armies, faced with the choice of joining the Cisalpine Republic or the Helvetic, they opted by a great majority to remain within the Swiss Union. The explanation for this is that, whereas the Cisalpine Republic was largely Italian in language, it was also centralist and authoritarian. Under the slogan *'Liberi e Svizzeri'* (Free and Swiss), which has remained famous in Ticino ever since, the improvised militia led by farmers now repulsed the Cisalpine Volunteers.

The Constitution of the Helvetic Republic divided Ticino into two cantons—Lugano and Bellinzona. The Italian language was raised with French to the status of an official language equal to German. Even so, the Ticinese were not altogether with the new régime. The inhabitants of the Leventina were crushed when they rose against the unified State so that Heinrich Zschokke, who in 1800 had tried to bring order to Ticino's anarchy, confirmed that the people on the far side of the Gotthard did not favour Switzerland to the extent supposed by the Constitution. The new Constitution of 1803, which put an end to the experiment of an indivisible Swiss Republic, reorganised the country along federal lines. Ticino was guaranteed control over its own affairs and the Leventina, which had inclined for a while towards integration with Uri, was promised to the new canton. Out of a period of complicated politics which followed throughout the nineteenth century, at least one fact emerges quite clearly: Ticino's wish to remain *Liberri e Swizzeri* never declined and the possibility of union with Italy was never postulated. The Ticinese may have taken a keen interest in the movement for Italian unity, often more than their Swiss neutrality allowed, but such enthusiasm did not cross the border as irredentism.

In the relationship between the Ticinese and Switzerland on the one hand, and with Italy on the other, there are peculiar ambiguities so that it is sometimes said that in Ticino nearly every Swiss and Italian problem exists in an exaggerated form. There is, first of all, the burden of the *Vögte* which robs the Ticino, unlike the Italian-speaking valleys in Graubünden, of any history which the Ticinese can regard as their own. Since 1800 the canton's link with Switzerland has become complicated by the political divisions of Ticino itself. The Liberals look back with pride upon the long years when their party had the upper hand, the Conservatives to the Restoration of 1815-30 and to the time between 1912 and 1940 when Federal Councillor Guiseppe Motta was in power. But the connection is always with a particular Switzerland, radical or conservative, rather than with Switzerland for itself alone. For many years the canton had no permanent capital and was divided above and below Monte Ceneri in two regions, one Catholic and Conservative, the other Liberal. Its political life was intense, with assassinations and the occasional *putsch* during the 1890s, and power shifting from one faction to another as a result of the smallest defections.

Much more than the people of Graubünden or Jura, the Ticinese have long been considered as outsiders. In the 1920s the celebrated Romance scholar Armino Janner wrote that, at best, they could be only 'adopted Swiss'. Confederates by dint of a political decision, their history had been that of 'a piece of Lombardian earth added to a completely different State by historical chance. As they have never fought, suffered or enthused in a complete relationship with the rest of the Swiss, in every thinking Ticinese lay the potential of an irredentist '—if one day he ceased to understand what it meant to be Swiss. Walsh, who visited the canton in the 1830s, was already shaking his head at the bitterness of the struggle between political parties and 'the spirit of faction' which has characterised the Ticinese up to the present time. Even the German democrat Wilhelm Hamm, who praised Ticino as one of the most liberal cantons of Switzerland, noted the internecine quarrels among parties and individuals which, on several occasions, have ended only after the intervention of Government troops: during a rebellion in 1890 against a conservative administration one member of the State Council was shot.

Ticino is remarkable in that, besides the Solothurn, it is the only Catholic canton which is radical in tradition and spirit. Its inhabitants have a peculiarly ambivalent attitude to the Church: they are not completely anti-clerical but they resist all attempts at interference in their daily affairs. They lack the religious fervour of Freiburg and have never shown the intolerance of Wallis. They seem to be fond of pomp and ritual (even socialist leaders take part in religious festivals), but are extremely disrespectful towards the Church at other times, especially towards its hierarchy. They have been described by Fritz-René Allemann as secret anarchist against all authority.

The Constitution of 1892 took account of Ticinese attitudes when it introduced proportional representation in the election of the cantonal Council, and this system has favoured minority parties such as the Socialists and Farmers' Party, up to the present. Although the smaller parties have only about 20% of the votes, they become the permanent spokesmen for both the major parties, Conservative and Radicals. It is still the individual, rather than the party, who counts at elections and corruption has not been unknown. The *italianità* of the Ticinese is expressed in politics as in no other sector of public life. They lack the talent for serious consideration of principles which is typical of the German Swiss, preferring a light-hearted, satirical approach which is the despair of their northern neighbours. Perhaps, as Fritz-René Allemann suggests, the prosaic Confederation needs such an element within its borders in order to counter-balance its excessive solemnity.

In the *Gran Consiglio,* the canton's Parliament, the ninety seats are shared among a variety of political parties, including the Christian Democrats (31), the Radicals (35), and the Socialists (12). The *Consiglio di Stato,* the cantonal Government, consists of five deputies. There is no separatist movement in Ticino. The main organisation which presses for the rights of the canton within the Swiss Confederation is *Conscienza Svizzera,* a study and information centre for Italian Switzerland.

As for Italy, Ticino reserved a very ambivalent attitude towards the new State to the South where their own language was spoken. The attraction of Italy is evident in the work of **Francesco Chiesa** (1871-1973), Ticino's most important author. Pointing out that Switzerland's French-speakers and German-speakers could, if they wished, withdraw into themselves and still survive as cultural entities, Chiesa claimed that Ticino, with a population of no more than 5% of the Confederation's population, needs identification with the culture of Italy in order to remain viable. 'Italian Switzerland is inevitably more Italian', he wrote 'than French Switzerland is French or German Switzerland German. The few can save **and preserve themselves only if they desire much and are worth much. Our only means of remaining Italian consists in** being Italian to the core'. From this view it was but a short **step towards sympathy for the fascist régime of Mussolini.** Chiesa's attitude did not spring from support for totalitarianism but from a fear that, if Mussolini was opposed by Ticino, 'the umbilical cord with the mother country' would be severed. As he announced after 1945, he would have been unable to take up any other position even towards a Communist Italy. Because there was 'no intellectual defence of the country' against Mussolini, there was no strong partisan movement in Ticino as there was in German-speaking cantons.

Although consistent, Chiesa's views during the 'thirties and 'forties were extreme. That they were unrepresentative of the views of the Ticinese is illustrated by the fact that during the Second World War, when Switzerland was officially neutral, they used to leave their lights on at night in order to point the way south for Allied bombers going into northern Italy. Even in *Risorgimento* times the Ticinese were not wholly in sympathy with the Italians: independent in spirit, they were in the habit of looking down their noses at their neighbours to the south, still under foreign domination, just as the German-speaking Swiss have a superior attitude towards the Germans. In fascism the people of the Ticino saw evidence to confirm their suspicions that the ability to remain free was lacking in the Italians. This attitude was re-inforced by class considerations, so that at best the Ticinese attitude towards Italy was a mixture of good will and contempt, at once a complex of inferiority and superiority. The total failure of irredentism now makes the fears of observers like Janner seem unreasonable, but only because Ticino's experience of Italian fascism made them feel more Swiss than ever before. Since 1939 the economic strength of Switzerland has made union with Italy seem unattractive and by now provides a very powerful argument against secession.

Nevertheless, Ticino is not without its problems. They are not strictly to do with language, for the Federal bargain has been well kept on the whole—the canton has its autonomy, its religion and language are protected—but they are inseparable from language and spring from the fact that the Ticinese are still overwhelmingly Italian-speaking and belong ethnically to the Italian people.

The problem of the first magnitude is immigration, both from German-speaking Switzerland and from Italy. The German Swiss like to speak of Ticino as 'the sun-room' or 'the southern balcony'. There is an element of truth in this idyllic comparison. Leaving the Gotthard tunnel, the traveller towards the south enters a region where vines, fig-trees and palms are grown, the *'Land von Unschuld und Reife'* (a land of innocence and fruition) described by Herman Hesse. The architecture here is quite distinct, with bell-towers and court-yards not to be found further north, and the people are more spontaneous and nonchalant in their gestures and speech. It is possible, of course, to exaggerate the reputation of Ticino as 'the merry south'. Certainly the regions on the far side of Monte Ceneri, around Lugano and Mendrisio remind the visitor of Tuscany, as do the districts around Lake Maggiore and the lower Ticino Valley which are known as 'the Riviera'. But there are other parts, such as the upper Ticino, Sopraceneri, the Blenio, Verzasca and Maggia Valleys, the mountain settlements of the Centovalli and the Sottoceneri, which are no different from Alpine hinterland—harsh, barren and a little monotonous, more like the higher valleys of the Grabünden. Nevertheless, German Swiss have found in Ticino a region to their liking and have visited it increasingly over the last century. Sunny, accessible, scenically beautiful and not very expensive, Ticino is a holiday place for week-enders and a retirement area for pensioners from the north, especially in the districts around the lakes where many thousands of villas have been built. Against tourists the canton can insulate itself but the German-speakers who settle there have brought their own tradesmen and businesses, with the result that Italian is becoming the language of a depressed sector of society. At the same time, the less picturesque valleys are deserted or taken over for hydro-electric schemes, while the lakes and rivers are suffering from more and more pollution.

Italian-speakers including immigrants from Italy, represented 5.3% of Switzerland's total population in 1888 and up to 1950 they rarely exceeded 6%. In 1960, however, they increased to 514,306 (9.5%) and to 11.9% in 1970. The immigration of Italians into Ticino dates from the end of the Second World War. Already in 1910 about 30% of the canton's population was Italian and it has been known to exceed 40% in recent years. Undamaged by the War, Ticino is among the cantons which attracts *Gastarbeiter* (guest-workers) from the south in their thousands. There were 285,000 Italians in Switzerland in 1950, 506,000 in 1960, 810,000 in 1965 and over a million in 1972.

At first these workers were welcome, for Switzerland was short of manual labour and their wage demands were moderate. By now the presence of foreign workers has become a source of widespread grievance—the so-called 'Swiss form of the colour problem'. The Italians, as a rule, are without rights and generally despised by the Swiss; the Ticinese would gladly treat them in the same way except that they too are in danger of being treated in this way. In the early days of immigration the Ticinese attitude of superiority was evident, but now they are anxious to avoid being confused by German-speakers with the dispossessed of Sicily and Naples. The number of Italians in Ticino has increased despite the stabilisation measures taken by the canton's Parliament in 1972. In June 1974 the Swiss rejected by a very small majority a proposal to limit the number of foreigners in every canton to 10%, and it was Ticino which stood to gain most from such measures.

The linguistic and cultural problems which the German-speakers bring to Ticino are immense. Very few learn Italian or are assimilated in any way. They build their own schools and run their own societies, so that their influence is often greater than their statistical strength, some 10% of the population, would imply. Ticino has no university of its own and many of its most talented youth have to live outside the canton. On the radio and television there is only a small number of programmes produced from within Ticino, mainly because while German Switzerland fosters the principle of particularism there is no such tradition in Italy. It is therefore difficult to steer a course which, while asserting the difference between Ticino and Italy, maintains the difference between the German Swiss and the Ticinese. Rivalry between the towns of Bellinzona, Lugano and Locarno prevents the cantonal authorities from speaking with one voice in cultural matters. Meanwhile, the situation is exacerbated by the Italians who cross the frontier to their places of work. It was Max Frisch, the dramatist, who summed up the Swiss dilemma when he said, 'We called out for manpower, but men came'. For these immigrants have to be housed, fed, transported and provided for the same extent as the citizens of Ticino. The Swiss Government has committed itself to reducing the number of foreigners in Switzerland by about 540,000 by 1977. It is believed in some quarters that the consequences of such moves would be disastrous for Swiss industry, the building and tourist industries in particular, and it was this fear which resulted in the decision during the autumn of 1974 to reject the Government's plans. Among organisations which have campaigned for better treatment for Italians in Ticino is the Catholic Workers' Movement which admits the necessity for a stabilised number of *Gastarbeiter* and demands equal protection in a more humane policy towards them.

The *'rivendicazioni ticinesi'*, the demands on Bern which Ticino has made from time to time, have not always been met by the Federal authorities with full sympathy. It is not that the canton has much to complain about which directly affects its political and linguistic status, for the acceptance of Italian as one of the State's official languages has never been questioned and the canton enjoys the same degree of autonomy as all the others. Indeed, in some respects Ticino has been fortunate in that one of its sons, Guiseppe Motta, the Catholic Conservative from the Leventina Valley, served as the canton's representative in Bern from 1911 to 1940 and was considered to be the dominant Swiss politician of his day. Those who criticised his foreign policy on the grounds that it was too sympathetic towards the fascist régime in Italy never disputed the fact that 'he contributed as much towards the helveticisation of Ticino as General Dufour did for Geneva'. Motta's words are still remembered: 'Ticino without Switzerland would lose in status and character; Switzerland without Ticino—that would be the same as mutilating the ideal of the Confederate State'.

Despite the preferential treatment accorded to Ticino in Motta's time, relations between the canton and Bern have not been without their fluctuations. When in 1803 Ticino achieved its independence within a Swiss framework and had secured it in 1814, its Government was faced with huge problems. The canton had little wealth of its own, its economy was crippled by taxes, it had only a rudimentary system of communications, no public education system and no modern administration. After 1848, when the Confederation began taking the taxes formerly reserved for the canton, Ticino's voice grew more strident. The claim by Enrico Celio, the canton's Federal Councillor, that peripheral areas required special treatment in legislation and commerce was largely ignored. Then, with the unification of Italy, Ticino's position grew even more unfavourable as the new State set up protective customs barriers on its frontiers, thus robbing the Swiss canton of its traditional markets. Ticino now turned to its neighbours beyond the Gotthard, contributing eagerly to the cost of building the railway which would link it with the north, only to find that Bern would impose its own tariffs at this point. Cut off from its markets to the north and to the south, Ticino's industry went into decline, and it was not until 1943 that the excessive transport costs over the Gotthard were lifted.

Since then the canton has shared vigorously in Switzerland's affluence. Its industries, particularly the manufacture of clothing and metal-processing, have flourished; power-stations and hydro-electric schemes have been built. Despite the economic boom in Ticino which has attracted attention in Switzerland during the last three decades, it remains true that the Ticinese are still employed at lower levels and that most professionals and technological specialists are German Swiss, as is the capital employed. Like other societies which have been neglected in the past and are now dependent on expertise from outside, the Ticinese prefer to educate their children in the humanities than for scientific or technological occupations. The canton's industry also remains highly sensitive to fluctuations in economic conditions: small setbacks, which in other cantons might slow down the rate of growth, cause stoppages and heavy unemployment in Ticino.

In agriculture too the canton has not developed like its neighbours to the north. The average unit of land here is about a third of the German Swiss, the result of a traditional system of gavelkind. In almost all the valleys, depopulation has been a problem for over a hundred years and in some, such as the Verasca Valley, the population is only a third of what it was in 1900. According to official estimates, the decrease in the agricultural districts up to 1950 was 37%—the highest in the whole of Switzerland. In 1960, a comparatively prosperous year, the excess number of births over deaths was 2·6% whereas in the rest of Switzerland it was 7·8%. No other canton had a lower number of marriages. This low birthrate, unusual for a predominantly Catholic canton, and the high rate of emigration, are no recent phenomena. Throughout the nineteenth century the Ticinese were famous abroad in the occupations traditionally associated with them—masons, chimney-sweeps, stable-hands and coachmen, chocolate-makers, plasterers and copper-smiths. When these crafts declined with the growth of industry in Switzerland and abroad, the Ticinese turned to new skills in German-speaking cantons. Much has been written in an attempt to explain that the motives for this emigration are not entirely economic, some observers suggesting that the Ticinese have an imaginative but unstable ethnic character which leads them, in the words of the writer Felice Filippini, to 'crazy and miraculous deeds which in other circumstances might have produced works of great significance but, in fact, have made of them a difficult people'.

Whatever the causes, the results of Ticinese emigration are obvious enough. Between 1850 and 1960 the population of Switzerland increased by 123% while Ticino's increased by only 67%, and many were Italians from Italy. It is not the Italians but the German-speaking Swiss, however, who constitute the most pressing problems in Ticino. There are, by now, many communities such as Orselina and Agra, where the permanent population is entirely German-speaking. Lugano, Locarno, Ascona and the surrounding villages have experienced a boom in land and property prices since 1945 comparable with that in the city of Zürich. The German-speaking Swiss who settle here may also be able to speak French, but few speak Italian. They tend to settle in small but well-defined areas which later spread to take in the surrounding countryside. Furthermore, they usually belong to the upper professional classes with wealth enough to follow their own life-style, oblivious to the communities around them even to the extent of having their children educated at private schools. It is said that the only Italian they hear is when the maid speaks to tradesmen calling at the door.

The culture which the Ticinese are anxious to defend against the influx of German-speakers is ancient and extensive. The canton has been for centuries the home of painters, sculptors and stone-masons—some of whom helped to build

Moscow's Kremlin and the most famous of whom was Vincenzo Vela of Ligometto. This tradition can be seen today in the architecture of Ticino's villages, such as Carona Breno, Bedigliora, Intragna and Bissone, where many fine buildings have been decorated by local craftsmen. At San Nicolao there is a splendid example of the Romanesque church of the early Middle Ages and every parish has something to show, a fresco or a chapel perhaps, as in the Engadine valleys of Graubünden. Apart from its architecture and rich folk-lore, Ticino boasts a substantial literature which during the last hundred years has shown signs of a new vitality. There are many painters' societies and exhibitions. Famous among Ticino's artists both inside and outside the canton are the painter Pietro Chiesa, the engraver Aldo Patocchi and the sculptors Vincenzo Vela, A. P. Pessina and Remo Rossi.

The most important Ticinese writer was Francesco Chiesa. Born at Sagno in 1871, he became the doyen of Italian writers in Switzerland and his hundredth birthday was celebrated throughout the canton in July 1971. A former journalist, Chiesa was for many years a headmaster but he also played a leading role in Ticino's cultural and political life after 1945. He began publishing his verse in 1897 and his prose works in 1913. Among his prose works are *Istorie e favole* (1913), *Racconti puerili* (1920), *Tempo di Marzo* (1925) and *La Scatola di pergamena* (1960); he also published six volumes of poetry including *Fuochi di primavera* (1919). Alone in his day as the defender of a Ticinese literature, Chiesa, who died in June 1973, is now acknowledged as the father of a distinct school of writers who emerged between the two World Wars, mainly as the product of Ticino's anti-fascist sentiments.

Encouraged by such magazines as *Svizzera Italiana, Quaderni Grigionitali* and *Cenobio,* and by a variety of prizes afforded by the State, such as *Libera Stampa,* these writers continued to take an interest in Italian culture after 1945 and to draw from it for their own purposes. Foremost among them were Felice Filippini (born 1917), who is also a painter, composer sculptor and head of *Radio della Svizzera Italiana,* and the poet Giorgio Orelli (born 1921). Since 1965 there has been increasing interest in the work of Ticinese writers, including Giovanni Orelli (born 1928), Plinio Martini (born 1923)

Amleto Pedroli (born 1920), Remo Fasan (born 1922) and Pio Fontana (born 1927). Most of these writers deal with contemporary themes and are particularly concerned with the problems of Ticino as a region with its own identity but in constant contact with the cultures of Switzerland and Italy. The cultural and intellectual centre is not Bellinzona but Lugano. The Confederation has already made it clear that it wishes to help Ticino solve its problems. Since 1942 the canton has received an annual grant for 'the preservation of its cultural and linguistic individuality'—although most of this goes to finance the schools. Grant-aid is also provided for *Radio della Svizzera Italiana.*

Provision for the Italian-speakers of Ticino on radio and television is made by the Swiss Broadcasting Company. There is a first programme devoted to information and entertainment and a second programme concentrating on music and cultural productions in Italian, as there are in German and French, while programmes are also broadcast regularly in Romansch. Out of a total of 19,421 hours broadcast on the first programme of the radio in 1970, 6,117 hours were in Italian (6,868 hours in German and 6,436 in French), that is 117 hours a week in Italian; on the second programme, out of a total of 11,409 hours, 3,359 were in Italian during 1970 (3,189 in German and 4,861 in French), or sixty-four hours a week in Italian. There is a complete television service in Italian: out of a total of 8,972 broadcasting hours in 1970, 2,793 hours (fifty-four per week) were in Italian (sixty per week in German and fifty-eight in French) on the first channel and two other channels began broadcasting from Lugano in 1974.

The number of books published in Italian in Switzerland is comparatively small: out of 6,065 new titles published in 1973, only 178 were in Italian (3,651 in German, 1,533 in French, thirty-six in Romansch and 667 in other languages). This figure represents an increase on the sixty-eight new titles published in Italian in 1959 and, of course, the Italian-speakers of Ticino are able to read books and periodicals published in Italy. Milan, which as a cultural, industrial and fashion centre equals Rome, is only an hour's train journey from Mendrisio. The Ticinese go into Italy regularly for their entertainment and touring companies from Milan perform in Lugano. Cultural circles in Ticino such as the women's organisation, the Lyceum Club, are in direct contact with their counterparts in Italy.

Attempts have been made to counteract the growing influence of German-speakers in Ticino. Between the two World Wars laws were passed to check the use of public inscriptions in German and to promote Italian for all official purposes, while the Federal Government has tried to prevent the purchase of land in Ticino by outsiders. There is some local opposition to such measures, especially from business men who see in the visitors and settlers an important source of livelihood and taxes. The dilemma of those who wish to maintain the *italianità* of Ticino was expressed by the councillor Biucchi in 1959 when he said, 'Ticino has preserved its own culture only in the mountain districts where the people live in poverty and where depopulation is therefore on the increase. Cultural protection and economic development do not easily go hand in hand. But mere resistance to the outside world will not solve Ticino's problems—the canton's own resources must be strengthened'.

THE JURASSIANS

The canton of Bern, in the north-west of Switzerland, is largely German-speaking. But in its northern parts, on the border with France and situated between the cantons of Neuchâtel and Solothurn, there is a region known as Jura where French is the predominant language. It comprises seven districts: Porrentruy, Delémont and Franches Montagnes in the extreme north are French-speaking and Catholic; Moutier, Courtelary and Neuveville to the south are French-speaking and Protestant. The seventh district is Laufental, a valley in the north-east near Basel, which is Catholic and German-speaking. The total population of Jura in 1974 was approximately 153,000 and that of Bern 1,006,000.

The natural sympathy between the Protestants of Bern and the people of the three southern districts, French-speaking but also Protestants, and the fact that no such feeling has ever existed on the part of the French-speaking, Catholic north, go back to the year 1000 when the King of Burgundy, Rudolph III, attempted to pacify the Catholic Church by presenting the Bishop of Basel with the gift of the abbey of Moutier-Grandval and all its assets, including about 540 square miles of land. This territory, where the principal towns are Delémont, Porrentruy, Moutier and Saint-Imier, corresponds to what is today Jura.

For centuries this little State, as it was then, was coveted by both France and the Leagues of High Germany, the forerunners of modern Switzerland. But it was not until the eighteenth century that Jura lost its independence. In 1735 and 1780 treaties were signed with the King of France, under which French troops were to be allowed to enter the region in the event of threatened invasion. Twelve years later, war having broken out between France and Austria, troops from the opposing sides clashed at Porrentruy. During the conflict the people of Jura proclaimed a republic, the *République Rauracienne*, named after a Gaullish tribe, the Rauraques, who had once settled in parts of Jura. They then voted for union with France, joining the young French Republic as the *département* of Mont-Terrible and later as part of Haut-Rhin.

But in 1813, after the fall of Napoleon I, the Treaty of Paris restored France to its former boundaries by making it relinquish its claim to Jura. The Jurassians protested strongly and sent a delegation to Louis XVIII to demand the maintenance of French sovereignty in the region, but without success. To compensate Bern for the loss of Vaud, today the canton north of Lake Geneva, and of Aargau near Zürich, Jura was handed back to Switzerland, without the consent of its inhabitants and to their great dismay.

Thus began the Swiss Jura question. For the next century and a half Jura was governed from Bern, in a canton of which it formed one fifth of the territory and had one eighth of the population. More individualist than the German-speakers of Bern, whose character is authoritarian in comparison, the Jurassians have a tradition of liberalism which allowed them to support the anarchism of Bakunin and Proudhon (who was himself a French-speaker from Jura) during the First Socialist International of 1872 against Karl Marx and his followers. In every generation since 1848, during eight military occupations, the *Kulturkampf* of 1874 and the Nazi period, the Jurassians protested against what they considered, as French-speakers living in a predominantly German-speaking canton, to be a process of Germanisation, whether brutal or surreptitious. It was for this reason that the writer Léon Froidevaux described his native Jura during the First World War as 'the Alsace of Switzerland'.

The relationship between the French-speakers of Jura and the rest of Bern is complicated by the fact that their German dialects have a special significance for the majority of the Swiss. After the obliteration of Latin in the seventh century, German was established by the Alemans over what is today about three quarters of Switzerland, from the linguistic boundaries dividing Valais, Fribourg and Bern to the frontier with Austria, from the Alpine watershed to Lake Constance and the Rhine, as well as parts of the Graubünden. German is spoken throughout this area, in nineteen out of Switzerland's twenty-five cantons, although mostly in its dialect forms. The Swiss dialects, despite increasing inter-mixture of populations and the influence of education and the mass media, have held their own with remarkable resilience against standard or High

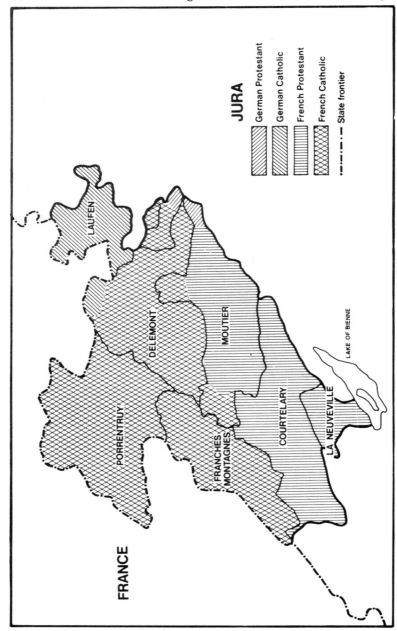

German, which is used only as the written form and for that reason is often described as *Schriftdeutsch.* The dialects, known collectively as *Schwyzerdütsch* (Swiss German), are to be heard not only in everyday conversations but also on public occasions, in administration and in church. They are an ancient residue of the Middle High German of the thirteenth and fifteenth centuries, having preserved much of their original pronunciation and vocabulary, particularly in the higher valleys. For the child, standard German is therefore more or less a different if not a foreign language—as different from Swiss German as High German is from, say, Dutch. Indeed, the dialects are such an important factor in the Swiss-German identity that they did much to strengthen the people's resistance to pan-Germanism and the Third *Reich.*

It is said sometimes that there is no Swiss *Umgangssprache,* (language of everyday use) for the man from Bern speaks *Bärndütsch* and the man from Zürich *Züritüütsch.* The only common form among speakers of Swiss German is *Grossratsdeutsch*—'the German of county councillors' but this, in fact, is written High German spoken according to the rules of dialect. It may therefore also be said that there is no Swiss German language, only an endless variety of dialects which are used according to geographical situations, class considerations and age-group. Nevertheless, the dialects show no signs of dying out. When, in the 1860s, the Swiss Dialect Dictionary was being planned, the object was to preserve the local peculiarities for the delight of later generations: the future, most believed, lay with High German. Yet by today more people speak Swiss German than ever before. The dialects are widely spoken in the Army, on radio, in law-courts, local councils, in churches and even in the schools. Despite this tenacity as a spoken form, Swiss German has only a smallish literature. The dramatist C. F. Hebel (1813-63), although not a Swiss, wrote lyrics in it and Rudolph von Tavel (1866-1934) wrote novels in Bernese. The novelist Jeremias Gotthelf (1797-1854) also broke into Bernese from time to time and his style is suffused by it. But the problem—that Swiss German is extremely difficult to write consistently—remains. This problem is not shared by French-speaking Switzerland, which has a completely different attitude to dialect: there dialect has for a long time been considered lower-class and Swiss German quite clearly despised.

In 1947, the traditional antagonism between Protestant, German-speaking Bern and the Catholic French-speakers in the northern districts of Jura was exacerbated by the canton's refusal to appoint George Moeckli, a French-speaking Jurassian, as Director of Public Works. During the controversy and in the euphoria of the German defeat which followed, a new movement called *Le Rassemblement Jurassien* was formed. Its aim was to rid Jura of domination from Bern and of the injustices in its social and cultural life since the so-called *Anschluss* of 1813. Soon afterwards it was opposed by another new organisation, *Les Patriotes Jurassiens,* which was mostly Protestant and wished to maintain connections with the canton of Bern. These two movements joined an already complicated array of older political parties and, within ten years, public opinion on the status of Jura was polarised and often very heated. That the problem was linguistic rather than religious in character is borne out by the fact that, while all other bodies joined in the debate, neither the Catholic Church nor the Protestant expressed an official view nor did they intervene in any way.

According to the *Rassemblement Jurassien,* which soon led a cross-section of public opinion, 'the Swiss Jura question' was not simply a matter of cultural and administrative justice, but also an economic problem. For example, its publications cited, quite accurately, that the rapid industrial expansion on the French side of the Belfort Gap, the geographical centre of the E.E.C., stopped short at the Swiss border, that the small town of Montbéliard in the Franche Comté was classed as one of the most prosperous and progressive towns in France with a growing population of 105,000 while the towns of Jura were losing their population from year to year, and that while Jura was more industrialised than the rest of the canton of Bern it was prevented from developing its investment by prohibitive taxes and lack of sufficient subsidies. On the other hand, its main platform was cultural and linguistic: 'the hegemony of Bern' had to be resisted because of its harmful effects on the status and numerical strength of French in the six districts where it was the majority language. The main organ of the *Rassemblement Jurassien* in the cultural sphere was the magazine *Sur Parole,* edited by the poet Jean Cuttat. One of the more notable, if less realistic features of all the movement's publications is a belief in *Francophonie,* a union of all French-speaking peoples.

Following a referendum in 1959 at which about half of the canton's population expressed itself in favour of a plebiscite on the future of Jura, the Bern Government reached the conclusion in 1965 that the only solution to a rapidly deteriorating situation was to prepare the way towards separation for all those districts which wanted it by organising a second referendum on the subject. According to the Swiss Federal Constitution (Article 43) separation would have to be achieved by voting, with all the citizens of Jura's seven districts taking part. The separatists of the *Rassemblement Jurassien* objected to this, however, claiming that only citizens with roots in the Jura over three generations, whether residents or living outside the region, should be entitled to vote—as was the case in 1848 when Neuchâtel, then a Prussian principality, decided to join Switzerland. Their fear was that, as in the referendum of 1959, recent immigrants from 'the old canton' of the German-speaking south, would vote against separation. But to have excluded German-speakers from the referendum would have been totally at variance with the clear provision of the Swiss Constitution which grants the right to vote on all subjects to the residents of the area, regardless of language, and to no one else. Eventually, the separatists accepted this regulation and then launched a lively campaign in preparation for the plebiscite.

There were other conditions which were accepted on all sides but which need not be described in order to illustrate the Swiss concept of democracy at work. The referendum could not be limited to a single question: are the residents of Jura in favour of the creation of a new canton? No matter what the over-all result might be, an opportunity had to be provided for any individual district not voting with the majority to ask for a second vote in order to decide its own future. Those communes lying along the boundary between the districts would have the chance of joining the neighbouring districts if they so wished. After the first vote a special system would be applied to the Laufental, which is German-speaking but separated from the rest of Bern by the French-speaking districts, to enable it to join one or other of its two neighbours, the canton of Basel Land or the canton of Solothurn. Lastly, in the event of a new canton of Jura being created, it would have to elect an assembly, its constitution would have to be approved by the Swiss Confederation and the entire population of Switzerland would be asked to vote on a change in the Federal Constitution, formally welcoming a twenty-sixth canton to its midst.

Meanwhile, between 1963 and 1970, pressure on the Bern authorities to solve the Jura question without further delay had been increasing rapidly. After a number of proposals for self-determination by the *Rassemblement Jurassien* had been rejected, many acts of violence were carried out against symbols of the Bern régime by the clandestine *Front de Libération Jurassien*. A military camp was burned down in 1963, troops were moved into the region in 1968, members of the young people's activist wing, which has over 2,000 members, the *Groupe Bélier,* were arrested and imprisoned for illegal activities, Government offices were occupied and ransacked.

In 1970 the Swiss Minister for Foreign Affairs, Fritz Wahlen, raised the Jura question in debate before the Federal Council during which the principle of autonomy for the region was agreed. A Commission was set up under the chairmanship of Max Petitpierre, a former President of Switzerland, which recommended recognition of the Jurassian people's rights to control their own affairs as an autonomous unit within the Swiss Confederation. In the same year a petition bearing the signatures of 6,000 Swiss citizens living outside Jura was presented to the Federal Government. The signatories, 'troubled by the persistence with which the Jurassians are demanding their independence, alarmed at seeing the aspirations of a minority stifled, and anxious about the danger that this state of affairs may hold for the future of the Confederation', called for measures which would allow Jura to assume 'its rightful place' as the twenty-sixth canton of Switzerland. To coincide with this important expression of support for the separatist cause, the *Rassemblement Jurassien*